Rick Steves

FLORENCE & TUSCANY

Rick Steves & Gene Openshaw

2015

CONTENTS

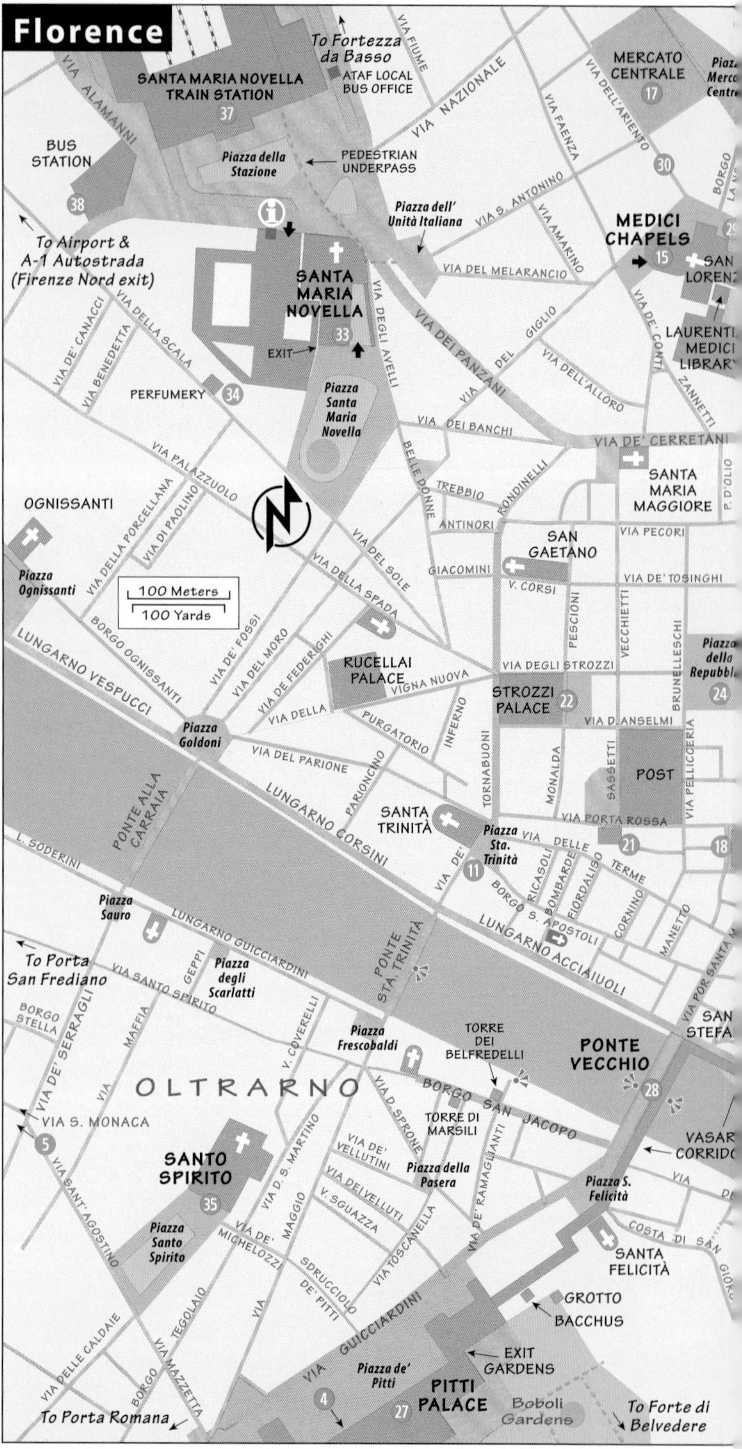
Florence
SANTA MARIA NOVELLA TRAIN STATION
37
To Fortezza da Basso
ATAF LOCAL BUS OFFICE
VIA FIUME
VIA NAZIONALE
MERCATO CENTRALE
17
VIA DELL'ARIENTO
VIA FAENZA
VIA ALAMANNI
BUS STATION
38
Piazza della Stazione
PEDESTRIAN UNDERPASS
30
To Airport & A-1 Autostrada (Firenze Nord exit)
Piazza dell' Unità Italiana
VIA S. ANTONINO
VIA AMARINO
MEDICI CHAPELS
15
VIA DEL MELARANCIO
SANTA MARIA NOVELLA
33
EXIT
VIA DEGLI AVELLI
VIA DEI PANZANI
VIA DEL GIGLIO
VIA DELL'ALLORO
VIA DE' CONTI
LAURENTIAN MEDICI LIBRARY
ZANNETTI
VIA DE' CANACCI
VIA BENEDETTA
VIA DELLA SCALA
PERFUMERY
34
Piazza Santa Maria Novella
VIA DEI BANCHI
VIA DE' CERRETANI
BELLE DONNE
TREBBIO
RONDINELLI
SANTA MARIA MAGGIORE
VIA PALAZZUOLO
OGNISSANTI
VIA DELLA PORCELLANA
VIA DI PAOLINO
ANTINORI
SAN GAETANO
VIA PECORI
Piazza Ognissanti
VIA DEL SOLE
VIA DELLA SPADA
GIACOMINI
V. CORSI
VIA DE' TOSINGHI
100 Meters
100 Yards
PESCIONI
VECCHIETTI
BRUNELLESCHI
Piazza della Repubblica
24
BORGO OGNISSANTI
VIA DE' FOSSI
VIA DEL MORO
VIA DE FEDERIGHI
RUCELLAI PALACE
VIGNA NUOVA
VIA DEGLI STROZZI
STROZZI PALACE
22
LUNGARNO VESPUCCI
VIA DELLA
PURGATORIO
INFERNO
VIA D. ANSELMI
Piazza Goldoni
VIA DEL PARIONE
TORNABUONI
MONALDA
SASSETTI
POST
VIA PELLICCERIA
PONTE ALLA CARRAIA
PARIONCINO
LUNGARNO CORSINI
SANTA TRINITÀ
VIA PORTA ROSSA
Piazza Sta. Trinità
VIA DELLE TERME
21
18
L. SODERINI
VIA DE'
11
BORGO S. APOSTOLI
RICASOLI
BOMBARDE
FIORDALISO
CORNINO
MANETTO
Piazza Sauro
LUNGARNO GUICCIARDINI
PONTE STA. TRINITÀ
LUNGARNO ACCIAIUOLI
To Porta San Frediano
VIA SANTO SPIRITO
GEPPI
Piazza degli Scarlatti
VIA POR SANTA MARIA
BORGO STELLA
VIA DE' SERRAGLI
MAFFIA
V. COVERELLI
Piazza Frescobaldi
TORRE DEI BELFREDELLI
PONTE VECCHIO
OLTRARNO
BORGO SAN JACOPO
28
VIA S. MONACA
5
VIA D. SPRONE
TORRE DI MARSILI
SANTO SPIRITO
VIA D. S. MARTINO
VIA DE' VELLUTINI
Piazza della Pasera
VIA DE' RAMAGLIANTI
VASARI CORRIDOR
VIA SANT'AGOSTINO
35
VIA DEI VELLUTI
V. SGUAZZA
Piazza S. Felicità
MAGGIO
VIA TOSCANELLA
COSTA DI SAN GIORGIO
Piazza Santo Spirito
VIA DE' MICHELOZZI
SDRUCCIOLO DE' PITTI
SANTA FELICITÀ
GROTTO
BACCHUS
VIA DELLE CALDAIE
TEGOLAIO
VIA MAZZETTA
VIA GUICCIARDINI
EXIT GARDENS
BORGO
Piazza de' Pitti
4
PITTI PALACE
27
Boboli Gardens
To Forte di Belvedere
To Porta Romana

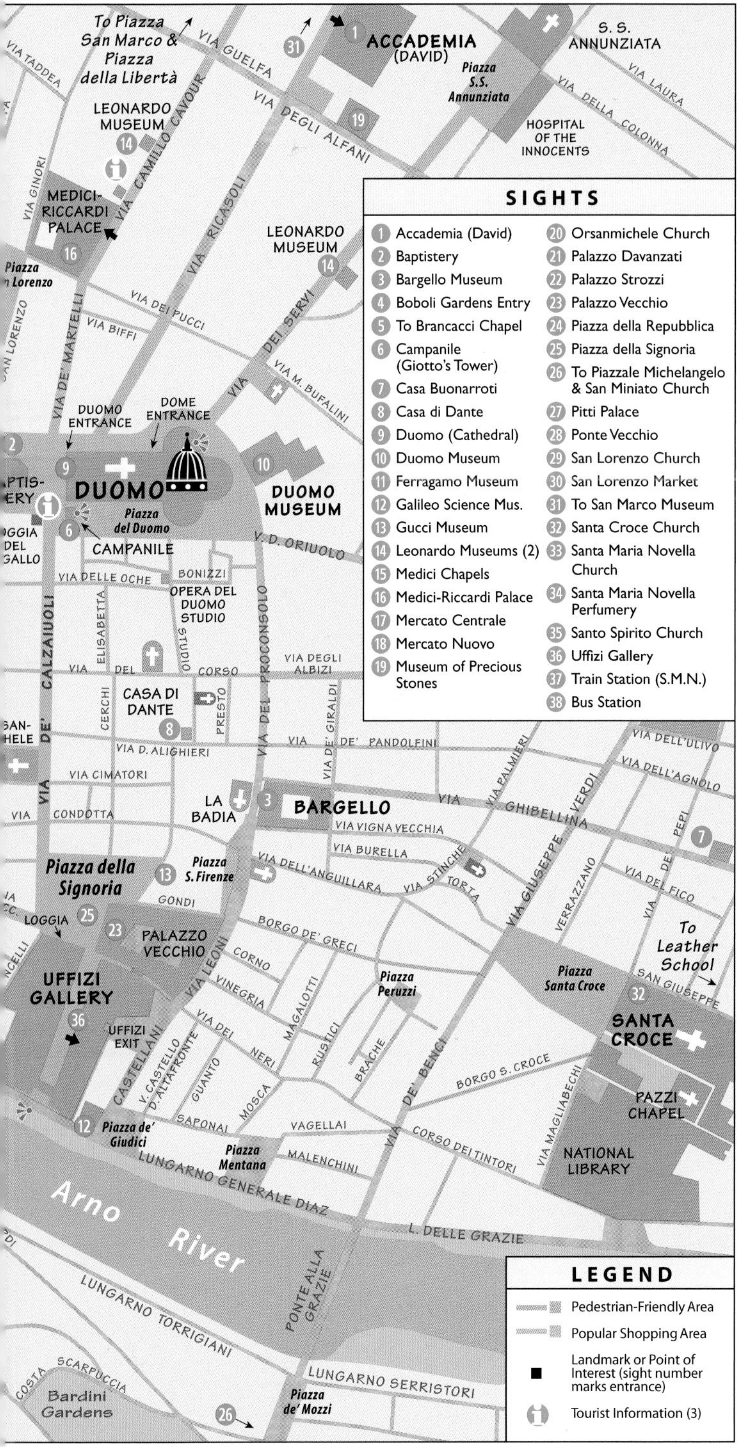

SIGHTS
1 Accademia (David)
2 Baptistery
3 Bargello Museum
4 Boboli Gardens Entry
5 To Brancacci Chapel
6 Campanile (Giotto's Tower)
7 Casa Buonarroti
8 Casa di Dante
9 Duomo (Cathedral)
10 Duomo Museum
11 Ferragamo Museum
12 Galileo Science Mus.
13 Gucci Museum
14 Leonardo Museums (2)
15 Medici Chapels
16 Medici-Riccardi Palace
17 Mercato Centrale
18 Mercato Nuovo
19 Museum of Precious Stones
20 Orsanmichele Church
21 Palazzo Davanzati
22 Palazzo Strozzi
23 Palazzo Vecchio
24 Piazza della Repubblica
25 Piazza della Signoria
26 To Piazzale Michelangelo & San Miniato Church
27 Pitti Palace
28 Ponte Vecchio
29 San Lorenzo Church
30 San Lorenzo Market
31 To San Marco Museum
32 Santa Croce Church
33 Santa Maria Novella Church
34 Santa Maria Novella Perfumery
35 Santo Spirito Church
36 Uffizi Gallery
37 Train Station (S.M.N.)
38 Bus Station
LEGEND
Pedestrian-Friendly Area
Popular Shopping Area
Landmark or Point of Interest (sight number marks entrance)
Tourist Information (3)
To Piazza San Marco & Piazza della Libertà
ACCADEMIA (DAVID)
Piazza S.S. Annunziata
S. S. ANNUNZIATA
HOSPITAL OF THE INNOCENTS
VIA TADDEA
VIA GUELFA
VIA DEGLI ALFANI
VIA LAURA
VIA DELLA COLONNA
LEONARDO MUSEUM
VIA CAMILLO CAVOUR
VIA GINORI
MEDICI-RICCARDI PALACE
VIA RICASOLI
Piazza San Lorenzo
VIA DEI PUCCI
VIA BIFFI
VIA DEI SERVI
VIA DE' MARTELLI
VIA M. BUFALINI
DUOMO ENTRANCE
DOME ENTRANCE
DUOMO
Piazza del Duomo
CAMPANILE
DUOMO MUSEUM
V. D. ORIUOLO
VIA DELLE OCHE
BONIZZI
OPERA DEL DUOMO STUDIO
VIA CALZAIUOLI
ELISABETTA
STUDIO
VIA DEL PROCONSOLO
VIA DEGLI ALBIZI
VIA DEL CORSO
CERCHI
CASA DI DANTE
PRESTO
VIA DE' GIRALDI
VIA DE' PANDOLFINI
VIA D. ALIGHIERI
VIA CIMATORI
VIA CONDOTTA
LA BADIA
BARGELLO
VIA GHIBELLINA
VIA PALMIERI
VIA GIUSEPPE VERDI
VIA DELL'ULIVO
VIA DELL'AGNOLO
VIA VIGNA VECCHIA
VIA BURELLA
VIA DE' PEPI
Piazza della Signoria
Piazza S. Firenze
VIA DELL'ANGUILLARA
VIA STINCHE
TORTA
VERRAZZANO
VIA DEL FICO
GONDI
LOGGIA
PALAZZO VECCHIO
BORGO DE' GRECI
To Leather School
CORNO
VIA LEONI
VINEGRIA
MAGALOTTI
Piazza Peruzzi
Piazza Santa Croce
SAN GIUSEPPE
UFFIZI GALLERY
UFFIZI EXIT
VIA DEI NERI
RUSTICI
BRACHE
VIA DE' BENCI
SANTA CROCE
CASTELLANI
V. CASTELLO D. ALTAFRONTE
GIUANTO
MOSCA
BORGO S. CROCE
VIA MAGLIABECHI
PAZZI CHAPEL
Piazza de' Giudici
SAPONAI
VAGELLAI
CORSO DEI TINTORI
Piazza Mentana
MALENCHINI
NATIONAL LIBRARY
LUNGARNO GENERALE DIAZ
Arno River
L. DELLE GRAZIE
LUNGARNO TORRIGIANI
PONTE ALLA GRAZIE
COSTA SCARPUCCIA
Bardini Gardens
LUNGARNO SERRISTORI
Piazza de' Mozzi

Tuscany
To Parma
To Milan
A-1
S-63
Bologna
EMILIA-ROMAGNA
LIGURIA
A-15
S-12
To Genoa
A-12
APUAN ALPS
S-64
Sestri Levante
Aulla
Levanto
Monterosso
Vernazza
Corniglia
Manarola
Riomaggiore
CINQUE TERRE
La Spezia
MARBLE QUARRIES
Abetone
S-445
A-1
Carrara
Lerici
Portovenere
Massa
Bagni di Lucca
Marina di Carrara
A-12
Pietra-santa
Montecatini
Pistoia
Prato
Collodi
Vespucci
Lucca
Viareggio
Lago Mass.
A-11
Vinci
Florence
Empoli
Arno R.
AMERICAN CEMETERY
Ligurian Sea
Pisa
San Miniato
S-2
Galileo
FiPiLi
Castellina
Elsa
Livorno
Poggibonsi
A-12
San Gimignano
Colle di Val d'Elsa
S-68
Volterra
Gorgona
Monteriggione
S-68
Cecina
Saline di Volterra
TUSCANY
S-1
S-73
Massa Marittima
SAN GALGANO
VIA AURELIA
S-439
Capraia
E-80
Piombino
Follonica
Braccagni
VILLA NAPOLEONE
Portoferraio
MONTE CAPANNE
Porto Azzurro
Grosseto
Corsica (France)
Marina di Campo
Castiglione della Pescaia
Elba
MAREMMA
Bastia
MONTE ARGENTARIO
Giglio
Mediterranean
LEGEND
A-24 Freeway
S-68 Major Road
High Speed Rail
Airport
Rail Line
Ruin, Museum, other Point of Interest

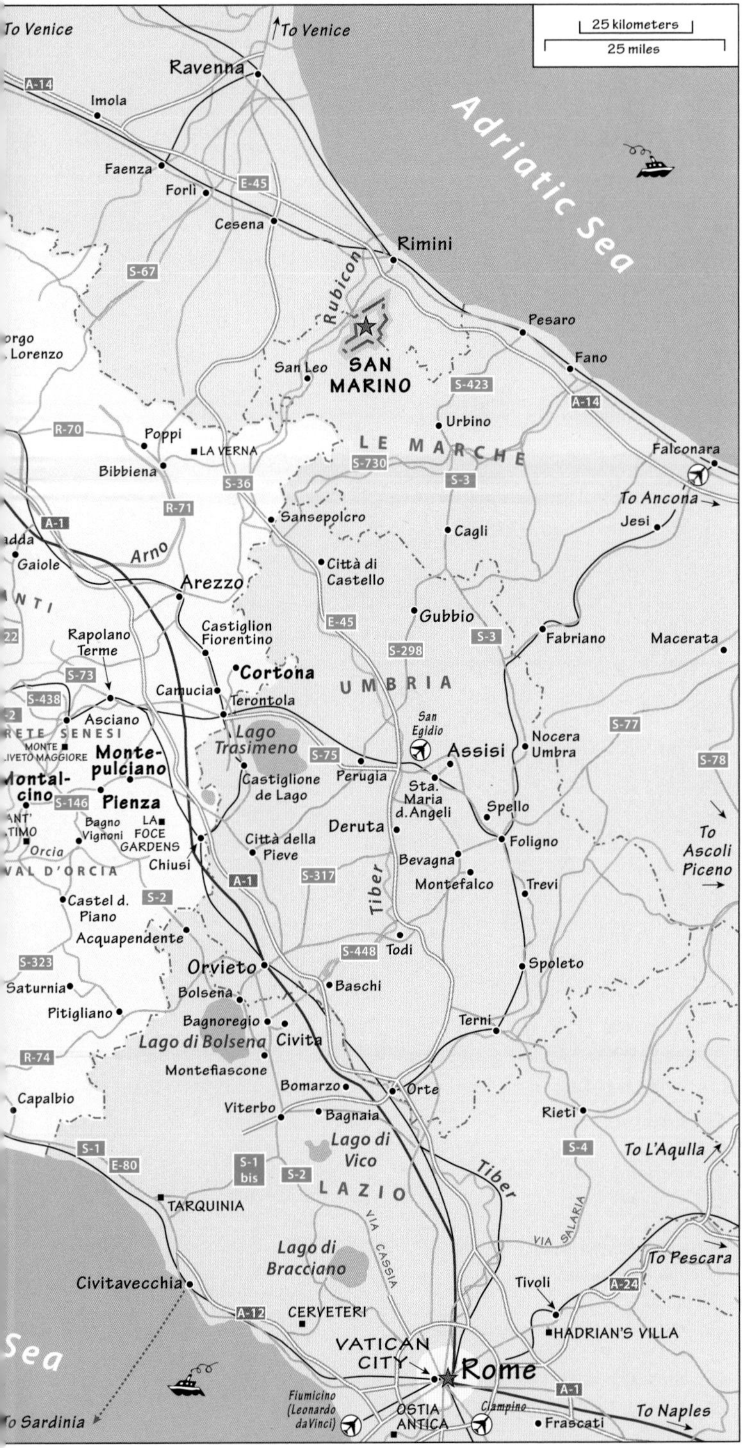

25 kilometers
25 miles
Adriatic Sea
To Venice
To Venice
Ravenna
Imola
Faenza
Forlì
Cesena
Rimini
Rubicon
SAN MARINO
San Leo
Pesaro
Fano
Urbino
LE MARCHE
Falconara
To Ancona
Jesi
Poppi
LA VERNA
Bibbiena
Sansepolcro
Cagli
Arno
Gaiole
Arezzo
Città di Castello
Gubbio
Fabriano
Macerata
Castiglion Fiorentino
Rapolano Terme
Cortona
Camucia
Terontola
UMBRIA
Asciano
Lago Trasimeno
San Egidio
Assisi
Nocera Umbra
Monte-pulciano
Castiglione de Lago
Perugia
Sta. Maria d.Angeli
Spello
Pienza
Bagno Vignoni
LA FOCE GARDENS
Deruta
Foligno
Chiusi
Città della Pieve
Bevagna
Montefalco
Trevi
To Ascoli Piceno
Orcia
VAL D'ORCIA
Tiber
Castel d. Piano
Acquapendente
Todi
Orvieto
Spoleto
Saturnia
Baschi
Bolsena
Pitigliano
Bagnoregio
Terni
Lago di Bolsena
Civita
Montefiascone
Bomarzo
Orte
Capalbio
Viterbo
Bagnaia
Rieti
Lago di Vico
To L'Aquila
Tiber
LAZIO
TARQUINIA
VIA CASSIA
VIA SALARIA
Lago di Bracciano
To Pescara
Civitavecchia
Tivoli
CERVETERI
HADRIAN'S VILLA
VATICAN CITY
Rome
Sea
Fiumicino (Leonardo daVinci)
OSTIA ANTICA
Ciampino
Frascati
To Naples
To Sardinia
A-14
E-45
S-67
S-423
A-14
R-70
S-730
S-3
S-36
R-71
A-1
E-45
S-298
S-3
S-73
S-438
S-75
S-77
S-78
S-146
S-317
A-1
S-2
S-323
S-448
R-74
S-1
E-80
S-1 bis
S-2
S-4
A-24
A-12
A-1

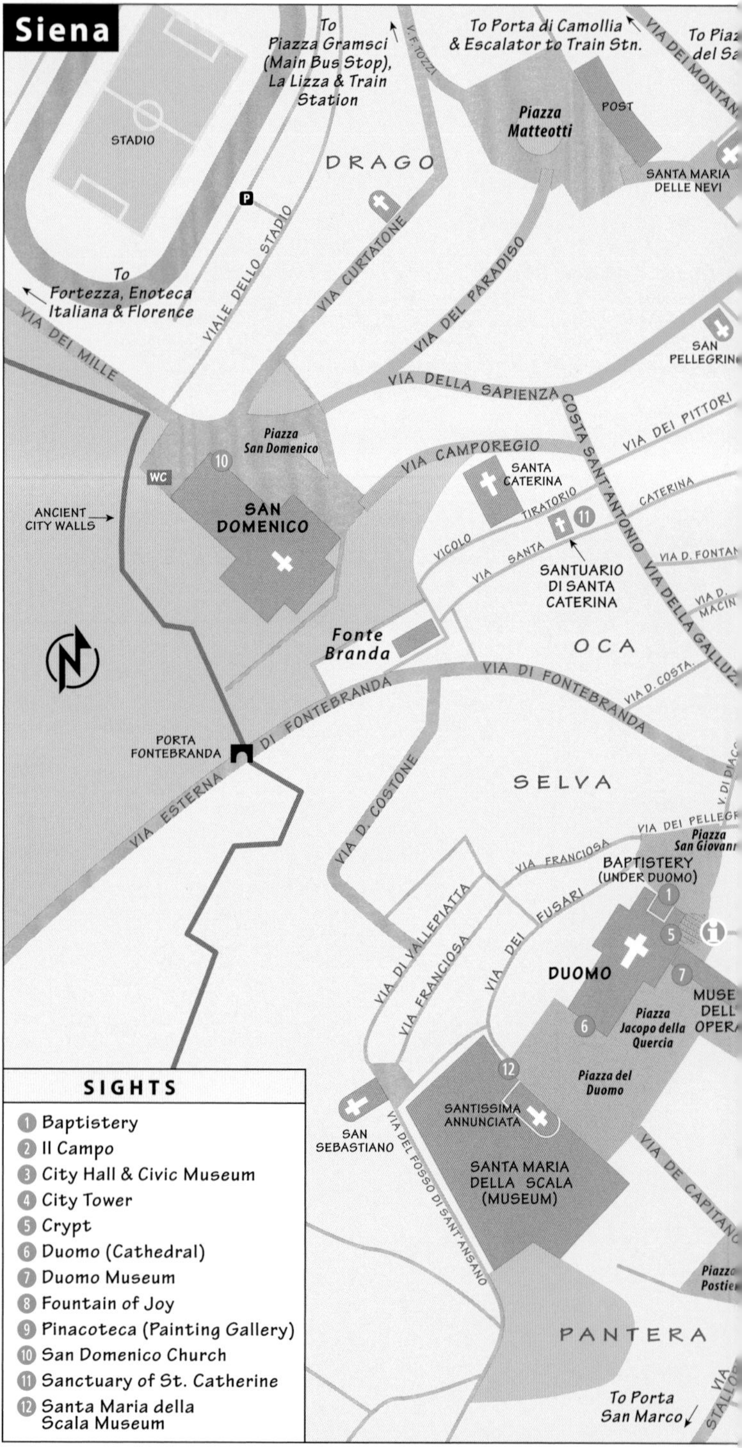
Siena
To Piazza Gramsci (Main Bus Stop), La Lizza & Train Station
To Porta di Camollia & Escalator to Train Stn.
V. F. TOZZI
VIA DEI MONTAN
Piazza Matteotti
POST
SANTA MARIA DELLE NEVI
STADIO
DRAGO
P
VIALE DELLO STADIO
VIA CURTATONE
VIA DEL PARADISO
To Fortezza, Enoteca Italiana & Florence
VIA DEI MILLE
SAN PELLEGRIN
VIA DELLA SAPIENZA
COSTA SANT'ANTONIO
VIA DEI PITTORI
Piazza San Domenico
VIA CAMPOREGIO
10
WC
SANTA CATERINA
SAN DOMENICO
VICOLO
TIRATORIO
11
CATERINA
ANCIENT CITY WALLS
VIA SANTA
SANTUARIO DI SANTA CATERINA
VIA D. FONTAN
VIA D. MACIN
VIA DELLA GALLUZ
Fonte Branda
OCA
VIA DI FONTEBRANDA
VIA D. COSTA.
PORTA FONTEBRANDA
DI FONTEBRANDA
VIA ESTERNA
VIA D. COSTONE
SELVA
V. DI DIACC
VIA DEI PELLEGR
Piazza San Giovanni
VIA FRANCIOSA
BAPTISTERY (UNDER DUOMO)
1
FUSARI
5
VIA DEI
VIA DI VALLEPIATTA
VIA FRANCIOSA
DUOMO
7
MUSE DELL OPER
6
Piazza Jacopo della Quercia
12
Piazza del Duomo
SANTISSIMA ANNUNCIATA
SAN SEBASTIANO
VIA DEL FOSSO DI SANT'ANSANO
SANTA MARIA DELLA SCALA (MUSEUM)
VIA DE CAPITANO
Piazza Postie
PANTERA
To Porta San Marco
VIA STALLO
SIGHTS
1 Baptistery
2 Il Campo
3 City Hall & Civic Museum
4 City Tower
5 Crypt
6 Duomo (Cathedral)
7 Duomo Museum
8 Fountain of Joy
9 Pinacoteca (Painting Gallery)
10 San Domenico Church
11 Sanctuary of St. Catherine
12 Santa Maria della Scala Museum

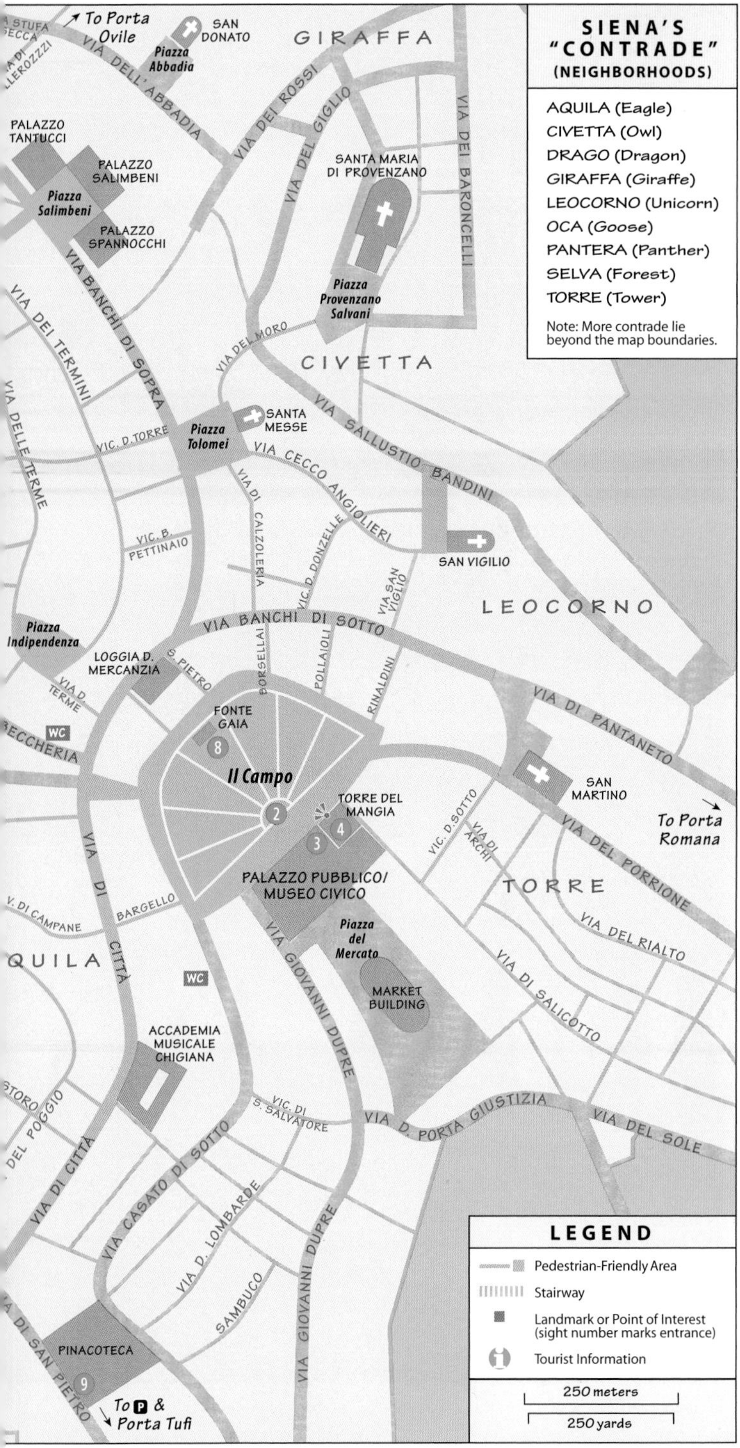
SIENA'S "CONTRADE" (NEIGHBORHOODS)
AQUILA (Eagle)
CIVETTA (Owl)
DRAGO (Dragon)
GIRAFFA (Giraffe)
LEOCORNO (Unicorn)
OCA (Goose)
PANTERA (Panther)
SELVA (Forest)
TORRE (Tower)
Note: More contrade lie beyond the map boundaries.
LEGEND
Pedestrian-Friendly Area
Stairway
Landmark or Point of Interest (sight number marks entrance)
Tourist Information
250 meters
250 yards
To Porta Ovile
SAN DONATO
Piazza Abbadia
GIRAFFA
VIA DELL'ABBADIA
VIA DEI ROSSI
VIA DEL GIGLIO
VIA DEI BARONCELLI
PALAZZO TANTUCCI
PALAZZO SALIMBENI
Piazza Salimbeni
PALAZZO SPANNOCCHI
SANTA MARIA DI PROVENZANO
Piazza Provenzano Salvani
VIA BANCHI DI SOPRA
VIA DEI TERMINI
VIA DELLE TERME
VIA DEL MORO
CIVETTA
SANTA MESSE
Piazza Tolomei
VIC. D. TORRE
VIA SALLUSTIO BANDINI
VIA CECCO ANGIOLIERI
VIA DI CALZOLERIA
VIC. D. DONZELLE
VIC. B. PETTINAIO
SAN VIGILIO
VIA SAN VIGLIO
LEOCORNO
VIA BANCHI DI SOTTO
Piazza Indipendenza
LOGGIA D. MERCANZIA
S. PIETRO
VIA D. TERME
BORSELLAI
POLLAIOLI
RINALDINI
VIA DI PANTANETO
WC
FONTE GAIA
8
Il Campo
2
TORRE DEL MANGIA
4
3
SAN MARTINO
To Porta Romana
VIC. D. SOTTO
VIA DI ARCHI
VIA DEL PORRIONE
PALAZZO PUBBLICO/ MUSEO CIVICO
TORRE
V. DI CAMPANE
BARGELLO
VIA DI CITTÀ
Piazza del Mercato
VIA DEL RIALTO
QUILA
WC
VIA GIOVANNI DUPRE
MARKET BUILDING
VIA DI SALICOTTO
ACCADEMIA MUSICALE CHIGIANA
VIC. DI S. SALVATORE
VIA D. PORTA GIUSTIZIA
VIA DEL SOLE
DEL POGGIO
VIA CASATO DI SOTTO
VIA DI CITTÀ
VIA D. LOMBARDE
VIA GIOVANNI DUPRE
SAMBUCO
PINACOTECA
9
VIA DI SAN PIETRO
To P & Porta Tufi

Pisa's Field of Miracles—the Duomo with its leaning Bell Tower

Tuscany—farmhouses, cypress trees, sunshine, and a timeless way of life

Michelangelo's David*—Accademia*

Tuscan hill town

Brunelleschi's Dome of the Duomo, Florence

Rick Steves

FLORENCE & TUSCANY 2015

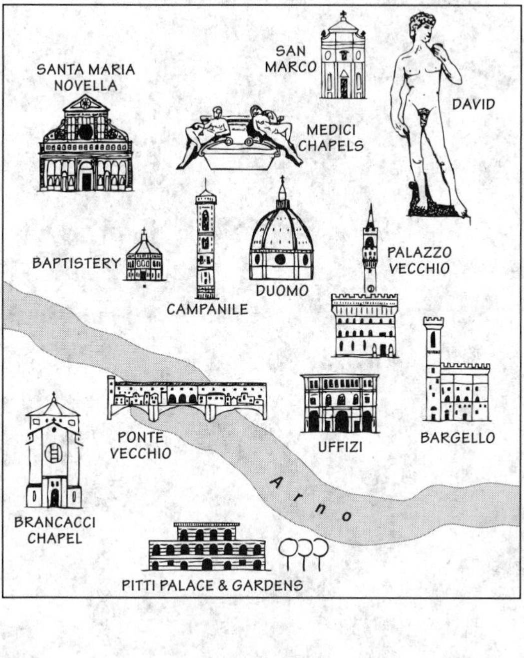

INTRODUCTION

Florence is Europe's cultural capital. As the home of the Renaissance and the birthplace of the modern world, Florence practiced the art of civilized living back when the rest of Europe was rural and crude. Democracy, science, and literature, as well as painting, sculpture, and architecture, were all championed by the proud and energetic Florentines of the 1400s.

When the Florentine poet Dante first saw the teenaged Beatrice, her beauty so inspired him that he spent the rest of his life writing poems to her. In the same way, the Renaissance opened people's eyes to the physical beauty of the world around them, inspiring them to write, paint, sculpt, and build.

Today, Florence is geographically small but culturally rich, with more artistic masterpieces per square mile than anyplace else. In a single day, you can look Michelangelo's *David* in the eyes, fall under the seductive sway of Botticelli's *Birth of Venus,* and climb the modern world's first dome, which still dominates the skyline.

Of course, there's a reality here, too. As the historic center becomes increasingly filled with visitors, rents are rising and locals are fleeing to the suburbs, threatening to make Florence a kind of Renaissance theme park. Sure, Florence is touristy. But where else can you stroll the same pedestrian streets walked by Michelangelo, Leonardo, and Botticelli while savoring the world's best gelato?

To round out your visit, see Florence and then escape to the Tuscan countryside. With its manicured fields, rustic farms, cypress-lined driveways, and towns clinging to nearly every hill, Tuscany is our romantic image of village Italy. Venture beyond the fringes of Florence and you'll find a series of sun- and wine-soaked villages, each with its own appeal. Stretching from the Umbrian border to the Ligurian Sea, the landscape changes from pastoral

Map Legend

Viewpoint	Airport	Tunnel
Entrance	Taxi Stand	Pedestrian Zone
Tourist Info	Tram Stop	Railway
Restroom	Bus Stop	Ferry/Boat Route
Castle	Metro Stop	Tram
Church	Parking	Stairs
Statue/Point of Interest	Gelato	Walk/Tour Route
Elevator	Park	Trail

Use this legend to help you navigate the maps in this book.

(Crete Senesi) to rocky (Chianti) to mountainous (the Montagnola) to flat and brushed with sea breezes (Pisa).

Each of Tuscany's time-passed villages seems to have its own claim to fame: Volterra (Etruscan ruins), San Gimignano (towers), Montalcino (wine), Montepulciano (artisans), Pienza (tidy Renaissance-planned streets), and so on. But Tuscany also has a variety of intriguing cities that fully engage even the most restless traveler. Siena huddles around one of Italy's coziest squares and finest cathedrals. Pisa boasts the famous Field of Miracles (with its Leaning Tower, an icon of all Italy) and a gritty working-class-meets-university-town bustle. And Lucca is graced with churches, towers, and a delightful city wall-turned-city park that's ideal for a stroll or pedal.

You'll discover that peaceful Tuscan villages and bustling Florence—with its rough-stone beauty, art-packed museums, children chasing pigeons, students riding Vespas, artisans sipping Chianti, and supermodels wearing Gucci fashions—offer many of the very things you came to Italy to see.

ABOUT THIS BOOK

Rick Steves Florence & Tuscany 2015 is a personal tour guide in your pocket. Better yet, it's actually two tour guides in your pocket: The co-author of this book is Gene Openshaw. Since our first "Europe through the gutter" trip together as high school buddies in the 1970s, Gene and I have been exploring the wonders of the Old World. An inquisitive historian and lover of European culture, Gene wrote most of this book's self-guided museum tours and neighborhood walks. Together, Gene and I keep this book up-to-date and accurate (though for simplicity, from this point we've shed our respective egos to become "I").

In this book, you'll find the following chapters:

Key to This Book

Updates

This book is updated every year—but things change. As soon as you pin down Italy, it wiggles. For the latest, visit www.ricksteves.com/update.

Abbreviations and Times

I use the following symbols and abbreviations in this book:

Sights are rated:

▲▲▲	Don't miss
▲▲	Try hard to see
▲	Worthwhile if you can make it
No rating	Worth knowing about

Tourist information offices are abbreviated as **TI,** and bathrooms are **WC**s. To categorize accommodations, I use a **Sleep Code** (described on page 633).

Like Europe, this book uses the **24-hour clock.** It's the same through 12:00 noon, then keeps going: 13:00, 14:00, and so on. For anything over 12, subtract 12 and add p.m. (14:00 is 2:00 p.m.).

When giving **opening times,** I include both peak season and off-season hours if they differ. So, if a museum is listed as "May-Oct daily 9:00-16:00," it should be open from 9 a.m. until 4 p.m. from the first day of May until the last day of October (but expect exceptions).

If you see a ✪ in a sight listing, it means that the sight is covered in much more detail elsewhere—either with its own self-guided tour, or as part of a self-guided walk.

For **transit** or **tour departures,** I first list the frequency, then the duration. So, a train connection listed as "2/hour, 1.5 hours" departs twice each hour and the journey lasts an hour and a half.

Orientation to Florence includes specifics on public transportation, helpful hints, local tour options, easy-to-read maps, and tourist information. The "Planning Your Time" section suggests a schedule for how to best use your limited time.

Sights in Florence describes the top attractions and includes their cost and hours.

The **Self-Guided Walks and Tours** take you through the core of Renaissance Florence, starting with Michelangelo's *David* and cutting through the heart of the city to Ponte Vecchio on the Arno River. You'll tour Tuscany's most fascinating museums and sights, including Florence's Accademia Gallery (home to Michelangelo's *David*), Uffizi Gallery, Bargello, Museum of San Marco, Duomo Museum, Palazzo Vecchio, Medici Chapels, Medici-Riccardi Palace, Church of Santa Maria Novella, Santa Croce Church, the

Oltrarno neighborhood (south of the Arno), Brancacci Chapel, Pitti Palace, and the Galileo Science Museum, as well as Siena's Duomo, Duomo Museum, and Civic Museum, and, in Pisa, the Leaning Tower, Duomo, and Field of Miracles.

Sleeping in Florence describes my favorite hotels, from good-value deals to cushy splurges.

Eating in Florence serves up a range of options, from inexpensive cafés to fancy restaurants.

Florence with Children includes my top recommendations for keeping your kids (and you) happy in Florence.

Shopping in Florence gives you tips for shopping painlessly and enjoyably, without letting it overwhelm your vacation or ruin your budget.

Nightlife in Florence is your guide to after-dark fun, including concerts, theaters, pubs, and clubs.

Florence Connections lays the groundwork for your smooth arrival and departure, covering transportation by train, bus, car, cruise ship, and by plane (with information on Florence's Amerigo Vespucci Airport).

Siena covers the highlights in this captivating Gothic city, from the stay-awhile central piazza to the 13th-century cathedral.

Pisa takes you beyond the Leaning Tower.

Lucca introduces you to the charms of this little-touristed, well-preserved city.

Three chapters on Tuscan hill towns—**Volterra and San Gimignano; Heart of Tuscany: Montepulciano, Pienza, and Montalcino;** and **Cortona**—bring you the best of village Italy.

The **Florentine and Tuscan History** chapter takes you on a whirlwind tour through the ages, covering two millennia, from ancient Tuscany to the present.

Practicalities is a traveler's tool kit, with our best travel tips and advice about money, sightseeing, staying connected, and using transportation. There's also a list of recommended books and films.

The **appendix** has nuts-and-bolts information, including useful phone numbers and websites, a festival list, a climate chart, a handy packing checklist, and Italian survival phrases.

Browse through this book, choose your favorite destinations, and link them up. Then have a terrific trip! Traveling like a temporary local, you'll get the absolute most out of every mile, minute, and dollar. As you visit places I know and love, I'm happy you'll be meeting my favorite Florentines.

Planning

This section will help you get started planning your trip—with advice on trip costs, when to go, and what you should know before you take off.

TRAVEL SMART

Many people travel through Italy thinking it's a chaotic mess. They feel that any attempt at efficient travel is futile. This is dead wrong—and expensive. Italy, which seems as orderly as spilled spaghetti, actually functions quite well. Only those who understand this and travel smart can enjoy Italy on a budget.

This book can save you lots of time and money. But to have an "A" trip, you need to be an "A" student. Read it all before your trip, noting holidays, specifics on sights, and days when sights are closed. You can wait in line for two hours to get into the Uffizi—or, by planning ahead (making reservations or buying the Firenze Card), you can walk right in. Saving Michelangelo's *David* for your trip finale is risky, and on Monday, impossible. (Florence's major sights, along with some minor ones, are closed on Mondays.) If you visit Siena as a short day trip, you'll miss the city's medieval magic at twilight. A smart trip is a puzzle—a fun, doable, and worthwhile challenge.

When you're plotting your itinerary, strive for a mix of intense and relaxed stretches. To maximize rootedness in Tuscany, minimize one-night stands. It's worth a drive after dinner to be settled into a town for two nights. Every trip—and every traveler—needs slack time (laundry, picnics, people-watching, and so on). Pace yourself. Assume you will return.

Reread this book as you travel, and visit local tourist information offices (abbreviated as TI in this book). Upon arrival in a new town, lay the groundwork for a smooth departure; get the schedule for the train or bus that you'll take when you depart. Drivers can figure out the best route to their next destination.

Update your plans as you travel. You can carry a small mobile device (phone, tablet, laptop) to find out tourist information, learn the latest on sights (special events, English tour schedules, etc.), book tickets and tours, make reservations, reconfirm hotels, research transportation connections, and keep in touch with your loved ones. If you don't want to bring a pricey device, you can use guest computers at hotels and make phone calls from landlines.

Enjoy the friendliness of your Tuscan hosts. Connect with the culture. Set up your own quest for the best gelato, piazza, *enoteca* (wine bar), or Renaissance painting or sculpture. Slow down and be open to unexpected experiences. Ask questions—most locals are eager to point you in their idea of the right direction. Keep a notepad in your pocket for confirming prices, noting directions, and organizing your thoughts. Wear your money belt, learn the currency, and figure out how to estimate prices in dollars. Those who expect to travel smart, do.

TRIP COSTS

Six components make up your total trip cost: airfare, surface transportation, room and board, sightseeing and entertainment, shopping and miscellany, and gelato.

Airfare: A basic, round-trip flight from the US to Florence can cost on average, about $1,000-2,000 total, depending on where you fly from and when (cheaper in winter or sometimes if flying into Milan or Rome). If Florence is part of a longer trip, consider saving time and money in Europe by flying into one city and out of another (for instance, into Florence and out of Paris). Overall, Kayak.com is the best place to start searching for transatlantic and intra-European flights on a combination of mainstream and budget carriers.

Surface Transportation: Most of Florence's sights, clustered in the downtown core, are within easy walking distance of each other. If you'd rather use taxis than walk, allow $80-100 over the course of a one-week visit (taxis can be shared by up to four people). The cost of round-trip, second-class train transportation to the recommended nearby destinations is affordable (about $11 for a train ticket to Pisa or Siena, and slightly less for a bus ticket to San Gimignano). For a one-way trip between Florence's airport and the city center, allow $8 by bus or $35 by taxi (can be shared). The other cities and villages covered in this book are made for walking. For more on public transportation and car rental, see "Transportation" in Practicalities.

Room and Board: You can thrive in Tuscany in 2015 on $135 a day per person for room and board. This allows $15 for lunch, $35 for dinner, and $85 for lodging (based on two people splitting the cost of a $170 double room that includes breakfast). Students and tightwads can enjoy Tuscany for as little as $65 a day ($30 for a bed, $35 for meals and snacks).

Sightseeing and Entertainment: Figure about $15 for major sights (Michelangelo's *David*, Uffizi Gallery), $5-10 for minor ones (museums, climbing church towers), and $25 for splurge experiences (e.g., walking tours and concerts). An overall average of $35 a day works for most people. Don't skimp here. After all, this category is the driving force behind your trip—you came to sightsee, enjoy, and experience Florence.

Shopping and Miscellany: Figure $3 per postcard, coffee, soft drink, or gelato. Shopping can vary in cost from nearly nothing to a small fortune. Good budget travelers find that this category

Tuscany at a Glance

▲▲▲**Florence** Art-packed, bustling city—starring Michelangelo's *David*, Renaissance paintings, and Brunelleschi's dome—with Ponte Vecchio spanning the flood-prone Arno River.

▲▲▲**Siena** Red-brick hilltop city known for its pageantry, Palio horse race, and a stunning traffic-free main square—great anytime but best after dark.

▲▲**Pisa** A city more famous for its iconic Leaning Tower than for its other equally impressive monuments on the gleaming white Field of Miracles.

▲▲**Lucca** Charming city with a lively (and flat) town center, ringed by intact old walls wide enough for biking and strolling.

▲▲**Volterra** Just far enough off the beaten path, surrounded by thick walls and hilly scenery, with a long Etruscan history and unusually interesting sightseeing for a small town.

▲▲**Montepulciano** Rugged town crowning a ridge, with dreamy vistas of the countryside and wine-tasting in inviting cantinas.

▲**San Gimignano** Epitome of a hill town, spiked with medieval towers offering superb views, popular with tourists who crowd the narrow alleys by day.

▲**Montalcino** Wine-lovers' paradise boasting a dramatic 14th-century castle, encircled by olive groves and famous vineyards.

Pienza Tiny Renaissance-planned architectural gem of a town nestled in the scenic hilly landscape of the Val d'Orcia.

Cortona Hillside town under the Tuscan sun, with historic churches and museums featuring Etruscan and Renaissance artifacts and art.

has little to do with assembling a trip full of lifelong, wonderful memories.

WHEN TO GO

Tuscany's best travel months (also its busiest and most expensive) are April, May, June, September, and October. These months combine the conveniences of peak season with pleasant weather.

Florence Almanac

Population: Approximately 420,000 people

Currency: Euro

City Layout: Florence is the capital of Tuscany and lies on the Arno River. It's divided into five administrative wards: the Historic Center, Campo di Marte, Gavinana, Isolotto, and Rifredi.

Best Viewpoints: Piazzale Michelangelo (and San Miniato Church, above it) overlooks the city and the Duomo from across the river. For other panoramic views of Florence, climb the Campanile or the Duomo's dome (next to each other) or the tower at Palazzo Vecchio.

Sweetest Festival: In late May, the city hosts an annual gelato festival, featuring tastings and demonstrations by gelato makers from all over Italy.

Tourist Tracks: From April to October, tourists outnumber Florence's local population. Each year, about 1.7 million tourists flock to the Uffizi Gallery to gaze at Botticelli's *Birth of Venus*.

Culture Count: A little over 90 percent of Florence's population is indigenously Italian and Roman Catholic. Immigrant groups are mostly European (3.5 percent) and East Asian (2 percent), with small percentages of North and South Americans and Northern Africans.

Famous Florentines: Florence, birthplace of the Renaissance, bred many great minds, including Michelangelo, Leonardo, Donatello, Brunelleschi, Machiavelli, Dante, and...Florence Nightingale, whose English parents named her after the city in which she was born.

Average Florentine: The average Florentine is 49 years old (7 years older than the average Italian) and will live until the age of 80. He/she is much more likely to have a leather jacket at home than a child (since less than 14 percent of the population is under 18).

The most grueling thing about travel in Tuscany is the summer heat in July and August, when temperatures hit the high 80s and 90s. Most mid-range hotels come with air-conditioning—a worthwhile splurge in the summer—but it's usually available only from June through September.

In April and October, you'll generally need a sweater or light jacket in the evening. In winter the temperatures can drop to the 40s or 50s (for more specifics, see the climate chart in the appendix). Off-season has none of the sweat and stress of the tourist season, but sights may have shorter hours, lunchtime breaks, and fewer activities. Confirm your sightseeing plans locally, especially when traveling off-season.

Rick Steves Audio Europe

If you're bringing a mobile device, be sure to check out **Rick Steves Audio Europe,** where you can download free audio tours and hours of travel interviews (via the Rick Steves Audio Europe app, www.ricksteves.com/audioeurope, iTunes, or Google Play).

My self-guided **audio tours** are user-friendly, easy to follow, fun, and informative, covering the major sights and neighborhoods in Florence: my Renaissance Walk, the Accademia, and the Uffizi Gallery. Compared to live tours, my audio tours are hard to beat: Nobody will stand you up, the quality is reliable, you can take the tour exactly when you like, and they're free.

Rick Steves Audio Europe also offers a far-reaching library of intriguing **travel interviews** with experts from around the globe.

KNOW BEFORE YOU GO

Your trip is more likely to go smoothly if you plan ahead. Check this list of things to arrange while you're still at home.

You need a **passport**—but no visa or shots—to travel in Italy. You may be denied entry into certain European countries if your passport is due to expire within three to six months of your ticketed date of return. Get it renewed if you'll be cutting it close. It can take up to six weeks to get or renew a passport (for more on passports, see www.travel.state.gov). Pack a photocopy of your passport in your luggage in case the original is lost or stolen.

Book rooms well in advance if you'll be traveling during peak season (summer) and any major holidays (see page 696).

Make museum reservations before your trip or buy a Firenze Card in Florence to avoid standing in long lines for the Uffizi (Renaissance paintings) and Accademia (Michelangelo's *David*). The Uffizi is often booked up a month or more in advance, while the Accademia is usually full at least a few days out. Reservations are explained on page 38, and the Firenze Card on page 34.

Call your **debit- and credit-card companies** to let them know the countries you'll be visiting, to ask about fees, request your PIN code (it will be mailed to you), and more. See page 626 for details.

Do your homework if you want to buy **travel insurance.** Compare the cost of the insurance to the likelihood of your using it and your potential loss if something goes wrong. Also, check whether your existing insurance (health, homeowners, or renters) covers you and your possessions overseas. For more information, see www.ricksteves.com/insurance.

Consider buying a **rail pass** after researching your options

How Was Your Trip?

Were your travels fun, smooth, and meaningful? If you'd like to share your tips, concerns, and discoveries, please fill out the survey at www.ricksteves.com/feedback. I value your feedback. Thanks in advance—it helps a lot.

(see page 678 and www.ricksteves.com/rail for all the specifics). If you're taking an **overnight train** and need a couchette *(cuccetta)* or sleeper—and you must leave on a certain day—consider booking it in advance through a US agent (such as www.ricksteves.com/rail, even though it may cost more than buying it in Italy). Other Italian trains, like the high-speed Frecce trains, require a seat reservation, but for these it's usually possible to make arrangements in Italy just a few days ahead. (For more on train travel, see the Practicalities chapter).

If you're planning on **renting a car** in Italy, bring your driver's license and an International Driving Permit (see page 683). Driving is prohibited in some city centers; if you drive in restricted areas marked with signage and monitored by cameras, you can be fined without a cop ever stopping you (see page 686).

If you plan to hire a **local guide,** reserve ahead by email. Popular guides can get booked up.

If you're bringing a **mobile device,** download any apps you might want to use on the road, such as translators, maps, and transit schedules. Check out **Rick Steves Audio Europe,** featuring travel interviews, audio tours, and other audio content about Florence and Tuscany (see page 9).

Check the **Rick Steves guidebook updates** page for any recent changes to this book (www.ricksteves.com/update).

Because **airline carry-on restrictions** are always changing, visit the Transportation Security Administration's website (www.tsa.gov) for a list of what you can bring on the plane and for the latest security measures (including screening of electronic devices, which you may be asked to power up).

Traveling as a Temporary Local

We travel all the way to Italy to enjoy differences—to become temporary locals. You'll experience frustrations. Certain truths that we find "God-given" or "self-evident," such as cold beer, ice in drinks, bottomless cups of coffee, and bigger being better, are suddenly not so true. One of the benefits of travel is the eye-opening realization that there are logical, civil, and even better alternatives. A willingness to go local ensures that you'll enjoy a full dose of Italian hospitality.

Europeans generally like Americans. But if there is a negative aspect to Italians' image of Americans, it's that we are loud, wasteful, ethnocentric, too informal (which can seem disrespectful), and a bit naive.

Think about the rationale behind "crazy" Italian decisions. For instance, many hoteliers turn off the heat in spring and can't turn on air-conditioning until summer. The point is to conserve energy, and it's mandated by the Italian government. You could complain about being cold or hot...or bring a sweater in winter, and in summer, be prepared to sweat a little like everyone else.

While Italians, flabbergasted by our Yankee excesses, say in disbelief, *"Mi sono cadute le braccia!"* ("I throw my arms down!"), they nearly always afford us individual travelers all the warmth we deserve. Judging from all the happy feedback I receive from travelers who have used this book, it's safe to assume you'll enjoy a great, affordable vacation—with the finesse of an independent, experienced traveler.

Thanks, and *buon viaggio!*

Rick Steves

Back Door Travel Philosophy

From *Rick Steves Europe Through the Back Door*

Travel is intensified living—maximum thrills per minute and one of the last great sources of legal adventure. Travel is freedom. It's recess, and we need it.

Experiencing the real Europe requires catching it by surprise, going casual..."Through the Back Door."

Affording travel is a matter of priorities. (Make do with the old car.) You can eat and sleep—simply, safely, and enjoyably—anywhere in Europe for $125 a day plus transportation costs. In many ways, spending more money only builds a thicker wall between you and what you traveled so far to see. Europe is a cultural carnival, and time after time, you'll find that its best acts are free and the best seats are the cheap ones.

A tight budget forces you to travel close to the ground, meeting and communicating with the people. Never sacrifice sleep, nutrition, safety, or cleanliness to save money. Simply enjoy the local-style alternatives to expensive hotels and restaurants.

Connecting with people carbonates your experience. Extroverts have more fun. If your trip is low on magic moments, kick yourself and make things happen. If you don't enjoy a place, maybe you don't know enough about it. Seek the truth. Recognize tourist traps. Give a culture the benefit of your open mind. See things as different, but not better or worse. Any culture has plenty to share.

Of course, travel, like the world, is a series of hills and valleys. Be fanatically positive and militantly optimistic. If something's not to your liking, change your liking.

Travel can make you a happier American, as well as a citizen of the world. Our Earth is home to seven billion equally precious people. It's humbling to travel and find that other people don't have the "American Dream"—they have their own dreams. Europeans like us, but with all due respect, they wouldn't trade passports.

Thoughtful travel engages us with the world. In tough economic times, it reminds us what is truly important. By broadening perspectives, travel teaches new ways to measure quality of life.

Globetrotting destroys ethnocentricity, helping us understand and appreciate other cultures. Rather than fear the diversity on this planet, celebrate it. Among your most prized souvenirs will be the strands of different cultures you choose to knit into your own character. The world is a cultural yarn shop, and Back Door travelers are weaving the ultimate tapestry. Join in!

FLORENCE
Firenze

ORIENTATION TO FLORENCE

The best of Florence lies on the north bank of the Arno River. The main historical sights cluster around the red-brick dome of the cathedral (Duomo). Everything is within a 20-minute walk of the train station, cathedral, or Ponte Vecchio (Old Bridge). The less famous but more characteristic Oltrarno area (south bank) is just over the bridge.

Though small, Florence is intense. Prepare for scorching summer heat, crowded narrow lanes and sidewalks, slick pickpockets, few WCs, steep prices, and long lines. Easy tourist money has corrupted some locals, making them greedy and dishonest (check your bill carefully).

FLORENCE: A VERBAL MAP

For a big and touristy city, Florence (pop. 420,000) is remarkably compact and easy to navigate. Most of the attractions lie just north of the Arno River, clustered in distinct zones. Here's a neighborhood-by-neighborhood rundown of the city:

Historic Core: The Duomo—with its iconic, towering dome—is the visual and geographical center of Florence; all other sights radiate out from here. The Duomo sits at the northeast corner of the oblong, grid-planned old town (immediately apparent on any map, and dating from Roman times). At the southeast corner is Piazza della Signoria—marked by the tower of Palazzo Vecchio (city hall) and adjacent Uffizi Gallery, with the Galileo Science Museum tucked just behind it. These two main landmarks are connected by the wide, pedestrianized, heavily tourist-trod Via de' Calzaiuoli, which bisects the old Roman town. To the west is a glitzy shopping zone (on the streets near Piazza della Repubblica), and to the east is a characteristic web of narrow lanes. This central axis—Duomo to Piazza della Signoria by way of Via de' Calzaiuoli—is the spine for Florentine sightseeing and the route of my self-guided Renaissance Walk.

Accademia/San Lorenzo (North of the Duomo): Via Cavour runs north from the Duomo, past the Medici-Riccardi Palace and through a nondescript urban zone. For the sightseer, the eastern part of this zone is dominated by the Accademia, with Michelangelo's *David;* nearby are the Museum of San Marco and the quintessentially Renaissance Piazza S.S. Annunziata. The western part clusters around the Church of San Lorenzo, with its Medici Chapels, and (a block north) Mercato Centrale, with the vendor stalls of San Lorenzo Market. The streets immediately surrounding Mercato Centrale (especially the pedestrianized Via Faenza) teem with mid-range and budget hotels, and trattorias catering exclusively to out-of-towners, creating a touristy area that's convenient, but insulates you from a more authentic slice of Florence.

Train Station/Santa Maria Novella (West of the Duomo): Northwest of the historic core, things get a bit more urban and dreary. This area, dominated by the train station and Church of Santa Maria Novella, specializes in inexpensive hotels and characteristic eateries. Closer to the river (especially around Strozzi Palace) is a posh shopping zone, with a more affordable mix of shops lining Via del Parione and Borgo Ognissanti.

Santa Croce (East of the Duomo): Tourists make the 10-minute trek from Piazza della Signoria east to Piazza Santa Croce, facing this neighborhood's main landmark, the Church of Santa Croce. Along the way—effectively across the street from the old town—is the Bargello, filling a former police station with some of Florence's best sculptures. The area stretching north and west from Santa Croce is increasingly authentic and workaday (especially along Via Pietrapiana and Borgo la Croce), offering an insightful glimpse at untouristy Florence just a short walk from the big sights.

Oltrarno (South of the River): Literally the "Other Side of the Arno River," this neighborhood opens up just across Ponte Vecchio from the main tourist zone. While the streets immediately around that bridge are jammed and tacky, two or three blocks away are pockets of Florence from a time before tourism. Many artisans still have workshops here, and open their doors to passing visitors. The Oltrarno is roughly divided in half by the giant Pitti Palace and surrounding gardens (Boboli and Bardini). To the west of the palace are the borderline-seedy Piazza di Santo Spirito (with its namesake church) and—a bit farther out—the Church of Santa Maria del Carmine, with its lavishly frescoed Brancacci Chapel. To the east of Pitti and the gardens, perched high on the hill, is the magnificent-view Church of San Miniato; just below that sits Piazzale Michelangelo (with Florence's most popular viewpoint), and tucked below and between there and the river is the lively and

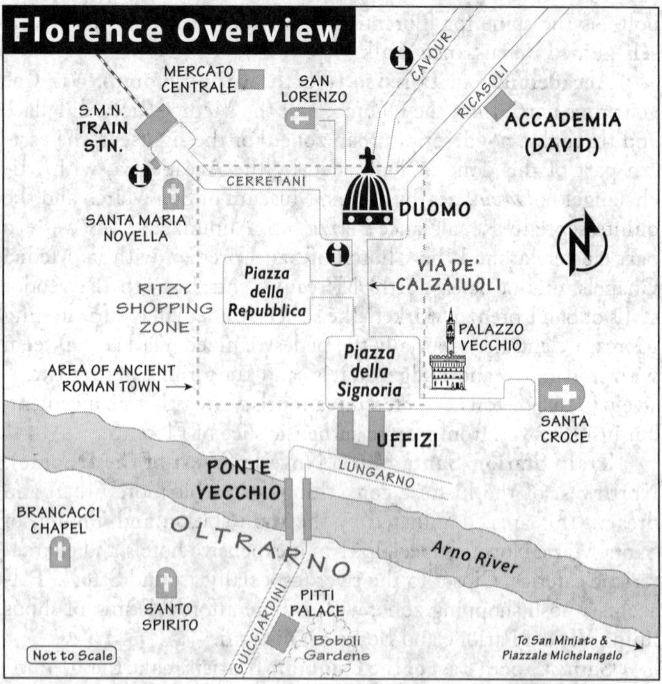

funky little San Niccolò neighborhood, with lively bars and trendy restaurants.

Farther Out: Everything mentioned above is within about a 30-minute walk of the Duomo. To venture farther, one popular choice is the adjacent, hilltop town of Fiesole (to the northeast, with archaeological sites and fine views). But in all directions, Florence is hemmed in by forested Tuscan hills with picturesque cypress-lined roads connecting lavish villas.

PLANNING YOUR TIME

Set up a good itinerary in advance. Do my recommended Renaissance Walk in the morning or late afternoon to avoid heat and crowds. Stop often for gelato.

Skipping Lines at Major Sights: The plans outlined here assume that you'll use my strategies to avoid wasting hours in line for the big attractions—especially the Uffizi Gallery and Accademia (starring Michelangelo's *David*). These sights nearly always have long ticket-buying lines, especially in peak season (April-Oct) and on holiday weekends. Crowds thin out on off-season weekdays. (Note that both of these major sights are closed on Monday.) Whatever time of year you visit, you have two easy options for skipping lines: **Make reservations** (see page 38) or buy a **Firenze**

Card (see page 34). Another place where you're likely to encounter lines are the Duomo sights, especially for climbing to the top of the dome or the Campanile (bell tower). These sights don't take reservations, but you can skip the lines at each one with a Firenze Card—or you can try visiting at a time when it's less crowded (I've noted these times, as well as more crowd-beating tips for several other sights, throughout this book).

The Firenze Card makes things very easy—just show up and flash your card—but it's very expensive. Because the card is valid for three days, it's not a good value if you're in town for just one or two days—buy one only if you want to pay a premium to skip lines. For a three-day visit with lots of sightseeing, the Firenze Card becomes (somewhat) more financially viable.

Closures: Some sights close early; see the early closing warning in the "Daily Reminder," later in this chapter. In general, Sundays and Mondays are not ideal for sightseeing, as many places are either closed or have shorter hours.

Florence in One Brutal Day

8:30	Accademia *(David).*
10:00	Take Renaissance Walk through town center and climb the Campanile or Duomo's dome.
12:00	Bargello (best statues).
13:30	Grab a quick lunch in or near Mercato Centrale.
14:00	Shopping at San Lorenzo Market (or elsewhere).
16:30	Uffizi Gallery (finest paintings).
19:30	Cross Ponte Vecchio and take the Oltrarno Walk (best local color) and have dinner across the river at 21:00.

Florence in Two Days

Day 1

8:30	Accademia *(David).*
10:00	Museum of San Marco (art by Fra Angelico).
12:00	Explore Mercato Centrale and have lunch there.
14:00	Medici Chapels (Michelangelo sculptures, closes early in winter).
16:30	Baptistery (closes at 14:00 on Sun).
17:00	Climb the Campanile or Duomo's dome.
18:00	Renaissance Walk through heart of old town (Duomo and Orsanmichele Church interiors closed in evening, but skippable).
20:00	Dinner in the old center.

Day 2

9:00	Bargello (great statues).

11:00 Galileo Science Museum or Santa Croce Church (opens at 14:00 on Sun). The Duomo Museum, with statues by Donatello and Michelangelo, is also a good choice (though closed through late 2015).
13:00 Lunch, then wander and shop.
15:00 Take a bike or walking tour.
17:00 Uffizi Gallery (best paintings).
19:00 Cross Ponte Vecchio for the Oltrarno Walk.
21:00 Dinner in Oltrarno.

Florence in Three (or More) Days

Day 1

8:30 Accademia *(David)*.
10:00 Museum of San Marco (Fra Angelico).
11:00 Explore San Lorenzo Market area, do some shopping, and browse for lunch in or near Mercato Centrale.
14:00 Medici Chapels (Michelangelo).
15:00 Baptistery (closes at 14:00 on Sun).
15:30 Climb the Campanile or Duomo's dome.
17:00 Renaissance Walk through heart of old town.
19:00 Explore and shop the Piazza della Signoria/Ponte Vecchio area.
20:00 Dinner in the old center.

If you'd like to squeeze in a walking or bike tour to get oriented, just spend a bit less time shopping and wandering.

Day 2

9:00 Bargello (top statues).
11:00 Galileo Science Museum or Santa Croce Church (opens at 14:00 on Sun).
13:00 Lunch, then wander and shop.
15:30 Uffizi Gallery (unforgettable paintings).
18:00 Cross Ponte Vecchio, take the Oltrarno Walk, and have dinner in Oltrarno.

Day 3

9:00 Whatever you didn't get to yesterday morning (Santa Croce or Galileo); also consider the Gucci Museum or other sights in the old center.

13:00 Lunch and time to shop, relax, or get to any sights you haven't seen yet (you could circle back to the daytime Oltrarno sights—Brancacci Chapel and Pitti Palace—or tour the Church of Santa Maria Novella, near the train station).

16:00 San Miniato Church (Gregorian chants generally at 18:30), Piazzale Michelangelo (city views), walk back into town.

Day 4

Side-trip to Siena (sights open daily; 1.25 hours away by bus), or consider an overnight stay to enjoy the town at twilight.

Day 5 (or More)

Visit your pick of Pisa, Lucca, and Tuscan hill towns—or take a cooking class.

ARRIVAL IN FLORENCE

For a rundown on Florence's train station, the bus station (next to the train station), and nearby airports—as well as tips for arriving by car or cruise ship—see the Florence Connections chapter.

TOURIST INFORMATION

Florence has two separate TI organizations.

The city TI has three different branches. The very crowded main branch is across the square from the **train station** (Mon-Sat 9:00-19:00, Sun 9:00-14:00; with your back to tracks, exit the station—it's 100 yards away, across the square in wall near corner of church at Piazza Stazione 4; tel. 055-212-245, www.firenzeturismo.it). Upstairs from this branch, drop by the easy-to-miss "Experience Florence" visitors center, with big touchscreens to help you virtually explore the city and plan an itinerary, and a surprisingly well-produced 3-D movie about the city, offering tasteful and evocative slices of Florentine life and lingering images of the big landmarks (free, 13 minutes, in Italian with English subtitles, open same hours as TI).

The smaller branch is very centrally located at **Piazza del Duomo,** at the west corner of Via Calzaiuoli (it's inside the Bigallo Museum/Loggia; Mon-Sat 9:00-19:00, Sun 9:00-14:00, tel. 055-288-496). They also have a branch at the **airport.**

The other TI, which covers both the city and the greater province of Florence, tends to be less crowded and more helpful. It's a couple of blocks **north of the Duomo,** just past Medici-Riccardi

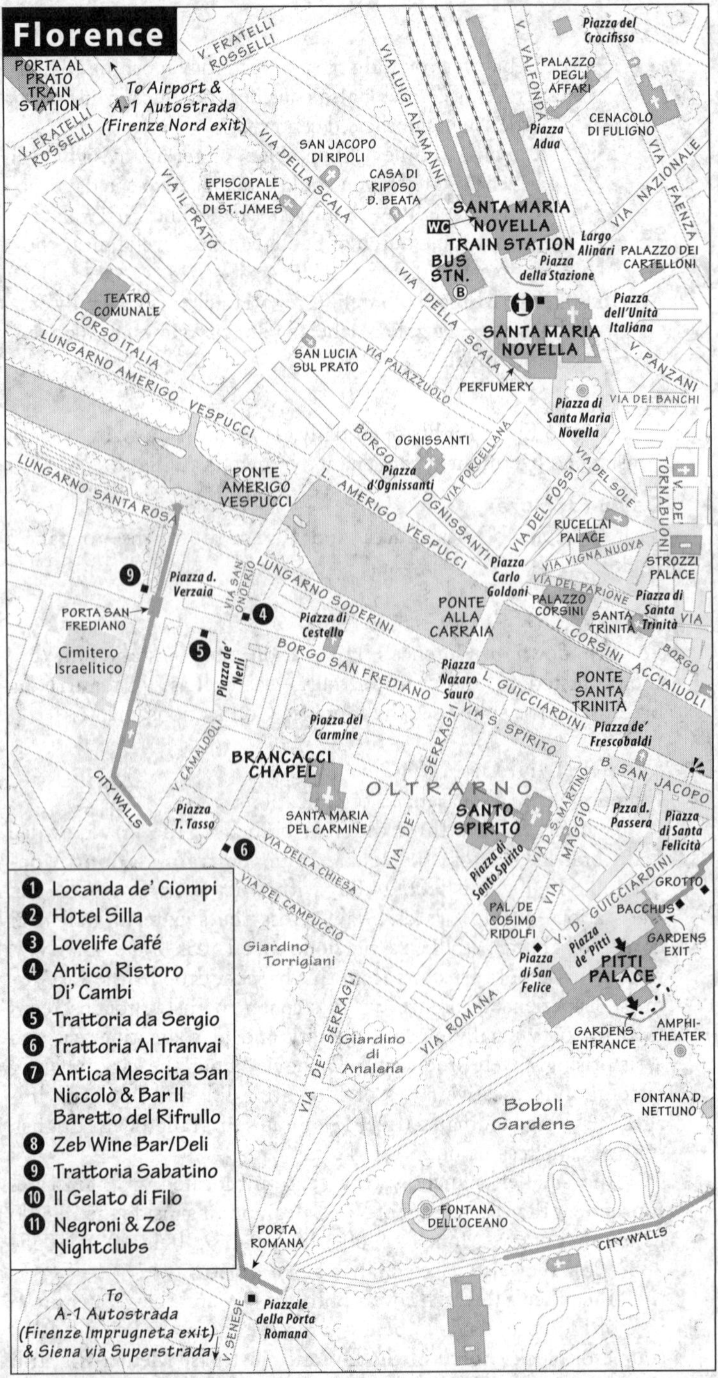
Florence
PORTA AL PRATO TRAIN STATION
To Airport & A-1 Autostrada (Firenze Nord exit)
V. FRATELLI ROSSELLI
VIA LUIGI ALAMANNI
V. VALFONDA
Piazza del Crocifisso
PALAZZO DEGLI AFFARI
CENACOLO DI FULIGNO
Piazza Adua
VIA FAENZA
VIA NAZIONALE
VIA DELLA SCALA
SAN JACOPO DI RIPOLI
CASA DI RIPOSO D. BEATA
EPISCOPALE AMERICANA DI ST. JAMES
VIA IL PRATO
WC
SANTA MARIA NOVELLA TRAIN STATION
BUS STN.
Largo Alinari
PALAZZO DEI CARTELLONI
Piazza della Stazione
TEATRO COMUNALE
CORSO ITALIA
LUNGARNO AMERIGO VESPUCCI
SAN LUCIA SUL PRATO
VIA PALAZZUOLO
SANTA MARIA NOVELLA
Piazza dell'Unità Italiana
V. PANZANI
PERFUMERY
Piazza di Santa Maria Novella
VIA DEI BANCHI
OGNISSANTI
BORGO OGNISSANTI
Piazza d'Ognissanti
VIA PORCELLANA
VIA DEL SOLE
V. DE' TORNABUONI
PONTE AMERIGO VESPUCCI
LUNGARNO SANTA ROSA
L. AMERIGO VESPUCCI
VIA DEL FOSSI
RUCELLAI PALACE
VIA VIGNA NUOVA
STROZZI PALACE
VIA DEL PARIONE
Piazza Carlo Goldoni
Piazza d. Verzaia
VIA SAN ONOFRIO
LUNGARNO SODERINI
PONTE ALLA CARRAIA
PALAZZO CORSINI
SANTA TRINITÀ
Piazza di Santa Trinità
PORTA SAN FREDIANO
Piazza di Cestello
L. CORSINI
BORGO ACCIAIUOLI
Cimitero Israelitico
Piazza de' Nerli
BORGO SAN FREDIANO
Piazza Nazaro Sauro
PONTE SANTA TRINITÀ
L. GUICCIARDINI
VIA S. SPIRITO
Piazza del Carmine
V. CAMALDOLI
VIA DE' SERRAGLI
Piazza de' Frescobaldi
BRANCACCI CHAPEL
OLTRARNO
B. SAN JACOPO
CITY WALLS
Piazza T. Tasso
SANTA MARIA DEL CARMINE
SANTO SPIRITO
VIA D. S. MARTINO
VIA MAGGIO
Pzza d. Passera
Piazza di Santa Felicità
VIA DELLA CHIESA
Piazza di Santo Spirito
V. D. GUICCIARDINI
GROTTO
VIA DEL CAMPUCCIO
PAL. DE COSIMO RIDOLFI
BACCHUS
Piazza de' Pitti
GARDENS EXIT
Giardino Torrigiani
Piazza di San Felice
PITTI PALACE
VIA ROMANA
GARDENS ENTRANCE
AMPHI-THEATER
Giardino di Analena
Boboli Gardens
FONTANA D. NETTUNO
FONTANA DELL'OCEANO
CITY WALLS
PORTA ROMANA
To A-1 Autostrada (Firenze Impruneta exit) & Siena via Superstrada
V. SENESE
Piazzale della Porta Romana
1 Locanda de' Ciompi
2 Hotel Silla
3 Lovelife Café
4 Antico Ristoro Di' Cambi
5 Trattoria da Sergio
6 Trattoria Al Tranvai
7 Antica Mescita San Niccolò & Bar Il Baretto del Rifrullo
8 Zeb Wine Bar/Deli
9 Trattoria Sabatino
10 Il Gelato di Filo
11 Negroni & Zoe Nightclubs

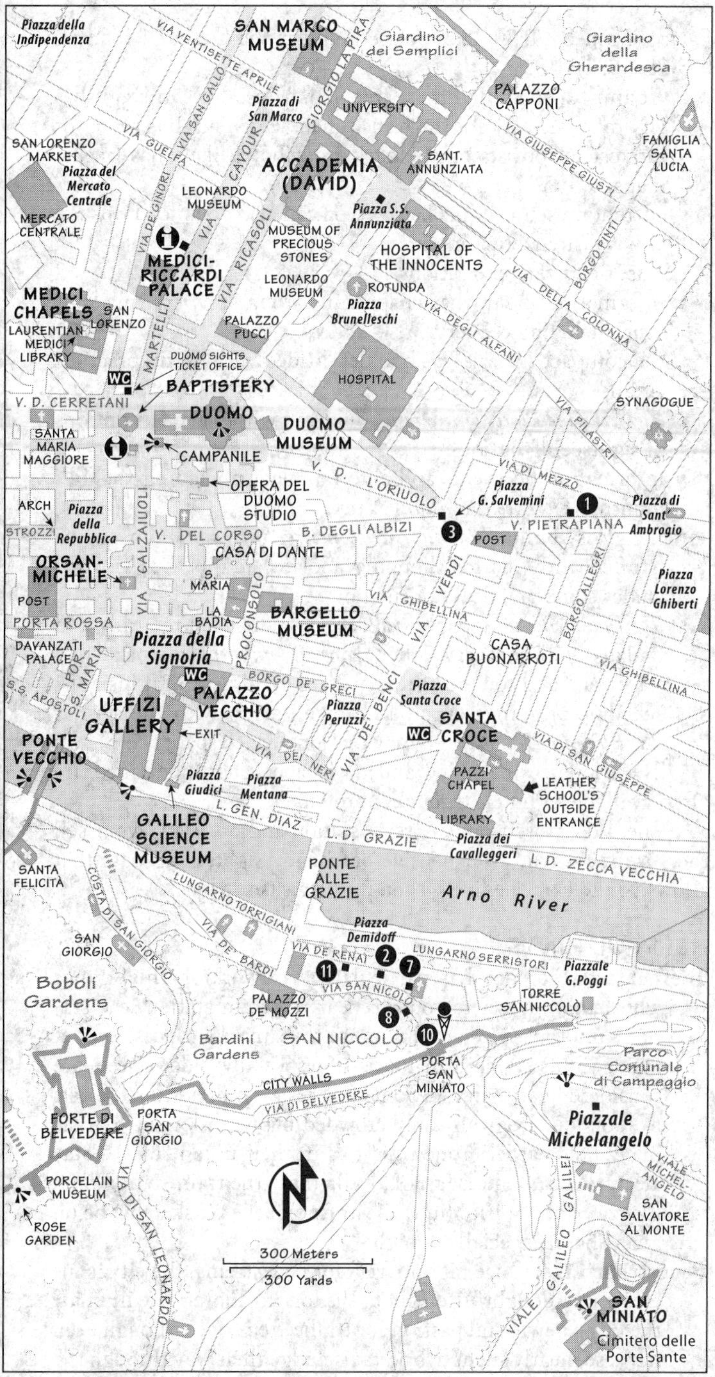
Piazza della Indipendenza
VIA VENTISETTE APRILE
SAN MARCO MUSEUM
Giardino dei Semplici
Giardino della Gherardesca
VIA GIORGIO LA PIRA
Piazza di San Marco
UNIVERSITY
PALAZZO CAPPONI
VIA SAN GALLO
VIA CAVOUR
VIA GUELFA
SAN LORENZO MARKET
Piazza del Mercato Centrale
MERCATO CENTRALE
ACCADEMIA (DAVID)
SANT. ANNUNZIATA
VIA GIUSEPPE GIUSTI
FAMIGLIA SANTA LUCIA
LEONARDO MUSEUM
VIA DE' GINORI
Piazza S.S. Annunziata
VIA RICASOLI
MUSEUM OF PRECIOUS STONES
HOSPITAL OF THE INNOCENTS
BORGO PINTI
MEDICI-RICCARDI PALACE
LEONARDO MUSEUM
ROTUNDA
Piazza Brunelleschi
VIA DELLA COLONNA
MEDICI CHAPELS
SAN LORENZO
LAURENTIAN MEDICI LIBRARY
MARTELLI
PALAZZO PUCCI
VIA DEGLI ALFANI
DUOMO SIGHTS TICKET OFFICE
WC
BAPTISTERY
HOSPITAL
V. D. CERRETANI
VIA PILASTRI
SYNAGOGUE
DUOMO
DUOMO MUSEUM
SANTA MARIA MAGGIORE
CAMPANILE
V. D. L'ORIUOLO
VIA DI MEZZO
OPERA DEL DUOMO STUDIO
Piazza G. Salvemini
1
Piazza di Sant' Ambrogio
ARCH
Piazza della Repubblica
STROZZI
V. DEL CORSO
B. DEGLI ALBIZI
3
V. PIETRAPIANA
POST
CASA DI DANTE
VIA CALZAIUOLI
ORSANMICHELE
S. MARIA
PROCONSOLO
VIA VERDI
BORGO ALLEGRI
Piazza Lorenzo Ghiberti
POST
VIA GHIBELLINA
PORTA ROSSA
LA BADIA
BARGELLO MUSEUM
DAVANZATI PALACE
Piazza della Signoria
CASA BUONARROTI
POR S. MARIA
WC
VIA GHIBELLINA
BORGO DE' GRECI
VIA DE' BENCI
Piazza Santa Croce
S.S. APOSTOLI
UFFIZI GALLERY
PALAZZO VECCHIO
Piazza Peruzzi
SANTA CROCE
WC
EXIT
PONTE VECCHIO
VIA DEI NERI
VIA DI SAN GIUSEPPE
PAZZI CHAPEL
LEATHER SCHOOL'S OUTSIDE ENTRANCE
Piazza Giudici
Piazza Mentana
GALILEO SCIENCE MUSEUM
L. GEN. DIAZ
LIBRARY
Piazza dei Cavalleggeri
L. D. GRAZIE
L. D. ZECCA VECCHIA
SANTA FELICITÀ
PONTE ALLE GRAZIE
Arno River
COSTA DI SAN GIORGIO
LUNGARNO TORRIGIANI
Piazza Demidoff
VIA DE' BARDI
SAN GIORGIO
VIA DE RENAI
2
LUNGARNO SERRISTORI
7
11
Piazzale G.Poggi
Boboli Gardens
VIA SAN NICCOLÒ
PALAZZO DE' MOZZI
TORRE SAN NICCOLÒ
8
Bardini Gardens
SAN NICCOLÒ
10
PORTA SAN MINIATO
Parco Comunale di Campeggio
CITY WALLS
VIA DI BELVEDERE
FORTE DI BELVEDERE
PORTA SAN GIORGIO
Piazzale Michelangelo
VIALE MICHELANGELO
PORCELAIN MUSEUM
VIA DI SAN LEONARDO
N
SAN SALVATORE AL MONTE
ROSE GARDEN
VIALE GALILEO
300 Meters
300 Yards
SAN MINIATO
Cimitero delle Porte Sante

Palace (Mon-Sat 8:30-18:30, closed Sun, at Via Cavour 1 red, tel. 055-290-832).

At any TI, you'll find these free, handy resources in English:

- city map (also ask for the transit map, which has bus routes of interest to tourists on the back; your hotel likely has freebie maps, too)
- current museum-hours listing (you can also download this list at www.firenzeturismo.it)
- a list of current exhibitions
- information about what's happening around town during your visit, including concerts
- the compact *Firenze Info* booklet, loaded with useful practical details
- *Firenze: The Places of Interest*, a fold-out with brief descriptions of sightseeing options
- information on events and entertainment, including the TI's monthly *Florence & Tuscany News*
- the glossy bimonthly *Florence Concierge Information* magazine (stuffed with ads for shopping and restaurants, but also includes some practical information)
- *The Florentine* newspaper (in English, published monthly and updated online every other Thu at www.theflorentine.net, for expats and tourists, great articles giving cultural insights, schedule of goings-on around town), along with the similar *The Florence Newspaper* (www.theflorencenewspaper.com).

The Florence magazine and newspapers just mentioned are often available at hotels throughout town.

The TIs across from the train station and on Via Cavour sell the **Firenze Card,** an expensive but handy sightseeing pass that allows you to skip the lines at top museums (see page 34).

HELPFUL HINTS

Theft Alert: Florence has particularly hardworking thief gangs who hang out where you do: near the train station, the station's underpass (especially where the tunnel surfaces), and at major sights. American tourists—especially older ones—are considered easy targets. Some thieves even dress like tourists to fool you. Logically, any crowded bus with lots of tourists likely holds at least one thief (it's in their union rules)—stay alert. Piazza Santa Maria Novella (near the train station) and Piazza Santo Spirito (in the Oltrarno) feel a bit sketchy; be on guard here, especially at night.

Pedestrian Tips: Once nightmarish for pedestrians, the city is increasingly delightful on foot. Visitors to Florence will enjoy the city's newfound passion for traffic-free zones (though even in these, nearly silent hybrid taxis nudge their way through the crowds with a persistent beep-beep-beep). However, particularly on trafficked streets, just getting from place to place can still be stressful: Chunky stone window frames and heavy iron grates around windows bully pedestrians off of the extremely narrow sidewalks and into the streets, which are temptingly empty...until a motor scooter or car whips around the corner at top speed. Walking down the street is a contact sport; Florentines think nothing of brushing, nudging, and bumping passersby, which can challenge those of us used to a bit more personal space.

Medical Help: There's no shortage of English-speaking medical help in Florence. To reach a doctor who speaks English, call **Medical Service Firenze** at 055-475-411 (mobile 339-297-0302); the phone is answered 24/7. Rates are reasonable. For a doctor to come to your hotel within an hour of your call, you'd pay €100-200 (higher rates apply on Sun, holidays, or for late visits). You pay only €50 if you go to the clinic when the doctor's in (Mon-Fri 11:00-12:00, 13:00-15:00 & 17:00-18:00, Sat 11:00-12:00 & 13:00-15:00, closed Sun, no appointment necessary, Via Roma 4, between the Duomo and Piazza della Repubblica).

Dr. Stephen Kerr is an English doctor specializing in helping sick tourists (drop-in clinic open Mon-Fri 15:00-17:00, other times by appointment, €50/visit, Piazza Mercato Nuovo 1, between Piazza della Repubblica and Ponte Vecchio, tel. 055-288-055, mobile 335-836-1682, www.dr-kerr.com). The TI has a list of other English-speaking doctors.

There are 24-hour **pharmacies** at the train station and on Borgo San Lorenzo (near the Baptistery).

Museum Strategies: If you want to see a lot of museums, the pricey Firenze Card—which saves you from having to wait in line or make reservations for the Uffizi and Accademia—can be a worthwhile investment (see page 34).

Visiting Churches: Some churches operate like museums, charging an admission fee to see their art treasures. Modest dress for men, women, and even children is required in some churches (including the Duomo, Santa Maria Novella, Santa Croce, Santa Maria del Carmine/Brancacci Chapel, and the Medici Chapels). I recommend no bare shoulders, short shorts, or short skirts at any church. Many churches let you borrow or buy a cheap, disposable poncho for instant respectability. Be respectful of worshippers and the paintings; don't use a flash. Churches usually close from 12:00 or 12:30 until 15:00 or 16:00.

Addresses: For reasons beyond human understanding, Florence has a ridiculously confusing system for street addresses, with separate numbering for businesses (red) and residences (black). In print, this designation is sometimes indicated by a letter following the number: "r" = red, for *rosso*; no indication or "n" = black, for *nero*. While usually black, B&B addresses can be either. The red and black numbers each appear in roughly consecutive order on streets, but bear no apparent connection with each other. The numbers are usually color-coded on street signs (red numbers are very fine, and the red hue has sometimes faded; the black numbers are thicker, bolder, and—mysteriously—sometimes blue). I'm lazy and don't concern myself with the distinction (if one number's wrong, I look nearby for the other) and can easily find my way around.

Chill Out: Schedule several breaks into your sightseeing when you can sit, pause, cool off, and refresh yourself with a sandwich, gelato, or coffee. Carry a water bottle to refill at Florence's twist-the-handle public fountains (near the Duomo dome entrance, around the corner from the "Piglet" at Mercato Nuovo, or in front of Pitti Palace). Try the *fontanello* (dispenser of free cold water, *frizzante* or *naturale*) on Piazza della Signoria, behind the statue of Neptune (on the left side of Palazzo Vecchio).

Internet Access: Virtually all Florence hotels have **Wi-Fi** free for guests, and many cafés and restaurants will tell you their network password if you buy something. The free Wi-Fi hotspot network you may see advertised is spotty, and the system for using it seems constantly in flux; pick up a brochure with details at the TI if you want to give it a try. If you need an Internet café with terminals, ask your hotelier or check the touristy area near San Lorenzo Market and the train station (especially along Via Faenza, a pincushion of tourist services).

Bookstores: For a good selection of brand-name guidebooks (including mine), try one of these shops. The first two are locally owned and carry only English books. **Paperback Exchange** has the widest selection and also deals in used books (Mon-Fri 9:00-19:30, Sat 10:30-19:30, closed Sun, just south of the Duomo on Via delle Oche 4 red, tel. 055-293-460). **B & M Books & Fine Art** is a bit smaller but also has a great Italian interest section (Tue-Sat 11:00-19:00, closed Sun-Mon, near Ponte alla Carraia at Borgo Ognissanti 4 red, tel. 055-294-575). **RED** (stands for "Read, Eat, Dream"), a flagship store for the Feltrinelli chain (the Italian Barnes & Noble) with a café and restaurant inside, has a small selection of English books (open long hours daily, on Piazza della Repubblica). For locations of these bookstores, see the map on page 320.

WCs: Public restrooms are scarce. Use them when you can, in any café or museum you patronize. Pay public WCs are typically

€1. Convenient locations include one at the Baptistery ticket office (near the Duomo); just down the street from Piazza Santa Croce (at Borgo Santa Croce 29 red); up near Piazzale Michelangelo; and inside the train station (near track 5). The free WC inside Palazzo Vecchio's courtyard (inside the ticket office, at the far end of the hall) is accessible even if you don't buy a ticket.

Laundry: The **Wash & Dry Lavarapido** chain offers long hours and efficient, self-service launderettes at several locations (about €8 for wash and dry, change machine but bring plenty of coins just in case, daily 8:00-22:00, tel. 055-580-480). These are close to recommended hotels: Via dei Servi 105 red (near *David*), Via del Sole 29 red and Via della Scala 52-54 red (between train station and river), Via Ghibellina 143 red (Palazzo Vecchio), and Via dei Serragli 87 red (across the river in Oltrarno neighborhood). For more options, ask your hotelier or the TI.

Bike Rental: The **city of Florence** rents bikes cheaply at the train station (€2/1 hour, €5/5 hours, €10/day, mobile 346-883-7821; information at any TI). **Florence by Bike** rents two-wheelers of all sizes (€3/hour, €9/5 hours, includes bike lock and helmet, child seat-€3 extra; Mon-Fri 9:00-13:00 & 15:30-19:30, Sat 9:00-19:00, Sun 9:00-17:00, closed Sun Nov-March; a 15-minute walk north of the Duomo at Via San Zanobi 120 red, tel. 055-488-992, www.florencebybike.it).

Travel Agency: While it's easy to buy train tickets to destinations within Italy at handy machines at the station, travel agencies can be more convenient and helpful for getting international tickets, reservations, and supplements. The cost may be the same, or there may be a minimal charge. Ask your hotelier for the nearest travel agency.

Updates to This Book: For updates to this book, check www.ricksteves.com/update.

GETTING AROUND FLORENCE

I organize my sightseeing geographically and do it all on foot. I think of Florence as a Renaissance treadmill—it requires a lot of walking. You likely won't need public transit, except maybe to head up to Piazzale Michelangelo and San Miniato Church for the view, or to Fiesole.

Buses: The city's full-size buses don't cover the old center well (the whole area around the Duomo is off-limits to motorized traffic). The TI hands out a map of transit routes (information also available on their website—www.firenzeturismo.it). Of the many bus lines, I find these to be of most value for seeing outlying sights:

Buses **#12** and **#13** go from the train station to Porta Romana,

Daily Reminder

Sunday: The Duomo's dome, Museum of Precious Stones, and Mercato Centrale are closed. The Baptistery's interior closes early, at 14:00.

A few sights are open only in the afternoon: Duomo (13:30-16:45), Santa Croce Church (14:00-17:30), Church of San Lorenzo (13:30-17:30 except closed Nov-Feb), Brancacci Chapel (13:00-17:00), and Church of Santa Maria Novella (12:00-17:00, from 13:00 Oct-June).

The Museum of San Marco and the Bargello are closed on the first, third, and fifth Sundays of the month. Palazzo Davanzati and the Medici Chapels close on the second and fourth Sundays. (Need a calendar to determine the ordinal order? Look in the appendix.)

Monday: The biggies are closed, including the Accademia *(David)* and the Uffizi Gallery, as well as the Pitti Palace's Palatine Gallery, Royal Apartments, and Gallery of Modern Art.

The Museum of San Marco and the Bargello close on the second and fourth Mondays. At Pitti Palace, the Boboli and Bardini Gardens, Argenti/Silverworks Museum, Costume Gallery, and Porcelain Museum close on the first and last Mondays. Palazzo Davanzati and the Medici Chapels are closed on the first, third, and fifth Mondays. San Lorenzo Market is closed Mondays in winter.

Target these sights on Mondays: the Duomo and its dome, Campanile, Baptistery, Medici-Riccardi Palace, Brancacci Chapel, Mercato Nuovo, Mercato Centrale, Casa Buonarroti, Galileo Science Museum, Palazzo Vecchio, and churches (including Santa Croce and Santa Maria Novella). Or take a walking tour.

Tuesday: Casa Buonarroti and the Brancacci Chapel are closed. The Galileo Science Museum closes early (13:00).

Wednesday: All sights are open, except for the Medici-Riccardi Palace and Santo Spirito Church.

up to San Miniato Church and Piazzale Michelangelo, and on to Santa Croce.

Bus **#7** goes from Piazza San Marco (near the Accademia and Museum of San Marco) to Fiesole, a small town with big views of Florence.

The train station and Piazza San Marco are two major hubs near the city center; to get between these two, either walk (about 15 minutes) or take bus #1, #6, #14, or #23.

Fun little **minibuses** (many of them electric—*elettrico*) wind through the tangled old center of town and up and down the river—just €1.20 gets you a 1.5-hour joyride. These buses, which

Thursday: All sights are open, though the following close early: Palazzo Vecchio (14:00) and off-season, the Duomo (16:00 May and Oct, 16:30 Nov-April).

Friday: All sights are open.

Saturday: All sights are open, but the Duomo's dome closes earlier than usual, at 17:40.

Early-Closing Warning: Some of Florence's sights close surprisingly early most days, as early as 13:50 for the following sights—the Bargello (unless it's hosting a special exhibit, when it closes at 17:00), Palazzo Davanzati, Medici Chapels (early closure off-season only), and the Museum of San Marco (on weekdays only, open later on Sat and when open on Sun). The Museum of Precious Stones closes at 14:00, as does Mercato Centrale (except in winter, when it stays open until 17:00 on Sat).

Late-Hours Relief: The Accademia and the Pitti Palace's Palatine Gallery, Royal Apartments, and Gallery of Modern Art are open until 18:50 (and the Uffizi until 18:35) daily except Monday.

Several sights are open until 19:00 on certain days: San Lorenzo Market (daily, but closed Mon in winter), the Duomo's dome (Mon-Fri), and the Baptistery (Mon-Sat, except first Sat of month until 14:00).

These sights are open until 19:30: Campanile (daily), and in summer, the Pitti Palace's Boboli and Bardini Gardens, Costume Gallery, Argenti/Silverworks Museum, and Porcelain Museum (daily except some Mon, June-Aug only). The San Miniato Church is open daily until 20:00 (closes at 19:00 in winter). Mercato Nuovo is open long hours daily.

In summer (April-Sept), the best late-hours sightseeing is at Palazzo Vecchio, which stays open until 24:00 (except on Thu, when it closes at 14:00); off-season, it's still open relatively late (Fri-Wed until 19:00).

run every 10 minutes from 7:00 to 21:00 (less frequent on Sun), are popular with sore-footed sightseers and eccentric local seniors.

Bus **#C1** stops behind Palazzo Vecchio and Piazza Santa Croce, then heads north, passing near San Marco and the Accademia before ending up at Piazza Libertà. On its southbound route, this bus also stops near the Church of San Lorenzo.

Bus **#C2** twists through the congested old center from the train station, passing near Piazza della Repubblica and Piazza della Signoria to Piazza Beccaria.

Bus **#C3** goes up and down the Arno River, with stops near Ponte Vecchio, the Carraia bridge to the Oltrarno (including Pitti Palace), and beyond.

Bus **#D** goes from the train station to Ponte Vecchio, cruises through the Oltrarno (passing Pitti Palace), and finishes at Ponte San Niccolò.

The minibuses connect many major parking lots with the historic center (tickets sold at machines at lots).

Buy bus tickets at tobacco shops *(tabacchi)*, newsstands, or the ATAF bus office on the west side of the train station (under the "digital" clock) on Piazza della Stazione (€1.20/90 minutes, €4.70/4 tickets, €5/24 hours, €12/3 days, €18/week, day passes aren't always available in tobacco shops, tel. 800-424-500, www.ataf.net). Be sure to validate your ticket in the machine on board. You can sometimes buy tickets on board, but you'll pay more (€2) and you'll need exact change. City buses are free with the Firenze Card (see page 34). Follow general bus etiquette: Board at front or rear doors, exit out the center.

Taxi: The minimum cost for a taxi ride is €5 (or €8.30 after 22:00, or €7 on Sundays); rides in the center of town should be charged as tariff #1. A taxi ride from the train station to the Duomo costs about €8. Taxi fares and supplements (e.g., €2 extra if you call a cab rather than hail one) are clearly explained on signs in each taxi. Look for an official, regulated cab: It should have a yellow banner on the door that says *Taxi/Comune di Firenze* with a red fleur-de-lis, and should be marked with one of the official phone numbers (4390 or 4242). Before getting in a cab at a stand or on the street, ask for an approximate cost (*"Più o meno, quanto costa?"* pew oh MEH-noh, KWAHN-toh KOH-stah). If you can't get a straight answer or the price is outrageous, wait for the next one. It can be hard to find a cab on the street; to call one, dial 055-4390 or 055-4242 (or ask your waiter or hotelier to call for you).

Tours in Florence

Tour companies big and small offer plenty of excursions that go out to smaller towns in the Tuscan countryside (the most popular day trips: Siena, San Gimignano, Pisa, and into Chianti country for wine-tasting). Florence city tours are readily available, but for most people, the city is really best on foot (and the book you're holding provides as much information as you'll get with a generic bus tour). To sightsee on your own, download my series of free audio tours that illuminate some of Florence's top sights and neighborhoods (see sidebar on page 9 for details).

For extra insight with a personal touch, consider the tour companies and individual Florentine guides listed here. Hardworking and creative, they offer a worthwhile array of organized sightseeing activities. Study their websites for details. If you're taking a city tour, remember that individuals save money with a scheduled public tour (such as those offered daily by Florencetown or ArtViva). If you're traveling as a family or small group, however, you're likely to save money by booking a private guide (since rates are hourly for any size of group).

WALKING (AND BIKING) TOURS

While I've outlined the general offerings for each company, check their websites or pick up their brochures to confirm specific times and prices.

ArtViva

This well-established company offers an intriguingly eclectic variety of tours. Most of their guides are native English speakers, and groups are small (maximum 18 adults). Popular choices include their overview tours ("Original Florence" 3-hour town walk for €29; "Florence in One Glorious Day" for €99 combines town walk and tours of the Uffizi and Accademia, more than 6 hours total), as well as their individual museum tours (Uffizi Gallery, €49, 2.25 hours; "Original *David*" Accademia tour, €36, 1 hour; all museum tours include admission). They also have cooking classes (see page 307), minibus tours around Tuscany and to the Cinque Terre, and some more unusual offerings: an Italian-language lesson taught while strolling the town, a "Haunting Florence" walk, a sommelier class, and an edgy "Sex, Drugs, and Renaissance" tour that examines the unseemly side of the city's history. For the full list, check their website or pick up their brochure. They offer a 10 percent discount for my readers: If booking online, go to www.artviva.com/ricksteves, and log in with username "ricksteves" and password "reader" (office near Piazza della Repubblica at Via de' Sassetti 1, second floor, above Odeon Cinema, Mon-Sat 8:00-18:00, Sun 8:30-13:30, tel. 055-264-5033 during day or mobile 329-613-2730 from 18:00-20:00, www.artviva.com).

Florencetown

This well-organized company runs a variety of English-language tours on foot or by bike. The boss, Luca Perfetto, offers student rates (10 percent discount) to anyone with this book, with an additional 10 percent off for second tours (if booking on their website, enter the code "RICKSTEVES" when prompted). Their most popular offerings are the "Walk and Talk Florence" tour that hits all the basic spots, including the Oltrarno neighborhood (€19, 2.5 hours), and the "I Bike Florence" tour, which gives you 2.5 hours on a vintage one-speed bike following a fast-talking guide on a blitz of the town's top sights (€25, helmets optional, 15 stops on both sides of the river; in bad weather, the bike tours go as a walking tour). They also have a cooking class that includes a market tour (see page 307). Their office is two blocks from Palazzo Vecchio at

Via de Lamberti 1 (find steps off Via de' Calzaiuoli on the river side of Orsanmichele Church); they also have a "Tourist Point" kiosk on Piazza della Repubblica, under the arches at the corner with Via Pellicceria (tel. 055-281-103, www.florencetown.com).

Walks Inside Florence

Two art historians—Paola Barubiani and Marzia Valbonesi—and their partners provide quality guided tours. Their company offers a daily 2.5-hour introductory tour (€55/person, 8 people maximum; outside except for a visit to see *David*—Accademia entry fee not included) and three-hour private tours (€180, €60/hour for more time, price is for groups of up to 6 people). They also offer an insightful shopping tour that features well-selected artisans; a guided evening walk; cooking classes with a market visit; private cruise excursions from the port of Livorno; an "art for foodies" tour that combines a visit to art highlights with a market tour; and more—see their website for details (ask about Rick Steves rate for any tour, Paola's mobile 335-526-6496, www.walksinsideflorence.com, paola@walksinsideflorence.it).

Florentia

Top-notch private walking tours—geared for thoughtful, well-heeled travelers with longer-than-average attention spans—are led by Florentine scholars. The tours range from introductory city walks and museum visits to in-depth thematic walks, such as the Oltrarno neighborhood, Jewish Florence, and family-oriented tours (tours start at €250, includes personal assistance by email as you plan your trip, reserve in advance, www.florentia.org, info@florentia.org).

Context Florence

This scholarly group of graduate students and professors leads "walking seminars," such as a 3.5-hour study of Michelangelo's work and influence (€80/person, plus museum admission) and a two-hour evening orientation stroll (€65/person). I enjoyed the fascinating three-hour fresco workshop (€75/person plus materials, you take home a fresco you make yourself). See their website for other innovative offerings: Medici walk, lecture series, food walks, family tours, and other programs throughout Europe (tel. 06-9672-7371, US tel. 800-691-6036, www.contexttravel.com, info@contexttravel.com).

Weekend Tour Packages for Students

Andy Steves (Rick's son) runs **WSA Europe,** offering three-day and longer guided and unguided packages—including accommodations, sightseeing, and unique local experiences—for budget travelers across 11 top European cities, including Florence (from €99, see www.wsaeurope.com for details).

COOKING CLASSES AND MARKET TOURS

Several of the above companies—as well as some dedicated culinary schools—offer cooking classes, sometimes including a shopping trip to pick up ingredients at a local market. This can be fun, memorable, educational, efficient (combining a meal with a "sightseeing" experience)...and delicious. For more on your options, see page 307 in the Eating in Florence chapter.

LOCAL GUIDES FOR PRIVATE TOURS

Alessandra Marchetti, a Florentine who has lived in the US, gives private walking tours of Florence and driving tours of Tuscany (€60-75/hour, mobile 347-386-9839, www.alessandramarchetti.com, aleoberm@tin.it).

Paola Migliorini, her husband Giuseppe, and their partners offer museum tours, city walking tours, private cooking classes, wine tours, and Tuscan excursions by van—you can tailor tours as you like (€60/hour without car, €70/hour in a van for up to 8 passengers, tel. 055-472-448, mobile 347-657-2611, www.florencetour.com, info@florencetour.com). They also do private shore excursions from the cruise-ship port of Livorno (€580 for up to 4 people, €680 for up to 6, €780 for up to 8, includes a driver/tour guide; also possible from La Spezia but more expensive).

Roberto Bechi, a top-notch guide based near Siena, can pick you up in Florence for off-the-beaten-path tours of the Tuscan countryside (see contact information on page 357).

HOP-ON, HOP-OFF BUS TOURS

Around town, you'll see big double-decker sightseeing buses double-parking near major sights. Tourists on the top deck can listen to brief recorded descriptions of the sights, snap photos, and enjoy a drive-by look at major landmarks (€20/1 calendar day, €25/48 hours, pay as you board, www.firenze.city-sightseeing.it). As the name implies, you can hop off when you want and catch the next bus (usually every 30 minutes, less frequently off-season). But since the most important sights are buried in the old center where big buses can't go, Florence doesn't really lend itself to this kind of tour bus. Look at the route map before committing.

DRIVING TOURS

500 Touring Club offers a unique look at Florence: from behind the wheel of one of the most iconic Italian cars, a vintage, restored Fiat 500. After a lesson in *la doppietta* (double-clutching), you'll head off in a guided convoy, following a lead car while listening to Italian oldies, with photo stops at the best viewpoints. Tours depart from a 15th-century villa on the edge of town; the tiny Fiats are restored models from the 1960s and

1970s. Itineraries vary from basic sightseeing to countryside excursions with wine-making and lunch; see their website for options (classic 2.5-hour tour-€70/person, US tel. 347/535-0030, Italian mobile 346-826-2324, Via Gherardo Silvani 149a, www.500touringclub.com, info@500touringclub.com, Andrea).

SIGHTS IN FLORENCE

In this chapter, Florence's most important museums have the shortest listings and are marked with a ✪. These sights are covered in much more detail in one of the self-guided tours included in this book. The Renaissance Walk chapter connects a number of Florence's major sights, from the Duomo to Ponte Vecchio over the Arno River.

Remember to check www.ricksteves.com/update for any significant changes that have occurred since this book was printed.

Opening Hours: Check opening hours carefully and plan your time well. Many museums have erratic hours (for example, closing on alternating Sundays and Mondays), and Florence—more than most cities—has a tendency to change these hours from season to season. Get the most up-to-date info at the TIs or online. The city TI has a convenient list of current hours for each sight; you can also download this list at www.firenzeturismo.it (click "Art & Museums," then select "Major museums and monuments of Florence" to find a link to opening times).

Price Hike Alert: Most of the major museums host special exhibits that boost the base admission price. Even if you only want to see the permanent collection, you're required to pay for the special exhibit. Consider yourself lucky if you happen to visit when admission is the normal price.

Sightseeing Strategies

Florence offers several options to help you bypass the lengthy ticket-buying lines that can plague its most popular sights in peak season.

You can spend less time in line and more time seeing the sights if you buy Florence's official sightseeing pass (the Firenze Card) or make advance reservations. I have all the details below, but here's...

The Bottom Line: The **Firenze Card** (at around $100 per person) is a major investment, but it's the easiest way to avoid lines at multiple sights. (And it's the *only* way to skip the often-long lines to ascend the Duomo's dome or tower.) Getting the card makes the most sense in peak season, from April through October, when crowds are worst; off-season travelers could do without it. You'll have to sightsee like mad for the full three-day validity period just to break even. Note that there are no Firenze Card discounts for seniors or families, though kids get in (mostly) free to sights; see "The Fine Print" at the end of the next section.

On a shorter visit (one or two days), or if you won't be entering too many sights, skip the Firenze Card and instead make **reservations** online for the Accademia and Uffizi, and if you want to climb the dome, try to hit it at a less-crowded time. However, if the price is not a problem, people in town for even just a few hours may find the Firenze Card worthwhile—simply to buy themselves line-skipping privileges.

There is also a €10 **combo-ticket** that covers Duomo-related sights: the Baptistery, dome, Campanile, Duomo Museum (closed for renovation through late 2015), and Santa Separata (the church crypt, inside the Duomo). Getting the combo-ticket only makes sense if you don't have a Firenze Card (which covers the same sights).

FIRENZE CARD

This three-day sightseeing pass gives you admission to many of Florence's sights, including the Uffizi Gallery and Accademia. Just as important, it lets you skip the ticket-buying lines without making reservations. With the card, you simply go to the entrance at a covered sight (look for the Firenze Card logo), show the card, and they let you in (though there still may be short delays at popular sights with bottleneck entryways or capacity limits). At some sights, you must first present your card at the ticket booth or information desk to get a physical ticket before proceeding to the entrance.

Cost and Coverage: The Firenze Card costs €72 and is valid for 72 hours from when you validate it at your first museum (e.g., Tue at 15:00 until Fri at 15:00). Validate your card only when you're ready to tackle the covered sights on three consecutive days. Make sure the sights you want to visit will be open (many sights are closed Sun or Mon; for details, see the "Daily Reminder" on page 26). The Firenze Card covers the regular admission price as well as any special-exhibit surcharges, and is good for one visit per sight. It also gives you free use of Florence city buses.

What's Included: To figure out if the card is a good deal for you, tally up the entry fees for what you want to see. Here's a sampling of popular sights and their ticket prices:

- Uffizi Gallery (€11, or €6.50 if no special exhibits, plus €4 fee if reserved ahead)
- Accademia (same as Uffizi, above)
- Palazzo Vecchio (€10 apiece for museum or tower, €14 for both)
- Bargello (€7, or €4 if no special exhibits)
- Medici Chapels (€9, or €8 if no special exhibits)
- Museum of San Marco (€4)
- Duomo sights: Baptistery, Campanile, dome climb, and—if open—Duomo Museum (€10)
- Pitti Palace sights: Palatine Gallery and Royal Apartments (€13; 8.50 if no special exhibits)

If you enter all of the above sights within three days—an ambitious plan—the Firenze Card will (just barely) pay for itself. If you see fewer sights, the card will cost you more than individual admissions (but will still save you time). The Firenze Card also covers a long list of minor sights that you might enjoy popping into, but wouldn't otherwise pay for. Of the Florence sights I list, the only ones *not* covered by the Firenze Card are the Church of San Lorenzo, the Bardini Gardens at Pitti Palace, and the fashion museums (Gucci and Ferragamo). For a complete list of included sights, see www.firenzecard.it. Expect some changeability in their coverage.

Where to Buy: Many outlets around town sell the card, including the TIs at the train station and at Via Cavour 1 red (a couple of blocks north of the Duomo) and at some sights: the Uffizi Gallery's door #2 (enter to the left of the ticket-buying line), back entrance of Santa Maria Novella (near the train station), Bargello, Palazzo Vecchio, Brancacci Chapel, and Strozzi Palace. Lines are shortest at Strozzi Palace, the Via Cavour TI (credit cards only), and the Church of Santa Maria Novella (facing the train station, at Piazza della Stazione 4); if you're doing the Uffizi first, door #2 is relatively quick. You can also pay for the card online (www.firenzecard.it), obtain a voucher, and pick up the card at any of the above locations.

The Fine Print: The Firenze Card is not shareable, and there are no family or senior discounts for Americans or Canadians. Children under 18 are allowed free into any state museum. However, at the Uffizi and Accademia, if they want to skip the lines with their Firenze Card-holding parents, children still must (technically) pay the €4 "reservation fee" (which can be paid on the spot—no need

Florence at a Glance

▲▲▲**Accademia** Michelangelo's *David* and powerful (unfinished) *Prisoners*. Reserve ahead or get a Firenze Card. **Hours:** Tue-Sun 8:15-18:50, closed Mon. See page 39.

▲▲▲**Duomo Museum** Underrated cathedral museum with sculptures (closed for renovation through late 2015). **Hours:** Normally Mon-Sat 9:00-19:30, Sun 9:00-13:45. See page 52.

▲▲▲**Bargello** Underappreciated sculpture museum (Michelangelo, Donatello, Medici treasures). **Hours:** Tue-Sat 8:15-17:00, until 13:50 if there are no special exhibits; also open first, third, and fifth Mon and second and fourth Sun of each month. See page 63.

▲▲▲**Uffizi Gallery** Greatest collection of Italian paintings anywhere. Reserve well in advance or get a Firenze Card. **Hours:** Tue-Sun 8:15-18:35, closed Mon. See page 57.

▲▲**Museum of San Marco** Best collection anywhere of artwork by the early Renaissance master Fra Angelico. **Hours:** Tue-Fri 8:15-13:50, Sat 8:15-16:50; also open 8:15-13:50 on first, third, and fifth Mon and 8:15-16:50 on second and fourth Sun of each month. See page 40.

▲▲**Medici Chapels** Tombs of Florence's great ruling family, designed and carved by Michelangelo. **Hours:** April-Oct Tue-Sat 8:15-16:50, Nov-March Tue-Sat 8:15-13:50; also open second and fourth Mon and first, third, and fifth Sun of each month. See page 45.

▲▲**Duomo** Gothic cathedral with colorful facade and the first dome built since ancient Roman times. **Hours:** Mon-Fri 10:00-17:00, Thu until 16:00 May and Oct, until 16:30 Nov-April; Sat 10:00-16:45, Sun 13:30-16:45. See page 47.

▲▲**Palazzo Vecchio** Fortified palace, once the home of the Medici family, wallpapered with history. **Hours:** Fri-Wed 9:00-19:00, until 24:00 April-Sept, Thu 9:00-14:00 year-round. See page 58.

▲▲**Galileo Science Museum** Fascinating old clocks, telescopes, maps, and three of Galileo's fingers. **Hours:** Wed-Mon 9:30-18:00, Tue 9:30-13:00. See page 62.

▲▲**Santa Croce Church** Precious art, tombs of famous Florentines, and Brunelleschi's Pazzi Chapel in 14th-century church. **Hours:** Mon-Sat 9:30-17:30, Sun 14:00-17:30. See page 64.

▲▲**Church of Santa Maria Novella** Thirteenth-century Dominican church with Masaccio's famous 3-D painting. **Hours:** Mon-Thu

9:00-17:30, Fri 11:00-17:30, Sat 9:00-17:00, Sun 12:00-17:00 July-Sept (from 13:00 Oct-June). See page 65.

▲▲Pitti Palace Several museums in lavish palace plus sprawling Boboli and Bardini Gardens. **Hours:** Palatine Gallery, Royal Apartments, and Gallery of Modern Art open Tue-Sun 8:15-18:50, closed Mon; Boboli and Bardini Gardens, Costume Gallery, Argenti/Silverworks Museum, and Porcelain Museum open daily June-Aug 8:15-19:30, April-May and Sept-Oct 8:15-18:30, March 8:15-17:30, Nov-Feb 8:15-16:30, closed first and last Mon of each month. See page 66.

▲▲Brancacci Chapel Works of Masaccio, early Renaissance master who reinvented perspective. **Hours:** Mon and Wed-Sat 10:00-17:00, Sun 13:00-17:00, closed Tue. Reservations required, though often available on the spot. See page 67.

▲▲San Miniato Church Sumptuous Renaissance chapel and sacristy showing scenes of St. Benedict. **Hours:** Daily Easter-mid-Oct 8:00-20:00, in winter 8:30-13:00 & 15:30-19:00, closed sporadically for special occasions. See page 70.

▲Piazza S.S. Annunziata Lovely square epitomizing Renaissance harmony, with Brunelleschi's Hospital of the Innocents, considered the first Renaissance building. See page 40.

▲Medici-Riccardi Palace Lorenzo the Magnificent's home, with fine art, frescoed ceilings, and Gozzoli's lovely Chapel of the Magi. **Hours:** Thu-Tue 9:00-18:00, closed Wed. See page 46.

▲Climbing the Duomo's Dome Grand view into the cathedral, close-up of dome architecture, and, after 463 steps, a glorious city vista. **Hours:** Mon-Fri 8:30-19:00, Sat 8:30-17:40, closed Sun. See page 50.

▲Campanile Bell tower with views similar to Duomo's, 50 fewer steps, and shorter lines. **Hours:** Daily 8:30-19:30. See page 51.

▲Baptistery Bronze doors fit to be the gates of paradise. **Hours:** Doors always viewable; interior open Mon-Sat 11:15-19:00 except first Sat of each month 8:30-14:00, Sun 8:30-14:00. See page 51.

▲Ponte Vecchio Famous bridge lined with gold and silver shops. **Hours:** Bridge always open (shops closed at night). See page 59.

▲Piazzale Michelangelo Hilltop square with stunning view of Duomo and Florence, with San Miniato Church just uphill. **Hours:** Always open. See page 69.

to reserve ahead). However, in practice, enforcement of this policy seems to vary.

ADVANCE RESERVATIONS

If you don't get a Firenze Card, it's smart to make reservations at the often-crowded Accademia and Uffizi Gallery. Some other Florence sights—including the Bargello, Medici Chapels, and Pitti Palace—have reservation systems, but it's not essential to book ahead for these. The Brancacci Chapel officially requires a reservation, but it's usually possible to walk right in and get an entry time on weekdays or any day off-season, especially before 15:30 (for details, see the Brancacci Chapel Tour chapter).

Accademia and Uffizi Reservations

Get reservations for these two top sights as soon as you know when you'll be in town. You can generally get an entry time for the Accademia a few days before your visit, but reserve for the Uffizi well in advance. Without a reservation at the Accademia and Uffizi, you can usually enter without significant lines from November through March after 16:00. But from April through October and on weekends, it can be crowded even late in the day. Any time of year, I'd consider reserving a spot.

There are several ways to make a reservation:

• **By Phone:** For either sight, reserve by phone before you leave the States (from the US, dial 011-39-055-294-883, or within Italy call 055-294-883; €4/ticket reservation fee; booking office open Mon-Fri 8:30-18:30, Sat 8:30-12:30, closed Sun). The reservation line is often busy. Be persistent. When you get through, an English-speaking operator walks you through the process—a few minutes later you say *grazie*, having secured an entry time and a confirmation number. Ten minutes before the appointed time, you'll present your confirmation number at the museum and pay cash for your ticket. You pay only for the tickets you pick up (e.g., if you reserved two tickets, but only you can go, you'll pay for just one ticket).

• **Online:** Using a credit card, you can reserve your Accademia or Uffizi visit online via the city's official site (€4/ticket reservation fee, www.firenzemusei.it—click on the gray "B-ticket" strip). You'll receive an immediate confirmation email, which is followed within three days by a voucher. Bring your voucher to the ticket desk to swap for an actual ticket.

Pricey middleman sites—such as www.uffizi.com and www.tickitaly.com—are reliable and more user-friendly than the official site, but their booking fees run about €10 per ticket. (When ordering from these broker sites, don't confuse Florence's Accademia with Venice's gallery of the same name.)

• **Through Your Hotel:** Some hoteliers are willing to book museum reservations for their guests (ask when you reserve your room); some offer this as a service, while others charge a small booking fee.

• **Private Tour:** Various tour companies—including the ones listed on page 29—sell tours that include a reserved museum admission.

• **Last-Minute Strategies:** If you arrive without a reservation, call the reservation number (see "By Phone," earlier); ask your hotelier for help; or head to a booking window, either at Orsanmichele Church (daily 9:00-16:00, along Via de' Calzaiuoli—see location on map on page V) or at the My Accademia Libreria bookstore across from the Accademia's exit (Tue-Sun 8:15-17:30, closed Mon, Via Ricasoli 105 red—see map on page 100). It's also possible to go to the Uffizi's official ticket office (use door #2 and skirt to the left of the long ticket-buying line—go ahead, you can really do this), ask if they have any short-notice reservations available, and pay cash. Any of these options will cost you the €4 reservation fee. Because the museums are closed on Mondays, the hardest day to snare a last-minute, same-day reservation is Tuesday—get an early start.

North of the Arno River

NORTH OF THE DUOMO

▲▲▲Accademia (Galleria dell'Accademia)

This museum houses Michelangelo's *David,* the consummate Renaissance statue of the buff, biblical shepherd boy ready to take on the giant. Nearby are some of the master's other works, including his powerful (unfinished) *Prisoners* and *St. Matthew,* as well as a *Pietà* (possibly by one of his disciples). Florentine Michelangelo Buonarroti, who would work tirelessly through the night, believed that the sculptor was a tool of God, responsible only for chipping away at the stone to let the intended sculpture emerge. Beyond the magic marble are some mildly interesting pre-Renaissance and Renaissance paintings, including a couple of lighter-than-air Botticellis, the plaster model of Giambologna's *Rape of the Sabine Women,* and a musical instrument collection with an early piano.

Cost and Hours: €11 (or €6.50 if there's no special exhibit), additional €4 for recommended reservation, covered by Firenze

Card; Tue-Sun 8:15-18:50, closed Mon, last entry 30 minutes before closing; audioguide-€6, Rick Steves audio tour available—see page 9, Via Ricasoli 60, reservation tel. 055-294-883, www.polomuseale.firenze.it. To avoid long lines in peak season, get the Firenze Card or make reservations (see page 38).

✪ See the Accademia Tour chapter.

▲Piazza S.S. Annunziata

This overlooked square, embodying the quintessence of Renaissance harmony, is tucked just a block behind the Accademia. Facing the square are two fine buildings: the 15th-century Santissima Annunziata church (worth a peek) and Filippo Brunelleschi's Hospital of the Innocents (Ospedale degli Innocenti), with terra-cotta medallions by Luca della Robbia. Built in the 1420s, the hospital is considered the first Renaissance building, and—with its mission to care for the least among society (impoverished, parentless children)—was also an important symbol of the increasingly humanistic, and humanitarian, outlook of Renaissance Florence.

I love sleeping on this square (at the recommended Hotel Loggiato dei Serviti) and picnicking here during the day (with the riffraff, who remind me of the persistent gap—today as in Medici times—between those who appreciate fine art and those just looking for some cheap wine). But in recent years, this piazza has been on the receiving end of some gentrification efforts. The Hospital of the Innocents is being turned into the Museo degli Innocenti, documenting the plight of the historical youngsters who lived here (due to open sometime in 2015; www.istitutodeglinnocenti.it).

▲▲Museum of San Marco (Museo di San Marco)

Located one block north of the Accademia, this 15th-century monastery houses the greatest collection anywhere of frescoes and paintings by the early Renaissance master Fra Angelico. The ground floor features the monk's paintings, along with some works by Fra Bartolomeo.

Upstairs are 43 cells decorated by Fra Angelico and his assistants. While the monk/painter was trained in the medieval religious style, he also learned and adopted Renaissance techniques and sensibilities, producing works that blended Christian symbols and Renaissance realism. Don't miss the cell of Savonarola, the charismatic monk who rode in from the Christian right, threw out the Medici, turned Florence into a theocracy, sponsored "bonfires of the vanities" (burning books, paintings, and so on), and was finally burned himself when Florence decided to change channels.

Cost and Hours: €4, covered by Firenze Card, Tue-Fri 8:15-13:50, Sat 8:15-16:50; also open 8:15-13:50 on first, third, and fifth Mon and 8:15-16:50 on second and fourth Sun of each month; last entry 30 minutes before closing, reservations possible but unnecessary, on Piazza San Marco, tel. 055-238-8608, www.polomuseale.firenze.it.

✪ See the Museum of San Marco Tour chapter.

Museum of Precious Stones (Museo dell'Opificio delle Pietre Dure)

This unusual gem of a museum features room after room of exquisite mosaics of inlaid marble and other stones. The Medici loved colorful stone tabletops and floors; you'll even find landscapes and portraits (find Cosimo I in Room I). Upstairs, you'll see wooden work benches from the Medici workshop (1588), complete with foot-powered power tools. Rockhounds can browse 500 different stones (lapis lazuli, quartz, agate, marble, and so on) and the tools used to cut and inlay them. Borrow the English descriptions in each room.

Cost and Hours: €4, covered by Firenze Card, Mon-Sat 8:15-14:00, closed Sun, last entry 30 minutes before closing, around corner from Accademia at Via degli Alfani 78, tel. 055-265-1357, www.opificiodellepietredure.it.

Church of San Lorenzo

This red-brick dome—which looks like the Duomo's little sister—was the parish church of the Medici and is the burial place of the family's founder, Giovanni di Bicci de' Medici (1360-1429). Brunelleschi designed the building, and Donatello worked on the bronze pulpits inside. The Medici Chapels, with Michelangelo's famous tomb sculptures, are part of the church complex (see listing, later).

Cost and Hours: €4.50, buy ticket just inside cloister to the left of the facade, €7 combo-ticket covers Laurentian Medici Library; Mon-Sat 10:00-17:30, Sun 13:30-17:30 March-Oct, closed Sun Nov-Feb; last entry 30

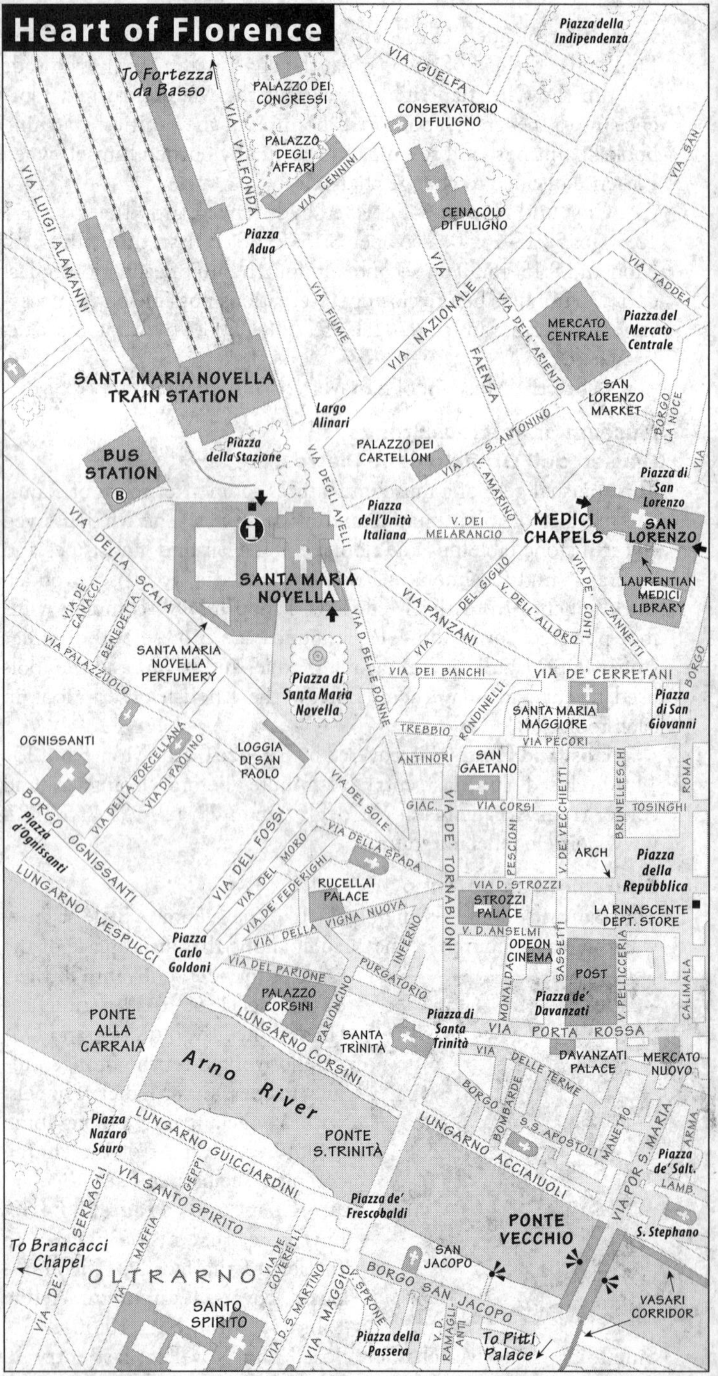
Heart of Florence
To Fortezza da Basso
Piazza della Indipendenza
VIA GUELFA
PALAZZO DEI CONGRESSI
CONSERVATORIO DI FULIGNO
PALAZZO DEGLI AFFARI
VIA VALFONDA
VIA CENNINI
CENACOLO DI FULIGNO
VIA LUIGI ALAMANNI
Piazza Adua
VIA FIUME
VIA NAZIONALE
VIA FAENZA
VIA DELL' ARIENTO
MERCATO CENTRALE
Piazza del Mercato Centrale
VIA TADDEA
SANTA MARIA NOVELLA TRAIN STATION
Largo Alinari
SAN LORENZO MARKET
BORGO LA NOCE
BUS STATION
Piazza della Stazione
PALAZZO DEI CARTELLONI
VIA S. ANTONINO
VIA DEGLI AVELLI
V. AMARINO
Piazza di San Lorenzo
Piazza dell'Unità Italiana
V. DEI MELARANCIO
MEDICI CHAPELS
SAN LORENZO
SANTA MARIA NOVELLA
LAURENTIAN MEDICI LIBRARY
VIA DELLA SCALA
VIA DE' CANACCI
VIA PANZANI
VIA DEL GIGLIO
V. DELL' ALLORO
VIA DE' CONTI
ZANNETTI
VIA BENEDETTA
SANTA MARIA NOVELLA PERFUMERY
VIA PALAZZUOLO
VIA D. BELLE DONNE
Piazza di Santa Maria Novella
VIA DEI BANCHI
VIA DE' CERRETANI
RONDINELLI
SANTA MARIA MAGGIORE
Piazza di San Giovanni
BORGO
OGNISSANTI
LOGGIA DI SAN PAOLO
TREBBIO
VIA PECORI
VIA DELLA PORCELLANA
VIA DI PAOLINO
ANTINORI
SAN GAETANO
VIA DEL SOLE
GIAC.
VIA CORSI
TOSINGHI
ROMA
BRUNELLESCHI
BORGO OGNISSANTI
Piazza d'Ognissanti
VIA DEL FOSSI
VIA DEL MORO
VIA DELLA SPADA
PESCIONI
V. DE' VECCHIETTI
ARCH
Piazza della Repubblica
LUNGARNO VESPUCCI
VIA DE' FEDERIGHI
RUCELLAI PALACE
VIA DE' TORNABUONI
VIA D. STROZZI
STROZZI PALACE
LA RINASCENTE DEPT. STORE
VIA DELLA VIGNA NUOVA
INFERNO
V. D. ANSELMI
Piazza Carlo Goldoni
ODEON CINEMA
SASSETTI
POST
V. PELLICCERIA
CALIMALA
VIA DEL PARIONE
PURGATORIO
PALAZZO CORSINI
PARIONCINO
MONALDA
Piazza de' Davanzati
PONTE ALLA CARRAIA
LUNGARNO CORSINI
SANTA TRÌNITÀ
Piazza di Santa Trìnità
VIA PORTA ROSSA
VIA DELLE TERME
DAVANZATI PALACE
MERCATO NUOVO
Arno River
BORGO S.S. APOSTOLI
BOMBARDE
MANETTO
VIA POR S. MARIA
ARMA
Piazza Nazaro Sauro
LUNGARNO GUICCIARDINI
PONTE S.TRINITÀ
LUNGARNO ACCIAIUOLI
Piazza de' Salt.
LAMB
VIA DE' SERRAGLI
VIA SANTO SPIRITO
GEPPI
Piazza de' Frescobaldi
PONTE VECCHIO
S. Stephano
To Brancacci Chapel
MAFFIA
VIA DE' COVERELLI
SAN JACOPO
OLTRARNO
VIA D. S. MARTINO
VIA MAGGIO
SPRONE
BORGO SAN JACOPO
VASARI CORRIDOR
SANTO SPIRITO
Piazza della Passera
V. D. RAMAGLIANTI
To Pitti Palace

SIGHTS

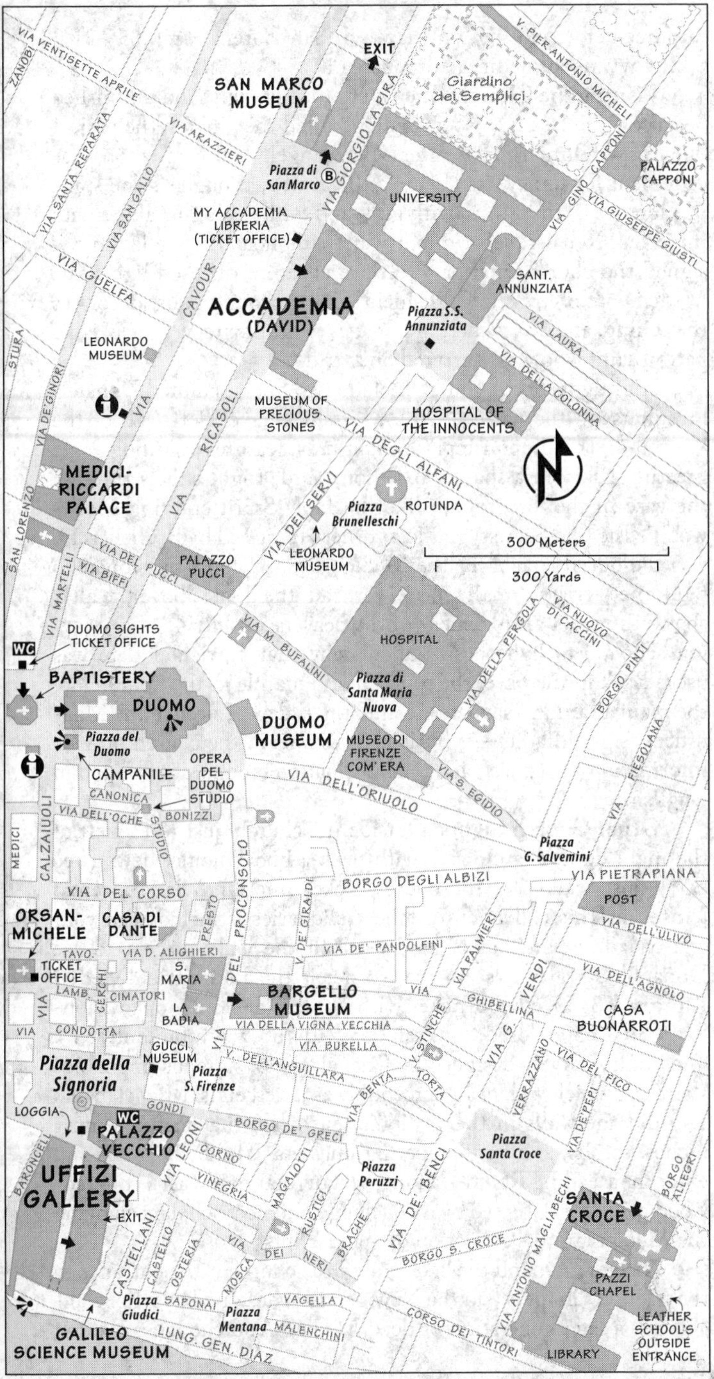

SAN MARCO MUSEUM
EXIT
Giardino dei Semplici
V. PIER ANTONIO MICHELI
VIA VENTISETTE APRILE
ZANOBI
VIA ARAZZIERI
VIA SANTA REPARATA
VIA SAN GALLO
Piazza di San Marco
VIA GIORGIO LA PIRA
UNIVERSITY
VIA GINO CAPPONI
PALAZZO CAPPONI
VIA GIUSEPPE GIUSTI
MY ACCADEMIA LIBRERIA (TICKET OFFICE)
VIA GUELFA
CAVOUR
ACCADEMIA (DAVID)
SANT. ANNUNZIATA
Piazza S.S. Annunziata
VIA LAURA
VIA DELLA COLONNA
LEONARDO MUSEUM
STURA
VIA DE' GINORI
VIA
VIA RICASOLI
MUSEUM OF PRECIOUS STONES
HOSPITAL OF THE INNOCENTS
VIA DEGLI ALFANI
MEDICI-RICCARDI PALACE
SAN LORENZO
VIA DEI SERVI
Piazza Brunelleschi
ROTUNDA
300 Meters
300 Yards
VIA DEL PUCCI
VIA BIFFI
VIA MARTELLI
PALAZZO PUCCI
LEONARDO MUSEUM
VIA NUOVO DI CACCINI
VIA DELLA PERGOLA
BORGO PINTI
WC
DUOMO SIGHTS TICKET OFFICE
VIA M. BUFALINI
HOSPITAL
BAPTISTERY
DUOMO
Piazza di Santa Maria Nuova
Piazza del Duomo
DUOMO MUSEUM
MUSEO DI FIRENZE COM' ERA
VIA FIESOLANA
CAMPANILE
OPERA DEL DUOMO STUDIO
VIA DELL'ORIUOLO
VIA S. EGIDIO
CANONICA
VIA DELL'OCHE
BONIZZI
STUDIO
MEDICI
CALZAIUOLI
PROCONSOLO
Piazza G. Salvemini
VIA PIETRAPIANA
BORGO DEGLI ALBIZI
POST
VIA DEL CORSO
V. DE' GIRALDI
VIA DELL'ULIVO
ORSAN-MICHELE
CASA DI DANTE
PRESTO
VIA PALMIERI
VIA DE' PANDOLFINI
TAVO.
VIA D. ALIGHIERI
TICKET OFFICE
S. MARIA
VIA DELL'AGNOLO
LAMB.
CERCHI
CIMATORI
BARGELLO MUSEUM
VIA GHIBELLINA
VIA G. VERDI
CASA BUONARROTI
LA BADIA
VIA DEL
VIA DELLA VIGNA VECCHIA
VIA CONDOTTA
VIA BURELLA
V. STINCHE
GUCCI MUSEUM
V. DELL'ANGUILLARA
VIA DEL FICO
Piazza della Signoria
Piazza S. Firenze
VIA BENTACORDI
TORTA
VERRAZZANO
VIA DE' PEPI
LOGGIA
GONDI
WC
PALAZZO VECCHIO
BORGO DE' GRECI
Piazza Santa Croce
VIA LEONI
CORNO
BARONCELLI
UFFIZI GALLERY
VINEGRIA
MAGALOTTI
Piazza Peruzzi
VIA DE' BENCI
BORGO ALLEGRI
EXIT
RUSTICI
BRACHE
SANTA CROCE
VIA ANTONIO MAGLIABECHI
CASTELLANI
CASTELLO
OSTERIA
VIA DEI NERI
MOSCA
BORGO S. CROCE
PAZZI CHAPEL
Piazza Giudici
SAPONAI
VAGELLA I
Piazza Mentana
MALENCHINI
CORSO DEI TINTORI
LEATHER SCHOOL'S OUTSIDE ENTRANCE
GALILEO SCIENCE MUSEUM
LUNG. GEN. DIAZ
LIBRARY

minutes before closing, on Piazza di San Lorenzo, tel. 055-214-042, www.operamedicealaurenziana.it.

Visiting the Church: The exterior is big, ugly, and unfinished because Pope Leo X (also a Medici) pulled the plug on the project due to dwindling funds—after Michelangelo had labored on a facade plan for four years (1516-1520). Inside, though, is the spirit of Florence in the 1420s, with gray-and-white columns and arches in perfect Renaissance symmetry and simplicity. Brunelleschi designed the church interior to receive an even, diffused light. The Medici coat of arms (a gold shield with six round balls) decorates the ceiling, and everywhere are images of St. Lawrence, the Medici patron saint who was martyred on a grill.

Highlights of the church include two finely sculpted Donatello pulpits (in the nave). In the Martelli Chapel (left wall of the left transept), Filippo Lippi's *Annunciation* features a smiling angel greeting Mary in a sharply 3-D courtyard. Light shines through the vase in the foreground, like the Holy Spirit entering Mary's womb. The Old Sacristy (far left corner), designed by Brunelleschi, was the burial chapel for the Medici. Bronze doors by Donatello flank the sacristy's small altar. Overhead, the dome above the altar shows the exact arrangement of the heavens on July 4, 1442, leaving scholars to hypothesize about why that particular date was used. Back in the nave, the round inlaid marble in the floor before the main altar marks where Cosimo the Elder—Lorenzo the Magnificent's grandfather—is buried. Assistants in the church provide information on request, and the information brochure is free and in English.

Other Church Sights: Outside the church, just to the left of the main door, is a **cloister** with peek-a-boo Duomo views (free entry, just walk past the church ticket line) and **San Lorenzo Museum.** This collection of fancy reliquaries is included in your church admission, but is hardly worth the walk, except to see Donatello's grave. Also in the cloister is the **Laurentian Medici Library** (€3, €7 combo-ticket with church, generally open Mon-Sat 9:30-13:30, closed Sun, tel. 055-210-760, www.bmlonline.it). The library, largely designed by Michelangelo, stars his impressive staircase, which widens imperceptibly as it descends. Michelangelo also did the walls in the vestibule (entrance) that feature empty niches, scrolls, and oddly tapering pilasters. Climb the stairs and enter the Reading Room—a long, rectangular hall with a coffered-wood ceiling—designed by Michelangelo to host scholars enjoying the Medici family's collection of manuscripts.

Nearby: Around the back end of the church is the entrance to the **Medici Chapels** and the New Sacristy, designed by Michelangelo for a later generation of dead Medici. And the lanes leading to Mercato Centrale (one block north) are clogged with the vendor stalls of **San Lorenzo Market.**

▲▲Medici Chapels (Cappelle Medicee)

The burial site of the ruling Medici family in the Church of San Lorenzo includes the dusky Crypt; the big, domed Chapel of Princes; and the magnificent New Sacristy, featuring architecture, tombs, and statues almost entirely by Michelangelo. The Medici made their money in textiles and banking, and patronized a dream team of Renaissance artists that put Florence on the cultural map. Michelangelo, who spent his teen years living with the Medici, was commissioned to create the family's final tribute.

Cost and Hours: €9 (or €8 if no special exhibits), covered by Firenze Card; April-Oct Tue-Sat 8:15-16:50, Nov-March Tue-Sat 8:15-13:50; also open second and fourth Mon and first, third, and fifth Sun of each month; last entry 30 minutes before closing; reservations possible but unnecessary, audioguide-€6, modest dress required, tel. 055-238-8602, www.polomuseale.firenze.it.

✪ See the Medici Chapels Tour chapter.

▲San Lorenzo Market

Florence's vast open-air market sprawls in the streets just north of the Church of San Lorenzo, between the Duomo and the train station (daily 9:00-19:00, closed Mon in winter). Until very recently, the stalls surrounded the church itself, but city gentrification efforts have pushed many of the vendors elsewhere. You'll likely find the highest concentration in the streets ringing Mercato Centrale, a block away. (However, as this is in flux—and highly controversial, with many vocal pro- and anti-market factions still sorting things out—you may have to ask around to find them).

Most of the leather stalls are run by Iranians selling South American leather that was tailored in Italy; a few more established, more reputable leather shops with permanent addresses are nearby. At stalls or shops, prices are soft—don't be shy about bargaining. (For much more advice about shopping for leather—including some recommendations of specific shops—see page 316 in the Shopping in Florence chapter.) Every night, in a poignant little parade that feels centuries old, the merchants fold their wares into their wheeled wooden stalls and push them through the city streets to their overnight parking spaces.

▲Mercato Centrale (Central Market)

Florence's giant iron-and-glass-covered central market, a wonderland of picturesque produce, is fun to explore. While the nearby San Lorenzo Market—with its garment and souvenir stalls in the streets—feels only a step up from a haphazard flea market, Mercato Centrale retains a Florentine elegance, particularly now that the upper level has been completely renovated and turned into an upscale food court. Wander around.

Downstairs, you'll see parts of the cow you'd never dream of eating (no, that's not a turkey neck), enjoy generous free samples, watch pasta being made, and have your pick of plenty of fun eateries sloshing out cheap and tasty pasta to locals (Mon-Fri 7:00-14:00, Sat 7:00-17:00, closed Sun).

Upstairs, the meticulously restored glass roof and steel rafters soar over a sleek and modern food court, serving up a bounty of Tuscan cuisine. This is clearly Florence's bid to have an upscale foodie market to call its own. For eating ideas downstairs, upstairs, and around the market, see page 291.

▲Medici-Riccardi Palace (Palazzo Medici-Riccardi)

Lorenzo the Magnificent's home is worth a look for its art. The tiny Chapel of the Magi contains colorful Renaissance gems such as the *Procession of the Magi* frescoes by Benozzo Gozzoli. The former library has a Baroque ceiling fresco by Luca Giordano, a prolific artist from Naples known as "Fast Luke" *(Luca fa presto)* for his speedy workmanship. While the Medici originally occupied this 1444 house, in the 1700s it became home to the Riccardi family, who added the Baroque flourishes.

Cost and Hours: €7, covered by Firenze Card, Thu-Tue 9:00-18:00, closed Wed, last entry 30 minutes before closing, ticket entrance is north of the main gated entrance, videoguide-€4, Via Cavour 3, tel. 055-276-0340, www.palazzo-medici.it.

✪ See the Medici-Riccardi Palace Tour chapter.

Leonardo Museums

Two different-but-similar entrepreneurial establishments—Le Macchine di Leonardo da Vinci and Museo Leonardo da Vinci—are several blocks apart and show off reproductions of Leonardo's ingenious inventions. Either one is fun for anyone who wants to crank the shaft and spin the ball bearings of Leonardo's fertile imagination. While there are no actual historic artifacts, each museum shows several dozen of Leonardo's inventions and experiments made into working models. You might see a full-size armored tank, walk into a chamber of mirrors, operate a rotating crane, or watch experiments in flying. The exhibits are described in English, and you're encouraged to touch and play with many of the models—it's great for kids. The Museo has larger scale models; Le Macchine has better visitor information.

Cost and Hours: Le Macchine di Leonardo da Vinci—€7, €2 discount with this book, April-Oct daily 9:30-19:30; Nov-March Mon-Fri 11:00-17:00, Sat-Sun 9:30-19:30; for €1 extra they'll throw in a slice of pizza and a Coke, in Galleria Michelangelo at Via Cavour 21; tel. 055-295-264, www.macchinedileonardo.com. **Museo Leonardo da Vinci**—€7, €0.50 discount with this book, daily April-Oct 10:00-19:00, Nov-March 10:00-18:00, Via dei Servi 66 red, tel. 055-282-966, www.mostredileonardo.com.

DUOMO AND NEARBY

While the Duomo itself is free to enter, several associated sights are all covered by a single €10 combo-ticket: the Baptistery, dome, Campanile, Duomo Museum (closed for renovation through late 2015), and Santa Separata (the church crypt, inside the Duomo). You can buy the ticket at automated machines around the Duomo area (credit cards only, require PIN); at the ticket office facing the Baptistery (at #7 on the square, across from entrance to the Baptistery); at the crypt inside the Duomo; and when it reopens, inside the Duomo Museum; as well as online (www.operaduomo.firenze.it). All of these sights are also covered by the Firenze Card (see page 34), which lets you skip the often-long lines for climbing the dome and/or the Campanile. To climb the dome or enter the Baptistery, you'll need to present your Firenze Card at a ticket office to get a free voucher.

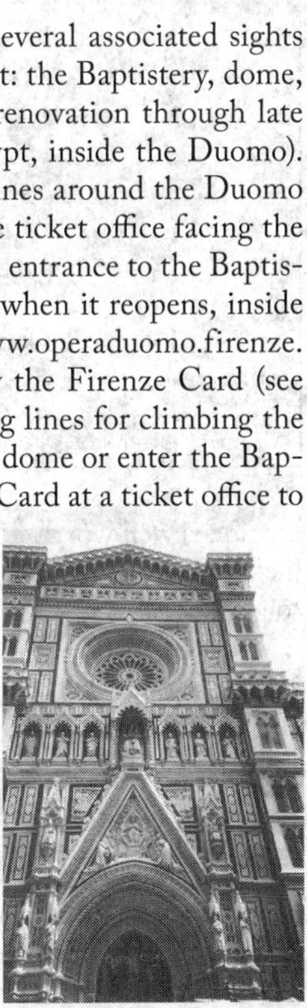

▲▲Duomo (Cattedrale di Santa Maria del Fiore)

Florence's Gothic cathedral has the third-longest nave in Christendom. The church's noisy Neo-Gothic facade (from the 1870s) is covered with pink, green, and white Tuscan marble. The cathedral's claim to artistic fame is Brunelleschi's magnificent dome—the first Renaissance dome and the model for domes to follow. While viewing it from the

Duomo Tour

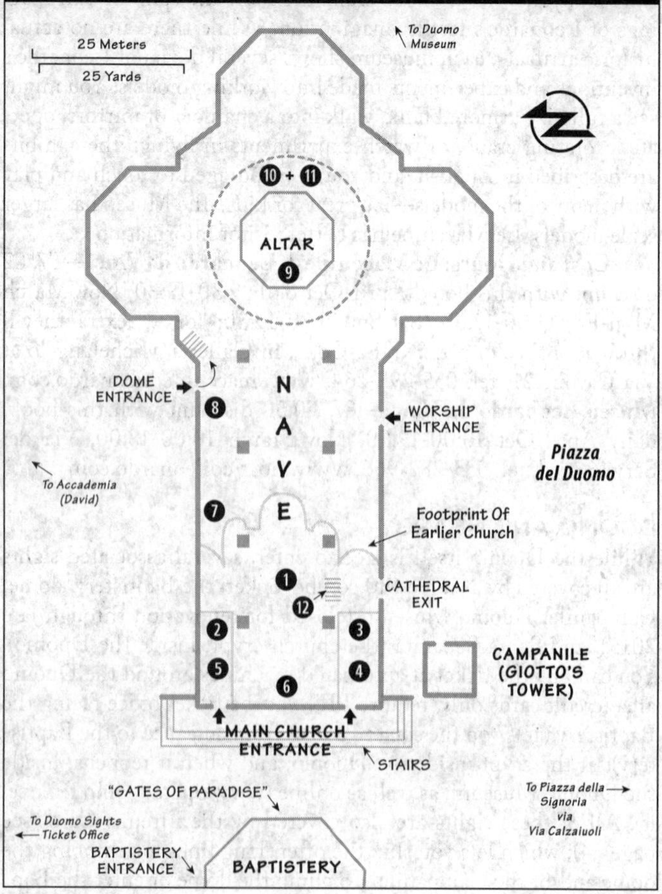

outside is well worth ▲▲, the massive but empty-feeling interior is lucky to rate ▲—it doesn't justify the massive crowds that line up to get inside.

Cost and Hours: Cathedral interior—free; Mon-Fri 10:00-17:00, Thu until 16:00 May and Oct, until 16:30 Nov-April; Sat 10:00-16:45, Sun 13:30-16:45, free English tours offered but fill up fast—ask inside the Duomo, modest dress code enforced, tel. 055-230-2885, www.operaduomo.firenze.it.

Audioguide: The €5 audioguide, rentable only inside the Duomo, covers the church interior and other associated sights (crypt, dome, and—when open—museum). To return the audioguide when you're done, find the no-wait entrance at the far-right end of the Duomo facade.

Lines: Because the church is free (and therefore not "covered" by the Firenze Card), lines can be long. Fortunately, the line moves fast—the average wait time is 10-15 minutes, and it rarely exceeds 30 minutes.

➲ **Self-Guided Tour:** Enter the Duomo (from Latin domus, as it's the "house" of God). ❶ Survey the huge nave—it's 500 feet long and 300 feet wide. The structural elements are unabashedly highlighted by the gray stone and cream-colored filling. In medieval times, engineers weren't accustomed to spanning such distances, so they used iron support bars between the columns to ensure stability. A church has been on this spot since the fall of Rome c. A.D. 500. (You can see part of the earlier church at the end of this tour.)

In 1296, the present church was begun under the architect ❷ Arnolfo di Cambio (see his bust on the left wall, inside a round medallion, second medallion from the entrance). Arnolfo, shown here holding the Duomo's blueprint, also built Palazzo Vecchio and Santa Croce Church. Construction continued under ❸ Giotto (his bust is on the right wall, opposite Arnolfo), who started the church's Campanile (and also helped to invent modern painting).

SIGHTS

By 1420, the nave was done, except for a 140-foot-wide hole in the roof over the altar. ❹ Filippo Brunelleschi (first medallion on the right wall) covered that with the famous dome that helped define the Renaissance. Finally, in the 19th century, the church was completed with a multicolored facade by ❺ Emilio de Fabris (mustachioed bust in the first medallion on the left wall).

Above the main entrance is a ❻ huge clock, painted by Paolo Uccello (1443). It still works. It's a 24-hour clock, starting with sunset as the first hour, and turning counterclockwise.

As you stroll down the nave, notice the equestrian portraits on your left. The church, originally financed by the city of Florence, honors great (secular) men, such as ❼ General John Hawkwood (on horseback; 1436, it's the second horse picture, colored green). Paolo Uccello wowed Florence by creating this 3-D illusion of an equestrian statue on the flat wall. Farther up the left (north) wall is a painting of Florence's great poet ❽ Dante, in a frilly stone frame. He holds his *Divine Comedy*, points toward Hell (Inferno), puts his back to Mount Purgatory, and turns toward Paradise—its skyline none other than that of Florence itself.

Continue all the way up to the very front of the church, beneath the brightly painted dome. The ❾ altar area is octagonal, echoing the shape of the Baptistery. At the base of the crucifix is a high-backed wooden chair—the cathedra of Florence's bishop, which makes the Duomo a "cathedral." Looking up, notice how the dome stretches halfway into the transepts—that was one big hole Brunelleschi had to cover. Look up 300 feet, into the dome, to see the expansive (if artistically uninteresting) ❿ *Last Judgment* by Giorgio Vasari and Federico Zuccari. From their graves, the dead rise into a multilevel heaven to be judged by a radiant Christ. Beneath Christ, Mary intercedes. Below them is the pagan god Kronos with the hourglass and a skeleton—symbolizing that mankind's time is up, and they (we) are entering eternity.

Just below that, on the base that supports the dome, is a ⓫ round stained-glass window by Donatello, showing The Coronation of the Virgin—demonstrating that human beings can eventually be exalted through the Christian faith.

Follow the crowds back toward the exit. Before leaving, if you have a combo-ticket for the Duomo sights (or want to buy one), consider a quick visit to the ⓬ crypt, with the footprint and miscellaneous historical fragments of an earlier church called Santa Reparata. But as there's little to see and it's sparsely explained, it's skippable. Brunelleschi's tomb is tucked unceremoniously (and free to view) in a corner of the crypt's bookstore.

▲Climbing the Duomo's Dome

For a grand view into the cathedral from the base of the dome, a peek at some of the tools used in the dome's construction, a chance to see Brunelleschi's "dome-within-a-dome" construction, a glorious Florence view from the top, and the equivalent of 463 plunges on a Renaissance StairMaster, climb the dome. While you're waiting in line—as you likely will (unless you have a Firenze Card)—spend a few minutes studying the precious Donatello sculpture above the recently restored side entrance door, called the Porta della Mandorla ("Door of the Almond"): Madonna and Bambino are carried by angels in an almond-shaped frame, above delicately carved barrel leaf and *Annunciation* mosaics by Nanni di Banco. Even the side door of this cathedral boasts priceless works by masters that would be the highlight of any other church. For more on the dome, see page 82 of the Renaissance Walk chapter.

Cost and Hours: €10 ticket covers all Duomo sights, covered by Firenze Card, Mon-Fri 8:30-19:00, Sat 8:30-17:40, closed Sun, last entry 40 minutes before closing, enter from outside church on north side, tel. 055-230-2885.

Crowd-Beating Tips: The line for the dome can be discouragingly long and slow-moving. The only way to skip the line is with the Firenze Card (but remember that you have to show your card at the ticket office near the Baptistery to get a voucher first). While difficult to predict, crowds may subside a bit at lunchtime (13:00-14:30) or near the end of the day. If it's just too long, consider ascending the campanile instead (see next).

SIGHTS

▲Campanile (Giotto's Tower)

The 270-foot bell tower has 50-some fewer steps than the Duomo's dome (but that's still 414 steps—no elevator); offers a faster, relatively less-crowded climb (with typically shorter lines); and has a view of that magnificent dome to boot. On the way up, there are several intermediate levels where you can catch your breath and enjoy ever-higher views. The stairs narrow as you go up, creating a mosh-pit bottleneck near the very top—but the views are worth the hassle. While the various viewpoints are enclosed by cage-like bars, the gaps are big enough to let you snap great photos.

Cost and Hours: €10 ticket covers all Duomo sights, covered by Firenze Card, daily 8:30-19:30, last entry 40 minutes before closing.

✪ See page 84 of the Renaissance Walk chapter.

▲Baptistery

Michelangelo said the bronze doors of this octagonal building were fit to be the gates of paradise. Check out the gleaming copies of Lorenzo Ghiberti's bronze doors facing the Duomo (the original panels are in the Duomo Museum—closed through late 2015). Making a breakthrough in perspective, Ghiberti used mathematical laws to create the illusion of receding distance on a basically flat surface.

The doors on the north side of the building were designed by Ghiberti when he was young; he'd won the honor and opportunity by beating Brunelleschi in a competition (the rivals' original entries are in the Bargello).

Inside, sit and savor the medieval mosaic ceiling, where it's always Judgment Day and Jesus is giving the ultimate thumbs-up and thumbs-down.

Cost and Hours: €10 ticket covers all Duomo sights, covered by Firenze Card (show your card at the ticket office to get a voucher), interior open Mon-Sat 11:15-19:00 except first Sat of month 8:30-14:00, Sun 8:30-14:00, last entry 30 minutes before closing, audioguide-€2, photos allowed inside, tel. 055-230-2885. The (facsimile) bronze doors are on the exterior, so they are always "open" and viewable.

✪ See page 84 of the Renaissance Walk. For more on the famous doors, see page 140 of the Bargello Tour chapter and page 163 of the Duomo Museum Tour chapter.

▲▲▲Duomo Museum (Museo dell'Opera del Duomo)

The underrated cathedral museum, behind the church, is great if you like sculpture; unfortunately, it will be closed through late 2015.

After it reopens, look for a late Michelangelo *Pietà* and statues from the original Baptistery facade. Upstairs, you'll find Brunelleschi's models for his dome, as well as Donatello's anorexic *Mary Magdalene* and playful choir loft. The museum features Ghiberti's original bronze "Gates of Paradise" panels (the ones on the Baptistery's doors today are copies).

Cost and Hours: €10 ticket covers all Duomo sights, covered by Firenze Card, Mon-Sat 9:00-19:30, Sun 9:00-13:45, last entry 45 minutes before closing, one of the few museums in Florence always open on Mon, audioguide-€5, guided tours available in summer (see page 159), Via del Proconsolo 9, tel. 055-282-226 or 055-230-7885, www.operaduomo.firenze.it.

✪ See the Duomo Museum Tour chapter.

BETWEEN THE DUOMO AND PIAZZA DELLA SIGNORIA

Casa di Dante (Dante's House)

Dante Alighieri (1265-1321), the poet who gave us *The Divine Comedy*, is the Shakespeare of Italy, the father of the modern Italian language, and the face on the country's €2 coin. However, most Americans know little of him, and this museum is not the ideal place to start. Even though it has English information, this small museum (in a building near where he likely lived) assumes visitors have prior knowledge of the poet. It's not a medieval-flavored house with period furniture—it's just a small, low-tech museum about Dante. Still, Dante lovers can trace his interesting life and works through pictures, models, and artifacts. And because the exhibits are as much about medieval Florence as they are about the man, novices can learn a little about the city Dante lived in.

Cost and Hours: €4, covered by Firenze Card, April-Sept daily 10:00-18:00; Oct-March Tue-Sun 10:00-17:00, closed Mon; last entry 30 minutes before closing, near the Bargello at Via Santa Margherita 1, tel. 055-219-416, www.museocasadidante.it.

➲ **Self-Guided Tour:** As you traverse the three floors of this museum, you'll walk through Dante's life—from starry-eyed youth to bitter exile, to the beatific legacy of his poetic genius. Some call Dante the father of the Renaissance. If you're new to the poet, this tour may help the museum seem less Dante-ing.

First Floor: Begin in Room I (straight ahead from the ticket desk). Dante was born into the noble Alighieri family (see his family tree) and baptized in the Baptistery (see old sketch of it). His plan in life was to be a doctor, symbolized by the glass cases of herbs.

Continue into Room II (on the left) to learn how Dante's life changed dramatically when he set eyes on Beatrice (look for a starry-sky picture of the event), and fell in love with her. They ended up marrying other people, but Beatrice remained Dante's muse, inspiring him to write lofty poetry.

In Room III, a model of Dante's Florence shows it as a walled city of many towers, housing feuding clans. Backtrack through Room I to reach Room IV, dedicated to the decisive Battle of Campaldino, in which Florence's army (including Dante) established the city's dominance.

Second Floor: Head upstairs and go straight into Room V. Dante entered civic life, serving as the ambassador to Pope Boniface VIII. Exhibits explain the confusing politics that divided Florence between the victorious Black Guelphs and the defeated Whites, which included Dante. Politically incorrect Dante was exiled (in glass case, see the *Book of the Nail*—"*Libro del Chiodo*"—that condemns him), and never again returned to his beloved Florence. Dante probably would have liked the flattering modern portrait of him (hanging high above the book). Opposite the book is a reconstruction of a medieval bedroom—peer through the glass to see a more realistic painting of him, in red, forlorn, having received the news of his exile, with his distinctive ear-flap cap, hooked nose, and jutting chin.

Dante roamed Italy and was received by nobles. In exile, he worked on his magnum opus, *The Divine Comedy* (a video of scenes from this work plays in Room VI). He died and was buried in Ravenna in 1321.

Top Floor: Dante's most enduring legacy is *The Divine Comedy.* The entire poem is displayed on the wall alongside pictures of Dante's cosmos: Hell (*inferno,* a spiral-shaped hole through the earth), Purgatory (*purgatorio,* a spiral-shaped mountain), and Paradise (*paradiso,* the concentric orbits of satellites that surround Earth). The display cases show off illuminated (illustrated) manuscripts of Dante's masterpiece, dating as far back as the 14th century.

▲Orsanmichele Church

In the ninth century, this loggia (covered courtyard) was a market used for selling grain (stored upstairs). Later, it was enclosed to make a church.

Outside are dynamic, statue-filled niches, some with accompanying symbols from the guilds that sponsored the art. Donatello's *St. Mark* and *St. George* (on the northeast and northwest corners) step out boldly in the new Renaissance style.

The interior has a glorious Gothic tabernacle (1359), which houses the painted wooden panel that depicts *Madonna delle Grazie* (1346). The iron bars spanning the vaults were the Italian Gothic answer to the French Gothic external buttresses. Look for the rectangular holes in the piers—these were once wheat chutes that connected to the upper floors. The museum upstairs (limited hours) displays most of the originals from the niches outside the building, by Ghiberti, Donatello, Brunelleschi, and others.

Cost and Hours: Free, daily 10:00-17:00 (except closed Mon in Aug), free upstairs museum open only Mon, niche sculptures always viewable from the outside. You can give the *Madonna della Grazie* a special thanks if you're in town when an evening concert is held inside the Orsanmichele (tickets sold on day of concert from door facing Via de' Calzaiuoli; also books Uffizi and Accademia tickets, ticket window open daily 10:00-17:00).

✪ See page 88 of the Renaissance Walk chapter.

▲Mercato Nuovo (a.k.a. the Straw Market)

This market loggia is how Orsanmichele looked before it became a church. Originally a silk and straw market, Mercato Nuovo still functions as a rustic yet touristy market (at the intersection of Via Calimala and Via Porta Rossa). Prices are soft, but San Lorenzo Market (listed earlier) is much better for haggling. Notice the circled X in the center, marking the spot where people landed after being hoisted up to the top and dropped as punishment for bankruptcy. You'll also find *Il Porcellino* (a statue of a wild boar nicknamed "The Piglet"), which people rub and give coins to ensure their return to Florence. This new copy, while only a few years old, already has a polished snout. At the back corner, a wagon sells tripe (cow innards) sandwiches—a local favorite (for more on this Tuscan taste treat, see page 290).

▲Piazza della Repubblica and Nearby

This large square sits on the site of the original Roman Forum. Florence was a riverside garrison town set below the older town of Fiesole—essentially a rectangular fort with the square marking the intersection of the two main roads (Via Corso and Via Roma). The square's lone column—nicknamed the "belly button of Florence"—once marked the intersection (the Roman streets were about nine feet below the present street level). Above ground, all that survives of Roman Florence is this column and the city's street plan. But beneath the stones lie the remains of the ancient city. Look at any map of Florence today, and you'll see the ghost of Rome in its streets: a grid-plan city center surrounded by what was the Roman wall. The Braille model of the city (in front of the Paszkowski café) makes the design clear.

The square was the site of the Jewish quarter in the 1500s; in 1571, Cosimo I had it walled in and made into a ghetto.

Today's piazza, framed by a triumphal arch, is a nationalistic statement celebrating the unification of Italy. (Because it's so new, the square is not a favorite of locals.) Florence, the capital of the newly united nation of Italy (1865-1870) until Rome was "liberated" (from the Vatican), lacked a square worthy of this grand new country. So in the 1860s, the city was spiffed up for its stint as

SIGHTS

the capital—the Jewish ghetto was razed, and the city walls were taken down to make grand European-style boulevards and open up an imposing, modern forum surrounded by stately circa-1890 buildings. Notice the proud statement atop the triumphal arch, which proclaims, "The squalor of the ancient city is given a new life." Atop the lone column stands a copy of a Donatello statue of a pagan goddess of abundance, overseeing the market with her cornucopia full of produce.

Between here and the river, you'll find characteristic parts of the medieval city that give a sense of what this neighborhood felt like before it was bulldozed. Back in the Middle Ages, writers described Florence as so densely built up that when it rained, pedestrians didn't get wet. Torches were used to light the lanes in midday. The city was prickly with noble families' towers (like San Gimignano) and had Romeo and Juliet-type family feuds. But with the rise of city power (c. 1300), no noble family was allowed to have an architectural ego trip taller than Palazzo Vecchio, and nearly all other towers were taken down.

Venerable cafés and stores line the square. During the 19th century, intellectuals met in cafés here. Gilli, on the northeast corner, is a favorite for its grand atmosphere and tasty sweets (cheap if you stand at the bar, expensive to sit down), while the recommended Paszkowski has good lunch options (see page 294).

The department store La Rinascente, facing Piazza della Repubblica, is one of the city's mainstays (WC on fourth floor; from the elevator, look left to find the stairs up to the bar with a rooftop terrace for great Duomo and city views).

Palazzo Strozzi

The former home of the wealthy Strozzi family, great rivals of the Medici, offers a textbook example of a Renaissance palace (built between 1489 and 1538). It feels like an attempt to one-up the Medici-Riccardi Palace just a few blocks away. Step into its grand courtyard and imagine how well-to-do families competed to commission grandiose structures (and artistic masterpieces) to promote their status and wealth. Today it hosts top-notch special exhibitions, usually uncrowded and well described in English. The courtyard also hosts a tranquil, shaded café.

Cost and Hours: Free entry to courtyard and café, both open daily 8:30-20:00; gallery price depends on changing exhibits—typically around €10, discounts with train or bus tickets, daily 9:00-20:00, Thu until 23:00, last entry one hour before closing; just west of Piazza della Repubblica at Piazza Strozzi, tel. 055-264-5155, www.palazzostrozzi.org.

▲Palazzo Davanzati

This five-story, late-medieval tower house offers a rare look at a noble dwelling built in the 14th century. Only the ground-floor loggia and first floor are open to visitors, though the remaining floors (more living quarters and the kitchen) can be visited with an escort (usually at 10:00, 11:00, and 12:00; call ahead to be sure there's space or ask when you arrive). Like other buildings of the age, the exterior is festooned with 14th-century horse-tethering rings made from iron, torch holders, and poles upon which to hang laundry and fly flags. Inside, though the furnishings are pretty sparse, you'll see richly painted walls, a long chute that functioned as a well, plenty of fireplaces, a lace display, and even an indoor "outhouse." While there's little posted information, you can borrow English descriptions in each room.

SIGHTS

Cost and Hours: €2, covered by Firenze Card, Tue-Sat 8:15-13:50; also open first, third, and fifth Sun and second and fourth Mon of each month; Via Porta Rossa 13, tel. 055-238-8610.

ON AND NEAR PIAZZA DELLA SIGNORIA

▲▲▲Uffizi Gallery

This greatest collection of Italian paintings anywhere features works by Giotto, Leonardo, Raphael, Caravaggio, Titian, and Michelangelo, and a roomful of Botticellis, including the *Birth of Venus.* Northern Renaissance masters (Dürer, Rembrandt, and Rubens) are also well represented. Start with Giotto's early stabs at Renaissance-style realism, then move on through the 3-D experimentation of the early 1400s to the real thing rendered by the likes of Botticelli and Leonardo. Finish off with the High Renaissance—Michelangelo, Rubens, and Titian. Because only 600 visitors are allowed inside the building at any one time, there's generally a very long wait. The good news: no Louvre-style mob scenes inside. The museum is nowhere near as big as it is great. Few tourists spend more than two hours inside. Nearly everything is displayed on one comfortable, U-shaped floor in chronological order from the 13th through 17th century. The left (east) wing, starring the Florentine Middle Ages to the Renaissance, is the best. The connecting cor-

ridor contains sculpture, and the right (west) wing focuses on the High Renaissance and Baroque.

Cost and Hours: €11 (or €6.50 if there's no temporary exhibit), extra €4 for recommended reservation, cash required to pick up tickets reserved by phone, covered by Firenze Card, Tue-Sun 8:15-18:35, closed Mon, last entry 30 minutes before closing, audioguide-€6, Rick Steves audio tour available—see page 9, museum info tel. 055-238-8651, reservation tel. 055-294-883, www.uffizi.firenze.it. To avoid the long ticket lines, get a Firenze Card (see page 34) or make reservations (see page 38).

✪ See the Uffizi Gallery Tour chapter.

In the Uffizi's Courtyard: Enjoy the courtyard (free), full of artists and souvenir stalls. (Swing by after dinner when it's completely empty.) The surrounding statues honor earthshaking Florentines: artists (Michelangelo), philosophers (Niccolò Machiavelli), scientists (Galileo), writers (Dante), cartographers (Amerigo Vespucci), and the great patron of so much Renaissance thinking, Lorenzo "the Magnificent" de' Medici. After hours, talented street musicians take advantage of the space's superior acoustics.

✪ See page 94 of the Renaissance Walk chapter.

Nearby: The **Loggia dei Lanzi,** across from Palazzo Vecchio and facing the square, is where Renaissance Florentines once debated the issues of the day; a collection of Medici-approved sculptures now stand (or writhe) under its canopy, including Cellini's bronze *Perseus.*

✪ See page 92 of the Renaissance Walk chapter.

▲▲Palazzo Vecchio

This castle-like fortress with the 300-foot spire dominates Florence's main square. In Renaissance times, it was the Town Hall, where citizens pioneered the once-radical notion of self-rule. Its official name—Palazzo della Signoria—refers to the elected members of the city council. In 1540, the tyrant Cosimo I made the building his personal palace, redecorating the interior in lavish style. Today the building functions once again as the Town Hall.

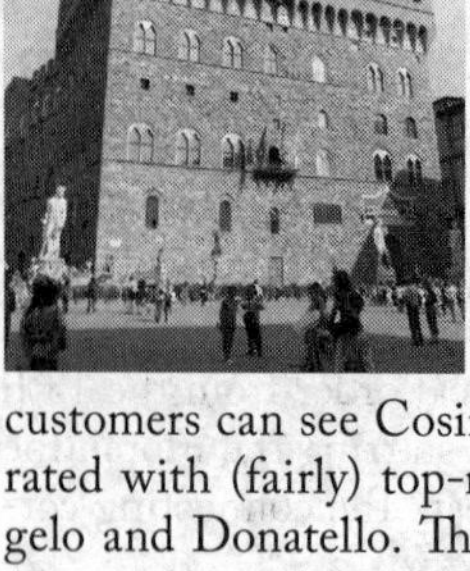

Entry to the ground-floor courtyard is free, so even if you don't go upstairs to the museum, you can step inside and feel the essence of the Medici. Paying customers can see Cosimo's (fairly) lavish royal apartments, decorated with (fairly) top-notch paintings and statues by Michelangelo and Donatello. The highlight is the Grand Hall (Salone dei

Cinquecento), a 13,000-square-foot hall lined with huge frescoes and interesting statues.

Cost and Hours: Courtyard—free to enter (and has WC), museum—€10, tower climb-€10 (418 steps), museum plus tower-€14, special exhibits can incur an optional, small additional fee, museum and tower covered by Firenze Card (first pick up ticket at ground-floor information desk before entering museum); Fri-Wed 9:00-19:00, until 24:00 April-Sept, Thu 9:00-14:00 year-round; tower keeps similar but shorter hours, ticket office closes one hour earlier, videoguide-€5, English tours available (see page 175), Piazza della Signoria, tel. 055-276-8224, http://museicivicifiorentini.comune.fi.it.

✪ See the Palazzo Vecchio Tour chapter.

▲Ponte Vecchio

Florence's most famous bridge has long been lined with shops. Originally these were butcher shops that used the river as a handy disposal system. Then, when the powerful and princely Medici built the Vasari Corridor (described next) over the bridge, the stinky meat market was replaced by the more elegant gold and silver shops that remain there to this day. A statue of Benvenuto Cellini, the master goldsmith of the Renaissance, stands in the center, ignored by the flood of tacky tourism.

For more about the bridge, see page 95 of the Renaissance Walk chapter and page 223 of the Oltrarno Walk chapter.

Vasari Corridor

This elevated and enclosed passageway, constructed in 1565, gave the Medici a safe, private commute over Ponte Vecchio from their Pitti Palace home to their Palazzo Vecchio offices. It's open only by special appointment, and while enticing to lovers of Florence, the actual tour experience isn't much. Entering from inside the Uffizi Gallery, you walk along a modern-feeling hall (wide enough to carry a Medici on a sedan chair) across Ponte Vecchio, and end in Pitti Palace. Half the corridor is lined with Europe's best collection of self-portraits, along with other paintings (mostly 17th- and 18th-century) that seem like they didn't make the cut to be hung on the walls of the Uffizi.

Entering the Corridor: Only a very limited number of tourists are allowed to enter the corridor (typically only for a few weeks each spring, requires a reservation and sells out far in advance; check the latest at www.uffizi.firenze.it). Barring that option, sev-

The Medici in a Minute and a Half

The Medici family—part *Sopranos,* part Kennedys, part John-D-and-Catherine-T art patrons—dominated Florentine politics for 300 years (c. 1434-1737). Originally a hardworking, middle-class family in the cloth, silk, and banking businesses, they used their wealth, blue-collar popularity, and philanthropy to rise into Europe's nobility, producing popes and queens.

1400s: The Princes

Lorenzo the Magnificent (ruled 1469-1492), Cosimo the Elder's grandson, epitomized the Medici ruling style: publicly praising Florence's constitution while privately holding the purse strings. A true Renaissance Man, Lorenzo's personal charisma, public festivals, and support of Leonardo, Botticelli, and teenage Michelangelo made Florence Europe's most enlightened city.

1494-1532: Exile in Rome

After Lorenzo's early death, the family was exiled by the Florentines. The Medici became victims of bank failure, Savonarola's reforms, and the Florentine tradition of democracy. They built a power base in Rome under Lorenzo's son (Pope Leo X, who made forays into Florence) and nephew (Pope Clement VII, who finally invaded Florence and crushed the republic).

1537-1737: The Grand Duchy—Mediocre Medici

Backed by Europe's popes and kings, the "later" Medici—descendants of Cosimo the Elder's brother—ruled Florence and Tuscany as just another duchy. Cosimo I was politically repressive but a generous patron of the arts, leaving his mark on Palazzo Vecchio, the Uffizi, and Pitti Palace. Cosimo II supported Galileo. Famous throughout Europe, the Medici married into Europe's royal families (Catherine and Marie de' Medici were queens of France), even while Florence declined as a political and economic power.

MEDICI FAMILY TREE

Giovanni de Medici (1360-1429)

Cosimo the Elder (1389-1464)
"Father of his country" ("Pater Patriae"). Wealthy businessman turned popular tyrant and patron of Donatello and Brunelleschi.

Piero the Gouty (1416-69)

Lorenzo the Magnificent
(1449-92) The model Renaissance Prince—charismatic, popular, friend of scholars and artists during Florence's height of power.

Giuliano
(1453-78) Lorenzo's little brother was murdered by a rival family in the Pazzi Conspiracy.

Piero the Unfortunate
(1472-1503) Exiled by Savonarola.

Giovanni
(1475-1521)
Became Pope Leo X, commissioned Raphael and excommunicated Luther.

Giuliano
Duke of Nemours
(1479-1516)
Michelangelo built his tomb in Medici Chapels.

Lorenzo II
(1492-1519) Tomb in Michelangelo's Medici Chapels.

Giulio
(1478-1534) Became Pope Clement VII whose armies installed the "Later Medici."

Catherine de' Medici
(1519-89) Through marriage, became Queen of France.

Several generations later...

Cosimo I (1519-74)
First Grand Duke of the "Later Medici" dynasty.

eral Florence tour operators offer guided visits of the corridor—typically a three-hour visit that also includes a tour of the Uffizi's collection: ArtViva (€98, tel. 055-264-5033, www.artviva.com) or Florencetown (€85, tel. 055-012-3994, www.florencetown.com). Both groups offer discounts to my readers (see page 29).

▲▲Galileo Science Museum (Museo Galilei e Istituto di Storia della Scienza)

When we think of the Florentine Renaissance, we think of visual arts: painting, mosaics, architecture, and sculpture. But when the visual arts declined in the 1600s (abused and co-opted by political powers), music and science flourished in Florence. The first opera was written here. And Florence hosted many scientific breakthroughs, as you'll see in this fascinating collection of Renaissance and later clocks, telescopes, maps, and ingenious gadgets. Trace the technical innovations as modern science emerges from 1000 to 1900. Some of the most talked-about bottles in Florence are the ones here that contain Galileo's fingers. Exhibits include various tools for gauging the world, from a compass and thermometer to Galileo's telescopes. Other displays delve into clocks, pumps, medicine, and chemistry. It's friendly, comfortably cool, never crowded, and just a block east of the Uffizi on the Arno River.

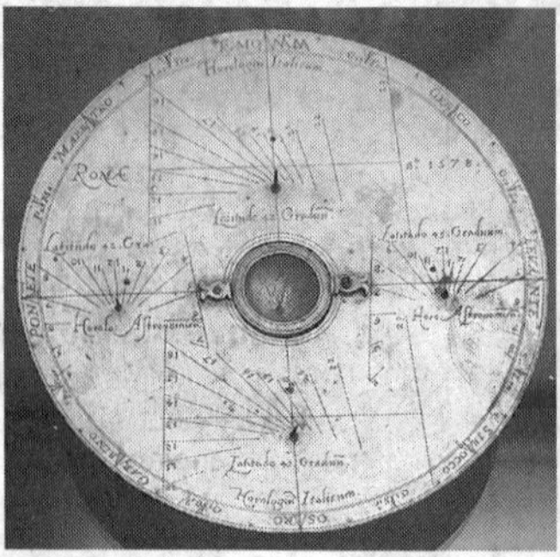

Cost and Hours: €9, €22 family ticket, cash only, covered by Firenze Card, Wed-Mon 9:30-18:00, Tue 9:30-13:00, last entry 30 minutes before closing, audioguide-€5, guided tours available—see page 257, Piazza dei Giudici 1, tel. 055-265-311, www.museogalileo.it.

✪ See the Galileo Science Museum Tour chapter.

▲Fashion Museums

Medici, Michelangelo, meh. If you've had enough of 15th-century Florence, delve into the 21st century at one of these fresh, well-presented, and stylish museums. While they thrill fashionistas who are on a pilgrimage to Florence, even those of us with a wardrobe furnished by The Gap may find these interesting.

The **Gucci Museum,** right on Piazza della Signoria, stylishly tells the story of the famous designer Guccio Gucci, who, in 1921, founded the company that has been synonymous with style for decades. Strolling this collection feels like window-shopping through history, with no option to buy. Seven rooms show off carefully curated items from the Gucci archives, while two more feature changing contemporary art exhibits, all watched over by the impeccably attired staff. Your visit begins on the ground floor, with a section dedicated to travel, a limited-edition 1979 Gucci Cadillac, all manner of top-of-the line travel cases...but, strangely, no Rick Steves 9" x 21" x 14" Rolling Carry-On. Then you'll head up for temporary exhibits of contemporary art; a small cinema (illustrating Gucci's dedication to film preservation); and exhibits on the company's unique Flora pattern, handbags from every era, and eveningwear—slinky gowns, each one identified with the celebrity who wore it on the red carpet. The top floor shows how the interlocking-clasp "GG" logo has evolved and been incorporated into fashion over time, displays Gucci home decor, and shows off several of the company's iconic bamboo-handle handbags. The suitably stylish café and bookshop are open even to those not visiting the museum (€6, daily 10:00-20:00, shop and café until 23:00, Piazza della Signoria 10, tel. 055-7592-3302, www.guccimuseo.com).

The **Ferragamo** flagship store has an interesting, nine-room **shoe museum.** The specific exhibit changes each year, but it's typically more fanciful and imaginative than the Gucci Museum...but, of course, it lacks that iconic Gucci logo (€6, daily 10:00-19:30, near Santa Trinità bridge at Piazza Santa Trinità 5, tel. 055-356-2417).

EAST OF PIAZZA DELLA SIGNORIA

▲▲▲Bargello (Museo Nazionale del Bargello)

This underappreciated sculpture museum is in a former police station-turned-prison that looks like a mini-Palazzo Vecchio. It has Donatello's very influential, painfully beautiful *David* (the first male nude to be sculpted in a thousand years), multiple works by Michelangelo, and rooms of Medici treasures. Moody Donatello, who embraced realism with his lifelike statues, set the personal and artistic style for many Renaissance artists to follow. The best pieces are in the ground-floor room at the foot of the outdoor staircase (with fine works by Michelangelo, Cellini, and Giambologna) and in the "Donatello room" directly above (with plenty by Donatello, including two different *Davids*, plus Ghiberti and Brunelleschi's revolutionary dueling door panels and yet another *David* by Verrocchio).

Cost and Hours: €7 (or €4 if no special exhibits), covered by Firenze Card, Tue-Sat 8:15-17:00—or until 13:50 if there's no special exhibit; also open these times on the first, third, and fifth Mon and the second and fourth Sun of each month; last entry 30 minutes before closing, reservations possible but unnecessary, audioguide-€6, Via del Proconsolo 4, reservation tel. 055-238-8606, www.polomuseale.firenze.it.

✪ See the Bargello Tour chapter.

▲▲Santa Croce Church

This 14th-century Franciscan church, decorated with centuries of precious art, holds the tombs of great Florentines. The loud

19th-century Victorian Gothic facade faces a huge square ringed with tempting shops and littered with tired tourists. Escape into the church and admire its sheer height and spaciousness. Your ticket includes the Pazzi Chapel and a small museum; the complex also houses a leather school.

Cost and Hours: €6, €8.50 combo-ticket with Casa Buonarroti, covered by Firenze Card, Mon-Sat 9:30-17:30, Sun 14:00-17:30, last entry 30 minutes before closing, audioguide-€6, modest dress required, 10-minute walk east of Palazzo Vecchio along Borgo de' Greci, tel. 055-246-6105, www.santacroceopera.it. The **leather school** is free and sells church tickets—handy when the church has a long line (daily 10:00-18:00, closed Sun in fall/winter, has own entry behind church plus an entry within the church, www.scuoladelcuoio.com).

✪ See the Santa Croce Tour chapter.

Casa Buonarroti (Michelangelo's House)

Fans enjoy a house standing on property once owned by Michelangelo. The house was built after Michelangelo's death by the artist's grand-nephew, who turned it into a little museum honoring his famous relative. Be warned: Michelangelo's descendants sold off many of the artist's drawings; you'll see a few of Michelangelo's early, less-than-monumental statues and sketches. The lack of any knockout pieces and the near-complete absence of English information make this sight best left to Michelangelo pilgrims.

Cost and Hours: €6.50, €8.50 combo-ticket with Santa Croce Church, covered by Firenze Card, Wed-Mon 10:00-17:00, closed Tue, English descriptions, Via Ghibellina 70, tel. 055-241-752, www.casabuonarroti.it.

Visiting the Museum: Climb the stairs to the first-floor landing, where you come face-to-face with portraits (by his contemporaries) of 60-year-old Michelangelo, the Buonarroti family walking sticks, and some leather shoes thought to be Michelangelo's.

The room to the left of the landing displays two relief panels, Michelangelo's earliest known sculptures. Teenage Michelangelo carved every inch of the *Battle of the Centaurs* (1490-1492). This squirming tangle of battling nudes shows his fascination with anatomy. He kept this in his personal collection all his life. *The Madonna of the Stairs* (c. 1490) is as contemplative as *Centaurs* is dramatic. Throughout his long career, bipolar Michelangelo veered between these two styles—moving or still, emotional or thoughtful, pagan or Christian.

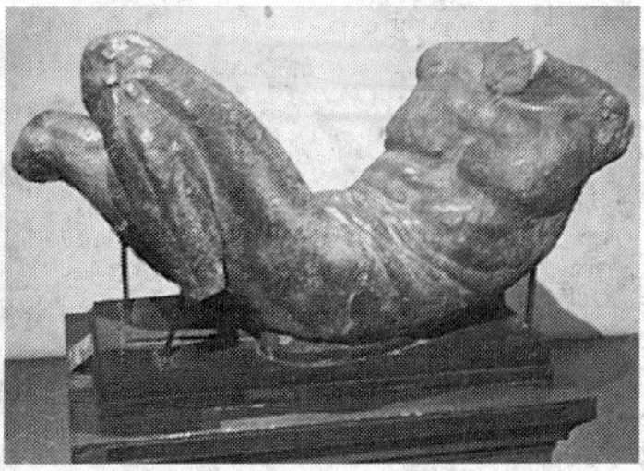

In an adjoining room is the big wooden model of a project Michelangelo took on but never completed: the facade of the Church of San Lorenzo (which remains bare brick to this day). The reclining river god was a model for one of the statues in the Medici Chapels.

The small room straight ahead from the landing is for the museum's vast collection of Michelangelo's sketches. To preserve the sensitive artworks, only a handful are displayed at a time. Vasari claimed that Michelangelo wanted to burn his preliminary sketches, lest anyone think him less than perfect.

The room to the right of the landing displays small clay and wax models—some by Michelangelo, some by pupils—that the artist used to sketch out ideas for his statues.

At the end of these displays is a hallway leading through several adjoining apartments, which seems pretty pointless since Michelangelo never actually lived here. On your way to the exit (via a side staircase), you'll pass by a scale model of the wooden cart used to transport the 12,000-pound *David* from the Duomo to Palazzo Vecchio.

And finally, true Michelangelomaniacs can complete their visit by exiting outside to gaze at Via Ghibellina 67 (next door to a *farmacia*). This humble doorway, lined with gray-green stone, was once the entrance to Michelangelo's actual residence, circa 1520.

SANTA MARIA NOVELLA SIGHTS NEAR THE TRAIN STATION

▲▲Church of Santa Maria Novella

This 13th-century Dominican church is rich in art. Along with crucifixes by Giotto and Brunelleschi, it contains every textbook's example of the early Renaissance mastery of perspective: *The Trinity* by Masaccio. The exquisite chapels trace art in Florence from

medieval times to early Baroque. The outside of the church features a dash of Romanesque (horizontal stripes), Gothic (pointed arches), Renaissance (geometric shapes), and Baroque (scrolls). Step in and look down the 330-foot nave for a 14th-century optical illusion.

Next to the church are the cloisters and the **museum,** located in the old Dominican convent of Santa Maria Novella. The museum's highlight is the breathtaking Spanish Chapel, with walls covered by a series of frescoes by Andrea di Bonaiuto.

Cost and Hours: Church and museum—€5, covered by Firenze Card, Mon-Thu 9:00-17:30, Fri 11:00-17:30, Sat 9:00-17:00, Sun 12:00-17:00 July-Sept (from 13:00 Oct-June), last entry 45 minutes before closing, audioguide-€5, modest dress required, main entrance on Piazza Santa Maria Novella, Firenze Card holders must enter behind the church at Piazza della Stazione 4, tel. 055-219-257, http://museicivicifiorentini.comune.fi.it or www.chiesasantamarianovella.it.

✪ See the Santa Maria Novella Tour chapter.

Nearby: The church also operates a top-of-the-line *parfumerie*, called **Farmacia di Santa Maria Novella** (enter around behind the church, daily 9:00-20:00, Via della Scala 16). Even non-shoppers enjoy exploring its elegant halls and heaven-scent. For details, see page 322 in the Shopping in Florence chapter.

SOUTH OF THE ARNO RIVER

The Oltrarno Walk chapter connects several of these sights, including Pitti Palace, Brancacci Chapel, and Santo Spirito Church.

▲▲Pitti Palace

The imposing Pitti Palace, several blocks southwest of Ponte Vecchio, has many separate museums and two gardens. The main reason to visit is to see the Palatine Gallery, but you can't buy a ticket for the gallery alone; to see it you'll need to buy ticket #1, which includes the Palatine Gallery, Royal Apartments, and Gallery of Modern Art. Ticket #2 covers the Boboli and Bardini Gardens, Costume Gallery, Argenti/Silverworks Museum (the Medici

treasures), and Porcelain Museum. Behind door #3 is a combo-ticket covering the whole shebang.

Cost and Hours: Ticket #1—€13 (€8.50 if no special exhibits), Tue-Sun 8:15-18:50, closed Mon, last entry 45 minutes before closing. Ticket #2—€10 (€7 if no special exhibits), daily June-Aug 8:15-19:30, April-May and Sept-Oct 8:15-18:30, March 8:15-17:30, Nov-Feb 8:15-16:30, closed first and last Mon of each month, last entry one hour before closing. Ticket #3—€11.50, valid 3 days, usually not available during special exhibitions. Reservations are possible but unnecessary, and everything is covered by the Firenze Card (except the Bardini Gardens—an additional €6 for cardholders). The €6 audioguide explains the sprawling palace. Tel. 055-238-8614, www.polomuseale.firenze.it.

✪ See the Pitti Palace Tour chapter.

▲▲Brancacci Chapel

For the best look at works by Masaccio (one of the early Renaissance pioneers of perspective in painting), see his restored frescoes here. Instead of medieval religious symbols, Masaccio's paintings feature simple, strong human figures with facial expressions that reflect their emotions. The accompanying works of Masolino and Filippino Lippi provide illuminating contrasts.

Cost and Hours: €6, cash only, covered by Firenze Card; free and easy reservations required, though it's usually possible to just show up and get an entry time on weekdays and any day off-season, especially if you arrive before 15:30; Mon and Wed-Sat 10:00-17:00, Sun 13:00-17:00, closed Tue, last entry 30 minutes before closing; free 20-minute film, videoguide-€2, knees and shoulders must be covered; in Church of Santa Maria del Carmine, on Piazza del Carmine in the Oltrarno neighborhood; reservations tel. 055-276-8224 or 055-276-8558, ticket desk tel. 055-284-361, http://museicivicifiorentini.comune.fi.it.

✪ See the Brancacci Chapel Tour chapter.

Nearby: The neighborhoods around the church are considered the last surviving bits of old Florence.

Santo Spirito Church

This church has a classic Brunelleschi interior—enjoy its pure Renaissance lines (and ignore the later Baroque altar that replaced the original). Notice Brunelleschi's "dice"—the stone cubes added above the column capitals that contribute to the nave's playful light-

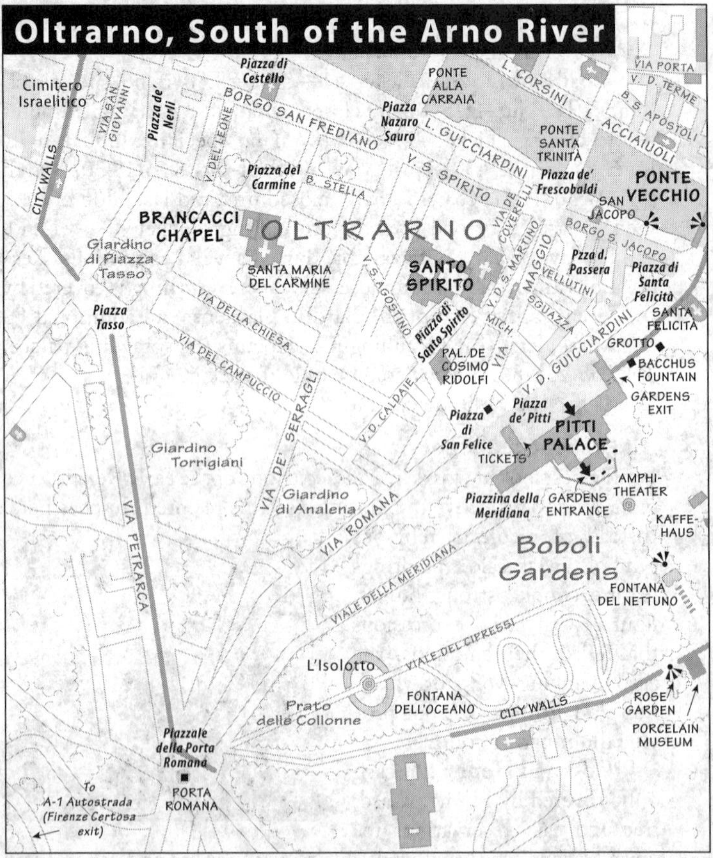

Oltrarno, South of the Arno River

ness. The church's art treasure is a painted, carved wooden crucifix attributed to 17-year-old Michelangelo. The sculptor donated this early work to the monastery in appreciation for allowing him to dissect and learn about bodies. The Michelangelo *Crocifisso* is displayed in the sacristy, through a door midway down the left side of the nave (if it's closed, ask someone to let you in). Copies of Michelangelo's *Pietà* and *Risen Christ* flank the nave (near the main door). Beer-drinking, guitar-playing rowdies decorate the church steps.

Cost and Hours: Free, Mon-Tue and Thu-Sat 9:30-12:30 & 16:00-17:30, Sun 11:30-12:30 & 16:00-17:30, closed Wed, Piazza di Santo Spirito, tel. 055-210-030, www.basilicasantospirito.it.

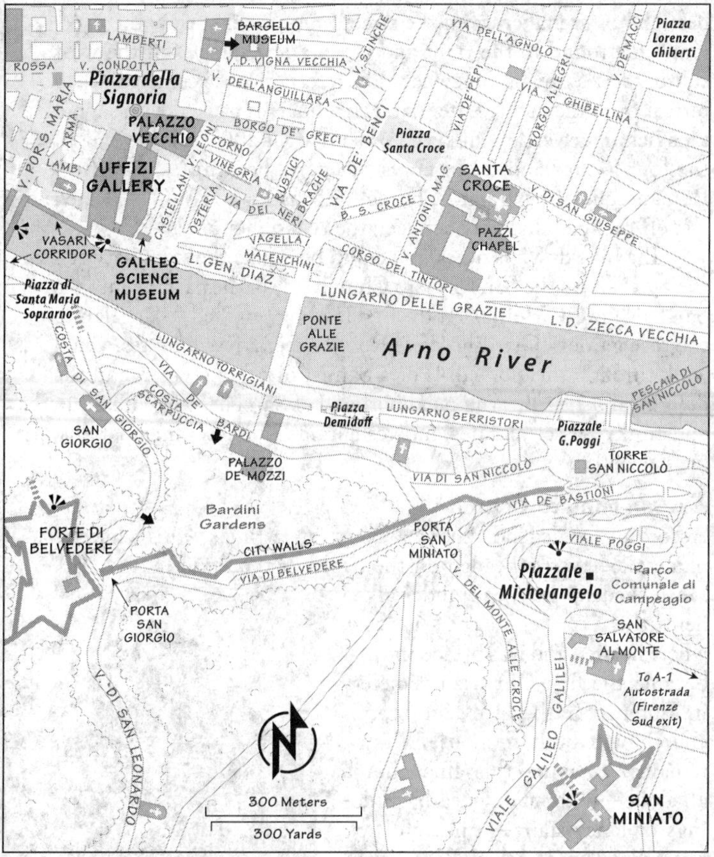

▲Piazzale Michelangelo

Overlooking the city from across the river (look for the huge bronze statue of *David*), this square has a superb view of Florence and the stunning dome of the Duomo.

It's worth the 30-minute hike, drive, or bus ride (either #12 or #13 from the southeast corner of the train station, between the pine trees and the bikes—takes 20-30 minutes, longer in bad traffic). It makes sense to take a taxi or ride the bus up and then enjoy the easy downhill walk back into town. An inviting café (open seasonally) with great views is just below the overlook. The best photos are taken from the street immediately below the overlook (go around to the right and down a few steps). Off the west side of the piazza is a somewhat hidden terrace, an excellent place to retreat from the mobs. After dark, the square is packed with school kids licking ice cream and each other. About 200 yards beyond all the tour groups and teenagers is the stark, beautiful, crowd-free, Romanesque San Miniato Church (next listing). A WC is located just off the road, halfway between the two sights.

The hike down is quick and enjoyable. Take the steps between the two bars on the San Miniato Church side of the parking lot (Via San Salvatore al Monte). At the first landing (marked #3), peek into the rose garden (Giardino delle Rose). After a few minutes, you'll walk through the old wall (Porta San Miniato) and emerge in the delightful little Oltrarno neighborhood of San Niccolò, with a fun and funky passel of cafés and restaurants (for recommendations, see page 305).

▲▲San Miniato Church

According to legend, the martyred St. Minias—this church's namesake—was beheaded on the banks of the Arno in A.D. 250. He picked up his head and walked here (this was before the #12 bus), where he died and was buried in what became the first Christian cemetery in Florence. In the 11th century, this church was built to house Minias' remains. Imagine this fine church all alone—without any nearby buildings or fancy stairs—a peaceful refuge where white-robed Benedictine monks could pray and work (their motto: *ora et labora*). The evening vesper service with the monks chanting in Latin offers a meditative worship experience—a peaceful way to end your visit.

Cost and Hours: Free, daily Easter-mid-Oct 8:00-20:00, in winter 8:30-13:00 & 15:30-19:00, closed sporadically for special occasions, tel. 055-234-2731, www.sanminiatoalmonte.it.

Getting There: It's about 200 yards above Piazzale Michelangelo. From the station, bus #12 takes you right to the San Miniato al Monte stop (hop off and hike up the grand staircase); bus #13 from the station takes you to Piazzale Michelangelo, from which you'll hike up the rest of the way.

Gregorian Chants: To experience this mystical medieval space at its full potential, time your visit to coincide with a prayer service of Gregorian chants. In general, these are held each evening at 18:30 and last 30 minutes—but as the schedule is subject to change, double-check with any TI, the church's website, or call ahead.

➲ **Self-Guided Tour:** For a thousand years, San Miniato Church—still part of a functioning monastery—has blessed the city that lies at the foot of its hill. Carved into the marble of its threshold of the left door is the Genesis verse *"Haec est Porta Coeli"* ("This is the Gate of Heaven").

Facade: The church's green-and-white marble facade (12th century) is classic Florentine Romanesque, one of the oldest in town. The perfect symmetry is a reminder of the perfection of God. The central mosaic shows Christ flanked by Mary and St. Minias. Minias, who was King of Armenia before his conversion, offers his secular crown to the heavenly king. The eagle on top, with bags of wool in his talons, reminds all who approach the church who paid for it—the wool guild.

Nave: Stepping inside, you enter the closest thing to a holy space that medieval Florentines could create. The "carpet of marble" dates from 1207. The wood ceiling is painted as it was originally. The glittering 13th-century golden mosaic that dominates the dome at the front of the nave repeats the scene on the church's facade: St. Minias offering his paltry secular crown to the king in heaven.

The Renaissance tabernacle front and center was commissioned by the Medici. It's résumé of early Renaissance humanism, with experiments in 3-D paintings (including St. Minias, in red) and a plush canopy of glazed terra-cotta panels by Luca della Robbia.

On the left side of the nave is an exquisite chapel dedicated to Cardinal Jacopo of Portugal. When 26-year-old Jacopo died in Florence (1459), his wealthy family mourned him by adding a chapel to the church (by cutting a hole in the church wall) and hiring the best artists of the day to decorate it. The family could enter their private chapel, take a seat on the throne (on the left), and meditate on the tomb of Jacopo (on the right).

Crypt: The church is designed like a split-level rambler, with staircases on either side of the altar, leading upstairs and down. Downstairs in the crypt, an alabaster window helps create a quiet and mysterious atmosphere. The forest of columns and capitals are all recycled...each from ancient Roman buildings and each different. The floor is paved with the tombstones of long-forgotten big shots. Look through the window in the marble altar to see St. Minias' name, carved on the box that holds his mortal remains.

Upstairs to the Sacristy: At the staircase to the right of the main altar, notice the sinopia on the wall. A sinopia is a pattern that guides the fresco artist and also allows the patron to have a peek at what the artist intends to create before it's set in plaster. There's a sinopia behind every surviving fresco in Florence.

Step upstairs and enter the sacristy (the room on the right), which is beautifully frescoed with scenes from the life of St. Benedict (circa 1350, by a follower of Giotto). Drop €2 into the electronic panel in the corner to light the room for five minutes. The elegantly bearded patron saint of Europe was the founder of the vast network of monasteries that gave the Continent some cohesiveness in the cultural darkness that followed the collapse of Rome. Benedict is shown as an active force for good, with his arm always outstretched: busy blessing, being kissed, preaching, helping, chasing the devil, bringing a man (crushed by a fallen tower) back to life, reaching out even on his death bed. Notice Benedict on the ramp, scooting up to heaven to be welcomed by an angel. And, overseeing everything, in the starry skies of the ceiling, are the four evangelists—each with his book, pen, and symbolic sidekicks.

Outside the Church: Before leaving, stroll through the cemetery behind the church (go right as you exit the church, head through the passage, and turn right again) to marvel at the showy crypts and headstones of Florentine hotshots from the last two centuries. *Pinocchio* fans take note: Author Carlo Lorenzini (pen name Collodi) was born in Florence and is buried here (from the bell tower, climb the steps to the wall and head right to the relatively nondescript Lorenzini family crypt at #37).

To get to Piazzale Michelangelo, head out and back down the grand staircase, savoring views of Florence along the way.

Near Florence

These two sights—the hilltop town of Fiesole, with grand views and ancient history, and the poignant American Cemetery—each sit just outside of Florence (in opposite directions).

Fiesole

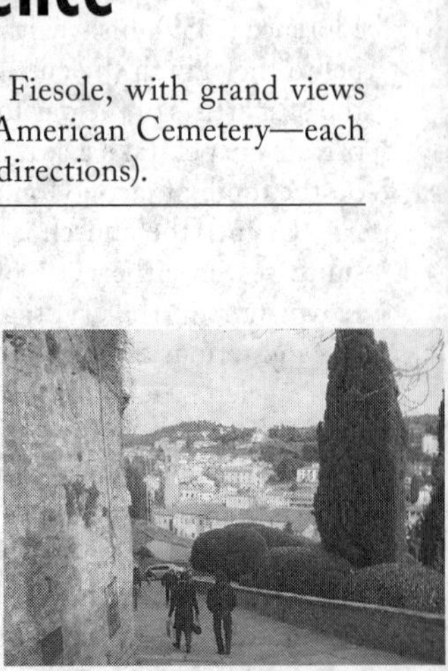

Perched on a hill overlooking the Arno valley, the tidy little town of Fiesole (fee-AY-zoh-lay) gives weary travelers a break in the action and—during the heat of summer—a breezy location from which to admire the city below. It's a small town with a main square, a few restaurants and shops, a few minor sights, and a great view. It's fitting that the E. M. Forster novel and the Merchant-Ivory film adaptation *A Room with a View* both have ties here.

The ancient Etruscans knew a good spot when they saw one, and chose to settle here, establishing Fiesole about 400 years before the Romans founded Florence. The Romans—more concerned with water access than with Fiesole's strategic, sky-high position—shifted the region's focus down into the valley, allowing Fiesole to evolve on a more relaxed track than bustling Florence. Wealthy Renaissance families in pre-air-conditioning days chose Fiesole as a preferred vacation spot, building villas in the surrounding hillsides. Later, 19th-century Romantics spent part of the Grand Tour admiring the vistas, much like the hordes of tourists do today. Most come here for the view—the actual sights pale in comparison to those in Florence. Shutterbugs visit in the morning for the best light, while some prefer the evening for sunset.

GETTING TO FIESOLE

It's only a half hour away by bus or taxi. From Florence's Piazza San Marco, take bus #7—enjoying a peek at gardens, vineyards, orchards, and villas—to the last stop, Piazza Mino (3-4/hour, fewer after 21:00 and on Sun, 30 minutes, €1.20, €2 if bought on bus, validate on board; departs Florence from Piazza San Marco to the right of the museum). As bus tickets can be tricky to buy in Fiesole (the lone tobacco stand that sells them can be unexpectedly closed), bring a return ticket with you from Florence—or be ready to pay extra to buy your ticket on board. Taxis from Florence cost about €25-35 (ride to the view terrace near La Reggia restaurant, then hike up to the Church of San Francesco—which is hard to reach by car—and finally explore downhill).

Orientation to Fiesole

From the bus stop on Piazza Mino, face the long side of the church (Duomo). The best view terrace, the Church of San Francesco, and La Reggia restaurant are to the left, up the steep, stone Via San Francesco. The TI and Archaeological Area are behind the Duomo, just to the right of the bell tower. Up the main drag to the right (Via Gramsci), you'll find the Alcedo *pasticceria* and the Coop supermarket. The small street to the far right (Via Giuseppe Verdi) leads up to a few more panoramic views in a residential neighborhood. And across the piazza is the restaurant Fiesolano.

Tourist Information: The TI is a two-minute walk from the bus stop, inside the ticket office for the Roman Archaeological Area—just head behind the church (daily April-Sept 10:00-19:00, March and Oct 10:00-18:00, Nov-Feb 10:00-14:00, Via Portigiani 3, tel. 055-596-1311, www.fiesoleforyou.it).

Market Day: Fiesole weekends often come with markets—produce on Saturday mornings, and all-day artisan markets on some Sundays.

Sights in Fiesole

ON OR NEAR THE MAIN SQUARE

Duomo

While this church has a drab, 19th-century exterior, the interior is worth a look. The cool, clean architecture—with round Romanesque arches and narrow slits for light—is enlivened by some glittering Gothic altarpieces and a wood-beamed ceiling. Over the main door, look for the blue-and-white glazed Giovanni della Robbia statue of St. Romulus (not the founder of Rome, but Fiesole's similarly named patron saint). Then climb up the stairs past the altar and bear right to find the smiling, head-cocked tomb of Bishop Salutati, which was carved by Mino da Fiesole, a talented student of Donatello's.

Cost and Hours: Free, daily 8:00-12:00, across Piazza Mino from the bus stop.

Archaeological Area and Museum

Florence has few visible Roman ruins—and archaeological finds are far, far better elsewhere in Italy—but if you're dying to see some local ancient history, Fiesole is probably your best chance. This overpriced and sparse but well-presented complex features a largely intact Roman theater, some less-intact fragments of other buildings, and a decent museum of local finds. And the valley view and peaceful setting are lovely. If you don't want to spring for the hefty entry fee, you can get a peek of the grounds from the café terrace just to the left of the turnstile.

Cost and Hours: €10, except Fri-Sun when an obligatory combo-ticket (€12) adds the Bandini Museum (see next listing), includes excellent videoguide, covered by Firenze Card; April-Sept daily 10:00-19:00, March and Oct daily 10:00-18:00; Nov-Feb Wed-Mon 10:00-14:00, closed Tue; behind the Duomo at Via Portigiani 1, www.museidifiesole.it.

Visiting the Ruins and Museum: First, you'll buy your ticket at the TI/ticket office (a half-block to the right, as you face the entrance). Be sure to borrow the included tablet videoguide, with ample English information and a well-produced virtual tour of the ruins before they were ruined. Then head inside, proceed straight ahead, and belly up to the railing.

At your feet is the area's chief attraction, its **Roman theater.** Occasionally used today for plays and concerts, the well-preserved theater held up to 2,000 people in its heyday. About half of what you see here has been rebuilt. More ruins sprawl nearby: To the right, marked by the three arches, are fragments of a bath complex; and to the left, in the trees, is what's left of a temple. While there's little to see, a pleasant loop walk connects everything.

The **museum,** located in the faux-temple within the Archaeological Area, imparts insight into Fiesole's Etruscan and Roman roots with well-displayed artifacts (borrow the English descriptions that supplement the videoguide). You'll see the standard items from Tuscany's many Etruscan museums: fragments of tombs (boxy bases and ornately decorated lids, depicting the departed lounging at an eternal banquet); bronze votive statues and tools; and jewelry. Upstairs are Attica-style black-and-red pottery vases. As this look originated in ancient Greece, their existence here is evidence of widely traveled Etruscan traders (who brought this style home with them). You'll also see several *bucchero* vases—a method for turning red clay into shiny black pottery pieces, in order to resemble highly prized bronze.

SIGHTS

Bandini Museum

This petite museum displays the wooden panels of lesser-known Gothic and Renaissance painters as well as the glazed terra-cotta figures of Andrea della Robbia.

Cost and Hours: €5, covered by €12 combo-ticket with Archaeological Area and Museum, also by Firenze Card, April-Sept Fri-Sun 10:00-19:00, closed Mon-Thu, shorter hours Oct-March, behind Duomo at Via Dupre 1.

UP THE HILL, AT THE TOP OF TOWN

To reach these sights, you'll have to huff your way about 10 minutes steeply up from the main square and bus stop. First you'll pass the recommended La Reggia restaurant, then the terrace, and finally (a few more vertical minutes up) the church complex.

▲▲Terrace and Garden with a View

Catch the sunset (and your breath) from the sweeping view terrace just above La Reggia restaurant. Florence stretches out from the Duomo's stately dome, with the Oltrarno and Piazzale Michelangelo in the background. And the hillsides all around are draped with vineyards and speckled with luxury villas of Renaissance bigwigs who knew how to maximize a great city view.

For overachievers in search of similar views—and a peek at residential Fiesole—climb up the opposite side of the square, along the equally steep road hugging the ridgeline.

Church of San Francesco

For even more hill-climbing, continue up from the view terrace to this charming little church. Its small scale and several colorful altar paintings make this church arguably more enjoyable than Fiesole's Duomo. Inside, you'll also find a quirky collection of souvenirs from local missionaries' travels.

Cost and Hours: Church—free, Mon-Sat 7:00-19:00, Sun 7:00-11:00 & 12:00-19:00, tel. 055-59-175; museum—free but donation suggested, flexible hours—usually Mon-Sat 9:30-12:00 & 15:00-18:30, Sun 15:00-18:30, may be closed Fri morning, tel. 055-59-175; both at Via San Francesco 13.

Visiting the Church: Before entering the church, poke in the doorway to the right for a look at the tranquil **cloister.** Climbing the nearby stairs (don't be shy), you'll find a hall of monastic cells, where Franciscan monks would meditate on colorful frescoes of bible stories. You'll see similar cells at the San Marco Museum, but these feel more lived-in.

Next head **inside** the church. The simple, clean interior allows the vibrant altar paintings that line the nave to really shine. Walking from the back to the front of this church is like flipping the pages of a Florentine Renaissance textbook: Notice how the altarpieces evolve from rigid, staged-looking late Gothic to fully flowering, more organic High Renaissance.

Within the church complex (to the left of the altar, find the door into the cloister, then head downstairs) is the eclectic, endearing little **Franciscan Ethnographic Missionary Museum** (Museo Missionario Etnografico Francescano). Consisting primarily of items that well-traveled Franciscan missionaries brought back from exotic lands to little Fiesole, it features an Egyptian mummy, ancient coins, and Chinese Buddhas and vases. It all sits upon some very old history: One wall of the museum is actually part of the third-century Etruscan town wall.

Eating in Fiesole

The first restaurant is right on Piazza Mino, where the bus from Florence stops; the other is near the view terrace above town.

Fiesolano, a local favorite, serves authentic Tuscan dishes at a fair price. They're particularly well-regarded for their Florentine steaks. Choose between the homey, cluttered interior, the few sidewalk tables facing the main square, or the shady garden terrace (€7-9 pizzas and pastas, €12-18 *secondi,* daily 12:30-14:30 & 19:30-23:30, Piazza Mino 9R, tel. 055-59-143, Leonardo).

Ristorante La Reggia degli Etruschi has some of the highest prices—and best views—in town, as long as you're willing to make the steep walk up. As you're paying for the panorama, it's essential to reserve a table at a window or on their terrace to fully enjoy the vista (€10-14 pastas, €18-20 *secondi*, daily 11:00-15:00 & 18:00-23:00, Via San Francesco 18, tel. 055-59-385).

Picnics: Fiesole is made-to-order for a scenic and breezy picnic. Grab a simple sandwich and a pastry at Fiesole's best *pasticceria,* **Alcedo** (head up the main drag from the bus stop to Via Gramsci 27, Tue-Sat 7:00-20:00, Sun 7:00-13:00, closed Mon). Round out your goodies across the street at the **Coop** supermarket (Mon-Sat 8:00-13:00 & 16:00-20:00, closed Sun) before backtracking to the panoramic terrace. Or, for more convenience and less view, picnic at the shaded park on the way to the view terrace (walk up Via San Francesco about halfway to the terrace, and climb the stairs to the right).

Florence American Cemetery and Memorial

The compelling sight of endless rows of white marble crosses and Stars of David recalls the heroism of the young Americans who fought so valiantly in World War II to free Italy (and ultimately Europe) from the grip of fascism. This particular cemetery is the final resting place of more than 4,000 Americans who died in the liberation of Italy. Climb the hill past the perfectly manicured lawn lined with grave markers, to the memorial, where maps and a history of the Italian campaign detail the Allied advance.

Cost and Hours: Free, daily 9:00-17:00; 7.5 miles south of Florence, off Via Cassia, which parallels the *superstrada* between Florence and Siena, 2 miles south of Florence Certosa exit on A-1 autostrada; buses from Florence stop just outside the cemetery; tel. 055-202-0020, www.abmc.gov.

If you don't have time to visit, you can see the cemetery as you drive by on the SR-2 highway from Florence to Siena (after you get on SR-2 south from the A-1 ring road, the cemetery will be on your right as you leave Florence).

RENAISSANCE WALK

From the Duomo to the Arno

After centuries of labor, Florence gave birth to the Renaissance. We'll start with the soaring church dome that stands as the proud symbol of the Renaissance spirit. Just opposite, you'll find the Baptistery doors that opened the Renaissance. Finally, we'll reach Florence's political center, dotted with monuments of that proud time. As great and rich as this city is, it's easily covered on foot. This walk through the top sights is less than a mile long, running from the Duomo to the Arno River.

Orientation

Length of This Walk: Allow two hours, including visits to the interiors of the Baptistery and Orsanmichele Church (but not the other sights mentioned). With limited time, you can skip the Medici-Riccardi Palace detour, and view the Baptistery and Orsanmichele Church from the outside.

Duomo (Cathedral): Free; Mon-Fri 10:00-17:00, Thu until 16:00 May and Oct, until 16:30 Nov-April; Sat 10:00-16:45, Sun 13:30-16:45. A modest dress code is enforced. See page 47 for crowd-beating tips.

Climbing the Dome: €10 ticket covers all Duomo sights; covered by Firenze Card—but get free voucher at ticket office opposite the Baptistery, at #7; Mon-Fri 8:30-19:00, Sat 8:30-17:40, closed Sun, last entry 40 minutes before closing, 463 steps.

Campanile (Giotto's Tower): €10 ticket covers all Duomo sights, covered by Firenze Card, daily 8:30-19:30, last entry 40 minutes before closing, 414 steps.

Baptistery: €10 ticket covers all Duomo sights; covered by Firenze Card—get free voucher at ticket office; interior open Mon-Sat 11:15-19:00 except first Sat of month 8:30-14:00, Sun 8:30-

14:00, last entry 30 minutes before closing. The facsimiles of the famous *Gates of Paradise* bronze doors on the exterior are always viewable (and free to see; the original panels are in the Duomo Museum).

Medici-Riccardi Palace: €7, covered by Firenze Card, Thu-Tue 9:00-18:00, closed Wed, last entry 30 minutes before closing, Via Cavour 3.

Orsanmichele Church: Free, daily 10:00-17:00 (except closed Mon in Aug), free upstairs museum open only Mon 10:00-17:00. The niche sculptures are always viewable from the outside. The church hosts evening concerts; tickets are sold on the day of the concert from the door facing Via de' Calzaiuoli. At the same ticket window, you can book tickets (often same-day) for the Uffizi and Accademia (€4 reservation fee applies).

Palazzo Vecchio: Courtyard—free, museum—€6.50, covered by Firenze Card, Fri-Wed 9:00-19:00, until 24:00 April-Sept, Thu 9:00-14:00 year-round, ticket office closes one hour earlier.

Information: There's a TI right on Piazza del Duomo (just south of Baptistery, at the corner of Via de' Calzaiuoli), and another one on Via Cavour 1, a couple of blocks north of the Duomo (immediately beyond the Medici-Riccardi Palace).

Audio Tour: You can download this chapter as a free Rick Steves audio tour (see page 9).

Services: Many cafés along the walk have WCs, and public pay toilets (€1) are at the ticket office opposite the Baptistery. You can refill your water bottle at public twist-the-handle fountains at the Duomo (left side, by the dome entrance), Palazzo Vecchio (behind the Neptune fountain), and on Ponte Vecchio.

Photography: In churches and other sights along this walk, photos without a flash are generally OK.

Eating: You'll find plenty of cafés, self-service cafeterias, bars, and gelato shops along the route. Along or near the path of this walk are several of my recommended eateries, including Self-Service Ristorante Leonardo (near the Duomo); the popular L'Antico Trippaio tripe-selling sandwich cart (also has non-tripe fare, a block east of Orsanmichele on Via Dante Alighieri; other cheap options are nearby); Cantinetta dei Verrazzano, a bakery/café with good *focacce* sandwiches; and Club del Gusto and All'Antico Vinaio (both on Via dei Neri, behind Palazzo Vecchio). For details on all of these places, see the Eating in Florence chapter. La Congrega is a nice little wine and coffee bar near the Duomo (see page 336).

Starring: Brunelleschi's dome, Ghiberti's doors, the Medici palaces, and the city of Florence—old and new.

OVERVIEW

The Duomo, the cathedral with the distinctive red dome, is the center of Florence and the orientation point for this walk. If you ever get lost, home's the dome. We'll start here, see several sights in the area, and then stroll down the city's pedestrian-only main street to Palazzo Vecchio and the Arno River. Consider prefacing this walk with a visit to the ultimate Renaissance Man: Michelangelo's *David* (✪ see the Accademia Tour chapter).

The Tour Begins

• *Stand in front of the Duomo as you get your historical bearings.*

The Florentine Renaissance

In the 13th and 14th centuries, Florence was a powerful center of banking, trading, and textile manufacturing. The resulting wealth fertilized the cultural soil. Then came the Black Death in 1348. Nearly half the population died, but the infrastructure remained strong, and the city rebuilt better than ever. Led by Florence's chief family—the art-crazy Medici—and propelled by the naturally aggressive and creative spirit of the Florentines, it's no wonder that the long-awaited Renaissance finally took root here.

The Renaissance—the "rebirth" of Greek and Roman culture that swept across Europe—started around 1400 and lasted about 150 years. In politics, the Renaissance meant democracy; in science, a renewed interest in exploring nature. The general mood was optimistic and "humanistic," with a confidence in the power of the individual.

In medieval times, poverty and ignorance had made life "nasty, brutish, and short" (for lack of a better cliché). The church was the people's opiate, and their lives were only a preparation for a happier time in heaven after leaving this miserable vale of tears.

Medieval art was the church's servant. The noblest art form was architecture—churches themselves—and other arts were considered most worthwhile if they embellished the house of God. Painting and sculpture were narrative and symbolic, designed to tell Bible stories to the devout and illiterate masses.

As prosperity rose in Florence, so did people's confidence in life and themselves. Middle-class craftsmen, merchants, and bankers felt they could control their own destinies, rather than be at the whim of nature. They

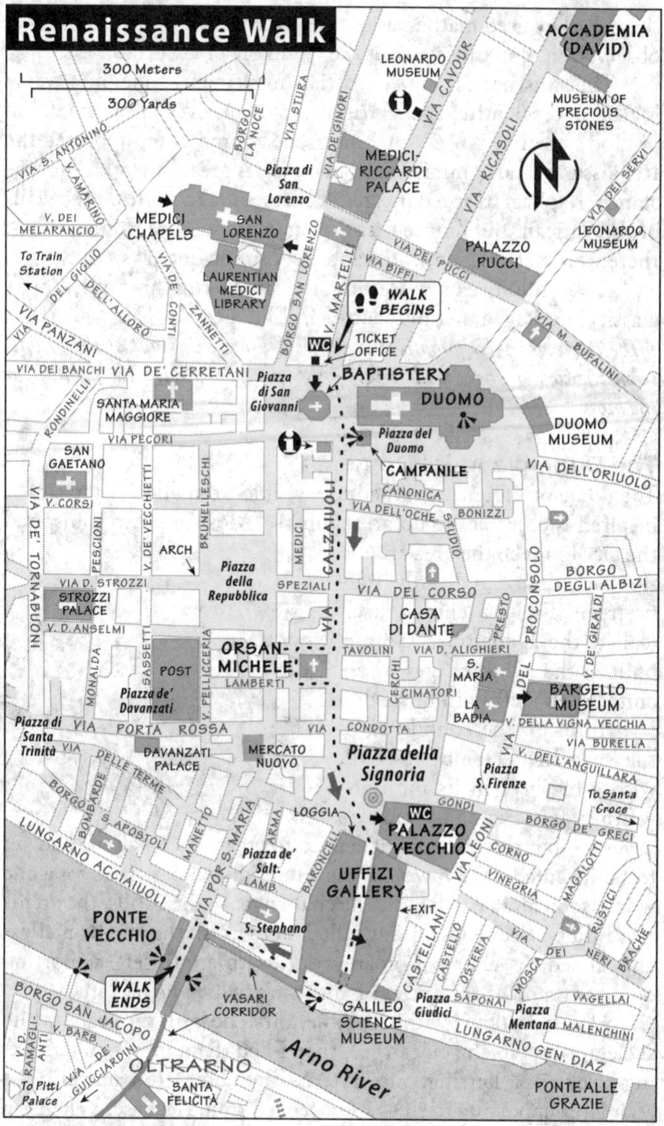

found much in common with the ancient Greeks and Romans, who valued logic and reason above superstition and blind faith.

Renaissance art was a return to the realism and balance of Greek and Roman sculpture and architecture. Domes and round arches replaced Gothic spires and pointed arches. In painting and sculpture, Renaissance artists strove for realism. Merging art and science, they used mathematics, the laws of perspective, and direct observation of nature to paint the world on a flat surface.

This was not an anti-Christian movement, though it was a logical and scientific age. Artists saw themselves as an extension of God's creative powers. At times, the church even supported the Renaissance and commissioned many of its greatest works—for instance, Raphael frescoed images of Plato and Aristotle on the walls of the Vatican. But for the first time in Europe since Roman times, there were rich laymen who wanted art simply for art's sake.

After 1,000 years of waiting, the smoldering fires of Europe's classical heritage burst into flames in Florence.

• *The dome of the Duomo is best viewed just to the right of the facade, from the corner of the pedestrian-only Via de' Calzaiuoli. Stand near the kiosk.*

The Duomo and Its Dome

The dome of Florence's cathedral—visible from all over the city—inspired Florentines to do great things. (Most recently, it inspired the city to make the area around the cathedral delightfully traffic-free.) The big church itself (called the Duomo) is Gothic, built in the Middle Ages by architects who left it unfinished.

Think of the confidence of the age: The Duomo was built with a big hole in its roof, just waiting for a grand dome to cover it—but the technology needed to create such a dome had yet to be invented. *No problema.* The Florentines knew that someone would soon be able to handle the challenge. In the 1400s, the architect Filippo Brunelleschi was called on to finish the job. Brunelleschi capped the church Roman-style—with a tall, self-supporting dome as grand as the ancient Pantheon's (which he had studied).

He used a dome within a dome. First, he built the grand white skeletal ribs, which you can see, then filled them in with interlocking bricks in a herringbone pattern. The dome grew upward like an igloo, supporting itself as it proceeded from the base. When the ribs reached the top, Brunelleschi arched them in and fixed them in place with the cupola at the top. His dome, built in only 14 years, was the largest since Rome's Pantheon.

Brunelleschi's dome was the wonder of the age, the model for many domes to follow, from St. Peter's to the US Capitol. People gave it the ultimate compliment, saying, "Not even the ancients could have done it." Michelangelo, setting out to construct the

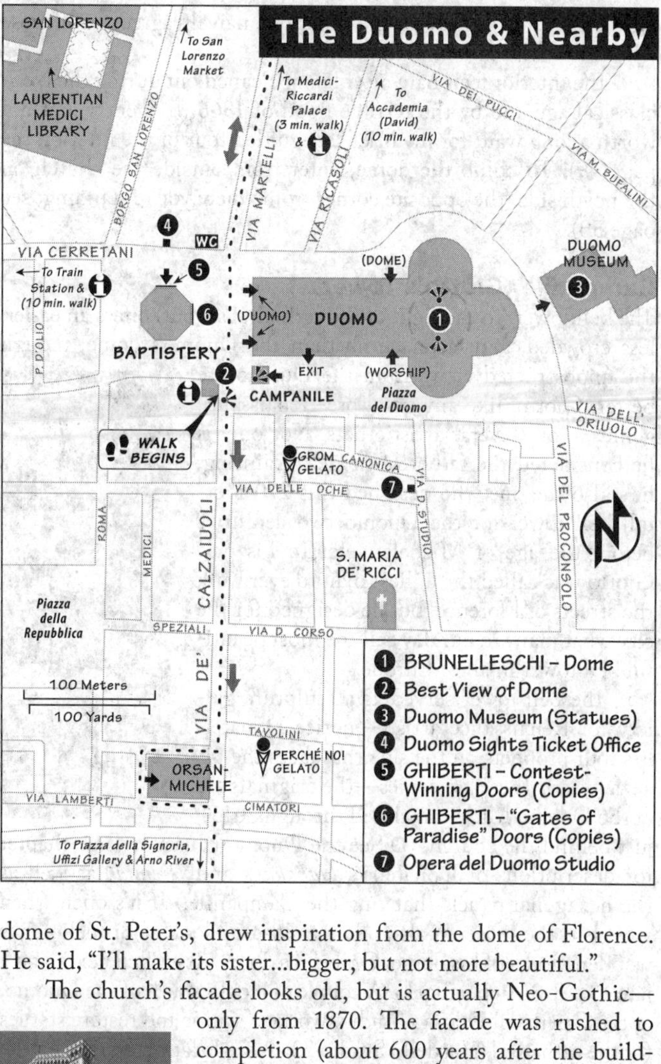

dome of St. Peter's, drew inspiration from the dome of Florence. He said, "I'll make its sister...bigger, but not more beautiful."

The church's facade looks old, but is actually Neo-Gothic—only from 1870. The facade was rushed to completion (about 600 years after the building began) to celebrate Italian unity, here in the city that for a few years served as the young country's capital. Its "retro" look captures the feel of the original medieval facade, with green, white, and pink marble sheets that cover the brick construction; Gothic (pointed) arches; and three horizontal stories decorated with mosaics and statues. Still, the facade is generally ridiculed. (While one of this book's authors thinks it's the most beautiful church

facade this side of heaven, the other one naively agrees with those who call it "the cathedral in pajamas.")

The interior feels bare after being cleaned out during the Neoclassical age and by the terrible flood of 1966 (free entry, but not worth a long wait; for my brief self-guided tour of the interior, see page 49). To climb the dome, enter from outside the church on the north side (the opposite corner from where you're standing; see page 50).

Campanile (Giotto's Tower)

The bell tower (to the right of the cathedral's front) offers an easier, less crowded, and faster climb than the Duomo's dome, though the unobstructed views from the Duomo are better. Giotto, like any good pre-Renaissance genius, wore several artistic hats. Not only is he considered the father of modern painting, he's also the one who designed this 270-foot-tall bell tower for the Duomo two centuries before the age of Michelangelo. In his day, Giotto was called the ugliest man to ever walk the streets of Florence, but he designed for the city what many in our day call the most beautiful bell tower in all of Europe.

The bell tower served as a sculpture gallery for Renaissance artists—notice Donatello's four prophets on the side that faces the piazza (west). These are copies—the originals are at the Duomo Museum (closed through 2015), just behind the church. (✪ See the Duomo Museum Tour chapter for descriptions of Donatello's *Habakkuk* and *Jeremiah* as well as the hexagonal panels that ring the Campanile.) If it's open when you visit, the museum also offers a close-up look at Brunelleschi's wooden model of his dome, Ghiberti's doors (described next), and a late *Pietà* by Michelangelo. A couple of blocks south of the Duomo, at the Opera del Duomo Studio, workers sculpt and restore statues for the cathedral (Via dello Studio 23a—see location on map on the previous page; you can peek through the doorway).

• *The Baptistery is the small octagonal building in front of the church. If you decide to go inside, get a ticket at the office across the piazza (Firenze Card holders need to get a voucher at the ticket office). If you just want to look at the exterior doors, there's no charge.*

Baptistery and Ghiberti's Bronze Doors

Florence's Baptistery is dear to the soul of the city. In medieval and Renaissance times, the locals—eager to link themselves to the classical past—believed (wrongly) that this was a Roman building. It is,

Ghiberti's Bronze Doors

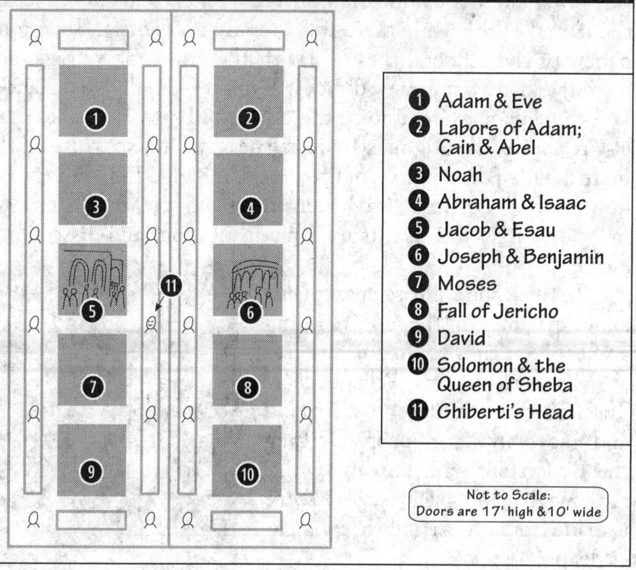

however, Florence's oldest building (11th century). Most festivals and parades either started or ended here.

Doors: The Baptistery's bronze doors bring us out of the Middle Ages and into the Renaissance. Some say the Renaissance began precisely in the year 1401, when Florence staged a competition to find the best artist to create the Baptistery's **north doors** (facing the ticket office; the door panels are being restored and may not be visible when you visit). Florence had strong civic spirit, with different guilds (powerful trade associations) and merchant groups embellishing their city with superb art. All the greats entered the contest, but 25-year-old Lorenzo Ghiberti won easily, beating out heavyweights such as Brunelleschi (who, after losing the Baptistery gig, was free to go to Rome, study the Pantheon, and later design the Duomo's dome). The original entries of Brunelleschi and Ghiberti—each showing the Old Testament story of the sacrifice of Isaac by Abraham—are in the Bargello, where you can judge them for yourself. Ghiberti's lithe, naked Isaac, even with his dad pointing a knife at his throat, is the picture of grace under pressure. Once awarded the prize, Ghiberti, a bit of a perfectionist, needed 20 years to finish the commission.

About the time Ghiberti completed the first set of doors, he was given another commission, in 1425, for the **east doors** (facing the church). This time there was literally no contest. The bronze panels of these doors (the ones with the crowd of tourists looking on) added a whole new dimension to art—depth. Michelangelo said these doors were fit to be the "Gates of Paradise." (These panels are copies; the originals are in the nearby Duomo Museum. For more detailed descriptions of the panels, see page 163.) Here we see how the Renaissance masters merged art and science. Realism was in, and Renaissance artists used math, illusion, and dissection to create it.

In the Jacob and Esau panel (just above eye level on the left), receding arches, floor tiles, and banisters create a background for a realistic scene. The figures in the foreground stand and move like real people, telling the Bible story with human details. Amazingly, this spacious, 3-D scene is made from bronze only a few inches deep.

Ghiberti spent 27 years (1425-1452) working on these panels. That's him in the center of the door frame, atop the second row of panels—the head on the left with the shiny male-pattern baldness.

Interior: You'll see a fine example of pre-Renaissance mosaic art (1200s-1300s) in the Byzantine style. Workers from St. Mark's in Venice came here to make the remarkable ceiling mosaics (of Venetian glass) in the late 1200s.

The Last Judgment on the ceiling gives us a glimpse of the medieval worldview. Life was a preparation for the afterlife, when you would be judged and saved, or judged and damned—with no in-between. Christ, peaceful and reassuring, blessed those at his right hand with heaven (thumbs up) and sent those on his left to hell (the ultimate thumbs-down), to be tortured by demons and gnashed between the teeth of monsters.

This hellish scene looks like something right out of the *Inferno* by Dante, who was dipped into the baptismal waters right here.

The rest of the ceiling mosaics tell the history of the world, from Adam and Eve (over the north/entrance doors, top row) to Noah and the Flood (over south doors, top row), to the life of Christ (second row, all around) to the life, ministry, and eventual beheading of John the Baptist (bottom row, all around)—all bathed in the golden glow of pre-Renaissance heaven.

• *Before we head south to the river, consider detouring a block north up Via de' Martelli (goes straight up from between the Duomo and Baptistery; turns into Via Cavour after a few blocks). At the intersection with Via dei Pucci is the imposing...*

Medici-Riccardi Palace

Renaissance Florence was ruled by the Medici, the rich banking family who lived in this building (for more on this family, see page 60). Studying this grand Florentine palace, you'll notice the lower walls are fortified, with elegant touches limited to the fancy upper stories. The Medici may have been the local Rockefellers, but having self-made wealth rather than actual noble blood, they were always a bit defensive. The Greek motifs along the eaves highlight the palace's Renaissance roots. Back then, rather than having parking spots, grand buildings came with iron rings to which you'd tether your horse.

You can step into the doorway at Via Cavour 1 and view the courtyard through an iron gate (though the entrance is farther up the street). If you pay admission, you get access to a quintessential Florentine palazzo with a courtyard and a couple of impressive rooms, most notably the sumptuous little Chapel of the Magi.

✪ See the Medici-Riccardi Palace Tour chapter.

• *Though we won't visit them on this walk, one block west of here are the Church of San Lorenzo (page 41) and Medici Chapels (✪ see the Medici Chapels Tour chapter); nearby, surrounding Mercato Centrale, are the leather-and-knickknack stalls of San Lorenzo Market. For now, return to the Duomo and continue south, entering the pedestrian-only street that runs from here toward the Arno River.*

Via de' Calzaiuoli

The pedestrian-only Via de' Calzaiuoli (kahlts-ay-WOH-lee) is lined with high-fashion shops, as Florence is a trendsetting city in trendsetting Italy. This street has always been the main axis of the city, and it was part of the ancient Roman grid plan that became

Florence. In medieval times, this street connected the religious center (where we are now) with the political center (where we're heading), a five-minute walk away. In the 20th century, this historic core was a noisy snarl of car traffic. But traffic jams have been replaced by potted plants, and now this is a pleasant place to stroll, people-watch, window-shop, lick the drips on your gelato cone, and wonder why American cities can't become more pedestrian-friendly.

And speaking of gelato...the recommended **Grom,** which keeps its *gelati* in covered metal bins, the old-fashioned way, is just a half-block detour away (take your first left, to Via delle Oche 24 red). Or you could drop by any of the several nearby gelato shops. *Perché no?* (Why not?)

Continue down Via de' Calzaiuoli. Two blocks down from the Baptistery, look right on Via degli Speziali to see a triumphal arch that marks **Piazza della Repubblica.** The arch celebrates the unification of Italy in 1870 and stands as a reminder that, in ancient Roman times, this piazza was the city center. For more on this square, see page 55.

• *A block farther, at the intersection with Via Orsanmichele, is the...*

Orsanmichele Church

The Orsanmichele Church provides an interesting look at Florence's medieval roots. It's a combo church/granary. Originally, this was an open loggia (covered porch) with a huge grain warehouse upstairs. The arches of the loggia were artfully filled in (14th century), and the building gained a new purpose—as a church. This was prime real estate on what had become the main drag between the church and palace.

The niches in the walls stood empty for decades before sponsors filled them in with statues. That role fell to the rising middle class of merchants and their guilds.

Florence in 1400 was a republic, a government working for the interests not of a king, but of these guilds (much as modern America caters to corporate interests). Over time, various guilds commissioned statues as PR gestures, hiring the finest artists of the generation. As a result, the statues that ring the church (generally copies of originals stored safely in nearby museums) function as a textbook of the evolution of Florentine art.

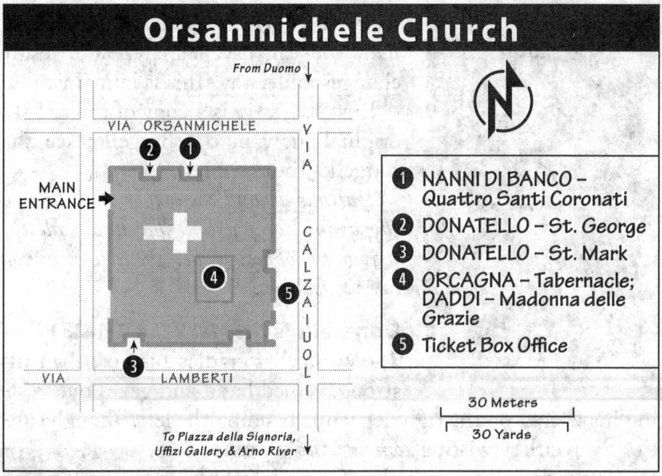

Orsanmichele Exterior

In earlier Gothic times, statues were set deep into church niches, simply embellishing the house of God. Here at the Orsanmichele Church, we see statues—as restless as man on the verge of the Renaissance—stepping out from the protection of the Church.

• *Head up Via Orsanmichele (to the right of the church) and circle the church exterior counterclockwise, looking out for these statues. Be careful not to stand right in the middle of the road—or at least keep an eye out for minibuses and horses. In the third niche is...*

Nanni di Banco's *Quattro Santi Coronati* (c. 1415-1417)

These four early Christians were sculptors martyred by the Roman emperor Diocletian because they refused to sculpt pagan gods. They seem to be contemplating the consequences of the fatal decision they're about to make. Beneath some of the niches, you'll find the symbol of the guilds that paid for the art. Art historians differ here. Some think the work was commissioned by the carpenters' and masons' guild. Others contend it was by the guys who did discount circumcisions.

• *The next niche holds...*

Donatello's *St. George*

George is alert, perched on the edge of his niche, scanning the horizon for dragons and announcing the new age with its new outlook. His knitted brow shows there's a drama unfolding. Sure, he's anxious, but he's also self-assured. Comparing this Renaissance-

style *St. George* to *Quattro Santi Coronati,* you can psychoanalyze the heady changes underway. This is humanism.

This *St. George* is a copy of the c. 1417 original (now in the Bargello; see the Bargello Tour chapter).

• *Continue around the corner of the church (bypassing the entrance for now), all the way to the opposite side. The first niche you come to features...*

Donatello's *St. Mark* (1411-1413)

The evangelist cradles his gospel in his strong, veined hand and gazes out, resting his weight on the right leg while bending the left. Though subtle, St. Mark's twisting *contrapposto* pose was the first seen since antiquity. Commissioned by the linen-sellers' guild, the statue has elaborately detailed robes that drape around the natural contours of his weighty body. When the guild first saw the statue, they thought the oversized head and torso made it top-heavy. Only after it was lifted into its raised niche did Donatello's cleverly designed proportions look right—and the guild accepted it. Eighty years after young Donatello carved this statue, a teenage Michelangelo Buonarroti stood here and marveled at it.

• *Backtrack to the entrance and go inside.*

Orsanmichele Interior

Here's a chance to step into Florence, circa 1350. The church has a double nave because it was adapted from a granary. Look for the pillars (on the left) with rectangular holes in them about three feet off the ground. These were once used as chutes for delivering grain from the storage rooms upstairs. Look up to see the rings hanging from the ceiling, likely used to make pulleys for lifting grain, and the iron bars spanning the vaults for support.

The fine **tabernacle** by Andrea Orcagna was designed exactly for this space: Like the biggest Christmas tree possible, it's capped by an angel whose head touches the ceiling. Take in the Gothic tabernacle's medieval elegance. What it lacks in depth and realism it makes up for in color, with an intricate assemblage of marble, glass, gold, and expensive lapis lazuli. Florence had just survived the terrible bubonic plague of 1348, which killed half the population. The elaborate tabernacle was built to display Bernardo Daddi's *Madonna delle Grazie,* which received plague survivors' grateful prayers. While it's great to see art in museums, it's even better to enjoy it in its original setting—"in situ"—where the artist intended it to be seen. When you view similar altarpieces out of context in the Uffizi, think back on the candlelit medieval atmosphere that surrounds this altarpiece.

Upstairs is a free museum (open only Mon 10:00-17:00) displaying most of the originals of the statues you just saw outside. Each one is identified by the subject, year, and sculptor, representing virtually every big name in pre-Michelangelo Florentine sculpture: Donatello, Ghiberti, Brunelleschi, Giambologna, and more.

Consider returning for one of the church's evening concerts; tickets are sold on the day of the concert from the door facing Via de' Calzaiuoli (see Orsanmichele Church map). You can also book tickets here for the Uffizi and Accademia.

• *The Bargello, with Florence's best collection of sculpture, is a few blocks east, down Via dei Tavolini. (✪ See the Bargello Tour chapter.) But let's continue down the mall 50 more yards, to the huge and historic square...*

Piazza della Signoria

The main civic center of Florence is dominated by Palazzo Vecchio, the Uffizi Gallery, and the marble greatness of old Florence littering the cobbles. Piazza della Signoria still vibrates with the echoes of the city's past—executions, riots, and great celebrations. There's even Roman history: Look for the **chart** showing the ancient city (on a waist-high, freestanding display to your right as you enter the square, in front of Chanel). Today, it's a tourist's world with pigeons, postcards, horse buggies, and tired hubbies. If it would make your weary companion happy, stop in at the recommended but expensive **Rivoire** café to enjoy its fine desserts, pudding-thick hot chocolate, and the best view seats in town. It's expensive—but if you linger, it can be a great value.

Before you towers Palazzo Vecchio, the palatial Town Hall of the Medici—a fortress designed to contain riches and survive the many riots that went with local politics. The windows

are just beyond the reach of angry stones, and the tower was a handy lookout post. Justice was doled out sternly on this square. Until 1873, Michelangelo's ***David*** stood where you see the replica today. The original was damaged in a 1527 riot (when a bench thrown from a palace window knocked its left arm off), but it remained here for several centuries, vulnerable to erosion and pollution, before being moved indoors for protection.

Step past the replica *David* through the front door into Palazzo Vecchio's courtyard (free). This palace was Florence's symbol of civic power. You're surrounded by art for art's sake—a cherub frivolously marks the courtyard's center, and ornate stuccoes and frescoes decorate the walls and columns. Such luxury represented a big change 500 years ago. For a self-guided tour of the palace, including more on this courtyard, ✪ see the Palazzo Vecchio Tour chapter.

• *Back outside, check out the statue-filled...*

Loggia dei Lanzi (a.k.a. Loggia della Signoria)

The loggia, once a forum for public debate, was perfect for a city that prided itself on its democratic traditions. But later, when the Medici figured that good art was more desirable than free speech, it was turned into an outdoor sculpture gallery. Notice the squirming Florentine themes—conquest, domination, rape, and decapitation. The statues lining the back are Roman originals brought back to Florence by a Medici when he moved home after living in Rome. Two statues in the front deserve a closer look.

At the right end of the loggia, ***The Rape of the Sabine Women*** (c. 1583)—with its pulse-quickening rhythm of muscles—is from the restless Mannerist period, which followed the stately and confident Renaissance. The sculptor, Giambologna, proved his mastery of the medium by sculpting three entangled bodies from one piece of marble. The composition is best viewed from below and in front. The relief panel below shows a wider view of the terrible scene. Note what looks like an IV tube on the arm of the horrified husband. It's an electrified wire that effectively keeps the pigeons away. (In the Accademia, you can see the plaster model of this statue that was used to guide Giambologna's workers in helping him create it.)

At the Palazzo Vecchio end, Benvenuto **Cellini's *Perseus*** (1545-1553), the loggia's most noteworthy piece, shows the Greek hero who decapitated the snake-headed Medusa. They say Medusa was so ugly she turned humans who looked at her to stone—though one of this book's authors thinks she's kinda cute.

• *Cross the square to the big* ***fountain of Neptune*** *by Bartolomeo Ammanati that Florentines (including Michelangelo) consider a huge waste of marble—though one of this book's authors... The guy on the horse, to the left, is Cosimo I, one of the post-Renaissance Medici.*

Find the round bronze plaque on the ground 10 steps in front of the fountain.

Savonarola Plaque

The Medici family was briefly thrown from power by an austere monk named Savonarola, who made Florence a constitutional republic. He organized huge rallies lit by roaring bonfires here on the square where he preached. While children sang hymns, the devout brought their rich "vanities" (such as paintings, musical instruments, and playing cards) and threw them into the flames.

But not everyone wanted a return to the medieval past. Encouraged by the pope, the Florentines fought back and arrested Savonarola. For two days, they tortured him, trying unsuccessfully to persuade him to see their side of things. Finally, on the very spot where Savonarola's followers had built bonfires of vanities, the monk was burned. The bronze plaque, engraved in Italian *("Qui dove...")*, reads, "Here, Girolamo Savonarola and his Dominican brothers were hanged and burned" in the year "MCCCCXCVIII" (1498). For help in deciphering Roman numerals, see page 699.

• *Stay cool, we have 200 yards to go. Follow the gaze of the fake* David *into the courtyard of the two-tone horseshoe-shaped building.*

Uffizi Courtyard

The top floor of this building, known as the *uffizi* (offices) during Medici days, is filled with the greatest collection of Florentine painting anywhere. It's one of Europe's top four or five art galleries (✪ see the Uffizi Gallery Tour chapter).

The Uffizi courtyard, filled with merchants and hustling young artists, is watched over by 19th-century statues of the great figures of the Renaissance. Tourists zero in on the visual accomplishments of the era—not realizing that it was multi-faceted. Let's pay tribute to the nonvisual Renaissance as well, as we wander through Florence's Renaissance Hall of Fame.

• *Stroll down the left side of the courtyard from Palazzo Vecchio to the river, noticing the following greats.*

Lorenzo de' Medici (the Magnificent) was a great art patron and cunning power broker. Excelling in everything except modesty, he set the tone for the Renaissance. His statue is tucked under the arcade, by a Uffizi doorway.

Giotto, holding the plan to the city's bell tower (which is named for him) was the great pre-Renaissance artist whose paintings foretold the future of Italian art.

Donatello, the sculptor who served as a role model for Michelangelo, holds a hammer and chisel.

Alberti wrote a famous book, *On Painting*, which taught early Renaissance artists the mathematics of perspective.

Leonardo da Vinci was a scientist, sculptor, musician, engineer...and not a bad painter either.

Michelangelo ponders the universe and/or stifles a belch.

Dante, with the laurel-leaf crown and lyre of a poet, says, "I am the father of the Italian language." He was the first Italian to write a popular work *(The Divine Comedy)* in the Florentine dialect, which soon became "Italian" throughout the country (until Dante, Latin had been the language of literature).

The poet **Petrarch** wears laurel leaves from Greece, a robe from Rome, and a belt from Walmart.

Boccaccio wrote *The Decameron,* stories told to pass the time during the 1348 Black Death.

The devious-looking **Machiavelli** is hatching a plot—his book *The Prince* taught that the end justifies the means, paving the way for the slick-and-cunning "Machiavellian" politics of today.

Vespucci (in the corner) was an explorer who gave his first name, Amerigo, to a fledgling New World.

Galileo (in the other corner) holds the humble telescope he used to spot the moons of Jupiter.

• *Pause at the Arno River, overlooking Ponte Vecchio.*

Ponte Vecchio

Before you is Ponte Vecchio (Old Bridge). A bridge has spanned this narrowest part of the Arno since Roman times. While Rome "fell," Florence never really did, remaining a bustling trade center along the river. To get into the exclusive little park below (on the north bank), you'll need to join the Florence rowing club.

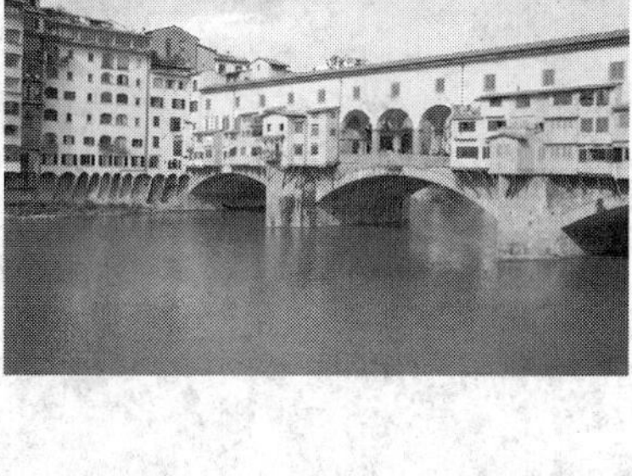

• *Finish your walk by hiking to the center of the bridge.*

A fine bust of the great goldsmith Cellini graces the central point of the bridge. This statue is a reminder that, in the 1500s, the Medici booted out the bridge's butchers and tanners and installed the gold- and silversmiths who still tempt visitors to this day. This is a very romantic spot late at night (when lovers gather, and a top-notch street musician performs). For more on this bridge, ✪ see the start of the Oltrarno Walk.

Look up to notice the protected and elevated passageway that led the Medici from Palazzo Vecchio through the Uffizi, across Ponte Vecchio, and up to the immense Pitti Palace, four blocks beyond the bridge. During World War II, the Nazi occupiers were ordered to blow up Ponte Vecchio. An art-loving German consul intervened and saved the bridge. The buildings at either end were destroyed, leaving the bridge impassable but intact. *Grazie.*

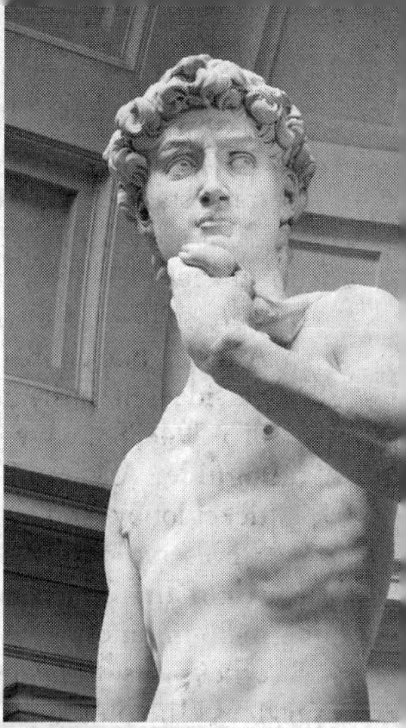

ACCADEMIA GALLERY TOUR

Galleria dell'Accademia

One of Europe's great thrills is seeing Michelangelo's *David* in the flesh at the Accademia Gallery. Seventeen feet high, gleaming white, and exalted by a halo-like dome over his head, *David* rarely disappoints, even for those with high expectations. And the Accademia doesn't stop there. With a handful of other Michelangelo statues and a few other interesting sights, it makes for an uplifting visit that isn't overwhelming. *David* is a must-see on any visit to Florence, so plan for it.

Orientation

Cost: €11 (or €6.50 if there's no temporary exhibit), additional €4 fee for recommended reservation; covered by Firenze Card.

Hours: Tue-Sun 8:15-18:50, closed Mon, last entry 30 minutes before closing.

Avoiding Lines: In peak season (April-Oct), it's smart to buy a Firenze Card or reserve ahead (see pages 34 and 38 for info on both options). Those with reservations or the Firenze Card line up at the entrance labeled *Reserved*. If you show up without a reservation or Firenze Card, and there's a long line at the *Not Reserved* entrance, try dropping by the My Accademia Libreria reservation office, just across the street from the exit, to see if they have any times available later that day (€4 reservation charge).

When to Go: In peak season, the museum is most crowded on Sun, Tue, and between about 11:00 and 13:00; in spring and fall, Sat is also quite busy. On off-season weekdays (Nov-March), you can sometimes get in with no reservation and no lines if you go before 8:30 or after 16:00.

Getting There: It's at Via Ricasoli 60, a 15-minute walk from the train station or a 10-minute walk northeast of the Duomo. Taxis are reasonable.

Information: Exhibits are explained in English, and a small bookstore sells guidebooks near the ticket booths at the entrance. Another bookstore (inside and near the exit) and several shops outside sell postcards, books, and posters. Reservation tel. 055-294-883, www.polomuseale.firenze.it.

Audioguide: A €6 audioguide (€10/2 people) is available in the ticket lobby. You can also download this chapter as a free Rick Steves **audio tour** (see page 9).

Length of This Tour: While *David* and the *Prisoners* can be seen in 30 minutes, allow an hour if you wish to linger and explore other parts of the museum.

Services: The museum has no bag-check service, and large backpacks are not allowed. WCs are downstairs near the entrance/exit.

Photography: No flash photography.

Cuisine Art: Gelateria Carabè, popular for its sumptuous *granite* (fresh-fruit Italian ices with a Sicilian flair), is a block toward the Duomo, at Via Ricasoli 60 red. My favorite place for a nearby picnic is the picturesque Renaissance Piazza S.S. Annunziata, just a block away; grab a takeout lunch at one of the places listed on page 298, and munch it on the square. That section also lists some restaurants.

Starring: Michelangelo's *David* and *Prisoners.*

The Tour Begins

• *From the entrance lobby, show your ticket, turn left, and look right down the long hall with* David *at the far end, under a halo-like dome. Yes, you're really here. With* David *presiding at the "altar," the* Prisoners *lining the "nave," and hordes of "pilgrims" crowding in to look, you've arrived at Florence's "cathedral of humanism."*

Start with the ultimate...

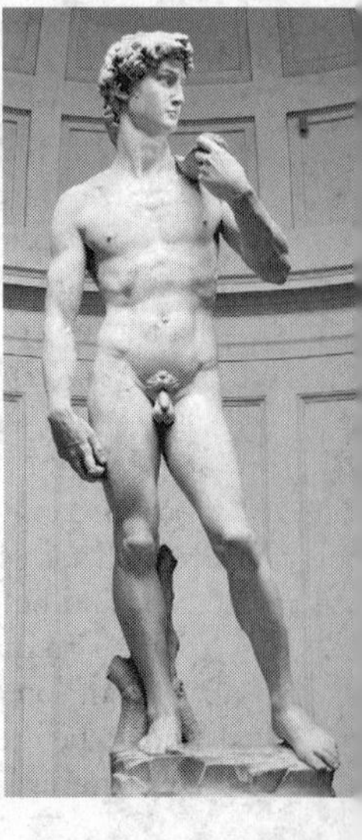

David (1501-1504)

When you look into the eyes of Michelangelo's *David,* you're looking into the eyes of Renaissance Man. This 17-foot-tall symbol of divine victory over evil represents a new century and a whole new Renaissance outlook. This is the age of Columbus and classicism, Galileo and Gutenberg, Luther and Leonardo—of Florence and the Renaissance.

In 1501, Michelangelo Buonarroti, a 26-year-old Florentine, was commissioned to carve a large-scale work for the Duomo. He was given a block of marble that other sculptors had rejected as too tall, shallow, and flawed to be of any value. But Michelangelo picked up his hammer and chisel, knocked a knot off what became *David*'s heart, and started to work.

The figure comes from a Bible story. The Israelites, God's chosen people, are surrounded by barbarian warriors led by a brutish giant named Goliath. The giant challenges the Israelites to send out someone to fight him. Everyone is afraid except for one young shepherd boy—David. Armed only with a sling, which he's thrown over his shoulder, David gathers five smooth stones from the stream and faces Goliath.

The statue captures David as he's sizing up his enemy. He stands relaxed but alert, leaning on one leg in a classical pose known as *contrapposto*. In his powerful right hand, he fondles the handle of the sling, ready to fling a stone at the giant. His gaze is steady—searching with intense concentration, but also with extreme confidence. Michelangelo has caught the precise moment when David is saying to himself, "I can take this guy."

Note that while the label on *David* indicates that he's already slain the giant, the current director of the Accademia believes, as I do, that Michelangelo has portrayed David facing the giant. Unlike most depictions of David after the kill, this sculpture does not show the giant's severed head. There's also a question of exactly how David's sling would work. Is he holding the stone in his right or left hand? Does the right hand hold the sling's pouch or the retention handle of a sling? Scholars debate Sling Theory endlessly.

David is a symbol of Renaissance optimism. He's no brute. He's a civilized, thinking individual who can grapple with and overcome problems. He needs no armor, only his God-given body and wits. Look at his right hand, with the raised veins and strong, relaxed fingers—many complained that it was too big and overdeveloped. But this is the hand of a man with the strength of God. No mere boy could slay the giant. But David, powered by God, could...and did.

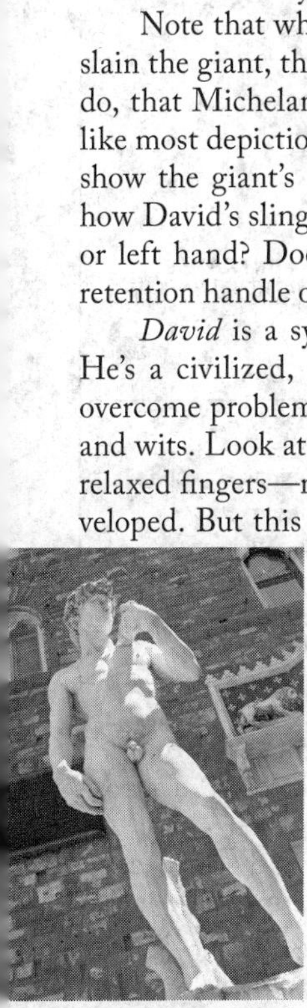

Originally, the statue was commissioned to stand along the southern roofline of the Duomo. But during the three years it took to sculpt, they decided instead to place it guarding the entrance of Town Hall— Palazzo Vecchio. (If the relationship between *David*'s head and body seems a bit out of proportion, it's because Michelangelo designed it to be seen "correctly" from far below the rooftop of the church.)

The colossus was placed standing up in

Accademia Overview

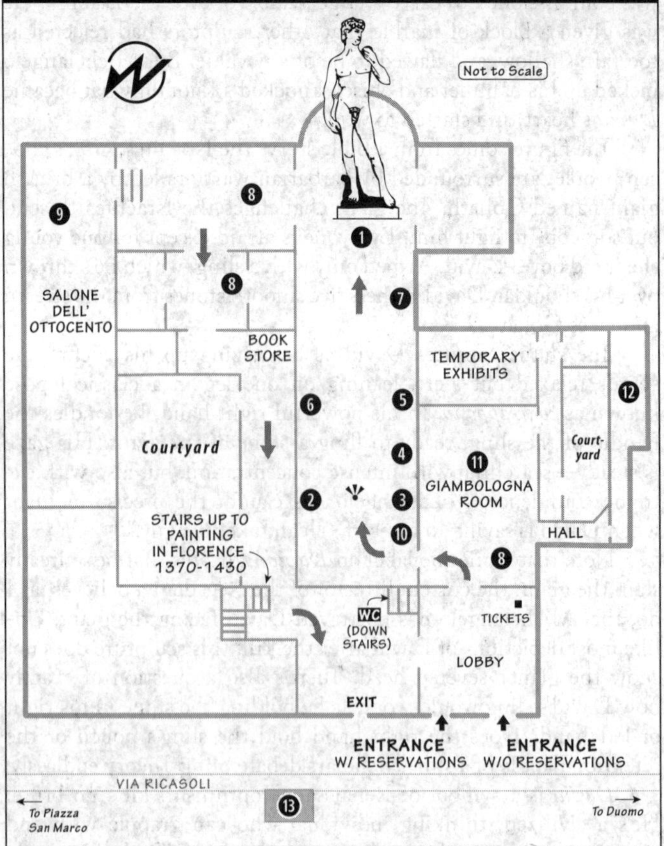

1 David
2 Awakening Prisoner
3 Young Prisoner
4 St. Matthew
5 Bearded Prisoner
6 Atlas Prisoner
7 Pietà
8 Paintings (3 Rooms)
9 Salone dell' Ottocento Statues
10 Bust of Michelangelo
11 Rape of the Sabine Women
12 Museum of Musical Instruments
13 My Accademia Libreria Reservation Office

a cart and dragged across rollers from Michelangelo's workshop (behind the Duomo) to Palazzo Vecchio, where it replaced a work by Donatello. There *David* stood—naked and outdoors—for 350 years. In the right light, you can see signs of weathering on his shoulders. Also, note the crack in *David*'s left arm where it was broken off during a 1527 riot near Palazzo Vecchio. In 1873, to conserve the masterpiece, the statue was finally replaced with a copy (see photo on page 99) and moved here. The real *David* now stands under a wonderful Renaissance-style dome designed just for him.

Circle *David* and view him from various angles. From the front, he's confident, but a little less so when you gaze directly into his eyes. Around back, see his sling strap, buns of steel, and Renaissance mullet. Up close, you can see the blue-veined Carrara marble and a few cracks and stains. From the sides, Michelangelo's challenge becomes clear: to sculpt a figure from a block of marble other sculptors said was too tall and narrow to accommodate a human figure.

Renaissance Florentines could identify with *David*. Like him, they considered themselves God-blessed underdogs fighting their city-state rivals. In a deeper sense, they were civilized Renaissance people slaying the ugly giant of medieval superstition, pessimism, and oppression.

• *Hang around a while. Eavesdrop on tour guides. The Plexiglas shields at the base of the statue went up after an attack by a frustrated artist, who smashed the statue's feet in 1991.*

Lining the hall leading up to David *are other statues by Michelangelo—his* Prisoners, St. Matthew, *and* Pietà. *Start with the* Awakening Prisoner, *the statue at the end of the nave (farthest from* David*). He's on your left as you face* David.

The *Prisoners* (*Prigioni*, c. 1516-1534)

These unfinished figures seem to be fighting to free themselves from the stone. Michelangelo believed the sculptor was a tool of God, not creating but simply revealing the powerful and beautiful figures that God had encased in the marble. Michelangelo's job was to chip away the excess, to reveal. He needed to be in tune with God's will, and whenever the spirit came upon him, Michelangelo worked in a frenzy, without sleep, often for days on end.

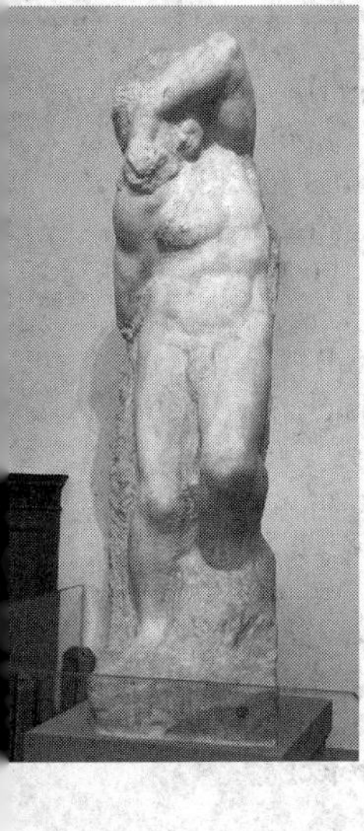

The *Prisoners* give us a glimpse of this fitful process, showing the restless energy of someone possessed, struggling against the rock that binds him. Michelangelo himself fought to create the image he saw in his mind's eye. You can still see the grooves from the chisel, and you can picture Michelangelo hacking away in a cloud of dust. Unlike most sculptors, who built a model and then marked up their block of marble to know where to chip, Michelangelo always worked freehand, starting from the

David, David, David, and *David*

Several Italian masters produced iconic sculptures of David—all of them different. Compare and contrast the artists' styles. How many ways can you slay a giant?

Donatello's *David* (1430, Bargello, Florence)

Donatello's *David* is young and graceful, casually gloating over the head of Goliath, almost Gothic in its elegance and smooth lines. While he has a similar weight-on-one-leg *(contrapposto)* stance as Michelangelo's later version, Donatello's *David* seems feminine rather than masculine. (For further description, see page 137 of the Bargello Tour chapter.)

Andrea del Verrocchio's *David* (c. 1470, Bargello, Florence)

Wearing a military skirt and armed with a small sword, Verrocchio's *David* is just a boy. The statue is only four feet tall—dwarfed by Michelangelo's monumental version. (For more, see page 137 of the Bargello Tour chapter.)

Michelangelo's *David* (1501-1504, Accademia, Florence)

Michelangelo's *David* is pure Renaissance: massive, heroic in size, and superhuman in

front and working back. These figures emerge from the stone (as his colleague Vasari put it) "as though surfacing from a pool of water."

The so-called ***Awakening Prisoner*** (the names are given by scholars, not Michelangelo) seems to be stretching after a long nap, still tangled in the "bedsheets" of uncarved rock. He's more block than statue.

On the right, the ***Young Prisoner*** is more finished. He buries his face in his forearm, while his other arm is chained behind him.

The *Prisoners* were designed for the never-completed tomb of Pope Julius II (who also commissioned the Sistine Chapel ceiling). Michelangelo may have abandoned them simply because the project itself petered out, or he may have deliberately left them unfinished. Having perhaps satisfied himself that he'd accomplished what he set out to do, and seeing no point in polishing them into their shiny, finished state, he went on to a new project.

strength and power. The tensed right hand, which grips a stone in readiness to hurl at Goliath, is more powerful than any human hand. It's symbolic of divine strength. A model of perfection, Michelangelo's *David* is far larger and grander than we mere mortals. We know he'll win. Renaissance Man has arrived.

Gian Lorenzo Bernini's *David* (1623, Borghese Museum, Rome)

Flash forward more than a century. In this self-portrait, 25-year-old Bernini is ready to take on the world, slay the pretty-boy Davids of the Renaissance, and invent Baroque. Unlike Michelangelo's rational, cool, restrained *David,* Bernini's is a doer: passionate, engaged, dramatic. While Renaissance *David* is simple and unadorned—carrying only a sling—Baroque Dave is "cluttered" with a braided sling, a hairy pouch, flowing cloth, and discarded armor. Bernini's *David,* with his tousled hair and set mouth, is one of us; the contest is less certain than with the other three Davids.

To sum up: Donatello's *David* represents the first inkling of the Renaissance; Verrocchio's is early Renaissance in miniature; Michelangelo's is textbook Renaissance; and Bernini's is the epitome of Baroque.

Walking up the nave toward *David,* you'll pass by Michelangelo's ***St. Matthew*** (1503), on the right. Though not one of the *Prisoners* series, he is also unfinished, perfectly illustrating Vasari's "surfacing" description.

The next statue (also on the right), the ***Bearded Prisoner,*** is the most finished of the four, with all four limbs, a bushy face, and even a hint of daylight between his arm and body.

Across the nave on the left, the ***Atlas Prisoner*** carries the unfinished marble on his stooped shoulders, his head still encased in the block.

As you study the *Prisoners,* notice Michelangelo's love and understanding of the human body. His greatest days were spent sketching the muscular, tanned, and sweating bodies of the workers in the Carrara marble quarries. The prisoners' heads and faces are the least-developed part—they "speak" with their poses. Comparing the restless, claustrophobic *Prisoners* with the serene and confident *David* gives an idea of the sheer emotional range in Michelangelo's work.

• *The unfinished threesome closest to* David *is the...*

Pietà

The figures struggle to hold up the sagging body of Christ. Michelangelo (or, more likely, one of his followers) emphasizes the heaviness of Jesus' dead body, driving home the point that this divine being suffered a very human death. Christ's massive arm is almost the size of his bent and broken legs. By stretching his body—if he stood up, he'd be more than seven feet tall—the weight is exaggerated.

• *After getting your fill of Michelangelo, consider taking a spin around the rest of the Accademia. Michelangelo's statues are far and away the highlight here, but the rest of this small museum—housed in a former convent/hospice—has a few bonuses.*

Paintings

Browse the pleasant-but-underwhelming collection of paintings in the hall near *David* and the adjoining corridor; you'll be hard-pressed to find even one by a painter whose name you recognize. (You'll find better art in the Giambologna Room; described on next page.)

Salone dell'Ottocento Statues

At the end of the hall to the left of *David* is a long room crammed with plaster statues and busts. These were the Academy art students' "final exams"—preparatory models for statues, many of which were later executed in marble. The black dots on the statues are sculptors' "points," guiding them on how deep to chisel. The Academy art school has been attached to the museum for centuries, and you may see the next Michelangelo wandering the streets nearby.

Bust of Michelangelo

At the end of the nave (farthest from *David*), a bronze bust depicts a craggy, wrinkled Michelangelo, age 89, by Daniele da Volterra. (Daniele, one of Michelangelo's colleagues and friends, is best known as the one who painted loincloths on the private parts of Michelangelo's nudes in the Sistine Chapel.) As a teenager, Michelangelo got his nose broken in a fight with a rival artist. Though Michelangelo went on to create great beauty, he was never classically handsome.

• Enter the room near the museum entrance dominated by a large, squirming statue.

Giambologna Room

This full-size plaster model of *Rape of the Sabine Women* (1582) guided Giambologna's assistants in completing the marble version in the Loggia dei Lanzi (on Piazza della Signoria, next to Palazzo Vecchio, described on page 91). A Roman warrior tramples a fighter from the Sabine tribe and carries off the man's wife. Husband and wife exchange one final, anguished glance. Circle the statue and watch it spiral around its axis. Giambologna was clearly influenced (as a plaque with photo points out) by Michelangelo's groundbreaking *Victory* in Palazzo Vecchio (1533-1534, described on page 180). Michelangelo's statue of a man triumphing over a fallen enemy introduced both the theme and the spiral-shaped pose that many artists imitated.

Browse the room clockwise (from the entrance) to locate minor **paintings** by artists you'll encounter elsewhere in Florence. Domenico Ghirlandaio's paintings of Renaissance Florence are behind the altar of the Church of Santa Maria Novella (see page 206). Francesco Granacci, a childhood friend of Michelangelo, assisted him on the Sistine Ceiling. Benozzo Gozzoli decorated the personal chapel of the Medici in the Medici-Riccardi Palace (see page 197). Filippino Lippi is known for his frescoes in the Brancacci Chapel and Church of Santa Maria Novella. And Botticelli's *Birth of Venus* hangs in the Uffizi (see page 118).

• From the Giambologna Room, head down a short hallway leading to a few rooms containing the...

Museum of Musical Instruments

Between 1400 and 1700, Florence was one of Europe's most sophisticated cities, and the Medici rulers were trendsetters. Musicians like Scarlatti and Handel flocked to the court of Prince Ferdinando (1663-1713). You'll see late-Renaissance cellos, dulcimers, violins, woodwinds, and harpsichords. (Listen to some on the computer terminals.)

As you enter, look for the two group paintings that include the prince (he's second from the right in both paintings, with the yellow bowtie) hanging out with his musician friends. The gay prince played a mean harpsichord, and he helped pioneer new variations. In the adjoining room, you'll see several experimental keyboards, including some by Florence's keyboard pioneer, Bartolomeo Cristofori. The tall piano on display (from 1739) is considered by some to be the world's first upright piano.

• Head one more time back up the nave to say goodbye to Dave, then turn left, and left again, to go through the bookstore toward the exit. From the

More Michelangelo

If you're a fan of earth's greatest sculptor, you won't leave Florence until there's a check next to each of these:

- **Bargello:** Several Michelangelo sculptures, including the *Bacchus* (pictured here; see the Bargello Tour chapter).

- **Duomo Museum:** Another moving *pietà* (see page 165); museum closed for renovation in 2015.
- **Medici Chapels:** The *Night* and *Day* statues, plus others done for the Medici tomb, located at the Church of San Lorenzo (see the Medici Chapels Tour chapter).
- **Laurentian Medici Library:** Michelangelo designed the entrance staircase and more, located at the Church of San Lorenzo (see page 41).
- **Palazzo Vecchio:** His *Victory* statue (see page 180).
- **Uffizi Gallery:** A rare Michelangelo painting (see page 126).
- **Casa Buonarroti:** Built on property Michelangelo once owned, at Via Ghibellina 70, containing some early works (see page 64).
- **Santa Croce Church:** Michelangelo's tomb (see page 64).
- **Santo Spirito Church:** Wooden crucifix thought to be by Michelangelo (see page 67).

bookstore, in good weather you can step out into the airy courtyard for some sun, fresh air, peace, and quiet...aaaah.

Before you leave—after the bookshop, but before the exit lobby—you'll see stairs up to the first floor, with one more exhibit. (I won't blame you if you skip this collection of altarpieces.) At the top, you'll find...

Florentine Paintings, 1370-1430

Here you'll find mostly altarpieces depicting saints and Madonnas, painted during the last gasp of the Middle Ages—the period after the Great Plague wracked Florence, but before Renaissance fever hit in full force. Gaze upon Lorenzo Monaco's *Man of Sorrows* (up the stairs, in the central hall, on the left side, from 1404): a green-skinned Christ accompanied by the instruments of his torture. Mentally contrast this somber scene with the confident optimism of Michelangelo's *David,* done a century later, in the full bloom of the Florentine Renaissance.

• *The tour is finished. From here, it's a 10-minute walk to the Duomo.*

UFFIZI GALLERY TOUR

Galleria degli Uffizi

In the Renaissance, Florentine artists rediscovered the beauty of the natural world. Medieval art had been symbolic, telling Bible stories. Realism didn't matter. But Renaissance people saw the beauty of God in nature and the human body. They used math and science to capture the natural world on canvas as realistically as possible.

The Uffizi Gallery (oo-FEED-zee) has the greatest overall collection anywhere of Italian painting. We'll trace the rise of realism and savor the optimistic spirit that marked the Renaissance.

My eyes love things that are fair,
and my soul for salvation cries.
But neither will to Heaven rise
unless the sight of Beauty lifts them there.
—Michelangelo Buonarroti, sculptor, painter, poet

Orientation

Cost: €11 (or €6.50 if there's no special exhibit), additional €4 fee for recommended reservation (if you've reserved tickets by phone, bring cash to pick them up), covered by Firenze Card.

Hours: Tue-Sun 8:15-18:35, closed Mon, last entry 30 minutes before closing.

Expect Changes: The Uffizi is undergoing a massive, years-long renovation that may affect your visit. Some of the items described in this chapter may be displayed in different rooms, on loan to other museums, or out for restoration—pick up a floor plan as you enter, and if you need help finding a particular piece of art, ask the guards in each room. Displaced masterpieces tend to be on display either at the end of the top-floor collection (rooms 43 and 45, after the Michelangelo rooms); or in the halls down on the first floor, which you'll see on your way to the exit (rooms 65-85, shuffled among the Raphael and Caravaggio rooms).

Avoiding Lines: To skip the notoriously long ticket-buying lines, either get a Firenze Card or reserve ahead (for details on both, see pages 34 and 38). During summer and on weekends, the Uffizi can be booked up a month or more in advance. Without a Firenze Card or reservation, you can usually enter without major lines from November through March after 16:00. But in peak season (April-Oct) and on weekends, the wait can be hours, and it can be crowded even late in the day. The busiest days are Tuesday, Saturday, and Sunday.

Getting There: It's on the Arno River between Palazzo Vecchio and Ponte Vecchio, a 15-minute walk from the train station.

Getting In: There are several entrances (see map on next page). Which one you use depends on whether you have a Firenze Card, a reservation, or neither.

Firenze Card holders enter at door #1 (labeled *Reservation Entrance*), close to Palazzo Vecchio. Read the signs carefully, as there are two lines at this entrance; get in the line for individuals, not groups.

People **buying a ticket on the spot** line up with everyone else at door #2, marked *Main Entrance.* (The wait can be hours long.)

To **buy a Firenze Card,** or to see if there are any same-day reservations available (€4 extra, but could save you time in the ticket line), enter door #2 to the left of the ticket-buying line (marked *Booking Service and Today;* don't be shy—just skirt around to the left of the long line).

UFFIZI

If you've **already made a reservation** and need to pick up your ticket, go to door #3 (labeled *Reservation Ticket Office,* across the courtyard from doors #1 and #2, and a bit closer to the river). Tickets are available for pick-up 10 minutes before your appointed time. If you booked online and have already prepaid, you'll just exchange your voucher for a ticket. If you (or your hotelier) booked by phone, give them your confirmation number and pay for the ticket (cash only). Once you have your ticket, walk briskly past the 200-yard-long ticket-buying line—pondering the IQ of this gang—to door #1. Show your ticket and walk in.

Information: English information is posted in many rooms. You can buy Uffizi guide-

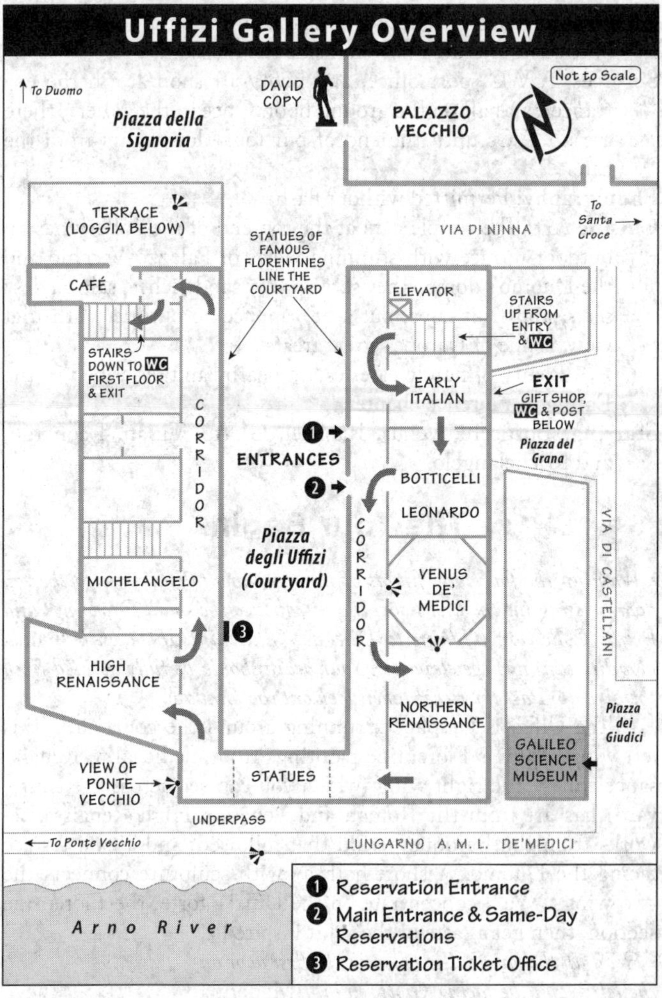

books (a nice souvenir) at the ground-floor bookstore (€12 small book, €16 bigger version). Museum info tel. 055-238-8651, reservation tel. 055-294-883, www.uffizi.firenze.it.

Audioguides: A 1.5-hour audioguide costs €6 (€10/2 people; must leave ID). You can also download this chapter as a free Rick Steves audio tour (see page 9).

Length of This Tour: Allow two hours. If you have less time, see the Florentine Renaissance rooms (Botticelli and Leonardo) and the High Renaissance section (Michelangelo, Raphael, and Titian).

Cloakroom: Baggage check is available in the entrance lobby. No bottled liquids are allowed inside the museum.

Services: A WC, post office, and book/gift shop are in the entrance/exit hall on the ground floor. Once in the gallery, there are no WCs until the end of our tour, downstairs from the café.

Photography: Permitted without flash.

Cuisine Art: The simple café at the top end of the gallery has an outdoor terrace with stunning views of Palazzo Vecchio and the Duomo's dome. They serve pricey sandwiches, salads, desserts, and fruit cups, but a €5 cappuccino outside, with that view, is one of Europe's great treats.

Plenty of handy eateries are nearby and described in the Eating in Florence chapter.

Starring: Botticelli, Venus, Raphael, Giotto, Titian, Leonardo, and Michelangelo.

The Tour Begins

• *Walk up the four long flights of the monumental staircase to the top floor, passing (at the first floor) the entrance to the small Drawings and Prints Collection (Gabinetto Disegni e Stampi). (Those with limited mobility can take the elevator.) Your brain should be fully aerated from the hike up. Past the ticket taker, look out the window.*

The Uffizi is U-shaped, running around the courtyard. This left wing contains Florentine paintings from medieval to Renaissance times. The right wing (which you can see across the courtyard) has art from the Roman and Venetian High Renaissance, works from the Baroque period that followed, and a café terrace facing the Duomo. A short hallway with sculpture connects the two wings. We'll concentrate on the Uffizi's forte, the Florentine section, then get a taste of the art it inspired.

• *Head up the long hallway, enter the first door on the left; you'll be facing Giotto's giant* Madonna and Child *(straight ahead).*

MEDIEVAL—WHEN ART WAS AS FLAT AS THE WORLD (1200-1400)

Giotto, Duccio, and Cimabue—A Trio of Madonnas with Child

In Giotto's painting, Mary and Baby Jesus sit on a throne in a golden never-never land symbolizing heaven. It's as if medieval Christians couldn't imagine holy people inhabiting our dreary material world. It took Renaissance painters to bring Mary down to earth and give

her human realism. For the Florentines, "realism" meant "three-dimensional." In this room, pre-Renaissance paintings show the slow process of learning to paint a 3-D world on a 2-D surface.

Before concentrating on the Giotto, look at some others in the room. The **crucifixion** (on your right as you face the Giotto) was medieval 3-D: paint a crude two-dimensional work, then physically tilt the head forward. Nice try.

The three similar-looking Madonna-and-Bambinos in this room—all painted within a few decades of each other in about the year 1300—show baby steps in the march to realism. **Duccio**'s piece (on the left as you face Giotto) is the most medieval and two-dimensional. There's no background. The angels are just stacked one on top of the other, floating in the golden atmosphere. Mary's throne is crudely drawn—the left side is at a three-quarter angle while the right is practically straight on. Mary herself is a wispy cardboard-cutout figure seemingly floating just above the throne.

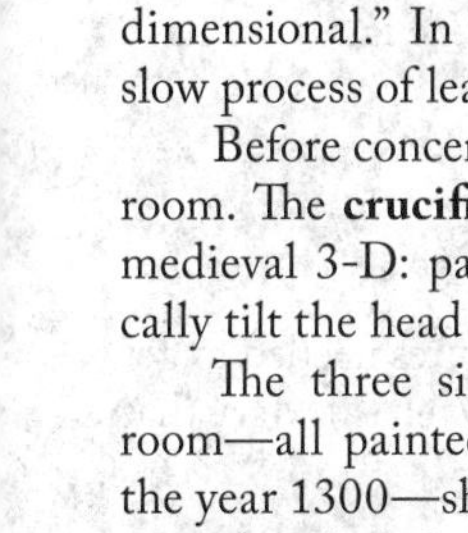

On the opposite wall, the work of **Cimabue**—mixing the iconic Byzantine style with budding Italian realism—is an improvement. The large throne creates an illusion of depth. Mary's foot actually sticks out over the lip of the throne. Still, the angels are stacked totem-pole-style, serving as heavenly bookends.

Giotto (JOT-oh) employs realism to make his theological points. He creates a space and fills it. Like a set designer, he builds a three-dimensional "stage"—the canopied throne—then peoples it with real beings. The throne has angels in front, prophets behind, and a canopy over the

top, clearly defining its three dimensions. The steps up to the throne lead from our space to Mary's, making the scene an extension of our world. But the real triumph here is Mary herself—big and monumental, like a Roman statue. Beneath her robe, she has a real live body, with knees and breasts that stick out at us. This three-dimensionality was revolutionary in its day, a taste of the Renaissance a century before it began.

Giotto was one of the first "famous" artists. In the Middle Ages, artists were mostly unglamorous craftsmen, like carpenters or cable-TV repairmen. They cranked out generic art and could have signed their work with a bar code. But Giotto was recognized as a genius, a unique individual. He died in a plague that devastated Florence. If there had been no plague, would the Renaissance have started 100 years earlier?

• *Enter Room 3, to the left as you face Giotto.*

Simone Martini (c. 1284-1344)—*Annunciation (Annunciazione)*

Simone Martini boils things down to the basic figures needed to get the message across: (1) The angel appears to sternly tell (2) Mary that she'll be the mother of Jesus. In the center is (3) a vase of lilies, a symbol of purity. Above is (4) the Holy Spirit as a dove about to descend on her. If the symbols aren't enough to get the message across, Simone Martini has spelled it right out for us in Latin: *"Ave Gratia Plena..."* or, "Hail, favored one, the Lord is with you." Mary doesn't exactly look pleased as punch.

This is not a three-dimensional work. The point was not to re-create reality but to teach religion, especially to the illiterate masses. This isn't a beautiful Mary or even a real Mary. She's a generic woman without distinctive features. We know she's pure—not from her face, but only because of the halo and symbolic flowers. Before the Renaissance, artists didn't care about the beauty of individual people.

Simone Martini's *Annunciation* has medieval features you'll see in many of the paintings in the next few rooms: (1) religious subject, (2) gold background, (3) two-dimensionality, and (4) meticulous detail.

• *Pass through Room 4, full of golden altarpieces, stopping at the far end of Room 5.*

Gentile da Fabriano (c. 1370-1427)—*Adoration of the Magi (Adorazione dei Magi)*

Look at the incredible detail of the Three Kings' costumes, the fine horses, and the cow in the cave. The canvas is filled from top to bottom with realistic details—but it's far from realistic. While the Magi worship Jesus in the foreground, their return trip home dangles over their heads in the "background."

This is a textbook example of the International Gothic style popular with Europe's aristocrats in the early 1400s: well-dressed, elegant people in a colorful, design-oriented setting. The religious subject is just an excuse to paint secular luxuries such as jewelry and clothes made of silk brocade. And the scene's background and foreground are compressed together to create an overall design that's pleasing to the eye.

Such exquisite detail work raises the question: Was Renaissance three-dimensionality truly an improvement over Gothic, or simply a different style?

• *Exit to your right and hang a U-turn left into Room 7.*

EARLY RENAISSANCE (MID-1400s)

Paolo Uccello (1397-1475)—*The Battle of San Romano (La Battaglia di San Romano)*

UFFIZI

In the 1400s, painters worked out the problems of painting realistically, using mathematics to create the illusion of three-dimensionality. This colorful battle scene is not so much a piece of art as an

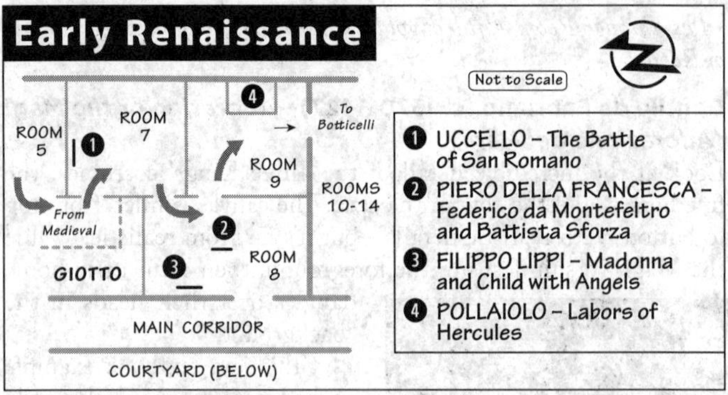

exercise in perspective. Paolo Uccello (oo-CHEL-loh) has challenged himself with every possible problem.

The broken lances at left set up a 3-D "grid" in which this crowded scene is placed. The fallen horses and soldiers are experiments in "foreshortening"—diminishing the things that are farther away from us (which appear smaller) to create the illusion of distance. Some of the figures are definitely A-plus material, like the fallen gray horse in the center and the white horse at the far right walking away. But some are more like B-minus work—the kicking red horse's legs look like ham hocks at this angle, and the fallen soldier at the far right would be child-size if he stood up.

And then there's the D-minus "Are you on drugs?" work. The converging hedges in the background create a nice illusion of a distant hillside maybe 250 feet away. So what are those soldiers the size of the foreground figures doing there? And jumping the hedge, is that rabbit 40 feet tall?

Paolo Uccello almost literally went crazy trying to master the three dimensions (thank God he was born before Einstein discovered one more). Uccello got so wrapped up in it he kind of lost... perspective.

UFFIZI

• *Enter Room 8. In the center of the room stands a double portrait.*

Piero della Francesca (c. 1412-1492)—*Federico da Montefeltro and Battista Sforza*

In medieval times, only saints and angels were worthy of being painted. In the humanistic Renaissance, however, even nonreligious folk like this husband and wife had their features preserved for posterity. Usually the man would have appeared on the left, with his wife at the right. But Federico's right side was definitely not his best—he lost his right eye and part of his nose in a tournament. Renaissance artists discovered the beauty in ordinary people and painted them, literally, warts and all.

• *On the wall behind the double portrait, next to the door, is...*

Fra Filippo Lippi (1406-1469)—*Madonna and Child with Angels (Madonna col Bambino e Angeli)*

Compare this Mary with the generic female in Simone Martini's *Annunciation*. We don't need the wispy halo over her head to tell us she's holy—she radiates sweetness and light from her divine face. Heavenly beauty is expressed by a physically beautiful woman.

Fra (Brother) Lippi, an orphan raised as a monk, lived a less-than-monkish life. He lived with a nun who bore him two children. He spent his entire life searching for the perfect Virgin. Through his studio passed Florence's prettiest girls, many of whom decorate the walls here in this room.

Lippi painted idealized beauty, but his models were real flesh-and-blood human beings. You could look through all the thousands of paintings from the Middle Ages and not find anything so human as the mischievous face of one of Lippi's little angel boys.

• *Enter Room 9, with two tiny works by Pollaiolo in the glass case between the windows.*

Antonio del Pollaiolo (c. 1431-1498)—*Labors of Hercules (Fatiche di Ercole)*

Hercules gets a workout in two small panels showing the human form at odd angles. The poses are the wildest imaginable, to show how each muscle twists and tightens. While Uccello worked on perspective, Pollaiolo studied anatomy. In medieval times, dissection of corpses was a sin and a crime (the two were the same then). Dissecting was a desecration of the human body, the temple of God.

But Pollaiolo was willing to sell his soul to the devil for artistic knowledge. He dissected.

There's something funny about this room that I can't put my finger on...I've got it—no Madonnas. Not one. (No, that's not a Madonna; she's a Virtue.)

We've seen how Early Renaissance artists worked to conquer reality. Now let's see the fruits of their work, the flowering of Florence's Renaissance.

• *Enter the large Botticelli room and take a seat.*

THE RENAISSANCE BLOSSOMS (1450-1500)

Florence in 1450 was in a Firenz-y of activity. There was a can-do spirit of optimism in the air, led by prosperous merchants and bankers and a strong middle class. The government was reasonably democratic, and Florentines saw themselves as citizens of a strong republic—like ancient Rome. Their civic pride showed in the public monuments and artworks they built. Man was leaving the protection of the church to stand on his own two feet.

Lorenzo de' Medici, head of the powerful Medici family, epitomized this new humanistic spirit. Strong, decisive, handsome, poetic, athletic, sensitive, charismatic, intelligent, brave, clean, and reverent, Lorenzo was a true Renaissance man, deserving of the nickname he went by—the Magnificent. He gathered Florence's best and brightest around him for evening wine and discussions of great ideas. One of this circle was the painter Botticelli (bot-i-CHEL-ee).

Sandro Botticelli (1445-1510)—*Allegory of Spring (Primavera)*

The Renaissance Blossoms

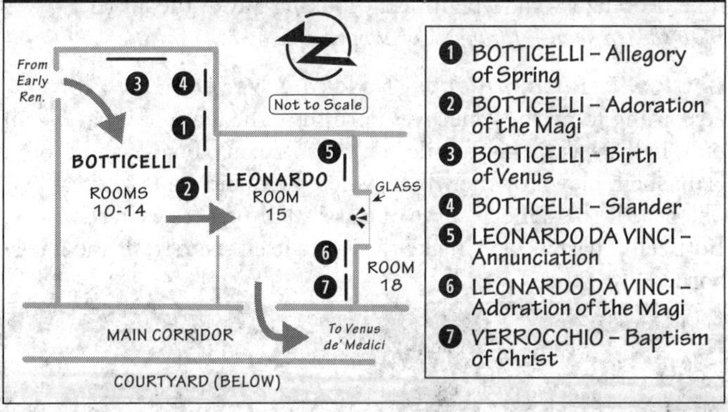

It's springtime in a citrus grove. The winds of spring blow in (Mr. Blue, at right), causing the woman on the right to sprout flowers from her lips as she morphs into Flora, or Spring—who walks by, spreading flowers from her dress. At the left are Mercury and the Three Graces, dancing a delicate maypole dance. The Graces may be symbolic of the three forms of love—love of beauty, love of people, and sexual love, suggested by the raised intertwined fingers. (They forgot love of peanut butter on toast.) In the center stands Venus, the Greek goddess of love. Above her flies a blindfolded Cupid, happily shooting his arrows of love without worrying about whom they'll hit.

Here is the Renaissance in its first bloom, its "springtime" of innocence. Madonna is out, Venus is in. Adam and Eve hiding their nakedness are out, glorious flesh is in. This is a return to the pre-Christian pagan world of classical Greece, where things of the flesh are not sinful. But this is certainly no orgy—just fresh-faced innocence and playfulness.

Botticelli emphasizes pristine beauty over gritty realism. The lines of the bodies, especially of the Graces in their see-through nighties, have pleasing, S-like curves. The faces are idealized but have real human features. There's a look of thoughtfulness and even melancholy in the faces—as though everyone knows that the innocence of spring will not last forever.

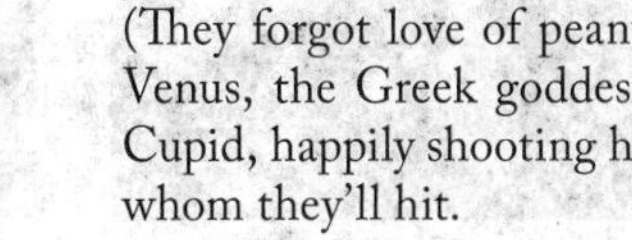

• *Look at the next painting to the right.*

Botticelli—*Adoration of the Magi (Adorazione dei Magi)*

Here's the rat pack of confident young Florentines who reveled in the optimistic pagan spirit—even in a religious scene. Botticelli included himself among the adorers, at the far right, looking vain in the yellow robe. Lorenzo is the Magnificent-looking guy at the far left.

• *On the left wall—thronged by admirers—you can't miss...*

Botticelli—*Birth of Venus (Nascita di Venere)*

According to myth, Venus was born from the foam of a wave. Still only half awake, this fragile, newborn beauty floats ashore on a clam shell, blown by the winds, where her maid waits to dress her. The pose is the same S-curve of classical statues (as we'll soon see). Botticelli's pastel colors make the world itself seem fresh and newly born.

This is the purest expression of Renaissance beauty. Venus' naked body is not sensual, but innocent. Botticelli thought that physical beauty was a way of appreciating God. Remember Michelangelo's poem: Souls will never ascend to heaven "...unless the sight of Beauty lifts them there."

Botticelli finds God in the details—Venus' windblown hair, her translucent skin, the maid's braided hair, the slight ripple of the wind god's abs, and the flowers tumbling in the slowest of slow motions, suspended like musical notes, caught at the peak of their brief life.

Mr. and Mrs. Wind intertwine—notice her hands clasped around his body. Their hair, wings, and robes mingle like the wind. But what happened to those splayed toes?

• *"Venus on the Half-Shell" (as many tourists call this) is one of the masterpieces of Western art. Take some time with it. Then find the small canvas on the wall to the right, near the* Allegory of Spring.

Botticelli—*Slander (La Calunnia)*

The spring of Florence's Renaissance had to end. Lorenzo died young. The economy faltered. Into town rode the monk Savonarola, preaching medieval hellfire and damnation for those who embraced the "pagan" Renaissance spirit. "Down, down with all gold and decoration," he roared. "Down where the body is food for the worms." He presided over huge bonfires, where the people threw in their fine clothes, jewelry, pagan books...and paintings.

Slander spells the end of the Florentine Renaissance. The architectural setting is classic Brunelleschi, but look what's taking place beneath those stately arches. These aren't proud Renaissance men and women but a ragtag, medieval-looking bunch, a Court of Thieves in an abandoned hall of justice. The accusations fly, and everyone is condemned. The naked man pleads for mercy, but the hooded black figure, a symbol of his execution, turns away. The figure of Truth (naked Truth)—straight out of *The Birth of Venus*—looks up to heaven as if to ask, "What has happened to us?" The classical statues in their niches look on in disbelief.

Botticelli listened to Savonarola. He burned some of his own paintings and changed his tune. The last works of his life were darker, more somber, and pessimistic about humanity.

The 19th-century German poet Heinrich Heine said, "When they start by burning books, they'll end by burning people." After four short years of power, Savonarola was burned in 1498 on his own bonfire in Piazza della Signoria, but by then the city was in shambles. The first flowering of the Renaissance was over.

• *Enter the next room. On the far wall, left of the door, is...*

Leonardo da Vinci (1452-1519)—*Annunciation (Annunciazione)*

UFFIZI

A scientist, architect, engineer, musician, and painter, Leonardo was a true Renaissance Man. He worked at his own pace rather than to please an employer, so he often left works unfinished. The two paintings in this room aren't his best, but even a lesser Leonardo is enough to put a museum on the map, and they're definitely worth a look.

In the *Annunciation,* the angel Gabriel has walked up to Mary, and now kneels on one knee like an ambassador, saluting her. See how relaxed his other hand is, draped over his knee. Mary, who's been reading, looks up with a gesture of surprise and curiosity.

Leonardo constructs a beautifully landscaped "stage" and puts his characters in it. Look at the bricks on the right wall. If you extended lines from them, the lines would all converge at the center of the painting, the distant blue mountain. Same with the edge of the sarcophagus and the railing. This subtle touch creates a subconscious feeling of balance, order, and spaciousness in the viewer.

Think back to Simone Martini's *Annunciation* to realize how much more natural, relaxed, and realistic Leonardo's version is. He's taken a miraculous event—an angel appearing out of the blue—and presented it in a very human way.

Leonardo da Vinci—*Adoration of the Magi* (*Adorazione dei Magi*)

Leonardo's human insight is even more apparent here, in this unfinished work (it may be under restoration during your visit). The poor kings are amazed at the Christ child—even afraid of him. They scurry around like chimps around a fire. This work is as agitated as the *Annunciation* is calm, giving us an idea of Leonardo's range. Leonardo was pioneering a new era of painting, showing not just the outer features but the inner personality.

The next painting to the right, ***Baptism of Christ***, is by Andrea del Verrocchio, Leonardo's teacher. Leonardo painted the angel on the far left when he was only a teenager. Legend has it that when Verrocchio saw that some kid had painted an angel better than he ever would...he hung up his brush for good.

Florence saw the first blossoming of the Renaissance. But when the cultural climate turned chilly, artists flew south to warmer climes. The Renaissance shifted to Rome.

• *Proceed past the Leonardo into the small hallway. Straight ahead is the doorway (with a glass barrier) to the Tribuna (a.k.a. Room 18). Gazing inside, you'll see the famous* Venus de' Medici *statue. (If this little hallway is extremely crowded, try going back out into the main hallway to find another glassed-in door there.)*

CLASSICAL SCULPTURE

If the Renaissance was the foundation of the modern world, the foundation of the Renaissance was classical sculpture. Sculptors, painters, and poets alike turned for inspiration to these ancient

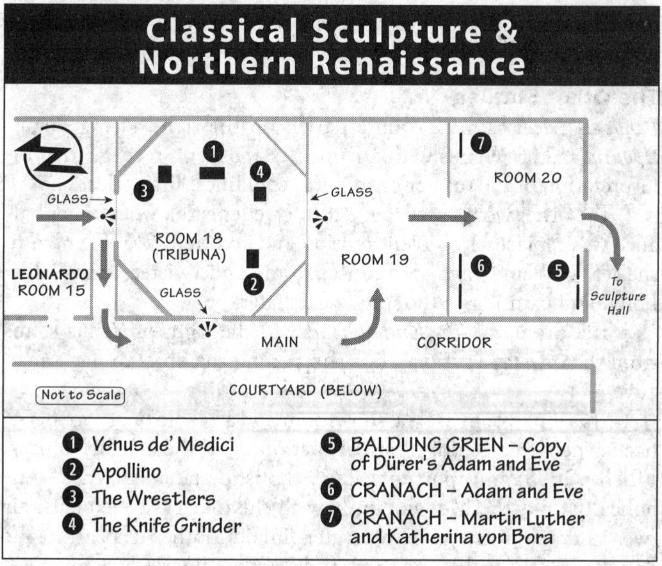

Greek and Roman works as the epitome of balance, 3-D perspective, human anatomy, and beauty.

Venus de' Medici (Venere dei Medici)

Is this pose familiar? Botticelli's *Birth of Venus* has the same position of the arms, the same S-curved body, and the same lifting of

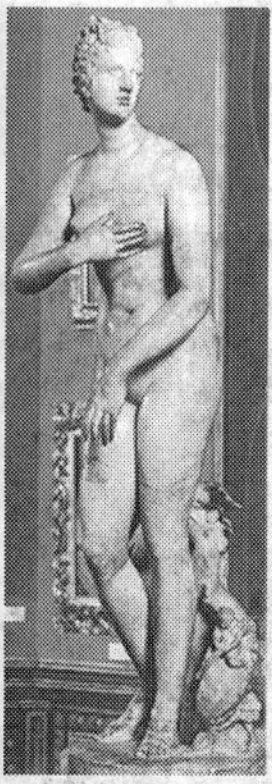

the right leg. A copy of this statue stood in Lorenzo the Magnificent's garden, where Botticelli used to hang out. This one is a Roman copy of the lost original by the great Greek sculptor Praxiteles. Balanced, harmonious, and serene, the statue embodies the attributes of Greece's "Golden Age," when balance was admired in every aspect of life.

Perhaps more than any other work of art, this statue has been the epitome of both ideal beauty and sexuality. In the 18th and 19th centuries, sex was "dirty," so the sex drive of cultured aristocrats was channeled into a love of pure beauty. Wealthy sons and daughters of Europe's aristocrats made the pilgrimage to the Uffizi to complete their classical education...where they swooned in ecstasy before the cold beauty of this goddess of love.

Louis XIV had a bronze copy made. Napoleon stole her away to Paris for himself. And in Philadelphia in the 1800s, a copy had to be kept under lock and key to prevent the innocent from catching the Venere-al disease. At first, it may be difficult for us to appreciate such passionate love of art, but if any generation knows the power of sex to sell something—be it art or underarm deodorant—it's ours.

The Other Statues

Venus de' Medici's male counterpart is on the right, facing Venus. *Apollino* (a.k.a. "Venus with a Penis") is another Greco-Roman interpretation of the master of smooth, cool lines: Praxiteles.

The other works are later Greek (Hellenistic), when quiet balance was replaced by violent motion and emotion. *The Wrestlers,* to the left of Venus, is a study in anatomy and twisted limbs—like Pollaiolo's paintings a thousand years later.

The drama of *The Knife Grinder* to the right of Venus stems from the off-stage action—he's sharpening the knife to flay a man alive.

This fine room was a showroom, or a "cabinet of wonders," back when this building still functioned as the Medici offices. Filled with family portraits, it's a holistic statement that symbolically links the Medici family with the four basic elements: air (weathervane in the lantern), water (inlaid mother of pearl in the dome), fire (red wall), and earth (inlaid stone floor).

• *Exit into the main hallway. Breathe. Sit. Admire the ceiling. Look out the window. See you in five.*

Back already? Now continue down the hallway. Enter the next room past the Tribuna, then turn right into Room 20.

NORTHERN RENAISSANCE

Baldung Grien (c. 1484-1545)—Copy of Dürer's *Adam and Eve*

The warm spirit of the Renaissance blew north into Germany. Albrecht Dürer (1471-1528), the famous German painter and engraver, traveled to Venice, where he fell in love with all things Italian. Returning home, he painted the First Couple in the Italian style—full-bodied, muscular (check out Adam's abs and Eve's knees), "carved" with strong shading, fresh-faced, and innocent in their earthly Paradise.

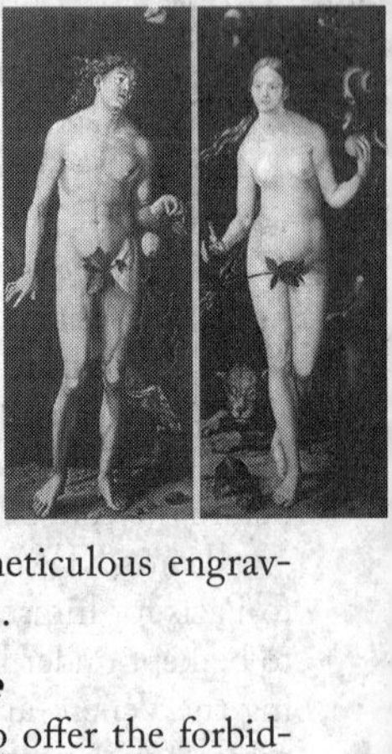

This copy of Dürer's original (it's in the Prado) by Hans Baldung Grien was a training exercise. Like many of Europe's artists—including Michelangelo and Raphael—Baldung Grien learned technique by studying Dürer's meticulous engravings, spread by the newly invented printing press.

Lucas Cranach (1472-1553)—*Adam and Eve*

Eve sashays forward, with heavy-lidded eyes, to offer the forbidden fruit. Adam stretches to display himself and his foliage to Eve.

The two panels are linked by smoldering eye contact, as Man and Woman awaken to their own nakedness. The Garden of Eden is about to be rocked by new ideas that are both liberating and troubling.

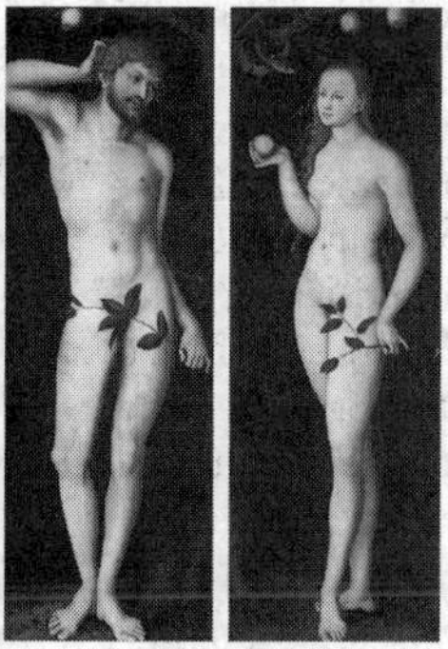

Though the German Lucas Cranach occasionally dabbled in the "Italian style," he chose to portray his Adam and Eve in the now-retro look of International Gothic.

They are slimmer than Dürer's, as well as smoother, more S-shaped, elegant, graceful, shapely, and erotic, with the dainty pinkies of the refined aristocrats who were signing Cranach's paycheck.

Though life-size, Adam and Eve are not lifelike, not monumental, not full-bodied or muscular, and are not placed in a real-world landscape with distant perspectives. Even so, Cranach was very much a man of the Renaissance, a friend of Martin Luther, and a champion of humanism.

• *Find a small, two-panel portrait featuring Martin Luther with his wife (or possibly a panel featuring Luther's colleague, Melanchthon; the museum rotates these two).*

Cranach—*Martin Luther*

Martin Luther—German monk, fiery orator, and religious whistle-blower—sparked a century of European wars by speaking out against the Catholic Church.

Luther (1483-1546) lived a turbulent life. In early adulthood, the newly ordained priest suffered a severe personal crisis of faith, before finally emerging "born again." In 1517, he openly protested against Church corruption and was excommunicated. Defying both the pope and the emperor, he lived on the run as an outlaw, watching as his ideas sparked peasant riots. He still found time to translate the New Testament from Latin to modern German, write hymns such as "A Mighty Fortress," and spar with the humanist Erasmus and fellow Reformer Zwingli.

In Cranach's portrait, Martin Luther (at age 46) is easing out of the fast lane. Recently married to an ex-nun, he has traded his monk's habit for street clothes, bought a house, had several kids... and has clearly been enjoying his wife's home cooking and home-brewed beer.

Cranach—*Katherina von Bora*

When "Katie" (well, Käthe) decided to leave her convent, the famous Martin Luther agreed to help find her a husband. She rejected his nominees, saying she'd marry no one...except Luther himself. In 1525, the 42-year-old ex-priest married the 26-year-old ex-nun "to please my father and annoy the pope." Martin turned his checkbook over to "my lord Katie," who also ran the family farm, raised their 6 children and 11 adopted orphans, and hosted Martin's circle of friends (including Cranach) at loud, chatty dinner parties.

• *Pass through the next couple of rooms, exiting to a great view of the Arno and Ponte Vecchio. Stroll through the...*

SCULPTURE HALL

A hundred years ago, no one even looked at Botticelli—they came to the Uffizi to see the sculpture collection. And today, these 2,000-year-old Roman copies of 2,500-year-old Greek originals are hardly noticed...but they should be. Only a few are displayed here now.

The most impressive is the male nude, ***Doriforo*** ("spear carrier"), a Roman copy of the Greek original by Polykleitos.

The purple statue in the center of the hall—headless and limbless—is a **female wolf** (*lupa,* c. A.D. 120) done in porphyry stone. This was the animal that raised Rome's legendary founders and became the city's symbol. Renaissance Florentines marveled at the ancient Romans' ability to create such lifelike, three-dimensional works. They learned to reproduce them in stone...and then learned to paint them on a two-dimensional surface.

• *Gaze out the windows from the hall for a...*

VIEW OF THE ARNO

Enjoy Florence's best view of the Arno and Ponte Vecchio. You can also see the red-tiled roof of the Vasari Corridor, the "secret" passage connecting Palazzo Vecchio, Uffizi, Ponte Vecchio, and Pitti Palace on the other side of the river—a half-mile in all. This was a private walkway, wallpapered in great art, for the Medici family's commute from home to work.

As you appreciate the view (best at sunset), remember that it's this sort of pleasure that Renaissance painters wanted you to get from their paintings. For them, a canvas was a window you looked through to see the wide world. Their paintings re-create natural perspective: Distant objects (such as bridges) are smaller, dimmer, and higher up the "canvas," while closer objects are bigger, clearer, and lower.

We're headed down the home stretch now. If your little U-feetsies are killing you, and it feels like torture, remind yourself that it's a pleasant torture and smile...like the *Marsia Rosso* statue next to you.

• *In the far hallway, turn left into the first room (#25) to find the works by Titian and Parmigianino.*

HIGH RENAISSANCE (1500-1550)

Titian (c. 1490-1576)—*Venus of Urbino (Venere di Urbino)*

Compare this *Venus* with Botticelli's newly hatched *Venus,* and you get a good idea of the difference between the Florentine and Venetian Renaissance. Botticelli's was pure, innocent, and otherworldly. Titian's should have a staple in her belly button. This isn't a Venus, it's a centerfold—with no purpose but to please the eye (and other organs). While Botticelli's allegorical *Venus* is a message, this is a massage. The bed is used.

Titian and his fellow Venetians took the pagan spirit pioneered in Florence and carried it to its logical hedonistic conclusion. Using bright, rich colors, they captured the luxurious life of happy-go-lucky Venice.

While other artists may have balanced their compositions with a figure on the left and one on the right, Titian balances his painting in a different way—with color. The canvas is split down the middle by the curtain. The left half is dark, the right half is lighter. The two halves are connected by a diagonal slash of luminous gold—the nude woman. The girl in the background is trying to find her some clothes.

By the way, visitors from centuries past also panted in front of this Venus. The Romantic poet Byron called it "*the* Venus." With her sensual skin, hey-sailor look, and suggestively placed hand, she must have left them blithering idiots.

• *Find a n-n-n-nearby painting...*

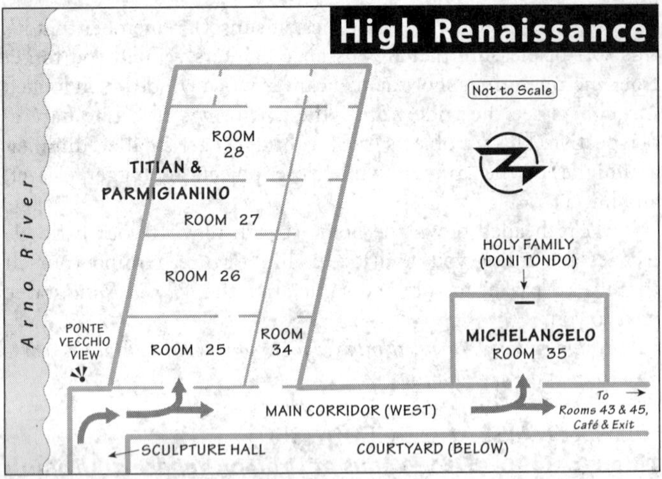

Parmigianino (1503-1540)—*Madonna with the Long Neck (Madonna della Collo Lungo)*

Once Renaissance artists had mastered reality, where could they go next?

Mannerists such as Parmigianino tried, by going beyond realism, exaggerating it for effect. Using brighter colors and twisting poses, they created scenes more elegant and more exciting than real life.

By stretching the neck of his Madonna, Parmigianino (like the cheese) gives her an unnatural, swanlike beauty. She has the same pose and position of hands as Botticelli's *Venus* and the *Venus de' Medici*. Her body forms an arcing S-curve—down her neck as far as her elbow, then back the other way along Jesus' body to her knee, then down to her foot. Baby Jesus seems to be blissfully gliding down this slippery slide of sheer beauty.

• *Return to the hallway and continue down a few steps to Room 35, the Michelangelo Room. Head for the round painting straight ahead from the door.*

Michelangelo Buonarroti (1475-1564)—*Holy Family (Sacra Famiglia)*, a.k.a. *Doni Tondo*

This is the only completed easel painting by the greatest sculptor in history. Florentine painters were sculptors with brushes; this shows it. Instead of a painting, it's more like three clusters of statues with some clothes painted on.

The main subject is the holy family—Mary, Joseph, and Baby Jesus—and in the background are two groups of nudes looking like classical statues. The background represents the old pagan world, while Jesus in the foreground is the new age of Christianity. The figure of young John the Baptist at right is the link between the two.

This is a "peasant" Mary, with a plain face and sunburned arms. Michelangelo shows her from a very unflattering angle—we're looking up her nostrils. But Michelangelo himself was an ugly man, and he was among the first artists to recognize the beauty in everyday people.

Michelangelo was a Florentine—in fact, he was like an adopted son of the Medici, who recognized his talent—but much of his greatest work was done in Rome as part of the pope's face-lift of the city. We can see here some of the techniques he used on the Sistine Chapel ceiling that revolutionized painting—monumental figures; dramatic angles (looking up Mary's nose); accentuated, rippling muscles; and bright, clashing colors (all the more apparent since both this work and the Sistine Chapel ceiling have recently been cleaned). These elements added a dramatic tension that was lacking in the graceful work of Leonardo and Botticelli.

Michelangelo painted this for his friend Agnolo Doni for 70 ducats. (Michelangelo designed, but didn't carve, the elaborate frame.) When the painting was delivered, Doni tried to talk Michelangelo down to 40. Proud Michelangelo took the painting away and would not sell it until the man finally agreed to pay double...140 ducats.

In the Uffizi, we've seen many images of female beauty: from ancient goddesses to medieval Madonnas and wicked Eves, from Botticelli's pristine nymphs to Titian's sensuous centerfold, from Parmigianino's cheesy slippery-slide to Michelangelo's peasant Mary. Their physical beauty expresses different aspects of the human spirit.

• *Consider your essential Uffizi tour over. But on your way to the exit, you'll pass by much more art, including one high-power stop—Raphael.*

But first, continue down the hallway—past the special exhibits and rooms where they temporarily display masterpieces from closed rooms—to the café. Here you can enjoy a truly aesthetic experience...

Little Capuchin Monk (Cappuccino)

This drinkable art form, born in Italy, is now enjoyed all over the world. It's called the "Little Capuchin Monk" because the coffee's frothy light- and dark-brown foam looks like the two-toned cowls of the Capuchin order. Sip it on the terrace in the shadow of the towering Palazzo Vecchio, and be glad we live in an age where you don't need to be a Medici to enjoy all this fine art. *Salute.*

• *When you're ready to move on, go down the staircase near the café, to the first floor. On your way down, you'll pass the WC (or you can just ride the elevator to the first floor). Like it or not, you'll be walking through dozens more rooms and a lot more art as you make your way to the exit* (Uscita).

FIRST FLOOR—MORE ART ON THE WAY TO THE EXIT

At the bottom of the staircase, you could detour left to the **Foreign Painters Section** to see a couple of **Rembrandt self-portraits** in Room 49.

Or, turning right, you enter Room 56, lined with ancient statues that inspired Renaissance painters. Continue through a half-dozen more rooms to Room 65, with **portraits by Bronzino** of Duke Cosimo I de' Medici, his wife, Eleonora, their cute bird-holding son, and their daughters.

• *Definitely stop in Room 66 for...*

UFFIZI

Raphael (Raffaello Sanzio, 1483-1520)—*Madonna of the Goldfinch (La Madonna del Cardellino)*

Raphael brings Mary and bambino down from heaven and into the real world of trees, water, and sky. He gives Baby Jesus (right) and John the Baptist a realistic, human playfulness. It's a tender scene painted with warm colors and a hazy background that matches the golden skin of the children.

Raphael perfected his craft in Florence, following the graceful style of Leonardo. In typical Leonardo fashion, this group of Mary, John the Baptist, and Jesus is arranged in the shape of a pyramid, with Mary's head at the peak.

Uffizi Gallery—First Floor

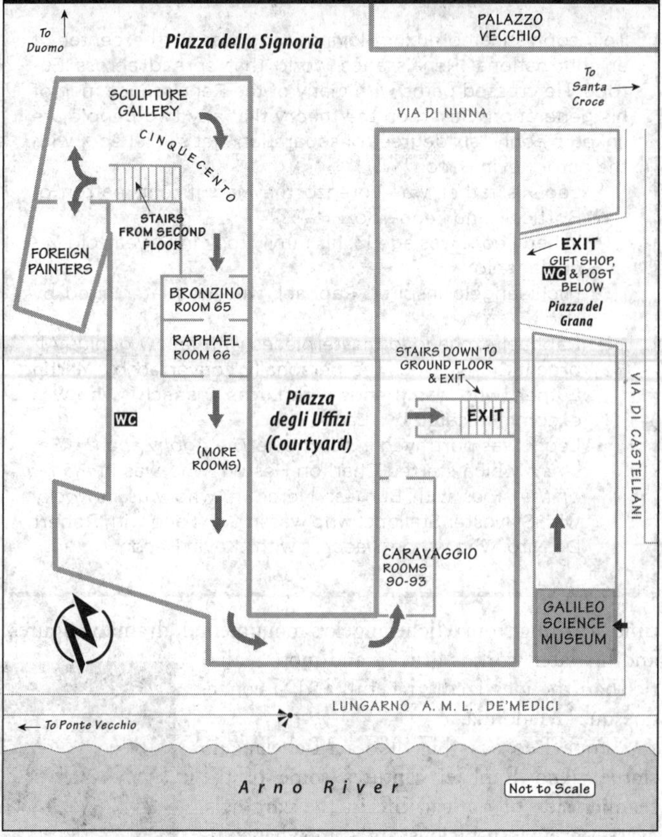

The two halves of the painting balance perfectly. Draw a line down the middle, through Mary's nose and down through her knee. John the Baptist on the left is balanced by Jesus on the right. Even the trees in the background balance each other, left and right. These things aren't immediately noticeable, but they help create the subconscious feelings of balance and order that reinforce the atmosphere of maternal security in this domestic scene—pure Renaissance.

• *On the wall to the left is...*

Raphael—*Leo X and Cardinals (Ritratta del Papa Leone X con i Cardinali)*

Raphael was called to Rome at the same time as Michelangelo, working next door in the Vatican apartments while Michelangelo painted the Sistine Chapel ceiling. Raphael peeked in from time to

Six Degrees of Leo X

This sophisticated, luxury-loving pope was at the center of an international Renaissance world that spread across Europe. He crossed paths with many of the Renaissance men of his generation. Based on the theory that any two people are linked by only "six degrees of separation," let's link Leo X with the actor Kevin Bacon:

- Leo X's father was Lorenzo the Magnificent, patron of Botticelli and Leonardo.
- When Leo X was age 13, his family took in 13-year-old Michelangelo.
- Michelangelo inspired Raphael, who was later hired by Leo X.
- Raphael exchanged masterpieces with fellow genius Albrecht Dürer, who was personally converted by Martin Luther (who was friends with Lucas Cranach), who was excommunicated by...Leo X.
- Leo X was portrayed in the movie *The Agony and the Ecstasy,* which starred Charlton Heston, who was in *Planet of the Apes* with Burgess Meredith, who was in *Rocky* with Sylvester Stallone, who was in *Cop Land* with Robert De Niro, who was in *Sleepers* with...Kevin Bacon.

time, learning from Michelangelo's monumental, dramatic figures, and his later work is grittier and more realistic than the idealized, graceful, and "Leonardoesque" Madonna.

Pope Leo X is big, like a Michelangelo statue. And Raphael captures some of the seamier side of Vatican life in the cardinals' eyes—shrewd, suspicious, and somewhat cynical. With Raphael, the photographic realism pursued by painters since Giotto was finally achieved.

The Florentine Renaissance ended in 1520 with the death of Raphael. Raphael (see his **self-portrait** near the window) is considered both the culmination and conclusion of the Renaissance. The realism, balance, and humanism we associate with the Renaissance are all found in Raphael's work. He combined the grace of Leonardo with the power of Michelangelo. With his death, the High Renaissance ended as well.

• *Continue on through a dozen more rooms to the exit. On your way, keep an eye out for any of the major paintings that may be temporarily displaced to this wing from upstairs (some may even be beyond the stairs down to the exit). Also keep an eye out for a room of works* *by **Caravaggio,** including the shocking ultra-realism of* Sacrifice of Isaac.

When you're ready to leave, the exit takes you back down to the WCs/bookstore/post office, and the way out to the street. You'll pop out behind the Uffizi, a block up from the river and very near the Galileo Science Museum and the Bargello (sculpture museum). When you re-enter the real world, you may see it with new eyes.

BARGELLO TOUR

The Renaissance began with sculpture. The great Florentine painters were "sculptors with brushes." You can see the birth of this revolution of 3-D in the Bargello (bar-JEL-oh), which boasts the best collection of Florentine sculpture. It's a small, uncrowded museum and a pleasant break from the intensity of the rest of Florence.

Orientation

Cost: €7 (or €4 without special exhibits), covered by Firenze Card.

Hours: Tue-Sat 8:15-17:00—or until 13:50 if there's no special exhibit; also open these times on the first, third, and fifth Mon and second and fourth Sun of each month; last entry 30 minutes before closing. You can reserve an entrance time, but it's unnecessary.

Getting There: It's located at Via del Proconsolo 4, a three-minute walk northeast of the Uffizi. Facing the Palazzo Vecchio, go behind the Palazzo and turn left. Look for a rustic brick building with a spire that looks like a baby Palazzo Vecchio. If lost ask, *"Dov'è Bargello?"* (doh-VEH bar-JEL-oh).

Getting In: You must pass through a metal detector to enter. No liquids are allowed in the museum.

Information: Tel. 055-238-8606, www.polomuseale.firenze.it.

Audioguide: You can rent one for €6 (€10/2 people).

Length of This Tour: Allow one hour. If your time is limited, be sure to see the Michelangelo statues on the ground floor and the Donatello *David* statues on the first.

Photography: Permitted only in the courtyard.

Cuisine Art: Inexpensive bars and cafés await in the surrounding streets. See recommended eateries on page 295.

Starring: Michelangelo, Donatello, Brunelleschi, Ghiberti, and four different *David*s.

The Tour Begins

COURTYARD

• *Buy your ticket and take a seat in the courtyard.*

The Bargello, built in 1255, was Florence's original Town Hall and also served as a police station *(bargello)*, and later a prison. The heavy fortifications tell us that keeping the peace in medieval Florence had its occupational hazards.

The Bargello, a three-story rectangular building, surrounds this cool and peaceful courtyard. The best statues are found in two rooms—one on the ground floor at the foot of the outdoor staircase, and another one flight up, directly above. We'll proceed from Michelangelo to Donatello to Verrocchio.

But first, meander around this courtyard and get a feel for sculpture in general and the medium of stone in particular. Sculpture is a much more robust art form than painting. Think of just the engineering problems of the sculpting process: quarrying and cutting the stone, transporting the block to the artist's studio, all the hours of chiseling away chips, then the painstaking process of sanding the final product by hand. A sculptor must be strong enough to gouge into the stone, but delicate enough to groove out the smallest details. Think of Michelangelo's approach to sculpting: He wasn't creating a figure—he was liberating it from the rock that surrounded it.

The Renaissance was centered on humanism—and sculpture is the perfect medium in which to express it. It shows the human form, standing alone, independent of church, state, or society, ready to create itself.

Finally, a viewing tip. Every sculpture has an invisible "frame" around it—the stone block it was cut from. Visualizing this frame helps you find the center of the composition.

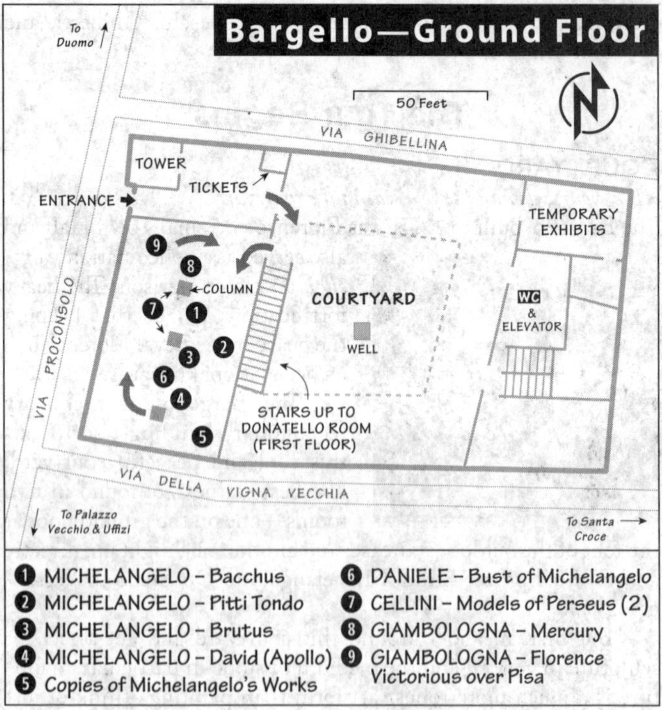

GROUND FLOOR

• *Head into the room at the foot of the courtyard's grand staircase. Enter, turn left, and watch for a party animal on the right.*

Michelangelo—*Bacchus* (*Baccho*, c. 1497)

Bacchus, the god of wine and revelry, raises another cup to his lips, while his little companion goes straight for the grapes.

Maybe Michelangelo had a sense of humor after all. Mentally compare this tipsy Greek god of wine with his sturdy, sober *David*, begun a few years later. Raucous *Bacchus* isn't nearly so muscular, so monumental... or so sure on his feet. Hope he's not driving. The pose, the smooth muscles, the beer belly, and swaying hips look more like Donatello's boyish *David*.

This was Michelangelo's first major commission. He often vacillated between showing man as strong and noble, or as weak and perverse. This isn't the nobility of the classical world, but the decadent side of orgies and indulgence.

• *Facing Bacchus' right cheek is a circular relief.*

Michelangelo—*Madonna and Child with John the Baptist* (*Madonna col Bambino e S. Giovannino,* c. 1505), a.k.a. *Pitti Tondo*

By 1504, Michelangelo had just finished his monumental, heroic statue *David.* In a complete change of pace, he turned to this quiet, small-scale marble work.

The Virgin Mary sits reading a book, while Baby Jesus and (probably) John the Baptist look on. The round *tondo* format gave Michelangelo a compositional opportunity. He combined the vertical (the upright Madonna) and the horizontal (her forearms and thighs), all enfolded in a warm family circle. Jesus curves lovingly around his mom, casually glancing at her book. Another dimension to the composition is depth: The bench Mary sits on juts outward, and her face rises from the stone in a cameo effect. Finally, Michelangelo added an element of surprise to the standard *tondo* by letting Mary's head pop out from the top of the frame.

The *tondo* is unfinished, giving us a chance to look at Michelangelo's work process. He started first with the easy stuff—Mary's robe and the bench, which are close to done. Mary's blouse is still in rough form, being chiseled out in Michelangelo's cross-hatch technique. Find the little details beginning to emerge—the small child at left and the tiny face in Mary's diadem. But called away to a bigger project in Rome, Michelangelo abandoned the not-quite-finished *tondo.*

• *Just steps away is...*

Michelangelo—*Brutus* (*Bruto,* 1540)

Another example of the influence of Donatello is this so-ugly-he's-beautiful bust by Michelangelo. His rough intensity gives him the look of a man who has succeeded against all odds, a dignified and heroic quality that would be missing if he were too pretty.

The subject is Brutus, the Roman who, for the love of liberty, murdered his friend and dictator, Julius Caesar *("Et tu...?").* Michelangelo could understand this man's dilemma. He himself was torn between his love of the democratic tradition of Florence and loyalty to his friends the Medici, who had become dictators.

So he gives us two sides of a political assassin. The right profile (the front view) is heroic. But the hidden side, with the drooping mouth and squinting eye, makes him more cunning, sneering, and ominous.

• *Farther along (you may have to jog around some special exhibits) is...*

Michelangelo—*David* (also known as *Apollo,* 1530-1532)

This restless, twisting man is either David or Apollo. (Is he reaching for a sling or a quiver?) Demure (and left unfinished), this statue is light years away from Michelangelo's famous *David* in the Accademia, which is so much larger than life in every way. We'll see three more *Davids* upstairs. As you check out each one, compare and contrast the artists' styles.

In the glass cases in the corner are small-scale copies of some of Michelangelo's most famous works. In this area, also look for a bust of Michelangelo by his fellow sculptor Daniele da Volterra, capturing his broken nose and brooding nature. (You may recognize this bust from the Accademia, which has a copy.)

• *Circling back clockwise toward the entrance, look for small statues in a glass case, by a pillar.*

Cellini—Models of *Perseus* (*Perseo,* 1545-1554)

The life-size statue of Perseus slaying Medusa, located in the open-air loggia next to the Palazzo Vecchio, is cast bronze. Benvenuto Cellini started with these smaller models (one in wax, one in bronze) to get the difficult process down. When it came time to cast the full-size work, everything was going fine...until he realized he didn't have enough metal! He ran around the studio, gathering up pewterware and throwing it in, narrowly avoiding a mess-terpiece.

Giambologna—*Mercury* (c. 1564-1580)

Catch this statue while you can—he's in a hurry to deliver those flowers. Despite all the bustle and motion, *Mercury* has a solid Renaissance core: the line of balance that runs straight up the center, from toes to hip to fingertip. He's caught in midstride. His top half leans forward, counterbalanced by his right leg in back, while the center of gravity rests firmly at the hipbone. Down at the toes, notice the cupid practicing for the circus.

Giambologna—*Florence Victorious over Pisa* (*Firenze Trionfa su Pisa,* c. 1529-1608)

This sculpture shows the fierce Florentine chauvinism that was born in an era when Italy's cities struggled for economic and political dominance... and Florence won.

• *To see the roots of Florence's Renaissance, climb the courtyard staircase to the next floor up and turn right into the large Donatello room.*

FIRST FLOOR

• *Entering the room, cross to the middle of the far wall, and check out the first of three* Davids *in this room (the one wearing the long skirt).*

Donatello—*David* (1408)

This marble sculpture is young Donatello's first take on the popular subject of *David* slaying Goliath. His dainty pose makes him a little unsteady on his feet. He's dressed like a medieval knight (fully clothed but showing some leg through the slit skirt). The generic face and blank, vacant eyes give him the look not of a real man but of an anonymous decoration on a church facade. At age 22, Donatello still had one foot in the old Gothic style. To tell the story of David, Donatello plants a huge rock right in the middle of Goliath's forehead.

• *From here, circle the room clockwise. The next statue is the same subject, by a different artist.*

Andrea del Verrocchio—*David* (c. 1470)

Verrocchio (1435-1488) is best known as the teacher of Leonardo da Vinci, but he was also the premier sculptor of the generation between Donatello and Michelangelo. Verrocchio's bronze *David* is definitely the shepherd "boy" described in the Bible. (Some have speculated that the statue was modeled on Verrocchio's young, handsome, curly-haired apprentice, Leonardo da Vinci.) David leans on one leg, not with a firm, commanding stance but a nimble one (especially noticeable from behind). Compare the smug smile of the victor with Goliath's "Oh, have I got a headache" expression.

• *Finally, near the corner, is...*

Donatello—*David* (c. 1430)

He's naked. Donatello sees David as a teenage boy wearing only a helmet, boots, and sword (this sculpture is often cited by scholars who think the artist, who never married, was homosexual). The

Donatello
(1386-1466)

Donatello was the first great Renaissance genius, a model for Michelangelo and others. He mastered realism, creating the first truly lifelike statues of people since ancient times. Donatello's work is highly personal. Unlike the ancient Greeks—but like the ancient Romans—he often sculpted real people, not idealized versions of pretty gods and goddesses. Some of these people are downright ugly. In the true spirit of Renaissance humanism, Donatello appreciated the beauty of flesh-and-blood human beings.

Donatello's personality was also a model for later artists. He was moody and irascible, purposely setting himself apart from others in order to concentrate on his sculpting. He developed the role of the "mad genius" that Michelangelo would later perfect.

smooth-skinned warrior sways gracefully, poking his sword playfully at the severed head of the giant Goliath. His *contrapposto* stance is similar to Michelangelo's *David,* resting his weight on one leg in the classical style, but it gives him a feminine rather than masculine look. Gazing into his coy eyes and at his bulging belly is a very different experience from confronting Michelangelo's older and sturdier Renaissance Man.

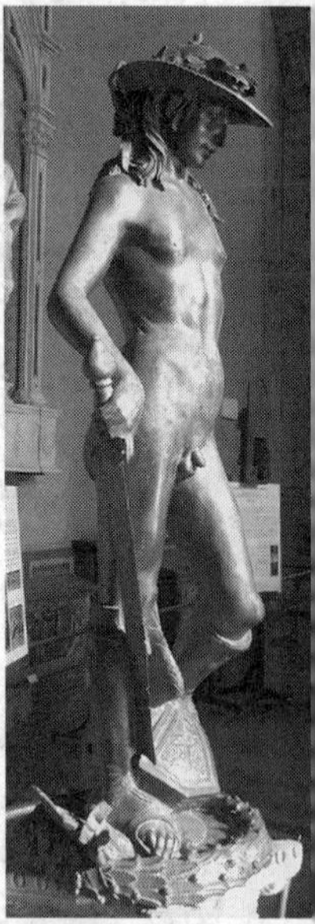

This bronze *David* paved the way for Michelangelo's. Europe hadn't seen a freestanding male nude like this in a thousand years. In the Middle Ages, the human body was considered a dirty thing, a symbol of man's weakness, something to be covered up in shame. The church prohibited exhibitions of nudity like this one and certainly would never decorate a church with it. But in the Renaissance, a new class of rich and powerful merchants appeared, and they bought art for personal enjoyment. Reading Plato's *Symposium,* they saw the ideal of Beauty in the form of a young man. This particular statue stood in the palace of the Medici (today's Medici-Riccardi Palace)...where Michelangelo, practically an adopted son, grew up admiring it.

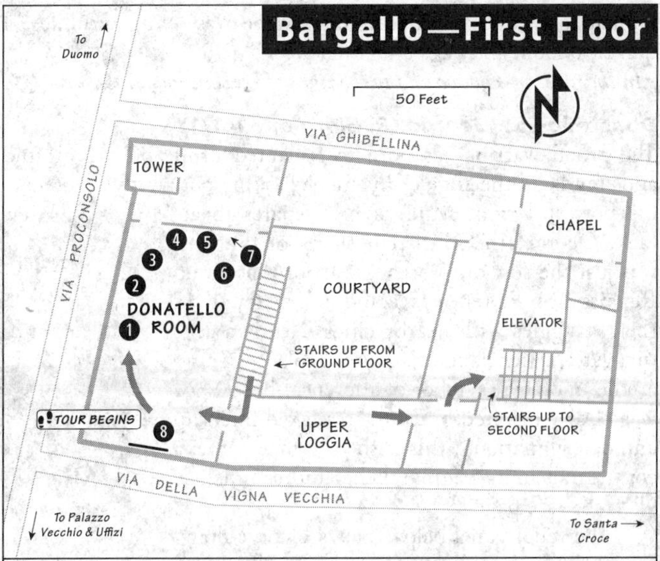

1. DONATELLO – David (1408)
2. VERROCCHIO – David (c. 1470)
3. DONATELLO – David (1430)
4. DONATELLO – Niccolò da Uzzano
5. DONATELLO – St. *George*
6. DESIDERIO – St. John the Baptist
7. GHIBERTI and BRUNELLESCHI – Abraham Sacrificing Isaac (2 versions)
8. DELLA ROBBIA – Terra-Cotta Relief Panels

Now's a good time to compare the four different *David*s that we've seen. Verrocchio's saucy, impertinent *David* has more attitude than Donatello's generic warrior, and is younger and more masculine than Donatello's girlish, gloating *David*. He's more vigorous than Michelangelo's unfinished *David/Apollo* but he's a far cry from Michelangelo's monumental version.

• *Along the wall behind the last* David *is...*

Donatello—*Niccolò da Uzzano* (c. 1420)

Not an emperor, not a king, not a pope, saint, or prince, this is one of Florence's leading businessmen, in a toga, portrayed in the style of an ancient Roman bust. In the 1400s, when Florence was inventing the Renaissance that all Europe would soon follow, there was an optimistic spirit of democracy that gloried in everyday people.

Donatello has portrayed this man as he was—with wrinkles, a quizzical look, and bags under his eyes.

• *In the niche just above and to the right of Uzzano, you'll see...*

Donatello—*St. George (S. Giorgio,* c 1417)

The proud warrior has both feet planted firmly on the ground and stands on the edge of his niche looking out alertly. He tenses his powerful right hand as he prepares to attack. George, the Christian slayer of dragons, was just the sort of righteous warrior that proud Renaissance Florentines could rally around in their struggles with nearby cities. Nearly a century later, Michelangelo's *David* replaced *George* as the unofficial symbol of Florence, but *David* was clearly inspired by *George*'s relaxed intensity and determination. (This is the original statue; a copy stands in its original niche at Orsanmichele Church—see page 89.)

The relief panel below shows George doing what he's been pondering. To his right, the sketchy arches and trees create the illusion of a distant landscape. Donatello, who apprenticed in Ghiberti's studio, is credited with teaching his master how to create 3-D illusions like this.

• St. John the Baptist, *begun by Donatello and finished by his student, is to the right.*

Desiderio da Settignano (and Donatello)—*St. John the Baptist (S. Giovannino,* c. 1455-1460)

John the Baptist was the wild-eyed, wildcat prophet who lived in the desert preaching, living on bugs 'n' honey, and baptizing Saviors of the world. The sculptor Settignano was a student of Donatello, the mad prophet of the coming Renaissance who might have identified with this original eccentric.

• *On the wall next to* George, *you'll find some bronze relief panels. Don't look at the labels just yet.*

Ghiberti and Brunelleschi—Baptistery Door Competition Entries

Some would say these two different relief panels represent the first works of the Renaissance. These two versions of *Abraham Sacrificing Isaac (Sacrificio di Isacco)* were finalists in a contest held in 1401 to decide who would create the bronze doors of the Baptistery. The contest sparked citywide excitement, which evolved into the Renaissance spirit. Lorenzo Ghiberti won and later did the doors

Ghiberti's panel, on the left, won.

known as the Gates of Paradise. Filippo Brunelleschi lost—fortunately for us—freeing him to design the Duomo's dome.

Both artists catch the crucial moment when Abraham, obeying God's orders, prepares to slaughter and burn his only son as a sacrifice. At the last moment—after Abraham has passed this test of faith—an angel of God appears to stop the bloodshed.

Let's look at the composition of the two panels: One is integrated and cohesive (yet dynamic), while the other is a balanced knickknack shelf of segments. Human drama: One has bodies and faces that speak. The boy's body is a fine classical nude in itself, so real and vulnerable. Abraham's face is intense and ready to follow God's will. Perspective: An angel zooms in from out of nowhere to save the boy in the nick of time.

Is one panel clearly better than the other? You be the judge. Pictured here are the two finalists for the Baptistery door competition—Ghiberti's and Brunelleschi's. Which do you like best?

It was obviously a tough call, but Ghiberti's was chosen, perhaps because his goldsmith training made him better suited for the technical end.

• *Cross all the way back to the far end of the room. Along the walls back near the entrance, you'll find several colorful terra-cotta reliefs.*

Luca della Robbia—Terra-Cotta Relief Panels

Mary and Baby Jesus with accompanying angels look their most serene in these panels by the master of painted, glazed porcelain. Polished blue, white, green, and yellow, they have a gentle and feminine look that softens the rough masculine stone of this room. Luca was just one of a family of della Robbias who pioneered art in terra-cotta.

THE REST OF THE BARGELLO

You've already seen the undisputed highlights of this compact museum. With more time, you can do some exploring. Browse around the rooms near the Donatello room, filled with ivories, jewelry, and dinnerware—objects that provide a look at life in Renaissance Florence.

Also consider strolling through the easy-to-miss second floor. To reach it, exit the Donatello room through the same door you entered. Cross to the rooms on the other side of the courtyard. Take your first left, then immediately turn right and find the carpeted staircase (marked *Al 2° Piano*) that leads to the second floor. (Note that the second floor is sometimes closed off-season.) Scattered through these rooms are medallions and terra-cotta panels of Mary with Baby Jesus, done by members of the Della Robbia clan, and an imposing armory collection. The most interesting room (sometimes closed at slow times) has large glass cases filled with miniature bronze models of famous statues. For example, look for small-scale, alternate versions of works by Giambologna, including his *Mercury* and *Rape of the Sabine Women*.

From swords to statues, from *Brutus* to Brunelleschi, from *David* to *David* to *David* to *David*—the Bargello's collection of civilized artifacts makes it clear why Florence dominated the Italian Renaissance.

MUSEUM OF SAN MARCO TOUR

Museo di San Marco

Two of Florence's brightest lights lived in the San Marco Monastery, a reminder that the Renaissance was not just a secular phenomenon. At the Museum of San Marco, you'll find these two different expressions of 15th-century Christianity—Fra Angelico's radiant paintings, fusing medieval faith with Renaissance realism, and Savonarola's moral reforms, fusing medieval faith with modern politics.

Orientation

Cost: €4, covered by Firenze Card.

Hours: Tue-Fri 8:15-13:50, Sat 8:15-16:50; also open 8:15-13:50 on first, third, and fifth Mon and 8:15-16:50 on second and fourth Sun of each month; last entry 30 minutes before closing. You can reserve an entrance time, but it's unnecessary.

Getting There: It's on Piazza San Marco, a block north of the Accademia, and several long blocks northeast of the Duomo (head up Via Ricasoli or Via Cavour). Piazza San Marco is a hub for many buses.

Information: Consider picking up the compact, worthwhile, official guide (€10) at the bookstore. Tel. 055-238-8608, www.polomuseale.firenze.it

Length of This Tour: Allow one hour.

Baggage Check: None is available, and large bags are not allowed in the museum (but if you ask nicely, the ticket-taker might watch your bag for you).

Photography: Prohibited.

Cuisine Art: Gelateria Carabè, known for its sumptuous *granite* (fresh-fruit Italian ices), is just a block away toward the

Duomo, at Via Ricasoli 60 red. For recommended eateries nearby, see page 298.

Starring: Fra Angelico's paintings and Savonarola's living quarters.

OVERVIEW

The ground floor features the world's best collection of Fra Angelico paintings. The upstairs contains the monks' cells (living quarters), decorated by Fra Angelico, and the cell of the most famous resident, Savonarola. Restoration is ongoing; expect that some paintings will be out and a room or two may be closed.

The Tour Begins

• *Buy your ticket and enter the courtyard/cloister.*

GROUND FLOOR

The Courtyard/Cloister

Stepping into the cloister, you can feel the spirituality of this place, a respite from the hubbub of modern Florence. You'll see Renaissance arches frame Gothic cross-vaulting—an apt introduction to a monastery built during an optimistic time, when Renaissance humanism dovetailed with medieval spirituality.

In 1439, Cosimo the Elder (the founder of the Medici ruling dynasty and Lorenzo the Magnificent's grandpa) hired the architect Michelozzo to build the monastery, and invited Fra Angelico's Dominican community to move here from Fiesole. Fra Angelico (c. 1400-1455) turned down an offer to be archbishop of Florence, instead becoming prior (head monk). He quickly began decorating the monastery walls with frescoes.

• *From the entrance, walk straight ahead. On the wall at the far end of the first corridor, in the corner of the cloister, is...*

Fra Angelico—*Crucifixion with St. Dominic (San Domenico in Adorazione del Crocifisso)*

The fresco by Fra Angelico shows Dominic, the founder of the order, hugging the bloody cross like a groupie adoring a rock star. Monks who lived here—including Fra Angelico, Savonarola, and Fra Bartolomeo—renounced money, sex, ego, and pop music to follow a simple, regimented life, meditating on Christ's ultimate sacrifice.

Fra Angelico considered painting to be a form of prayer. He worked to bridge the gap between the infinite (Christ) and the finite (a

SAN MARCO

Museum of San Marco—Ground Floor

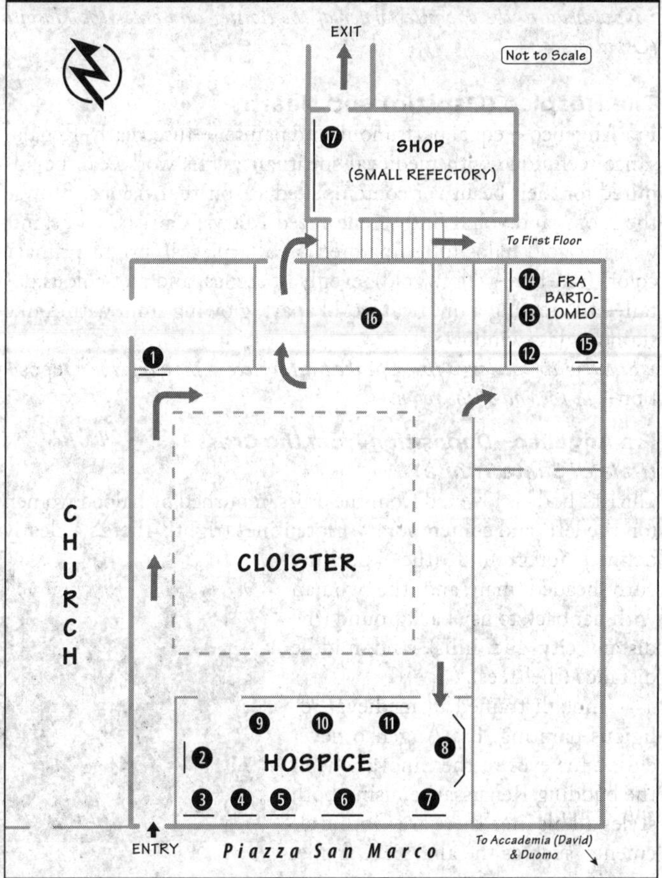

1. FRA ANGELICO – Crucifixion with St. Dominic
2. FRA ANGELICO – Deposition from the Cross
3. FRA ANGELICO – Triptych of St. Peter Martyr
4. FRA ANGELICO – Wedding & Funeral of the Virgin
5. FRA ANGELICO – Last Judgment
6. FRA ANGELICO – Door Panels of a Cupboard for Silver
7. FRA ANGELICO – Lamentation
8. FRA ANGELICO – Altarpiece of the Linen-Drapers
9. FRA ANGELICO – Annalena Altarpiece
10. FRA ANGELICO – San Marco Altarpiece
11. FRA ANGELICO – Bosco ai Frati Altarpiece
12. FRA BARTOLOMEO – Ecce Homo
13. FRA BARTOLOMEO – St. Dominic
14. FRA BARTOLOMEO – St. Thomas Aquinas
15. FRA BARTOLOMEO – Portrait of Savonarola
16. FRA ANGELICO – Crucifixion with Saints
17. GHIRLANDAIO – Last Supper

mortal's ability to relate to God) by injecting an ethereal atmosphere into his frescoes.

• *Now head to the opposite corner of the cloister and enter the Hospice (Ospizio).*

The Hospice (Ospizio) and Nearby

Fra Angelico—equal parts monk and painter—fused early-Renaissance technique with medieval spirituality. His works can be admired for their beauty or contemplated as spiritual visions. Browse the room, and you'll find serene-faced Marys, Christs, and saints wearing gold halos (often painted on altarpieces), bright primary colors (red-blue-yellow/gold), evenly lit scenes, and meticulous detail—all creating a mystical world apart, glowing from within like stained-glass windows.

• *Start with the large three-peaked altarpiece—showing the* Deposition—*at the end of the room.*

Fra Angelico—*Deposition from the Cross (Pala di Santa Trinità)*

Christ's body is lowered from the cross, mourned by haloed women (on the left) and contemporary Florentines (right). There's a clearly defined foreground (the kneeling, curly-headed man and the woman with her back to us), background (the distant city and hills), and middle distance (the trees).

Though trained in medieval religious painting, Fra Angelico never closed his eyes to the innovations of the budding Renaissance, using both styles all his life. There are Gothic elements, such as the altarpiece frame, inherited from his former teacher (who painted the pinnacles on top). The holy wear halos, and the stretched-out "body of Christ" is symbolically "displayed" like the communion bread.

But it's truly a Renaissance work. The man in green, lowering Christ, bends forward at a strongly foreshortened (difficult to draw) angle. Christ's toes, kissed by Mary Magdalene, cross the triptych wall, ignoring the frame's traditional three-arch divisions. Fra Angelico was boldly "coloring outside the lines" to create a single, realistic scene.

And the holy scene has been removed from its golden heaven and placed in the first great Renaissance landscape—on a lawn, among flowers, trees, cloud masses, real people, and the hillsides of Fiesole overlooking Florence. Fra Angelico, the ascetic monk, refused to renounce one pleasure—his joy in the natural beauty of God's creation.

• *Moving counterclockwise around the room, you'll find the following works (among others). First, turn left to find...*

Fra Angelico—*Triptych of St. Peter Martyr (Trittico di San Pietro Martire)*

In this early, more "medieval" work, Fra Angelico sets (big) Mary and Child in a gold background flanked by (small) saints standing obediently in their niches. When he joined the Dominican community in Fiesole, the artist took the name Giovanni (as he was known in his lifetime), and he wore the same attire as these famous Dominicans (including St. Dominic, far left, and St. Thomas Aquinas, far right)—white robe, blue cape, and tonsured haircut.

Peter Martyr (next to Mary, with bloody head) exemplified the unbending Dominican spirit. Attacked by heretics (see the scene above Peter), he was hacked in the head with a dagger but died still preaching, writing with his own blood: *"Credo in Deum"* ("I believe in God").

• *Continuing counterclockwise, look at the two small panels sharing one long frame.*

Fra Angelico—*Wedding* and *Funeral of the Virgin (Sposalizio, Funerali della Vergine)*

Fra Angelico's teenage training was as a miniaturist, so even these small predella panels (part of a larger altarpiece) are surprisingly realistic. The folds in the clothes, the gold-brocade hemlines, and the precisely outlined people are as though etched in glass. Notice the Renaissance perspective tricks he was exploring, setting the wedding in front of receding buildings and the funeral among candles that get shorter at the back of the scene.

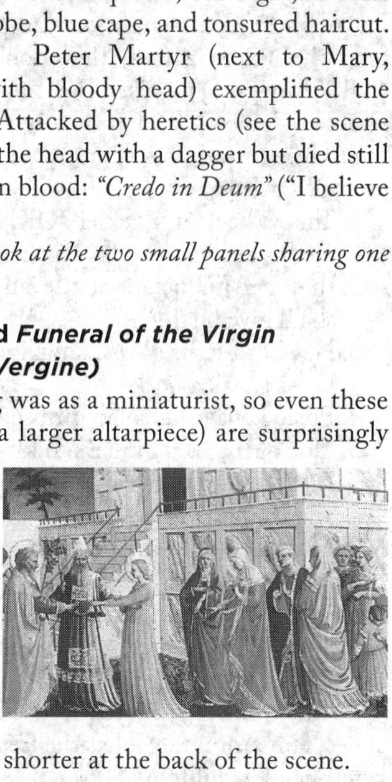

• *Next up is...*

Fra Angelico—*Last Judgment (Giudizio Universale)*

Despite the Renaissance, Florence in the 1420s was still a city in the Christian universe described by Dante. Hell (to the right) is a hierarchical barbecue where sinners are burned, boiled, and

tortured by a minotaur-like Satan, who rules the bottom of the pit. The blessed in heaven (left) play ring-around-the-rosy with angels. In the center, a row of open tombs creates a 3-D highway to hell, stretching ominously to that final Judgment Day.

• *On the other side of the pillar are several panels. Look at the one on the left.*

Fra Angelico (and Assistants)—*Door Panels of a Cupboard for Silver (Pannelli dell'Armadio degli Argenti)*

The first nine scenes in this life of Christ (the big panel on the left end) are by Fra Angelico himself (the rest by assistants). Like storyboards for a movie, these natural, realistic, and straightforward panels "show" through action, they don't just "tell" through symbols. (The Latin inscription beneath each panel is redundant.) The miraculous is presented as an everyday occurrence.

1. The Wheel of Ezekiel (OK, that's medieval symbolism) prophesies Christ's coming.
2. In the Annunciation, the angel gestures to tell Mary that she'll give birth.
3. Newborn Jesus glows, amazing his parents, while timid shepherds sneak a peek.
4. Precocious Jesus splays himself and says, "Cut me."
5. One of the Magi kneels to kiss the babe's foot.
6. In the temple, the tiny baby is dwarfed by elongated priests and columns.
7. Mary and the baby ride, while Joseph carries the luggage.
8. Meanwhile, babies are slaughtered in a jumble of gore, dramatic poses, and agonized faces.
9. The commotion contrasts with the serenity of the child Jesus in the temple.

This work by 50-year-old Fra Angelico—master of many styles, famous in Italy—has the fresh, simple, and spontaneous storytelling of a children's book.

• *Near the left end of this wall is...*

Fra Angelico—*Lamentation (Compianto sul Cristo Morto)*

This painting of the executed Christ being mourned silently by loved ones was the last thing many condemned prisoners saw during

their final hours. It once hung in a church where the soon-to-be executed were incarcerated.

The melancholy mood is understated, suggested by a series of horizontal layers—Christ's body, the line of mourners, the city walls, landscape horizon, layered clouds, and the crossbar. It's as though Christ is being welcomed into peaceful rest, a comforting message from Fra Angelico to the condemned.

"Fra Angelico" (Angelic Brother) is a nickname that describes the artist's reputation for sweetness, humility, and compassion. It's said he couldn't paint a Crucifixion without crying. In 1984, he was beatified by Pope John Paul II and made patron of artists.

• *At the end of the room hangs...*

Fra Angelico—*Altarpiece of the Linen-Drapers (Tabernacolo dei Linaioli)*

Check out the impressive size and marble frame (by Ghiberti, of baptistery-door fame), which attest to Fra Angelico's worldly success and collaboration with the Renaissance greats. The monumental Mary and Child, as well as the saints on the doors, are gold-backed and elegant, to please conservative patrons. In the three predella panels below, Fra Angelico gets to display his Renaissance chops, showing haloed saints mingling with well-dressed Florentines amid local cityscapes and landscapes. (Find Ghiberti in the left panel, kneeling, in blue.)

• *On the long wall are three similar-looking altarpieces. Move left to right, watching the...*

Evolution of the *Sacra Conversazione*

Fra Angelico (largely) invented what became a common Renaissance theme: Mary and Child surrounded by saints "conversing" informally about holy matters. Four examples in this room show how Fra Angelico, exploring Renaissance techniques, developed the idea over his lifetime.

Fra Angelico—*Annalena Altarpiece (Pala d'Annalena)*

In the *Annalena Altarpiece* (c. 1435)—considered Florence's first true *Sacra Conversazione*—the saints flank Mary in a neat line, backed by medieval gold in the form of a curtain. Everyone is either facing out or in profile—not the natural poses of a true crowd. There's little eye contact, and certainly no "conversation."

Mary and Jesus direct our eye to Mary's brooch, the first in a series of circles radiating out from the center: brooch, halo, canopy arch, circle of saints. Set in a square frame, this painting has the circle-in-a-square composition that marks many *Sacra Conversaziones*.

Fra Angelico—*San Marco Altarpiece (Pala di San Marco)*

Cosimo the Elder commissioned this painting (c. 1440) as the centerpiece of the new church next door. (Note: The *San Marco Altarpiece* may be under restoration at the time of your visit.) For the dedication Mass, Fra Angelico theatrically "opens the curtain," revealing a stage set with a distant backdrop of trees, kneeling saints in the foreground, and a crowd gathered around Mary and Child at center stage on a raised, canopied throne. The carpet makes a chessboard-like pattern to establish 3-D perspective. The altarpiece was like a window onto a marvelous world where the holy mill about on earth as naturally as mortals.

To show just how far we've come from Gothic, Fra Angelico gives us a painting-in-a-painting—a crude, gold-backed Crucifixion.

Fra Angelico—*Bosco ai Frati Altarpiece (Pala di Bosco ai Frati)*

This altarpiece (c. 1450) is Fra Angelico's last great work, and he uses every stylistic arrow in his quiver: the detailed friezes of the miniaturist; medieval halos and gold backdrop; monumental, naturally posed figures in the style of Masaccio (especially St. Francis, on the left, with his relaxed *contrapposto*); 3-D perspective established by the floor tiles; and Renaissance love of natural beauty (the trees and sky).

Fra Angelico's bright colors are eye-catching. The gold backdrop sets off the red-pink handmaidens, which set off Jesus' pale skin. The deep blue of Mary's dress, frosted with a precious gold hem, turns out at her feet to show a swath of the green inner lining, suggesting the 3-D body within.

Despite Renaissance realism, Fra Angelico creates a world of his own—perfectly lit, with no moody shadows, dirt, frayed clothing, or imperfections. The faces are certainly realistic, but they express no human emotion. These mortals, through sacrifice and meditation, have risen above the petty passions celebrated by humanist painters, to achieve a serenity that lights them from within.

• *From here, we'll circle the cloister counterclockwise. Exit the Hospice back into the courtyard, walk to the end of the corridor, and enter the next set of rooms (marked* Lavabo e Refettorio*). The small room on the left has paintings and fresco fragments by...*

Fra Bartolomeo

Fra Bartolomeo (1472-1517) lived and worked in this monastery a generation after the "Angelic" brother. ***Ecce Homo*** shows the kind of Christ that young, idealistic Dominican monks (like Fra Bartolomeo) adored in their meditations—curly-haired, creamy-faced, dreamy-eyed, bearing the torments of the secular world with humble serenity.

• *From Jesus, the third panel on the right is...*

Fra Bartolomeo—*St. Dominic (San Domenico)*

St. Dominic holds a finger to his lips—"Shh! We have strict rules in my order." Dominic (c. 1170-1221), a friend of St. Francis of Assisi, formed his rules after seeing the austere *perfetti* (perfect ones) of the heretical Cathar sect of southern France. He figured they could only be converted by someone just as extreme, following Christ's simple, possession-free lifestyle. Nearing 50, Dominic made a 3,400-mile preaching tour—on foot, carrying his luggage—from Rome to Spain to Paris and back. Dominic is often portrayed with the star of revelation over his head.

• *Two more panels to the right is...*

Fra Bartolomeo—*St. Thomas Aquinas (San Tommaso d'Aquino)*

St. Thomas Aquinas (c. 1225-1274, wearing a hood)—the intellectual giant of the U. of Paris—used logic and Aristotelian models to defend and explain Christianity (building the hierarchical belief system known as Scholasticism). He's often shown with a heavy build and the sun of knowledge burning in his chest.

• *As you face the door, to the left you'll see...*

Fra Bartolomeo—*Portrait of Savonarola (Ritratto di Fra' Girolamo Savonarola)*

This is the famous portrait—in profile, hooded, with big nose and clear eyes, gazing intently into the darkness—of the man reviled as the evil opponent of Renaissance goodness. Would it surprise you to learn that it was Savonarola who inspired Fra Bartolomeo's art? Bartolomeo was so moved by Savonarola's sermons that he burned his early nude paintings (and back issues of *Penthouse*), became a monk, gave up painting for a few years...then resurfaced to paint the simple, sweet frescoes we see here.

• *Leaving the world of Fra Bartolomeo, return to the courtyard and continue to the next room* (Capitolo), *which contains the large wall fresco...*

Fra Angelico—*Crucifixion with Saints (Crocifissione dell'Angelico)*

This Crucifixion, against a bleak background, is one of more than 20 versions of Christ's torture/execution in the monastery. It was in this room that naughty monks were examined and judged.

Among the group of hermits, martyrs, and religious extremists who surround the cross, locate Dominic (kneeling at the foot of the cross, in Dominican white robe, blue cape, and tonsured hair, with star on head), Peter Martyr (kneeling in right corner, with bloody head), and Thomas Aquinas (standing behind Peter, with jowls and sun on chest).

The bell in the room is the original church bell, the one that rang a warning to Savonarola the night he was arrested. (The mob was so enraged that they exiled the bell for 10 years.)

• *Return to the courtyard, go through the next door, and head upstairs to the first floor.*

FIRST FLOOR

The Monks' Living Quarters and Fra Angelico's Frescoes

This floor is lined with the cells (bedrooms) of those who lived in the monastery: monks (in the corridor to your left), novice monks (farther down), and lay people and support staff (to your right). We'll see Savonarola's quarters in the far corner. Each room was frescoed by Fra Angelico or his assistants.

After a long day of prayer, meditation, reading, frugal meals, chopping wood, hauling water, translating Greek, attending Mass, and more prayer, a monk retired to one of these small, bare, lamp-lit rooms. His "late-night TV" was programmed by the prior—Fra Angelico—in the form of a fresco to meditate on before sleep. In monastic life, everything is a form of prayer. Pondering these scenes, monks learned the various aspects of worship: humility, adoration, flagellation, reflection, and so on.

All in all, 43 cells were decorated in the early 1440s by Fra Angelico and his assistants. Many feature a crucifix and St. Dominic, but each shows Dominic in a different physical posture (kneeling, head bowed, head raised, hands folded), which the monks copied in order to attain a more spiritual state.

• *At the top of the staircase, you'll come face-to-face with Fra Angelico's* Annunciation.

❶ Fra Angelico—*Annunciation (Annunciazione):* Sway back and forth and watch the angel's wings sparkle (from glitter mixed into the fresco) as he delivers "the good news" to the very humble and accepting Virgin. Mary is under an arcade that's remarkably similar to the one in the monastery courtyard. Fra Angelico brings this scene home to the monks quite literally.

Paintings such as this one made Fra Angelico so famous that the pope called on him to paint the Vatican. Yet this work, like the other frescoes here, was meant only for the private eyes of humble monks. Monks gathered near the *Annunciation* for common prayers, contemplating Christ's life from beginning *(Annunciation)* to end (*Crucifixion with St. Dominic,* over your left shoulder). The caption reads: Remember to say your Hail Marys.

• *From the* Annunciation, *take a few steps to the left, and look down the (east) corridor lined with monks' cells. Some of Fra Angelico's best work is found in the 10 cells along the left-hand side. Begin with the first of these cells.*

❷ *Noli me Tangere:* The resurrected Jesus, appearing as a hoe-carrying gardener, says, "Don't touch me" and gingerly sidesteps

Museum of San Marco—First Floor

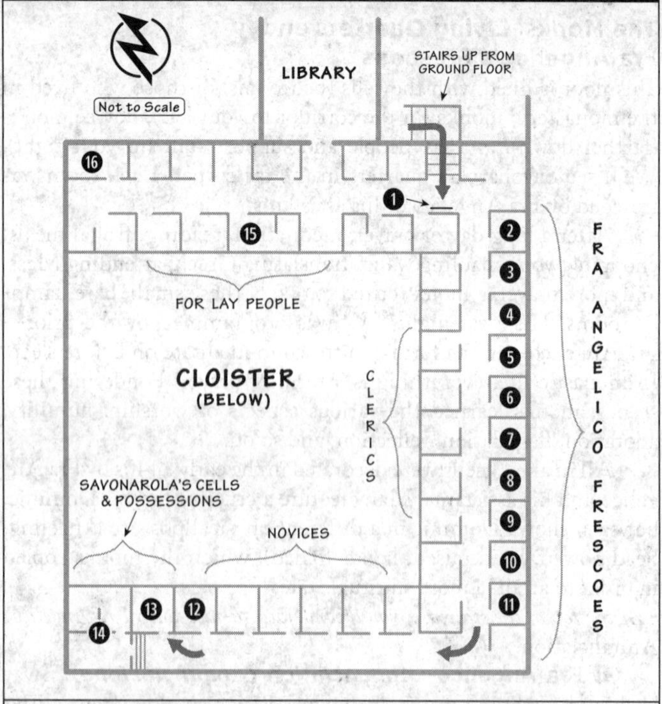

1. Annunciation
2. Noli me Tangere
3. Lamentation
4. Annunciation
5. Crucifixion
6. Birth of Jesus
7. Transfiguration
8. The Mocking of Christ
9. The Empty Tomb
10. Mary Crowned
11. Presentation in the Temple
12. Savonarola's Banner
13. Savonarola's Cloak & Crucifix
14. Savonarola's Cells
15. Kiss of Judas
16. Cosimo the Elder's Cells

Mary Magdalene's grasp. The flowers and trees represent the blossoming of new life, and they're about the last we'll see. Most scenes have stark, bare backgrounds, to concentrate the monk's focus on just the essential subject.

❸ ***Lamentation:*** Christ and mourners are a reverse image of the *Lamentation* downstairs. Christ levitates, not really supported by the ladies' laps. The colors are muted grays, browns, and pinks. Dominic (star on head)

stands contemplating, just as the monk should do, by mentally transporting himself to the scene.

❹ ***Annunciation:*** The painting's arches echo the room's real arch. (And they, in turn, harmoniously "frame" the "arch" of Mary and the angel bending toward each other to talk.) Peter Martyr (bloody head) looks on.

You can't call these cells a wrap until you've found at least six crosses, three Dominics, three Peters, and a Thomas Aquinas. Ready...go.

❺ ***Crucifixion:*** That's one cross. And another Dominic.

❻ ***Birth of Jesus:*** And there's your second Peter.

❼ ***Transfiguration:*** Forsaking Renaissance realism, Fra Angelico emphasizes the miraculous. In an aura of blinding light, Christ spreads his arms cross-like, dazzling the three witnesses at the bottom of the "mountain." He's joined by disembodied heads of prophets, all spinning in a circle echoed by the room's arch. These rooms, which housed senior monks, have some of the most complex and intellectually demanding symbolism.

❽ ***The Mocking of Christ:*** From Renaissance realism to Dalí surrealism. Dominic, while reading the Passion, conjures an image of Christ—the true king, on a throne with a globe and scepter—now blindfolded, spit upon, slapped, and clubbed by...a painting of medieval symbols of torment. This must have been a puzzling riddle from the Master to a fellow monk.

❾ ***The Empty Tomb:*** The worried women are reassured by an angel that "he is risen." Jesus, far away in the clouds, seems annoyed that they didn't listen to him.

❿ ***Mary Crowned:*** ...triumphantly in heaven, while Dominic, Peter, Aquinas, Francis, and others prepare to celebrate with high-fives.

⓫ ***Presentation in the Temple:*** Baby Jesus is swaddled like a mummy. And there's your final Peter.

• *Continue around the bend—Savonarola's three rooms are at the far end of the corridor.*

Savonarola's Cells (Celle del Savonarola)

Girolamo Savonarola (1452-1498) occupied the cluster of rooms at the end of the hall. But before you climb the three steps to his cells, stop at the last two rooms along the hall (on the right). Here you'll find a number of his possessions, including ⓬ fragments of a **banner** *(Lo Stendardo del Savonarola)* and ⓭ his **blue cloak** and personal **crucifix.** Savonarola's life changed dramatically at 22, when he heard a sermon on repentance. He traded his scholar's robes for the blue cloak of a simple Dominican monk. He quickly became known for his asceticism, devotion, and knowledge of the Bible. His followers rallied around this banner, painted with a gruesome Crucifixion scene in the Fra Angelico style. They paraded through the streets reminding all that Christ paid for their worldly Renaissance sins.

• *Now enter* ⓮ ***Savonarola's Cells.***

First Room

The **portrait bust** shows the hooded monk, whose personal charisma and prophetic fervor led him from humble scholar to celebrity preacher to prior of San Marco to leader of Florence to controversial martyr. The **relief** under the portrait bust shows Savonarola at his greatest moment. He stands before the Florence city council and pledges allegiance to Florence's constitution, assuming control of the city after the exile of the Medici (1494). Reviled as a fanatical, regressive tyrant and praised as a saint, reformer, and champion of democracy, Savonarola was a complex man in a position of great power during turbulent times.

Various **paintings** depict Savonarola in action, including one by Federico Andreotti, which shows the powerful monk reproaching two troublemakers in his study.

• *The next room is Savonarola's...*

Study (Studiolo)

Seated at this **desk,** in his ecclesiastical folding **chair,** Savonarola scoured his Bible for clues to solve Florence's civic strife.

In 1482 at age 30, the monk had come to San Marco as a lecturer. He was bright, humble...and boring. Then, after experiencing divine revelations, he spiced his sermons with prophecies of future events...which started coming true. His sermons on Ezekiel, Amos, Exodus, and the Apocalypse predicted doom for the Medici family. He made brazen references to the pope's embezzling and stable of mistresses, and preached hope for a glorious future after city and church were cleansed.

Packed houses heard him rail against the "prostitute church... the monster of abomination." Witnesses wrote that "the church echoed with weeping and wailing," and afterward "everyone wandered the city streets dazed and speechless." From this humble desk, he corresponded with the worldly pope, the humanist Pico della Mirandola, and fans, such as Lorenzo the Magnificent, who begrudgingly admired his courage.

Lorenzo died, the bankrupt Medici were exiled, and Florence was invaded by France...as Savonarola had prophesied. In the power vacuum, the masses saw Savonarola as a moderate voice who championed a return to Florence's traditional constitution. He was made head of a Christian commonwealth.

• *Finally, step into the...*

Room with Savonarola's Possessions (Le Reliquie di Savonarola)

Savonarola's personal moral authority was unquestioned, as his simple **wool clothes** and **rosary** attest.

At first, his rule was just. He cut taxes, reduced street crime, shifted power from rich Medici to citizens, and even boldly proposed banning Vespas from tourist zones.

However, Savonarola had an uncompromising and fanatical side, as his **hair-shirt girdle** suggests. His government passed strict morality laws against swearing, blasphemy, gambling, and ostentatious clothes, which were enforced by gangs of thuggish teenagers. At the height of the Christian Republic, during Lent of 1497, followers built a huge "bonfire of vanities" on Piazza della Signoria, where they burned wigs, carnival masks, dice, playing cards, musical instruments, and discredited books and paintings.

In 1498, several forces undermined Savonarola's Republic: scheming Medici, crop failure, rival cities, a pissed-off pope threatening excommunication for Savonarola and political isolation for Florence, and a public tiring of puritanism. Gangs of opponents (called *Arrabbiati*, "Rabid Dogs") battled Savonarola's supporters (the "Weepers"). Meanwhile, Savonarola was slowly easing out of public life, refusing to embroil the church in a lengthy trial, retiring to his routine of study, prayer, and personal austerity.

Egged on by city leaders and the pope, a bloodthirsty mob marched on San Marco to arrest Savonarola. *Arrabbiati* fought monks with clubs (imagine it in the **courtyard** out the window), while the church bells clanged and the monks shouted, *"Salvum fac populum tuum, Domine!"* ("Save thy people, Lord!"). The *Arrabbiati* stormed up the stairs to this floor, and Savonarola was handed over to the authorities. He was taken to Palazzo Vecchio, tortured, tried, and sentenced.

On May 23, 1498 (see the **painting** *Supplizio del Savonarola in Piazza della Signoria*), before a huge crowd in front of Palazzo Vecchio (where today a memorial plaque is embedded in the pavement of the Piazza della Signoria), Savonarola was publicly defrocked, then publicly forgiven by a papal emissary. Then he was

hanged—not Old West-style, in which the neck snaps, but instead slowly strangled, dangling from a rope, while teenage boys hooted and threw rocks.

The crowd looked upon the lifeless body of this man who had once captivated their minds, as they lit a pyre under the scaffold—see the **stick *(palo)*** from the fire. The flames rose up, engulfing the body, when suddenly...his arm shot upward!—like a final blessing or curse—and the terrified crowd stampeded, killing several. Savonarola's ashes were thrown in the Arno.

THE REST OF THE MUSEUM

The corridor near Fra Angelico's *Annunciation* has the library (also designed by Michelozzo), which contains music and other manuscripts. In a cell across the hall and a bit to the right is Fra Angelico's ⓯ ***Kiss of Judas*** fresco—a theme that proved prophetic, since it was outside that cell that Savonarola was arrested. At the end of the corridor (right side) are ⓰ **Cosimo the Elder's cells.** As the builder of this monastery, he often retired here for spiritual renewal. Inside, the painting of the Magi includes a kneeling Magus kissing the baby's little holy toes—a portrait of Cosimo.

• *To exit, return to the stairway and descend. Take a right at the bottom into a bookshop decorated with a fine Ghirlandaio* Last Supper *fresco (are you as tired as John is?). WCs are in the next hallway. Pass through corridors filled with a hodgepodge of architectural fragments and on to the exit. On the street, turn right, then right again, and you'll see the Campanile of the Duomo.*

DUOMO MUSEUM TOUR

Museo dell'Opera del Duomo

This fine museum is—unfortunately—closed for renovation at least through late 2015. However, if it has reopened by the time you visit, it's a treat: Brunelleschi's dome, Ghiberti's bronze doors, and Donatello's statues—these creations define the 1400s (the Quattrocento) in Florence, when the city blossomed and classical arts were reborn. All are featured at the Duomo Museum, plus a Michelangelo *Pietà* that was intended as his sculptural epitaph. While copies now decorate the exteriors of the Duomo (cathedral), Baptistery, and Campanile (bell tower, called Giotto's Tower), the original sculptured masterpieces of the complex are now restored and displayed safely indoors, filling the Duomo Museum. This museum is a delight, though it's overlooked by most visitors to Florence.

Orientation

Closure Warning: The museum is undergoing a major renovation and is scheduled to be closed entirely until late 2015. When it reopens, many of the details listed here—and throughout this tour—are likely to have changed.

Cost: €10 ticket covers all Duomo sights, covered by Firenze Card.

Hours: Mon-Sat 9:00-19:30, Sun 9:00-13:45, last entry 45 minutes before closing. This is one of the few museums in Florence that's open every Monday. It also stays open later than most.

Getting There: The museum is across the street from the Duomo on the east side (the opposite end from the Baptistery), at Via del Proconsolo 9.

Information: Tel. 055-282-226 or 055-230-7885, www.operaduomo.firenze.it

Tours: The audioguide costs €5. Guided English tours are gen-

Duomo Museum—Ground Floor

1. Roman Sarcophagi, Etruscan Fragments, Chronological Chart & Baptistery Statues
2. Madonna with the Glass Eyes
3. Statue of Pope Boniface VIII
4. DONATELLO – St. John the Evangelist
5. Scale Model of Duomo's Facade
6. Room of Altarpieces & Reliquaries
7. John the Baptist's Finger
8. GHIBERTI – "Gates of Paradise" Doors
9. MICHELANGELO – Pietà

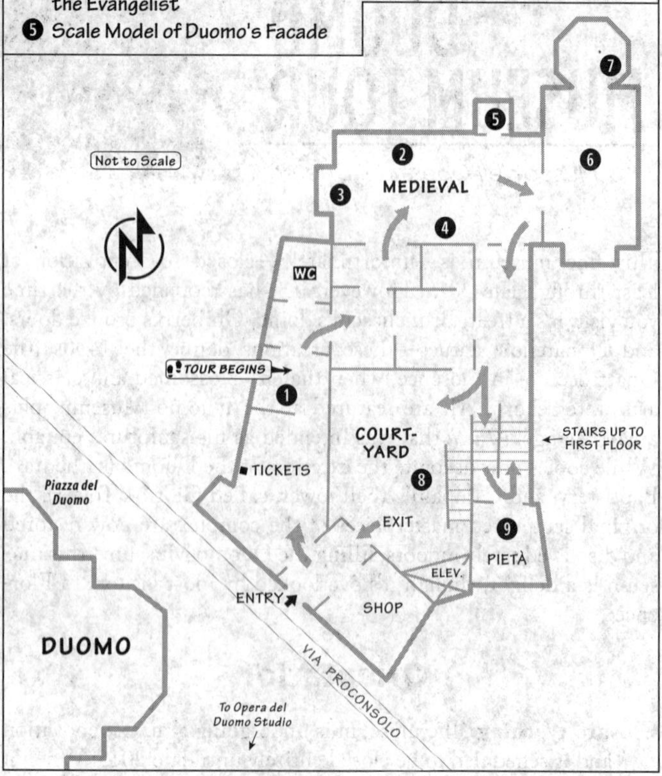

erally offered daily in summer for €3 (as they use volunteer guides, schedules vary—stop by or call to ask).

Length of This Tour: Allow 1.5 hours. With limited time, focus on Ghiberti's doors, Michelangelo's *Pietà,* Donatello's sculptures, and the pair of finely carved choir lofts *(cantorie).*

Photography: Allowed, but no flash around paintings.

Starring: Brunelleschi, Ghiberti, Donatello, and Michelangelo.

The Tour Begins

Ghiberti's doors are on the ground floor, while Donatello's statues are on the first floor. The *Pietà* is on a landing halfway between floors.

GROUND FLOOR

The Medieval Cathedral

• *Browse the first few small rooms.*

Roman sarcophagi, Etruscan fragments, a chronological chart, and broken Baptistery statues attest to the 2,000-year history of Florence's Duomo, Baptistery, and Campanile. The Baptistery was likely built on the site of a pagan Roman temple. It was flanked by a humble church that, by the 1200s, was not big enough to contain the exuberant spirit of a city growing rich from the wool trade and banking. In 1296, the cornerstone was laid for a huge church—today's Duomo—intended to be the biggest in Christendom.

• *The first large room features statues from the original facade (1296-1587). You'll see a tall, seated pope and a cheery Virgin-and-Child known as the...*

Madonna with the Glass Eyes (Madonna in Trono col Bambino)

The architect Arnolfo di Cambio designed this statue to sit in a niche on the church's exterior. The building was dedicated to Mary—starry-eyed over the birth of Baby Jesus. She sits, crowned like a chess-set queen, above the main door, framed with a dazzling mosaic halo. She's accompanied (to our right) by St. Zenobius, Florence's first bishop during Roman times, whose raised hand consecrates the formerly pagan ground as Christian.

Statue of Pope Boniface VIII

Despised by Dante for his meddling in politics, this pope paid 3,000 florins to get his image in a box seat on the facade. His XL shirt size made him look correct when viewed from below. Though the statue is stylized, Arnolfo realistically shows the pope's custom-made, extra-tall hat and bony face. (Most of the room's statues are straight-backed, to hang on the facade.)

• *On the long wall opposite the Madonna, find...*

Donatello—*St. John the Evangelist (San Giovanni Evangelista)*

A hundred years later, Arnolfo's medieval facade became a showcase for Renaissance sculptors.

John sits gazing at a distant horizon, his tall head rising high above his massive body. This visionary foresees a new age...and the coming Renaissance. The right hand is massive—as relaxed as though it were dangling over the back of a chair, but full of powerful tension. Like the mighty right hand of Michelangelo's *David,* and the beard of Michelangelo's *Moses,* this work is a hundred years ahead of its time.

At 22 years old, Donatello (c. 1386-1466) sculpted this work just before becoming a celebrity for his inspiring statue of *St. George* (original in the Bargello, copy on the exterior of the Orsanmichele Church). Donatello, like most early Renaissance artists, was a blue-collar worker, raised as a workshop apprentice among knuckle-dragging musclemen. He proudly combined physical skill with technical know-how to create beauty (Art + Science = Renaissance Beauty). His statues are thinkers with big hands who can put theory into practice.

• *To the right of the Madonna, in an adjoining room, find a...*

Scale Model of the Duomo's Original Facade

In Renaissance times, this is what the Duomo would have looked like. (The model, by Franco Gizdulich, is 1:20.) The glassy-eyed Madonna was over the main doorway, Pope Boniface was to the left, high up, and Donatello's St. John was to the left, farther down. You can see that only the bottom third was ever completed with marble facing—the upper part was bare brick. Had Arnolfo's design been completed, the three-story facade would have looked much like today's colorful, Neo-Gothic version, with pointed arches and white, pink, and green marble, studded with statues and gleaming

with gold mosaics. In 1587, the still-incomplete facade was torn down.

• *Up a few steps at the end of the long statue room is a...*

Room of Altarpieces and Reliquaries

These medieval altarpieces, which once adorned chapels and altars inside the Duomo, show saints and angels suspended in a gold never-never land. In the adjoining room, the ornate reliquaries hold bones and objects of the saints (Peter's chains, Jerome's jawbone, and so on), many bought from a single, slick 14th-century con artist preying on medieval superstition.

In the 1400s, tastes changed, and these symbols of crude medievalism were purged from the Duomo and stacked in storage. Soon artists replaced the golden heavenly scenes with flesh-and-blood humans who inhabited the physical world of rocks, trees, and sky... the Renaissance.

• *Go into the little chapel at the far end of this room. The first glass case on the right as you enter the chapel contains...*

John the Baptist's Finger in a Reliquary (Reliquario di un Dito Indice di San Giovanni)

The severed index finger of the beheaded prophet is the most revered relic of all the holy body parts in this museum.

• *Pass through a few more rooms into the ground-floor courtyard, where you'll find...*

Ghiberti's Baptistery Doors

The Renaissance began in 1401 with a citywide competition to build new doors for the Baptistery. Lorenzo Ghiberti (c. 1378-1455) won the job and built the doors (now on the Baptistery's north side), which everyone loved. He then was hired to make another set of doors—these panels—for the main entrance facing the Duomo. These bronze "Gates of Paradise" (1425-1452) revolutionized the way Renaissance people saw the world around them.

The original 10 panels from the Gates of Paradise were moved from the Baptistery to the museum to better preserve them. (Copies now adorn the Baptistery itself—see the graphic on page 85 for the original layout.) But even indoors, corrosive oxides gathered between the bronze panels and their gilding. After years of restoration, the doors are now back on display. The panels are under glass to protect against natural light and gassed with nitrogen to protect them from oxygen and humidity.

• *Here's a description of a few of the panels:*

Joseph and Benjamin (Storie di Giuseppe e Beniamino)

With just the depth of a thumbnail, Ghiberti creates a temple in the round that's inhabited by workers. This round temple wowed Florence. Armed with the rules of perspective, Ghiberti rendered reality with a mathematical precision we don't normally impose on what we see, when our eyes and minds settle for ballpark estimates about relative size and distance. For Florentines, suddenly the world acquired a whole new dimension—depth.

Adam and Eve (La Creazione e Storie di Adamo ed Eva)

Ghiberti tells several stories in one panel—a common medieval technique—using different thicknesses in the relief. In the sketchy

background (very low relief), God in a bubble conducts the Creation. In the center (a little thicker), Eve springs from Adam's side. Finally, in the lower left (in high relief), an elegantly robed God pulls Adam, as naked as the day he was born, from the mud.

Ghiberti welcomed the innovations of other artists. See the angel flying through an arch (right side). This arch is in very low relief but still looks fully 3-D because it's rendered sideways, using the perspective tricks of painting. Ghiberti learned the technique from one of his employees, the young Donatello.

Jacob and Esau (Storie di Giacobbe ed Esau)

The "background" arches and the space they create are as interesting as the scenes themselves. At the center is the so-called vanishing point on the distant horizon, where all the arches and floor tiles converge. This calm center gives us an eye-level reference point for all the figures. Those closest to us, at the bottom of the panel, are big and clearly defined. Distant figures are smaller, fuzzier, and higher up.

Ghiberti has placed us about 20 feet away from the scene, part of this casual crowd of holy people—some with their backs to us—milling around an arcade.

Labors of Adam, and Cain and Abel (Il Lavoro dei Progenitori e Storie di Caino e Abele)

On one mountain, we see Cain and Abel offering a sacrifice at the top, Adam waving at the bottom, and the first murder in between. In early panels such as this one (pictured at right) Ghiberti used only a sketchy landscape as a backdrop for human activities.

Ghiberti, the illegitimate son of a goldsmith, labored all his working life (more than 50 years) on the two Baptistery doors. Their execution was a major manufacturing job, requiring a large workshop of artists and artisans for each stage of the process: making the door frames that hold the panels, designing and making models of the panels (forming them in wax in order to cast them in bronze), gilding the panels (by bathing them in powdered gold dissolved in mercury, then heating until the gold and bronze blended), polishing the panels, mounting them, installing the doors...and signing paychecks for everyone along the way. Ghiberti was as much businessman as artist.

Solomon and the Queen of Sheba (Salomone e la Regina di Saba)

The receding arches stretch into infinity, giving the airy feeling that we can see forever. All of the arches and steps converge at the center of the panel, where the two monarchs meet, uniting their respective peoples. Ghiberti's subject was likely influenced by the warm ecumenical breeze blowing through Florence in 1439, as religious leaders convened here in an attempt to reunite the eastern (Constantinople) and western (Rome) realms of Christendom.

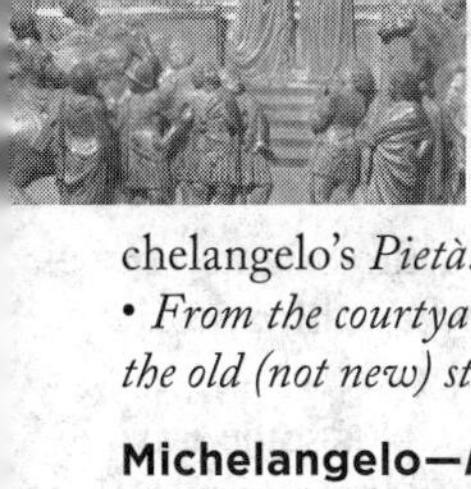

If the Renaissance began in 1401 with Ghiberti's doors, it ended in 1555 with Michelangelo's *Pietà*.

• *From the courtyard, look for two staircases almost side by side. Ascend the old (not new) staircase to the first landing, where you'll find...*

Michelangelo—*Pietà* (1547-1555)

The aging Michelangelo (1475-1564) designed his own tomb, with this as the centerpiece. He was depressed by old age, the recent death of his soul mate, and the grim reality that by sculpting this statue he was writing his own obituary. Done on his own dime, it's fair to consider this an introspective and very personal work.

Three mourners tend the broken body of the crucified Christ. We see Mary, his mother (the shadowy figure on our right); Mary Magdalene (on the left, polished up by a pupil); and Nicodemus, the converted Pharisee, whose face is clearly that of Michelangelo himself. The polished body of Christ stands out from the unfinished background. Michelangelo (as Nicodemus), who spent a lifetime bringing statues to life by "freeing" them from the stone, looks down at what could be his final creation, the once-perfect body of Renaissance Man that is now twisted, disfigured, and dead.

Seen face-on, the four figures form a powerful geometric shape: a circle inside a triangle, split down the middle by Christ's massive (but very dead) arm. Seen from the right side, they seem to interact with each other, their sketchy faces changing emotions from grief to melancholy to peaceful acceptance.

Fifty years earlier, a confident Michelangelo had worked here on these very premises, skillfully carving *David* from an imperfect block. But he hated this marble for the *Pietà;* it was hard and grainy, and gave off sparks when hit wrong. (The chisel grooves in the base remind us of the sheer physical effort it must have taken for a senior citizen to sculpt this.) Worst of all, his housekeeper kept bugging him with the same question that Pope Julius II used to ask about the Sistine Chapel—"When will you finish?" Pushed to the edge, Michelangelo grabbed a hammer and attacked the flawed marble statue, hacking away and breaking off limbs, then turned to the servant and said, "There! It's finished!" (An assistant later repaired some of the damage, but cracks are still visible in Christ's left arm and only leg.)

• *Continue upstairs to the first floor, entering a large room lined with statues and two balconies. Donatello's prophets are at the far end.*

FIRST FLOOR

Room of the *Cantorie*

The room displays two choir boxes *(cantorie)* and the original 16 statues (by several sculptors) from the bell tower's third story, where copies stand today.

Donatello did several statues of the prophets, plus some others in collaboration. (Some of the statues may be under restoration during your visit.)

Donatello ("Little Donato") invented the Renaissance style

Duomo Museum—First Floor

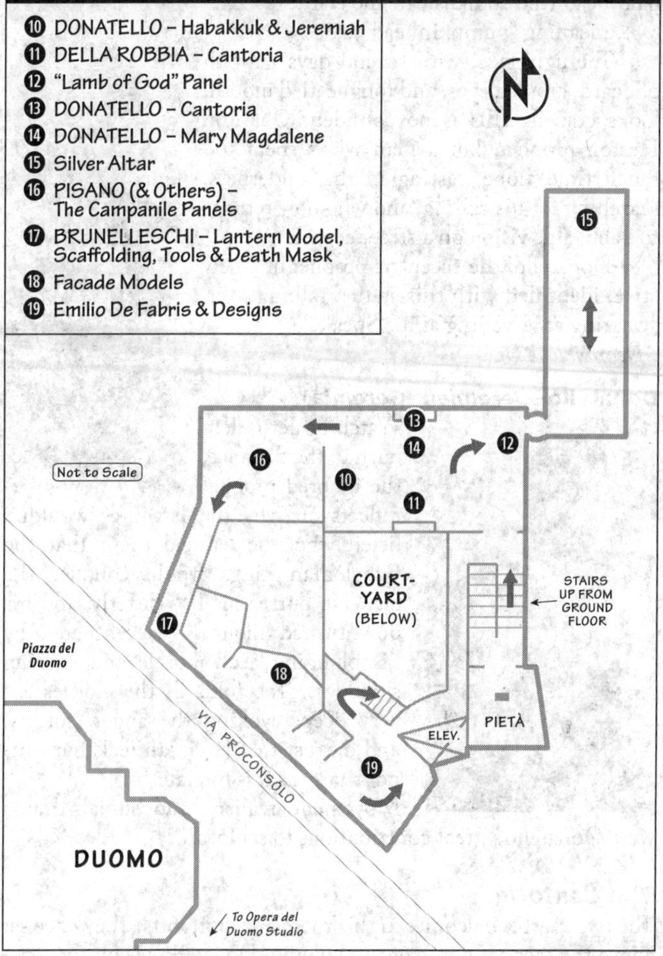

that Michelangelo would later perfect—powerful statues that are ultra-realistic, even ugly, sculpted in an "unfinished" style by an artist known for experimentation and his prickly, brooding personality. Both men were famous but lived like peasants, married only to their work.

Donatello—*Habakkuk (Abacuc)*

Donatello's signature piece shows us the wiry man beneath the heavy mantle of a prophet. Habakkuk's rumpled cloak falls down the front, dividing the body lengthwise. From the deep furrows emerges a bare arm with well-defined tendons and that powerful

right hand. His long, muscled neck leads to a bald head (the Italians call the statue *Lo Zuccone,* meaning "pumpkinhead").

The ugly face, with several days' growth of beard, crossed eyes, and tongue-tied mouth, looks crazed. This is no confident Charlton Heston prophet, but a man who's spent too much time alone, fasting in the wilderness, searching for his calling, and who now returns to babble his vision on a street corner.

Donatello, the eccentric prophet of a new style, identified with this statue, talking to it, swearing at it, yelling at it: "Speak!"

• *Nearby, look for...*

Donatello—*Jeremiah (Geremia)*

Watching Jerusalem burn in the distance, the ignored prophet reflects on why the Israelites wouldn't listen when he warned them that the Babylonian kings would conquer the city. He purses his lips bitterly, and his downturned mouth is accentuated by his plunging neck muscle and sagging shoulders. The folds in the clothes are very deep, evoking the anger, sorrow, and disgust that Jeremiah feels but cannot share, as it is too late.

Movement, realism, and human drama were Donatello's great contributions to sculpture.

The *Cantorie*

The two marble balconies in this room are choir lofts. They once sat above the sacristy doors of the Duomo. Donatello's is on the right (from the entrance); Luca della Robbia's on the left. Della Robbia's is a reconstruction from casts, with the original 10 panels displayed below.

Luca della Robbia—*Cantoria* (1430-c. 1438)

After almost 150 years of construction, the cathedral was nearly done, and the Opera del Duomo, the workshop in charge, began preparing the interior for the celebration. Brunelleschi hired a little-known sculptor, 30-year-old Luca della Robbia, to make this balcony choir-box *(cantoria)* for singers in the cathedral. It sums up the exuberance of the Quattrocento. The panels are a celebration of music, song, and dance performed by toddlers, children, and teenagers.

The *cantoria* brings Psalm 150 ("Praise ye the Lord") to life like a YouTube video. Starting in the upper left, the banner reads *"Laudate D.N.M."*—"Praise the Lord"—while children laugh and dance to the sound of trumpets *("sono Tubae")* and guitars, autoharps, and tambourines *("Psaltero... Cythera... Timpano")*. In the next level down, kids dance ring-around-the-rosy, a scene in the round on an almost-flat surface, showing front, back, and in-between poses. At bottom right, the Psalm ends: "Everybody praise the Lord!" Della Robbia's choir box was a triumph, a celebration of Florence's youthful boom time.

The Della Robbia family is best known for their colorful glazed terra-cotta, such as the **round "Lamb of God" panel** (over your left shoulder), by Luca's nephew.

Donatello—*Cantoria* (1433-c. 1440)

If Della Robbia's balcony looks like afternoon recess, Donatello's looks like an all-night rave. Donatello's figures are sketchier, murky, and filled with frenetic activity, as the dancing kids hurl themselves around the balcony. Imagine candles lighting this as the scenes seem to come to life. If the dance feels almost pagan, there's a reason.

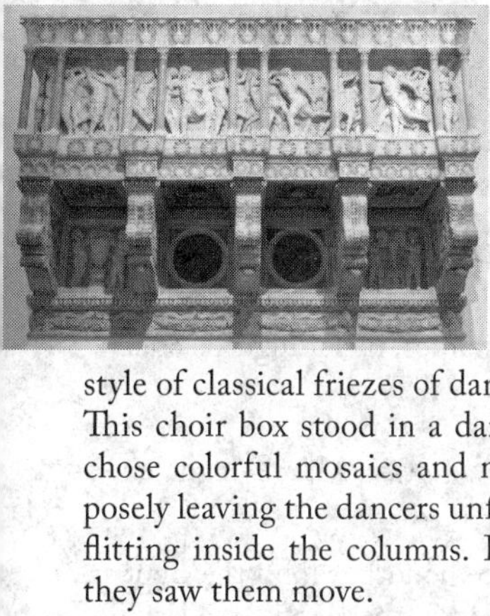

Recently returned from a trip to Rome, Donatello carved in the style of classical friezes of dancing *putti* (chubby, playful toddlers). This choir box stood in a dark area of the Duomo, so Donatello chose colorful mosaics and marbles to catch the eye, while purposely leaving the dancers unfinished and shadowy, tangled figures flitting inside the columns. In the dim light, worshippers swore they saw them move.

• *Beneath Donatello's* cantoria *is a statue of...*

Pop. 100,000...But Still a Small Town

At the dawn of the Renaissance, Florence was bursting with creative geniuses, all of whom knew each other and worked together. For example, after Ghiberti won the bronze-door competition, Brunelleschi took teenage Donatello with him to Rome. Donatello returned to join Ghiberti's workshop. Ghiberti helped Brunelleschi with dome plans. Brunelleschi, Donatello, and Luca della Robbia collaborated on the Pazzi Chapel. And so on, and so on.

Donatello—*Mary Magdalene* (*Maddalena,* c. 1455)

Carved from white poplar, originally painted with realistic colors (like the medieval crucifix displayed in the next room), this statue is less a Renaissance work of beauty than a medieval object of intense devotion.

Mary Magdalene—the prostitute rescued from the streets by Jesus—folds her hands in humble prayer. Her once-beautiful face and body have been scarred by fasting, repentance, and the fires of her own remorse. The matted hair sticks to her face; veins and tendons line the emaciated arms and neck. The rippling hair suggests emotional turmoil within. But from her hollow, tired eyes, a new beauty shines, an enlightened soul that doesn't rely on the external beauty of human flesh.

The man who helped rebirth the classical style now shocked Florence by turning his back on it. Picking up a knife, he experimented in the difficult medium of woodcarving, where subtlety can get lost when the wood splits off in larger-than-wanted slivers.

Sixty-five-year-old Donatello had just returned to Florence, after years away. His city had changed. Friends were dying (Brunelleschi died before they could reconcile after a bitter fight), favorite pubs were overrun with frat boys, and Florence was gaga over Greek gods in pretty, gleaming marble. Donatello fell into a five-year funk, completing only two statues, including this one.

THE REST OF THE MUSEUM

• *Enter the adjoining room (to the right as you face* Mary Magdalene*).*

Silver Altar

The exquisite half-ton silver altarpiece honoring John the Baptist, which dominates this room, once stood in the Baptistery. Each of the immaculately restored silver panels depicts an episode from John the Baptist's life: birth, baptizing Jesus, and so on. Around the right side are his execution and the presentation of his disembodied head to Herod during a feast.

• *Pass back through the large room of the* cantorie *and into the next room. Work clockwise from the entrance.*

Andrea Pisano (and others)—*The Campanile Panels* (c. 1334-1359)

These 28 hexagonal and 28 diamond-shaped, blue-glazed panels decorated the Duomo's Campanile, seven per side (where copies stand today). The original design scheme was perhaps Giotto's, but his successor, Andrea Pisano, and assistants executed most of the panels.

The panels celebrate technology, showing workers, inventors, and thinkers. Allegorically, they depict humanity's long march to "civilization"—a blend of art and science, brain and brawn. But realistically, they're snapshots of that industrious generation that helped Florence bounce back ferociously from the Black Death of 1348.

The lower, **hexagonal panels** (reading clockwise from the entrance) show God starting the chain of creation by inventing (1) man and (2) woman, then (3) Adam and Eve continuing the work, (4) Jabal learning to domesticate sheep, (5) Jubal blowing a horn, inventing music...

• *Continuing along the next wall...*

(6) Tubalcain the blacksmith and (7) Noah inventing wine and Miller Time. (8) An astronomer sights along a quadrant to chart the heavens and the (round, tilted-on-axis, pre-Columbian) earth, (9) a master builder supervises his little apprentices building a brick wall, (10) a doctor holds a flask of urine to the light for analysis (yes, that's what it is), and so on.

• *Skip ahead to the fourth wall, the second panel.*

(20) The invention of sculpture, as a man chisels a figure to life.

The upper **diamond-shaped panels,** of marble on blue majolica (tin-glazed pottery tinged blue with copper sulfate), add religion (sacraments and virtues) to the civilization equation.

• *Enter the next, narrow room to find tools, scaffolding, and, at the end of the corridor, a wooden model of the cathedral dome's lantern.*

Model of the Lantern (Cupola di S. Maria del Fiore)

Look at this model of the dome's top portion (or look out the window—if it's open—at the real thing). Brunelleschi's dome, a feat of engineering that was both functional and beautiful, put mathematics in stone. It rises 330 feet from the ground, with eight white, pointed-arch ribs, filled in with red brick and capped with a "lantern" (cupola) to hold it all in place.

In designing the dome, Brunelleschi faced a number of challenges: The dome had to cover a gaping 140-foot hole in the roof of the church (a drag on rainy Sundays), a hole too wide to be spanned by the wooden scaffolding that traditionally supported a dome under construction. (An earlier architect suggested supporting the dome with a great mound of dirt inside the church...filled with coins, so peasants would later cart it away for free.) In addition, the eight-sided "drum" that the dome was to rest on was too weak to support its weight, and there were no side buildings on the church on which to attach Gothic-style buttresses.

The solution was a dome within a dome, leaving a hollow space between to make the structure lighter. And the dome had to be self-supporting, both while being built and when finished, so as not to require buttresses.

Brunelleschi used wooden models such as these to demonstrate his ideas to skeptical approval committees.

Scaffolding

Although no scaffolding supported the dome itself, the stonemasons needed exterior scaffolding to stand on as they worked. Support timbers were stuck into postholes in the drum (some are visible on the church today).

The dome rose in rings. First, the workers stacked a few blocks of white marble to create part of the ribs, then connected the ribs with horizontal crosspieces before filling in the space with red brick, in a herringbone pattern. When the ring was complete and self-supporting, they'd move the scaffolding up and do another section.

Tools

The dome weighs 80 million pounds—as much as the entire population of Florence—so Brunelleschi had to design special tools and machines to lift and work all that stone. (The lantern alone—which caps the dome—is a marble building nearly as tall as the Baptistery.) You'll see sun-dried bricks, brick molds, rope, a tool belt, compasses, stone pincers, and various pulleys for lifting. Brunelleschi also designed a machine (not on display) that used horses to turn a shaft that reeled in rope, lifting heavy loads.

The dome was completed in 16 short years, capping 150 years of construction on the church. Brunelleschi enjoyed the dedication ceremonies, but he died before the lantern was completed. His legacy is a dome that stands as a proud symbol of man's ingenuity, proving that art and science can unite to make beauty.

• *Facing the lantern model, find...*

Brunelleschi's Death Mask *(Maschera Funebre)*

Filippo Brunelleschi (1377-1446) was uniquely qualified to create the dome. Trained in sculpture, he gave it up in disgust after losing

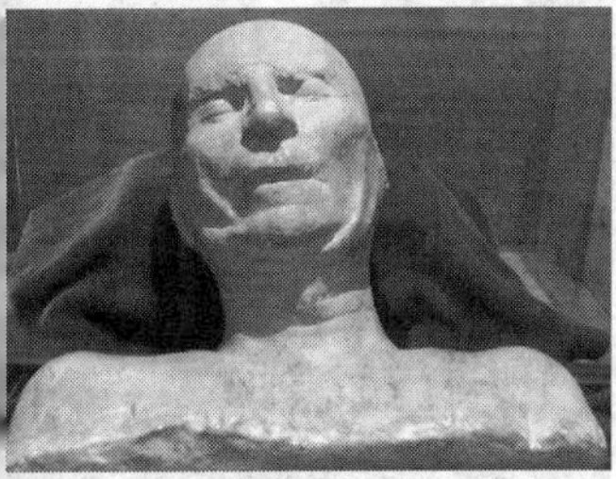

the Baptistery-door gig. In Rome, he visualized placing the Pantheon on top of Florence's Duomo, and dissected the Pantheon's mathematics and engineering.

Back home, he astounded Florence with a super-realistic painting of the Baptistery, as seen from the Duomo's front steps. Florentines lined up to see the painting (now lost) displayed side by side with the real thing, marveling at the 3-D realism. (Brunelleschi's mathematics of linear perspective were later expanded and popularized by Alberti.)

In 1420 Brunelleschi was declared *capomaestro* of the dome project. He was a jack-of-all-trades and now master of all as well, overseeing every aspect of the dome, the lantern, and the machinery to build them. Despite all his planning, it's clear from documentary evidence that he was making it up as he went along, exuding confidence to workers and city officials while privately improvising.

• *The models you'll find two rooms farther along represent the...*

Facade from the 16th to the 19th Centuries

The church wasn't done. In 1587, the medieval facade by Arnolfo was considered hopelessly outdated and torn down like so much old linoleum. But work on a replacement never got off the ground, and the front of the church sat bare for nearly 300 years while church fathers debated proposal after proposal (like the models in this room) by many famous architects. Most versions champion the Renaissance style to match Brunelleschi's dome, rather than Gothic to fit the church.

• *Two rooms later, we reach the conclusion to the Duomo's long history.*

The 19th-Century Facade

Finally, in the 1800s, as Italy was unifying and filled with a can-do spirit, there was a push to finish the facade. **Emilio De Fabris (portrait)** won a competition, and began to build a neo-Gothic facade that echoed the original work of Arnolfo. The new-old facade was dedicated in 1887. Notice that even De Fabris changed designs as he went—the spikes along the roofline in some of the designs are not there today.

Critics may charge that De Fabris' facade is too retro, but it was the style of the church beloved by Ghiberti, Donatello, Brunelleschi, and the industrious citizens of Florence's Quattrocento, who saw it as Florence's finest art gallery.

THE OPERA DEL DUOMO TODAY

If you climb the stairs to the sparse third-floor landing, you might see lab-coated workers busy in the restoration studio. They belong to the Opera del Duomo, the organization that does the continual work required to keep the cathedral's art in good repair (*opera* is Italian for "work").

For another behind-the-scenes peek, make one more stop after leaving the Duomo Museum: Head to the left around the back of the Duomo to find Via dello Studio (near the south transept), then walk a block toward the river to #23a (freestanding yellow house on the right; see map on page 83). You can look through the open doorway of the **Opera del Duomo art studio** and see workers sculpting new statues, restoring old ones, or making exact copies. They're carrying on an artistic tradition that dates back to the days of Brunelleschi. The "opera" continues.

PALAZZO VECCHIO TOUR

With its distinctive castle turret and rustic stonework, this fortified "Old Palace"—Florence's past and present Town Hall—is a Florentine landmark. The highlight of the interior is the Grand Hall: With a Michelangelo sculpture and epic paintings of great moments in Florentine history, it was the impressive epicenter of Medici power. The richly decorated rooms of the royal apartments—though hardly the most sumptuous royal quarters in Europe—show off some famous art, creative decorative flourishes, and aristocratic curiosities. It's open very late in summer, making it a fine after-dinner sightseeing option.

While there are plenty of sightseeing options here, this tour focuses on the "museum" part of the palace.

Orientation

Cost: Courtyard—free, museum—€10, tower climb—€10, museum plus tower-€14; special exhibits can incur an optional, small additional fee. Both the museum and tower are covered by the Firenze Card (for the museum, get your ticket at the ground-floor information desk before heading upstairs; for the tower, simply present your card at the base of the stairs).

Hours: Museum—April-Sept Fri-Wed 9:00-24:00, Thu 9:00-14:00; Oct-March Fri-Wed 9:00-19:00, Thu 9:00-14:00; tower—April-Sept Fri-Wed 9:00-21:00, Thu 9:00-14:00; Oct-March Fri-Wed 10:00-17:00, Thu 10:00-14:00; last entry to museum or tower one hour earlier. The tower is closed in rainy or other inclement weather.

Information: Tel. 055-276-8224, http://museicivicifiorentini.comune.fi.it.

Tours: A videoguide is available for €5 (€8/2 people). Tours in

English are offered daily, last 1.25 hours, and cost €2. The tour schedule varies, and it's wise to reserve in advance (tel. 055-276-8224).

Tower Climb: Ascending Florence's landmark civic tower requires climbing 418 steps from ground level—though if you're touring the museum first, you'll already be about halfway there. (And if you have a museum ticket, you can ride the elevator up that far—ask.) The entrance to the tower is at the very end of the museum tour, on the second floor. If you're skipping the museum and doing only the tower, use the staircase opposite the one that leads up to the museum (on the left as you enter the courtyard).

Activities for Kids: The palace's family program offers an ever-changing range of activities, usually requiring reservations—check online at www.palazzovecchio-familymuseum.it, call the tours number above, or ask at the reception by the ticket office (no activities after 17:00). See the ✪ Florence with Children chapter for more details.

Nighttime Terrace Visits: In summer, you can join an escort for an un-narrated walk along the "patrol path"—the balcony that runs just below the crenellated top of the building (€2 plus regular admission ticket, every 30 minutes between 21:00 and 23:00, no tours Oct-March). Note that this tour doesn't go to the top of the tower.

Length of This Tour: One hour.

Starring: The spacious grand hall known as the Salone dei Cinquecento, lavish royal apartments, and statues by Michelangelo and Donatello.

The Tour Begins

• *Stand in Florence's main square, Piazza della Signoria, and take in the palace's grand facade.*

Exterior

Around the year 1300, the citizens of Florence broke ground on a new Town Hall, designed by Arnolfo di Cambio, who also did the Duomo. Arnolfo's design expanded on an earlier palace on the site, turning its small tower into today's 308-foot spire and increasing the building's architectural footprint, which is why the tower ended up slightly off-center.

In Renaissance times, Florence was a proud, self-governing Republic, and this building is where its governing council *(signo-*

ria) met. The entrance sported a statue that symbolized the city's independent spirit—Michelangelo's *David.* (The statue standing here today is a copy—the original *David* was moved to the Accademia for safekeeping in 1873.) The palace's imposing, castle-like exterior announced to all of Europe's kings, popes, princes, and tyrants that Florence was determined to remain an independent city governed by its citizens.

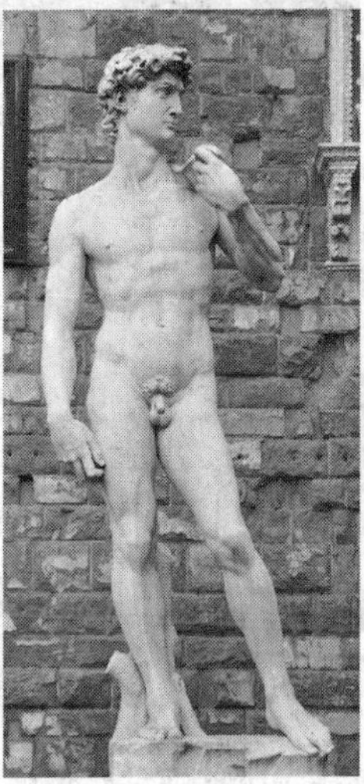

But then came Cosimo I, who changed everything. (See a statue of him riding a horse, left of the palace.) In the 1530s, Cosimo assumed power and turned Florence's republic into a tyrannical dukedom. He and his wife Eleonora moved into Palazzo Vecchio and transformed it from a symbol of the people to a luxury palace of the aristocracy. Let's go in and see what kind of extreme makeover they did to the place.

• *Enter the courtyard (free admission), walking past the fake* David *and Bandinelli's* Hercules and Cacus.

Courtyard

This courtyard has long been a showcase for great Florentine art—art that made a statement to the city's populace.

Anchoring the courtyard is a copy of *Putto with Dolphin*, an innovative work of Renaissance 3-D by Verrocchio, Leonardo da Vinci's teacher. With a twisting spiral form, this statue was one of the first intended to be equally enjoyable from any angle—an improvement on medieval statues that only worked when seen from the front. It stands where the original used to, spouting water piped in from the Boboli Gardens.

Verrocchio's cherub took the place of Donatello's bronze *David* (now in the Bargello, and described on page 137), an even more groundbreaking statue—the first male nude sculpted in a thousand years. Donatello's *David* also made a bold populist statement, with an inscription on the base that said, "Behold, a boy defeated a tyrant, so fight on, citizens!"

Stroll around. The faded maps indicate foreign-policy concerns

of the Duchy of Tuscany. The squiggly wall painting (called "grotesque") was all the rage around 1500, inspired by ancient Roman art, which was being excavated at the time.

While Palazzo Vecchio's exterior and courtyard reflect the tastes and ideas of the Florentine Republic, most of the interior decoration dates from a later era. When Florence came under the rule of Cosimo I de' Medici, he suspended the city council and ruled as a "Grand Duke." He transformed this building from a civic center of the people into his personal palatial residence.

• *To see the rest of the palace, you'll have to buy a ticket at the desk deeper in the complex. After buying your ticket, start your tour with a quick look at the free* ***Tracce di Firenze exhibit****, near the ticket office. Compare the big painting of the city "Fiorenza" (from 1490) with the version at the opposite end of the room (from 1936) to see how much—or how little—the city has changed over the centuries.*

Now head upstairs, following signs to the Museo. *(Firenze Card holders must get a paper ticket on the ground floor before ascending.) On the first floor, enter one of the highlights of the palace, the 13,000-square-foot...*

Grand Hall (Salone dei Cinquecento)

This vast room—170' by 75'—is also called the Salone dei Cinquecento (Hall of Five Hundred). Originally built under Savonarola in 1494 to house the Florentine Republic's 500 Grand Councilors, it was expanded under Cosimo I to accommodate 500

party-goers. The ceiling and huge wall paintings, all by Giorgio Vasari and his assistants, are a celebration of the power of Florence, specifically the power of the Medici. Consider this magnificent room in its proper context: In an age when there was no mass media to use as a mouthpiece, this was how a fabulously wealthy person waged a public-relations campaign (and kept the people down).

Cosimo I is the star here, looking down from the circular medallion in the center of the ceiling. He's dressed as an emperor, with his highness-ness affirmed by the crown of the Holy Roman Emperor and blessed by the staff and cross of the pope. He's circled by a kaleidoscope of symbols of Florentine craft and art guilds, and the shields of his domain, all asserting his power.

In the square frame, find the letters "SPQF." In place of the Roman motto of SPQR (*Senatus Populusque Romanus*—the Senate and People of Rome), Cosimo used "SPQF," implying that Florence is the new Rome. From the stage at the far end of the room, Cosimo sat on his throne, overseeing his fawning subjects.

But now sitting in the front of the room is a statue of **Pope Leo X,** looking down from his own throne. The son of Lorenzo the Magnificent, Leo X was the first of three Medici popes. When he became pope in 1513, the family suddenly had religious authority and some seriously good connections, helping them eventually become bankers to the Vatican.

Giorgio Vasari's wall paintings show great Florentine victories: over Pisa in 1497 (on the left) and over Siena in 1555 (on the right). In the Pisa paintings, check out the third painting from the left: In the upper-left corner you can see the Field of Miracles, with its church and Leaning Tower. In the Siena paintings, watch the Florentines storm Siena's gate by lantern light. Vasari's style features crowded canvases, contorted bodies in every imaginable pose, bright color, and a "flat" surface design. If you're into Mannerism, this is your Sistine Chapel.

While Vasari's battle scenes are impressive, they pale in comparison to what some scholars believe was first painted on these walls. Around 1500, this hall was the scene of a painting contest between two towering geniuses—young Michelangelo and aging Leonardo da Vinci. Unfortunately, Michelangelo never got around to starting his proposed *Battle of Cascina* (and his paper sketch of it is lost to history). But Leonardo may have painted the *Battle of Anghiari* here. Art historians have long suspected that this famous-but-unseen Leonardo masterpiece lies hidden beneath Vasari's *Battle of Marciano* (on the Siena wall, third painting from the left). Vasari himself may have hinted at it to later scholars by painting an enigmatic clue: a banner (40 feet up, hard to find without binoculars) that reads *Cerca trova*—"He who seeks, finds."

Underneath Siena, in the middle of the right wall, stands **Michelangelo's *Victory*** (*La Vittoria*, 1533-1534), showing a young man triumphing over an older man. It was designed to ornament the never-finished tomb of Pope Julius II in St. Peter's Basilica in Rome. *Victory* was the prototype of the hall's many spiral-shaped statues by other artists. Taking their cue from Michelangelo, later artists twisted and contorted their sculpted figures into almost ridiculous acrobatics. Six of the statues are the *Labors of Hercules*.

• *From here, we enter the royal apartments that housed Cosimo I and his family and guests. Be aware that some rooms on our tour may be temporarily closed to visitors—the palace is a working city hall, after all.*

Exit the Grand Hall in the back-right corner, and enter the first of the royal apartments, known as the...

Apartments of Leo X

In 1540, Cosimo I and his wife Eleonora of Toledo moved into Palazzo Vecchio, turning the Town Hall into their private residence. They set about redecorating with frescoes and coffered ceilings in the Mannerist style. They wanted each room to have a theme. These rooms were dedicated to great members of the Medici family who preceded Cosimo I.

Loop clockwise through these apartments. The first room (immediately to the left as you enter this wing) honors Cosimo the Elder, who launched the Medici dynasty in the 1400s. You'll see Cosimo portrayed on the ceiling, including one scene where he greets Brunelleschi and Ghiberti. (Find all the details on the information charts in each room.)

Cosimo I de' Medici
(1519-1574)

This palace is all about Cosimo I de' Medici. His presence is everywhere. In the famous statue on the square outside the palace, he sits like a Roman emperor astride a horse. Inside, in the Grand Hall, he looms high above in a ceiling painting. And his aesthetic vision is on full display in the Royal Apartments, which were personally decorated with care by Cosimo and his high-maintenance wife Eleonora.

Cosimo's Medici forebears had been Florentine big shots, but Cosimo was the first to have a royal title, after the pope made him a Grand Duke in 1569. Don't confuse Grand Duke Cosimo I with his equally famous ancestor, Cosimo the Elder, who established the Medici dynasty a century earlier. To see how Cosimo I fits into the Medici family tree, see the chart on page 60.

Before Cosimo I took charge, the loggia in front of the palace (Loggia dei Lanzi) had been used as a gathering place, where Florentines discussed the issues of the day. Cosimo changed it into an art gallery, swapping out public discourse for statues that personified the power and strength of his family. Perseus, holding the head of Medusa, sent a clear message about how the Medici dealt with their enemies.

It was Cosimo I who moved the family out of the Medici-Riccardi Palace and into these digs—officially called Palazzo della Signoria. Cosimo left the exterior as-is, which is why it still looks like a medieval fortress. But he completely revamped the inside, updating it to match the outlook of the Renaissance. Later, when his wife Eleonora complained about needing a fancier place with a bigger yard, they moved across the river to the Pitti Palace, where she could stroll the sprawling Boboli Gardens. The Vasari Corridor was built over Ponte Vecchio to connect the two palaces. After they'd moved out, Palazzo della Signoria began to be known as the "old" palace—Palazzo "Vecchio."

The next room is dedicated to the greatest of the Medici, Lorenzo the Magnificent, shown in the central ceiling painting on a throne in his purple robe. Here you feel the passion of this avid patron of the arts. Lorenzo died in 1492, when Florence was at its pinnacle (and a self-governing republic), when the New World was still a mystery, and the center of European power hadn't yet moved to Spain, France, and England. Enjoy the fine examples of the erotic, mystical, and fanciful art of his time. After Lorenzo

Giorgio Vasari
(1511-1574)

Giorgio Vasari—painter, architect, and writer—has been dismissed by history as a Renaissance hack, a man who was equally mediocre at many things. But his influence on Renaissance history is undeniable.

During his lifetime, Vasari enjoyed respect and accumulated a considerable fortune. He was consistently employed by patrons in the Medici family in Florence and Rome. In Florence, you'll see his mark everywhere. His huge frescoes color the main hall of Palazzo Vecchio and the dome of the Duomo (see page 47). His oil paintings hang in the Church of Santa Maria Novella (see page 209) and the Uffizi Gallery. He built the tomb for his hero Michelangelo in Santa Croce Church (page 214). As an architect, he designed the Uffizi Gallery and the Vasari Corridor over Ponte Vecchio, which connects the Uffizi with the Pitti Palace.

Vasari is most famous, though, as the first Italian art historian. His book, *The Lives of the Artists,* was an early work that chronicled the Renaissance (with a bias that favored Florentine painters, sculptors, and architects). For that classic alone, we can say *"Grazie tante!"*

the Magnificent died, the Medici were exiled from Florence for 20 years.

Continue into the final room to see what came next. The room honors Lorenzo's son, who was exiled but eventually became Pope Leo X. A wall painting shows Leo's triumphal return to Florence, where citizens celebrate outside Palazzo Vecchio. Note Michelangelo's *David* guarding the entrance.

• *From here, go up the staircase to the second floor, then turn left, entering the...*

Apartments of the Elements (Quartiere degli Elementi)

As Cosimo considered himself an enlightened Renaissance Man, he wanted his apartments decorated in the spirit of the classical world. Each of his personal living rooms has a name, usually derived from the ceiling and wall paintings.

The first room (with paintings by Vasari and assistants) depicts the four classical elements. On the left wall (as you enter) is "Water," showing the birth of Venus from the foam of the waves.

Next is "Fire," with Vulcan at the forge hammering away while cupids pump the bellows and sharpen their arrows. "Earth" shows the abundant cornucopia of the world's produce. And on the ceiling, representing "Air," are scenes from the sky—the chariots of the sun and moon, and Cronos defeating Saturn to create the world.

Circle counterclockwise around this wing, starting with the balcony that offers a stunning view of Piazzale Michelangelo (closed in winter). One room displays Verrocchio's original *Putto with Dolphin* (1476), from the courtyard downstairs. The statue originally stood in the Medici family's rural villa before Cosimo I brought it to Palazzo Vecchio. It may have captured the newlywed couple's innocent joy and abandon as they moved into their new home together.

• *Return to the top of the stairs and cross over to the Apartments of Eleonora of Toledo. On the way, you'll pass along a* ***balcony*** *overlooking the Grand Hall. Gaze out over the opulence and imagine it filled by a lavish Medici wedding celebration with a 500-person guest list. Now enter the apartments, starting in the Green Room.*

Private Apartments of Eleonora di Toledo

Eleonora of Toledo (1522-1562) married Cosimo I in 1539. Their marriage united the Medici clan with royal bloodlines all over Europe. The following year, the couple moved out of the Medici-Riccardi Palace (as it's now known) and settled in here. As Florence's "first lady," Eleonora used her natural grace and beauty to mollify Florentine democrats chafing under Cosimo's absolutist rule.

In the Green Room (Sala Verde), you'll find the Chapel of Eleonora, brightly painted by Agnolo Bronzino (1540-1565). After serving as their artistic wedding planner, Bronzino became Cosimo and Eleonora's court painter. The chapel's ceiling features St. Michael with a sword, battling a demon; St. John with his symbolic eagle; St. Francis receiving the stigmata; and St. Jerome with his companion the lion. In the center is the three-faced Trinity. Bronzino and Vasari were the two big stars of the Mannerist style, and this palace was their enormous blank canvas.

Before leaving the Green Room, find the other little room (likely Eleonora's private study) and a door, locked tight with a padlock, which leads onto the Vasari Corridor. From here, Eleonora and Cosimo could enter a private passageway that led through the Uffizi, across Ponte Vecchio, and into their other home across the river—the Pitti Palace.

Continue through the next half-dozen rooms, making your

Palazzo Vecchio—Second Floor

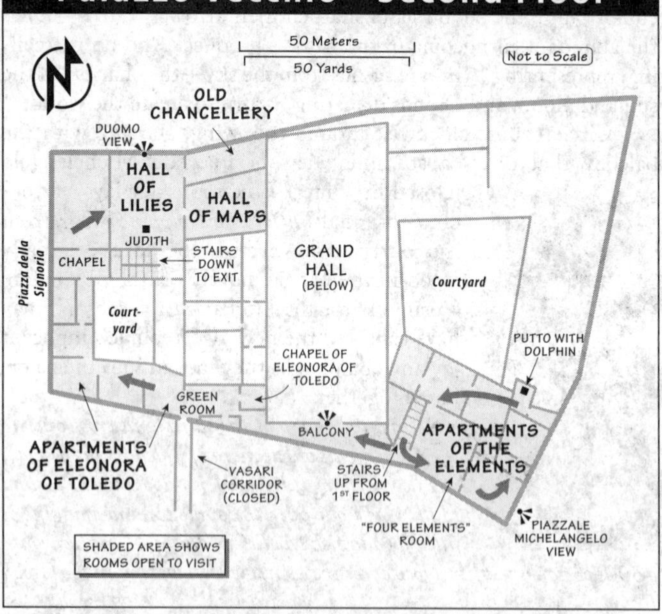

way to the large Hall of Lilies. Each of these rooms features virtuous women of history, thus putting Eleonora in their company. In the Room of the Sabines, the ceiling painting shows the Sabine women bravely stepping between their men and the enemy Romans to appeal for peace. In the next room, Esther kneels before the Persian king to plead for her Jewish people. Next, Penelope spins at her wheel, faithfully awaiting the return of her lost husband Odysseus. The Penelope Room also has a *Madonna and Child* by Botticelli.

• *Continue through these rooms (passing by* ***Dante's Death Mask****) to reach the large hall with the high, gilded ceiling.*

Hall of Lilies (Sala dei Gigli)

The coffered ceiling (from the 1460s) sports the fleur-de-lis—the three-petaled lily that's the symbol of Florence. Check out the great view of the Duomo out the window, and compare it with a painting on the wall (by Ghirlandaio) showing a glimpse of the Duomo, circa 1482. (Can't find the Duomo in the painting? Let the lion point the way.)

The room's highlight is Donatello's 11-piece bronze, *Judith and Holofernes*—cast in 1457, when the artist was in his prime. It shows a Biblical scene easily interpreted by its Renaissance audience: the victory of the weak-but-virtuous Judith over Holofernes the tyrant. The statue was commissioned by Cosimo the Elder to use as a fountain in the garden of the Medici-Riccardi Palace (note the holes in the cushion's corners). Since then, it's served as Florentine propaganda, displayed to justify the strength of whoever was in power. The Medici saw themselves as the noble Judith slaying their (drunken, sleepy) enemies. But when the Medici were driven out by Savonarola in the 1490s, the Florentines took the statue from the Medici-Riccardi Palace and placed it at Palazzo Vecchio's doorway (where the fake *David* now stands) as a symbol of their triumph over the corrupt family. A decade later, it was replaced by Michelangelo's *David*, the symbol of Florence victorious.

• *End your tour with a visit to two nearby rooms.*

Old Chancellery and Hall of Geographical Maps

The **Old Chancellery** (Sala delle Cancelleria) was once the office of Niccolò Machiavelli (1469-1527). Ponder the bust and portrait of the man who faithfully served the Florentine Republic as a civil servant from 1498 to 1512, while the Medici were exiled as tyrants. When the Medici returned to power (under Pope Leo X), they tortured and exiled Machiavelli. He then wrote *The Prince,* a poly-sci treatise about how a ruler can ruthlessly gain and maintain power. Ironically, Machiavelli's cautionary advice soon came to be exploited by the man who would end the Florentine Republic for good—Grand Duke Cosimo I.

Finally, the **Hall of Geographical Maps** (Sala delle Carte Geografiche, the palace's former wardrobe) is full of maps made in a fit of post-1492 fascination with the wider world. Most date from about 1560 and show how serious cartography had become in the first 70 years after Columbus landed in the New World. They also say a great deal about what 16th-century Europeans did—and didn't—know about faraway lands. For example, Cosimo's huge *mappa mundi* globe was obviously made before the discovery of Australia. On other maps, some Texans and Southern Californians can even find their hometowns (far right corner of the hall, upper level). Florentines excelled at creating and publishing maps—which is why, even though Columbus beat the Florentine Amerigo

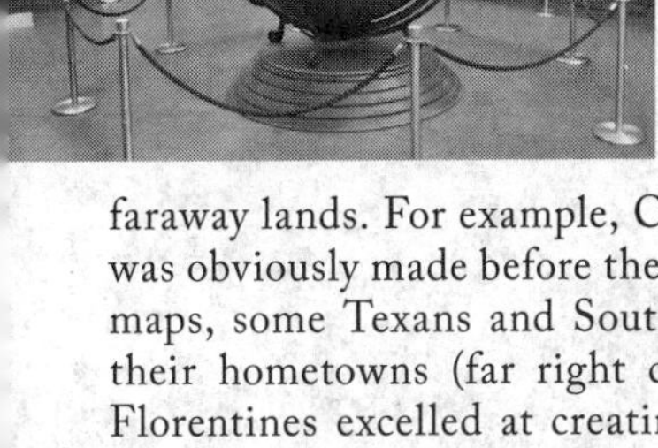

Vespucci to the New World, our continent isn't called "North Columbia."

• *To exit, return to the Hall of Lilies; the door on the left leads to a landing. From here, more than 200 stairs lead up to the top of the* ***tower*** *(show your ticket or Firenze Card to ascend); the stairs leading down take you to the courtyard and exit. You're at the center of Florence—the city awaits.*

MEDICI CHAPELS TOUR

Cappelle Medicee

The Medici Chapels contain tombs of Florence's great ruling family, from Lorenzo the Magnificent to those less so. The highlight is a chapel designed by Michelangelo when he was at the height of his creative powers. This is Renaissance Man's greatest "installation," a room completely under one artist's control, featuring innovative architecture, tombs, and sculpture. His statues tell of a middle-aged man's brooding meditation on mortality, the fall of the Medici Golden Age, and the relentless passage of time—from *Dawn* to *Day* to *Dusk* to *Night.*

Orientation

Cost: €9 (or €8 if there are no special exhibits), covered by Firenze Card.

Hours: April-Oct Tue-Sat 8:15-16:50, Nov-March Tue-Sat 8:15-13:50; also open second and fourth Mon and first, third, and fifth Sun of each month; last entry 30 minutes before closing. Reservations are possible but unnecessary.

Crowd Alert: The bottleneck entrance (tickets and metal detector) can make for a slow entry. If you have a Firenze Card, let them know and they'll likely let you skip to the front of the security line.

Dress Code: No tank tops, short shorts, or short skirts.

Getting There: It's at the back (west end) of the Church of San Lorenzo—the one with the smaller dome on Florence's skyline (five-minute walk northwest of Duomo). See page 41 for more about the Church of San Lorenzo.

Information: Tel. 055-238-8602, www.polomuseale.firenze.it.

Audioguide: €6 (€10/2 people).

Length of This Tour: Allow 45 minutes. With limited time, make a beeline to Michelangelo's New Sacristy.
Services: WCs are midway up the staircase that leads from the Crypt to the Chapel of Princes. Look for the camouflaged doorway.
Photography: Prohibited.
Starring: Michelangelo's statues *Day, Night, Dawn,* and *Dusk.*

OVERVIEW

The Medici Chapels consist of three burial places: the unimpressive Crypt; the large and gaudy Chapel of Princes; and—the highlight—Michelangelo's New Sacristy, a room completely designed by him to honor four Medici. Due to restoration work, scaffolding in the Chapel of Princes may obscure some (lesser) sights when you visit.

For a quick overview of the Medici family tree, see page 60.

The Tour Begins

• *Enter the Chapel and buy tickets. Immediately after you show your ticket, you're in...*

The Crypt

This gloomy, low-ceilinged room with gravestones underfoot reminds us that these "chapels" are really tombs. You'll see a few Lorenzos buried in this room (after all, "Laurentius," or Lawrence, was the family's patron saint)...but none that is "Magnificent" (he's later). The collection of ornate silver and gold reliquaries is appropriately macabre and worth a quick look.

• *Head upstairs via the staircase. First find your way into the large, domed, multicolored chapel, which is* not *by Michelangelo.*

Chapel of Princes (La Cappella dei Principi, 1602-1743)

The impressive **dome** overhead (seen from outside, it's the big, red-brick "mini-Duomo") tops an octagonal room that echoes the Baptistery and Duomo drum. It's lined with six tombs of Medici rulers and is decorated everywhere with the **Medici coat of arms**—a shield with six balls thought to represent the pills of doctors *(medici),* reputedly their original occupation. Along with many different-colored marbles, geologists will recognize jasper, porphyry, quartz, alabaster, coral, mother-of-pearl, and lapis lazuli.

Sixteen shields ring the room at eye level, each representing one of the Tuscan cities ("Civitas") ruled by Florence's dukes. Find Florence, with its fleur-de-lis ("Florentiae"), and Pisa ("Pisarum"), both just left of the altar.

The bronze **statues** honor two of the "later" Medici, the cultured but oppressive dukes who ruled Florence after the city's glorious Renaissance. In the first niche to the right (as you face the altar) stands Ferdinando I (ruled 1587-1609), dressed in an ermine cape and jewels. He started the work on this Chapel of Princes and tore down the Duomo's medieval facade. His son, Cosimo II (ruled 1609-1621, to the right), appointed Galileo "first professor" of science at Pisa U., inspiring him to label the moons of Jupiter "the Medici Stars."

The **altar** was finished in 1939 for a visit from Hitler and Mussolini. The altar itself is the only Christian symbolism in this spacious but stifling temple to power, wealth, and mediocre Medici.

(*Psst.* A room behind the altar—though it may be blocked by scaffolding—displays relics and the pastoral staff of Pope Leo X, who was Lorenzo the Magnificent's son and Michelangelo's classmate.)

• *Continue down the hall, passing statues of Roman armor with worms sprouting out, to Michelangelo's New Sacristy.*

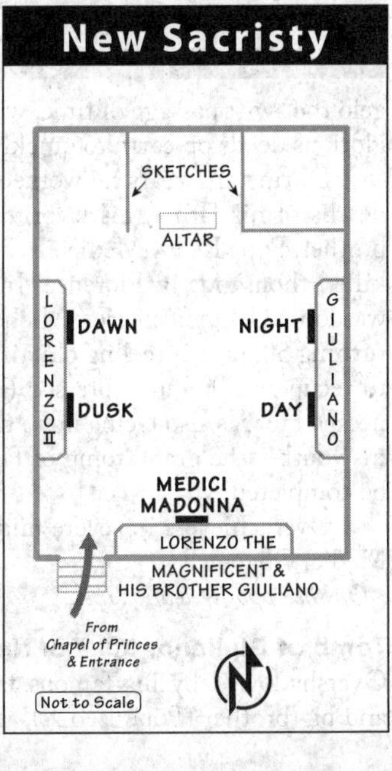

Michelangelo's New Sacristy (Sacrestia Nuova)

The entire room—architecture, tombs, and statues—was designed by Michelangelo over a 14-year period (1520-1534) to house the bodies of four of the Medici family. Michelangelo, who spent his teen years in the Medici household and personally knew three of the four family members buried here, was emotionally attached to the project. This is the work of a middle-aged man (he started at age 45 and finished at 59) reflecting on his contemporaries dying around him, and on his own mortality.

• *There are tombs decorated with statues against three of the walls, and an altar on the fourth. Start with the tomb on the left wall (as you enter and face the altar).*

Tomb of Lorenzo II, Duke of Urbino

Lorenzo II—the grandson of Lorenzo the Magnificent—is shown as a Roman general, seated, elbow resting on a Medici-bank money box, and bowing his head in contemplation. He had been the model for Machiavelli's *The Prince,* and when he died at 27 (of tuberculosis and syphilis) without a male heir, the line of great princes stretching back to Cosimo the Elder died with him.

His sarcophagus, with a curved, scrolled lid, bears the reclining statues that Michelangelo named *Dusk* and *Dawn*. ***Dusk*** (the man), worn out after a long day, slumps his chin on his chest and reflects on the day's events. ***Dawn*** (the woman) stirs restlessly after a long night, with an anguished face, as though waking from a bad dream. *Dusk* and *Dawn,* with their counterparts *Day* and *Night* (opposite wall), represented to Michelangelo the swift passage of time, which kills everyone and causes our glorious deeds on earth to quickly fade.

During the years he worked here, Michelangelo suffered the deaths of his father, his favorite brother, and his unofficial stepbrother, Pope Leo X Medici. In addition, plagues in 1522 and 1527 killed thousands in Florence. In 1527, his adopted city of Rome was looted by mercenaries. Michelangelo's letters reveal that, upon turning 50, he was feeling old, tired ("If I work one day, I need four to recuperate"), and depressed (he called it *mio pazzo,* "my madness"). He was also facing up to the sad fact that the masterpiece of his youth—the grand tomb of Pope Julius II—was never going to be completed.

Overachievers in severe midlife crises may wish to avoid the Medici Chapels.

• *On the opposite wall is the...*

Tomb of Giuliano, Duke of Nemours

Overshadowed by his famous father (Lorenzo the Magnificent) and big brother (Pope Leo X), **Giuliano** led a wine-women-and-

song life, dying young without a male heir. His statue as a Roman general, with scepter, powerful Moses-esque pose, and alert, intelligent face, looks in the direction of the Madonna statue, as though asking forgiveness for a wasted life. The likeness is not at all accurate. Michelangelo said, "In a thousand years, no one will know how they looked."

Giuliano's "active" pose complements the "contemplative" one of Lorenzo, showing the two elements (thought + action) that Plato and Michelangelo believed made up the soul of man.

Night (the woman) does a crossover sit-up in her sleep, toning the fleshy abs that look marvelously supple and waxlike, not like hard stone. She's highly polished, shimmering, and finished with minute details. Michelangelo's females—musclemen with coconut-shell breasts—are generally more complete and (some think) less interesting than his men.

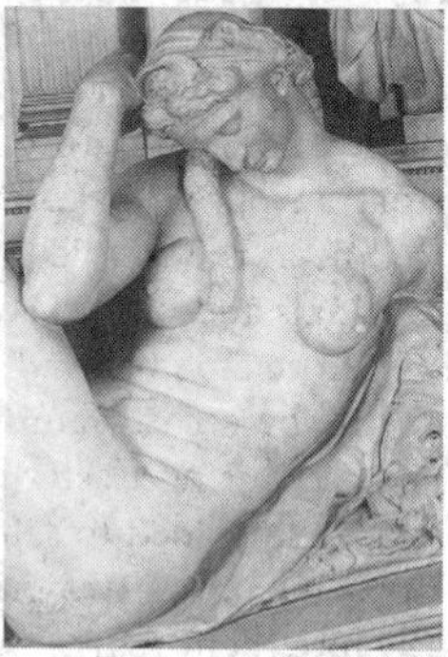

Michelangelo was homosexual. While his private sex life (or lack thereof) remains a mystery, his public expressions of affection were clearly weighted toward men. Some say he was less interested in female bodies and felt he could easily sum them up in a statue.

Day (the man) works out a crick in his back, each limb twisting a different direction, turning away from us. He looks over his shoulder with an expression (suspicious? angry? arrogant?) forever veiled behind chisel marks suggestive of Impressionist brush strokes. In fact, none of the four reclining statues' faces expresses a clear emotion, as all are turned inward, letting body language speak.

If, as some say, Michelangelo purposely left these statues "unfinished" while liberating them from their stone prison, it certainly adds mystery and a contrast in color and texture. *Night*'s moonlit clarity and *Day*'s rough-hewn grogginess may also reflect Michelangelo's own work schedule—a notorious day-sleeper and guilt-ridden layabout ("Dear to me is sleep") who, when inspired (as a friend wrote), "works much, eats little, and sleeps less."

Among *Night*'s symbols (the crescent moon on her forehead, owl under knee, and poppies underfoot) is a grotesque **mask** with, perhaps, a self-portrait. Michelangelo, a serious poet (so much so that he almost considered sculpting his "day job"), has *Night* say in one of his poems: "As long as shame and sorrow exist / I'd rather not see or hear / So speak softly and let me sleep."

Day, Night, Dawn, and *Dusk*—brought to life in this room where Michelangelo had his workshop, and where they've been ever since—meditate eternally on Death, squirming restlessly, unable to come to terms with it.

• *On the entrance wall is the...*

Tomb of Lorenzo the Magnificent and His Brother Giuliano

As the tomb was never completed, all that really marks where The Magnificent One's body lies is a marble slab, now topped with a statue of the Madonna flanked by saints. Perhaps Michelangelo was working up to the grand finale to honor the man who not only was the greatest Medici, but who also plucked a poor 13-year-old Michelangelo from an obscure apprenticeship to dine at the Medici table with cardinals and kings.

Lorenzo's beloved younger brother, Giuliano, died in 1478 in a "hit" by a rival family, stabbed to death before the altar of the Duomo during Easter Mass. (Lorenzo, wounded, drew his sword and backpedaled to safety. Enraged supporters grabbed the assassins—including two priests planted there by the pope—and literally tore them apart.)

The **Medici Madonna,** unlike many Michelangelo women, is thin, vertical, and elegant, her sad face veiled under chisel marks. Aware of the hard life her son has ahead of him, she tolerates the squirming, two-year-old Jesus, who seems to want to breast-feed. Mary's right foot is still buried in stone, so this unfinished statue was certainly meant to be worked on more. The saints **Cosmas** and **Damian** were done by assistants.

The Unfinished Project

The Chapel project (1520-1534) was plagued by delays: design changes, late shipments of Carrara marble, the death of patrons, Michelangelo's other obligations (including the Laurentian Medici Library next door), his own depression, and...revolution.

In 1527, Florence rose up against the Medici pope and declared itself an independent republic. Michelangelo, torn between his love of Florence and loyalty to the Medici of his youth, walked a fine line. He continued to work for the pope while simultaneously designing fortified city walls to defend Florence from the pope's troops. In 1530, the besieged city fell, republicans were rounded up and executed, and Michelangelo went into hiding (perhaps in the chapel basement, down the steps to the left of the altar). Fortunately, his status as both an artist and a staunch Florentine spared him from reprisals.

In 1534, a new pope enticed Michelangelo to come back to Rome with a challenging new project: painting the *Last Judgment* over the altar in the Sistine Chapel. Michelangelo left, never to return to the Medici Chapels. Assistants gathered up statues and fragments from the chapel floor (and the Madonna from Michelangelo's house) and did their best to assemble the pieces according to Michelangelo's designs.

• *The apse is the area behind the altar. This has the best view of the chapel as a whole.*

Sketches on the Walls of the Apse

Michelangelo's many design changes and improvisational style come to life in these (dimly lit and hard to see behind Plexiglas) black chalk and charcoal doodles, presumably by Michelangelo and assistants.

• *Starting on the left wall and working clockwise at about eye level...*

Look at all the marks: hash marks counting off days worked, a window frame for the Laurentian Medici Library, scribbles, a face, an arch, a bearded face, and (on the right wall) a horse, a nude figure crouching under an arch, a twisting female nude with her dog, and a tiny, wacky, cartoon Roman soldier with shield and spurs. You really do get a sense of Michelangelo and staff working, sweating, arguing, and just goofing off as the hammers pound and dust flies.

The Whole Ensemble—Michelangelo's Vision

The New Sacristy was the first chance for Michelangelo to use his arsenal of talents—as sculptor, architect, and Thinker of Big Ideas—on a single multimedia project. The resulting "installation" (a 20th-century term) produces a powerful overall effect that's different for everyone—"somber," "meditative," "redemptive," "ugly."

The room is a cube topped with a Pantheon-style dome, with three distinct stories—the heavy tombs at ground level, upper-level windows with simpler wall decoration, and the dome, better-lit and simpler still. The whole effect draws the eye upward, from dark and "busy" to light and airy. (It's intensified by an optical illusion—Michelangelo made the dome's coffers, the upper windows, and round lunettes all taper imperceptibly at the top so they'd look taller and higher.)

The white walls are lined in gray-brown-green stone. The half columns, arches, and triangular pediments are traditional Renaissance forms, but with no regard for the traditional "orders" of the time (matching the right capital with the right base, the correct width-to-height ratio of columns, upper story taller than lower, etc.). Michelangelo had Baroque-en the rules, baffling his contemporaries and pointing the way to a new, more ornate style that used old forms as mere decoration.

Finally, Michelangelo, a serious Neo-Platonist, wanted this room to symbolize the big philosophical questions that death presents to the living. Summing up these capital-letter concepts (far, far more crudely than was ever intended), the room might say:

Time (the four reclining statues) kills Mortal Men (statues of Lorenzo and Giuliano) and mocks their Glory (Roman power symbols). But if we Focus (Lorenzo and Giuliano's gaze) on God's Grace (Madonna and Child), our Souls (both Active and Contemplative parts) can be Resurrected (the Chapel was consecrated to this) and rise from this drab Earth (the dark, heavy ground floor) up into the Light (the windows and lantern) of Heaven (the geometrically perfect dome), where God and Plato's Ideas are forever Immortal.

And that, folks, is a Mouthful.

MEDICI-RICCARDI PALACE TOUR

Palazzo Medici-Riccardi

Cosimo the Elder, the founder of the ruling Medici family dynasty, lived here with his upwardly mobile clan, including his grandson, Lorenzo the Magnificent. Besides the immediate family, the palace also hosted many famous Florentines: teenage Michelangelo, who lived almost as an adopted son; Leonardo da Vinci, who played the lute at Medici parties; and Botticelli, who studied the classical sculpture that dotted the gardens. The historical ambience is captured in a few well-preserved rooms and in a 15th-century fresco that brings the colorful Medici world to life.

Orientation

Cost: €7, covered by Firenze Card.

Hours: Thu-Tue 9:00-18:00, closed Wed, last entry 30 minutes before closing.

Crowd Alert: While the palace is rarely mobbed, you may encounter a slight bottleneck at the tiny Chapel of the Magi (Cappella di Benozzo Gozzoli). Only 10 people are allowed in at a time, but the line moves quickly.

Getting There: It's one block north of the Duomo at Via Cavour 3. The ticket entrance is a bit north of what appears to be the main entrance (which is often gated shut).

Information: The €1.50 brochure available at the entrance is worth considering. Tel. 055-276-0340, www.palazzo-medici.it.

Audioguide: The €4 videoguide includes 25 minutes of commentary and interactive maps.

Length of This Tour: Allow an hour. With limited time, focus on the Chapel of the Magi.

Photography: Photography without a flash is OK, except in the Chapel of the Magi, where photos are not allowed.

Starring: Cosimo the Elder and Lorenzo the Magnificent as depicted in Gozzoli's colorful Magi frescoes.

The Tour Begins

Exterior

Cosimo the Elder hired the architect Michelozzo to build the palace (1444), whose three-story facade set the tone for the rest of Florence—rough stones at bottom, rising to smooth and elegant on top. Two generations later, Michelangelo added the distinctive "kneeling windows" (with scrolls), an innovation that later cropped up on palaces the world over. In the 1700s, the palace was extended northward (keeping the same style) by its next owners, the Riccardi family.

• *Buy your ticket, pass through one small courtyard, and continue into the...*

Courtyard

As with many Italian homes, the courtyard served as an open-air meeting point and "living room" for the extended family. The statue of Orpheus (who calmed wild animals with his harp) reminded visitors that the Medici family calmed wild Florence with smart and soothing politics. Find the family shield above the arches, with the six pills of these doctors *(medici)*-turned-cloth merchants-turned-international bankers. The Riccardi family later gilded this Renaissance lily with Baroque decor and adorned this courtyard with their collection of classical sculpture. Temporary exhibits (included in your ticket) often inhabit rooms adjoining the courtyard.

Garden

Pop into the fragrant garden with its greenhouse for lemon trees. This tiny oasis is a mere fraction of the once-spacious gardens that stretched for a city block to the north. In the past, the grounds were studded with many more fountains and statues, including the *Venus de' Medici* (Uffizi). Donatello's *David* (Bargello) likely stood in the courtyard. Teenage Michelangelo studied sculpture and liberal arts in the family school located in the gardens.

At the far end of the garden and down the stairs is the Museo degli Marmi, included with your ticket. At some point, you may want to visit its small collection of rare busts of ancient gods (Hercules, or Ercole), philosophers, emperors (Caracalla), and ordinary citizens (a *bambino* and the handsome Riccardi Athlete).

• *Enter the room to Orpheus' left.*

Lorenzo's Workshop

This room was once Lorenzo the Magnificent's public office. It now houses a multimedia *Star Wars*-meets-art history setup that allows you to see close-ups of Gozzoli's Magi frescoes. (Like *Star Wars,* this once-cutting-edge technology now seems quaint.) Stand on the lighted square and use your arm to point at marked areas of the large video screen. It zooms in, and a narrator explains the selected detail. A smaller plasma screen takes you through what Lorenzo's workshop would have been like in 1492.

• *Check out any temporary exhibits (in the room to Orpheus' right), then head upstairs. From the corner of the courtyard, a stairway leads to the...*

Chapel of the Magi (Cappella di Benozzo Gozzoli)

This sumptuous little room was the nuclear family's private chapel, where they could kneel at the altar and pray to a *Madonna and Child* by Fra Filippo Lippi (where a copy stands now). At the time, it was rare and highly prestigious for a family to have a private chapel (this is one of only three in Florence). But Cosimo the Elder was the pope's banker—he even bankrolled one of the Crusades. He could afford it.

The three walls around the altar display *The Journey of the Magi* (the three kings—one king per wall) by Benozzo Gozzoli (1459).

Each wall has a dominant color of white, green, or red: the Medici family colors.

On the biggest wall, ❶ a curly-haired young king, dressed in white and riding a white horse, leads a parade of men through a rocky landscape. (Some scholars have suggested that the young Magus may be Lorenzo the Magnificent, but others dismiss the idea. Lorenzo is pictured elsewhere—read on.) The scene takes you not to Bethlehem, but to 15th-century Medici-populated Tuscany. Riding behind the king is ❷ Piero the Gouty, Lorenzo the Magnificent's dad (wearing a red hat, on a gray-white horse). Accompanying him is his father, ❸ Cosimo the Elder, who founded the family dynasty and hired Gozzoli to paint this room (in red hat, riding a modest brown donkey). In the line of young men behind them is Piero's 10-year-old son and future ruler—❹ Lorenzo the Magnificent (sixth in from the left, in red cap with scoop nose and brown bowl-cut hair; he looks to the right with an intense gaze). Little Lorenzo grew up surrounded by these beautiful frescoes that celebrate the natural world. One day, he would commission his own great art.

Above Lorenzo (and slightly to the right) is ❺ Gozzoli himself. The sour-faced man in the cap above Gozzoli is ❻ Pope Pius II, often called "the first humanist" (see "Piccolomini Library" on page 380). Lost? Ask the attendant where they are: *"Dov'è* (doh-VEH) *Benozzo Gozzoli? Dov'è Cosimo? Dov'è Lorenzo?"*

The next wall (working clockwise) sets the king and his entourage in a green, spacious, and obviously Tuscan landscape. The men wear colorful clothes that set trends throughout Europe. Every year on Epiphany (January 6), the Medici men would actually dress up like this and parade through the streets to celebrate the holiday of the three kings.

On the last wall, notice that the white-bearded king on his white donkey (far left) got cut off when the room was later remodeled. But the fresco was preserved—find the horse's ass on the other side of the doorway.

Gozzoli's crystal-clear, shadowless scenes reflect the style of his teacher, Fra Angelico. The portraits are realistic, showing the leading characters of 1459 Florence.

The room itself functioned both as a chapel and as the place where Cosimo the Elder received VIPs. By portraying his own family in this religious setting, Cosimo made a classy display of cool power and sophistication. When learned rival powers came here, they thought, "Damn, these Medici are good."

• Exit the Gozzoli room into several...

Palatial Rooms with Temporary Exhibitions

Though the displays change often, the rooms themselves give a small sense of the former luxury of the palace—chandeliers, tapestries, claw-foot chairs, and such. From roughly 1400 to 1700, the city of Florence set the tone for fashion and interior decor throughout Europe. This palace was ground zero of international style.

• Eventually you'll reach a room displaying a painting in a glass case.

Fra Filippo Lippi—*Madonna and Child*

Lippi's cheek-to-cheek *Madonna and Child* demonstrates his specialty—humanizing the son of God and the Virgin. Baby Jesus' transparent shirt, Mary's transparent scarf, and their transparent halos make this late Lippi work especially ethereal. Mary's eyes are sad, while Jesus stares into his spiritual future. She gives him a tender hug before he's off on his mission.

• Several rooms branching off the Lippi room are government offices.

The Palace as Civic Center

Today, the palace is a functioning county government building. As you wander around, notice the bureaucrats at work. Occasionally, the provincial council meeting room (Sala Quattro Stagione) is open for viewing. You'll see a few dozen modern-looking seats for the council members, amid chandeliered elegance. The tapestries on the wall depict the four seasons *(quattro stagione).*

• Complete your visit in the nearby...

Luca Giordano Room

This Baroque, Versailles-like former reception hall was added by the Riccardi family. The ceiling (*The Apotheosis of the Medici Family,* frescoed in 1685 by the Naples artist Luca Giordano) features Medici big shots (with starbursts over their heads) frolicking with Greek gods. Walk slowly toward the center of the room and watch as the Medici appear to rise up into heaven to be crowned by Zeus. Ringing the base of the ceiling are various

Greek myths—find Poseidon with his trident (to the left) and Hades carrying off Persephone (to the right). Claiming her place among the ancients, the blue-robed woman over the entrance is Florence, who re-birthed the classical world.

• *Your tour is done. Now head back out into the modern world and take your place among the ancients—and youth—of Florence.*

SANTA MARIA NOVELLA TOUR

Chiesa di Santa Maria Novella

The Church of Santa Maria Novella, chock-full of groundbreaking paintings and statues, is a reminder that the Renaissance was not simply a secular phenomenon. Many wealthy families paid for chapels inside this church that today are appreciated for their fine art.

Masaccio's fresco *The Trinity* (1427), the first painting of modern times to portray three-dimensional space, blew a "hole in the wall" of this church. From then on, a painting wasn't just a decorated panel, but a window into the spacious 3-D world of light and color. With Masaccio's *Trinity* as the centerpiece, the church traces Florentine art from the medieval era to the Quattrocento (1400s) to the onset of Baroque.

Orientation

Cost: €5 covers church and museum (in the adjoining cloister), covered by Firenze Card.

Hours: Mon-Thu 9:00-17:30, Fri 11:00-17:30, Sat 9:00-17:00, Sun 12:00-17:00 July-Sept (from 13:00 Oct-June), last entry 45 minutes before closing.

Dress Code: No bare shoulders, short skirts, or short shorts for adults. Clothing must cover the knees. Free poncho-like coverings are available.

Getting There: It's on Piazza Santa Maria Novella, across the street from (and south of) the train station.

Getting In: To buy tickets, enter the courtyard to the right of the church's main door. Inconveniently, Firenze Card holders must walk behind the church and enter through the doorway at Piazza della Stazione 4 (near the TI).

Information: Tel. 055-219-257, www.chiesasantamarianovella.it.

Audioguide: €5 (€8/2 people).

Santa Maria Novella

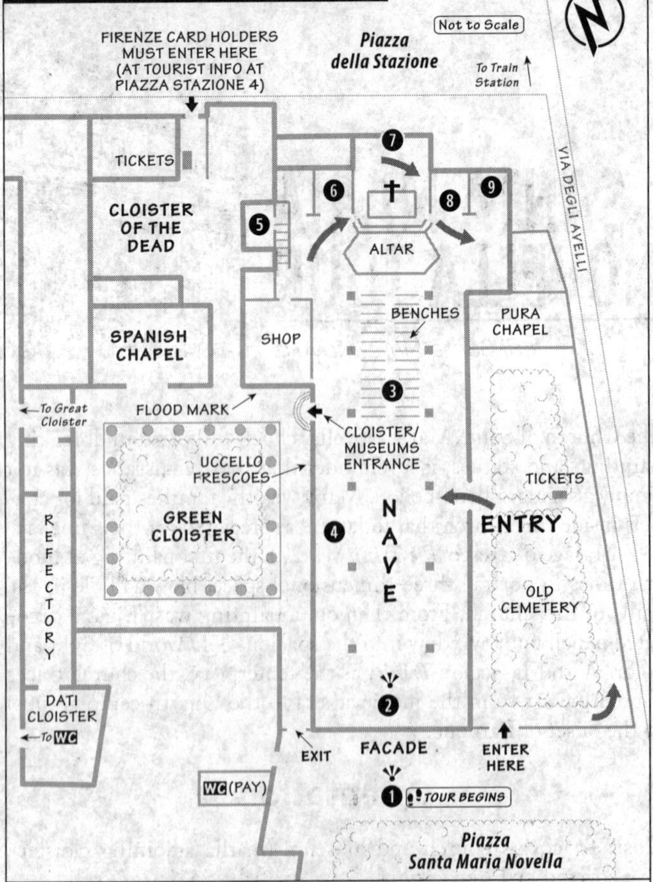

1. *View of Facade*
2. *View down the Nave*
3. *GIOTTO – Crucifixion*
4. MASACCIO – The Trinity
5. *ORCAGNA BROTHERS – Hell, Purgatory & Heaven*
6. BRUNELLESCHI – Crucifixion
7. GHIRLANDAIO – Fresco Cycles of Mary and John the Baptist
8. FILIPPINO LIPPI – St. Philip at the Temple of Mars & St. John the Evangelist Raising Drusiana
9. VASARI – Madonna of the Rosary

Length of This Tour: Allow 45 minutes. Masaccio's *Trinity* and Ghirlandaio's Mary and John the Baptist fresco cycles are a must.

Services: Free WCs are inside the museum. Pay WCs (€1) are to the left of the church facade.

Photography: Prohibited.

Eating: For recommended restaurants in the area, see page 301.

Nearby: A block away from the church is a fancy **perfumery** (Farmacia di Santa Maria Novella). This store, which feels like a small museum, is free and fun to visit (see listing on page 322).

Starring: The early Renaissance—Masaccio, Giotto, Brunelleschi, and Ghirlandaio.

The Tour Begins

❶ Exterior Facade

The green-and-white marble facade (1456-1470) by Leon Battista Alberti contains elements of Florence's whole history: Romanesque (horizontal stripes, like the Baptistery), Gothic (pointed arches on the bottom level), and Renaissance (geometric squares and circles on the upper level).

The church itself is cross-shaped, with a high central nave and low-ceilinged side aisles. The scrolls on the facade help bridge the two levels.

Before stepping inside, turn around and survey Piazza Santa Maria Novella. This marked the Dominican Quarter, just outside the city walls, while the Franciscans flanked the city on the opposite side of town at Santa Croce. The monks here built a hospice (the fine arcade opposite the church), ran a pharmacy (around the corner), and for centuries provided a kind of neighborhood clinic (which still functions as an emergency room—notice the ambulances parked on the right).

The obelisks at either end of the square were commissioned by Cosimo I (a 16th-century Medici duke—don't confuse him with Cosimo the Elder). His symbol was the turtle, and turtles seem to be holding up the obelisks, which served as end posts for a racetrack. Imagine high-energy horse races in this square as jockeys rode bareback, to the delight of Florentine spectators.

• *Enter the courtyard to the right of the main door, passing through the cemetery, where you'll pay to enter. As you go inside the church, Masaccio's* Trinity *is on the opposite wall from the entrance. But we'll start our tour at the central doorway in the facade, looking down the long nave to the altar. (Inconveniently, Firenze Card holders must enter from the back of the church, pass through the museum/cloisters, and enter the basilica from the opposite side—see the map.)*

❷ Interior View down the Nave

From the wall facing the altar, the long, 330-foot nave looks even longer, thanks to a 14th-century perspective illusion. The columns converge as you approach the altar, the space between them gets smaller, the arches get lower, and the floor gets higher, creating the illusion that the nave stretches farther into the distance than it actually does. Gothic architects were aware of the rules of perspective, just not how to render them on a two-dimensional canvas.

• *Hanging from the ceiling in the middle of the nave is a painting by...*

❸ Giotto—*Crucifixion*

The altarpiece by Giotto (c. 1266-1337) originally stood on the main altar. Stately and understated, it avoids the gruesome excesses of many medieval crucifixes. The tragic tilt of Christ's head, the parted lips, and the stretched rib cage tell more about human suffering than an excess of spurting blood.

On either side of the crossbar, Mary and John sit in a golden, iconic heaven, but they are fully human, turned at a three-quarter angle, with knowing, sympathetic expressions. Giotto, the proto-Renaissance experimenter in perspective, creates the illusion that Christ's hands are actually turned out, palms down, and not hammered flat against the cross. Still, it would be another century before painters could fully make 3-D realism a reality.

• *Masaccio's* Trinity *is on the left wall, about midway along the nave (opposite the entrance). For the best perspective, stand about 20 feet from it, then take four steps to your left, standing on the shield with a crown. Masaccio positioned it to be seen by the faithful as they dipped fingers into a (missing) font and crossed themselves—"Father, Son, and Holy Ghost."*

❹ Masaccio—*The Trinity* (1425-1427)

In his short but influential five-year career, Masaccio (1401-1428) was the first painter since ancient times to portray Man in Nature—real humans with real emotions, in a spacious three-dimensional world. (Unfortunately for tourists, his best portrayal of 3-D space is here, but his best portrayal of humans is in the Brancacci Chapel across the river.)

With simple pinks and blues (now faded), Masaccio creates the illusion that we're looking into a raised, cube-shaped chapel (about nine feet tall) topped with an arched ceiling and framed at the entrance with classical columns. Inside the chapel, God the Father stands on an altar, holding up the cross of Christ. (Where's the dove of the Holy Spirit? Why is God's "white collar" crooked?) John looks up at Christ while Mary looks down at us. Two donors (husband and wife, most likely) kneel on the front step outside the chapel, their cloaks spilling out of the niche. Below this fake chapel sits a fake tomb with the skeleton of Adam; compare it with the real tomb and niche to the right.

The checkerboard-coffered ceiling creates a 3-D tunnel effect, with rows of panels that appear to converge at the back, the panels getting smaller, lower, and closer together. Earlier painters had played with tricks like this, but Masaccio went further. He gave such thought to the proper perspective that we, as viewers, know right where we stand in relation to this virtual chapel.

He knew that, in real life, the rows of coffers would, if extended, stretch to the distant horizon. Lay a mental ruler along them, and you'll find the "vanishing point"—where all the lines intersect—all the way down below the foot of the cross. Masaccio places us there, looking "up" into the chapel.

Having fixed where the distant horizon is and where the viewer is, Masaccio draws a checkerboard grid in between, then places the figures on it (actually underneath it) like chess pieces. What's truly amazing is that young Masaccio seemed to grasp this stuff intuitively—as a "natural"—eyeballing it and sketching freehand what later artists would have to work out with a pencil and paper.

What Masaccio learned intuitively, Brunelleschi analyzed mathematically, and Alberti (who did the facade) codified in his famous 1435 treatise, *On Painting*. Soon, artists everywhere were drawing Alberti checkerboards on the ground, creating spacious, perfectly lit, 3-D scenes filled with chess-piece humans.

• *The Orcagna Chapel is at the far end of the left transept. As you approach, view the chapel from a distance. This is the illusion that Masaccio tried to create—of a raised chapel set in a wall with people inside—using only paint on a flat surface. Climb the steps to see...*

❺ Orcagna Brothers—Frescoes of the Last Judgment (1340-1357)

In 1347-1348, Florence was hit with the terrible Black Death (bubonic plague) that killed half the population. Here, in the Orcagna Chapel, the fading frescoes from that grim time show hundreds of figures, and not a single smile.

It's the Day of Judgment (center

wall), and God (above the stained-glass window) spreads his hands to divide the good from the evil. God has selected Dante as the interior decorator for heaven and hell. (Find Dante all in white, with his ear-flap cap, among the crowd to the left of the window, about a third of the way up.) Notice that God is bigger than the angels, who dwarf the hallowed saints, who are bigger than ordinary souls such as Dante, mirroring the feudal hierarchy of king, nobles, knights, and serfs.

In *Heaven* (left wall), Hotel Paradiso is *completo*, stacked with gold-haloed saints. *Hell* (faded right wall) is a series of layers, the descending rings of Dante's Inferno. A river of fire runs through it, dividing *Purgatory* (above) and *Hell* (below). At the bottom of the pit, where dogs and winged demons run wild, naked souls in caves beg for mercy and get none.

• *In a chapel to the left of the church's main altar, you'll find...*

❻ Filippo Brunelleschi—Crucifixion

Filippo Brunelleschi (1377-1446)—architect, painter, sculptor—used his skills as an analyst of nature to carve (in wood) a perfectly realistic *Crucifixion*, neither prettified nor with the grotesque exaggeration of medieval religious objects. His Christ is buck naked, not particularly muscular or handsome, with bulging veins, armpit hair, tensed leg muscles, and bent feet. The tilt of Christ's head frees a tendril of hair that directs our eye down to the wound and the dripping blood, dropping straight from his side to his thigh to his calf—a strong vertical line that sets off the curve of Christ's body. Brunelleschi carved this to outdo a crucifix his friend Donatello had done elsewhere. He thought Donatello's Christ looked like an agonized peasant; Brunelleschi's was a dignified noble. (BTW, Donatello was impressed.)

• *In the choir area behind the main altar are Ghirlandaio's 21 frescoes, stacked seven to a wall. We'll concentrate on just the six panels on the bottom.*

❼ Domenico Ghirlandaio—Fresco Cycles of Mary and John the Baptist (1485-1490)

At the peak of Florence's power, wealth, and confidence, Domenico Ghirlandaio (1449-1494) painted portraits of his fellow Florentines in their Sunday best, inhabiting video-game landscapes of mixed classical and contemporary buildings, rubbing shoulders with saints and angels. The religious subjects get lost in the colorful scenes of everyday life—perhaps a metaphor for how Renaissance humanism was marginalizing religion.

• *Start with the left wall and work clockwise along the bottom. The first scene shows the...*

Expulsion of Joachim from the Temple

Proud, young Florentine men (the group at left) seem oblivious to bearded, robed saints rushing from the arcade. There's Ghirlandaio himself (in the group on the right) looking out at us, with one hand proudly on his hip and the other gesturing, "I did this." The scene is perfectly lit, almost shadow-free, allowing us to look deep into the receding arches.

• *The next scene, on the right, is the...*

Birth of the Virgin

Five beautiful young women, led by the pregnant daughter of Ghirlandaio's patron, parade up to newborn Mary. The pregnant girl's brocade dress is a microcosm of the room's decorations. Dancing babies in the room's classical frieze celebrate Mary's birth, obviously echoing Donatello's beloved *cantoria* in Florence's Duomo Museum.

True, Ghirlandaio's works are "busy"—each scene crammed with portraits, designs, fantasy architecture, and great costumes—but if you mentally frame off small sections, you discover a collection of mini-masterpieces.

• *On the lowest part of the center wall, flanking the stained-glass window, are two matching panels.*

Giovanni Tornabuoni and His Wife Francesca Kneeling

Giovanni Tornabuoni, who paid for these frescoes, was a successful executive in the Medici Company (and Lorenzo the Magnificent's uncle). However, by the time these frescoes were being finished, the Medici bank was slipping seriously into the red, and soon the family had to flee Florence, creditors on their heels.

• *On the right wall...*

Mary Meets Elizabeth

In a spacious, airy landscape (with the pointed steeple of Santa Maria Novella in the distance), Mary and Elizabeth embrace, uniting their respective entourages. The parade of ladies in contemporary dress echoes the one on the opposite wall. This panel celebrates youth, beauty, the city, trees, rocks, and life.

A generation after Brunelleschi and Alberti, all artists—including the near-genius Ghirlandaio—had mastered perspective tricks. Here, Alberti's famed checkerboard is laid on its side, making a sharply receding wall to create the illusion of great distance.

Ghirlandaio employed many assistants in his productive workshop: "Johnson, you do the ladies' dresses. Anderson, you're great at birds and trees. And Michelangelo...you do young men's butts." The three small figures leaning over the wall (above Mary and Elizabeth) were likely done by 13-year-old Michelangelo, an apprentice here before being "discovered" by Lorenzo the Magnificent. Relaxed and natural, they cast real shadows, as true to life as anyone in Ghirlandaio's perfect-posture, face-the-camera world.

Ghirlandaio was reportedly jealous of talented Michelangelo (who was contemptuous of Ghirlandaio), but, before they parted ways, Michelangelo learned how to lay fresco from the man who did it as well as anyone in Florence.

• *On the far right, find the...*

Appearance of an Angel to Zechariah

In a crowded temple, old Zechariah is going about his business, when an angel strolls up. "Uh, excuse me..." The event is supposedly miraculous, but there's nothing supernatural about this scene: no clouds of fire or rays of light. The crowd doesn't even notice the angel. Ghirlandaio presents the holy in a completely secular way.

• *In the chapel to the right of the altar, Filippino Lippi did the frescoes on the left and right walls. Look first at the right wall, lower level...*

❽ Filippino Lippi

St. Philip at the Temple of Mars

In an elaborate shrine, a statue of the angry god Mars waves his broken lance menacingly. The Christian Philip points back up at him and says, "I'm not afraid of him—that's a false god." To prove it, he opens a hole in the base of the altar, letting out a little dragon, who promptly farts (believe it when you see it), causing the pagan king's son to swoon and die. The overcome spectators clutch their foreheads and noses.

If Ghirlandaio was "busy," Lippi is downright hyperactive, filling every square inch with something frilly—rumpled hair, folds in clothes, dramatic gestures, twisting friezes, windblown flags, and flatulent dragons.

• *On the left wall, lower level, is...*

St. John the Evangelist Raising Drusiana from the Dead

The miracle takes place in a spacious 3-D architectural setting, but Lippi has all his actors in a chorus line across the front of the stage. Filippino Lippi (1457-1504, the son of the more famous Fra Filippo Lippi) was apprenticed to Botticelli and exaggerated his bright colors, shadowless lighting, and elegant curves.

The sober, dignified realism of Florence's Quattrocento was ending. Michelangelo would extend it, building on Masaccio's spacious, solemn, dimly lit scenes. But Lippi championed a style (later called Mannerism, which led to Baroque) that loved color, dramatic excitement, and the exotic.

• *In the next chapel to the right of the altar, on the central wall, find...*

❾ Giorgio Vasari—Madonna of the Rosary

The picture-plane is saturated with images from top to bottom. Saints and angels twist and squirm around Mary (the

SANTA MARIA NOVELLA

red patch in the center), but their body language is gibberish, just an excuse for Vasari to exhibit his technique.

Giorgio Vasari (1511-1574) was a prolific artist. As a Mannerist, he copied the "manner" of, say, a twisting Michelangelo statue, but violated the sober spirit, multiplying by 100 and cramming the canvas. I've tried to defend Vasari from the art critics who unanimously call his art superficial and garish...but doggone it, they're right. With Vasari, who immortalized the Florentine Renaissance with his writing, the Renaissance ended.

• *Exit the church out the left side, descending stairs into the* museo *part of the visit. Pause at the bottom of the steps and take in the peaceful Green Cloister.*

Museum of Santa Maria Novella

The church was part of a Dominican monastery. Imagine monks circling this shaded courtyard (cloister), as well as several adjoining ones.

At the bottom of the steps, find a **small plaque** on the wall that marks the height of the 1966 flood ("Il 4 Novembre 1966..."). The horrendous flood of the Arno inundated the church and monastery with eight feet of water, destroying the precious frescoes that once lined the Green Cloister. The greatest losses (on the east wall) were **frescoes by Paolo Uccello** depicting, ironically, the Great Flood. Nearby, check out the gravestones of the **Cloister of the Dead.**

The highlight of the museum is its breathtaking **Spanish Chapel** (a.k.a. the Sala Capitular). Once the former chapter house of the monastery, the sheer size of the vault put this place on the map when it was built in the 1320s (it became known as the Spanish Chapel after Cosimo I gave it to his bride Eleonora of Toledo). Covering the chapel's walls is Andrea di Bonaiuto's 14th-century fresco series, *Allegory of the Active and Triumphant Church and of the Dominican Order* (c. 1365). The fresco is a visual Sunday-school class—complete with Peter's fishing boat. Follow the long and tricky road to salvation, ending high above, where the saved are finally greeted by Peter at his gate.

On the left wall, find the 13th-century Dominican theologian Thomas Aquinas (dark robe) seated in glory amid virtues, authors of books of the Bible, and angels. The central wall tells the Passion story: Christ carries his cross (lower left), is crucified between two thieves (center), then rises triumphant (right) to trample and spook the demons of death. On the right wall, the pinkish church was inspired by designs for the Duomo, which was then under construction. Using the museum's chart, find medieval celebrities in the fresco, including Dante and Beatrice, and artists Giotto and Cimabue. Along the bottom of the fresco, dogs fight off the wolves of heresy. They're led by St. Dominic, whose fiercely loyal Dominicans (*Dominicanus* in Latin) rightly earned their medieval play-on-words nickname of "Domini canes"—God's dogs.

SANTA CROCE TOUR

Chiesa di Santa Croce

Santa Croce, one of Florence's biggest and oldest churches, gives us a glimpse into the medieval roots of the Renaissance. The church was the centerpiece of a monastery for Franciscans; it was built by Arnolfo di Cambio, who also designed the Duomo, and frescoed by Giotto, the proto-Renaissance pioneer.

In the cloisters is a small chapel that some consider the finest example of early Renaissance architecture. The church was host to many famous Florentines, including Michelangelo and Galileo, who are both buried here. Today, the church complex houses a leather school, a display on the disastrous 1966 flood, and a museum housed in the monks' former dining hall.

Orientation

Cost: €6 (or €8.50 combo-ticket with nearby Casa Buonarroti), includes the church, Pazzi Chapel, museum, and cloisters; covered by Firenze Card. The leather school is always free.

Hours: Church—Mon-Sat 9:30-17:30, Sun 14:00-17:30, last entry 30 minutes before closing. Leather school—daily 10:00-18:00, closed Sun in Nov-March.

Expect Changes: The arrangement of the various exhibits inside the church complex has been in flux in recent years, so you may find that some items differ from what's described here; use the map and the helpful staff to find your way around.

Crowd-Beating Tips: A limited number of people are allowed to enter at one time, sometimes resulting in waits of up to 40 minutes in summer. Firenze Card holders have a priority line. Otherwise, go early or late in the day, or use the...

Back Door Entrance: The leather school, tucked in the back of the church, is never crowded, and also sells entrance tickets to the

church, letting you skip the line. It's less than a five-minute walk away: Head west along the left side of the church, and enter the doorway at Via San Giuseppe 5 red (labeled *Leather School of Florence*). Follow *Scuola del Cuoio* signs through the small garden and humble parking lot to the low-key back entrance of the school. Don't be shy—they want you to visit their store. Once inside, pass through the workshops and displays to the room with the cash register, and tell the cashier you want a church ticket. From here, you can enter directly into the church (go down the hallway to pop out at #11 on the Santa Croce map; from there, make your way to the nave to start this tour).

Dress Code: A modest dress code (no short shorts or bare shoulders) is enforced. A vending machine at the entrance dispenses disposable ponchos for €1.

Getting There: It's a 10-minute walk east of Palazzo Vecchio along the street called Borgo de' Greci.

Information: Tel. 055-246-6105, www.santacroceopera.it. The leather school has its own website (www.scuoladelcuoio.com).

Audioguide: €6 (€8/2 people).

Length of This Tour: Allow one hour. With less time, focus on the tombs of VIFs (Very Important Florentines) and the Giotto frescoes.

Photography: Permitted in most areas, without flash.

Eating: Recommended eateries are nearby (see page 300).

Shopping: While the church's leather school is famous, it's also pricey; other leather shops abound in this area, including several cut-rate outfits and the pricier, recommended **Altelier Classe.** An excellent fragrance shop, **Aqua Flor,** is also nearby. And to break out of the touristy rut, head a few blocks north and east to shop with the Florentines along **Via Pietrapiana** and **Borgo La Croce.** For more on all of these options, see the Shopping in Florence chapter.

Starring: Tombs of Michelangelo and Galileo, Giotto's frescoes, St. Francis' robe, and Brunelleschi's Pazzi Chapel.

The Tour Begins

• *Begin on the square in front of the church.*

Piazza Santa Croce

Santa Croce Church was built from 1294 to 1442. Architect Arnolfo di Cambio's design was so impressive, the city also hired him to do the Duomo and Palazzo Vecchio.

The church's colorful marble facade, left unfinished for centuries, was finally added in the 1850s. A statue of the medieval poet Dante adorns the church steps.

The church presides over a vast square ringed with a few old palazzos, notably the late Renaissance building at the far end. Piazza Santa Croce has always been one of Florence's gathering spots, for Carnival, May Day, and community events. If you're here in the third week of June, the square is covered with dirt and surrounded by bleachers for the annual soccer/rugby match, which pits neighborhood against neighborhood while commemorating games played here as long ago as the 16th century.

If you were here on November 4, 1966, you would have found the square covered with 15 feet of water. The Arno flooded that day, submerging the church steps and rising halfway up the central doorway. (More on the flood later.)

• *Buy your ticket and enter. Start at the far end of the nave (farthest from the altar). Face the altar and gaze down the long nave.*

The Nave

The effect here is one of great spaciousness. The nave is 375 feet long, lined with columns that are tall, slender, and spaced far apart, supporting wide, airy arches. As in most Gothic churches, there's no attempt to hide the structural skeleton of columns and pointed arches. Instead, they're the stars of this show, demonstrating the mathematical perfection of the design and the builders' technical prowess.

The Tombs

Hundreds of people are buried in the Santa Croce complex, including 276 of them under your feet, marked by plaques in the floor. More famous folk line the walls.

• *Nearby, find the tombs of two particularly well-known people.*

On the left wall (as you face the altar), near the back door, is the **tomb of Galileo Galilei** (1564-1642), the Pisan who lived his last years under house arrest near Florence. His crime? Defying the Church by saying that the earth revolved around the sun. His

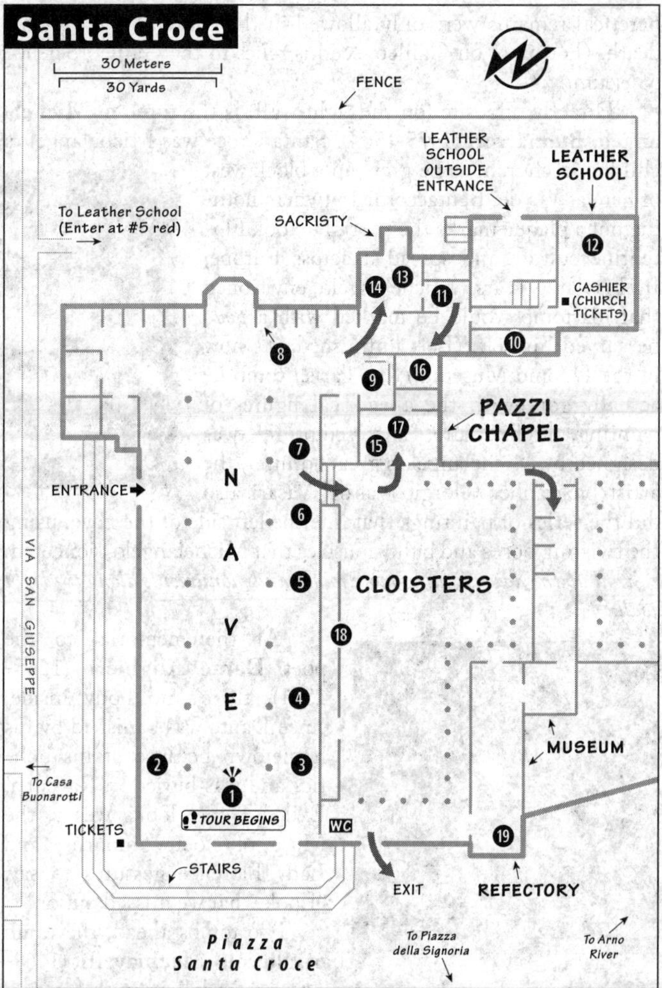

1. View down the Nave
2. Galileo's Tomb
3. Michelangelo's Tomb
4. Dante's Memorial
5. Machiavelli's Tomb
6. DONATELLO – Annunciation
7. Rossini's Tomb
8. GIOTTO – Death of St. Francis
9. GADDI – Frescoes in the Baroncelli Chapel
10. IL BRONZINO – Descent into Limbo
11. MONACO – St. James the Greater
12. Leather School
13. St. Francis' Tunic
14. CIMABUE – Crucifixion
15. Bookshop & Parigi Exhibit (lower level)
16. Flood Photos (lower level)
17. Pazzi Chapel
18. Romantic Graves Gallery
19. GADDI – Tree of the Cross and Last Supper

heretical remains were only allowed in the church long after his death. (For more on Galileo, see his relics in the Galileo Science Museum.)

Directly opposite (on the right wall) is the **tomb of Michelangelo Buonarroti** (1475-1564). Santa Croce was Michelangelo's childhood church, as he grew up a block west of here at Via dei Bentaccordi 15 (where nothing but a plaque marks the spot). He took Florentine culture and spread it across Europe. In his later years, Michelangelo envisioned that his tomb would be marked with a *pietà* he carved himself. (Left unfinished, it's now in the Duomo Museum.) The garish tomb he actually got—with the allegorical figures of painting, architecture, and sculpture—was designed by Michelangelo's great admirer, the artist/biographer Giorgio Vasari. Vasari also did the series of paintings that line the left side of the nave, using the twisting poses and bulky muscles that Michelangelo pioneered.

• *Stroll up the nave, finding more tombs and monuments along the right wall.*

At the memorial to the poet **Dante Alighieri** (1265-1321), there's no body inside, since Dante was banished by his hometown because of his politics and was buried in Ravenna. Exiled Dante looks weary, the Muse of Poetry mourns, and Lady Florence gestures to say, "Look what we missed out on."

Two tombs ahead, the **tomb of Niccolò Machiavelli** (1469-1527) features Lady Justice presenting a medallion with his portrait on it. Machiavelli, a champion of democratic Florence, opposed the Medici as tyrants. When they returned to power, he was arrested and tortured. He retired to his farm to write *The Prince,* a how-to manual on hardball politics.

A few steps farther along, Donatello's carved gray-and-gold **relief** (1430-1435) depicting the Annunciation shows a kneeling angel gently breaking the news to an astonished Mary. Notable for its then-unprecedented realism, the wispy Mary (on the right) is

SANTA CROCE

considered one of the artistic breakthroughs that marked the beginning of the long-overdue Renaissance.

Two tombs up is **Gioacchino Rossini** (1792-1868), the Italian composer of many operas and the *William Tell Overture* (a.k.a. the *Lone Ranger* theme). Rossini died in Paris, but his body was later moved here, to his homeland, during a wave of Italian nationalism in the late 19th century.

• *Head for the main altar. In the first chapel to the right of the altar are the...*

Giotto Frescoes in the Bardi Chapel (c. 1325)

The left wall has the famous *Death of St. Francis.* With simple but eloquent gestures, Francis' brothers bid him a sad farewell. One folds his hands and stares longingly at Francis' serene face. Another bends to kiss Francis' hand, while others raise their arms in grief. It's one of the first expressions of human emotion in modern painting. It's also one of the first to create a real three-dimensional grouping of figures. Giotto places three kneeling men (with their backs to us) in the foreground, puts some others standing behind Francis, and turns the rest to profile.

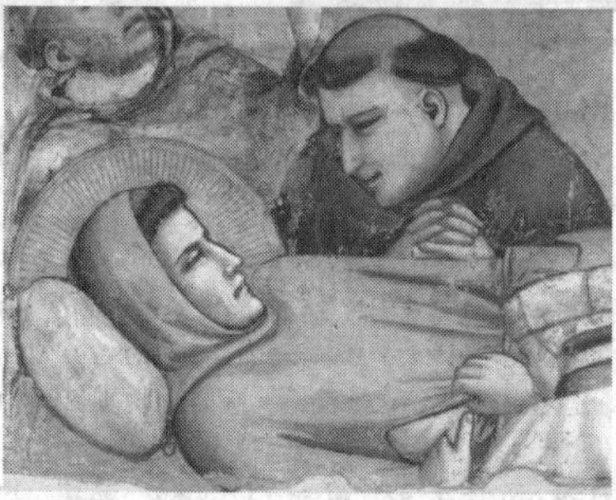

Giotto and his army of assistants were hired to plaster much of the church in colorful frescoes. But over the years, most were chiseled off, replaced by more modern works (like Vasari's). This chapel was only whitewashed over, and the groundbreaking frescoes were rediscovered in the 19th century.

• *Facing the altar, turn right, and head into the right (south) transept. At the far end, enter the chapel decorated with colorful frescoes.*

Gaddi Frescoes in the Baroncelli Chapel (c. 1328-1338)

After assisting Giotto in the Bardi Chapel, Taddeo Gaddi (1300-1366)—Giotto's beloved godson—was charged with painting this chapel. His lively frescoes cover both the wall to the left (as you enter), and the wall straight ahead (with stained-glass windows by Gaddi and an altar by Giotto).

Start with the wall to the left. The story of Mary, the mother of Jesus, unfolds from top to bottom, left to right. At the very top (under the pointed arch), is a temple scene. Mary's future dad, Joachim (with a beard and a halo), is turned away from the temple because he's childless. Ashamed, he retreats to the wilderness (right side), where an angel promises him a daughter. Overjoyed, Joachim rushes to his wife, Anna, and they embrace (next level down, left panel). Anna soon gives birth to baby Mary (badly damaged panel, right side). Still a child, Mary climbs the steps of the temple (bottom level, left panel; most of her body is missing from peeling plaster) to the chief priest (cone-shaped hat), who would raise her.

When it comes time for Mary to marry, the priest assembles all the eligible bachelors (bottom-right panel). Joseph's staff sprouts leaves and a dove (center of scene, to left of priest), signaling that he is chosen. In the foreground, a sore loser bends over and breaks his own staff.

Mary's life continues on the altar/stained-glass wall. At the top left, an angel swoops down to tell Mary that she'll give birth to Jesus. Perhaps Gaddi's most impressive scene is just below: A sleeping shepherd is awakened by an angel, who announces that Christ is born. Gaddi, an early pioneer in lighting effects, placed these windows where the natural light coming through would mix with the supernatural light from the radiant angel. (It's said that Gaddi studied solar eclipses to the point of near-blindness.) Finally, Mary's story comes to its culmination (right of window): She gives birth to the Son of God in a stable.

• *From here, you'll head down a nearby hallway (exit the chapel and do an immediate U-turn right, into a long hallway) to see a few interesting rooms. This part of the church has been in flux recently, so the exact route may vary. But most likely, at the end of the hallway, two small rooms highlight works that were recently (finally) restored, decades after flood damage: the Medici Chapel shows off Il Bronzino's* Descent into Limbo (Discesa al Limbo), *while another room displays Lorenzo Monaco's painting of St. James the Greater* (San Jacopo il Maggiore).

Also in this area, you can pay a visit to Santa Croce's famous Leather School. (If, for some reason, the hallway is closed, you can still visit the school through its own entrance, a short walk away; for directions, see the start of this chapter.)

Leather School (Scuola del Cuoio)

After World War II, the Franciscan monks created a "Boys Town" here to give war orphans a trade: making leather products. It was the first shop of what is now a popular leather district. The Gori family of merchants helped found the school and the grandson still runs it today. Wander through the former dorms for monks, watch the leatherworking in action, and browse the finished products—for sale, of course. Angled mirrors let you look over the shoulders of the busy leatherworkers. At the start of the long hallway, see the photos of visiting celebrities, from popes, Jimmy Stewart, and "Miss" Barbara Bush to Ozzy Osbourne and Robert Downey, Jr. If you're in the market for leather, be aware that this shop—while top-quality—has some of the highest prices in Florence (for leather-buying tips, see page 316).

• Head back toward the main part of the church. Along the way (on the right from the main hallway), be sure to step into the large room called the...

Sacristy

In a glass case along the wall, find a bit of **St. Francis' tunic** (*Parte della Tonaca,* scrunched up in a small gold frame). Francis (c. 1182-1226), a monk from nearby Assisi, caused a stir by challenging the decadence of Church government and society in general. Adopting the poor, wandering lifestyle of Jesus Christ, he preached a message of non-materialism and love. His charismatic presence and stirring sermons attracted many followers, including the monks who founded Santa Croce. Francis' humanistic outlook and appreciation for the beauty of nature helped sow the seeds that would bloom into the Florentine Renaissance. Also displayed is a Papal Bull *(Regula Ordinis),* which finally legitimized the once-controversial Franciscan movement.

Cimabue's *Crucifixion* (1423) was heavily damaged in the 1966 flood (which we'll learn more about soon), and most of Christ's face and body were washed away. Rescued and restored (as best they could), it became a symbol of the flood's destruction and the international community's efforts to rebuild the historic city.

• Return to the nave and exit between the Rossini and Machiavelli tombs into the delightful cloister (open-air courtyard). Descend the stairs and go in the first door on the left.

Bookshop and Small Cloister

This recently restored space is shared by a fine bookshop and a modern, engaging exhibit about **Pietro Parigi** (1892-1990), a woodcut artist who made his name as a book illustrator and creator

SANTA CROCE

of theater posters. Parigi grew up in this church, inspired by the same artistic treasures you're enjoying today. You'll see several of his expressive, minimalist prints, as well as some of the original woodblocks he used to make them.

Head out the far end of the bookshop to enter a tranquil, small cloister (possibly closed in bad weather), where you'll see modern pillars with photos of **flood damage.** Located close to the Arno, Santa Croce was especially hard-hit by the devastating flood of November 1966. Water spilled into the church complex (including the museum/refectory we'll see later), carrying off furnishings and artwork, and leaving several feet of mud in its wake. Cimabue's famous *Crucifixion*—which we just saw in the sacristy—was badly damaged, but salvageable.

• *Head back out through the bookshop into the large cloister, turn left, then look (on your left) for the door into the...*

Pazzi Chapel

Begun in 1430 by Brunelleschi, this small chapel captures the Renaissance in miniature. As with his Duomo dome, Brunelleschi was inspired by Rome's ancient Pantheon. The circle-in-square design reflects the ancient Romans' (and Renaissance Florentines') belief in the unity and harmony of perfect shapes. Notice how the color scheme of white plaster and gray sandstone accentuates the architectural lines, so that only a little decoration is needed. The creamy colors help diffuse the light from the dome's windows, making the chapel evenly lit and meditative. The four medallions showing the evangelists (at the base of the dome) may be by Donatello; the medallions of apostles (on the walls) are by Luca della Robbia. While originally used as a monk's assembly room (chapter house), this later became the Pazzi family's private chapel. Imagine how modern this chapel must have seemed after Brunelleschi capped it with a dome.

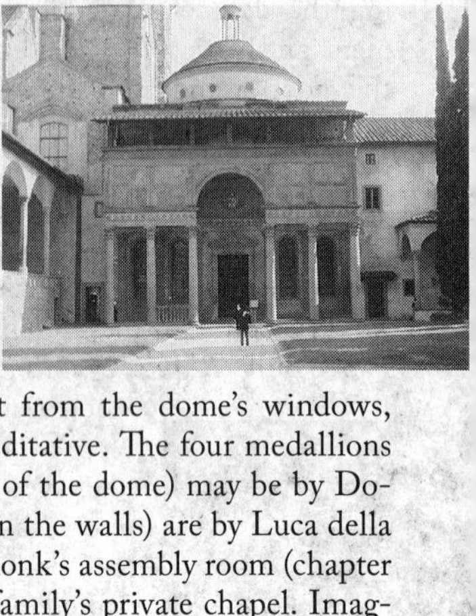

• *Exiting into the big cloister, notice the long building on the right (below the gallery) that houses the Romantic Graves Gallery; this collection of 19th-century headstones is also included in your church admission. To your left is the entrance to the...*

Museum (Museo) and Refectory

Stroll through several rooms of paintings, statues, medieval altarpieces, frescoes, and ceramic altarpieces by Andrea della Rob-

Floods in Florence

Summer visitors to Florence gaze at the lazy green creek called the Arno River and have a tough time imagining it being a destructive giant. But rare, powerful flooding is a part of life in this city. The Arno River washed away Ponte Vecchio in 1177 and 1333. And on November 4, 1966, a huge rainstorm turned the Arno into a wall of water, inundating the city with mud stacked as high as 20 feet. Nearly 14,000 families were left homeless, and tens of thousands of important frescoes, paintings, sculptures, and books were destroyed or damaged.

Almost as impressive as the flood was the huge outpouring of support, as the art-loving world came to the city's rescue. While money poured in from far and wide, volunteers, nicknamed "mud angels," mopped things up. After the flood, scientists made great gains in restoration techniques as they cleaned and repaired masterpieces from medieval and Renaissance times. Cimabue's *Crucifixion,* now displayed in Santa Croce's Refectory, is a prime example.

You'll see plaques around town showing the high-water marks from 1966 (about six feet high at the Duomo). Now that a dam has tamed the Arno, kayakers glide peacefully on the river, sightseers enjoy the great art with no thought of a flood, and locals...still get nervous after every heavy rain.

bia until you come out into the large room that was originally the monks' refectory, or dining hall, under heavy timber beams.

The refectory's entire far wall is frescoed with the impressive, 1,300-square-foot *Tree of the Cross and Last Supper*, by Taddeo Gaddi. A crucifix sprouts branches blossoming with medieval symbolism, which dining monks ate up. Francis kneels at the base of the cross and makes sympathetic eye contact with Jesus. In one of the scenes that flank the cross (upper left), Francis has a vision in which he receives the stigmata—the same wounds in his hands, feet, and side that Christ suffered when he was crucified. Beneath the Tree of the Cross is the Last Supper, a scene that gave the monastery's residents the illusion that they were eating in the symbolic company of Jesus and the apostles.

OLTRARNO WALK

A Loop Trip South from Ponte Vecchio

Staying in the tourist zone leaves you with an incomplete impression of Florence. Most of its people live and work outside the touristy center. The best place to get a sense of rustic, old Florence is in the Oltrarno neighborhood, south of the Arno River. While the essence of the Oltrarno is best enjoyed by simply wandering, this walk gives you a structure in which to cover its highlights.

We'll start at Ponte Vecchio, walk to the Pitti Palace, explore some colorful (and slightly seedy) back streets, pass by the Brancacci Chapel, and return to where we started—Ponte Vecchio. This walk is a helpful way to link some of the Oltrarno sights worth seeing.

Orientation

Pitti Palace: Various combo-tickets cover different parts of the palace and range from €7 to €11.50 (more with special exhibitions). The Palatine Gallery is open Tue-Sun 8:15-18:50, closed Mon.

Santo Spirito Church: Free, Mon-Tue and Thu-Sat 9:30-12:30 & 16:00-17:30, Sun 11:30-12:30 & 16:00-17:30, closed Wed.

Santa Maria del Carmine: Free, daily 8:00-12:00 & 17:00-18:30.

Brancacci Chapel: €6, cash only, Mon and Wed-Sat 10:00-17:00, Sun 13:00-17:00, closed Tue; free reservations are required, but on weekdays and any day off-season, it's usually possible to get a time right away, especially if you come before 15:30 (reservation tel. 055-276-8224 or 055-276-8558, English spoken).

When to Go: What you'll see on this walk varies with the time of day, but mornings and evenings are best. Mid-afternoon is sleepy, and many shops and churches are closed. Most of the artisan shops are closed on weekends. In the evening, cafés, restaurants, and strolling people—both locals and tourists—leave the strongest impression, but most shops close by 19:00 or 19:30.

Getting There: Start at Ponte Vecchio, which crosses the Arno River (a 10-minute walk south of the Duomo).

Length of This Tour: Allow about an hour, not including visits to church interiors, the Brancacci Chapel, or the Pitti Palace. With less time, finish the walk early, at Piazza Santo Spirito.

Eating: You'll pass a number of recommended restaurants, described on page 302.

Shopping: The Oltrarno is a great shopping destination for jewelry, clothes, leather goods, woodwork, prints, home decor, and more. Two streets, Borgo San Jacopo and Via di Santo Spirito, are lined with shops. For a rundown of several shops worth popping into here—including several right along the route of this walk—see page 329 in the Shopping in Florence chapter.

Starring: Views of the Arno, Florence's medieval past, present-day artisans at work, and few tourists.

The Tour Begins

• *Start in the middle of Ponte Vecchio.*

Ponte Vecchio

The Arno River separates the city center from the Oltrarno—the neighborhood on the "other" *(altro)* side of the river. The two sides have historically been connected by this oldest bridge—Ponte Vecchio (current version built in 1345)—lined with its characteristic shops.

Florence was born on the north bank (founded by the Romans in the first century B.C.), and since the 1200s, the Oltrarno has been the city's poorer, working-class cousin. As the Oltrarno grew in medieval times, the wooden walls were replaced by stone, and two more bridges were added, connecting it with the city center. Looking upstream (east), you'll see the lone crenellated tower that marks the wall that once defined the medieval city. By Michelangelo's day, the Oltrarno had grown enough that this bridge was about mid-Florence.

Look above to see the Vasari Corridor (the yellow wall with the round windows), which was named for its architect, Giorgio Vasari. This was the personal passageway built for the Medici family to give them a private

OLTRARNO

commute from the Uffizi (center of city government) to the Pitti Palace, their palatial home (which we'll see a bit later). The corridor, built in five months in 1565, drilled straight through people's homes. The only detour is where it curves around the tower at the end of the bridge. (The family who owned that tower must have had a lot of clout.) With Medici princes prancing back and forth in their corridor, the smells of the traditional shops had to go. That's when Ponte Vecchio's original merchants—butchers and fishmongers—were replaced by today's gold- and silversmiths.

Ponte Vecchio has seen a lot of turmoil. The plaque above the crowds on the uphill side honors Gerhard Wolf, the German consul in Florence who is credited with saving the bridge (as well as other

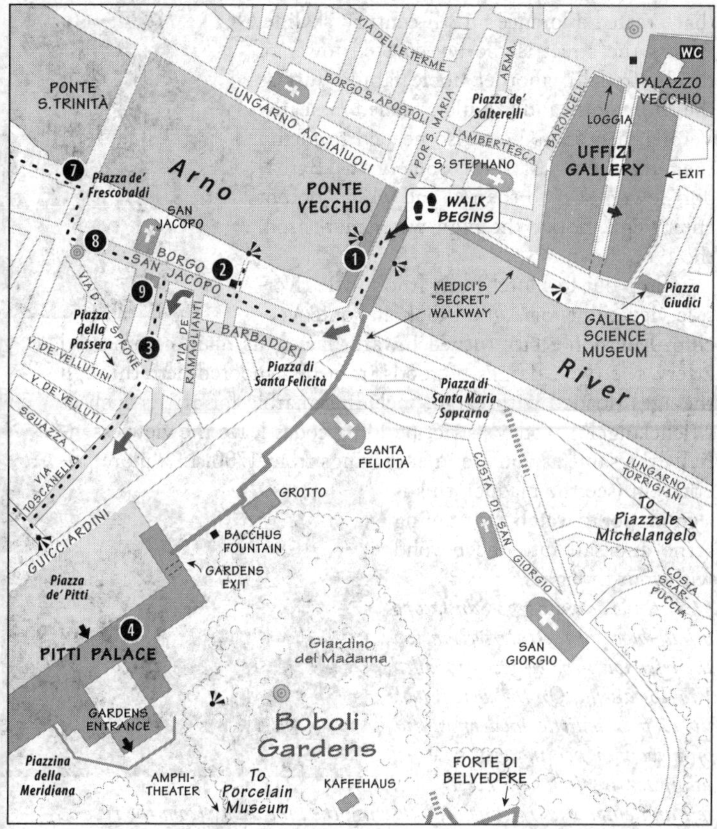

art treasures) from destruction during World War II. In August 1944, as Hitler's occupying troops fled the city, they were ordered to destroy all of Florence's bridges to cover their retreat. Ponte Santa Trinità was demolished (rebuilt in 1958), and Ponte Vecchio was next in line. But thankfully, Wolf understood the bridge's historic value, and instead of destroying it, he had the buildings at either end blown up to render the bridge unusable. The flood of 1966, which later inundated the city, destroyed still more bridges and dramatically thrust entire trees like spears through buildings on Ponte Vecchio.

• Cross the bridge, turn right on Borgo San Jacopo, and walk one block. You'll pass ugly buildings from the 1950s, built after the damage from WWII-era bombs. Stop at the twin towers.

Torre dei Barbadori, Torre dei Belfredelli, and Photo Op

The tower of the Barbadori family is typical of countless towers

that created Florence's 12th-century skyline. Across the street is the ivy-covered tower of the Belfredelli, another noble family. Just as the Montagues and Capulets feuded in nearby Verona, neighbors here also needed to fortify their mansions. At the corner of the Barbadori tower, next to the red and white "do not enter" sign, notice the high-water mark from the 1966 flood.

Step out to Hotel Lungarno's little riverside viewpoint for a good look at Ponte Vecchio. Envision a city turned inward, facing its main commercial artery, the river. Barges of goods from Pisa moored here through the ages (loaded with cargo, including marble for artists such as Michelangelo). Today's strict building codes leave the view essentially the same as you see in engravings from 1700. In a more poetic vein (see the plaque), this is a good spot to watch the rippling Arno and sail into the beyond with your thoughts.

• *Continue down Borgo San Jacopo a half-block to the intersection (on the left) with the tiny street called Via Toscanella. On the corner, look up to find a little modern statue of a woman holding her nose—a dumpster is often left here. Turn left and enter Via Toscanella, following the lane away from the river... and deeper into the Oltrarno. Notice how Via Toscanella opens up a bit wider 20 yards down. In the 1950s, this former pedestrian-only promenade was widened to accommodate modern traffic.*

Via Toscanella

You're on a quiet and characteristic lane typical of the Oltrarno. A high stone wall hides a private garden (common in this city). The street is named for the family of Paolo Toscanelli (1397-1482), the scientist who used Brunelleschi's dome as a giant sundial and convinced Columbus to reach the East by sailing west. For a glimpse of the clothing styles of today's locals, look up at their laundry.

The little square ahead is **Piazza della Passera.** Also known as Canto ai Quattro Leoni, the piazza was officially renamed "Passera" (sparrow) in 2005. The legend goes that in 1348, the inhabitants of this neighborhood tried to help a sick little bird, which then brought the plague to the city. Some Florentines opt for a more titillating interpretation—the area around the square was occupied by brothels, and the word *passera* is somewhat vulgar slang for the female genitalia.

The recommended **Trattoria 4 Leoni** dominates the square, and the classic little **Caffè degli Artigiani** is a reminder of the earthy pride of this once rustic district, now gaining affluence as it becomes trendier. Demographically, the Oltrarno is an interesting melting pot of traditional craftspeople, immigrants, retired people, and yuppies.

Continue down Via Toscanella. You'll pass artisan shops on this and neighboring streets. Their doors are open to welcome browsers. Be comfortable stepping in and enjoying the proud work of the artisan. It's polite to say *"Buon giorno"* and *"Ciao."* "Can I take a look?" is *"Posso guardare?"* (POH-soh gwahr-DAH-ray). Long a working-class neighborhood, the Oltrarno is where artisans still ply the traditional trades of their forebears. You'll find handmade furniture, jewelry, leather items, shoes, pottery, and picture frames in a centuries-old style. Craftsmen bind books and make marbled paper. Antique pieces are refurbished by people who've become curators of the dying techniques of gilding, engraving, etching, enameling, mosaics, and repoussé metal work. It was in artisan workshops like these that boys like Leonardo, Michelangelo, and little Sandy Botticelli apprenticed.

• *Continue to the end of Via Toscanella and turn left. You'll soon see the stony facade of a huge palace.*

Pitti Palace

The massive palace, with its rusticated stonework so pleasing to noble egos, sits conveniently in front of the quarry from where all that stone was cut. This behemoth shows the Renaissance aesthetics of symmetry and mathematical order on a giant scale. In the 15th century, the Oltrarno became a fashionable spot for Florentine nobles to build palaces.

Originally built for the Pitti family (15th century), the palace was later bought and enlarged by the Medici (16th century). In the 1860s, when Florence briefly ruled Italy as the interim capital, the palace was the "White House" for the ruling Savoy family. While stark on the outside, it is much warmer on the inside, and its bulk hides the lush Boboli Gardens. It's been a museum since the early 1900s (✪ see the Pitti Palace Tour chapter).

• *Turn 180 degrees and—with your back to the Pitti Palace—double back down the street called Sdrucciolo de' Pitti (enjoy wrapping your tongue around that "sdr"). Continue west, crossing busy Via Maggio. You'll come to a big church facing a square.*

Piazza Santo Spirito

Piazza Santo Spirito, with its bald-faced church, is the community center, hosting a colorful produce market in the morning. Later in the day, bohemians and winos move in to drink and strum guitars on the church steps. Steer clear of any seedy characters camping out near the fountain.

Santo Spirito Church is worth a visit (see page 67) for its Brunelleschi-designed interior and crucifix by Michelangelo. As a teenager, Michelangelo was allowed to dissect bodies from the adjacent monastic mortuary in order to learn the secrets of anatomy—something he considered key to portraying bodies accurately. As thanks, he made the crucifix.

The church's blank facade prompted the neighborhood to have a contest to design a fun finish: The nearby **Ricchi Caffè** displays the hundred or so entries on its walls. Choose your favorite while enjoying an ice cream or drink.

• ***To end the walk here:*** *To return to the Arno River, face Santo Spirito Church and walk north, along the right side of the church, up Via del Presto di San Martino. At the end of the block, turn right and enter a busy five-way intersection, Piazza de' Frescobaldi. From here, you'll see Ponte Santa Trinità arcing over the Arno, decorated with statues on the end. You can finish the walk here, in the middle of Florence, free to explore. (You could head back to Ponte Vecchio along two enticing shopping streets, Via di Santo Spirito, which turns into Borgo San Jacopo; for specifics, see page 330.)*

To continue the walk: *From the far end of Piazza Santo Spirito (opposite the church), turn right on Via Sant'Agostino. Stroll westward for 5-10 minutes, enjoying more people-watching and browsing the small antique and fashion shops, until you reach a big square.*

Porta San Frediano

Porta San Frediano (c. 1333) is one of the gates in Florence's medieval wall, which stretches impressively from here to the river. This gate straddled the road to Pisa. In medieval times, a three-quarter-mile-wide strip outside the wall was cleared to deny attackers any cover. The tower, originally twice as high, was built when gravity ruled warfare. During the Renaissance, gunpowder became the weapon of choice, and the tower—now just an easy target—was lopped. Florence's symbol, the lily (fleur-de-lis), decorates the top of the tower. The 40-foot doors weigh 16 tons each, and are studded with fat iron nails to withstand battering rams. Take a close look at the hardware. Touch it. Clang a ring.

Piazza del Carmine

Piazza del Carmine (the ugliest square in Florence) hosts the Church of Santa Maria del Carmine, with its famous Brancacci Chapel and Masaccio frescoes. Just a few years ago, most of Europe's main squares were parking lots just like this. Now this square is an exception.

Step into Santa Maria del Carmine. Redone after a 1714 fire, the church offers a good look at textbook Baroque art. Don't miss the impressive 3-D work on the ceiling. Just as the Renaissance originated in Florence and went from here to Rome, Baroque originated in Rome and went from there to Florence. The adjacent Brancacci Chapel is covered with frescoes by Masaccio—some of the most exquisite art in Florence (✪ see the Brancacci Chapel Tour chapter).

• *With your back to the church, head straight, toward the river. At Borgo San Frediano, consider detouring a few blocks left to see the* ***Porta San Frediano*** *city gate (see sidebar). Otherwise, turn right onto Borgo San Frediano, then take the first left to Ponte alla Carraia.*

For a drink, snack, or treat, you have a couple of options: First, before turning onto Ponte alla Carraia, watch for ***La Cité Libreria Café,*** *a cool local hangout with a leftist vibe and a good* aperitivo *scene in the evening (20 red on Borgo San Frediano). Or, facing the bridge, drop into* ***Gelateria la Carraia*** *for an ice-cream cone.*

From the Carraia bridge, turn right and walk along the river toward Ponte Vecchio to the next square...

Piazza de' Frescobaldi

At this small square, along the river, two statues flank Ponte Santa Trinità. The elegant Palazzo Frescobaldi faces the river. A block up from the river, on the corner, look for the picturesque little Medici-era fountain that decorates a flatiron corner.

Before moving on, just stand at the intersection, watch traffic come and go, and marvel at how the chaos all seems to work out fine.

• *Now, with your back to the river, cross the square and turn left, down Borgo San Jacopo.*

Torre dei Marsili

See how quickly the rough-around-the-edges neighborhood becomes an upscale, pedestrian-friendly lane of fashion stores, antique and jewelry shops, and nice restaurants. Stop at #17 (on the right), at **Torre dei Marsili,** to admire the terra-cotta figurines above the door, especially the fine Annunciation scene.

• *A few steps past the tower are Via Toscanella and the twin towers, and—just like that—we're back at Ponte Vecchio. Ciao.*

BRANCACCI CHAPEL TOUR

Cappella Brancacci

In the Brancacci (bran-KAH-chee) Chapel, Masaccio created a world in paint that looked like the world we inhabit. For the first time in a thousand years, Man and Nature were frozen for inspection. Masaccio's painting techniques were copied by many Renaissance artists, and his people—sturdy, intelligent, and dignified, with expressions of understated astonishment—helped shape Renaissance men and women's own self-images.

Orientation

Cost: €6, cash only, covered by Firenze Card.

Hours: Mon and Wed-Sat 10:00-17:00, Sun 13:00-17:00, closed Tue, last entry 30 minutes before closing.

Reservations: Reserving an entry time is required (and free), but on weekdays and any day off-season, it's often possible to walk right in and get an entry time, especially if you come before 15:30. Officially, reservation times begin every 20 minutes, with a maximum of 30 visitors per time slot (you have 20 minutes inside the chapel). But when it's not too busy, they generally let people come and go at will and stay as long as they like.

If you want to find out beforehand if there's a long line, you can call ahead to the ticket desk (tel. 055-284-361).

Firenze Card users don't need a reservation at all and can walk in whenever they like.

To reserve in advance, call the chapel a day ahead (tel. 055-276-8224 or 055-276-8558, English spoken, call center open Mon-Sat 9:30-13:00 & 14:00-17:00, Sun 9:30-12:30). If the line is busy, keep trying; it's best to call in the afternoon. You can also try via email—info.museoragazzi@comune.fi.it.

Dress Code: Modest dress (covered shoulders and knees—a scarf will do) is requested when visiting the church and chapel (if it's very hot, they might be lenient—-but better not to chance it).

Getting There: The Brancacci Chapel is in the Church of Santa Maria del Carmine, on Piazza del Carmine, in the Oltrarno neighborhood south of the Arno River. It's about a 20-minute walk or short taxi ride (about €11) from downtown Florence. From Ponte Vecchio, cross to the Oltrarno side, turn right on Borgo San Jacopo, walk 10 minutes, then turn left into Piazza del Carmine. (✪ See the previous Oltrarno Walk chapter for a nice walking route.)

Getting In: The chapel is accessible only through the paid entrance to the right of the church.

Information: Tel. 055-284-361, http://museicivicifiorentini.comune.fi.it.

Film: Your ticket includes a 20-minute film (English subtitles) on the chapel, the frescoes, and Renaissance Florence. The film's computer animation brings the paintings to 3-D life—they appear to move—while narration describes the events depicted in the panels. The film takes liberties with the art, but it's visually interesting and your best way to see the frescoes close up.

Audioguide: A good videoguide describes the frescoes (€2, leave ID as deposit). You're allowed to keep it for 25 minutes. I'd view most of it in the courtyard—then you can maximize your time face to face with the art inside. I'd skip the videoguide if the film (described earlier) is showing.

Length of This Tour: Allow 30 minutes (plus 30 minutes if you see the film or rent the videoguide).

Photography: Allowed without a flash.

Starring: Masaccio, Masolino, and Filippino Lippi.

OVERVIEW

The chapel has frescoes that tell the story of Peter—half are by Masaccio and half by either Masolino or Filippino Lippi (the son of Filippo Lippi). Although Masaccio is the star, the panels by his colleagues are interesting and provide a good contrast in styles. Masaccio's works are sprinkled among the others, mostly on the left and center walls.

The panels are displayed roughly in the order they were painted, from upper left to lower right—the upper six by Masaccio and Masolino (1424-1425), the lower ones by Masaccio (1426-1427) and Filippino Lippi (1481-1485).

It's best to read this chapter before you enter, because if it's busy, you'll have only 20 minutes in the chapel.

Brancacci Chapel

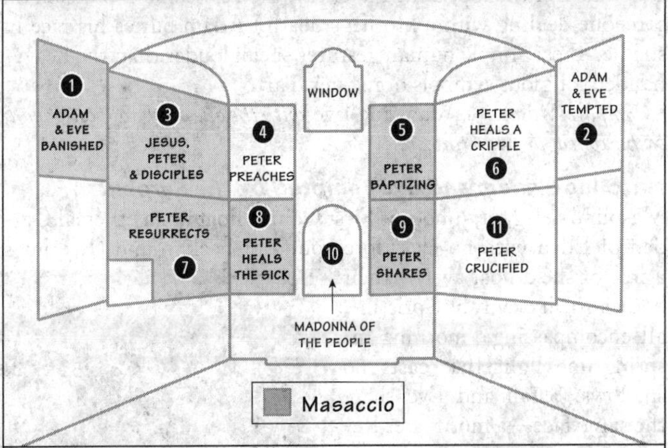

1. MASACCIO – Adam and Eve Banished from Eden
2. MASOLINO – Adam and Eve Tempted by the Serpent
3. MASACCIO – Jesus, Peter & Disciples Pay the Tribute Money
4. MASOLINO – Peter Preaches to a Crowd
5. MASACCIO – Peter Baptizing Converts
6. MASOLINO – Peter Heals a Cripple and Resurrects Tabitha
7. MASACCIO – Peter Resurrects the Son of Theophilus
8. MASACCIO – Peter Heals the Sick with his Shadow
9. MASACCIO – Peter Shares the Wealth with the Poor
10. ANONYMOUS – The Madonna of the People
11. FILIPPINO LIPPI – Peter Crucified

The Tour Begins

THE CHAPEL

• *Start with the left wall, the small panel in the upper left.*

Masaccio—*Adam and Eve Banished from Eden*

Renaissance man and woman—as nude as they can be—turn their backs on the skinny, unrealistic, medieval Gate of Paradise and take their first step as mortal humans in the real world. For the first time in a thousand years of painting, these figures cast a realistic shadow, seemingly lit by the same light we are—the natural light through the Brancacci Chapel's window.

Eve wails from deep

within. (The first time I saw her, I thought Eve's gaping mouth was way over the top, until I later saw the very same expression on someone dealing with a brother's death.) Adam buries his face in shame. These simple human gestures speak louder than the heavy-handed religious symbols of medieval art.

• *Compare Masaccio's* Adam and Eve *with the one on the opposite wall, by his colleague Masolino.*

Masolino—*Adam and Eve Tempted by the Serpent*

Masolino's elegant, innocent First Couple float in an ethereal Garden of Eden with no clear foreground or background (Eve hugs a tree or she'd float away). Their bodies are lit evenly by a pristine, all-encompassing, morning-in-springtime light that casts no shadows. Satan and Eve share the same face—a motif later Renaissance artists would copy.

In 1424, Masolino da Panicale (1383-1435) was hired by the Brancacci family to decorate this chapel with the story of Peter (beginning with the Original Sin that Peter's "Good News" saves man from). Masolino, a 40-year-old contractor with too many other commitments, invited 23-year-old Masaccio (1401-1428) to help him. The two set up scaffolding and worked side by side—the older, workmanlike master and the younger, intuitive genius—in a harmonious collaboration. They just divvied up the panels, never (or rarely) working together on the same scene.

• *Return to the left wall, upper level. From here, we'll work clockwise around the chapel. After* Adam and Eve, *the second panel is...*

Masaccio—*Jesus, Peter, and the Disciples Pay the Tribute Money*

The tax collector (in red miniskirt, with his back to us) tells Jesus that he must pay a temple tax. Jesus gestures to say, "OK, but the money's over there." Peter, his right-hand man (gray hair and beard, brown robe), says, "Yeah, over there." Peter goes over there to the lake (left side of panel), takes off his robe, stoops down at an odd angle, and miraculously pulls a coin from the mouth of a fish. He puts his robe back on (right side of panel) and pays the man.

Some consider this the first modern painting, placing real humans in a real setting, seen from a single viewpoint—ours. Earlier painters had done far more detailed landscapes than Masaccio's sketchy mountains, lake, trees, clouds, and buildings, but they never fixed where the viewer was in relation to these things.

Masaccio tells us exactly where we stand—near the crowd, farther from the trees, with the sun to our right casting late-afternoon shadows. We're no longer detached spectators, but an extension of the scene. Masaccio lets us stand in the presence of the human Jesus. While a good attempt at three-dimensionality, Masaccio's work is far from perfect. Later artists would perfect mathematically what Masaccio eyeballed intuitively.

The disciples all have strong, broad-shouldered bodies, but each face is unique. Blond, curly-haired, clean-shaven John is as handsome as the head on a Roman coin (Masaccio had just returned from Rome). Thomas (far right, with a five-o'clock shadow) is intense. Their different reactions—with faces half in shadow, half in light—tell us that they're divided over paying the tax.

Masaccio's people have one thing in common—a faraway look in the eye, as though hit with a spiritual two-by-four. They're deep in thought, reflective, and awestruck, aware they've just experienced something miraculous. But they're also dazzled, glazed over, and a bit disoriented, like tourists at the Brancacci Chapel.

• *Continuing clockwise, we move to the next panel, on the center wall.*

Masolino—*Peter Preaches to a Crowd*

Masolino and Masaccio were different in so many ways, but they were both fans of Giotto (c. 1266-1337), who told stories with simple gestures and minimal acting, adding the human drama by showing the reaction of bystanders. Here, the miraculous power of the sermon is not evident in Peter (who just raises his hand) but in the faces of the crowd. The lady in the front row is riveted, while others close their eyes to meditate. The big nun (far right) is skeptical, but wants to hear more. The tonsured monk's mouth slips open in awe, while the gentleman to the left finds it interesting enough to come a little closer.

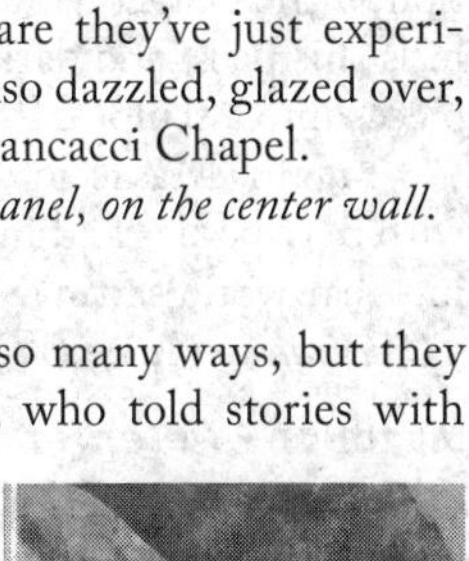

Masolino never mastered 3-D space like Masaccio. Peter's extreme profile is a cardboard cutout, his left leg stands too high to plant him realistically on flat ground, the people in the back have their gazes fixed somewhere above Peter, and the "Masacciesque" mountains in the background remain just that, background.

• *Continuing clockwise to the other side of the window, come to...*

Masaccio—*Peter Baptizing Converts*

A muscular man kneels in the stream to join the cult of Jesus. On the bank (far right), another young man waits his turn, shivering in his jockstrap. Among the crowd, a just-baptized man wrestles with his robe, while the man in blue, his hair still dripping, buttons up.

The body language is eloquent: The strongman's humility, the shivering youth's uncertainty, and the bowed heads of the just-baptized communicate their reflection on the life-altering choice they've just made.

Masaccio builds these bodies with patches of color (an especially effective technique in fresco, where colors can bleed together). He knew that a kneeling man's body, when lit from the left (the direction of the chapel window), would look like a patchwork of bright hills (his pecs) and dark crevasses (his sternum). He assembles the pieces into a sculptural, 3-D figure, "modeled" by light and shade.

Again, Masaccio was the first artist to paint real humans—with 3-D bodies and individual faces, reflecting inner emotions—in a real-world setting.

• *Continue clockwise to the right wall.*

Masolino—*Peter Heals a Cripple* (left side) and *Resurrects Tabitha* (right side)

Masolino takes a crack at the 3-D style of his young partner, setting two separate stories in a single Florentine square, defined by an arcade on the left and a porch on the right. Crude elements of the future Renaissance style abound: The receding buildings establish the viewer's point of reference; the rocks scattered through the square define 3-D space; there are secular details in the background (mother and child, laundry on a balcony, a monkey on a ledge); and the cripple (left) is shown at an odd angle (foreshortening). Masaccio may have helped on this panel.

But the stars of the work are the two sharply dressed gentlemen strolling across the square, who help to divide (and unite) the two stories of Peter. The patterned coat is a textbook example of the International Gothic style that was the rage in Florence—elegant, refined, graceful, with curvy lines creating a complex, pleasing pattern. The man walking is at a three-quarters angle, but Masolino shows the coat from the front to catch the full display. The picture is evenly lit, with only a hint of shadow, accentuating the colorful clothes and cheerful atmosphere.

In mid-project (1426), Masolino took another job in Hungary, leaving Masaccio to finish the lower half of the chapel. Masolino never again explored the Renaissance style, building a successful career with the eternal springtime of International Gothic.

• *Move to the lower level. Start on the left wall with the second panel and work clockwise.*

Masaccio—*Peter Resurrects the Son of Theophilus*

Peter (in that same brown robe... like Masaccio, who was careless about his appearance) raises the boy from the world of bones, winning his freedom from stern Theophilus (seated in a niche to the left).

The courtyard setting is fully 3-D, Masaccio having recently learned a bit of the mathematics of perspective from his (older) friends Brunelleschi and Donatello. At the far right of the painting are three of the Quattrocento (1400s) giants who invented painting perspective (from right to left): Brunelleschi, who broke down reality mathematically; Alberti, who popularized the math with his book, *On Painting;* and Masaccio himself (looking out at us), who opened everyone's eyes to the powerful psychological possibilities of perspective.

Little is known of Masaccio's short life. "Masaccio" is a nickname (often translated as "Lumbering Antonio") describing his personality—stumbling through life with careless abandon, not worrying about money, clothes, or fame...a lovable doofus. Imagine the absent-minded professor, completely absorbed in his art.

Next to Masaccio's self-portrait is a painting within a painting of Peter on a throne. On a flat surface with a blank background,

Masaccio has created a hovering hologram, a human more 3-D than even a statue made in medieval times.

"Wow," said Brother Philip, a 20-year-old Carmelite monk stationed here when Masaccio painted this. Fra Filippo ("Brother Philip") Lippi was inspired by these frescoes and went on to become a famous painter himself. At age 50, while painting in a convent, he fell in love with a young nun, and they eloped. Nine months later, "Little Philip" was born, and he too grew to be a famous painter—Filippino Lippi, who in 1481 was chosen to complete the Brancacci Chapel.

Filippino Lippi painted substantial portions of this fresco, including the group in the far left (five heads but only eight feet).

• *Moving clockwise to the center wall, you'll see...*

Masaccio—*Peter Heals the Sick with his Shadow*

Peter is a powerful Donatello statue come to life, walking toward us along a Florentine street. Next to him, in the red cap, is bearded Donatello, Masaccio's friend and mentor.

Masaccio inspired more than painters. He gave ordinary people a new self-image of what it was to be human. Masaccio's people are individuals, not generic Greek gods, not always pretty (like the old bald guy) but still robust and handsome in their own way. They exude a seriousness that makes them very adult. Compare these street people with Masolino's two well-dressed dandies, and you see the difference between Florence's working-class, urban, "democratic" spirit (Guelphs) and the courtly grace of Europe's landed gentry (Ghibellines).

• *The next panel, on the other side of the altar, is...*

Masaccio—*Peter Shares the Wealth with the Poor*

Early Christians practiced a form of communal sharing. The wealthy Ananias lies about his contribution, and he drops dead at Peter's feet. Peter takes the missing share and gives it to a poor lady who can't even afford baby pants. The shy baby, the grateful woman, and the admiring man on crutches show Masaccio's blue-collar sympathies.

The scene reflects an actual event in Florence—a tax-reform measure to make things equal for everyone. Florentines were championing a new form of government where, if we all contribute our fair share through taxes, we don't need kings and nobles.

• *The altar under the window holds a painting that is not by Masaccio, Masolino, or Lippi.*

Anonymous (possibly Coppo di Marcovaldo)—
The Madonna of the People

This medieval altarpiece replaces the now-destroyed fresco by Masaccio that was the centerpiece of the whole design—Peter's crucifixion.

With several panels still unfinished, Masaccio traveled to Rome to meet up with Masolino. Masaccio died there (possibly poisoned) in 1428, at age 27. After his death, the political and artistic climate changed, the chapel was left unfinished (the lower right wall), and some of his frescoes were scraped off whole (his *Crucifixion of Peter*) or in part (in *Peter Resurrects the Son of Theophilus,* several exiled Brancaccis were erased from history, later to be replaced).

Finally, in 1481, new funding arrived and Filippino Lippi, the son of the monk-turned-painter, was hired to complete the blank panels and retouch some destroyed frescoes.

• *The right wall, lower section, contains two panels by Filippino Lippi. The first and biggest is...*

Filippino Lippi—*Peter Crucified*

Lippi completes the story of Peter with his upside-down crucifixion. Lippi tried to match the solemn style of Masaccio, but the compositions are busier, and his figures are less statuesque, more colorful and detailed. Still, compared with Lippi's other, more hyperactive works found elsewhere, he's reined himself in admirably here to honor the great pioneer.

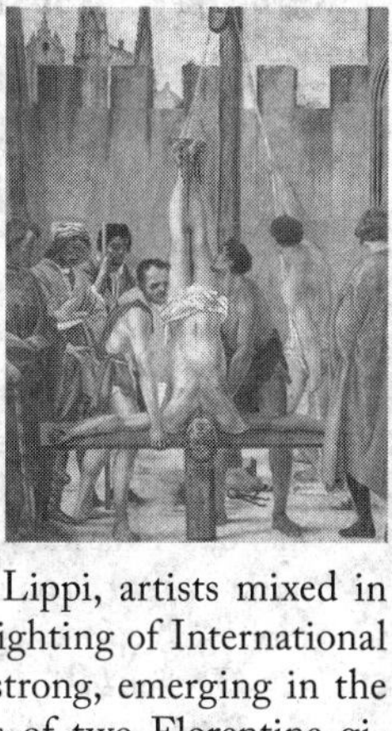

In fact, while Masaccio's perspective techniques were enormously influential, learned by every Tuscan artist, his sober style was not terribly popular. Another strain of Tuscan painting diverged from Masaccio. From Fra Filippo Lippi to Botticelli, Ghirlandaio, and Filippino Lippi, artists mixed in the bright colors, line patterns, and even lighting of International Gothic. But Masaccio's legacy remained strong, emerging in the grave, statuesque, harsh-shadow creations of two Florentine giants—Leonardo da Vinci and Michelangelo.

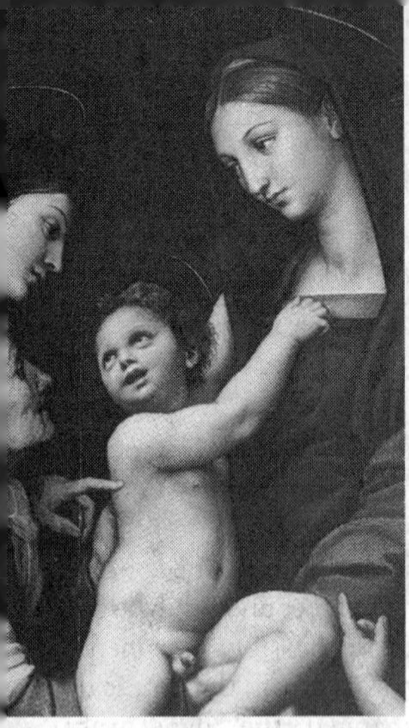

PITTI PALACE TOUR

Palazzo Pitti, Galleria Palatina

Pitti Palace offers many reasons for a visit: the palace itself, with its imposing exterior and lavish interior; the second-best collection of paintings in town; the statue-dotted Boboli Gardens; and a host of secondary museums. However, seeing it all is impossible, and choosing where to spend your time can be confusing. While famous, Pitti Palace exhausts tourists.

Do yourself a favor and stay focused on the highlights: Stick to the Palatine Gallery, which has the painting collection, plus the sumptuous rooms of the Royal Apartments. The paintings pick up where the Uffizi leaves off, at the High Renaissance. Lovers of Raphael's Madonnas and Titian's portraits will find some of the world's best at Pitti Palace. For fashionistas, the Costume Museum is worth a peek. And if it's a nice day, take a stroll in the Boboli Gardens, a rare and inviting patch of extensive green space within old Florence.

Orientation

Cost: Everything—except the Bardini Gardens (€6)—is covered by the Firenze Card. Otherwise, you have three ticketing options:

Ticket #1 (the tour described in this chapter) costs €13 (€8.50 if no special exhibitions). This ticket covers the recommended Palatine Gallery, Royal Apartments, and Gallery of Modern Art. You can't buy a ticket for just the Palatine Gallery.

Ticket #2 is €10 (€7 if no special exhibitions) and covers the Boboli and Bardini Gardens, Costume Gallery, Argenti/Silverworks Museum (the Medici treasures), and Porcelain Museum.

Pitti Palace & Boboli Gardens

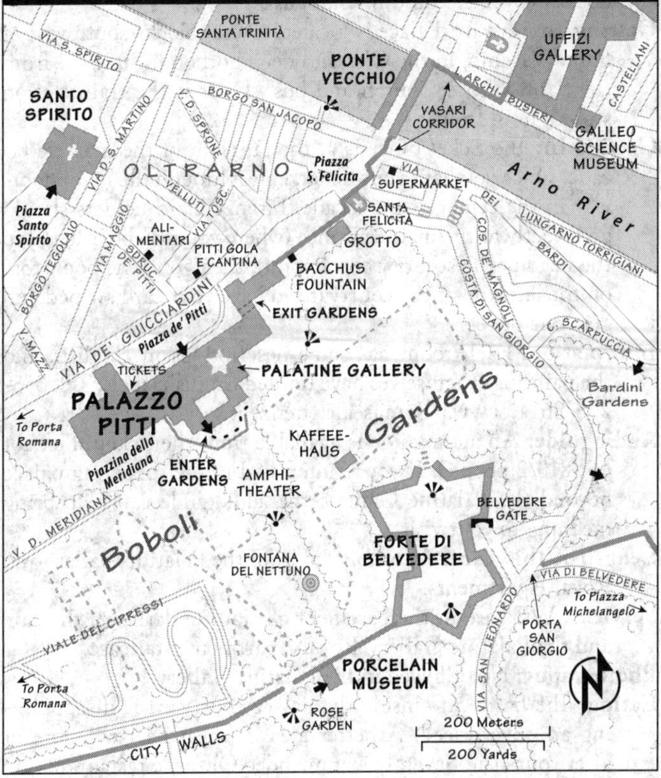

Ticket #3, a combo-ticket covering all of the above, costs €11.50 but is usually not available during special exhibitions (valid 3 days).

Hours: The "ticket #1" sights (Palatine Gallery, Royal Apartments, and Gallery of Modern Art) are open the same hours year-round: Tue-Sun 8:15-18:50, closed Mon, last entry 45 minutes before closing.

The "ticket #2" sights (Boboli and Bardini Gardens, Costume Gallery, Argenti/Silverworks Museum, and Porcelain Museum) vary depending on the season: daily June-Aug 8:15-19:30, April-May and Sept-Oct 8:15-18:30, March 8:15-17:30, Nov-Feb 8:15-16:30; closed first and last Mon of each month, last entry one hour before closing.

Avoiding Lines: Reservations are generally not necessary. But if there's a long line, you can try asking at window 3 at the ticket office (marked "Reservation Desk") if they'll let you make a €3 reservation on the spot (not always possible). You can also skip lines if you have a Firenze Card (but remember that the card doesn't cover the Bardini Gardens).

Getting There: Pitti Palace is located several blocks southwest of Ponte Vecchio, in the Oltrarno neighborhood. Bus #C3 from the Santa Croce Church and bus #D from the train station stop right in front.

Getting In: The ticket office is at the far right of the massive facade. Once you have your ticket, enter through the main doorway in the center of the facade. Firenze Card holders should go directly to the main entrance (where you may be ushered to the head of the security checkpoint); then go to the bookstore on the left side of the courtyard to have your card swiped and get your tickets.

Information: Each room has some descriptions in English, and the paintings themselves have limited English labels. Tel. 055-238-8614, www.polomuseale.firenze.it.

Audioguide: An audioguide is available from the ticket office for €6 (€10/2 people). If you're interested in the sprawling palace beyond the Palatine Gallery, the audioguide can help bring meaning to your visit.

Length of This Tour: Allow one hour for the Palatine Gallery and Royal Apartments.

Services: WCs are in the basement corridor underneath the café and the Palatine Gallery/Royal Apartments staircase.

Photography: Not allowed in the Palatine Gallery.

Eating: The basic café inside the palace courtyard is disappointing and overpriced. A better idea is to eat nearby before or after your visit. Several recommended Oltrarno restaurants are a few blocks away (see page 302). Across the piazza is a cozy wine-by-the-glass *enoteca*, Pitti Gola e Cantina, which also serves €10 *antipasti* plates, €9-13 lunches, and €14 homemade pastas (food served 13:00-24:00, closed Tue, Piazza Pitti 16, tel. 055-212-704). For picnics, a tiny *alimentari* is a half-block from the palace (€3-5 made-to-order sandwiches, Sdrucciolo de' Pitti 6), and a supermarket is a short walk away, near Ponte Vecchio (see page 306). A drinking fountain is in front of the palace, at the base of the square, across the street from Banca Toscana.

Shopping: The area around Pitti Palace is a busy shopping zone, with no shortage of high-profile shops. (The recommended **La Pelle** leather shop is between here and Ponte Vecchio.) I enjoy browsing two different streets near Pitti Palace: the narrow lane called **Sdrucciolo de' Pitti,** directly across from the entrance courtyard; and, a block north, the very local-feeling **Via Romana** (which conveniently connects the palace entrance with the rear gate of Boboli Gardens). For tips on exploring these shopping zones, see page 329 in the Shopping in Florence chapter.

Starring: Raphael, Titian, and the most ornate palace you can tour in Florence.

The Tour Begins

The plain and brutal Pitti Palace facade is like other hide-your-wealth palace exteriors in Florence. The Pitti family (rivals of the Medici family) began building it in 1458 but ran out of money. It sat unfinished until the Medici bought it, expanded it, and moved in during the mid-1500s, choosing to keep the name. It's an imposing facade—more than two football fields long, made of heavy blocks of unpolished stone, and set on a hill. For nearly two centuries (1549-1737), this palace was arguably Europe's cultural center, setting trends in the arts, sciences, and social mores.

• *Enter the palace through the central doorway and into the courtyard. From here, all of the sights are well marked: The Palatine Gallery entrance is to your right, the Boboli Gardens entrance is straight ahead, and the Argenti/Silverworks Museum is to the left. Climb several flights of stairs to the Palatine Gallery (Galleria Palatina).*

PALATINE GALLERY

• *Enter Room 1 of the Palatine Gallery. (If there's a temporary exhibit, your visit may begin in the large white ballroom, which then leads into Room 1.)*

The collection is all on one floor. To see the highlights, walk straight down the spine through a dozen or so rooms. (Avoid the rooms that branch off to the side.) At the far end, make a U-turn left and double back. After the Palatine Gallery, the route flows naturally into the even-more-lavish rooms of the Royal Apartments.

You'll walk through one palatial room after another, with frescoed ceilings that celebrate the Medici family and give the rooms their names (the Venus Room, Apollo Room, and so on). The walls sag with floor-to-ceiling paintings in gilded frames, stacked three and four high, different artists and time periods all jumbled together. Use the information folders in each room to help find the featured paintings. Even with their help, it's still difficult to pick out the masterpieces from the minor pieces. Focus on my recommended highlights first, then let yourself browse.

Rooms 1 and 2

• *Immediately to your right as you enter is the...*

Pitti Palace—Palatine Gallery

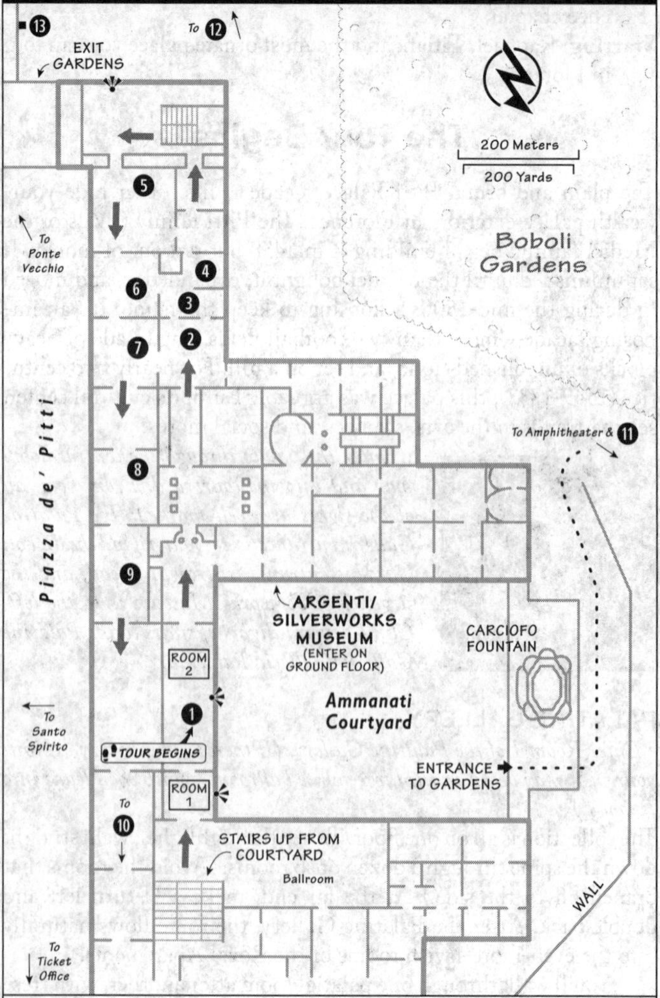

1. Bust of Cosimo I & Garden Views
2. FILIPPO LIPPI – Madonna and Child
3. RAPHAEL – Holy Family
4. Napoleon's Bathroom
5. RAPHAEL – Portrait of a Woman
6. RAPHAEL – Madonna of the Grand Duke; Tommaso Inghirami; Agnolo and Maddalena Doni; Madonna with Child and St. John the Baptist
7. RAPHAEL – Veiled Woman
8. TITIAN – Mary Magdalene; Portrait of a Man
9. TITIAN – Portrait of a Lady; Pietro Aretino; The Concert; CANOVA – Venus Italica
10. To Royal Apartments
11. To Porcelain Museum & City Views
12. To Grotto of Buontalenti
13. Bacchus Fountain

Bronze Bust of Cosimo I

Thank Cosimo I de' Medici (1519-1574, with beard and crown) for this palace. Cosimo I (not to be confused with Cosimo the Elder, the 15th-century founder of the Medici clan) was the first Grand Duke, and the man who revived the Medici family's dominance a generation after the death of Lorenzo the Magnificent. Cosimo I's wife, Eleonora, bought the palace from the Pittis and convinced him and their 11 children to move there from their home in the Palazzo Vecchio. They used their wealth to expand Pitti, building the gardens and amassing the rich painting collection. This would be the Medici family home for the next 200 years.

• *Look out the windows to enjoy...*

Views of Boboli Gardens

Dotted with statues and fountains, the gardens seem to stretch forever. The courtyard below (by Ammanati) is surrounded by the palace on three sides; the fourth side opens up theatrically onto the gardens, which rise in terraces up the hillside. Cosimo I and his descendants could look out their windows at eye level onto the garden's amphitheater, ringed with seats around an obelisk that once stood in the Temple of Ramses II in Egypt. At this amphitheater, the Medici enjoyed plays and spectacles, including perhaps the first opera, *Euridice* (1600).

From the amphitheater, the central axis of the Boboli Gardens stair-steps up to the top of the hill (where there are great views of Florence and beyond). The gardens' expansive sightlines, sculpted foliage, geometric patterns, Greek statues, and bubbling fountains would serve as the model a century later for the gardens at Versailles.

• *Continue straight ahead through a handful of rooms until you reach a green-and-gold room virtually wallpapered with paintings.*

Sala di Prometeo (Room 17)

• *Inside this room, look for the fireplace topped with a round-framed painting.*

Fra Filippo Lippi—*Madonna and Child* (c. 1452)

This pure, radiant Virgin cradles a playful Jesus as he eats a pomegranate. Lippi's work combines medieval piety with new Renaissance techniques. It may be Florence's first *tondo* (circular artwork), an innovative format that soon became a Renaissance staple. Seed-eating Jesus adds a human touch, but the pomegranate was also a medieval symbol for new life and the Resurrection. In medieval style, the background relates episodes from different places and times, including Mary's birth to Anne (in bed, at left) and the meeting of Mary's parents (distant background, right). But these stories are set in rooms that are textbook Renaissance 3-D, with floor tiles and ceiling coffers that create the illusion of depth. The ladies bringing gifts to celebrate Mary's birth add another element of everyday Renaissance realism.

Compare Lippi's Madonna with two by Lippi's star pupil, **Botticelli** (one on the left wall, one on the right, both hung high). Botticelli borrowed much from Lippi, including the same facial features, pale skin, precise lines, and everyday details.

• *The next room is the...*

Sala di Ulisse (Room 22)

This was the Grand Duke's bedroom. One of Cosimo I's favorite paintings hangs above the fireplace.

Raphael—*Holy Family (Sacra Famiglia,* a.k.a. *Madonna dell'Impannata,* 1512-1514)

This work introduces us to the range of this great artist. There's the creamy, rosy beauty of the Virgin alongside the gritty wrinkles of St. Anne/Elizabeth. At first glance, it seems like a stately scene, until you notice that Jesus is getting tickled. Everyone is in motion—gazes pointed in all different directions—but they're also posed in a harmonious pyramid, with Jesus' crotch at the center. Little John the Baptist sticks a foot in our face and points to Jesus as The One. Also typical of the always-busy Raphael: The work was probably completed by some of his 50-plus assistants.

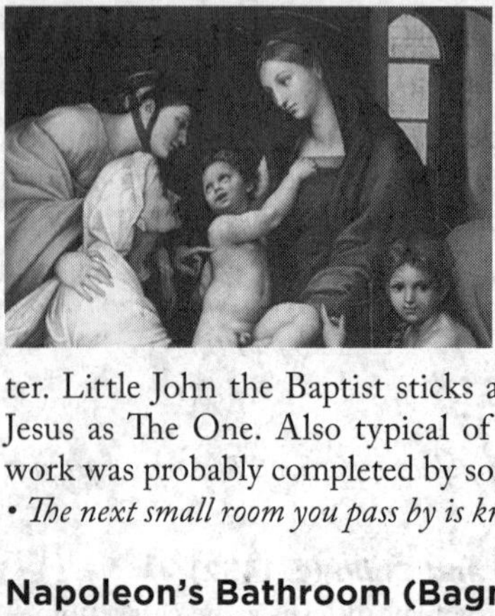

• *The next small room you pass by is known as...*

Napoleon's Bathroom (Bagno di Napoleone)

The white-marble luxury and sarcophagus-shaped bathtub were intended for the great French conqueror, Napoleon Bonaparte, when he ruled Florence (1799-1814). Napoleon installed his little sister

Elisa as Grand Duchess, and she spent her years here redecorating the palace, awaiting her brother's return. But Napoleon was not destined to meet this water loo. After he was toppled from power, the palace returned to its previous owners.

Over the centuries, the palace hosted several rulers: 200 years of Medici (c. 1549-1737); 100 years of Austrians (the Habsburg-Lorraines, 1737-1860); 15 years of Napoleon (1799-1814); and 60 years under the Savoys, Italy's first royal family (1860-1919), who made Pitti their "White House" when Florence was briefly the capital of modern Italy.

• *Pass through the final rooms and exit out the far end into the stairwell (with some handy benches). Ahhh. Admire the views of the Duomo, Palazzo Vecchio, and green hills of Fiesole in the distance. The Medici could commute from here to downtown Florence by way of a private, covered passageway (Vasari Corridor) that goes from Pitti Palace and across Ponte Vecchio to the Palazzo Vecchio. If you look down into the Boboli Gardens, you can see the melted-frosting entrance to the Buontalenti Grotto.*

As you continue on through the second half of the collection, the first room you enter is the...

Sala dell' Iliade (Room 27)

This is the first of several former staterooms, used for grand public receptions. For centuries, Europe's nobles, ladies, and statesmen passed through these rooms as they visited the Medici. They wrote home with wonder about the ceiling frescoes and masterpiece-covered walls. The ceiling frescoes depict the Greek gods cavorting with Medici princes, developing the idea of rule by divine right—themes that decades later would influence the decoration of Versailles. Turn your attention to the painting by the entrance door.

Raphael—*Portrait of a Woman* (*Ritratto di Donna,* a.k.a. *La Gravida,* 1505-1506)

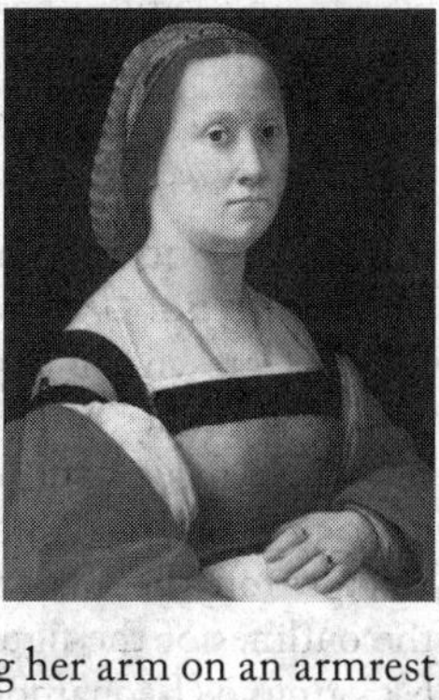

This rather plain-looking woman has one hand on her stomach and a serious expression on her face. She's pregnant. Though she is no Madonna, and her eyes don't sparkle, the woman has presence. Raphael's sober realism cuts through the saccharine excesses of the surrounding paintings.

As one of Raphael's earliest portraits, from his time in Florence, it shows the influence of Leonardo da Vinci. Like Mona Lisa, she's a human pyramid turned at a three-quarters angle, supporting her arm on an armrest

Raphael
(1483-1520)

Raphael (like most Renaissance greats, known by a single name) is considered the culmination of the High Renaissance. (Note that the museum uses his Italian name Raffaello, or Raffaello Sanzio.) He combined symmetry, grace, beauty, and emotion. With his debonair personality and lavish lifestyle, Raphael also epitomized the worldly spirit of the Renaissance.

Raphael lived a charmed life. Handsome and sophisticated, he quickly became a celebrity in the Medici family's high-living circle of bankers, princes, and popes. He painted masterpieces by day and partied by night. Both in his life and art, he exuded what his contemporaries called *sprezzatura*—an effortless, unpretentious elegance. In a different decade, he might have been thrown out of the Church as a great sinner, but his love affairs and devil-may-care personality were perfectly in keeping with the optimism of the times.

Raphael employed a wide range of styles and techniques, but there are some recurring elements. His paintings are bathed in an even light, with few shadows. His brushwork is smooth and blended, and colors are restrained. Works from the Florence years (1504-1508) show Leonardo's influence: Mona Lisa poses,

that's almost at the level of the frame itself. It's as if she's sitting near the edge of an open window, looking out at us.

• *Enter the next room, straight ahead.*

Sala di Saturno (Room 28)

This room boasts the second-biggest Raphael collection in the world—the Vatican beats it by one. A half-dozen Raphael paintings ring the room at eye level, ranging from dreamy soft-focus Madonnas to down-to-earth, five-o'clock-shadow portraits.

• *Next to the door you just came through, find...*

Raphael—*Madonna of the Grand Duke* (*Madonna del Granduca,* 1505)

Raphael presents Mary in an unusually simple pose—standing, while she cradles baby Jesus under his bum. With no background, the whole focus is on Mother, lost in thought, and Child, looking right at us. Mary's dreamy face and Jesus' golden body seem to emerge from the shadows. Try as you might, you can't quite discern the outlines of the figures, as they blend seamlessly into the dark background (Leonardo's sfumato technique).

sfumato brushwork (soft outlines), and lots of sweet Madonnas and Holy Families in a pyramid format. On the other hand, Raphael's portraits are never saccharine. The poses are natural, and individual quirks are never glossed over. He captures the personality without a hint of caricature.

In his later years, Raphael experimented with more complex compositions and stronger emotions. In group scenes, Raphael wants you to follow his subjects' gazes as they exchange glances or look off in different directions. This adds a sense of motion and psychological tension to otherwise well-balanced scenes. Raphael's compositions always have a strong geometric template. Figures are arranged into a pyramid or a circle. Human bodies are composed of oval faces, cylindrical arms, and arched shoulders. Subconsciously, this creates the feeling that God's created world is geometrically perfect. But Raphael always lets a bit of messy reality spill over the lines so his scenes don't appear static. His work comes across as simple and unforced...*sprezzatura.*

When Raphael died in 1520, he was one of Europe's most celebrated painters (along with Michelangelo and Titian). His style went out of fashion with the twisted forms of Mannerism and over-the-top drama of Baroque. The 1700s saw a revival, and today's museums are stuffed with sappy Madonnas by Raphael's many imitators. It's easy to dismiss his work and lump him in with his wannabes. Don't. This is the real deal.

The apparently simple pose is actually a skillful, geometric composition. Mary's head and flowing mantle form a triangle.

The triangle's base is, first, the neckline of her dress, then her belt, then the horizontal line formed by her arm and Jesus' thighs. The geometric symmetry is enlivened by an off-kilter touch of reality: Mary's head tilts ever-so-slightly to the side.

This Madonna radiates tenderness and holiness, the divine embodied in human form. The iconic face, the pale colors, the simple pose, the geometric perfection—all are classic Raphael.

• *Now survey a few more paintings, moving clockwise through the room. At the right end of the same wall as the* Madonna del Granduca *is...*

Raphael—*Portrait of Tommaso Inghirami* (c. 1510)

Wearing his bright red Cardinal's suit, Tommaso was the friend and librarian of the Medici pope, Leo X. Raphael captures him during an unposed moment, as he pauses to think while writing. Without glossing over anything, Raphael shows us the man just as he was, complete with cleft chin, jowls, lazy eye, and all.

• *On the next wall, look for...*

Raphael—Companion Portraits of Agnolo and Maddalena Doni (c. 1505-1506)

These portraits are as crystal clear as the *Madonna del Granduca* is hazy. They're a straightforward look at an upwardly mobile Florentine couple. He was a successful businessman in the textile trade (who commissioned Michelangelo's *Holy Family* in the Uffizi), and she was the daughter of one of the city's richest families. Raphael places them right at the edge of the picture plane, showing off his fine clothes and her jewelry.

• *Immediately to the left of the door leading to the next room is...*

Raphael—*Madonna with Child and St. John the Baptist* (*Madonna dell' Seggiola*, c. 1514-1516)

This colorful, round painting (also known as the *Madonna of the Chair*) is one of Raphael's best-known and most-copied works. Mary hugs Baby Jesus, squeezing him along with little John the Baptist. This Mary is no distant Madonna; she wears a peasant's scarf and a colorful dress and looks directly out at us with a cheerful half-smile. The composition plays on the theme of circles and spheres. The whole canvas is patterned after round sculpture-relief *tondi.* Mary's halo is a circle, her scarf forms a half-circle, and her face is an oval. The pudgier-than-normal

Bambino exaggerates the overall roundness of the scene. Mother and child fit together like interlocking half-circles. As in a cameo, the figures seem to bulge out from the surface, suggesting roundness. Bathed in a golden glow, Mary enfolds her child into the safe circle of motherly love.

• *Head into the next room.*

Sala di Giove (Room 29)

Here in the throne room, the Grand Duke once saw visitors beneath a ceiling fresco showing Jupiter receiving legendary guests.

• *To the left of the door leading into the next room is...*

Raphael—*Veiled Woman (La Velata,* 1514-1515)

The dark-haired beauty's dark eyes stare intently at the viewer. The elaborate folds of her shiny silk dress contrast with her creamy complexion. It's a study in varying shades of white and brown, bathed in a diffuse golden glow. A geometric perfection underlies this woman's soft, flesh-and-blood beauty: Her ovoid face, almond eyes, arch-shaped eyebrows, and circular necklace are all framed by a triangular veil. She is the very picture of perfection...except for that single wisp of loose hair that gives her the added charm of human imperfection.

Who is she? She may be the same woman Raphael depicted topless for a painting in Rome and as a Virgin (in Dresden). The biographer Vasari claims (and scholars debate) that La Velata is Raphael's beloved girlfriend Margherita Luti, known to history as La Fornarina, or the baker's daughter. Raphael became so obsessed with her that he had to have her near him to work. Vasari says that Raphael's sudden and premature death at age 37 came after a night of wild sex with her. Whoever La Velata is, she's one of the beauties of Western art.

• *Pass through the Sala di Marte (Room 30) and into the Sala di Apollo (Room 31). Two paintings by Titian flank the entrance door.*

Sala di Apollo (Room 31)

Titian—*Mary Magdalene (La Maddalena,* c. 1530-1535)

According to medieval lore (but not the Bible), Mary Magdalene was a prostitute who repented when she heard the message of Jesus. Titian captures her right on the cusp between whore and saint. She's naked, though covered by her hair, which she pulls around her like a cloak as she gazes heavenward, lips parted. Her hair is a rainbow of red, gold, and brown, and her ample flesh radiates gold. The rippling locks (echoed by gathering clouds in the background) suggest the inner turmoil and spiritual awakening of this passionate soul.

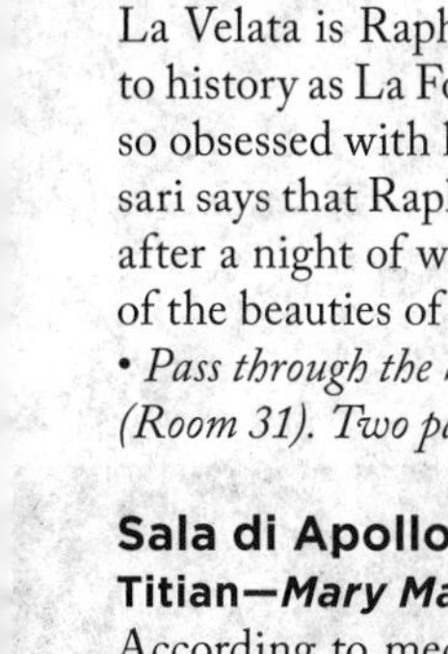

Among the upper classes in Renaissance times, Mary Magdalene was a symbol of how sensual enjoyment (food, money, sex) could be a way of celebrating God's creation. The way this Mary Magdalene places her hand to her breast and gathers her hair around her is also the classic "Venus Pudica" pose of many ancient Greek statues. It's simultaneously a gesture of modesty and a way of drawing attention to her voluptuous nudity.

Titian—*Portrait of a Man (Ritratto Virile,* c. 1545)

This unknown subject has so mesmerized viewers that his portrait has become known by various monikers, including *The Young Englishman, The Gray-Eyed Nobleman,* and *Doctor McDreamy's Evil Twin.* The man is dressed in dark clothes and set against a dim background, so we only really see his face and hands, set off by a ruffled collar and sleeves. He nonchalantly places his hand on his hip while holding a glove, and stares out. The man is unforgettable, with a larger-than-life torso and those piercing blue-gray eyes that gaze right at us with extreme intensity. Scholars have speculated that the man could be a well-known lawyer...eternally cross-examining the museumgoers.

• *In the next room, you'll find several more Titians.*

Sala di Venere (Room 32)

• *Survey the room in a clockwise order. First up, turn around and face the door you just came through. Immediately to the right is...*

Titian—*Portrait of a Lady* (*Ritratto di Donna,* a.k.a. *La Bella,* c. 1536)

Titian presents a beautiful *(bella)* woman in a beautiful dress to create a beautiful ensemble of colors: the aqua-and-brown dress, the gold necklace, pearl earrings, creamy complexion, auburn hair, and dark jewel-like eyes. She embodies the sensual, sophisticated, high-society world that Titian ran around in. The woman is likely Titian's Venus of Urbino, standing up and with her clothes on (see page 125). Scholars speculate on who she really was; perhaps she's Eleonora the Duchess of Urbino, or the mistress of the previous Duke, or maybe she's just a paid model that Titian found to be... beautiful.

• *At the right end of the same wall is...*

Titian—*Portrait of Pietro Aretino* (c. 1545)

The most notorious and outrageous figure in Renaissance high society was the writer Pietro Aretino (1492-1556). In 1527, he fled Rome, having scandalized the city with a collection of erotic/pornographic sonnets known as the *Sixteen Ways* (or sex positions). He took refuge in luxury-loving Venice, where he befriended Titian, a fellow connoisseur of eroticism and the arts. Titian and Aretino were both commoners, but they moved easily in court circles: Titian the diplomat and Aretino the fiery satirist who tweaked the noses of arrogant princes. (In fact, Aretino was part of the Rat Pack of rowdy Medici that included the father of Cosimo I.)

This portrait captures the self-confidence that allowed Aretino to stand up to royalty. Titian portrays him with the bearded face of an ancient satyr (a lecherous, untamed creature in Greek mythology). His torso is huge, like a smoldering volcano of irreverence that could erupt at any moment. Rather than the seamless brushstrokes and elaborate detail of Titian's earlier works, the figure of Aretino is composed of many rough strokes of gold and brown paint. Around age 60, Titian radically altered his style, adopting this "unfinished" look that the Impressionists would elaborate on centuries later. Aretino joked when he saw the portrait, "It breathes and moves as I do in the flesh. But perhaps [Titian] would have spent more time on my fine clothes—the robe, the silk, the gold chain—if I'd paid him more." Aretino gave the portrait to Cosimo I as a gift.

• *On the facing wall, just over the small table, find...*

Titian—*The Concert* (*Concerto,* 1510-1512)

An organ-playing man leans back toward his fellow musician (a monk), who's put down his cello to tap him on the shoulder. A young dandy in fancy clothes and a feathered cap looks on. The meaning of the work is a puzzle, perhaps intentionally so. Titian may have collaborated on this early painting with his colleague Giorgione, who specialized in enigmatic works used by cultured hosts as conversation starters.

Maybe it's just a slice-of-life snapshot of Venetian musicians briefly united in their common task. Or maybe it's a philosophical metaphor, in which a middle-aged man, blithely engaged in the gay music of his youth, is interrupted by a glimpse at his future—the bass notes and receding hairline of old age.

• *In the middle of the Sala di Venere stands...*

Canova—*Venus Italica* (*Venere,* 1810)

This pure white marble statue of Venus looks like the *Venus de' Medici* with a sheet (see page 121). Like the Medici Venus, she's nude, modestly crossing her hands in front of her (the "Venus Pudica" pose), while turning her head to the side. But Canova's Venus clutches a garment, which only highlights her naked vulnerability.

In 1796, a young French general named Napoleon Bonaparte toured the Uffizi and fell in love with the *Venus de' Medici*. A few

Titian
(c. 1490-1576)

Titian the Venetian (the museum uses his Italian name Tiziano or Tiziano Vecellio) captures the lusty spirit of his hometown. Titian was one of the most prolific painters ever, cranking out a painting a month for almost 80 years. He excelled in every subject: portraits of kings, racy nudes for bedrooms, creamy-faced Madonnas for churches, and pagan scenes from Greek mythology. He was cultured and witty, a fine musician and businessman—an all-around Renaissance kind of guy. Titian was famous and adored by high society, including Cosimo I and other Medici.

Titian's style changed over his long career. In his youth, he painted alongside Giorgione, even working on the same canvases (scholars still debate who did what). When he reached middle age, he found his voice: bright colors (particularly the famed "Titian red"), large-scale canvases, exuberant motion, and complex compositions, rebelling against the strict symmetry of early Renaissance. In his sixties, his technique became more impressionistic. He applied the paint in rough, thick brushstrokes, even using his fingers. In these late works, his figures don't pop from the background; instead, they blend in, creating a moody atmosphere.

Throughout his life, his bread and butter were portraits of Europe's movers and shakers—kings, popes, countesses, mistresses, artists, and thinkers. Without ever making the people who sat for him more handsome or heroic than they were, he captured both their outer likeness and their inner essence. Their clothes and accessories tell us about their social circle, so collectively, his portraits are a chronicle of the Renaissance in all its sensual glory.

years later, when he conquered Italy, he carried Venus off with him to Paris. To replace it, the great Venetian sculptor Canova was asked to make a copy. He refused to make an exact replica, but he agreed to do his own interpretation, combining motifs from many ancient Venuses of the Pudica (modest) and Callipigia (ample derriere) styles. Canova's *Venus Italica* stood in the Uffizi until Napoleon was conquered and *Venus de' Medici* returned.

• *From here, the rooms of the Palatine Gallery lead into the...*

ROYAL APARTMENTS

These 14 rooms (of which only a few are open at any one time) are where Florence's aristocrats lived in the 18th and 19th centuries. The decor reflects both Italian and French styles. In the 16th century, the two countries cross-pollinated when Catherine de' Medici (Lorenzo the Magnificent's great-granddaughter) married the king of France. Soon power shifted northward, which is why many of these rooms mimic the Versailles style, rather than vice versa. You'll see rooms of different themes and color schemes. Each room features the style of a particular time period. Ogle the velvety wallpaper, heavy curtains, white-and-gold stucco ceilings, chandeliers, and Louis XIV-style chairs, canopied beds, clocks, and candelabras. Gazing over it all are portraits of some of the people who lived in these rooms. Here, you get a real feel for the splendor of the dukes' world.

THE REST OF PITTI PALACE

If you've got the energy and interest, it'd be a Pitti to miss the palace's other offerings: the Boboli and Bardini Gardens, Argenti/Silverworks Museum (the Medici treasures), Costume Gallery, and Porcelain Museum (all covered by ticket #2; the Firenze Card covers everything except the Bardini Gardens).

Other Palatine Gallery Works

Art lovers can hunt down Titian's *Portrait of Filippo II of Spain* and *Portrait of Ippolito de' Medici;* Giorgione's *Three Ages of Man;* Caravaggio's *Sleeping Cupid* and *Portrait of Antonio Martelli (Cavaliere di Malta);* and many more.

Gallery of Modern Art

On the second floor, this gallery features Romantic, Neoclassical, and Impressionist works by 19th- and 20th-century Tuscan painters.

Costume Gallery

Also on the second floor, this fine collection displays centuries' worth of men's and women's fashions, with thoughtful explanations about the philosophical underpinnings of clothing styles. This is worth a linger for those interested in fashion, and interesting to anybody. The darkened room at the far end of the exhibit displays the clothes that Cosimo I and Eleonora of Toledo were buried in (later retrieved from their tombs and preserved—a rare chance to see original 16th-century garments).

Argenti/Silverworks Museum

This Medici treasure chest (on the ground and mezzanine floors) holds items such as jeweled crucifixes, exotic porcelain, rock-crystal goblets, and gilded ostrich eggs, made to entertain fans of the applied arts.

Boboli and Bardini Gardens

For those eager to escape the halls upon halls of fancy apartments, two adjoining gardens are located behind the palace. Enter the Boboli Gardens directly from Pitti Palace's courtyard. The less-visited Bardini Gardens are higher up and farther out behind the Boboli, rising in terraces toward Piazzale Michelangelo. Both gardens are similar, providing a pleasant and shady refuge from the city heat, with statues, fountains, and scenic vistas down tree-lined avenues.

A few fun little sights are in the low-lying area to the far left as you enter the Boboli Gardens. First, near the end of the palace, is the much-photographed **Bacchus Fountain** (Fontana di Bacco, 1560), starring Cosimo I's fat dwarf jester straddling a turtle—a fitting metaphor for this heavyweight palace.

Just beyond Bacchus is the **Grotto of Buontalenti,** an artificial cave crusted with fake stalactites and copies of Michelangelo's *Prisoners,* which once stood here (and are now in the Accademia). Playful figures—a hunter with his dog, goats, a monster—seem to morph into existence from the cottage cheese-like walls. At the top of the hour (check posted schedules), the grotto gates are opened for five minutes of frolicking among the statues.

You can also stroll up the steep terraces directly behind the palace. From the top, you're greeted by a panoramic view of the palace and Oltrarno churches (but only peek-a-boo views of the old town center, the Palazzo Vecchio, and Duomo). On your way up, you'll pass the **amphitheater** (ringed with statues). At the top, just beyond the hillcrest, is a pleasant **rose garden** with bucolic views of the rolling Tuscan hills (punctuated by cypress trees). The small building adjoining the rose garden houses the **Porcelain Museum,** with a modest and sparsely described collection of ducal dinnerware. From here, you can follow signs around to the **Belvedere Fortress,** with even higher and better views, and the Belvedere Gate, which leads to the Bardini Gardens.

GALILEO SCIENCE MUSEUM TOUR

Museo Galilei e Istituto di Storia della Scienza

Enough art, already! Forget the Madonnas and Venuses for a while to ponder weird contraptions from the birth of modern science. The same spirit of discovery that fueled the artistic Renaissance helped free the sciences from medieval mumbo jumbo. This museum offers a historical overview of technical innovations from roughly A.D. 1000 to 1900, featuring early telescopes, clocks, experiments, and Galileo's fingers in a jar.

English majors will enjoy expanding their knowledge. Art lovers can admire the sheer beauty of functional devices. Engineers will be in hog heaven among endless arrays of gadgets. Everyone will be fully amused by my feeble attempts to explain technical concepts. And admission to the museum gives you access to one of the marvels of modern science: air-conditioning.

Orientation

Cost: €9, €22 family ticket covers two adults and two kids ages 18 and under, cash only, tickets good all day, covered by Firenze Card.

Hours: Wed-Mon 9:30-18:00, Tue 9:30-13:00, last entry 30 minutes before closing.

Getting There: The museum is located one block east of the Uffizi on the north bank of the Arno River at Piazza dei Giudici 1.

Information: Tel. 055-265-311, www.museogalileo.it. Excellent English descriptions are posted throughout. Engaging video screens in many rooms illustrate the inventions and scientific principles (with information in English).

Tours: The well-produced €5 **audioguide** offers both a highlights tour as well as dial-up info (with video) on each exhibit. The 1.5-hour English-language **guided tour** covers the collection plus behind-the-scenes areas, and includes hands-on demonstrations of some of the devices (€50 flat fee for 2-14 people, cash only, doesn't include museum entry, book at least a week in advance, great for kids, tel. 055-234-3723, groups@museogalileo.it).

Length of This Tour: Allow one hour (or more, especially for those interested in science).

Photography: Permitted without a flash.

Starring: Galileo's telescopes, experiment models, and fingers.

The Tour Begins

The collection is on the first and second floors. Take advantage of the helpful English-speaking docents. They're available to answer questions about how these scientific gadgets work. In fact, the staff is happy that you're there to see this museum, and not just lost on your way to the Uffizi.

• *Buy your ticket and head up the stairs to the first floor, Room I.*

Room I: The Medici Collections

In this room, you immediately get a sense of the variety of devices to be found in the collection: everything from a big wooden quadrant and maps to optical illusions and old science books. These belonged to that trend-setting family, the Medici, who always seemed at the forefront of Europe's arts and sciences. Many of the objects we'll see measured the world around us—the height of distant mountains, the length of a man's arm, the movement of the sun and stars across the sky. In fact, one of the bold first steps in science was to observe nature and measure it. What scientists found was that nature—seemingly ever-changing and chaotic—actually behaves in an orderly way, following rather simple mathematical formulas.

Room II: Astronomy and Time

This room has (triangle-shaped) quadrants and (round) astrolabes. In medieval times, sailors used these to help them find their way at sea. They mapped the constellations as a starting point. Next they had to figure out where they stood in relation to those stars.

Quadrants: A *quad*-rant is one-*fourth* of a 360-degree circle, or 90 degrees. You'd grab this wedge-shaped object by its

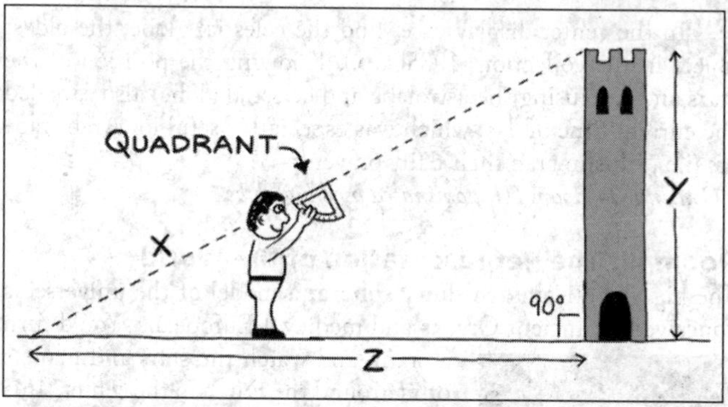

curved edge, point it away from you, and sight along the top edge toward, say, a distant tower or star. Then you'd read the scale etched along the curved edge to find how many degrees above the horizon the object was.

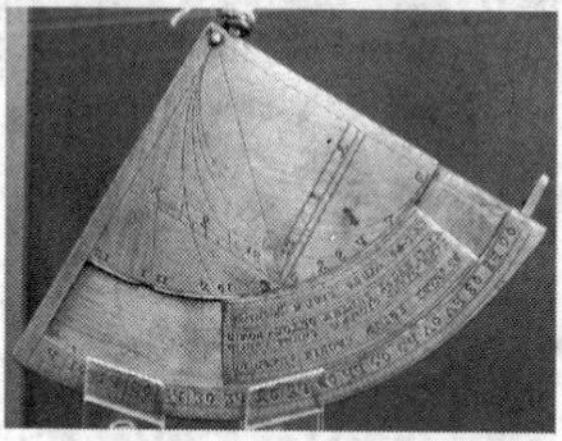

The quadrant *(quadrante)* measured the triangle formed by you, the horizon, and a distant object. Once you knew at least three of the triangle's six variables (three angles and three sides), you could calculate the others. (That's trigonometry.) Armed with this knowledge, you could use the quadrant to measure all kinds of things. On land, you could calculate how high or how far away a building was. At sea, you could figure your position relative to the sun and stars.

Astrolabes: Astrolabes—invented by the ancient Greeks and pioneered by medieval Arab sailors—combined a quadrant with a map of the sky (a star chart), allowing you to calculate your position against the stars without doing all of the math. You'd hang the metal disk from your thumb and sight along the central crossbeam, locate a star, then read its altitude above the horizon on the measuring scale etched around the rim.

Next, you'd enter this information by turning a little handle on the astrolabe's face. This set the wheels-within-wheels into motion, and the constellations would spin across a backdrop of coordinates. You'd keep turning until the astrolabe mirrored the current heavens. With your known coordinates dialed in, the astrolabe calculated the unknowns, and you could read out your position along the rim.

In the center display case, find the celestial globe, the oldest object in the collection (1085 A.D.). Knowing the position of the stars and sun (using the astrolabe and celestial globe) also revealed the current time of day, which was especially useful for Arab traders (i.e., Muslims) in their daily prayers.

• *Continue to Room III, dominated by a big globe.*

Room III: The Representation of the World

The big globe is an **armillary sphere,** a model of the universe as conceived by ancient Greeks and medieval Europeans. You'd turn a crank and watch the stars and planets orbit around the Earth in the center. This Earth-centered view of the universe—which matches our common-sense observations of the night sky—was codified by Ptolemy, a Greek-speaking Egyptian of the second century A.D.

Ptolemy (silent P) summed up Aristotle's knowledge of the heavens and worked out the mathematics explaining their movements. His math was complex, especially when trying to explain the planets, which occasionally lag behind the stars in their paths across the night sky. (We now know it's because fast-orbiting Earth passes the outer planets in their longer, more time-consuming orbits around the sun.)

Ptolemy's system dominated Europe for 1,500 years. It worked most of the time and fit well with medieval Christianity's human-centered theology. But, finally, Nicolaus Copernicus (and Galileo) made the mental leap to a sun-centered system. This simplified the math, explained the movement of planets, and—most importantly—changed Earthlings' conception of themselves forever.

Thanks to Columbus' voyages, the Europeans' world suddenly got bigger and rounder. Increasingly, maps began to portray the spherical world on a flat surface.

• *Pass through Room IV (with more globes and a map where south is up) and enter...*

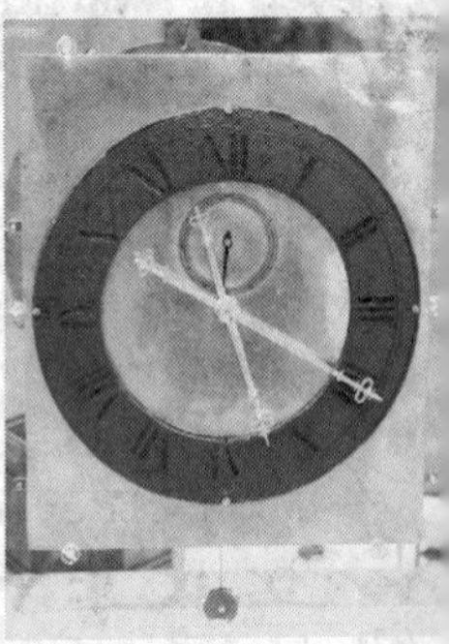

Room V: The Science of Navigation

This room has more quadrants and maps, plus a new navigational feature: clocks. By measuring time accurately, sailors could not only establish their latitude (north-south on the globe), but also their longitude (east-west).

In the 1700s, with overseas trade booming, there was a crying need for an accurate and durable clock to help in navigation. Sighting by the stars told you your latitude but was less certain on whether you were near Florence, Italy (latitude 44), or Portland, Maine (also latitude 44). You needed a way to time Earth's 24-hour rotation, to know exactly where you were on that daily journey—that is, your longitude. Reward money was offered for a good clock that could be taken to sea, and scientists sprang into action.

The longitude problem was finally solved—and a £20,000 prize won—by John Harrison of England (1693-1776), who developed the "chronometer" (not in this museum), a spring-driven clock that was set in a suspension device, to keep it horizontal. It was accurate within three seconds a day, far better than any clock displayed here.

• *Room VI (The Science of Warfare) displays not weapons but surveyors' tools, crucial for plotting the trajectory of, say, a cannonball. Next up is one of the museum's highlights.*

Room VII: Galileo's New World

Galileo Galilei (1564-1642) is known as the father of modern science. His discoveries pioneered many scientific fields, and he was among the first to blend mathematics with hands-on observation of nature to find practical applications. Raised in Pisa, he achieved fame teaching at the University of Padua before working for the Grand Duke of Florence. The museum displays several of his possessions (lens, two telescopes, compass, and thermometer), models illustrating his early experiments, and his fingers, preserved in a jar.

• *Immediately to the right, look for the case containing...*

Galileo's Telescopes: Galileo was the first Earthling to see the moons of Jupiter. With a homemade telescope, he looked through the lens and saw three moons lined up next to Jupiter. This discovery also irked the Church, which insisted that all heavenly bodies orbited the Earth. You could see Jupiter's moons with your own eyes if you simply looked through the telescope, but few church scholars bothered to do so, content to believe what they'd read in ancient books.

Galileo built these telescopes, based on reports he'd read from Holland. He was the first person to seriously study the heavens with telescopes. Though these only magnified the image about 30

times ("30 power," which is less than today's binoculars), he saw Jupiter's four largest moons, Saturn's rings, the craters of the moon (which he named "seas"), and blemishes (sunspots) on the supposedly perfect sun.

• *In the same case is a...*

Pendulum Clock Model: Galileo's restless mind roamed to other subjects. It's said that during a church service in Pisa, Galileo looked up to see the cathedral's chandelier swaying slowly back and forth, like a pendulum. He noticed that a wide-but-fast arc took the same amount of time as a narrow-but-slow arc. "Hmmm. Maybe that regular pendulum motion could be used to time things..."

• *The last case on this wall contains a...*

Thermoscope: Galileo also invented the thermometer (or thermoscope—similar to the museum's 19th-century replica), though his glass tube filled with air would later be replaced by thermometers filled with mercury.

• *Across the room is a giant model of an...*

Inclined Plane: The large wooden ramp figures in one of the most enduring of scientific legends. Legend has it that Galileo dropped cannonballs from the Leaning Tower of Pisa to see whether heavier objects fall faster than lighter ones, as the ancient philosopher Aristotle (and most people) believed. In fact, Galileo probably didn't drop objects from the Leaning Tower, but likely rolled them down a wooden ramp like this reconstructed one.

Rolling balls of different weights down the ramp, he timed them as they rang the bells posted along the way. (The bells are spaced increasingly far apart, but a ball—accelerating as it drops—will ring them at regular intervals.) What Galileo found is that—if you discount air resistance—all objects fall at the same rate, regardless of their weight. (It's the air resistance, not the weight, that makes a feather fall more slowly than a cannonball.)

He also found that falling objects accelerate at a regular rate (9.8 meters per second faster every second), summed up in a mathematical formula (distance is proportional to the time squared).

Galileo pioneered the art of experimentation. He built devices that could simulate nature on a small scale in a controlled laboratory setting, where natural forces could be duplicated and measured. In the following rooms, we'll see many of the experimental tools and techniques he inspired.

• *And last but not least, in the glass case perched on the column at the end of the benches, look for...*

Galileo's Fingers: Galileo is perhaps best known as a martyr

for science. He popularized the belief (conceived by the Polish astronomer Nicolaus Copernicus in the early 1500s) that the Earth orbits around the sun. At the time, the Catholic Church (and most of Europe) preached an Earth-centered universe. At the age of 70, Galileo was hauled before the Inquisition in Rome and forced to kneel and publicly proclaim that the Earth did not move around the sun. As he walked away, legend has it, he whispered to his followers, "But it does move!"

A century after his death, Galileo's followers preserved his finger bone *(Dito Medio della Mano Destra di Galileo)*, displayed on an alabaster pedestal, as a kind of sacred relic in this shrine to science. (This case also holds two other fingers and a tooth that were rediscovered a few years ago.) Galileo's beliefs eventually triumphed over the Inquisition, and, appropriately, we have his right middle finger raised upward for all those blind to science.

• *Room VIII has early glassware and thermometers (which you'll explore in greater depth in Room XV). Continue on to...*

Room IX: Exploring the Physical and Biological World

This room has both telescopes (for observing objects far away) and microscopes (to see the world up close).

A **telescope** is essentially an empty tube with a lens at the far end to gather light, and another lens at the near end to magnify the image. The farther apart the lenses, the greater the magnification, which is why telescopes have increased in size over time. The longest ever built was 160 feet, but the slightest movement would jiggle the image.

Galileo used a "refracting telescope," made with lenses that bend (refract) light. Later on, scientists started using "reflecting telescopes," which were often thick-barreled, with the eyepiece sticking out the side. These telescopes use mirrors (not lenses) to bounce light rays back and forth through several lenses, thereby increasing magnification without the long tubes and distortion of refractors.

• *Ascend to the second floor and enter Room X.*

Room X: The Lorraine Collections (Medical Science)

Look at the big table with all the drawers and jars in the glass case in the center of the room. Back when the same guy who cut your

hair removed your appendix, medicine was crude. In the 1700s, there were no anesthetics beyond a bottle of wine, nor was there any knowledge of antiseptics. The best they could do was resort to the healing powers of herbs and plants. Consider what was thought to be therapeutic in the 1700s: cocaine, anise, poisonous plants like belladonna, tea, and ipecac.

The room also displays models detailing the varieties of complications that could arise during childbirth. Not a pretty sight, but crucial to finding ways to save lives.

Room XI: The Spectacle of Science

This room is filled with odd-looking devices used by scientists to instruct and amaze. Chief among them, in the middle of the room, are the turn-the-crank machines dealing with electricity.

Electromagnetism: Lightning, magnets, and static cling mystified humans for millennia. Little did they know that these quite different phenomena are all generated by the same invisible force—electromagnetism.

In the 1700s, scientists began to study, harness, and play with electricity. As a popular party amusement, they devised big static electricity-generating machines. You turned a crank to spin a glass disk, which rubbed against silk cloth and generated static electricity. The electricity could then be stored in a glass Leyden jar (a jar coated with metal and filled with water). A metal rod sticking out of the top of the jar gave off a small charge when touched, enough to create a spark, shock a party guest, or tenderize a turkey (as Ben Franklin attempted one Thanksgiving). But such static generators could never produce enough electricity for practical use.

• *In the corner near where you entered, look for a...*

Model for Demonstrating Newton's Mechanics: Isaac Newton (1642-1727) explained all of the universe's motion ("mechanics")—from spinning planets to rolling rocks—in a few simple mathematical formulas.

The museum's collision balls (the big wooden frame with hanging balls—labeled "Elastic and Inelastic Collisions Apparatus"), a popular desktop toy in the 1970s, demonstrate Newton's three famous laws.

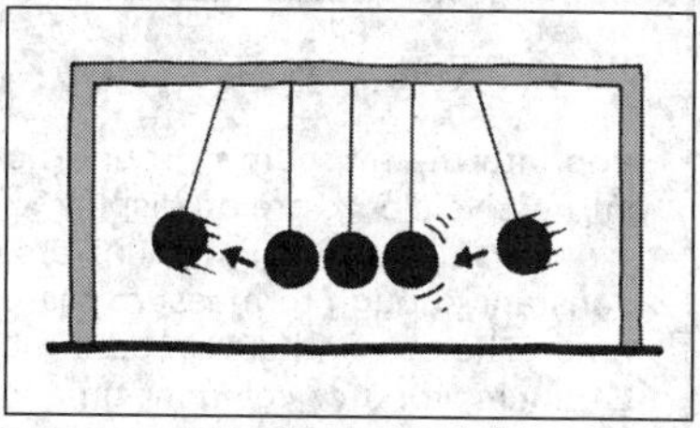

1. Inertia: The balls just sit there unless something moves them, and once they're set in motion, they'll keep moving the same way until something stops them.
2. Force = Mass × Acceleration: The harder you strike the balls, the more they accelerate (change speeds). Strike with two balls to pack twice the punch.
3. For every action, there's an equal and opposite reaction: When one ball swings in and strikes the rest, the ball at the other end swings out, then returns and strikes back.

• *Rooms XII and XIII have devices formerly used to teach the "new" physics of Newton. In Room XIII is a famous model.*

Room XIII: The Archimedes Screw Model

Back in third-century B.C. Greece, Archimedes—the man who gave us the phrase "Eureka!" ("I've found it!")—invented a way to pump water that's still occasionally used today. It's a screw in a cylinder. Simply turn the handle and the screw spins, channeling the water up in a spiral path (as seen in the video in Room XII). Dutch windmills powered big Archimedes screws to push water over dikes, reclaiming land from the sea.

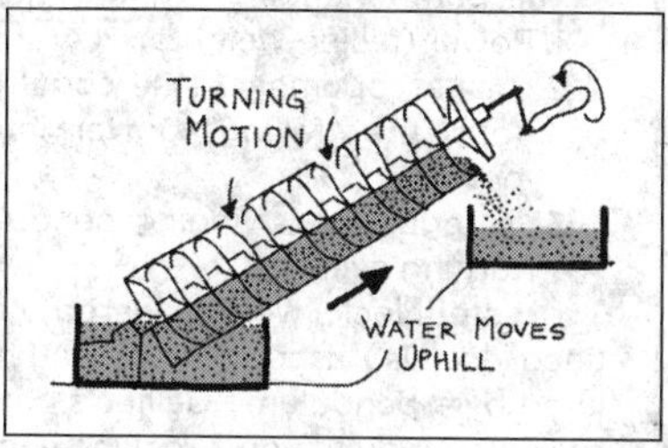

Room XIV: Precision Instruments

This room shows the development of big reflecting **telescopes** and finer **microscopes.**

One day, a Dutchman picked something from his teeth, looked at it under his crude microscope, and discovered a mini-universe, crawling with thousands of "very little animalcules, very prettily a-moving" (i.e., bacteria and protozoa). Antonie van Leeuwenhoek (1632-1723) popularized the microscope, finding that

Tick, Tock, Clocks

Pop into the museum's ground-floor bookshop, where some impressive clocks are on display.

In an ever-changing universe, what is constant enough to measure the passage of time? The sun and stars passing over every 24 hours work for calendar time, but not for hours, minutes, or seconds. Since the time of the Greeks, man used sundials, or the steady flow of water or sand through an opening, but these were only approximate.

In medieval times, humans invented mechanical clocks that work similarly to the classic grandfather clock. The clock is powered by suspended weights that slowly "fall," producing enough energy to turn a series of cogwheels that methodically move the clock hands around the dial. The whole thing is regulated by a pendulum rocking back and forth, once a second. A clock has three essential components:

1. Power (falling weights).
2. An "escapement" (the cogs that transform the "falling" power into turning power).
3. A regulator (swinging pendulum) that keeps the gears turning evenly.

Later clocks were powered by a metal spring that slowly uncoiled (also used in most watches). The power was regulated by a pendulum—Galileo's contribution. Unfortunately, a rocking pendulum on a rocking ship wasn't going to work.

During the so-called Age of Reason (1600s) and Age of Enlightenment (1700s), the clock was the perfect metaphor for the orderly workings of God's well-crafted universe. So, wondered the philosophers/scientists, would the universe eventually wind down like an old clock? In fact, in every energy exchange (as stated in the second law of thermodynamics), a certain amount of energy is transformed into nonrecyclable heat, meaning a perpetual motion machine is impossible. This principle of entropy (the trend toward dissipation of energy) has led philosophers to ponder the eventual cold, lifeless fate of the universe itself.

fleas have fleas, semen contains sperm, and one-celled creatures are our fellow animals.

Microscopes can be either simple or compound. A simple one is just a single convex lens—what we'd call a magnifying glass. A compound microscope contains two (or more) lenses in a tube, working like a telescope: One lens magnifies the object, and the eyepiece lens magnifies the magnified image. Van Leeuwenhoek opted for a simple microscope (not in this museum), since early compound ones often blurred and colored objects around the edges. His glass bead-size lens could make a flea look 275 times bigger.

Room XV: Atmosphere and Light

Even nature's most changeable force—the weather—was analyzed by human reason, using thermometers and barometers.

Thermometers: You'll see many interesting thermometers—spiral ones, tall ones, and skinny ones on distinctive bases. All operate on the basic principle that heat expands things. So, liquid in a closed glass tube will expand and climb upward as the temperature rises.

Galileo's early thermoscope was not hermetically sealed, so it was too easily affected by changing air pressure. So scientists experimented with various liquids in a vacuum tube—first water, then alcohol. Finally, Gabriel Fahrenheit (1686-1736) tried mercury, the densest liquid, which expands evenly. He set his scale to the freezing point of a water/salt/ice mixture (zero degrees) and his own body temperature (96 degrees). With these parameters, water froze at 32 degrees and boiled at 212 degrees. Anders Celsius (1701-1744) used water as the standard, and called the freezing point 0 and the boiling point 100.

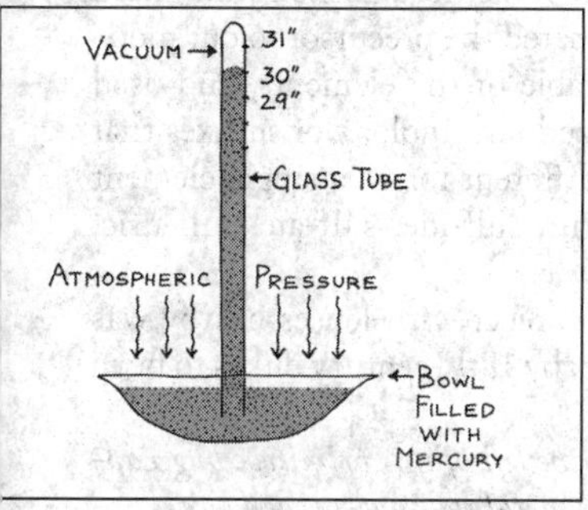

Barometers: To make a barometer, take a long, skinny glass tube (like the ones in the wood frames), fill it with liquid mercury, then turn it upside-down and put the open end into a bowlful of more mercury. The column of mercury does not drain out, because the air in the room "pushes back," pressing down on the surface of the mercury in the bowl.

Changing air pressure signals a shift in the weather. Hot air expands, pressing down harder on the mercury's surface, thereby causing the mercury column to rise above 30 inches; this indicates the "pushing away" of clouds and points to good, dry weather. Low pressure lets the mercury drop, warning of rain. If you have a barometer at home, it probably has a round dial with a needle (or a digital readout), but it operates on a similar principle.

• *In the next room, you'll find (among magnets, generators, and small machines) a couple of early batteries.*

Room XVI: Electricity

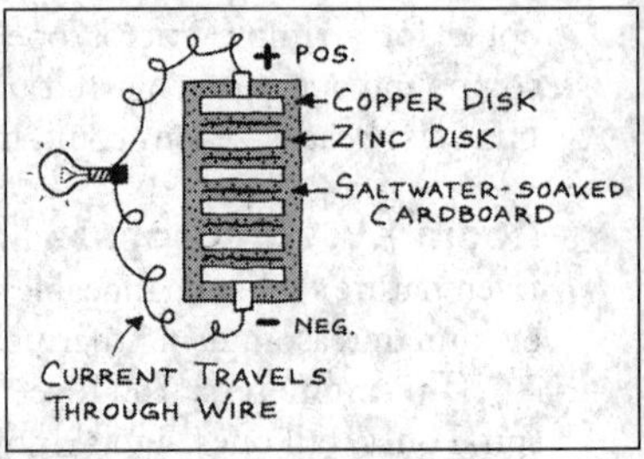

Alessandro Volta (1745-1827) built the first battery in Europe. (Although the museum does not have one of Volta's batteries, it does have similar devices.) A battery generates electricity from a chemical reaction. Volta (and others) stacked metal disks of zinc and copper between disks of cardboard soaked with salt water. The zinc slowly dissolves, releasing electrons into the liquid. Hook a wire to each end of the battery, and the current flows. When the zinc is gone, your battery is dead.

England's Michael Faraday (c. 1831) created the first true electric motor, which could generate electricity by moving a magnet through a coil of copper wire. Faraday shocked the world (and occasionally himself), and his invention soon led to the production of electricity on a large scale.

Room XVII: Making Science Useful

Chemistry: Antoine Lavoisier (1743-1794) was the Galileo of chemistry, introducing sound methodology and transforming the mumbo jumbo of medieval alchemy into hard science. He created the precursor to our modern periodic table of the elements, and used the standardized terminology of suffixes that describe the different forms a single element can take (sulfur, sulf-ide, sulf-ate, sulf-uric, etc.).

The large object-with-lenses nearby was used, I believe, by 18th-century dukes to burn bugs.

• *In the case to the left of this primitive bug zapper, look for the metal rod in a wooden box.*

Standard Meter: Much of the purpose of science is to use constants to measure an ever-changing universe. For centuries, one of these constants was the meter-long metal rod, established in 1790 as the fundamental unit by which all distances are measured.

The rod is exactly one meter. Or 39.37 inches. Or 1/1,000th of the distance from the Galileo Science Museum to *David.* Or 1/10,000,000th of the distance from the equator to the North Pole. Or, according to the updated definition from 1960, a meter is the length of 1,650,763.73 wavelengths in a vacuum of the orange-red radiation of krypton 86. Ain't science wonderful?

• *On the way out, Room XVIII is filled with novelty pieces—a barometer hidden in a walking stick, a portable pharmacy kit, and an early air-conditioner (ventilator/fan). Downstairs, you'll pass through a fun kids' zone with hands-on exhibits and touchscreens, and (just before the shop) lots of clocks from various historical periods.*

SLEEPING IN FLORENCE

Contents

Competition among hotels is stiff. When things slow down, fancy hotels drop their prices and become a much better value for travelers than the cheap, low-end places. For information and tips on pricing, getting deals, making reservations, seasonal differences (peak season versus off-season), and much more, see page 632 of the Practicalities chapter.

I like hotels that are handy to the great sights. Nearly all of my recommended accommodations are located in the center of Florence. If arriving by train, you can either walk (usually around 10 minutes) or take a taxi (roughly €6-8) to reach most of my recommended accommodations, as buses don't cover the city center very well.

Florence is notorious for its mosquitoes. If your hotel lacks air-conditioning, request a fan and don't open your windows, especially at night. Many hotels furnish a small plug-in bulb *(zanzariere)*—usually set in the ashtray—that helps keep the blood-suckers at bay. If not, you can purchase one cheaply at any pharmacy *(farmacia)*.

Museumgoers take note: Your hotelier may be able to reserve entry times for you at the Uffizi Gallery and the Accademia (Michelangelo's *David*). This can be handy if you don't plan to get a Firenze Card, and don't want to bother with reserving these sights yourself (for both options, see page 34). If interested, ask about it when you book your room. Most likely the hotelier will book your museum visits by phone, then give you a confirmation number that you'll take to the museum, where you'll pay cash for your ticket. Your hotel may charge a fee for this service.

North of the Arno River

NEAR THE DUOMO

All of these places are within a block of Florence's biggest church and main landmark. While touristy—and expensive—this location puts just about everything in town at your doorstep.

$$$ Palazzo Niccolini al Duomo, one of five elite Historic Residence Hotels in Florence, is run by Niccolini da Camugliano. The lounge (where free chamomile tea is served in the evenings) is palatial, but the 12 rooms, while splendid, vary wildly in size. If you have the money and want a Florentine palace to call home, this can be a good bet (Db-€240, bigger rooms up to €500, ask for 10 percent Rick Steves discount when you book directly with the hotel, check online to choose a room and consider last-minute deals, elevator, air-con, free guest computer, Wi-Fi, Via dei Servi 2, tel. 055-282-412, www.niccolinidomepalace.com, info@niccolinidomepalace.com).

$$$ Hotel Duomo's 24 rooms are modern and comfortable enough, but you're paying for the location and the views—the Duomo looms like a monster outside the hotel's windows. If staying here, you might as well spring the extra €20 for a "superior" room with a view (Sb-€110, Db-€180, Tb-€230, 10 percent discount with this book if you pay cash, air-con, elevator, Wi-Fi, Piazza del Duomo 1, fourth floor, tel. 055-219-922, www.hotelduomofirenze.it, info@hotelduomofirenze.it; Paolo and Gilvaneide).

$$ Residenza dei Pucci rents 13 pleasant rooms (each one different) spread over three floors. The decor, a mix of soothing earth tones and aristocratic furniture, makes this place feel upscale for this price range (Sb-€135, Db-€150, Tb-€170, Qb suite-€238, 10 percent discount with this book if you pay cash, air-con, no elevator, Wi-Fi, reception open 9:00-20:00, shorter hours off-season—let them know if you'll arrive late, Via dei Pucci 9, tel. 055-281-886, www.residenzadeipucci.com, info@residenzadeipucci.com, friendly Mirella and Marina).

$$ Soggiorno Battistero rents seven simple, airy rooms, most with great views, overlooking the Baptistery and the Duomo square. Request a view or a quieter room in the back when you book, but keep in mind there's always some noise in the city center. It's a pristine and minimalist place run by Italian Luca and his American wife Kelly, who makes the hotel particularly welcoming

(Sb-€83, Db-€110, Tb-€145, Qb-€155, 5 percent discount if you book directly with the hotel and pay cash, breakfast served in room, air-con available June-Aug, elevator, Wi-Fi, Piazza San Giovanni 1, third floor, tel. 055-295-143, www.soggiornobattistero.it, info@soggiornobattistero.it).

$$ Residenza Giotto B&B offers the chance to stay on Florence's upscale shopping drag, Via Roma. Occupying the top floor of a 19th-century building, this place has six bright, slightly scruffy rooms and a terrace with knockout views of the Duomo's tower. Reception is generally open 9:00-17:00; let them know your arrival time in advance (Sb-€90, Db-€139, view rooms-€10 extra, extra bed-€25, 10 percent discount if you book direct and pay cash, air-con, elevator, Wi-Fi, Via Roma 6, tel. 055-214-593, www.residenzagiotto.it, info@residenzagiotto.it, Giorgio).

$$ La Residenza del Proconsolo B&B, run by helpful Mariano, has five older-feeling rooms a minute from the Duomo (three rooms have Duomo views). The place lacks public spaces, but the rooms are quite large and nice—perfect for eating breakfast, which is served in your room (Sb-€90, Db-€120, Tb-€140, slightly larger "deluxe" with view-€20 more, air-con, no elevator, Wi-Fi, Via del Proconsolo 18 black, tel. 055-264-5657, mobile 335-657-4840, www.proconsolo.com, info@proconsolo.com).

NORTH OF THE DUOMO

North of Mercato Centrale

After dark, this neighborhood can feel a little deserted, but I've never heard of anyone running into harm here. It's a short walk from the train station and an easy stroll to all the sightseeing action. While workaday, it's practical, with plenty of good budget restaurants and markets nearby.

$$ Relais Grand Tour has five charming rooms on a nondescript street between the train station and the Accademia. This cozy B&B will make you feel right at home; it's thoughtfully appointed and the owners, Cristina and Giuseppe, live there. The delightful and spacious suites come with a garden ambience on the ground floor (Db-€115, suite-€135, 10 percent discount with this book if you book directly with hotel and pay cash, includes breakfast voucher for the corner bar—or skip it to save €7/person, skip daily cleaning to save €11/day, air-con, Wi-Fi, Via Santa Reparata 21, tel. 055-283-955, www.florencegrandtour.com, info@florencegrandtour.com). They run another more romantic, pricier place a couple of blocks away.

$$ Galileo Hotel, a comfortable business hotel with 31 rooms on a chaotic and congested street, is run with familial warmth (Sb-€100, Db-€130, Tb-€160, Qb-€190, ask for 10 percent Rick Steves discount when you book directly with hotel and pay cash, quadru-

Sleep Code

(€1 = about $1.40, country code: 39)

Abbreviations

S = Single, **D** = Double/Twin, **T** = Triple, **Q** = Quad, **b** = bathroom, **s** = shower only

Price Rankings

$$$ Higher Priced—Most rooms €160 or more.

$$ Moderately Priced—Most rooms between €100-160.

$ Lower Priced—Most rooms €100 or less.

Unless otherwise noted, credit cards are accepted, staff speak basic English, breakfast is included, and Wi-Fi is generally free. Florence charges a hotel tax of €1 per star (according to the hotel's official star rating) per person per night, which is generally not included in the rates I've quoted—a couple staying at a three-star hotel would pay €3 each, or €6 total, per night. Prices change; verify current rates online or by email. For the best prices, always book directly with the hotel.

ple-paned windows effectively shut out street noise, air-con, elevator, guest computer, Wi-Fi, Via Nazionale 22a, tel. 055-496-645, www.galileohotel.it, info@galileohotel.it).

$$ Hotel Il Bargellino, run by Bostonian Carmel and her Italian husband Pino, is in a residential neighborhood within walking distance of the center. They rent 10 summery rooms decorated with funky antiques and Pino's modern paintings. Guests enjoy Leopoldo, the parrot, and relaxing on the big, breezy, momentum-slowing terrace adorned with plants and lemon shrubs (S-€45, D-€90, Db-€100, €5 more for room facing terrace, book directly with hotel and ask for Rick Steves rate, extra bed-€25, no breakfast, Wi-Fi, north of the train station at Via Guelfa 87, tel. 055-238-2658, www.ilbargellino.com, carmel@ilbargellino.com).

$ Casa Rabatti is the ultimate if you always wanted to have a Florentine mama. Its four simple, clean rooms are run with warmth by Marcella. This is a great place to practice your Italian, since Marcella loves to chat and speaks minimal English. Seeing nearly two decades of my family Christmas cards on their walls, I'm reminded of how long she has been keeping budget travelers happy (D-€50, Db-€60, €25 extra per bed in shared quad or quint, prices good with this book, cash only but secure reservation with credit card, no breakfast, fans available, Wi-Fi, 5 blocks from station at Via San Zanobi 48 black, tel. 055-212-393, casarabatti@inwind.it).

$ Hotel Enza rents 18 straightforward rooms, some recently

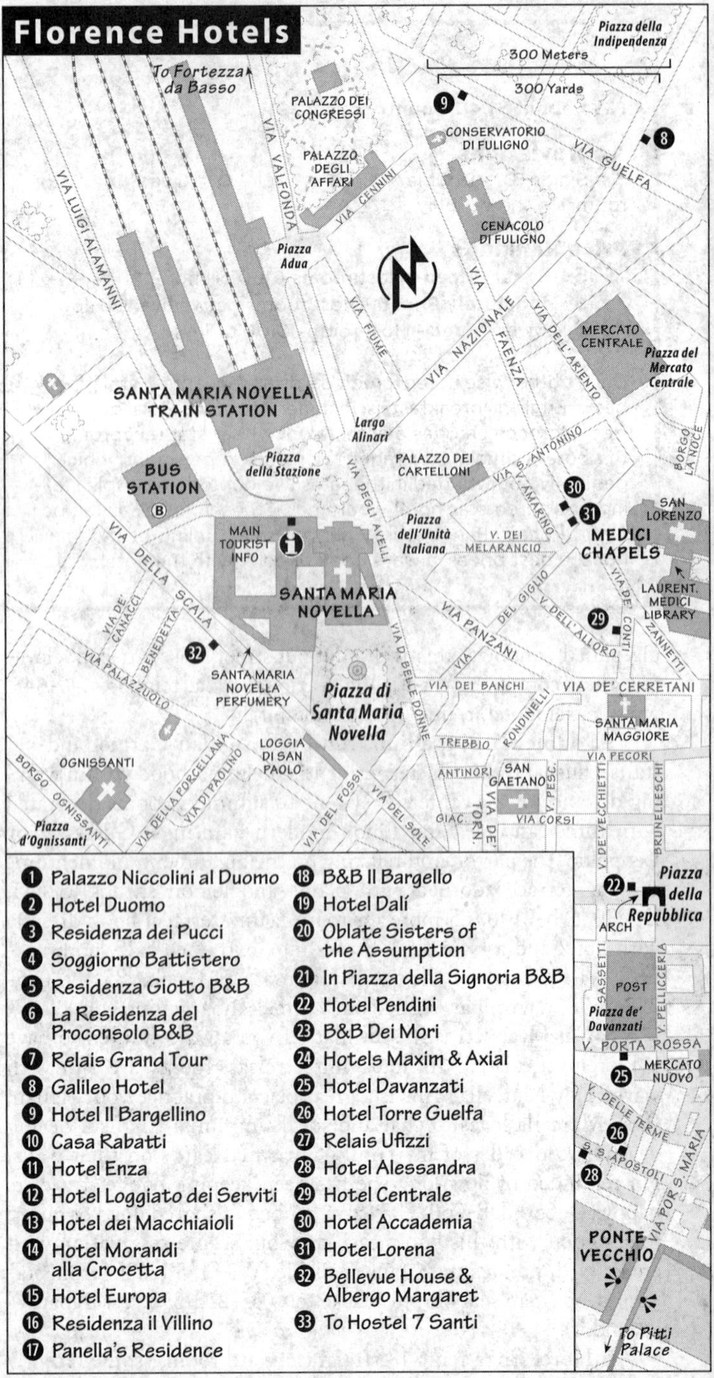

Florence Hotels
Piazza della Indipendenza
300 Meters
300 Yards
To Fortezza da Basso
PALAZZO DEI CONGRESSI
PALAZZO DEGLI AFFARI
VIA VALFONDA
VIA CENNINI
CONSERVATORIO DI FULIGNO
VIA GUELFA
CENACOLO DI FULIGNO
VIA LUIGI ALAMANNI
Piazza Adua
VIA FIUME
VIA NAZIONALE
VIA FAENZA
VIA DELL'ARIENTO
MERCATO CENTRALE
Piazza del Mercato Centrale
SANTA MARIA NOVELLA TRAIN STATION
Largo Alinari
BORGO LA NOCE
BUS STATION
Piazza della Stazione
PALAZZO DEI CARTELLONI
VIA S. ANTONINO
V. AMARINO
SAN LORENZO
VIA DEGLI AVELLI
MAIN TOURIST INFO
Piazza dell'Unità Italiana
V. DEI MELARANCIO
MEDICI CHAPELS
VIA DELLA SCALA
SANTA MARIA NOVELLA
VIA DEL GIGLIO
V. DELL'ALLORO
VIA DE' CONTI
LAURENT. MEDICI LIBRARY
VIA DE' CANACCI
BENEDETTA
VIA PANZANI
ZANNETTI
VIA PALAZZUOLO
SANTA MARIA NOVELLA PERFUMERY
Piazza di Santa Maria Novella
VIA D. BELLE DONNE
VIA DEI BANCHI
RONDINELLI
VIA DE' CERRETANI
SANTA MARIA MAGGIORE
TREBBIO
OGNISSANTI
LOGGIA DI SAN PAOLO
VIA DELLA PORCELLANA
VIA DI PAOLINO
ANTINORI
SAN GAETANO
VIA PECORI
BORGO OGNISSANTI
VIA DEL FOSSI
VIA DEL SOLE
GIAC.
VIA DE' TORN.
V. PESC.
VIA CORSI
V. DE' VECCHIETTI
BRUNELLESCHI
Piazza d'Ognissanti
Piazza della Repubblica
ARCH
SASSETTI
V. PELLICCERIA
POST
Piazza de' Davanzati
V. PORTA ROSSA
MERCATO NUOVO
V. DELLE TERME
S. S. APOSTOLI
VIA POR S. MARIA
PONTE VECCHIO
To Pitti Palace
1 Palazzo Niccolini al Duomo
2 Hotel Duomo
3 Residenza dei Pucci
4 Soggiorno Battistero
5 Residenza Giotto B&B
6 La Residenza del Proconsolo B&B
7 Relais Grand Tour
8 Galileo Hotel
9 Hotel Il Bargellino
10 Casa Rabatti
11 Hotel Enza
12 Hotel Loggiato dei Serviti
13 Hotel dei Macchiaioli
14 Hotel Morandi alla Crocetta
15 Hotel Europa
16 Residenza il Villino
17 Panella's Residence
18 B&B Il Bargello
19 Hotel Dalí
20 Oblate Sisters of the Assumption
21 In Piazza della Signoria B&B
22 Hotel Pendini
23 B&B Dei Mori
24 Hotels Maxim & Axial
25 Hotel Davanzati
26 Hotel Torre Guelfa
27 Relais Ufizzi
28 Hotel Alessandra
29 Hotel Centrale
30 Hotel Accademia
31 Hotel Lorena
32 Bellevue House & Albergo Margaret
33 To Hostel 7 Santi

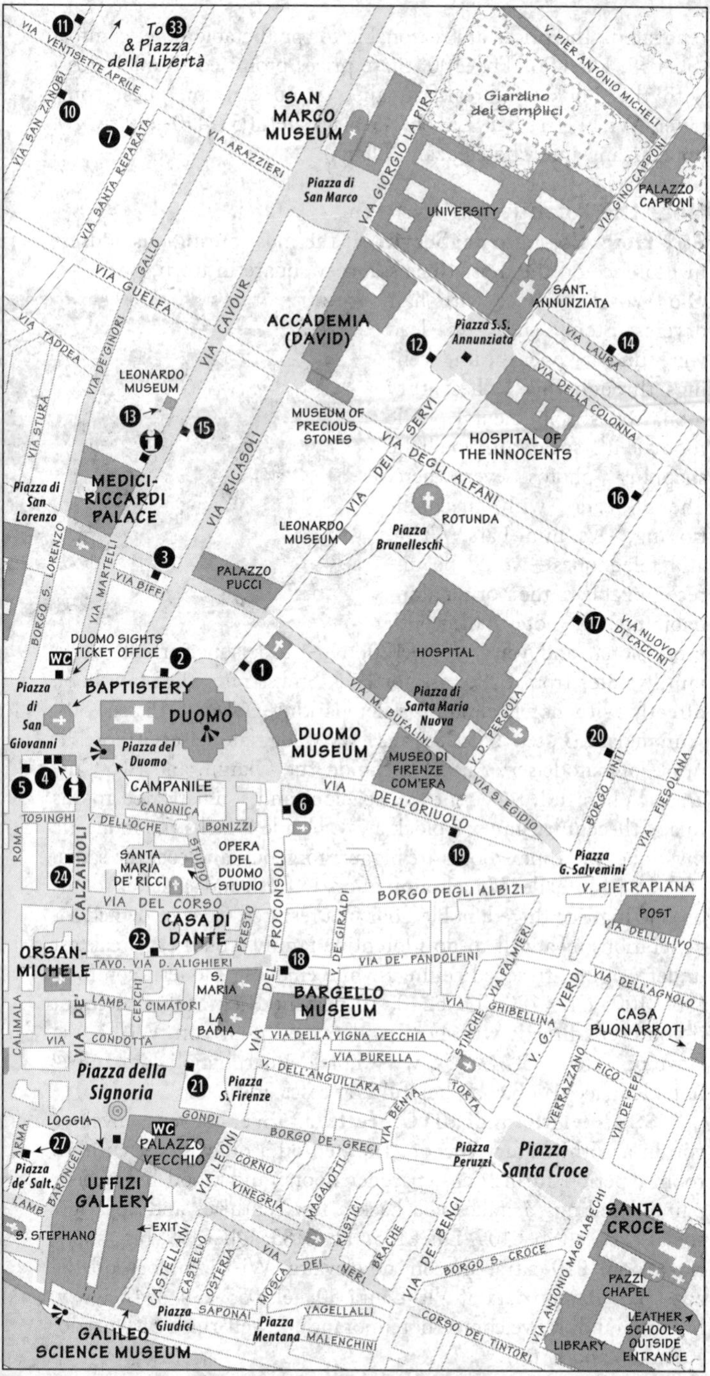
11
To 33
& Piazza
della Libertà
VIA VENTISETTE APRILE
VIA SAN ZANOBI
10
7
VIA SANTA REPARATA
VIA ARAZZIERI
SAN
MARCO
MUSEUM
Piazza di
San Marco
VIA GIORGIO LA PIRA
Giardino
dei Semplici
V. PIER ANTONIO MICHELI
VIA GINO CAPPONI
PALAZZO
CAPPONI
UNIVERSITY
VIA GUELFA
GALLO
VIA TADDEA
VIA DE' GINORI
VIA CAVOUR
ACCADEMIA
(DAVID)
Piazza S.S.
Annunziata
SANT.
ANNUNZIATA
12
14
VIA LAURA
VIA DELLA COLONNA
LEONARDO
MUSEUM
13
15
VIA STURA
MUSEUM OF
PRECIOUS
STONES
VIA DEI SERVI
HOSPITAL OF
THE INNOCENTS
VIA DEGLI ALFANI
Piazza di
San
Lorenzo
MEDICI-
RICCARDI
PALACE
VIA RICASOLI
16
ROTUNDA
LEONARDO
MUSEUM
Piazza
Brunelleschi
3
BORGO S. LORENZO
VIA MARTELLI
VIA BIFFI
PALAZZO
PUCCI
17
VIA NUOVO
DI CACCINI
DUOMO SIGHTS
TICKET OFFICE
WC
2
1
HOSPITAL
Piazza
di
San
Giovanni
BAPTISTERY
DUOMO
VIA M. BUFALINI
Piazza di
Santa Maria
Nuova
V. D. PERGOLA
20
Piazza del
Duomo
DUOMO
MUSEUM
MUSEO DI
FIRENZE
COM'ERA
5
4
CAMPANILE
VIA S. EGIDIO
BORGO PINTI
VIA FIESOLANA
CANONICA
6
VIA DELL'ORIUOLO
TOSINGHI
V. DELL'OCHE
BONIZZI
19
ROMA
CALZAIUOLI
STUDIO
OPERA
DEL
DUOMO
STUDIO
SANTA
MARIA
DE' RICCI
24
PROCONSOLO
Piazza
G. Salvemini
BORGO DEGLI ALBIZI
V. PIETRAPIANA
VIA DEL CORSO
V. DE' GIRALDI
POST
CASA DI
DANTE
PRESTO
23
ORSAN-
MICHELE
TAVO.
VIA D. ALIGHIERI
18
VIA DE' PANDOLFINI
VIA PALMIERI
VIA DELL'ULIVO
S.
MARIA
DEL
BARGELLO
MUSEUM
VERDI
VIA DELL'AGNOLO
LAMB.
CERCHI
CIMATORI
LA
BADIA
VIA
GHIBELLINA
V. G.
CASA
BUONARROTI
CALIMALA
VIA DE'
VIA
CONDOTTA
VIA DELLA VIGNA VECCHIA
STINCHE
VIA BURELLA
VERRAZZANO
FICO
Piazza della
Signoria
21
Piazza
S. Firenze
V. DELL'ANGUILLARA
TORTA
VIA DE PEPI
VIA BENTACORDI
GONDI
LOGGIA
27
WC
PALAZZO
VECCHIO
BORGO DE' GRECI
ARMA.
Piazza
de' Salt.
BARONCELLI
VIA LEONI
CORNO
Piazza
Peruzzi
Piazza
Santa Croce
UFFIZI
GALLERY
LAMB.
VINEGRIA
MAGALOTTI
VIA DE' BENCI
SANTA
CROCE
S. STEPHANO
EXIT
CASTELLANI
CASTELLO
OSTERIA
RUSTICI
BRACHE
BORGO S. CROCE
VIA ANTONIO MAGLIABECHI
VIA
DEI
NERI
MOSCA
PAZZI
CHAPEL
Piazza
Giudici
SAPONAI
VAGELLALLI
Piazza
Mentana
MALENCHINI
CORSO DEI TINTORI
LEATHER
SCHOOL'S
OUTSIDE
ENTRANCE
LIBRARY
GALILEO
SCIENCE MUSEUM

renovated. The prices are reasonable for predictable hotel comfort (Sb-€55, Db-€80, Tb-€100, these prices promised through 2015 with this book, no breakfast, air-con, no elevator, guest computer, Wi-Fi, Via San Zanobi 45 black, tel. 055-490-990, www.hotelenza.it, info@hotelenza.it, Diana).

Near the Accademia

$$$ Hotel Loggiato dei Serviti, at the most prestigious address in Florence on the most Renaissance-y square in town, gives you Old World romance with hair dryers. Stone stairways lead you under open-beam ceilings through this 16th-century monastery's monumental public rooms—it's so artful, you'll be snapping photos everywhere. The 38 cells—with air-conditioning, TVs, mini-bars, Wi-Fi, and telephones—would be unrecognizable to their original inhabitants. The hotel staff is both professional and warm (Sb-€120, Db-€160, superior Db-€190, family suites from €280, ask for Rick Steves rate when you book directly with hotel, elevator, valet parking-€21/day, Piazza S.S. Annunziata 3, tel. 055-289-592, www.loggiatodeiservitihotel.it, info@loggiatodeiservitihotel.it; Simonetta, Gianni, and two Chiaras). When full, they rent five spacious and sophisticated rooms in a 17th-century annex a block away. While it lacks the monastic mystique, the annex rooms are bigger, gorgeous, and cost the same.

SLEEPING

$$$ Hotel dei Macchiaioli offers 15 fresh and spacious rooms on one high-ceilinged, noble floor in a restored palazzo owned for generations by a well-to-do Florentine family. You'll eat breakfast under original frescoed ceilings while enjoying modern comforts (Sb-€100, Db-€180, Tb-€240, 10 percent Rick Steves discount if you book directly with hotel and pay cash, air-con, Wi-Fi, Via Cavour 21, tel. 055-213-154, www.hoteldeimacchiaioli.com, info@hoteldeimacchiaioli.com, helpful Francesca and Paolo).

$$ Hotel Morandi alla Crocetta, a former convent, envelops you in a 16th-century cocoon. Located on a quiet street with 12 rooms, period furnishings, parquet floors, and wood-beamed or painted ceilings, it takes you back a few centuries and up a few social classes (Sb-€105, Db-€155, Tb-€185, Qb-€199, big "superior" room-€30 extra, air-con, no elevator, Wi-Fi, a block off Piazza S.S. Annunziata at Via Laura 50, tel. 055-234-4747, www.hotelmorandi.it, welcome@hotelmorandi.it, well-run by Maurizio, Rolando, and Ertol).

$$ Hotel Europa, family run since 1970, has a welcoming atmosphere fostered by cheery Miriam, Roberto, and daughters Priscilla and Isabel. The breakfast room is spacious, and most of the 12 rooms have views of the Duomo (Sb-€89, Db-€150, Tb-€180, Qb-€250, 10 percent discount if you pay cash, mention Rick Steves to get their best available room, air-con, elevator, Wi-Fi, Via Cavour 14, tel. 055-239-6715, www.webhoteleuropa.com, firenze@webhoteleuropa.com).

EAST OF THE DUOMO

While convenient to the sights and offering a good value, these places are mostly along nondescript urban streets, lacking the grit, charm, or glitz of some of my other recommended neighborhoods.

$$ Residenza il Villino has 10 charming rooms and a picturesque, peaceful little courtyard. The owner, Neri, has turned part of the hotel into a mini-museum of early Italian fashion. As it's in a "little villa" (as the name implies) set back from the street, this is a quiet refuge from the bustle of Florence (Sb-€105, small Db-€120, Db-€135, family suite that sleeps up to 5—price upon request, book directly with hotel for best prices, 5 percent discount with this book if you pay cash, air-con, guest computer, Wi-Fi, just north of Via degli Alfani at Via della Pergola 53, tel. 055-200-1116, www.ilvillino.it, info@ilvillino.it).

$$ Panella's Residence, once a convent and today part of owner Graziella's extensive home, is a classy B&B, with five chic, romantic, and ample rooms, antique furnishings, and historic architectural touches (Db-€155, bigger "deluxe" Db-€180, extra bed-€40, book direct and mention Rick Steves for these prices, discounts for cash and stays of 3 or more nights, air-con, Wi-Fi, Via della Pergola 42, tel. 055-234-7202, mobile 345-972-1541, www.panellaresidence.com, panella_residence@yahoo.it).

$$ B&B Il Bargello is a home away from home, run by friendly and helpful Canadian expat Gabriella. Hike up three long flights (no elevator) to reach six smart, relaxing rooms. Gabriella offers a cozy communal living room, kitchen access, and an inviting rooftop terrace with close-up views of Florence's towers (Db-€110, ask for Rick Steves rate when you book directly with hotel and pay cash; fully equipped apartment across the hall-€180/2 people, €10 more per extra person; air-con, free guest computer, Wi-Fi, 20 yards off Via Proconsolo at Via de' Pandolfini 33 black, tel. 055-215-330, mobile 339-175-3110, www.firenze-bedandbreakfast.it, info@firenze-bedandbreakfast.it).

$ Hotel Dalí has 10 cheery rooms in a nice location for a great price. Samanta and Marco, who run this guesthouse with a charming passion and idealism, are a delight to know (S-€40, D-€70, Db-€85, extra bed-€25, request quiet room when you book, nearby apartments sleep 2-6 people, no breakfast, fans but no air-con, elevator, Wi-Fi, free parking, 2 blocks behind the Duomo at Via dell'Oriuolo 17 on the second floor, tel. 055-234-0706, www.hoteldali.com, hoteldali@tin.it).

$ Locanda de' Ciompi, overlooking the inviting Piazza dei Ciompi antique market in a young and lively neighborhood, is just right for travelers who want to feel like a part of the town. Alessio and daughter Lisa have five rooms that are tidy, lovingly maintained, and affordable (S with private b down hall-€73, Db-€90, bigger superior Db-€96, Tb-€140, 10 percent discount with this book if you book directly with hotel and pay cash, includes breakfast at nearby bar, air-con, Wi-Fi, 8 blocks behind the Duomo at Via Pietrapiana 28—see map on page 20, tel. 055-263-8034, www.bbflorencefirenze.com, info@bbflorencefirenze.com).

$ Oblate Sisters of the Assumption run an institutional 30-room hotel in a Renaissance building with a dreamy garden, great public spaces, appropriately simple rooms, and a quiet, prayerful ambience (Sb-€55, Db-€94, Tb-€141, Qb-€188, cash only, single beds only, family discounts available, air-con, elevator, Wi-Fi in lobby with suggested donation, €10/day limited parking—request when you book, Borgo Pinti 15, tel. 055-248-0582, sroblateborgopinti@virgilio.it, sisters are likely to speak French but not English, Sister Theresa is very helpful).

SOUTH OF THE DUOMO

Between the Duomo and Piazza della Signoria

Buried in the narrow, characteristic lanes in the very heart of town, these are the most central of my accommodations recommendations (and therefore a little overpriced). While worth the extra cost for many, given Florence's walkable, essentially traffic-free core, nearly every hotel I recommend can be considered central.

$$$ In Piazza della Signoria B&B, overlooking Piazza della Signoria, is peaceful, refined, and homey at the same time. Fit for a honeymoon, the 10 rooms come with all the special touches and little extras you'd expect in a top-end American B&B, and the service is sharp and friendly. However, the rates are high, and the "partial view" rooms, while slightly larger, require craning your neck to see anything—not worth the extra euros. Guests enjoy socializing at the big, shared breakfast table (viewless Db-€250, partial-view Db-€280, full-view "deluxe" Db-€300, Tb-€280, partial-view Tb-€300, ask for 10 percent discount when you book direct with this book, family apartments, lavish bathrooms, air-con, tiny elevator, guest computer, Wi-Fi, Via dei Magazzini 2, tel. 055-239-9546, mobile 348-321-0565, www.inpiazzadellasignoria.com, info@inpiazzadellasignoria.com, Sonia and Alessandro).

$$$ Hotel Pendini, with three stars and 44 rooms (most of them recently renovated and plush), fills the top floor of a grand building overlooking Piazza della Repubblica that was built to celebrate Italian unification in the late 19th century. This place just feels classy; as you walk into the lobby, it's as if you're walking back in time (Sb-€139, Db-€189, deluxe Db with square view and noise-€239, air-con, elevator, guest computer, Wi-Fi, Via degli Strozzi 2, tel. 055-211-170, www.hotelpendini.it, info@hotelpendini.it).

$$ B&B Dei Mori, a peaceful haven with a convivial and welcoming living room, rents five colorful rooms ideally located on a quiet pedestrian street near Casa di Dante—within a five-minute walk of the Duomo, the Bargello, or Piazza della Signoria. Accommodating Daniele (Danny) and his staff pride themselves on offering personal service, including lots of tips on dining and sightseeing in Florence (D-€110, Db-€130, minimum two-night stay, 10 percent discount for Rick Steves' readers—ask when you book directly with the hotel, less inviting overflow apartment, air-con-€5, no elevator, Wi-Fi, reception open 8:00-19:00, Via Dante Alighieri 12, tel. 055-211-438, www.deimori.com, deimori@bnb.it).

$$ Hotel Maxim is reasonably priced considering its prime location on the main pedestrian drag. While the 26 rooms are straightforward, its narrow, painting-lined halls and cozy lounge have old Florentine charm (Sb-€75, Db-€130, Tb-€160, Qb-€180, book directly with hotel and use promo code "RICK" for 10 percent discount, air-con, elevator, guest computer, Wi-Fi, Via de' Calzaiuoli 11, tel. 055-217-474, www.hotelmaximfirenze.it, reservation@hotelmaximfirenze.it, Chiara).

$$ Hotel Axial, two floors below their sister Hotel Maxim, has a more businesslike feel and 14 rooms that are only slightly nicer for the higher rates (Sb-€90, bigger "superior" Sb-€114, Db-€149, book directly with hotel and use promo code "RICK" for 10 percent discount, air-con, elevator, guest computer, Wi-Fi, Via de' Calzaiuoli 11, tel. 055-218-984, www.hotelaxial.it, info@hotelaxial.it, Nicola).

Near Ponte Vecchio

This sleepy zone is handy to several sights and some fine shopping streets (from top-end boutiques to more characteristic hole-in-the-wall shops), though it's accordingly pricey and lacks a neighborhood feel of its own.

$$$ Hotel Davanzati, bright and shiny with artistic touches, has 25 cheerful rooms with all the comforts. The place is a family affair, thoughtfully run by friendly Tommaso and father Fabrizio, who offer drinks and snacks each evening at their candlelit happy hour, plus lots of other extras (Sb-€132, Db-€199, Tb-€259, family rooms available, these rates good with this book though prices soft off-season, 10 percent discount if you pay cash, free loaner laptop in every room, free on-demand videos—including Rick Steves' Italy shows—on your room TV, air-con, Wi-Fi, next to Piazza Davanzati at Via Porta Rossa 5—easy to miss so watch for low-profile sign above the door, tel. 055-286-666, www.hoteldavanzati.it, info@hoteldavanzati.it).

$$$ Hotel Torre Guelfa has grand—almost royal—public spaces and is topped by a fun medieval tower with a panoramic rooftop terrace (72 stairs take you up—and back—720 years). Its 31 pricey rooms vary wildly in size and layout. Room 315, with a private terrace (€260), is worth reserving several months in advance (Db-€190, higher prices for bigger rooms, ask for Rick Steves discount, family deals, check their website for promotions, air-con, elevator, guest computer, Wi-Fi, a couple blocks northwest of Ponte Vecchio, Borgo S.S. Apostoli 8, tel. 055-239-6338, www.hoteltorreguelfa.com, info@hoteltorreguelfa.com, Niccolo and Barbara).

$$$ Relais Uffizi is a peaceful little gem, offering a friendly welcome and 15 classy but well-worn rooms tucked away down a tiny alleyway off Piazza della Signoria. The lounge has a huge window overlooking the action in the square below (Sb-€120, Db-€180, Tb-€220, more for deluxe rooms, air-con, elevator, guest computer, Wi-Fi; from the square, go down the tiny Chiasso de Baroncelli lane—right of the loggia—and look for Chiasso del Buco 16 on your right; tel. 055-267-6239, www.relaisuffizi.it, info@relaisuffizi.it, charming Alessandro and Elizabetta).

$$ Hotel Alessandra, a lesser value, is 16th-century, tranquil, and sprawling, with 27 big, old-school rooms and a tiny Arno-view terrace (S with private bathroom down the hall-€88, Sb-€110, Db-€150, "superior" Db with Arno view-€30 extra, Tb-€195, Qb-€215, 5 percent cash discount, air-con, 30 steps to the elevator, guest computer, Wi-Fi, Borgo S.S. Apostoli 17, tel. 055-283-438, www.hotelalessandra.com, info@hotelalessandra.com, Anna and son Andrea).

BETWEEN THE DUOMO AND THE TRAIN STATION

This touristy zone has lots of budget and mid-range hotels catering to an international clientele, stacks of basic trattorias, and easy access to major sights (just steps from the Medici Chapels, Church of San Lorenzo, and Mercato Centrale, and only a bit farther to the biggies). The mostly pedestrianized Via Faenza is the spine of this neighborhood, with lots of tourist services.

$$$ Hotel Centrale is indeed central, just a short walk from the Duomo. The 31 spacious but overpriced rooms—with a tasteful mix of old and new decor—are over a businesslike conference center (Db-€190, bigger superior Db-€237, Tb-€236, suites available, 10 percent discount with this book, ask for Rick Steves rate when you reserve, 20 percent discount if booked two months in advance, air-con, elevator, guest computer, Wi-Fi, Via dei Conti 3, check in at big front desk on ground floor, tel. 055-215-761, www.hotelcentralefirenze.it, info@hotelcentralefirenze.it, Margherita and Roberto).

$$ Hotel Accademia has 21 old-school rooms and a floor plan that defies logic. While it's overpriced and getting a bit long in the tooth, the location is convenient (small Sb-€70, Db-€145, Tb-€170, 10 percent discount with this book if you book directly with the hotel and pay cash, air-con, no elevator, guest computer, Wi-Fi, Via Faenza 7, tel. 055-293-451, www.hotelaccademiafirenze.com, info@hotelaccademiafirenze.com, Tea).

$ Hotel Lorena, just across from the Medici Chapels, has 19 simple, well-worn rooms (six of which have shared bathrooms) and a tiny lobby. Though it feels a bit like a youth hostel, it's cheap, well-located, and run with care by the Galli family (S-€45, Sb-€65, D-€75, small Db-€80, Db-€90, Tb-€120, very flexible rates, cash only, breakfast-usually €5 extra but free for Rick Steves readers, air-con, Wi-Fi, Via Faenza 1, tel. 055-282-785, www.hotellorena.com, info@hotellorena.com).

NEAR THE TRAIN STATION

These fine, charming little budget options are on a grimy urban street that's across Piazza Santa Maria Novella from the train station. The church's sweet-smelling perfumery is just across the street.

$$ Bellevue House, a great budget option, is a third-floor (no elevator) oasis of tranquility, with six spacious, old-fashioned rooms flanking a long, mellow-yellow lobby. It's a peaceful time warp thoughtfully run by the Michel family (Db-€110, Tb-€120, Qb-€140, 10 percent discount if you book directly with hotel and stay two nights, no breakfast, air-con, Wi-Fi, Via della Scala 21, tel. 055-260-8932, www.bellevuehouse.it, info@bellevuehouse.it; Luciano, Susan, and Alessandro).

$ Albergo Margaret, homey yet minimalist, doesn't have a public lounge or offer breakfast. Run by the Cristantielli family, it has seven tidy, simple rooms (Ss-€55, D-€50, Ds-€70, Db-€90, 10 percent discount if you book directly with hotel and pay cash, extra bed-€10, air-con in most rooms, Wi-Fi, near Santa Maria Novella at Via della Scala 25, tel. 055-210-138, www.hotel-margaret.it, info@hotel-margaret.it; Francesco, Anna, and

Graziano). Graziano also rents an apartment upstairs (for up to 5 people; prices on request).

HOSTEL AWAY FROM THE CENTER

This hostel, northeast of downtown, is a bus ride from the action. A far more central hostel is in the Oltrarno (see listing at the end of this chapter).

$ Hostel 7 Santi calls itself a "travelers' haven." It fills a former convent, but you'll feel like you're in an old school. Still, it offers some of the best cheap beds in town, is friendly to older travelers, and comes with the services you'd expect in a big, modern hostel, including Wi-Fi and self-serve laundry. It's in a more residential neighborhood near the Campo di Marte stadium, about a 10-minute bus ride from the center (200 beds in 60 rooms, mostly 4- or 6-bed dorms with a floor of doubles and triples, €16-18/dorm bed, Sb-€45, Db-€60, Tb-€70, Qb-€80, includes sheets and towels, breakfast and dinner available but cost extra, no curfew, guest computer, Wi-Fi; Viale dei Mille 11—from train station, take bus #10, #17, or #20, direction: Campo di Marte, to bus stop Chiesa dei Sette Santi; tel. 055-504-8452, www.7santi.com, info@7santi.com).

South of the Arno River, in the Oltrarno

Across the river in the Oltrarno area, between Pitti Palace and Ponte Vecchio, you'll find small, traditional crafts shops, neighborly piazzas, and family eateries. The following places are an easy walk from Ponte Vecchio. Only the first two are real hotels—the rest are a ragtag gang of budget alternatives.

$$$ Hotel Silla is a classic three-star hotel with 36 cheery, spacious rooms. On the opposite side of the river from Santa Croce Church, it has a breezy terrace and faces the river, overlooking a small park, with free coffee and tea for guests in the late afternoon. The surrounding neighborhood can be a bit noisy (Db-€170, bigger "superior" Db-€200, Tb-€230, book directly with hotel and use promo code "RICK" for 10 percent discount, extra bed-€35, air-con, elevator, guest computer, Wi-Fi, parking-€19/day, Via dei Renai 5—see map on page 20, tel. 055-234-2888, www.hotelsilla.it, hotelsilla@hotelsilla.it; Laura, Chiara, Massimo, and Stefano).

$$ Hotel la Scaletta has 36 recently remodeled, bright rooms hiding in a tortured floor plan, plus a fabulous rooftop terrace overlooking the Boboli Gardens (Db-€160, slightly more for new "superior" rooms, third bed-€30, family suite that sleeps up to 5-€270, breakfast-€10, air-con, elevator, guest computer, Wi-Fi, Via de'

Guicciardini 13, tel. 055-283-028, www.hotellascaletta.it, info@hotellascaletta.it).

$ Soggiorno Alessandra has five bright, comfy, and smallish rooms. Because of its double-paned windows, you'll hardly notice the traffic noise (D-€70, Db-€75, Tb-€95, Qb-€125, includes basic breakfast in room, air-con-€5, no elevator, Wi-Fi, just past the Carraia Bridge at Via Borgo San Frediano 6, tel. 055-290-424, www.soggiornoalessandra.it, info@soggiornoalessandra.it, Alessandra).

$ Casa Santo Nome di Gesù is a grand, 25-room convent whose sisters—Franciscan Missionaries of Mary—are thankful to rent rooms to tourists. Staying in this 15th-century palace, you'll be immersed in the tranquil atmosphere created by a huge, peaceful garden, generous and prayerful public spaces, and smiling nuns. As with the Istituto Gould, next, it's a good value and understandably popular—it's best to reserve a couple of months in advance (Db-€85, Tb-€115, Qb-€135, book direct to avoid fees, no air-con but rooms have fans, elevator, Wi-Fi in common areas, memorable convent-like breakfast room, 1:00 in the morning curfew, parking-€10, Piazza del Carmine 21, tel. 055-213-856, www.fmmfirenze.it, info@fmmfirenze.it).

SLEEPING

$ Istituto Gould is a Protestant Church-run place with 40 clean and spartan rooms that have twin beds and modern facilities. It's located in a 17th-century palace overlooking a beautiful garden courtyard. The complex also houses kids from troubled homes, and proceeds raised from renting rooms help fund that important work (Sb-€55, Db-€60, €20 more for garden rooms that are quieter and have air-con, Tb-€84, Qb-€100, breakfast-€6, non-air-con rooms have fans, Wi-Fi in lobby, Via dei Serragli 49, tel. 055-212-576, www.istitutogould.it, foresteriafirenze@diaconiavaldese.org). You must arrive when the office is open (Mon-Fri 8:45-13:00 & 15:00-19:30, Sat 9:00-13:30 & 14:30-18:00, no live check-in on Sundays but they'll email you a code).

Hostel: **$ Ostello Santa Monaca** is a well-run, institutional-feeling hostel a long block east of the Brancacci Chapel. As clean as its guests, its 114 beds in 13 rooms (2- to 22-bed dorms) attract a young backpacking crowd (€18-26/bed, includes sheets and towel, 10:00-14:00 lock-out, 2:00 in the morning curfew, guest computer, Wi-Fi, self-serve laundry, kitchen, bike rental, Via Santa Monaca 6, tel. 055-268-338, www.ostellosantamonaca.com, info@ostellosantamonaca.com).

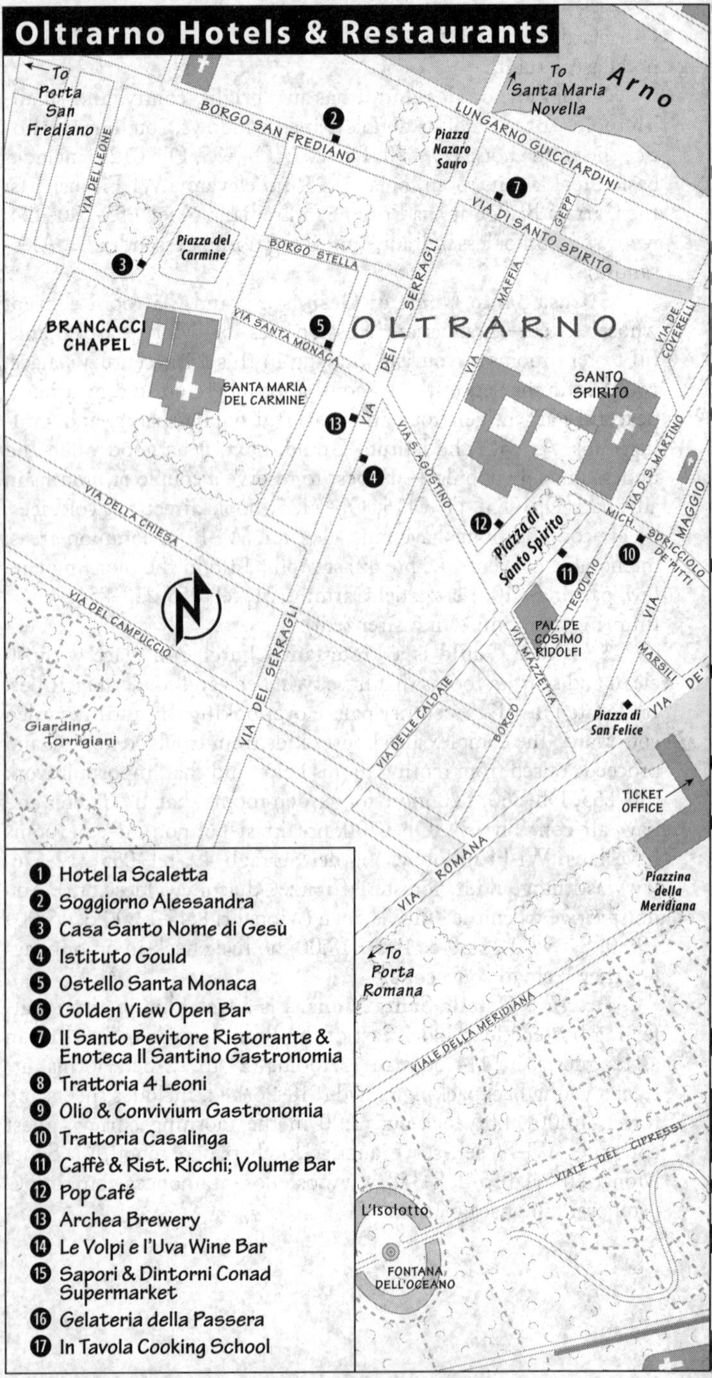
Oltrarno Hotels & Restaurants
To Porta San Frediano
To Santa Maria Novella
Arno
BORGO SAN FREDIANO
Piazza Nazaro Sauro
LUNGARNO GUICCIARDINI
VIA DEL LEONE
VIA DI SANTO SPIRITO
GEPPI
Piazza del Carmine
BORGO STELLA
SERRAGLI
MAFFIA
BRANCACCI CHAPEL
VIA SANTA MONACA
OLTRARNO
VIA DE' COVERELLI
DEI
SANTA MARIA DEL CARMINE
SANTO SPIRITO
VIA
VIA S. AGOSTINO
VIA D. S. MARTINO
VIA DELLA CHIESA
MICH.
MAGGIO
Piazza di Santo Spirito
SDRUCCIOLO DE' PITTI
TEGOLAIO
VIA DEL CAMPUCCIO
PAL. DE COSIMO RIDOLFI
VIA MAZZETTA
VIA MARSILI
VIA DEI SERRAGLI
VIA DELLE CALDAIE
BORGO
VIA DE'
Giardino Torrigiani
Piazza di San Felice
TICKET OFFICE
VIA ROMANA
Piazzina della Meridiana
To Porta Romana
VIALE DELLA MERIDIANA
VIALE DEL CIPRESSI
L'Isolotto
FONTANA DELL'OCEANO
1 Hotel la Scaletta
2 Soggiorno Alessandra
3 Casa Santo Nome di Gesù
4 Istituto Gould
5 Ostello Santa Monaca
6 Golden View Open Bar
7 Il Santo Bevitore Ristorante & Enoteca Il Santino Gastronomia
8 Trattoria 4 Leoni
9 Olio & Convivium Gastronomia
10 Trattoria Casalinga
11 Caffè & Rist. Ricchi; Volume Bar
12 Pop Café
13 Archea Brewery
14 Le Volpi e l'Uva Wine Bar
15 Sapori & Dintorni Conad Supermarket
16 Gelateria della Passera
17 In Tavola Cooking School

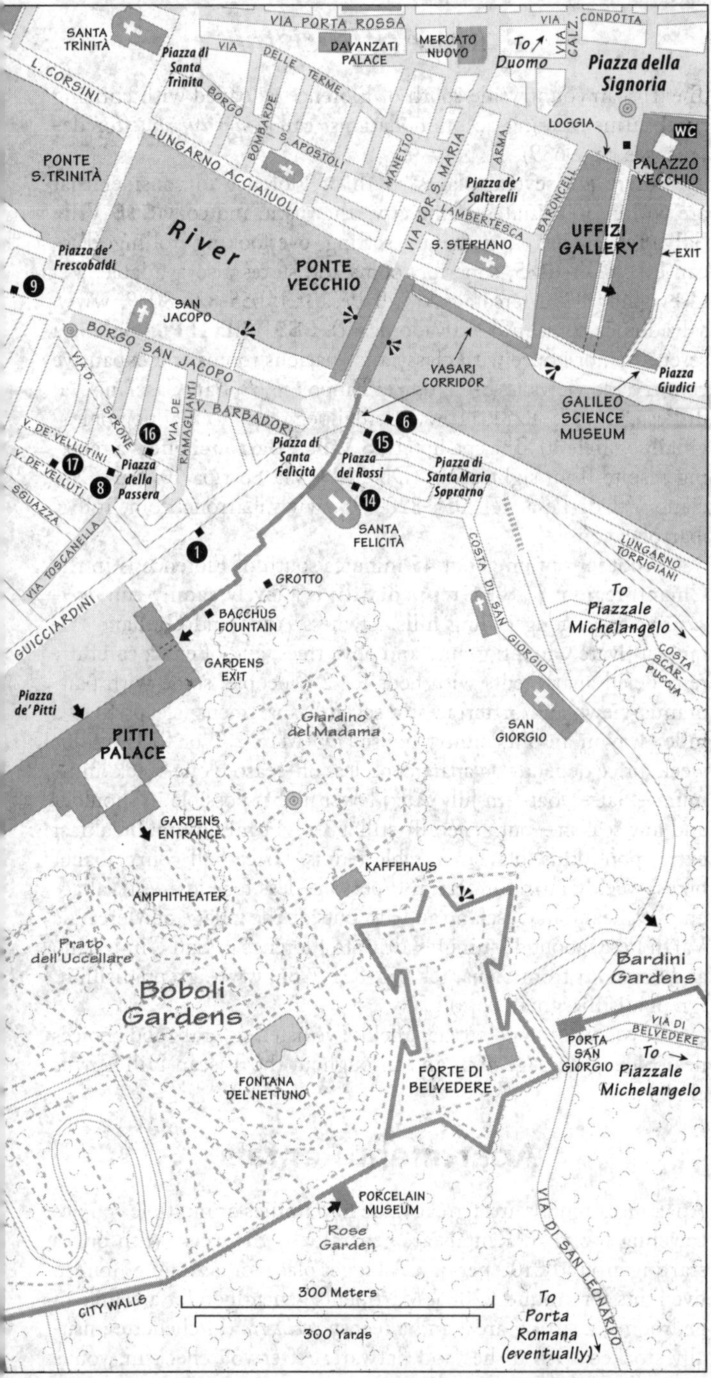
VIA PORTA ROSSA
SANTA TRÌNITÀ
Piazza di Santa Trìnita
DAVANZATI PALACE
MERCATO NUOVO
To Duomo
VIA CONDOTTA
VIA CALZ.
Piazza della Signoria
VIA DELLE TERME
L. CORSINI
BORGO
BORGO S. APOSTOLI
BOMBARDE
MANETTO
VIA POR S. MARIA
ARMA
LOGGIA
WC
PALAZZO VECCHIO
PONTE S. TRINITÀ
LUNGARNO ACCIAIUOLI
Piazza de' Salterelli
LAMBERTESCA
BARONCELLI
UFFIZI GALLERY
EXIT
S. STEPHANO
River
Piazza de' Frescobaldi
PONTE VECCHIO
9
SAN JACOPO
BORGO SAN JACOPO
VASARI CORRIDOR
Piazza Giudici
GALILEO SCIENCE MUSEUM
VIA D. SPRONE
VIA DE RAMAGLIANTI
V. BARBADORI
6
15
16
V. DE' VELLUTINI
V. DE' VELLUTI
17
8
Piazza della Passera
SGUAZZA
Piazza di Santa Felicità
Piazza dei Rossi
Piazza di Santa Maria Soprarno
14
SANTA FELICITÀ
VIA TOSCANELLA
1
COSTA DI SAN GIORGIO
LUNGARNO TORRIGIANI
GROTTO
BACCHUS FOUNTAIN
GUICCIARDINI
To Piazzale Michelangelo
COSTA SCARPUCCIA
GARDENS EXIT
Piazza de' Pitti
PITTI PALACE
Giardino del Madama
SAN GIORGIO
GARDENS ENTRANCE
KAFFEHAUS
AMPHITHEATER
Prato dell'Uccellare
Bardini Gardens
Boboli Gardens
VIA DI BELVEDERE
PORTA SAN GIORGIO
To Piazzale Michelangelo
FORTE DI BELVEDERE
FONTANA DEL NETTUNO
PORCELAIN MUSEUM
Rose Garden
VIA DI SAN LEONARDO
300 Meters
300 Yards
CITY WALLS
To Porta Romana (eventually)

SLEEPING

Rural *Agriturismi*

The Tuscan countryside south of Florence is loaded with enticing rural farms offering accommodations, called *agriturismi* (for details, see page 639).

There are several places south of Florence to consider that are within 30 minutes of the city. The rustic and cozy **$$$ Villa Salvadonica** has a gorgeous setting overlooking rolling Tuscan hills (Db-€185, superior rooms and suites also available, Via Grevigiana 82, Mercatale Val di Pesa, tel. 055-821-8039, www.salvadonica.com, info@salvadonica.it). **$$$ Villa Il Poggiale** is a serene manor house with classy and spacious rooms and expansive countryside views (Db-€170, Via Empolese 69, San Casciano Val di Pesa, tel. 055-828-311, www.villailpoggiale.it, villailpoggiale@villailpoggiale.it). The spa hotel **$$ Villa I Barronci** offers a relaxing respite from sightseeing (Db-€129, Via Sorripa 10, San Casciano Val di Pesa, tel. 055-820-598, www.ibarronci.com, info@ibarronci.com).

Another option about 45 minutes south of Florence is in the Chianti region: **$$$ I Greppi di Silli** is a lovely, family-run *agriturismo* set among rolling hills. Owners Anna and Giuliano Alfani cultivate Chianti grapes and olive trees, and offer six carefully remodeled apartments with beds for 2-6 people, some with panoramic views and/or terraces; a seventh apartment (sleeps 8) is a mile away in an old country house (Db-€115-280 or €735-1,900/week, price depends on apartment, less off-season; one-week minimum—Sat-to-Sat—in July-Aug, fewer nights possible in shoulder and low season—but generally still a 3-night minimum; breakfast extra, pool, kids' play area, table tennis, bocce ball court, loaner bikes, weekly farm dinners-€30/person—less for kids, Via Vallacchio 19, near San Casciano and just outside the village of Mercatale Val di Pesa, about 45 minutes' drive to Florence or San Gimignano and one hour from Siena, tel. 055-821-7956, www.igreppidisilli.it, igreppidisilli@gmail.com).

If you want to go farther afield, I've listed several good choices near Siena (see page 403) and throughout the Tuscan Hill Towns chapters.

Apartment Rentals

Apartment rentals are a great value for families or multiple couples traveling together. Rentals are generally by the week, with prices starting around €100 per day. A bigger place for a group of four to five rents for around €200. Apartments generally offer a couple of bedrooms, a sitting area, and a teensy *cucinetta* (kitchenette), usually stocked with dishes and flatware. After you check in, you're basically on your own. While you won't have a doorman to carry your bags or a maid to clean your room each day, you will get an inside peek at an Italian home, and you can save lots of money—especially if you take advantage of the cooking facilities—with no loss of comfort.

Cross-Pollinate, an online booking agency, represents B&Bs and apartments in a handful of European cities, including Florence. Unlike huge aggregator websites like HomeAway or VRBO, Cross-Pollinate handpicks its listings. Search their website for a listing you like, then submit your reservation online. If the place is available, you'll be charged a small deposit and emailed the location and check-in details. Policies vary from owner to owner, but in most cases you'll pay the balance on arrival in cash. Florence listings range from €55 to €250 per night, and minimum stays vary from one to three nights (US tel. 800-270-1190, Italy tel. 06-9936-9799, www.cross-pollinate.com, info@cross-pollinate.com).

Frederick of **Tournights** runs a similar apartment-finding service in Florence (www.tournights.com, info@tournights.com).

EATING IN FLORENCE

Contents

As a big city jammed with tourists, Florence has plenty of good restaurants—but even more bad ones. In this chapter, I've recommended a cross-section of what I feel are reliably good eateries, from cafeterias and sandwich shops to classic Italian trattorias and foodie splurges. Be warned that my readers fill many of the mom-and-pop eateries listed here. If you want to steer away from my readers, grab another spot—but to really escape from the crowds, you need to get away from the town center. The Oltrarno, just across the river, is a good compromise: far enough away to not feel completely overrun by tourists, but close enough for an easy commute by foot. And in general, value and flavors are often better in smaller Tuscan towns, where the rustic simplicity of ingredient-driven local cuisine really shines.

You may have the best luck finding local ambience at lunch, since that's when many restaurants in the center cater to office workers. For dinner, those same places fill with tourists early; then, after about 21:00, the tourists are replaced by locals dining later.

For an overview of restaurants, other types of eateries, and Florentine cuisine, along with tips on tipping, see "Eating" in the Practicalities chapter. Remember, restaurants like to serve what's fresh. If you're into flavor, go for the seasonal best bets—featured in the *piatti del giorno* ("specials of the day") section on menus. For dessert, it's gelato (see sidebar later in this chapter).

To save money and time for sights, keep lunches fast and simple, eating at one of the countless sandwich shops and stands, pizzerias, or self-service cafeterias. Picnicking is easy—there's no shortage of corner *supermercatos,* or you can picnic your way through Mercato Centrale. You'll find a unique range of sandwich options in Florence. In addition to the basic *panino* (here, that's usually on a baguette), *crostini* (open-faced sandwich on toasted baguette), and *semel* (a big, puffy roll), you'll see places advertising *schiaccata* (sandwich made with a "squashed," focaccia-like bread). Florence is home to many carts selling tripe sandwiches—a prized local specialty; for details, see the "Florentine Food Carts Have Got Some Guts" sidebar.

Foodies should consider purchasing Elizabeth Minchilli's excellent app, Eat Florence, which has thorough descriptions of all things food-related in the city (www.elizabethminchilliinrome.com). While there's a fair amount of overlap with my listings, Elizabeth's choices skew a bit more upscale than mine, and her extensive descriptions of each place offer more nuance than my quick snapshots.

If you'd like to combine a meal with the opportunity to learn how to cook some Italian dishes, see the end of this chapter for a rundown of some of the many cooking classes offered in Florence.

North of the Arno River

MERCATO CENTRALE

Florence's Industrial Age, steel-and-glass Mercato Centrale (Central Market) has undergone an exciting resurgence in recent years. The ground floor has always been a fun-to-explore food wonderland of vendors selling meat, fish, produce, and other staples to a mostly local clientele, plus some lunch-only food counters. But in 2014, the upstairs—long a gloomy and neglected no-man's land—underwent a complete refurbishment and is now poised to become a global foodie mecca, with a chichi food court and several restaurants that are open late into the evening. As this is a rapidly gentrifying scene, expect changes as this space continues to evolve.

Ground Floor: The market zone, with lots of raw ingredients and a few humble food counters, is open only through lunchtime (Mon-Fri 7:00-14:00, Sat 7:00-17:00, closed Sun). Buy a picnic of fresh mozzarella cheese, olives, fruit, and crunchy bread to munch on the steps of the nearby Church of San Lorenzo. The fancy deli, **Perini,** is famous for its quality (pricey) products and enticing display. But for a sit-down meal, head for the venerable **Nerbone in the Market.** Join the shoppers and workers who crowd up to the

Florentine Food Carts Have Got Some Guts

While on a lunch break from chipping trapped statues out of blocks of marble, Michelangelo would swing by the market and dig into a bun stuffed with stewed organs. Offal sandwiches originated as an affordable source of protein for working-class Florentines. While this longstanding tradition nearly faded away a few years back, the recent worldwide foodie trend for "nose-to-tail" eating has kicked off a renaissance of food carts selling this prized local delicacy.

Tourists may find it hard to stomach, but Florentines' favorite quick lunch is a *panino* (sandwich) of *trippa* or *lampredotto*—the second and fourth stomach of a cow, respectively—slow-boiled to tender perfection. Less common variations include *poppo*—udder, and *nervetti*—tendons. While these are worth trying (be brave), most carts also offer *bollito* (stewed beef), and some have *porchetta* (roast pork with herbs).

When you order, the food-cart proprietor pulls the lid off of a gently simmering pot, forks out some tender meat, and—if you're lucky—dips the bun in the broth to enhance the flavor. Topping things off are one or both of the two standard sauces: spicy, red *salsa piccante* and *salsa verde,* a tangy parsley sauce.

As it's been for centuries, these food stands are most commonly found at or near markets. Good places include **Nerbone in the Market** at Mercato Centrale; **L'Antico Trippaio,** tucked in the tight streets between the Duomo and Palazzo Vecchio; the locally beloved ***lampredotto* cart** at Mercato Nuovo; or anywhere else that locals are excited about. Come on, have some guts...give it a try.

bar to grab their €4-7 plates, and then find a stool at the cramped shared tables nearby. Of the several cheap market diners, this feels the most authentic (lunch menu served Mon-Sat 12:00-14:00, sandwiches available from 8:00 until the bread runs out, closed Sun, cash only, inside Mercato Centrale on the side closest to the Church of San Lorenzo, mobile 339-648-0251).

Upstairs: Under a gleaming glass roof and stylish giant wicker lampshades, a dozen upscale food counters (each labeled with the type of food and proprietor—a *Who's Who* of Florentine chefs and restaurant-world insiders) let you browse for your perfect meal. Grab what you want—pizza, pasta, fish, meat, *salumi, lampredotto,* wine, and so on—and pull up a stool at one of the food-court tables between the stalls. Higher up, there are also restaurants with designated seating and table service: A more casual pizzeria on one side, and a more formal place on the other. The eateries up here are open much longer hours than the traditional, downstairs places—they're fine for lunch or dinner (daily 10:00-24:00, www.mercatocentrale.it). Before choosing, be sure to browse a full circuit around the scene to know your options.

Near Mercato Centrale

If you can't find what you want in the market itself, consider one of these alternatives on the surrounding streets. My recommended eateries are all within a few blocks of each other, and each has its own distinct vibe, so scout around to choose your favorite. As this area is close to the "tourist ghetto" zone—near many hotels and San Lorenzo Market—these eateries skew to an especially touristy clientele.

Trattoria Mario's has been serving hearty lunches to market-goers since 1953 (Fabio and Romeo are the latest generation). Their simple formula: no-frills, bustling service, old-fashioned good value, and shared tables. It's *cucina casalinga*—home cooking *con brio*. This place is high-energy and jam-packed. Their best dishes often sell out first, so go early. If there's a line, put your name on the list (€5-6 pastas, €8 *secondi*, cash only, Mon-Sat 12:00-15:30, closed Sun and Aug, no reservations, Via Rosina 2, tel. 055-218-550).

EATING

Casa del Vino, Florence's oldest operating wine shop, offers glasses of wine from among 25 open bottles (see the list tacked to the bar). Owner Gianni, whose family has owned the Casa for more than 70 years, is a class act. Gianni's *carta dei panini* lists delightful €3.50 sandwiches and €1 crostini; the *I Nostri Panini* (classic sandwiches) richly reward adventurous eaters. Their €4-5 *taglierini* (sampler platters) offer nibbles of various local *salumi* (cured meats) and cheeses. During busy times, it's a mob scene. You'll eat standing outside alongside workers on a quick lunch break (Mon-Fri 9:30-20:00 year-round, Sat 9:30-17:00 Sept-June only, closed Sun year-round and Sat in summer, near Mercato Centrale at Via dell'Ariento 16 red, tel. 055-215-609).

Trattoria Zà-Zà screams "tourist trap" with big photo menus, touts out front, and covered terrace seating on a little square facing Mercato Centrale. And yet, for some reason, it remains a top recommendation among locals. Maybe it's because they offer a family-friendly festival of standard Tuscan dishes, such as *ribollita* and *bistecca alla fiorentina,* plus a variety of big, splittable €8 salads. Arrive early (before 19:30), make a reservation, or stand in line. Choose between the colorful interior or the outdoor piazza. Understand your itemized bill, and don't mistake their outside seating with the neighboring restaurant's (€8-11 pastas, €11-16 *secondi*, daily 11:00-23:00, Piazza del Mercato Centrale 26 red, tel. 055-215-411, www.trattoriazaza.it). Their **bar/osteria,** nearby, has

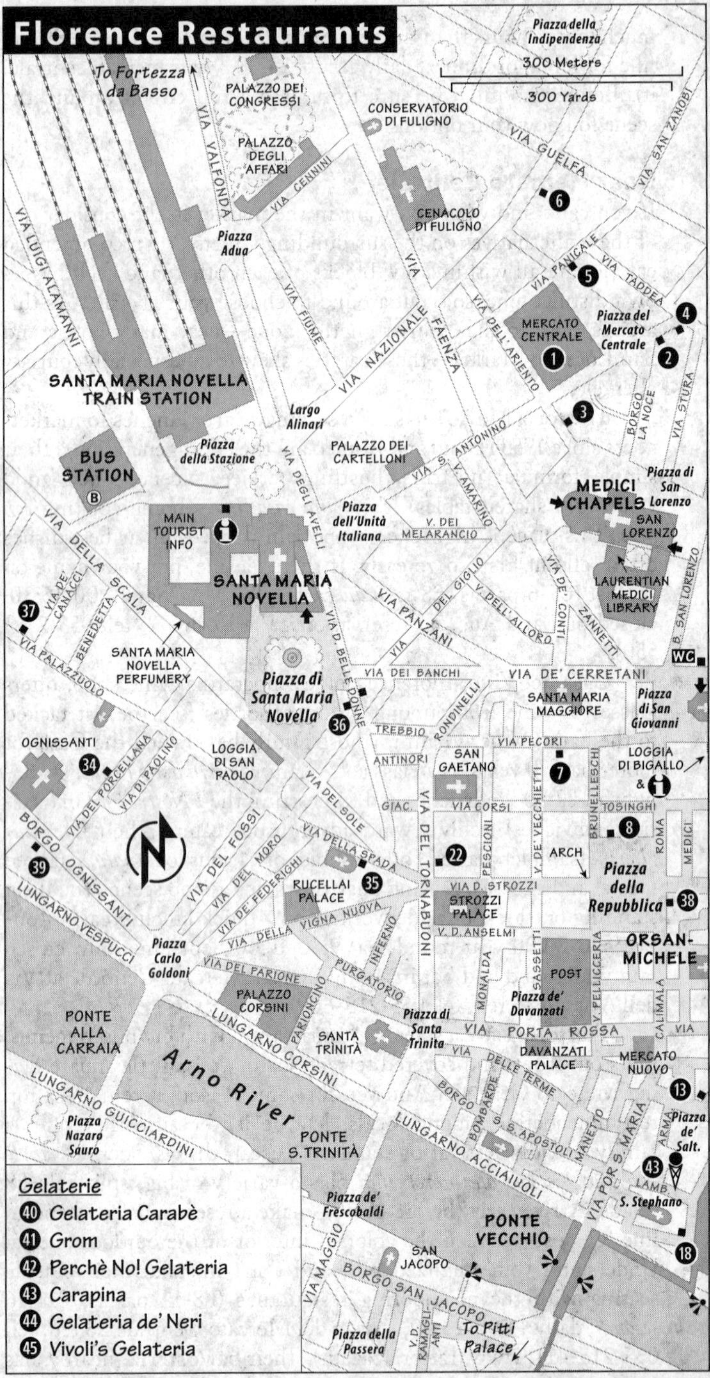
Florence Restaurants
Piazza della Indipendenza
300 Meters
300 Yards
To Fortezza da Basso
PALAZZO DEI CONGRESSI
PALAZZO DEGLI AFFARI
CONSERVATORIO DI FULIGNO
CENACOLO DI FULIGNO
VIA GUELFA
VIA SAN ZANOBI
VIA VALFONDA
VIA CENNINI
VIA LUIGI ALAMANNI
Piazza Adua
VIA FIUME
VIA NAZIONALE
VIA FAENZA
VIA PANICALE
VIA TADDEA
VIA DELL' ARIENTO
MERCATO CENTRALE
Piazza del Mercato Centrale
BORGO LA NOCE
VIA STURA
SANTA MARIA NOVELLA TRAIN STATION
Largo Alinari
Piazza della Stazione
BUS STATION
PALAZZO DEI CARTELLONI
VIA S. ANTONINO
V. AMARINO
VIA DEGLI AVELLI
Piazza dell'Unità Italiana
V. DEI MELARANCIO
MEDICI CHAPELS
Piazza di San Lorenzo
SAN LORENZO
LAURENTIAN MEDICI LIBRARY
B. SAN LORENZO
MAIN TOURIST INFO
SANTA MARIA NOVELLA
VIA DELLA SCALA
VIA DE' CANACCI
BENEDETTA
VIA PALAZZUOLO
SANTA MARIA NOVELLA PERFUMERY
VIA PANZANI
VIA DEL GIGLIO
V. DELL' ALLORO
VIA DE' CONTI
ZANNETTI
VIA D. BELLE DONNE
Piazza di Santa Maria Novella
VIA DEI BANCHI
VIA DE' CERRETANI
WC
SANTA MARIA MAGGIORE
Piazza di San Giovanni
RONDINELLI
TREBBIO
ANTINORI
SAN GAETANO
VIA PECORI
LOGGIA DI BIGALLO &
OGNISSANTI
VIA DEL PORCELLANA
VIA DI PAOLINO
LOGGIA DI SAN PAOLO
VIA DEL SOLE
GIAC.
VIA CORSI
TOSINGHI
BRUNELLESCHI
V. DE' VECCHIETTI
PESCIONI
VIA DEL TORNABUONI
ROMA
MEDICI
ARCH
Piazza della Repubblica
BORGO OGNISSANTI
VIA DEL FOSSI
VIA DEL MORO
VIA DE' FEDERIGHI
VIA DELLA SPADA
RUCELLAI PALACE
VIA DELLA VIGNA NUOVA
VIA D. STROZZI
STROZZI PALACE
V. D. ANSELMI
ORSAN-MICHELE
LUNGARNO VESPUCCI
Piazza Carlo Goldoni
VIA DEL PARIONE
INFERNO
PURGATORIO
MONALDA
SASSETTI
POST
V. PELLICCERIA
CALIMALA
PALAZZO CORSINI
PARIONCINO
Piazza de' Davanzati
PONTE ALLA CARRAIA
LUNGARNO CORSINI
SANTA TRÌNITÀ
Piazza di Santa Trìnita
VIA PORTA ROSSA
VIA
DAVANZATI PALACE
MERCATO NUOVO
Arno River
VIA DELLE TERME
BORGO
BOMBARDE
S. S. APOSTOLI
MANETTO
VIA POR S. MARIA
ARMA
Piazza de' Salt.
LUNGARNO GUICCIARDINI
Piazza Nazaro Sauro
PONTE S. TRINITÀ
LUNGARNO ACCIAIUOLI
LAMB.
S. Stephano
Piazza de' Frescobaldi
PONTE VECCHIO
VIA MAGGIO
SAN JACOPO
BORGO SAN JACOPO
Piazza della Passera
V.D. RAMAGLIANTI
To Pitti Palace
1
2
3
4
5
6
7
8
13
18
22
34
35
36
37
38
39
43
Gelaterie
40 Gelateria Carabè
41 Grom
42 Perchè No! Gelateria
43 Carapina
44 Gelateria de' Neri
45 Vivoli's Gelateria

EATING

1 Mercato Centrale Eateries
2 Trattoria Mario's & Trattoria Zà-Zà
3 Casa del Vino
4 Pepò
5 Trattoria la Burrasca
6 Mostodolce Beer Hall
7 Self-Service Rist. Leonardo
8 Paszkowski Café
9 EATaly
10 Turkuaz Döner Kebab
11 Istanbul Döner Kebab
12 Veggy
13 Rivoire Café
14 Osteria Vini e Vecchi Sapori
15 Frescobaldi Ristorante & Wine Bar
16 Cantinetta dei Verrazzano
17 I Fratellini
18 'Ino Wine Bar
19 L'Antico Trippaio, Pizzeria Totò & Supermarket
20 Da' Vinattieri
21 Il Cernacchino
22 Panini Tartufati Procacci
23 Due Sorsi e un Boccone
24 La Mescita Fiaschetteria
25 Il Centro Supermercati
26 Pasticceria Robiglio
27 To Antica Trattoria da Tito
28 Ristorante Cafaggi
29 Ristorante del Fagioli
30 Trattoria Anita
31 Trattoria l'cche C'è C'è
32 All'Antico Vinaio
33 Club del Gusto
34 Trattoria Sostanza-Troia
35 Trattoria Marione
36 Trattoria al Trebbio
37 Trattoria "da Giorgio"
38 Caffè La Terrazza
39 Sesio Bar
Gelateria
To 27
VIA VENTISETTE APRILE
SAN MARCO MUSEUM
VIA ARAZZIERI
Piazza di San Marco
VIA GIORGIO LA PIRA
UNIVERSITY
VIA SANTA REPARATA
VIA SAN GALLO
VIA CAVOUR
VIA GUELFA
ACCADEMIA (DAVID)
VIA DE' GINORI
LEONARDO MUSEUM
MUSEUM OF PRECIOUS STONES
V. D. ALFANI
VIA RICASOLI
MEDICI-RICCARDI PALACE
ROTUNDA
VIA DEI SERVI
Piazza Brunelleschi
VIA DEI PUCCI
VIA BIFFI
PALAZZO PUCCI
LEONARDO MUSEUM
VIA MARTELLI
HOSPITAL
VIA M. BUFALINI
DUOMO SIGHTS TICKET OFFICE
BAPTISTERY
DUOMO
Piazza di Santa Maria Nuova
DUOMO MUSEUM
MUSEO DI FIRENZE COM' ERA
Piazza del Duomo
CAMPANILE
VIA DELL'ORIUOLO
CANONICA
VIA DELL'OCHE
BONIZZI
STUDIO
SANTA MARIA DE' RICCI
OPERA DEL DUOMO STUDIO
VIA DEL PROCONSOLO
B. D. ALBIZI
VIA CALZAIUOLI
VIA DEL CORSO
CASA DI DANTE
PRESTO
V. DE' GIRALDI
V. DE' PANDOLFINI
V. TAVO.
VIA D. ALIGHIERI
S. MARIA
CERCHI
CIMATORI
LA BADIA
BARGELLO MUSEUM
CONDOTTA
VIA DELLA VIGNA VECCHIA
VIA BURELLA
Piazza della Signoria
Piazza S. Firenze
V. DELL'ANGUILLARA
VIA BENTA.
GONDI
LOGGIA
WC
PALAZZO VECCHIO
BORGO DE' GRECI
Piazza Santa Croce
VIA DI SAN GIUSEPPE
UFFIZI GALLERY
VIA LEONI
CORNO
VINEGIA
MAGALOTTI
RUSTICI
Piazza Peruzzi
V. D. BENCI
SANTA CROCE
EXIT
VIA CASTELLANI
CASTELLO
OSTERIA
VIA MOSCA
VIA DE' NERI
BRACHE
B. S. CROCE
PAZZI CHAPEL
Piazza Giudici
SAPONAI
VAGELLA I
Piazza Mentana
MALENCHINI
CORSO DEI TINTORI
LEATHER SCHOOL'S OUTSIDE ENTRANCE
GALILEO SCIENCE MUSEUM
LUNG. GEN. DIAZ
LIBRARY

a similar menu (with a few differences, including more *taglieri* options—cheese-and-meat plates), a trendier-feeling interior, and a smaller, more open outdoor-dining zone.

Pepò, a colorful and charmingly unpretentious space tucked just around the corner from the Zà-Zà glitz, handles its neighbor's overflow admirably. With a short menu of simple but well-prepared Florentine classics, it's an easy neighborhood fallback where you won't feel like you've settled for second-best (€9-10 pastas, €11-14 *secondi,* daily 12:00-14:30 & 19:00-22:30, Via Rosina 4/6 red, tel. 055-283-259).

Trattoria la Burrasca is Flintstone-chic. Friendly Elio and his staff offer a limited menu with good-value seasonal specials of Tuscan home cooking. It's small, with just 14 tables—and often a copy of this guidebook on every one (it's typically filled with my readers). If Archie Bunker were Italian, he'd eat at this trattoria for special nights out (€6-7 pastas, €8-14 *secondi,* no cover or service charge, Tue-Sun 12:00-15:00 & 19:00-22:30, closed Mon, Via Panicale 6, north corner of Mercato Centrale, tel. 055-215-827).

Beer Hall: To get a taste of Italy's growing obsession with microbrews, nurse a pint at the rollicking **Mostodolce,** a *"birrificio artigianale"* (craft brewery). They serve nine different craft beers—their own production—and basic €6-10 pub grub to appreciative, raucous, youthful patrons who pin their drawings to the walls and spill out onto the street (daily 11:00-24:00, Via Nazionale 114 red, tel. 055-230-2928).

QUICK MEALS NEAR THE DUOMO

Self-Service Ristorante Leonardo is an inexpensive, air-conditioned, quick, and handy cafeteria. It feels no-frills and old-school, but the food is better than many table-service eateries in this part of town. Stefano and Luciano (like Pavarotti) run the place with enthusiasm and put out free pitchers of tap water. It's just a block from the Duomo, southwest of the Baptistery (€5 *primi*, €6-7 main courses, lots of veggies, daily 11:45-14:45 & 18:45-21:45, closed Sat Nov-March, upstairs at Via Pecori 11, tel. 055-284-446).

Paszkowski, a grand café on Piazza della Repubblica, serves up inexpensive, quick lunches. At the display case, order a salad or €6 plate of pasta or cooked veggies (or half-and-half for €7), pay the cashier, and find a seat upstairs. Better yet, eat at one of the tables on the square—you can sit on the right side of the terrace for no extra charge...but note that the full-table service prices are much more expensive (daily 7:00-24:00, lunch served 12:00-15:00, closed Mon off-season, Piazza della Repubblica 35 red—northwest corner, tel. 055-210-236).

Gourmet Mini-Mall with Food Counters: **EATaly** is an outpost of the small but growing chain of foodie mini-malls that are popping up in big Italian cities (as well as in New York City, thanks to part-owner Mario Batali). This slick, modern space just a half-block from the Duomo offers several food options under one roof: a soft-serve gelato counter and tempting pastry shop (just inside the door); a grocery store for top-end Italian ingredients and kitchen gadgets; and, in back, a cluster of food counters serving €9-12 pastas and pizzas and €10-16 *secondi,* including daily specials. If you don't have time to browse the markets and corner stores, this could be a handy place for a pricey, one-stop surgical strike to assemble a gourmet picnic or to stock up on edible souvenirs (Mon-Sat 9:00-22:30, Sun 10:00-22:30, restaurants closed before 12:00 and 15:30-19:00, Via de' Martelli 22 red, tel. 055-015-3601).

Döner Kebab: A good place to try this cheap Middle Eastern specialty is **Turkuaz,** a couple of blocks northeast of the Duomo (Via dei Servi 65; see sidebar on page 296).

NEAR PIAZZA DELLA SIGNORIA

Piazza della Signoria, the scenic square facing Palazzo Vecchio, is ringed by beautifully situated yet touristy eateries serving overpriced, bad-value, and probably microwaved food. If you're determined to eat on the square, have pizza at Ristorante il Cavallino or bar food from the Irish pub next door. Piazza della Signoria's saving grace is **Rivoire** café, famous for its fancy desserts and thick hot chocolate (€7). While obscenely expensive, it has the best view tables on the square. Stand at the bar with the locals and pay way less (Tue-Sun 7:30-24:00, closed Mon, tel. 055-214-412).

Dining near the Piazza

Osteria Vini e Vecchi Sapori, half a block north of Palazzo Vecchio, is a colorful eatery serving Tuscan food with a fun, accessible menu of delicious €8-10 pastas and €9-15 *secondi* (Mon-Sat 12:30-14:30 & 19:30-22:30, closed Sun, reserve for dinner; facing the bronze equestrian statue in Piazza della Signoria, go behind its tail into the corner and to your left; Via dei Magazzini 3 red, tel. 055-293-045, run by Mario while wife Rosanna cooks and son Thomas serves).

Frescobaldi Ristorante and Wine Bar, the showcase of Italy's aristocratic wine family, is a good choice for a formal dinner in Florence. Candlelight reflects off glasses of wine, and high-vaulted ceilings complement the sophisticated dishes. They offer the same seasonal menu in three different dining areas: cozy interior, tight wine bar, and breezy terrace. If coming for dinner, make a reservation and dress up (€11-15 appetizers and pastas, €19-26 *secondi,* lighter wine-bar menu at lunch, daily 12:00-14:30 & 19:00-22:30, closed the middle of Aug, air-con, half a block north of Palazzo

Cheap, Fast, and Not a Hint of Pasta

If you're on the move and crave a cheap, filling, healthy alternative to the typical plate of noodles or ham-and-cheese *panino,* you have some good options.

My favorite is the *döner kebab:* slow-roasted, ultra-thin-sliced chicken or veal stuffed into pita bread *(panino)* or a wrap *(piadina),* along with tomatoes, onions, lettuce, tangy yogurt sauce, and (optional) hot chili sauce. A vegetarian alternative is falafel (a fried garbanzo-bean patty) served with the same works. Dishes cost about €3-5, and shops are generally open from 11:00 in the morning until midnight. Kebab shops with more traffic tend to be better bets—their meat and toppings are that much fresher. A handy place is **Turkuaz** (two blocks from the Duomo at Via dei Servi 65); or try **Istanbul Döner Kebap** (Via dei Benci 18 red, just south of Santa Croce).

You can cover all the health-food bases at **Lovelife,** a simple, informal place with green salads, couscous and rice dishes, quiches, fruits, smoothies, and juices. Order at the counter, then eat at one of their few tables downstairs or take your meal to go (€4-5 meals, Mon-Fri 8:30-19:30, Sat 12:00-19:00, closed Sun, east of the Duomo at Via dell'Oriuolo 26 red—see map on page 20, tel. 055-263-8027).

Veggy is a hole-in-the-wall serving €5 *piadine* and *bruschette,* big €7 salads, and fruit and veggie "shakes" to go (daily 10:00-19:00, steps north of the Duomo at Via dei Servi 8 red, tel. 348-651-0507).

Several stands selling fresh fruit, juice, and "smoothies" are found throughout the center. Try **Il Chiosco** (The Kiosk), which faces the southeast corner of the Duomo (sporadic hours but usually daily 9:00-19:00, closed Nov-Feb, Piazza delle Pallattole). Another stand is south of Piazza della Repubblica, on the corner of Via Porta Rossa and Via Pellicceria.

Vecchio at Via dei Magazzini 2-4 red, tel. 055-284-724, www.deifrescobaldi.it, Duccio).

Cheap, Simple Eats near the Piazza

Cantinetta dei Verrazzano, a long-established bakery/café/wine bar, serves delightful sandwich plates in an old-time setting. Their *selezione Verrazzano* is a fine plate of four little crostini (like mini-bruschetta) proudly featuring different breads, cheeses, and meats from the Chianti region (€7.50). The *tagliere di focacce,* a sampler plate of mini-focaccia sandwiches, is also fun (€16 for big plate for two). Add a €6 glass of Chianti to either of these dishes to make a fine, light meal. Office workers pop in for a quick lunch, and it's traditional to share tables. Be warned: Prices can add up here in a hurry (Mon-Sat 8:00-21:00, Sun 10:00-16:30, no reservations taken, just off Via de' Calzaiuoli, across from Orsanmichele Church at Via dei Tavolini 18, tel. 055-268-590). They also have benches and tiny tables for eating at take-out prices. Simply step to the back and point to a hot *focacce* sandwich (€3), order a drink at the bar, and take away your food or sit with Florentines and watch the action while you munch. For dessert, consider their tempting display case of delicious cakes.

I Fratellini is a hole-in-the-wall where the "little brothers" have served peasants 29 different kinds of sandwiches and cheap glasses of Chianti wine (see list on wall) since 1875. Join the local crowd to order, then sit on a nearby curb to eat, placing your glass on the wall rack before you leave (€3 sandwiches, daily 9:00-19:30 or until the bread runs out, closed Sun in winter, 20 yards in front of Orsanmichele Church on Via dei Cimatori, tel. 055-239-6096). Be adventurous with the menu (easy-order by number). Consider *finocchiona e caprino* (#15, a Tuscan salami and soft goat cheese), *lardo di Colonnata* (#22, cured lard aged in Carrara marble), and *cinghiale* (#19, spicy boar salami) sandwiches. Order the most expensive wine they're selling by the glass (€5 for a medium pour of Brunello; bottles are labeled).

EATING

Wine Bar near Ponte Vecchio: **'Ino** is a mod little shop filled with gifty edibles. Alessandro and his staff serve €5-8 sandwiches and €3.50 glasses of wine—you'll munch your meal while perched on a tiny stool. They can also make a fine €9-12 *piatto misto* of cheeses and meats with bread (daily 11:30-16:30, immediately behind Uffizi Gallery courtyard on Ponte Vecchio side, between olive tree and river, Via dei Georgofili 7 red, tel. 055-219-208).

Cheap Takeout on Via Dante Alighieri: Three handy places line up on this street, just a couple of blocks from the Duomo. **L'Antico Trippaio,** a food cart, is a fixture in the town center. Cheap and authentic as can be, this is where locals come daily for €4-7 sandwiches *(panini)*, featuring specialties like *trippa* (tripe), *lampredotto*, and a list of more appetizing options, including *bollito* (for more on these, see sidebar on page 290). Lisa, Maurizio, and Roberto offer a free plastic glass of rotgut Chianti with each sandwich for travelers with this book (daily 9:00-21:00, on Via Dante Alighieri, mobile 339-742-5692). **Pizzeria Totò,** just next to the tripe stand, has good €2.50-3 slices (daily 10:30-23:00, Via Dante Alighieri 28 red, tel. 055-290-406). And a few steps in the opposite direction is a **Metà supermarket,** with cheap drinks and snacks and a fine *antipasti* case inside (daily 8:30-21:30, Sun from 9:00, Via Dante Alighieri 20-24). If you pick up lunch at any of these, the best people-watching place to enjoy your sandwich is three blocks away, on Piazza della Signoria.

More Sandwich Shops in the Historic Center: Two additional handy, well-regarded places to grab a €4 sandwich are **Da' Vinat-**

tieri, just a half-block from the Duomo (*schiaccata* sandwiches plus *trippa* and *lampredotto*, daily 10:00-19:30, next to Casa di Dante at Via Santa Margherita 4 red); and **Il Cernacchino** (*panino* sandwiches, Mon-Sat 9:30-19:30, closed Sun, just north of Palazzo Vecchio at Via della Condotta 38 red, tel. 055-294-119). For something substantially more upscale, yet still affordable, stop by **Panini Tartufati Procacci**—right along Florence's most genteel boutique-browsing street. This wine bar, with a swanky, circa-1885 atmosphere, specializes in pungent truffle-scented ingredients: €5 *panini* and €9-18 sampler plates of *salumi* and cheeses. While the platters are pricey, the sandwiches may be Florence's cheapest way to dine on truffles (Mon-Sat 10:00-20:00, closed Sun, Via Tornabuoni 64 red, tel. 055-211-656).

NEAR THE ACCADEMIA

There aren't many appealing sit-down restaurants in the boring streets near the Accademia (though two excellent choices, Da Tito and La Cafaggi, aren't too far away and are worth a detour—described later). But hungry tourists looking for a quick lunch between sightseeing stops find plenty of options. My favorite plan is to picnic in the ultimate Renaissance square: Grab a take-out bite at one of these places, then hike around the block and join the bums on **Piazza S.S. Annunziata,** the first Renaissance square in Florence (don't confuse this with the less-interesting Piazza San Marco, closer to the supermarket). There's a fountain for washing fruit on the square. Grab a stony seat anywhere you like, and savor one of my favorite cheap Florence eating experiences.

Due Sorsi e un Boccone ("Two Sips and a Bite"), just around the corner from *David*, serves just that: €1 glasses of house wine and €3.50 savory or sweet crêpes and made-to-order *schiacciate* (sandwiches on flattened, foccacia-like bread). Order your food to go, or squeeze into the tight interior (just a few counters and tall stools). It's run with a fresh, youthful attitude and jammed with local students at lunchtime (Mon-Fri 11:00-19:00, closed Sat-Sun, Via degli Alfani 105 red, mobile 334-264-0931).

La Mescita Fiaschetteria is a characteristic hole-in-the-wall a few steps farther down the same street, where locals and students enjoy €5-6 pasta plates, €6-8 *secondi,* or hearty €2.50 sandwiches with good €1.50 house wine. The place can either be mobbed by students or a peaceful time warp, depending on when you stop by. Mirco and Alessio are gregarious to the point of being a bit pushy... order carefully and check your bill (Mon-Sat 10:45-16:00, closed Sun, Via degli Alfani 70 red, mobile 338-992-2640).

Il Centro Supermercati, a handy supermarket a half-block north of the Accademia, has a curbside sandwich bar (Panineria); you'll order your sandwich at the bar, then head inside the supermarket to pick up any other provisions and pay (Mon-Sat 8:30-20:00, Sun 10:00-15:00, sandwich counter may close earlier, Via Ricasoli 109 red).

Sit-Down Lunch in a Classy Café: **Pasticceria Robiglio,** a smart little café, opens up its stately dining area and sets out a few tables on the sidewalk for lunch. They have a small menu of daily pasta and *secondi* specials, and seem determined to do things like they did in the elegant, pre-tourism days. Before you leave, be tempted by their pastries—famous among Florentines (generous €9-10 plates, a great €8 *niçoise*-like "fantasy salad," pretty pastries, smiling service, daily 12:00-15:00, longer hours as a café, a block toward the Duomo off Piazza S.S. Annunziata at Via dei Servi 112 red, tel. 055-212-784).

Memorable Restaurants a Bit Farther from the Accademia

These two places—within a 5- to 10-minute walk of the Accademia—are worth going out of your way for to get a memorable meal.

Antica Trattoria da Tito, a 10-minute hike from the Accademia along Via San Gallo, can be fun if you want a long, drawn-out event of a meal with a local crowd and smart-aleck service. The boss, Bobo, serves quality traditional food and lots of wine. While the food is good, there's no pretense—it's just a playground of Tuscan cuisine with "no romance allowed." The music is vintage 1980s and can be loud. To gorge on a feast of *antipasti* (cold cuts, cheeses, a few veggies, and bruschetta), consider ordering *fermami* (literally "stop me")—for €17, Bobo brings you food until you say, *"Fermami!"* A couple can get *fermami*, desserts, and a nice bottle of wine for around €60 total. As this is a popular place, they say that reservations are "almost obligatory" (€6-10 pastas, €10-18 *secondi*, €17 *gran tagliere*—big plate of cheese and meat, travelers with this book get a free after-dinner drink, Mon-Sat 12:30-15:00 & 19:00-23:00, closed Sun, Via San Gallo 112 red, tel. 055-472-475, www.trattoriadatito.it).

Ristorante Cafaggi fills a bright, sophisticated-but-not-snobby space on a drab street between the Accademia and Mercato Centrale. With a vaguely 1950s vibe, it feels like it's been retro since before it was "retro." Family-run since 1922, with Grandma and Grandpa still puttering around and lending a hand, this place feels devoted to good cuisine, with a thoughtfully planned menu and recipes posted on their website. The service can be a bit shy; the emphasis here is their generations-old passion for Florentine food. In addition to flawlessly executed renditions of many of the local favorites described on page 657, notice that the menu includes more challenging-yet-authentic dishes, such as tripe and brains (€8-10 pastas, €12-16 *secondi,* Mon-Sat 12:30-15:00 & 19:00-22:00, closed Sun, Via Guelfa 35 red, tel. 055-294-989, www.ristorantecafaggi.com).

BETWEEN PALAZZO VECCHIO AND SANTA CROCE CHURCH

Ristorante del Fagioli, an enthusiastically run eatery where you can sense the heritage, just feels real. The dad, Gigi, commands the kitchen while family members Antonio, Maurizio, and Simone keep the throngs of loyal customers returning. The cuisine: home-style bread-soups, hearty steaks, and other Florentine classics. Don't worry—while *fagioli* means "beans," that's the family name, not the extent of the menu (€9-12 pastas and *secondi,* cash only, Mon-Fri 12:30-14:30 & 19:30-22:30, closed Sat-Sun, reserve for dinner, a block north of the Alle Grazie bridge at Corso dei Tintori 47, tel. 055-244-285).

Trattoria Anita, midway between the Uffizi and Santa Croce, feels old-school, with wood paneling and rows of wine bottles. Brothers Nicola, Gianni, and Maurizio offer a good-value lunch special: three hearty Tuscan courses for €10 on weekdays (€7-8 pastas, €7-13 *secondi,* Mon-Sat 12:00-14:30 & 19:00-22:15, closed Sun, on the corner of Via Vinegia and Via del Parlagio at 2 red, tel. 055-218-698).

Trattoria I'cche C'è C'è (EE-kay chay chay; dialect for "whatever there is, there is") is a small, tourist-crammed, family-style restaurant where fun-loving Gino, his wife Mara, and their son Jacopo serve functional Florentine dishes. It's worth considering for budget travelers who want an affordable sit-down meal in a lively locale—their €13 three-course, fixed-price meal is a good deal, if high cuisine is not your priority (also €7-12 pastas, €12-18 *secondi,* Tue-Sun 12:30-14:30 & 19:30-22:30, closed Mon and two weeks in Aug, midway between Bargello and river at Via Magalotti 11 red, tel. 055-216-589).

Quick Lunch Places behind Palazzo Vecchio: Via dei Neri, which runs behind Palazzo Vecchio and the Uffizi exit toward Santa Croce, seems to specialize in sightseers seeking lunch between landmarks. Clearly the most popular is **All'Antico Vinaio,** a photogenic Florentine favorite, which offers two options: You can either stand in the street, grabbing a €5 sandwich and pouring your own wine (€2/glass), or head across the street to their *osteria* to sit down and order from a more extensive menu (Mon-Sat 12:00-23:00, Sun 12:00-16:00, Via dei Neri 65 red, tel. 055-238-2723). If Vinaio is just too overrun, a few doors down is the quieter **Club del Gusto,** with friendly owner/chef Paolo. Grab a salad or sandwich to carry away, or enjoy a made-to-order pasta plate at a table in back

(€5 *crostini* and pastas, €6 small *secondi*, daily 9:00-24:00, Via dei Neri 50 red, tel. 348-090-3142).

NEAR THE CHURCH OF SANTA MARIA NOVELLA

Trattoria Sostanza-Troia, characteristic and well-established, is famous for its beef. Hearty steaks and pastas are splittable. Whirling ceiling fans and walls strewn with old photos evoke earlier times, while the artichoke pies remind locals of Grandma's cooking. Crowded, shared tables with vinyl tablecloths give the place the feel of a simple bistro. Reservations are always a good idea but essential for dinner, during which they offer two seatings, at 19:30 and 21:00 (€9-11 pastas, €12-18 *secondi,* cash only, lunch served Mon-Sat 12:30-14:00, closed Sun, closed Sat off-season, Via del Porcellana 25 red, tel. 055-212-691).

Trattoria Marione serves sincerely home cooked-style meals to a mixed group of tourists and Florentines beneath hanging ham hocks. The ambience is happy, crowded, food-loving, and a bit frantic (€9-12 pastas, €10-13 *secondi,* daily 12:00-17:00 & 19:00-23:00, Via della Spada 27 red, tel. 055-214-756, Fabio).

Trattoria al Trebbio serves traditional food, especially rabbit and steak, in a throwback Florentine setting. Inside, enjoy the old movie posters and garlands of garlic, or grab one of the few tables outside (€7-10 pastas, €10-14 *secondi,* daily 12:00-15:00 & 19:00-23:00, half a block off of Piazza Santa Maria Novella at Via delle Belle Donne 47 red, tel. 055-287-089, Antonio).

Trattoria "da Giorgio" is a family-style diner on a sketchy street serving up piping-hot, simple home cooking to happy locals and tourists alike. Their three-course, fixed-price meal, including water and a drink, is a great value (€13 at lunch, €14 at dinner). Choose from among the daily specials or the regular menu. This place is completely without pretense—ideal for a cheap but fun night out (Mon-Sat 12:00-14:30 & 18:30-22:00, closed Sun, Via Palazzuolo 100 red, tel. 055-284-302, Silvano).

HIDDEN ROOFTOP CAFÉ TERRACES WITH HIGH PRICES AND SPECTACULAR VIEWS

If you're willing to pay way too much to nurse a drink surrounded by Florentine splendor, head to one of these rooftop terraces.

Caffè La Terrazza, at the top of La Rinascente department store overlooking Piazza della Repubblica (and described on page 327), is the slightly more lowbrow, more affordable option, with one of the best views in Florence of the nearby Duomo, which looms gloriously on the horizon (€6 coffee drinks).

Sesio, perched on the top floor of the luxurious Westin Hotel on Piazza Ognissanti, charges outrageous prices for cocktails (€15 and up; €6 coffee drinks) with amazing views of the Florence sky-

Gelato

Italy's best ice cream is in Florence. But beware of scams at touristy joints on busy streets that turn a simple request for a cone into a €10 "tourist special" rip-off. To avoid this, survey the size options and specify what you want—for example, *un cono da tre euro* (a €3 cone). For more gelato tips, see page 652.

All of these places, which are a cut above, are open daily for long hours.

Near the Accademia: A Sicilian choice on a tourist thoroughfare, **Gelateria Carabè** is particularly famous for its luscious granite—Italian ices made with fresh fruit. A *cremolata* is a granita with a dollop of gelato—a delicious combination (from the Accademia, it's a block toward the Duomo at Via Ricasoli 60 red).

Near the Duomo: **Grom** used to be a strictly boutique *gelateria,* but its smart and aggressive expansion plan has now conquered Italy and beyond (with branches in New York City and Malibu). While they tout their organic ingredients and seasonally changing menu, that claim carries a bit less weight coming from a global chain. But the quality is still reasonably good—as the line you'll frequently see here attests—and the location is handy to the Duomo area (Via delle Oche 24 red). Just up Via Cavour from the Duomo, the **EATaly** foodie superstore has a unique soft-serve gelato counter just inside the door (Via de' Martelli 22 red).

line. As you're at the eastern edge of town, the city lines up before you: Duomo, Palazzo Vecchio, Ponte Vecchio, Pitti Palace. To turn your pricey drink into a light dinner, come by during their *aperitivo* happy hour (19:00-21:00), when your €15 drink includes access to a little buffet, giving you something to nibble as the sun sinks low in the sky and bathes the skyline in a spotlight (daily 12:00-24:00, Piazza Ognissanti 3, tel. 055-27151). This is a nice finale to a shopping stroll down Borgo Santi Apostoli and Borgo Ognissanti (see page 326 in the Shopping in Florence chapter).

South of the Arno River, in the Oltrarno

In general, dining in the Oltrarno offers a more authentic experience; although it's quite close to the old center, tourists imagine that it's another world and tend to stay away. At many of these places, Florentines may even outnumber my readers. For locations, see the map on page 284.

Near Orsanmichele Church: **Perchè No!** is located dead-central—just off the busy main pedestrian drag, Via de' Calzaiuoli—and it's surprisingly good, much better than similar-seeming places nearby. They serve up a few unusual flavors, to boot (Via dei Tavolini 19).

Near Ponte Vecchio: **Carapina** is a mod *gelateria* with some pleasantly atypical flavors, seasonal ingredients, and a loyal following (Via Lambertesca 18 red).

Near the Church of Santa Croce: Florentines flock to **Gelateria de' Neri,** with an enticingly wide array of flavors (Via dei Neri 9 red). Nearby, the venerable **Vivoli's** still has great gelato—but it's more expensive, and stingy in its servings. Before ordering, try a free sample of their rice flavor—*riso* (opposite the Church of Santa Croce, go down Via Torta a block and turn right on Via Stinche).

Across the River: If you want an excuse to check out the little village-like neighborhood across the river from Santa Croce (or are walking to Piazzale Michelangelo), enjoy a gelato at the tiny **Il Gelato di Filo** (named for Filippo and Lorenzo) at Via San Miniato 5 red, a few steps toward the river from Porta San Miniato (see map on page 20). Foodies and connoisseurs rank Filo as one of Florence's best (and in this city, that's really saying something). Gelato chef Edmir is proud of his fruity sorbet as well. Closer to the main sights (roughly between Pitti Palace and Brancacci Chapel), **Gelateria della Passera** is another good, popular, classy choice (Via Toscanella 15).

DINING OR DRINKING WITH A PONTE VECCHIO VIEW

Golden View Open Bar is a lively, trendy bistro, good for a romantic meal or just a salad, pizza, or pasta with fine wine and a fine view of Ponte Vecchio and the Arno River. Its white, minimalist interior is a stark contrast to atmospheric old Florence. Reservations for window tables are essential unless you drop in early for dinner (€10 pizzas, €11-16 pastas, big €13 salads, €20-30 *secondi,* daily 11:30-24:00, impressive wine bar, 50 yards east of Ponte Vecchio at Via dei Bardi 58, tel. 055-214-502, mobile 333-475-7400, www.goldenviewopenbar.com, run by Antonio, Marco, and Tommaso). They have four seating areas (with the same menu and prices) for whatever mood you're in: a riverside pizza place, a classier restaurant, a jazzy lounge, and a wine bar (they also serve a buffet of appetizers free with your €10-12 drink from 19:00 to 21:30). Mixing their fine wine, river views, and live jazz makes for a wonderful evening (jazz Mon, Wed, Fri, and Sat nights at 21:00).

DINING WELL IN THE OLTRARNO

Of the many good and colorful restaurants in the Oltrarno, these are my favorites. You can survey most of them while following the route in the ✪ Oltrarno Walk chapter before making a choice. Reservations are a good idea in the evening.

Il Santo Bevitore Ristorante, lit like a Rembrandt painting and filled with dressy tables, serves creative Tuscan cuisine. They're enthusiastic about matching quality produce from the area with the right wine. This is a good break from the big, sloppy plates of pasta you'll get at many Florence eateries (€9-12 pastas, €8-12 meat-and-cheese *taglieri,* €10-18 *secondi,* good wine list by the glass or bottle, daily 12:30-14:30 & 19:30-22:30, closed Sun for lunch, come early or make reservations, no outside seating, Via di Santo Spirito 64, tel. 055-211-264, www.ilsantobevitore.com). Their smaller wine bar next door, **Enoteca Il Santino Gastronomia,** feels like the perfect after-work hangout for foodies who'd like a glass of wine and some light food. Tight, cozy, and atmospheric, one wall is occupied by the bar, where you can assemble an €8-12 *tagliere* of local cheeses and *salumi* (also available to take away). They also have a few €6-8 hot dishes. Both the food and the wine are locally sourced from small producers (daily 12:30-23:00, Via di Santo Spirito 60 red, no reservations, tel. 055-230-2820).

Trattoria 4 Leoni creates the quintessential Oltrarno dinner scene, and is understandably popular with tourists. The Tuscan-style food is made with an innovative twist and an appreciation for vegetables. You'll enjoy the fun energy and characteristic seating, both outside on the colorful square, Piazza della Passera, and inside, where you'll dine in exposed-stone sophistication. While the wines by the glass are pricey, the house wine is good (€10-14 *primi,* €12-15 *secondi,* daily 12:00-24:00, dinner reservations smart; from Ponte Vecchio walk four blocks up Via de' Guicciardini, turn right on Via dello Sprone, then slightly left to Via de' Vellutini 1; tel. 055-218-562, www.4leoni.com).

Antico Ristoro Di' Cambi is a meat lover's dream—thick with Tuscan traditions, rustic touches, and T-bone steaks. The bustling scene has a memorable, beer-hall energy. As you walk in, you'll pass a glass case filled with red chunks of Chianina beef that's priced by weight (for the famous *bistecca alla fiorentina,* €40/kilo, standard serving is half a kilo per person). Before you OK your investment, they'll show you the cut and tell you the weight. While the steak comes nearly uncooked, it's air-dried for 21 days so it's not really raw, just very tasty and tender—it'll make you happy you're at the top of the food chain. Sit inside the convivial woody interior or outside on a square (€8-10 pastas, €10-18 *secondi,* Mon-Sat 12:00-14:30 & 18:30-22:30, closed Sun, reserve on weekends and to sit outside, Via Sant'Onofrio 1 red, one block south of Ponte

Amerigo Vespucci, see map on page 20, tel. 055-217-134, www.anticoristorodicambi.it, run by Stefano and Fabio, the Cambi cousins).

Olio & Convivium Gastronomia is primarily a catering company for top-end events, and this is where they showcase their cooking. It started as an elegant deli whose refined olive-oil-tasting room morphed into a romantic, aristocratic restaurant. Their three intimate rooms are surrounded by fine *prosciutti,* cheeses, and wine shelves. It can seem intimidating and a little pretentious, but well-dressed foodies will appreciate this place for its quiet atmosphere. Their list of €14-25 *gastronomia* plates offers an array of taste treats and fine wines by the glass (€14-18 pastas, €20-22 *secondi,* stylish €18 lunches with wine, Tue-Sun 12:00-14:30 & 19:00-22:30, closed Mon, strong air-con, Via di Santo Spirito 4, tel. 055-265-8198, Tommaso).

Trattoria da Sergio is a tiny eatery about a block before Porta San Frediano, one of Florence's medieval gates. It has charm and a strong following, so reservations are a must. The food is on the gourmet side of home-cooking—mama's favorites with a modern twist—and therefore a bit more expensive (€9-10 *primi,* €12-18 *secondi,* Mon-Sat 12:00-14:00 & 19:30-22:45, Sun 12:00-14:00 only, Borgo San Frediano 145 red, see map on page 20, tel. 055-223-449, Sergio and Marco).

Trattoria Al Tranvai, with tight seating and small dark-wood tables, looks like an old-time tram filled with the neighborhood gang. A 10-minute walk from the river at the edge of the Oltrarno, it feels like a small town's favorite eatery (€8-10 pastas, €10-13 *secondi,* Mon 19:00-24:00, Tue-Sat 12:30-14:30 & 19:30-22:30, closed Sun; from the Brancacci Chapel, go south on Via del Leone 5 minutes to Piazza T. Tasso 14 red—see map on page 20; tel. 055-225-197, www.altranvai.it).

Via di San Niccolò: This charming little street—the Oltrarno's "hipster corner"—can be a fun place for young foodies to explore. There's a convivial neighborhood pizzeria, an *enoteca,* a rollicking and youthful bar (Il Baretto del Rifrullo), and a *gelateria* scooping up some of Florence's best ice cream (Neri—see page 292). For those looking to dine, two eateries anchor the square: **Antica Mescita San Niccolò,** with traditional decor but a modern approach, feels like the grandkids took over Nonno's trattoria. Technically a wine bar, they also serve up Tuscan standbys. Check out their cellar, which is built in what was a thousand-year-old church crypt (€9 pastas, €14 *secondi,* daily 12:00-24:00, Via San Niccolò 60 red, tel. 055-234-2836). **Zeb** is a tight, mod, minimalist wine-bar/deli with one long counter (just two dozen seats) flanked by tall stools. Although the name is short for *zuppe e bolliti* ("soup and boiled meats"), they dish up all types of well-executed and elegantly presented Florentine food. The chalkboard menu lists homemade pastas and meat and fish *secondi*. Portions are large and fun to share. While smiley Mama Guiseppina is charming, her son Alberto—who interacts with the English-speaking clients—didn't quite inherit her warmth. The clientele is a mix of tipsy regulars and international foodies seeking a slightly fresher take on Italian classics. Dinner reservations are smart (€8-12 pastas and *secondi*, Mon-Tue 9:30-20:00, Thu-Sat 9:30-22:30, Sun 9:30-17:00, closed Wed, Via San Miniato 2 red, tel. 055-234-2864, www.zebgastronomia.com).

EATING CHEAPLY IN THE OLTRARNO

Trattoria Sabatino, farthest away and least touristy of my Oltrarno listings, is a spacious, brightly lit mess hall. You get the feeling it hasn't changed much since it opened—in 1956. It's disturbingly cheap, with family character and a simple menu—a super place to watch locals munch, especially since you'll likely be sharing a table. You'll find it just outside Porta San Frediano, a 15-minute walk from Ponte Vecchio (€4 pastas, €5-6 *secondi*, Mon-Fri 12:00-14:30 & 19:15-22:00, closed Sat-Sun, Via Pisana 2 red, see map on page 20, tel. 055-225-955, www.trattoriasabatino.it, little English spoken). Let eating here be your reward after following the stroll in my ✪ Oltrarno Walk chapter.

EATING

Trattoria Casalinga, an inexpensive standby, comes with aproned women bustling around the kitchen. Florentines and tourists alike pack the place and leave full and happy, with euros to spare for gelato (€7 pastas, €9-11 *secondi*, Mon-Sat 12:00-14:30 & 19:00-22:00, after 20:00 reserve or wait, closed Sun and Aug, just off Piazza di Santo Spirito, near the church at Via de' Michelozzi 9 red, tel. 055-218-624, www.trattorialacasalinga.it, Andrea and Paolo).

Caffè Ricchi has fine gelato, homemade desserts, shaded outdoor tables, and €4 pasta dishes at lunch (self-service or to go). After noting the plain facade of the Brunelleschi church facing the square, step inside the café and pick your favorite picture of the many ways the church might be finished (daily 7:00-24:00, until 21:00 in winter, tel. 055-280-830). **Ristorante Ricchi,** its sister restaurant next door, is more formal, has a larger menu, and also has tables on the square.

Le Volpi e l'Uva, a wine bar just steps from Ponte Vecchio, has a limited menu of *affettati* (cold cuts), cheese, and *crostone* (hearty bruschetta)—a nice spot for a light lunch (for details, see the listing on page 335).

Supermarket: Sapori & Dintorni Conad, just over Ponte Vecchio and to the left, has all you need for a picnic (Mon-Sat 8:30-21:00, Sun 9:30-21:00).

Cooking Classes

Tuscany has some of Italy's best food, and Florence is a natural place to learn a thing or two from this region's prodigious culinary tradition. Cooking classes range from multi-day or multi-week courses for professional and semi-professional chefs, to two- or three-hour crash courses for tourists. If you're an efficiency fiend like I am, these are a great use of time: You're combining a unique Italian experience (learning to cook, say, pasta from scratch) with a satisfying meal, all in just a few hours.

In my experience, the best casual cooking classes are taught by trained chefs with actual restaurant experience (rather than hobbyists or unemployed Florentines embarking on a second career); take place in a real kitchen environment (rather than a stuffy classroom or "show" kitchen); have a spirit of fun and interaction; involve smaller groups (allowing more personal interaction with the instructor); and—perhaps most importantly—are hands-on rather than demonstration-based.

You'll typically spend a couple of hours cooking, then sit down to a hard-earned (if not always flawlessly executed) meal. They'll send you on your way with the recipes you prepared that day, ready to try to re-create them at home. Some classes also include a shopping trip to the market. While this adds an engaging dimension to your cooking experience, it also adds time and expense, and (some think) draws the focus away from the actual cooking.

The options listed below represent only a few of your many choices. As this is a fast-changing scene, if you're serious about taking a cooking class in Florence, it's worth doing some homework online (compare websites, read reviews) and booking well ahead.

Through a Cooking School: **In Tavola** hits a good balance: It's a dedicated cooking school in the heart of the Oltrarno, where trained, Italian but English-speaking chefs quickly demonstrate each step before setting you loose to try your hand. The kitchen feels functional and real (in a good way), but you'll sit down to eat in the cozy wine cellar (classes ranging from €53-73/person, multi-lesson professional courses available, ideally book well ahead but you can try calling last-minute, between Pitti Palace and Brancacci Chapel at Via dei Velluti 18/20 red, tel. 055-217-672, www.intavola.org, info@intavola.org, Fabrizio and American Jennifer).

Through a Tour Operator: Several reputable walking-tour companies in Florence offer a variety of cooking classes. **ArtViva** offers a range of hands-on cooking classes: three-course (€59/person), four-course (€68/person), pasta (€53/person), and pastry (€55/person; 10 percent discount with this book—log in at www.artviva.com/ricksteves with username "ricksteves" and password "reader"; tel. 055-264-5033). **Florencetown**'s five-hour experience starts

EATING

with a trip to Mercato Centrale, then settles into their kitchen for a cooking lesson (€85/person; also 3-hour pizza- and gelato-making class for €45/person; 10 percent discount with the code "RICK-STEVES," chef Giovanni, Via de Lamberti 1, tel. 055-281-103, www.florencetown.com). Both of these companies are described on page 29.

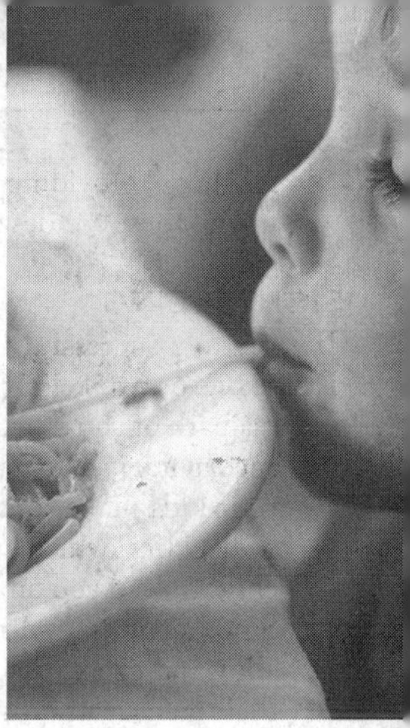

FLORENCE WITH CHILDREN

With relatively few kid-friendly activities, Florence may not be the ideal destination for a family vacation. But it does offer enough entertainment to keep kids occupied for a few days. Spend the morning hiking up to Piazzale Michelangelo or the top of the Duomo's dome. In the afternoons, wander the city's streets and squares looking for quirky sculptures or visit various interactive museums. Here are a few ideas for family fun in the art capital of Europe.

Trip Tips

EATING

Florence offers plenty of food options for children. Try these tips to keep your kids content throughout the day.

- For a refreshing respite from the midday heat, take a gelato break or go to an air-conditioned, kid-friendly place for lunch.
- Picnic lunches and dinners work well. For ready-made picnics, drop by a *rosticceria* (deli), a sandwich shop, or a cheap take-out pizzeria (*diavola* is the closest thing on the menu to pepperoni).
- Eat dinner early (at about 19:00) to dodge the romantic crowd. Restaurants are less kid-friendly after 21:00. Skip the famous places. Look instead for self-service cafeterias, bars (children are welcome), or fast-food restaurants where kids can move around without bothering others. Eating *al fresco* is fun; try places on squares where kids can run free while you dine. You can nearly always get some kind of plain noodles.
- For fast and kid-approved meals in the old center, there are plenty of hamburger and pizza joints. For a good cafeteria, try Self-Service Ristorante Leonardo (a block from the Duomo). *Gelaterie* such as Perchè No! (Via dei Tavolini 19) are brash

and neon, providing some of the best high-calorie memories in town. These are described in the Eating in Florence chapter.

SIGHTSEEING

The key to a successful Florence family vacation is to slow down. Tackle one or two key sights each day, mix in a healthy dose of pure fun at a park or square, and take extended breaks when needed.

- Incorporate your child's interests into each day's plans. Let your kids make some decisions, such as choosing lunch spots or deciding which stores or museums to visit. Deputize your child to lead you on my self-guided walks and museum tours.
- Since a trip is a splurge for parents, kids should enjoy a larger allowance, too. Provide ample money and ask your kids to buy their own treats, postcards, and trinkets within that daily budget.
- Buy your child a trip journal, and encourage him or her to write down observations, thoughts, and favorite sights and memories. This journal could end up being your child's favorite souvenir.
- It's good to have a "what if" procedure in place in case something goes wrong, such as getting separated in a crowd. Give your kids a business card from your hotel, your own contact information (if you brought a mobile phone), and a few euros to cover the cost of a phone call if they don't have their own mobile phones.
- If you allow kids to explore a museum or neighborhood on their own, be sure to establish a clear meeting time and place.
- Seek out kid-friendly sights, such as the Leonardo Museums, the Galileo Science Museum, or Palazzo Vecchio (all described later). If you're visiting art museums with younger children, you could hit the gift shop first so you can buy postcards; then hold a scavenger hunt to find the pictured artwork.
- Italy's national museums generally offer free admission to children under 18—always ask before buying tickets for your kids.
- Long museum lines add insult to injury for the preteen dragged into another old building filled with more old paintings. Book ahead to avoid lines whenever possible, especially at the Uffizi and Accademia; see page 38. Or you could get a Firenze Card (€72/adult for 3 days) to bypass lines. In this case, your kids (who get in free) can skip the line with you—but at busy and crowded sights like the Uffizi and Accademia, you may have to pay €4 for an on-the-spot reservation for them (for details on the Firenze Card, see page 34).
- Guidebooks can make history more accessible for kids. Try *Florence: Just Add Water* (excellent for travelers ages 10 to adult), easy to find in the US or in Florence (see bookstores

listed on page 24). The pocket-size, spiral-bound *Kids Go Europe: Treasure Hunt Florence,* available in the US, encourages youngsters to journal and sketch.

- Context Florence offers a children's tour program run by scholarly guides who make the city's great art and culture accessible to a younger audience (see page 30). Local guide Alessandra Marchetti also does kid-tailored tours (see page 31).

TRANSPORTATION

- Families with kids can sometimes get price breaks on train tickets; see page 671 for details.

Top Sights and Activities

MUSEUMS AND CHURCHES

Leonardo Museums

After touring a bunch of hands-off museums, squirming kids will enjoy the hands-on activities at either Le Macchine di Leonardo da Vinci or Museo Leonardo da Vinci. They can burn off some of that human energy while powering modern re-creations of the brilliant scientist's machines (see page 46).

Cost and Hours: Admission to each museum is €7 for adults (with this book, Le Macchine offers adults a €2 discount; the Museo offers €0.50 off), €5 for kids ages 6 and older, free for kids under 6. **Le Macchine di Leonardo da Vinci**—April-Oct daily 9:30-19:30; Nov-March Mon-Fri 11:00-17:00, Sat-Sun 9:30-19:30; for €1 extra they'll throw in a slice of pizza and a Coke, in Galleria Michelangelo at Via Cavour 21, tel. 055-295-264, www.macchinedileonardo.com. **Museo Leonardo da Vinci**—daily April-Oct 10:00-19:00, Nov-March 10:00-18:00, Via dei Servi 66 red, tel. 055-282-966, www.mostredileonardo.com.

Palazzo Vecchio

With a number of interactive activities for kids, this palace can be a good place for the whole family to explore together. For kids ages six and up, the palazzo rents family kits—turtle-shaped backpacks filled with materials for helping kids learn about the Medici and uncover interesting details about the place. The palace's family program (Museo dei Ragazzi) offers a variety of activities for kids as young as four all the way up to teenagers (usually requires reservations). Enjoy brief performances portraying Medici history, or help your kids paint their very own frescoes. As the offerings are always in flux, call or email, or drop by to find out what your options are (✪ see the Palazzo Vecchio Tour chapter).

Cost and Hours: €10, free for those under age 18, covered by Firenze Card, family kit-€5; kids' programs may involve a small additional charge (usually €2) and run Fri-Wed 9:00-17:00, Thu 9:00-14:00; tel. 055-276-8224, www.musefirenze.it/en, info@muse.comune.fi.it.

Galileo Science Museum

See several of Galileo's fingers on display, plus cool old telescopes and early chemical and science lab stuff. Engaging video screens illustrate scientific principles. Be warned that some parents find the museum's displays on childbirth too graphic for kids (✪ see the Galileo Science Museum tour chapter).

Cost and Hours: €9, €22 family ticket covers two adults and two kids ages 18 and under, cash only, covered by Firenze Card, Wed-Mon 9:30-18:00, Tue 9:30-13:00, last entry 30 minutes before closing, audioguide-€5, Piazza dei Giudici 1, tel. 055-265-311, www.museogalileo.it.

Duomo Dome Climb (Cattedrale di Santa Maria del Fiore)

Climbing the dome of the cathedral is almost like climbing an urban mountain—you'll spiral up in a strange dome-within-a-dome space, see some musty old tools used in the construction, get a bird's-eye peek into the nave from way up, and then pop out to see the best city view in town.

Cost and Hours: €10 ticket covers dome climb and all Duomo sights, covered by Firenze Card, Mon-Fri 8:30-19:00, Sat 8:30-17:40, closed Sun, last entry 40 minutes before closing, modest dress code enforced, enter from outside church on north side, tel. 055-230-2885, www.operaduomo.firenze.it.

Bargello (Museo Nationale del Bargello)

While kids are likely to be more familiar with Michelangelo's *David*, they may prefer the works at the Bargello. This underappreciated sculpture museum in a former police-station-turned-prison hosts Florence's most interesting collection of statues—with many bizarre poses (✪ see the Bargello Tour chapter).

Cost and Hours: €7, €4 if no special exhibits, covered by Firenze Card, Tue-Sat 8:15-17:00, or until 13:50 if no special exhibit; also open the same times on the first, third, and fifth Mon and the second and fourth Sun of each month; last entry 30 minutes before closing, audioguide-€6, Via del Proconsolo 4, reservation tel. 055-238-8606, www.polomuseale.firenze.it.

Uffizi Courtyard

This courtyard, filled with artists and souvenir stalls, is ringed by statues of all the famous Florentines (Amerigo Vespucci, Machiavelli, Leonardo, and so on)—great for putting faces on a sweep through history (see page 94 of the Renaissance Walk chapter).

Museum of Precious Stones

Find 500 different kinds of stones on display, demonstrating the fascinating techniques of inlay and mosaic work.

Cost and Hours: €4, covered by Firenze Card, Mon-Sat 8:15-14:00, closed Sun, last entry 30 minutes before closing, around corner from Accademia at Via degli Alfani 78, tel. 055-265-1357, www.opificiodellepietredure.it.

PARKS AND SQUARES

Boboli and Bardini Gardens

These adjacent gardens outside the Pitti Palace are landscaped wonderlands. While designed to give adults a break from the city, they're kid-friendly, too. Tickets to the gardens cover the Costume Gallery, Argenti/Silverworks Museum, and Porcelain Museum at Pitti Palace (✪ see the Pitti Palace Tour chapter).

Cost and Hours: Choose ticket #2 for Boboli and Bardini Gardens—€10 (€7 if no special exhibitions); Boboli is covered by Firenze Card, but Bardini is not; daily June-Aug 8:15-19:30, April-May and Sept-Oct 8:15-18:30, March 8:15-17:30, Nov-Feb 8:15-16:30; closed first and last Mon of each month, last entry 45 minutes before closing, tel. 055-238-8614, www.polomuseale.firenze.it.

Parco delle Cascine

Originally constructed as a hunting ground and farm for the Medici family, Florence's sprawling public park has lots of grass, historic monuments, and a playground. For a fee, families can cool off in the park's outdoor swimming pool, the Pavoniere.

Cost and Hours: Park—free and open year-round; swimming pool—€9 for adults, €7 for kids ages 4-12, open May-Aug daily 10:00-18:00, until 18:30 on Sat-Sun, tel. 055-362-233.

Getting There: Head west of the old center along the north side of the river (10-minute walk).

Piazza d'Azeglio

This peaceful and breezy park, complete with playground, can be a welcome refuge from touring madness (open daily, dawn to dusk).

Getting There: It's a 15-minute walk east from the Duomo. Or take bus #12 or #13 from the train station or the Piazza San Marco bus stop just north of the Duomo.

Piazzale Michelangelo

Older children may enjoy hiking up to this panoramic piazza for the superb view of Florence and the Duomo. Bring a picnic and eat lunch on the somewhat hidden terrace, just off the west side of the piazza.

Getting There: It's a 30-minute hike up to the square, but the downhill walk back into town is easy and enjoyable. See page 69 for info on alternative transportation.

Piazza della Repubblica

For kids running on their gelato buzz well into the evening hours, this vibrant piazza has a sparkling carousel and lively street musicians.

MORE EXPERIENCES

Open-Air Markets

Florence's various markets are fun for kids (✪ see the Shopping in Florence chapter). Remember to haggle.

Florencetown's "I Bike Florence" Tour

This tour, led by a quick-talking guide, is a 2.5-hour, 15-stop blitz of the town's top sights. Families with younger children are provided with tandem bikes.

Cost and Hours: €25 for ages 12 and over, 10 percent discount for students, children under 6 ride free, tours run daily March-Oct at 10:00 and 15:00, also at 18:00 May-Sept, helmets optional, Via de Lamberti 1, tel. 055-012-3994, www.florencetown.com.

CHILDREN

Leaning Tower of Pisa

This side-trip from Florence is probably the most interesting for kids (✪ see the Leaning Tower Tour chapter). Note that kids under age eight aren't allowed to climb the tower.

Cost and Hours: €18 to go inside and climb to the seventh-floor viewing platform, the belfry is not accessible; daily April-Sept 8:00-20:00, Oct 9:00-19:00, Nov-Feb 10:00-17:00, March 9:00-18:00, ticket office opens 30 minutes early, last entry 30 minutes before closing, timed entry, reservations recommended, www.opapisa.it.

SHOPPING IN FLORENCE

Florence may be one of Europe's most enticing shopping towns—it's been known for its sense of style since the Medici days. Many people spend entire days (or lifetimes) shopping here. While most businesses are as staid and stately as the city itself, a sampling of creative, funky shops will help you appreciate the younger side of Florence.

Hours: Smaller stores are generally open 9:00-13:00 and 15:30-19:30, usually closed on Sunday, often closed on Monday (or at least Monday morning), and sometimes closed for a couple of weeks around August 15. Bigger stores have similar hours, without the afternoon break. Many stores also have promotional stalls in the market squares.

Information: For shopping ideas, ads, and a list of markets, see *The Florentine* newspaper or *Florence Concierge Information* magazine (free from TI and many hotels). For authentic, locally produced wares, look for shops displaying the ***Esercizi Storici Fiorentini*** seal, with a picture of Palazzo Vecchio's tower. At these city-endorsed "Historical Florentine Ventures," you may pay a premium, but you can be assured of quality (for a list of shops, see www.esercizistorici.it).

Tax Refunds: For details on how to get VAT refunds and comply with customs regulations, see page 628.

Tours: If you're serious about shopping, consider a shopping-oriented tour; see my suggestions under "Tours in Florence" on page 28.

Department Stores: Typical chain department stores are **Coin,** the Italian equivalent of Macy's (Mon-Sat 10:00-20:00, Sun 10:30-20:00, on Via de' Calzaiuoli, near Orsanmichele Church); the similar, upscale **La Rinascente** (Mon-Sat 9:00-21:00, Sun 10:30-20:00, on Piazza della Repubblica); and **Oviesse,** a discount clothing chain, the local JCPenney (Mon-Sat 9:00-19:30, Sun 10:00-19:30, near train station at intersection of Via Panzani and Via del Giglio).

Bargaining: At Florence's many street markets (such as San Lorenzo Market), and even at many mid-range leather shops, prices are very soft. The first price you're quoted is an opening volley; sometimes if you simply show small signs of reluctance, you'll be offered a better price. Feel free to push back with a much lower offer. (And you'll often get a discount if you buy two or more of something.) Some vendors are willing to help you deal with the red tape to get your VAT refunded, while others just give you a discount equivalent to the tax to avoid the hassle. Vendors may also sweeten the deal if you offer to pay cash.

Calling in Reinforcements: If you end up going overboard on Florentine finds, you can buy a cheap extra suitcase at the various open-air market stalls (including San Lorenzo Market). A big suitcase with wheels costs about €25 and should last just long enough to haul your purchases home.

What to Buy

Many shoppers in Florence put leather at the top of their list: jackets, handbags, wallets, shoes, and so on. With its inimitable sense of style, richly perfumed leather shops, and notoriously persuasive sales clerks, Florence has a way of turning leather browsers into leather buyers. Other popular items include fragrances (perfumes and colognes) and cosmetics; paper products (marbled paper, stationery, blank books); art reproductions; and edible souvenirs.

SHOPPING

LEATHER *(CUOIO)*

Florence's long leatherworking tradition was born at Santa Croce Church, where Franciscan monks perfected the art of binding gorgeously illustrated manuscripts. Over the centuries, the skill evolved into a more fashion-forward form of leatherworking—today's designer shoes, jackets, and handbags. You'll see leather for sale all over Florence. But the prices—and the stakes—are high, so it pays to be an informed consumer. I'll cover some general leather-buying tips; then I'll recommend a few particular shops. While this advice is focused primarily on leather jackets, much of it also applies to handbags, shoes, and other items.

Leather-Buying Tips

An Italian leather jacket or bag is a major purchase. If you're serious about buying a big-ticket item, do some homework before you leave home. Visit importers and boutiques in your area to find out what they charge so that you can smartly comparison-shop when you get to Florence. While the memory of buying a leather jacket in Italy creates a big intangible value, given the less-than-favorable euro-to-dollar exchange rate, it could be more economical to just buy your jacket at home.

Don't expect to get a good-quality, authentic leather, "made in Italy" jacket for less than about €250-350. Top-quality and designer jackets can cost much more—and there's a big difference in quality between a €100 jacket, a €250 jacket, and a €500 jacket. Think carefully about your budget before you head out.

If you want to spend only €100-200, there are plenty of merchants around town (particularly at San Lorenzo Market stalls) willing to help you part with your money. But if you pay a lower price, you're likely sacrificing quality, craftsmanship, and durability.

Remember, bargaining is common, and the prices are as soft as that famously supple Italian leather. Don't be shy. Except at the top-of-the-line designers, assume that the first quoted price is just a starting point.

A major concern of leather buyers is whether the item is made in Italy or abroad. Because any item that is even partially assembled in Italy can be legally labeled "Made in Italy," many leather producers—including some globally famous brands—make their bags abroad, then bring them home for a few final stitches. And even leather that is truly worked, start to finish, in Italy, may originate in South America or elsewhere.

When evaluating leather, here are a few things to look for: Leather should smell like, well, leather—not chemicals. (Some vendors tout their "vegetable-tanned" wares, meaning they use only organic treatments.) But that "genuine leather" smell can be faked as well. Don't be fooled by other tricks, either, such as holding a lighter or match against the leather to show that it doesn't burn. Some leather imitators also pass this test.

The "touch test" is important: The leather should feel soft and pliable. If it's rough and thick, it's probably lower-quality (or imitation). Crumple the leather to see how well it rebounds. If it remains wadded or wrinkled, it's not top-notch.

Examine the seams and stitching for flaws, consider the quality of the liner, and test the zippers to be sure they'll last. (American men find themselves fumbling with "backwards" Italian zippers, which run along the left rather than the right.)

Consider the fit. Italians prefer their jackets more fitted than

Americans, and their idea of the "right size" may feel snug to you. If you're shopping for a jacket in summer, remember you'll be wearing it over a heavy sweater in the winter. Don't let a salesperson talk you into a jacket that doesn't fit. ("Italians like to roll their sleeves up" is one of many lines vendors may employ to try to get you to splurge on a jacket that doesn't fit properly.) Better leather shops can alter your jacket on the spot, or have you swing by to pick it up later. They may even offer to custom-make a jacket for you and ship it to you at home—though, both for matters of fit and finances, this is a bit risky, and should only be agreed to with a shop that has a stellar reputation.

Where to Buy Leather Jackets

When Italians want to shop for affordable leather, they go to suburban outlet malls (such as The Mall, with outlet stores for many top-name Italian designers, about 15 miles southeast of the Duomo, www.themall.it). Or they head for a leather factory (Piero Tucci is one of many with a good reputation, www.pierotucci.com). But this isn't practical for a carless tourist on a short visit. Most leather shops within walking distance of the old core of Florence cater to tourists and well-heeled locals, so true bargains are rare. In these neighborhoods, you basically have four options (in increasing order of price):

1) buy a cheap, likely imitation, almost certainly made-in-China jacket from a street vendor;

2) visit a hole-in-the-wall shop with slightly better quality, though still somewhat ambiguous origin;

3) find a mid-range leather "factory" or gallery with a good reputation, authentic made-in-Italy merchandise, and higher prices; or

4) go designer, at one of the big-name boutiques all around town—Gucci, Prada, or their dozens of competitors.

Note that the lines separating these categories are blurry; many of the street stalls in category 1 are actually outposts of shops in category 2, and some of the vendors in category 3 make jackets for the big names in category 4. For most travelers, one of the middle two approaches works best; if you can afford it, I'd lean toward option 3 to get something that will last for years.

Here are a few specific shops with good reputations:

La Pelle, straight ahead from the Oltrarno end of Ponte Vecchio, stocks a fine variety of good-quality leather coats (€300-400); the welcome is warm but not too aggressive (Via Guicciardini 11 red, tel. 055-292-031, www.lapellesrl.it).

Atelier Classe sits down a mostly neglected alley near Piazza Santa Croce. While surrounding streets teem with cut-rate leather, this boutique feels classier—but the prices are accordingly higher (€400-600 for a basic jacket, on-site alterations possible, closed

Sun and Mon morning until 14:00, Via Torta 16 red, tel. 055-268-145, www.atelierclasse.com). They also have a shoe store two doors down.

Davide Cesari sits along the embankment on the north side of the Arno, just steps from Ponte Vecchio. They make jackets for some well-known American brands. It feels tasteful but a bit pushy (€250-400 jackets, Lungarno Acciaiuoli 32 red, tel. 055-282-019).

Noi, facing Piazza Davanzati, comes with an even harder sell than the others listed here, but the quality is reputable (Via Porta Rossa 65 red, tel. 055-210-319, www.noi-firenze.com).

Michelangelo is a bit less expensive than the others (mid-range €250-350 jackets) and the quality feels less assured. Somewhere between "hard-sell" and "soft-sell," it's burrowed down a side street from the San Lorenzo Market chaos (daily 10:00-19:00, Via Giovan Battista Zannoni 9/11 red, tel. 055-285-497, www.lagalleriamichelangelo.com).

On Borgo La Noce: To step down a notch, you could browse the aggressive shops that line Borgo La Noce between the Church of San Lorenzo and Mercato Centrale. While these shops—including **Massimo Leather, Raffaello,** and **Pelletteria La Noce**—have their fans (likely because of their somewhat lower prices and gregarious/"helpful" sales clerks), they feel a bit less upmarket than the ones listed above.

Sales: Yet another option is to simply shop sales. Even big-name designers will deeply discount last year's models. Consider bargain-hunting at department stores, and watch for sales notices posted in boutique windows.

Where to Buy Leather Bags

Many of the tips above also apply to handbags and shoes. And some of the leather jacket shops listed above also sell bags.

The venerable **Leather School** (Scuola del Cuoio) at **Santa Croce Church**—described on page 218—is the most famous place to buy leather in Florence. The quality is unsurpassed, but prices are extremely high. Don't plan to buy unless you're looking to splurge on a top-end, lifetime purchase (figure €150 for a small purse; a personalized monogram costs just a bit extra). But even for browsers, it's worth a visit as the most accessible place to watch leather workers hard at work. Note that the leather school produces mostly handbags, briefcases, travel cases, wallets, and belts—not jackets or shoes (daily 10:00-18:00, artisans at work Mon-Fri 10:00-17:30, closed Sun off-season, enter around behind Santa Croce Church at Via San Giuseppe 5 red, or from inside the church; 055-244-533, www.scuoladelcuoio.com).

Of Florence's many mid-range shops specializing in bags, **Via de Ginori 23r** is well worth a browse. Conveniently located just a

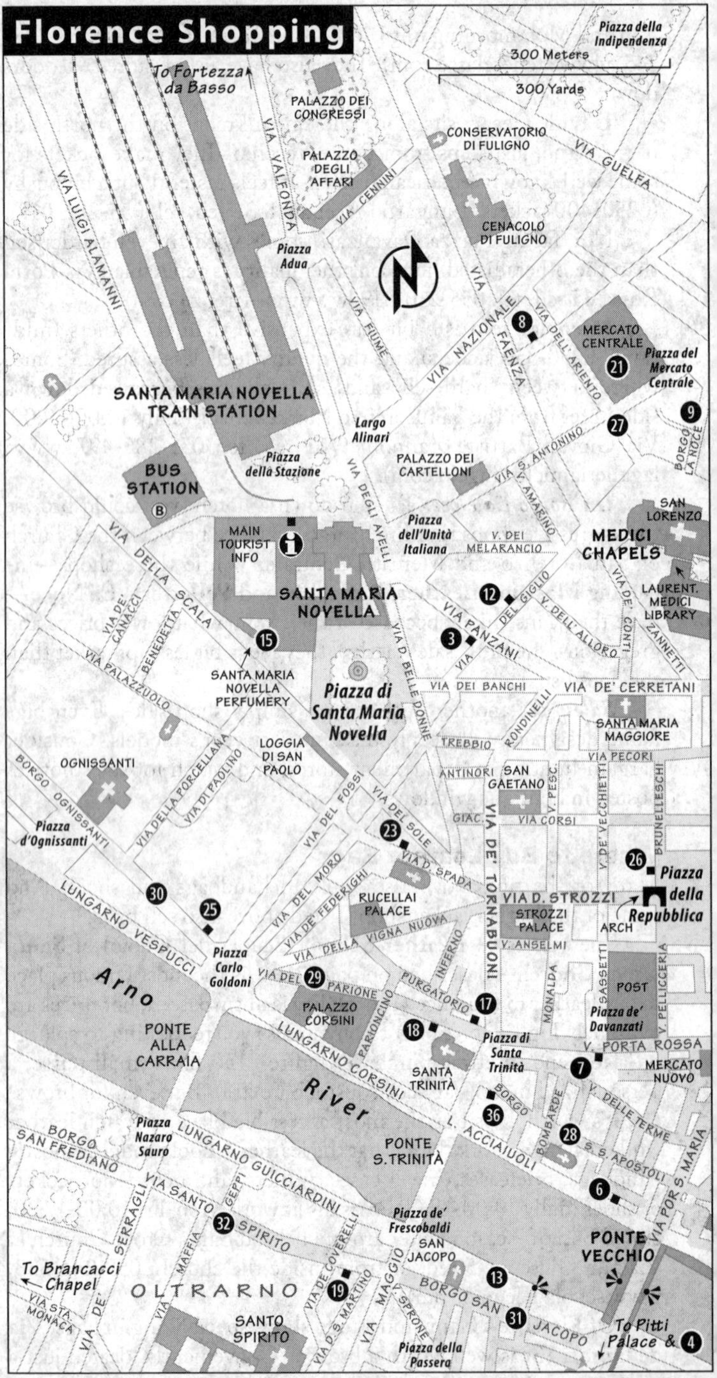
Florence Shopping
To Fortezza da Basso
PALAZZO DEI CONGRESSI
PALAZZO DEGLI AFFARI
Piazza della Indipendenza
300 Meters
300 Yards
CONSERVATORIO DI FULIGNO
CENACOLO DI FULIGNO
VIA GUELFA
VIA LUIGI ALAMANNI
VIA VALFONDA
VIA CENNINI
Piazza Adua
VIA FIUME
VIA NAZIONALE
VIA FAENZA
VIA DELL'ARIENTO
MERCATO CENTRALE
Piazza del Mercato Centrale
SANTA MARIA NOVELLA TRAIN STATION
Largo Alinari
BUS STATION
Piazza della Stazione
PALAZZO DEI CARTELLONI
VIA S. ANTONINO
V. AMARINO
BORGO LA NOCE
SAN LORENZO
MEDICI CHAPELS
LAURENT. MEDICI LIBRARY
MAIN TOURIST INFO
VIA DEGLI AVELLI
Piazza dell'Unità Italiana
V. DEI MELARANCIO
VIA DELLA SCALA
SANTA MARIA NOVELLA
VIA DEL GIGLIO
V. DELL'ALLORO
VIA DE' CONTI
ZANNETTI
VIA PANZANI
VIA D. BELLE DONNE
VIA DE' CANACCI
BENEDETTA
VIA PALAZZUOLO
SANTA MARIA NOVELLA PERFUMERY
Piazza di Santa Maria Novella
VIA DEI BANCHI
RONDINELLI
VIA DE' CERRETANI
SANTA MARIA MAGGIORE
TREBBIO
LOGGIA DI SAN PAOLO
OGNISSANTI
BORGO OGNISSANTI
VIA DELLA PORCELLANA
VIA DI PADLINO
ANTINORI
SAN GAETANO
VIA PECORI
V. PESC.
V. DE' VECCHIETTI
BRUNELLESCHI
VIA DEI FOSSI
VIA DEL SOLE
GIAC.
VIA CORSI
Piazza d'Ognissanti
VIA DEL MORO
VIA DE' FEDERIGHI
VIA D. SPADA
VIA DE' TORNABUONI
VIA D. STROZZI
Piazza della Repubblica
LUNGARNO VESPUCCI
RUCELLAI PALACE
STROZZI PALACE
ARCH
VIA DELLA VIGNA NUOVA
INFERNO
V. ANSELMI
Arno
Piazza Carlo Goldoni
VIA DEL PARIONE
PURGATORIO
MONALDA
SASSETTI
POST
V. PELLICCERIA
PALAZZO CORSINI
PARIONCINO
Piazza de' Davanzati
PONTE ALLA CARRAIA
LUNGARNO CORSINI
Piazza di Santa Trinità
V. PORTA ROSSA
MERCATO NUOVO
SANTA TRINITÀ
River
BORGO
BOMBARDE
V. DELLE TERME
Piazza Nazaro Sauro
LUNGARNO GUICCIARDINI
PONTE S. TRINITÀ
L. ACCIAIUOLI
S. S. APOSTOLI
VIA POR S. MARIA
BORGO SAN FREDIANO
VIA SANTO SPIRITO
GEPPI
SERRAGLI
Piazza de' Frescobaldi
SAN JACOPO
PONTE VECCHIO
VIA MAFFIA
VIA DE' COVERELLI
VIA MAGGIO
To Brancacci Chapel
OLTRARNO
VIA D. S. MARTINO
BORGO SAN JACOPO
SPRONE
VIA STA. MONACA
VIA DE'
SANTO SPIRITO
Piazza della Passera
To Pitti Palace & 4
8
21
9
27
12
3
15
23
26
30
25
29
17
18
7
36
28
6
32
13
19
31

Department Stores
1 Coin
2 La Rinascente
3 Oviesse
Leather
4 To La Pelle
5 Atelier Classe
6 Davide Cesari
7 Noi
8 Michelangelo
9 Borgo La Noce Shops
10 S. Croce Leather School
11 Via de Ginori 23r (Bags)
12 Furò e Punteruolo (Bags)
13 Roberta (Bags)
14 Gilardini (Shoes)
Perfume & Cosmetics
15 Farmacia di S. Maria Novella
16 Aqua Flor
Paper, Stationery & Prints
17 Parione
18 Alberto Cozzi
19 L'Ippogrifo
20 Fabriano Boutique
Food
21 Mercato Centrale
22 EATaly
Gifts & Books
23 MIO Concept Store
24 Paperback Exchange
25 B & M Books
26 RED Bookstore
Shopping Areas
27 San Lorenzo Market
28 Borgo Santi Apostoli
29 Via del Parione
30 Borgo Ognissanti
31 Borgo San Jacopo
32 Via di Santo Spirito
33 Piazza Santa Croce
34 To Via Pietrapiana & Borgo La Croce
35 Gucci Museum
36 Ferragamo Museum
VIA VENTISETTE APRILE
VIA SAN ZANOBI
VIA SANTA REPARATA
VIA GUELFA
GALLO
VIA TADDEA
VIA DE' GINORI
VIA STURA
LEONARDO MUSEUM
MEDICI-RICCARDI PALACE
Piazza di San Lorenzo
BORGO S. LORENZO
VIA MARTELLI
VIA BIFFI
DUOMO SIGHTS TICKET OFFICE
WC
Piazza di San Giovanni
BAPTISTERY
DUOMO
Piazza del Duomo
CAMPANILE
DUOMO MUSEUM
VIA M. BUFALINI
Piazza di Santa Maria Nuova
MUSEO DI FIRENZE COM'ERA
V. D. PERGOLA
VIA S. EGIDIO
VIA DELL'ORIUOLO
BORGO PINTI
VIA FIESOLANA
Piazza G. Salvemini
To
TOSINGHI
V. DELL'OCHE
CANONICA
BONIZZI
ROMA
CALZAIUOLI
SANTA MARIA DE' RICCI
OPERA DEL DUOMO STUDIO
STUDIO
VIA DEL CORSO
CASA DI DANTE
PRESTO
PROCONSOLO
BORGO DEGLI ALBIZI
V. PIETRAPIANA
POST
VIA DELL'ULIVO
ORSAN-MICHELE
TAVO.
VIA D. ALIGHIERI
V. DE' GIRALDI
VIA DE' PANDOLFINI
VIA PALMIERI
VIA DELL'AGNOLO
S. MARIA
LA BADIA
BARGELLO MUSEUM
VIA GHIBELLINA
V. G. VERDI
CASA BUONARROTI
CALIMALA
LAMB.
CIMATORI
CERCHI
VIA DE'
VIA CONDOTTA
VIA DELLA VIGNA VECCHIA
VIA BURELLA
STINCHE
Piazza della Signoria
Piazza S. Firenze
V. DELL'ANGUILLARA
TORTA
VERRAZZANO
FICO
VIA DE' PEPI
LOGGIA
GONDI
PALAZZO VECCHIO
BORGO DE' GRECI
VIA BENTACORDI
Piazza Peruzzi
Piazza Santa Croce
ARMA
Piazza de' Salt.
BARONCELLI
UFFIZI GALLERY
VIA LEONI
CORNO
VINEGRIA
MAGALOTTI
RUSTICI
VIA DE' BENCI
VIA ANTONIO MAGLIABECHI
SANTA CROCE
LAMB.
S. STEPHANO
EXIT
CASTELLANI
CASTELLO
OSTERIA
VIA MOSCA
DEI NERI
BRACHE
BORGO S. CROCE
PAZZI CHAPEL
Piazza Giudici
SAPONAI
Piazza Mentana
VAGELLAI
MALENCHINI
CORSO DEI TINTORI
LEATHER SCHOOL'S OUTSIDE ENTRANCE
LIBRARY
GALILEO SCIENCE MUSEUM

SHOPPING

couple of blocks from the San Lorenzo Market, this family-run shop carries a tasteful collection of stylish yet practical bags—some of their own production, some from other local suppliers—and a line of eco-friendly bags made from recycled tires (Mon 15:30-19:30, Tue-Sat 10:00-14:00 & 15:00-19:30, closed Sun, may be closed Sat afternoon in summer, Via de Ginori 23 red, tel. 055-239-8031).

Not far away, **Furò e Punteruolo** ("Flatknife and Awl") sells a small selection of wallets, purses, and handbags in a more rustic style. Paulo makes everything by hand on the premises (closed Mon morning, Via del Giglio 29 red, mobile 348-437-0867).

Across the river in the Oltrarno, a couple of blocks from Ponte Vecchio, **Roberta** is another popular choice for fashionable but moderately priced leather handbags (Mon-Sat 10:00-19:30, closed Sun, also closed Mon Nov-Feb, Borgo San Jacopo 74 red, tel. 055-284-017, www.robertafirenze.com).

Where to Buy Leather Shoes

I dare not wade into this highly subjective topic. But for a reliable local standby, consider **Gilardini,** just steps from the Duomo and Baptistery. This classic and classy shop sells a variety of Italian leather shoes, for women or men (Sun-Mon 15:30-19:30, Tue-Sat 9:30-19:30, Via Cerretani 8 red, tel. 055-212-412, www.gilardinishoes.it).

PERFUME AND COSMETICS

Long ago, as part of their service to the community, Dominican friars typically served as pharmacists (a.k.a. chemists or alchemists). And—back in an age when "medicine" meant potions and herbal remedies—the pharmacy at the Dominican church of Santa Maria Novella was a local trendsetter in the art of fragrance. In the centuries since, perfumes and colognes have taken off in a big way in other parts of this fashion-forward city. Below are two fragrance experiences—both elegant, but quite different: The big, staid, church-run perfumery, and a smaller, more intimate alternative.

The **Farmacia di Santa Maria Novella** has long been run by the Dominicans of Santa Maria Novella. Thick with the lingering aroma of centuries of spritzes, this palatial perfumery and cosmetics shop started as the herb garden of the Santa Maria Novella monks. Well-known even today for its top-quality products, it is extremely Florentine. It's as formal as it is historic, with dressy, no-nonsense clerks. Pick up the history sheet from the rack, and wander deep into the shop. The main sales room, where you can sample more than 60 perfumes—as well as face creams, body lotions, and talcum powders—was originally a chapel; the middle (green) room offers potpourris and incenses for the home; and the historic third room, which sells herbal products, is where the pharmacy was originally established in 1612. From here, you can peek at one of Santa Maria Novella's cloisters with its dreamy frescoes and imagine a time before Vespas and tourists. If you get serious about buying, pick up an electronic card, which the clerks load up with your selections. When you're ready to check out, bring it back to the bunker-like perfume room to pick up your purchases (€80/bottle perfumes, daily 9:00-20:00, a block from Piazza Santa Maria Novella, 100 yards down Via della Scala at #16, tel. 055-216-276, www.smnovella.com).

Aqua Flor is a rare shop where the master perfumer sells his wares in the same space where he makes them. Hidden away on a side street between Piazza della Signoria and Piazza Santa Croce, Aqua Flor uses only natural extracts to pull out subtle but warmly pungent aromas, free of the acrid artificial edge of many mass-market fragrances. They're generous with samples, and the space is enjoyable to simply be in. In one of the three cavernous rooms, you'll see Sileno's "organ"—the giant cabinet stocked with little jars and bottles—where, like a musician, he finds just the right combination of notes (€40/bottle eaux de toilette, €90/bottle perfumes, they can also create a custom fragrance just for you, daily 10:00-19:00, Borgo Santa Croce 6, tel. 055-234-3471, www.florenceparfum.com). After your visit, be sure to dip into the courtyard of the sprawling palazzo-turned-condominium complex that houses the shop.

PAPER, STATIONERY, AND PRINTS

Long known as a literary center, Florence offers traditional marbled stationery (whose edge is dipped carefully into a bath of swirling pigments) and leatherbound journals, plus reproductions of old documents, prints, maps, and manuscripts.

On Via del Parione, Just North of the River: This street seems to specialize in high-quality stationery shops. At the start of the street, facing Piazza di Santa Trinità, **Parione** has been selling a classy selection of marbled paper, stationery, and paper boxes since 1923 (closed Sun, Via del Parione 10 red, tel. 055-215-684, www.parione.it). A few doors down, **Alberto Cozzi** is a big shop with a colorfully cluttered window display of marbled paper products (Via del Parione 35 red, tel. 055-294-968).

In the Oltrarno: **L'Ippogrifo** makes stylish, high-quality prints of mostly Florentine scenes, which are a notch above the mass-produced posters you'll see around town (closed Sun, at Via di Santo Spirito 5 red, tel. 055-213-255, www.stampeippogrifo.com). **Legatoria La Carta** is a workshop producing all manner of marbled paper products, from blank books to desk sets. It's a few short blocks down Via Romana from Pitti Palace's entrance, and just a block from the Boboli Gardens' rear entrance (Mon-Sat 9:30-17:30, closed Sun, Via Romana 58 red, tel. 055-094-8043, www.legatoria-lacarta.com). Both of these shops are located on shopping streets; to see what's nearby, check "In the Oltrarno," later in this chapter.

Modern Style in the Historical Center: **Fabriano Boutique,** tucked in the twisty streets between the Duomo and the river, is part of a top-end chain selling attractive, high-quality office supplies—leatherbound office tools, modern stationery, and more (daily 10:00-20:00, Via del Corso 59 red, www.fabrianoboutique.com).

FINE-ART SOUVENIRS

You'll find no shortage of places to buy reproductions of your favorite Florentine art (posters, calendars, books, prints, and so on). Major museums—such as the **Uffizi** and **Accademia**—have excellent bookstores. The bookstore at the **Duomo Museum** (closed through late 2015) is well-stocked and a bit less crowded than the shops at some of the bigger sights.

EDIBLE GOODIES

Mercato Centrale is a prime spot for stocking up on culinary souvenirs (Mon-Fri 7:00-14:00, Sat 7:00-17:00, closed Sun, a block north of the Church of San Lorenzo). Classic purchases include olive oil and balsamic vinegar, unusually shaped and colored pasta, dried porcini mushrooms, spices, and jars of pestos and sauces (such as pesto *genovese* or *tartufo*—truffle).

EATaly, an outpost of the gourmet mini-mall chain that's sweeping Italy, is a convenient place to pick up pricey, premium consumable souvenirs (see listing on page 294).

Wines: While many bring home a special bottle of Chianti Classico or Brunello di Montalcino, I take home only the names of my favorite wines—and buy them later at my hometown wine shop. Remember that all liquids—wine, olive oil, or otherwise—need to be placed in checked luggage.

FUNKY, ARTSY SOUVENIRS

Clet Abraham, a French-born street artist now living in Florence, has gained an international reputation for his clever alterations to traffic signs. Most commonly, he adds his flourishes to the dull "no entry" signs, a horizontal white bar in a red circle. In his most iconic piece—which you'll see around the city—he's added a figure that looks like it's sneaking off with the white bar. His message: Think before you blindly follow regulations. While you can debate whether these works blur the line between vandalism and art, Clet's Banksy-like creativity is hard to deny. The Clet gallery, where you can buy stickers and other fun things, is in the Oltrarno's lively, youthful San Niccolò neighborhood, just a few steps from some recommended restaurants (Mon-Sat 9:30-18:00, closed Sun, Via dell'Olmo 8 red).

MIO Concept Store features an artsy and eclectic collection of gifts, home decor, gadgets, jewelry, and accessories that feels like a hipster home sale (Tue-Sat 10:00-13:30 & 14:30-19:00, Mon 15:00-19:00 only, closed Sun, in a nondescript urban zone between the train station and Piazza della Signoria at Via delle Spada 34 red, tel. 055-264-5543, www.mio-concept.com).

MORE SOUVENIR AND SHOPPING IDEAS

For a list of bookstores, see page 24. Other souvenir ideas include silk ties, scarves, Tuscan ceramics, and wood-carved bowls and spoons. Goofy knickknacks featuring Renaissance masterpieces are popular: Botticelli mouse pads, Raphael lipstick-holders, and plaster *David*s.

Best Shopping/Browsing Areas

To fully explore and enjoy Florence as a shopper, make a point to break out of the heavily traveled tourist zones right in the heart of town—the **Santa Croce** area; **Ponte Vecchio's** gold and silver shops; the old, covered **Mercato Nuovo** (three blocks north of Ponte Vecchio, described on page 55); and, to a lesser extent, the streets near the **Accademia.** But just a short walk away, you'll find several pleasant streets and neighborhoods with a (somewhat) more authentic and innovative array of shops.

Each of the descriptions in this section is designed as a lightly guided shopping stroll, which you could use as a refreshing break between weighty sightseeing stops. As this section is meant for casual window-shoppers, I've listed only the address and a brief description for each shop. They tend to follow the same general opening hours described at the beginning of this chapter: some close for a mid-afternoon break, and many close for part or all of the day on Sunday and/or Monday. Most shops mentioned here have good websites, or at least Facebook pages—simply search the name if you want more details before visiting. And, of course, as in any town, there's a high degree of turnover among merchants; expect that some of the shops noted here will go out of business before your visit.

SAN LORENZO MARKET

The market stalls between the Church of San Lorenzo and Mercato Centrale are no secret—this is ground zero for tourists seeking cheap, cut-rate souvenirs. And it's a fun area to browse and bargain.

While the vendors used to clog the streets around the Church of San Lorenzo, in recent years urban renewal initiatives have forced most of the stalls into the narrow streets around Mercato Centrale, just a couple of blocks away—a trend that may continue in the future. Wherever you find the stalls, they're filled with lower-end leather, clothing, T-shirts, handbags, and souvenirs (daily 9:00-19:00, closed Mon in winter).

Mercato Centrale (Central Market) itself is a giant covered food market, with a top-end food court upstairs (see "Edible Goodies," earlier).

IN THE HISTORIC CENTER, JUST NORTH OF THE RIVER

An enticing string of streets—Borgo Santi Apsotoli, Via del Parione, and Borgo Ognissanti—runs parallel to the river one block inland, from near the Uffizi westward. I've narrated the most interesting shops on these three progressive streets, from east to west. Near the start of this stretch, you'll find jewelry shops, fashion boutiques, and touristy but good-quality shops selling stationery and other local products; farther along, more home-decor stores are mixed in.

Borgo Santi Apostoli

SHOPPING

This narrow and fairly touristy street begins just one short block up from Ponte Vecchio. Among the fashion boutiques, designer handbag shops, and jewelers is **Gatto Bianco** ("White Cat," on the right, at #12 red), which sells big, chunky, modern-style jewelry. At #20 red, **T. Pestelli** is a fascinating silverwork shop where Tommaso creates finely detailed jewelry and small sculptures. Continuing along, you'll pass several antiques and art shops. After about two blocks, on the right (#42 red), is an outpost of **Angela Caputi,** another local jeweler whose oversized, colorful resin accessories has earned her a loyal following. Just after that, set back on the little square on the left, is **La Bottega dell'Olio,** a boutique selling olive oil and beautiful hand-carved wooden bowls, spoons, and other kitchen utensils (Piazza del Limbo 4 red). Also on the left (#37 red) is **Sola a Firenze** ("Only in Florence"), with a tasteful collection of cards, prints, and paintings, as well as silverwork and jewelry made by the family. Near the end of the street (#45 red), the stylish and upscale **Viajiyu** sells a selection of their own pricey, fashionable shoes and will custom-make some for you (www.viajiyu.com). Fill-

Florence's Upscale Boutique Streets

Florence is a bastion of high fashion, where budget travelers can enjoy high-end window-shopping. The entire area between the river and the cathedral is busy with inviting boutiques that show off ritzy Italian fashions. The highest concentration of shops is along Via dei Calzaiuoli, Via de' Tornabuoni, and the streets in between (particularly around Piazza della Repubblica). In recent years, city officials have been pedestrianizing and sprucing up more and more streets in this area in an attempt to cement Florence's status as a high-fashion destination. (Many locals grouse that in so doing, they've forced out more characteristic, low-rent mom-and-pop shops that have thrived here for generations.)

Via dei Calzaiuoli mixes tourist-rip-off pizza and gelato joints with upscale chain boutiques.

Via de' Tornabuoni is a delightfully pedestrianized, flower-lined street where Prada and Gucci face each other, like bitter rivals, kicking off a string of Italian designers and international chains—Boss, Sisley, Zara, Liu Jo. The bottom half of the street features the big Italian "-i" designers (Gucci, Armani, Fendi, Tiffan-i); a pillar marks the intersection with the lower-rent, and more characteristic, Borgo Santi Apostoli (described later) and the Ferragamo store (and its shoe museum).

Piazza della Repubblica has several fine shops, including the upscale La Rinascente department store, with its Duomo-view café terrace (see page 55).

If you head under that piazza's arch and down **Via degli Strozzi,** you'll pass big names—Dolce & Gabbana, Louis Vuitton, Cartier, and Bulgari—on the way to the fine Palazzo Strozzi (a good place for a coffee break; described on page 56) and the intersection with Via de' Tornabuoni, the pedestrian street mentioned above.

Fashion lovers shouldn't miss the **Gucci Museum,** with a prime address on Piazza della Signoria (and described on page 62).

ing the stately 800-year-old building next door is the flagship store for the famous shoemaker **Ferragamo,** with its endearing shoe museum in the basement (Via de' Tornabuoni 2; see description on page 62).

Ferragamo marks the end of Borgo Santi Apostoli, where it opens up into the triangular Piazza Santa Trinità. Leaving this square to the right (away from the river) is **Via de' Tornabuoni,** arguably Florence's most inviting top-of-the-line boutique browsing street. Recently pedestrianized, it's lined with oversized flower pots, well-heeled shoppers, and international designers. But to keep within our budget, we'll continue straight ahead through Piazza Santa Trinità, jogging a bit right to angle up...

Via del Parione

Though we're gradually leaving the high-fashion district, this street still boasts plenty of trendy boutiques, handbag shops, and salons. Two good paper shops (both described earlier, under "Paper, Stationery, and Prints") kick off this street: first, **Parione** (on the right, #10 red), then **Alberto Cozzi** (on the left, #35 red). **Letizia Firoini** (on the right, #60 red) lovingly crafts handmade puppets, most of them based on traditional *commedia dell'arte* figures. Across the street (#37 red), **Bazzanti** is a sprawling space with bulky statues for the home and garden.

At the end of the street, you'll pop out at a lively three-way intersection. Across the street are a trio of engaging shops: **Marioluca Giusti** sells high-quality plastic plates, glasses, and other tableware that look stylish but are durable enough for a backyard picnic (Via Lunga 133); **A. Bianda Coltelleria** is a classy gentlemen's shop, selling pocketknives and shaving gear (Via della Vigna Nuova 86 red); and **La Piccola T-Shirteria** sells unique Florentine-hipster loungewear (Via della Vigna Nuova 84 red, www.lapiccolatshirteria.com).

From here, you have two options. If you take a sharp right and head up **Via della Vigna Nuova,** you'll head back to the main upscale shopping zone (Via de' Tornabuoni) by way of several smaller boutiques. Along here, step into Conto Luce (#89 red), with colorful, creative, even goofy household stuff. But mostly this street is all about the clothes—it's a great place to shop for stylish, more affordable everyday fashion, with a few splurge boutiques mixed in (Petit Bateau, at #16 red, is the perfect place to outfit the li'l sailor in your life).

Or, for a look at Florentine home decor, you can carry on through the small square and continue straight ahead, up...

Borgo Ognissanti

On the right, just before the start of this street, is the landmark **Münstermann**, a venerable *parafarmacia* (not-quite-pharmacy) selling old-fashioned lotions, creams, oils, ointments, soaps, and men's shaving gear. Step into the time-warp interior, which smells like Grandpa's aftershave (Piazza Goldoni 2 red). Continuing up Borgo Ognissanti, on the right (#2 red), look for **100% Birbe,** a small, lovable children's store with toys and toddler decor. Next door is Florence's premier English bookstore, **B&M Books** (#4 red; see listing under "Helpful Hints" on page 22). Carry on, passing clothes boutiques, art galleries, and **Giotto Ceramiche** (#15 red), with Tuscan ceramics—large and small—for the home. From here, the street takes on a clear home-furnishing flavor, with antiques, furniture stores, and home-accessory depots that offer a glimpse into outfitting a contemporary local home. **Kartell** (#52 red) specializes in bold, colorful, minimalist design and decor. Two doors down, **Tela Lintea** (#56 red) has more traditional linens and home furnishings. Step across to the left side of the street, then look back across and up to the dramatic facade of #26, which is in the Liberty Style (Italian-style Art Nouveau).

Soon you'll emerge into Piazza Ognissanti, watched over by its namesake church—which feels endearingly scruffier and more lived-in than the city's many famous houses of worship. Also overlooking the square is the Westin Hotel; for a memorable (if pricey) finale to your shopping stroll, strut into the fancy lobby, ride the elevator to the sixth-floor café terrace, and spend too much on a drink with one of the best panoramic views of Florence (described on page 301).

IN THE OLTRARNO

Across the river, a short walk past the tourist crowds takes you to some less-discovered zones that are worth exploring. I've focused on two areas: near Pitti Palace, and the main street parallel to the river (Borgo San Jacopo to Via di Santo Spirito).

The Oltrarno is known for its artisanal workshops, where craftspeople make and sell finely handmade items on their premises. I've listed the shops that are easily accessible to browsers. For a more in-depth look at Oltrarno workshops, pick up the brochure called "A Tour of Artisan Workshops," which you may find at the TI or at participating shops. Various local tour operators also do tours of Oltrarno workshops (see "Tours in Florence" on page 28).

Near Pitti Palace

Both of these streets—within a very short walk of Pitti Palace—make a pleasant break between sights.

Sdrucciolo de' Pitti: Directly across from the big courtyard in front of Pitti Palace, poke down the narrow alley called Sdrucciolo de' Pitti. While more touristy (just steps from a big sight), and therefore pricey, it's a convenient place to drop into a cluster of fine little shops. One short block down the lane, on the left, is **La Casa della Stampa** (#11 red), a cramped prints shop cluttered with old printing presses and a "bargain bin" of tattered antique documents. Just past that is **Giulia Materia** (#13 red), a hipster design boutique with colorful and creative clothes, cloth bags, and blank books. Next is **Le Telerie Toscane** (#15 red), with textiles—placemats, towels, table runners, and tablecloths—with Tuscan designs that feel less mass-produced than the ones sold at cheap souvenir stands. And across the street, **Argenteria Donato Zaccaro** (#12-14 red) sells silver jewelry and other goods.

Via Romana: Running southwest from Pitti Palace into a sleepy residential quarter, this workaday street features an eclectic mix of art galleries, antique shops, and creative boutiques that offer a change of pace from the generally traditional offerings in the Oltrarno. (You can also visit this street on your way home from the Boboli Gardens—the back exit of Boboli puts you at the far end of Via Romana, so you can follow this walk backward to the Pitti Palace entry.)

Facing the palace, turn right and walk past the **Oro Nero** shop (Piazza de Pitti 1 red), which sells a wide array of "Black Gold" (as its name means): artisanal chocolates and teas (you'll encounter another tea shop later on this walk). Continuing straight past the shop and through the small, busy Piazza San Felice, you'll start down Via Romana. On the left, **Anita Russo** (#13 red), a ceramics studio, sells pottery pieces made by Anita herself. Across the street, **Erboristeria Boboli** (#12 red)—a fragrant shop with herbal/organic lotions, fragrances, candles, and so on—is worth a whiff. Passing some clothing boutiques, you'll reach (on the right, at #26 red) **Tealicious,** where Laura curates a fragrant selection of exotic teas, including some unusual flavor combinations. A block farther on the left (at #39 red), **Tabescè** produces quirky, modern, Murano-style glass jewelry and funky art objects that appeal to hipsters. And across the street is the characteristic **Legatoria La Carta** marbled paper shop and book bindery (#58 red; see full listing earlier). Soon after, you reach the rear entrance to Boboli Gardens; Via Romana continues past this point, but there are fewer interesting shops.

Along the River

Borgo San Jacopo and Via di Santo Spirito, running parallel to the river through the heart of the Oltrarno, are lined with fine shops. The first stretch (Borgo San Jacopo)—with its proximity to Ponte Vecchio—feels quite touristy, with jewelry and clothing stores and souvenir shops, while Via di Santo Spirito feels increasingly more local, with several home-decor places. Crossing Ponte Vecchio from the historical center, turn right and head down...

Borgo San Jacopo: The shops along here are heavy on leather, fashion boutiques, jewelry, textiles, and prints. The **Ortiga Sicilia** fragrance shop (#12 red) is the latest venture of one of the founders of Crabtree & Evelyn, who now lives just around the corner. **Le Sorelle** (#30 red) is a fun home and garden shop. **Domi Textile & Design** (#38 red) carries top-quality but pricey Busatti linens for the home. **Fantasie Florentine** (#50 red)—a cluttered stationery and souvenir shop—marks the lane leading to a fine Arno perch for viewing Ponte Vecchio. Soon after and across the street, **Argentiere Pagliai** (#41 red) is a fine, old-school Oltrarno silversmith with a real workshop in the back; while there's not much to browse inside, the window displays are worth a look. Passing a few more hole-in-the-wall jewelry shops, you'll reach **Roberta,** with leather handbags (for details, see listing earlier); their second shop, a few doors down, has more bags, plus scarves and ties. You'll come to the busy cross-street Via Maggio, passing a characteristic fountain on your left. Crossing Via Maggio straight ahead, you'll start down...

Via di Santo Spirito: From here, the shops get a bit less touristy, with more real artisans mixed in. Passing the recommended Olio and Convivium wine and olive oil bar on the right, look across the street for **L'Ippogrifo,** a print shop (#5 red; see listing earlier). Then comes a stretch of furniture, antique, and home-decor shops—less practical for souvenir-hunting, but satisfying for window-shopping...and getting ideas for back home. There's also a smattering of fashion boutiques along here. On the right (at #16 red), watch for the cluttered, hole-in-the-wall **La Bottega di Mastro Geppetto,** with Pinocchio-themed window displays up front, but a handmade wooden frame store in back. (Written and published in Florence in 1883, the original Pinocchio stories are often appropriated by local merchants for their touristic currency. You'll notice a chain of tacky, Pinocchio-themed but made-in-China wooden toy stores around Florence that act as magnets for tourists. At least this shop actually carves wood on the premises.)

Fiorile (#26 red) is a florist and housewares shop that feels like a hidden gem with modern style; it may just inspire you to pick up a bouquet for your hotel room. Next door, **Studio Puck** (#28 red) sells prints and frames with a unique, fresh take that offers a change of pace from the traditional Florentine designs. On the left (#15 red), **Castorina** produces delicate, hand-carved wooden sculptures, frames, furniture, table legs, and so on—some gilded, others unfinished. Step inside to smell the sawdust and watch the masters hard at work in the back. Near the end of the street on the right (#58 red), **Angela Caputi** produces big, bold, colorful, but lightweight resin jewelry; she also has a shop across the river, on Borgo Santi Apostoli. Just beyond at #62 red, peek in the window at **Francesco,** an old-school cobbler's shop, which makes shoes right here. The busy cross-street marks the end of Via di Santo Spirito—and of our walk.

But for a look at one more artisan shop, turn left (away from the river) up Via dei Serragli, a busier street with more antiques and housewares. About a block up on your right is **Bianchi Lamberto e Duccio** (#10 red). Here a father-and-son team produces bronze and brass frames, door knockers, and other design features. Duccio, the son, speaks good English and enjoys explaining the family business.

NEAR PIAZZA SANTA CROCE

The area around Santa Croce Church is another popular, if touristy, shopping zone. And you're just a few steps away from a lower-impact, more local residential zone to the north and east. The farther you get from the church, the more real Florentines you'll be sharing the streets with.

Touristy Shops at Piazza Santa Croce and Nearby: The piazza in front of Santa Croce Church is bordered by a high concentration of shops. Leather vendors, in particular, cling to the church, trying to entice customers who suffered sticker shock at the church's **leather school** (for more on the Santa Croce Leather School, see page 218). These shops target tired sightseers, making this a handy, if not particularly affordable or authentic area to buy leather. The most leather shops are along **Borgo de Greci,** the heavily touristed corridor linking Piazza della Signoria and Piazza Santa Croce. For something with a bit better quality, head a couple of short blocks north to **Atelier Classe** (see listing earlier). An excellent perfume shop, **Aqua Flor,** is also nearby, just down Via Borgo Santa Croce (see listing earlier).

Shop with the Florentines (Via Pietrapiana and Borgo La Croce): To get off the beaten path, walk about 10 minutes northeast of Santa Croce, to the axis formed by Via Pietrapiana, Borgo La Croce, and Via Gioberti. This authentic-feeling area isn't about artsy souvenirs, but about getting a glimpse at what Florentines buy for day-to-day life.

Short but bustling **Via Pietrapiana** is lined with shops, and dominated by a big, Renaissance loggia that marks the entrance to a park filled with the quirky, grubby **Piazza di Ciompi flea market,** which blurs the boundary between antiques and junk (daily 9:00-19:30, bigger the last Sun of each month). Also along this street, at #67 red, is the **Sotto Sotto** fashion outlet, where local bargain hunters browse last year's deeply discounted designer fashions (closed Sun, www.sottosotto.it).

Heading east on Via Pietrapiana, you'll reach Piazza Sant'Ambrogio, with its namesake church. To the right of the church, **Borgo La Croce** teems with local shoppers. Stroll this mostly pedestrianized street two blocks to the big piazza, passing stores selling housewares, kitchen gadgets, linens, haircuts, clocks, everyday fashion, shoes, home decor, organic body products, ceramics, pets, candy, antiques, and bridal wear. This is the most interesting strip in the area, but at its far end, you could continue straight ahead through the big square and across the busy street, and proceed down **Via Gioberti**—which is wider, less pedestrian-friendly, and lined with more everyday shops, including inexpensive fashion chain stores.

NIGHTLIFE IN FLORENCE

With so many American and international college students in town, Florence by night can have a frat-party atmosphere. For me, nighttime is for eating a late meal, catching a concert, strolling through the old-town pedestrian zone and piazzas with a gelato, or hitting one of the many pubs.

The latest on nightlife and concerts is listed in several publications available free at the TI, such as *The Florentine* monthly (the online version is updated weekly at www.theflorentine.net). The TI can give you a rundown of the day's musical events. Also check www.firenzeturismo.it. The monthly *Firenze Spettacolo,* which has an English section—www.firenzespettacolo.it) is sold cheap at newsstands.

STROLLING AFTER DARK

The **historic center** has a floodlit ambience that's ideal for strolling. The entire pedestrian zone around the Duomo and along Via de' Calzaiuoli, between the Uffizi and the Duomo, is lively with people.

Piazza della Repubblica, lined with venerable 19th-century cafés, offers good people-watching. In the evening, it's a hub of activity, with opera singers, violinists, harpists, bizarre street performers, and a cover band that plays cheesy tunes for the seating area of one of the piazza's bars.

Ponte Vecchio is a popular place to enjoy river views (and kiss), and often has a street musician after dark who encourages passersby to dance.

A few areas feel creepy after dark. Use good judgment. I'd skip the seedy area north of Mercato Centrale.

SIGHTSEEING

Certain sights in Florence stay open later, allowing you to extend your sightseeing into the evening. You can get a pre-dinner workout by climbing the Duomo's dome (Mon-Fri until 19:00) or Campanile (daily until 19:30). Or you can do some early-evening sightseeing at the Accademia (Tue-Sun until 18:50), Uffizi (Tue-Sun until 18:35), Duomo Museum (Mon-Sat until 19:30, but closed for renovation through late 2015), and others. Palazzo Vecchio is open until 24:00 from April through September (except on Thu). For a list of late-night sights, see page 26.

SUNSETS

For the perfect end to the day, watch the sun descend over the Arno River from any of the bridges, especially Ponte Vecchio. Piazzale Michelangelo, perched on a hilltop across the river (bus #12 or #13 from the train station), is also awesome for sunset-watching; it's packed with Romeos and Juliets on weekend evenings. The nearby San Miniato Church (200 yards uphill) is quieter and comes with the same commanding view. If you're going after dark, it's more efficient to zip up there by taxi (rather than take a one-hour round-trip hike). While side-tripping out to Fiesole for the sunset is popular (described on page 72), I'd stick with Piazzale Michelangelo.

LIVE MUSIC

Frequent **live concerts** enhance Florence's beautiful setting. In the summertime, piazzas host a wide range of performers, including pop bands on temporary stages. The lovely sounds of classical music fill churches year-round for special performances. At the TI, ask about current musical events, and keep an eye open for posters as you wander around town.

Orsanmichele Church regularly holds concerts under its Gothic arches. Tickets are sold on the day of the concert from the door facing Via de' Calzaiuoli.

Orchestra della Toscana presents classical concerts from November to May in Teatro Verdi (€13-16, box office open Mon-Sat 10:00-13:00 & 16:00-19:00, closed Sun, near Bargello at Via Ghibellina 97, tel. 055-212-320, www.orchestradellatoscana.it or www.teatroverdionline.it).

St. Mark's English Church offers opera music several nights each week from February through October (with fewer dates in the winter). Check the website or call to see what's playing (full opera performance-€35, opera concerts-€25, Via Maggio 18, mobile 340-811-9192, www.concertoclassico.info).

Santo Stefano Church hosts concerts almost nightly at 21:15 (€12, on Piazza Santo Stefano, near north end of Ponte Vecchio, tel. 055-289-367, mobile 330-885-951, www.notearmoniche.com).

Dinner Theater at Teatro del Sale is a quirky place for dinner and theater. Every night (except Sun-Mon) at 19:30 they kick off a buffet with a fun array of tasty dishes for an hour and a half. Then they take away the tables, and there's an hour-long show. Sometimes the show is great for non-Italian speakers—and sometimes it's not (call or check their website). The old theater is not technically a restaurant, so you'll pay a €7 membership fee to "join" the association, plus €30 for the evening, including drinks (10 blocks behind the Duomo, northeast of Santa Croce at Via dei Macci 111, tel. 055-200-1492, www.teatrodelsale.com).

The recommended **Golden View Open Bar** complements its Arno River views with live jazz (Mon, Wed, Fri, and Sat at 21:00; near Ponte Vecchio—see listing on page 303).

The **Box Office** sells tickets for rock concerts and theater productions in Italian (Mon-Fri 10:00-19:00, Sat 9:00-14:00, closed Sun, east of Santa Croce Church at Via delle Vecchie Carceri 1, tel. 055-210-804, www.boxofficetoscana.it).

Ponte Vecchio often hosts a fine street musician late each evening in summer. He plugs in his amp, while young people get comfortable on the curb. There's generally a street concert nightly in the **Uffizi courtyard.**

DRINKS

Wine Bars: An *enoteca* is fun for sampling regional wines and enjoying munchies, especially pre-dinnertime. Throughout the old town, *enoteche* serve fine Italian wines by the glass with memorable atmospheres. **Le Volpi e l'Uva,** specializing in small, often organic wine producers, has a cozy interior and romantic seating on a quiet little piazza. They have 40 open bottles to choose from and a short menu of appropriate dishes. For maximum tasting, they are happy to arrange a flight of half-glasses and make a little plate of mixed *affettati* (cold cuts) and cheeses (Mon-Sat 11:00-21:00, closed Sun, 65 yards south of Ponte Vecchio—walk through Piazza Santa Felicità to Piazza dei Rossi 1, tel. 055-239-8132, www.levolpieluva.com, run by wine experts Riccardo, Ciro, and Emilio).

Pubs: Irish and English pubs abound in Florence, attracting a mixed crowd of locals and tourists. Most are open late daily. Popular ones include **The Old Stove** (Via Pellicceria 2 red, south of Piazza della Repubblica), **Angie's Pub** (Via dei Neri 35 red, east of the Uffizi), **The Fiddlers Elbow** (Piazza Santa Maria Novella 7 red), and the **Dublin Pub** (Via Faenza 27, near the Mercato Centrale).

Microbreweries: Italy is experiencing a craft beer fad, and Florence has several places where you can join in. Handy to many recommended hotels (and near Mercato Centrale) is **Mostodolce,** with a lively, youthful atmosphere, nine of their own beers on tap, and pub grub (see listing on page 294). Or head across the river to **Archea Brewery,** a small pub that brews several of their own varieties, with a few other Italian-produced beers on tap (daily 17:00-24:00, opens at 18:00 in winter, Via de'Serragli 44 red, a 5-minute walk west of Piazza di Santo Spirito, tel. 055-219-671, Carmine).

LATE-NIGHT LOCAL SCENES

American university students in Florence seem to do more drinking than studying during their semesters abroad. Despite the college party vibe, there is something for everyone in Florence after-hours.

As elsewhere in Italy, many bars have a nightly *aperitivo*, a spread of snacks intended to tide you over until dinner. For the price of a drink, anyone can sample a dish, and the frugal can stretch it to a light meal.

Piazza Santa Croce: It's a hangout at night, often with concerts in front of the church. The epicenter of American student partying is around this square, where you'll find lots of bars and more foreigners than Italians. The neighboring Via de' Benci is busy with trendy night spots. **Moyo,** a slick, gold-lit lounge, is popular with a hip—and young—local crowd (no cover, €5-8 drinks, open daily until late, *aperitivo* 19:00-22:30, dancing from 22:30, free Wi-Fi, just off Piazza Santa Croce at Via de' Benci 23 red, tel. 055-247-9738, www.moyo.it). There are tables outside, if you want to hear yourself talk, and another inviting lounge next door.

Near the Duomo: La Congrega Lounge Bar, a tiny wine/champagne/coffee bar, is a handy little retreat day or night tucked into a tiny lane, 20 yards off Via de' Calzaiuoli. It offers a chic mix of old and new (daily 9:00-24:00, *aperitivo* 18:00-21:00, between the Duomo and Piazza della Repubblica at Via Tosinghi 3/4 red, tel. 055-287-267, Maya).

Near Piazza della Repubblica: Slowly feels anything but slow, with loud DJ music and a trendy vibe (€10 drinks, *aperitivo* with mellow music 18:30-22:00, DJ after about 22:30, south of Piazza della Repubblica at Via Porta Rossa 63 red, tel. 055-265-5354). Just a few steps up the square, **YAB** ("You Are Beautiful") is the dance club of choice, with the action often not starting until midnight (€13-16 cover, Via Sassetti 5 red, www.yab.it).

Piazza Demidoff: To rub elbows with the locals, head across the river toward tiny Piazza Demidoff (cross the bridge east of

Ponte Vecchio and turn left, about a 10-minute walk). These two places have outdoor seating, chichi interiors, late hours (until 2:00 in the morning), and Florentines flaunting their latest shoe purchases: **Negroni** (opens Mon-Fri at 8:30, Sat-Sun at 19:00, Via dei Renai 17 red, tel. 055-243-647) and **Zoe** (opens Mon-Sat at 9:00, Sun at 18:00, Via dei Renai 13 red, tel. 055-243-111).

San Niccolò: Just a few steps around the corner from Piazza Demidoff, Via di San Niccolò has a compact and enjoyable cluster of nighttime hangouts. The bar called **Il Baretto del Rifrullo** is the center of attention, with a lively and sophisticated yet youthful setting (open daily until late, free Wi-Fi, Via San Niccolò 55 red, tel. 055-234-262). Various restaurants—and some of Florence's best gelato, at the recommended Neri—are just steps away. For a more complete rundown of this area, see page 305.

Piazza di Santo Spirito: This square—long known for its riffraff and druggies—has become a more mainstream place to enjoy the evening. It's lined with popular bars and restaurants, including the busy bar **Volume** (€6-8 drinks, daily 9:00-24:00, *aperitivo* 18:30-22:00, see map on page 284 for location). On the opposite side of the square, **Pop Café** feels trendy, though it's plastic-plate simple, with students getting comfortable on the curbs and cobbles (€5-7 drinks, daily 9:00-24:00, *aperitivo* 19:00-22:00, Piazza di Santo Spirito 18, tel. 055-217-475).

MOVIES

Find first-run films in their original languages—including English—at Odeon Cinema, a beautiful historic movie house right downtown, a half-block west of Piazza della Repubblica (Piazza Strozzi, tel. 055-214-068, www.odeonfirenze.com; for schedule of original-language films, look under *"Original Sound"*).

FLORENCE CONNECTIONS

Florence is Tuscany's transportation hub, with fine train, bus, and plane connections to virtually anywhere in Italy. The city has several train stations, a bus station (next to the main train station), and an airport (and Pisa's airport is nearby). Livorno, on the coast west of Florence, is a major cruise-ship port for passengers visiting Florence, Pisa, and other nearby destinations.

By Train

Florence's main train station is called **Santa Maria Novella** (*Firenze S.M.N.* on schedules and signs). Florence also has two suburban train stations: **Firenze Rifredi** and **Firenze Campo di Marte.** Note that some trains don't stop at the main station—before boarding, confirm that you're heading for S.M.N., or you may overshoot the city. (If this happens, don't panic; the other stations are a short taxi ride from the center.)

SANTA MARIA NOVELLA STATION

Built in Mussolini's "Rationalism" style back between the wars, in some ways the station seems to have changed little—notice the 1930s-era lettering and architecture. As at any busy train station, be on guard: Don't trust "porters" who want to help you find your train or carry your bags (they're not official), and politely decline offers of help using the automated ticket machines by anyone other than uniformed staff.

To orient yourself to the station and nearby services, stand with your back to the tracks. Look left to see the green cross of a 24-hour pharmacy *(Farmacia)* and a small food court (marked *Bar & Snack*). Baggage storage *(deposito bagagli)* is also to the left, halfway down track 16 (€6/5 hours, then cheaper per hour after that, daily 6:00-23:00, passport required, maximum 40 pounds, no explosives—sorry). Directly ahead of you is the main hall (*salone biglietti,* with Trenitalia ticket windows; for information, use window #18 or #19—take a number). WCs (€1) are to the right, near the head of track 5. The high-speed Italo information office and Trenitalia Frecciaclub (first-class lounge) are opposite track 5, near the exit.

To reach the **TI,** walk away from the tracks and exit the station; it's straight across the square, 100 yards away, by the stone church.

Buying Tickets: If you need tickets to travel within Italy, there's no reason to stand in line at a window. Take advantage of the user-friendly, "Fast Ticket" *(Biglietto Veloce)* machines that display schedules, issue tickets, and even make reservations for rail-pass holders. Some take only credit cards; others take cards and cash. Using them is easy—just tap "English."

Be aware there are two train companies: Trenitalia, with most connections, has green-and-white machines (toll tel. 892-021, www.trenitalia.it); the red machines are for their high-speed competitor, Italo (no rail passes accepted, cheaper the further in advance you book, tel. 06-0708, www.italotreno.it).

To get international tickets, you'll need to either go to a ticket window (in the main hall) or a travel agency. For more on train travel in Italy—including your ticket-buying options—see page 671.

Cheap Eats: The food court near track 16 includes places to get pizza, *panini*, and simple salads, plus a McDonald's. The handiest supermarket is the classy Sapori & Dintorni Conad, across the busy street toward the Duomo (Mon-Sat 8:30-21:00, Sun 9:30-20:00, Largo Alinari 6/7).

Getting to the Duomo and City Center

The Duomo and town center are to your left (with your back to the tracks). Out the doorway to the left, you'll find city buses and the taxi stand. **Taxis** cost about €6-8 to the Duomo, and the line moves fast, except on holidays. **Buses** generally don't cover the center well and probably aren't the best way to reach your hotel (walking could be faster), but if you need to take one, buy a ticket at the ATAF ticket office outside (go straight ahead out the side door and look for the kiosk in the middle of the street). Minibus #C2 (which runs through the middle of town) departs from across the square, at the corner beyond the TI and Santa Maria Novella underpass; however, by the time you walk to the stop, you're already halfway to downtown.

To **walk** into town (10-15 minutes), exit the station through the main hall and head straight across the square outside (toward the Church of Santa Maria Novella). On the far side of the square, keep left and head down the main Via dei Panzani, which leads directly to the Duomo.

Train Connections

From Florence by Train to: Pisa (2-3/hour, 45-75 minutes), **Lucca** (2/hour, about 1.5 hours), **Siena** (direct trains hourly, 1.5-2 hours; bus is better because Siena's train station is far from the center), **Camucia-Cortona** (hourly, 1.5 hours), **Livorno** (hourly, 1.25 hours, some change in Pisa), **La Spezia** (for the Cinque Terre, 5/day direct, 2.5 hours, otherwise nearly hourly with change in Pisa), **Milan** (hourly, 1.75 hours), **Venice** (hourly, 2-3 hours, may transfer in Bologna; often crowded—reserve ahead), **Assisi** (8/day direct, 2-3 hours), **Orvieto** (hourly, 2 hours, some with change in Campo di Marte or Rifredi station), **Rome** (at least hourly, 1.5 hours, most connections require seat reservations), **Naples** (hourly, 3 hours), **Brindisi** (8/day, 8 hours with change in Bologna or Rome), **Interlaken** (5/day, 5.5-6 hours, 2-3 changes), **Frankfurt** (1/day, 12 hours, 1-3 changes), **Paris** (3/day, 10-15 hours, 1-2 changes, important to reserve overnight train ahead), **Vienna** (1 direct overnight train, or 5/day with 1-3 changes, 10-16 hours).

Note that the departures listed above are operated by Trenitalia; Italo offers additional high-speed connections to major Italian cities (including **Milan, Padua, Venice, Rome,** and **Naples;** see page 671).

By Bus

The BusItalia bus station (100 yards west of the Florence train station on Via Santa Caterina da Siena) is a big, old-school lot with numbered stalls and all the services you'd expect. Schedules for regional trips are posted, and TV monitors show imminent departures. Bus service drops dramatically on Sunday. Generally it's best to buy bus tickets in the station, as you'll pay 30 percent more if you buy tickets onboard. Bus info: tel. 800-373-760 (Mon-Fri 9:00-15:00, closed Sat-Sun), www.fsbusitalia.it.

As some Tuscan towns (including Volterra and Montepulciano) have few connections, day-trippers with more money than time could consider a guided tour such as those offered by ArtViva (see page 29). Otherwise, check the schedule online before heading to the station.

Getting to the Train Station and City Center: Exit the station through the main door, and turn left along the busy street toward the brick dome. The train station is on your left, while downtown Florence is straight ahead and a bit to the right.

From Florence by Bus to: San Gimignano (hourly, less on

Sun, 1.5-2 hours, change in Poggibonsi), **Siena** (about 2/hour, 1.25-hour *rapida/via superstrada* buses are faster than the train, avoid the slower *ordinaria* buses, www.sienamobilita.it), **Volterra** (4/day Mon-Sat, 1/day Sun, 2 hours, change in Colle di Val d'Elsa to CPT bus #770, www.cpt.pisa.it), **Montepulciano** (1-2/day, 2 hours, change in Bettolle, LFI bus, www.lfi.it), Florence's **Amerigo Vespucci Airport** (2/hour, 30 minutes, pay driver and immediately validate ticket, usually departs from platform 1, first bus leaves for airport from Florence at 5:30).

By Taxi

For small groups with more money than time, zipping to nearby towns by taxi can be a good value (e.g., €120 from your Florence hotel to your Siena hotel).

A more comfortable alternative is to hire a private car service. Florence-based **Transfer Chauffeur Service** has a fleet of modern vehicles with drivers who can whisk you between cities, to and from the cruise ship port at Livorno, and through the Tuscan countryside for around the same price as a cab (tel. 338-862-3129, www.transfercs.com, marco.masala@transfercs.com, Marco). **Prestige Rent** also has friendly, English-speaking drivers and offers similar services (office near Piazza della Signoria at Via Porta Rossa 6 red, tel. 055-398-6598, mobile 333-842-4047, www.prestigerent.com, usa@prestigerent.com, Saverio).

By Car

The autostrada has several exits for Florence. Get off at the Nord, Sud, or Certosa exits and follow signs toward—but not into—the Centro.

Don't even attempt driving into the city center. Florence has a traffic-reduction system that's complicated and confusing even to locals. Every car passing into the "limited traffic zone" (*Zona Traffico Limitato,* or *ZTL*) is photographed; those who haven't jumped through bureaucratic hoops to get a permit can expect to receive a €100 ticket in the mail (and an "administrative" fee from the rental company). If you get lost and cross the line several times...you get several fines. The no-go zone (defined basically by the old medieval wall, now a boulevard circling the historic center of town—watch for *Zona Traffico Limitato* signs) is roughly the area between the river, main train station, Piazza della Libertà, Piazza Donatello, and Piazza Beccaria; across the river, in the Oltrarno, the area around Pitti Palace and Santo Spirito is also a ZTL. Confusingly, several streets are classified ZTL only at certain times of day; at the beginning of each block, watch for a stoplight with instructions (in

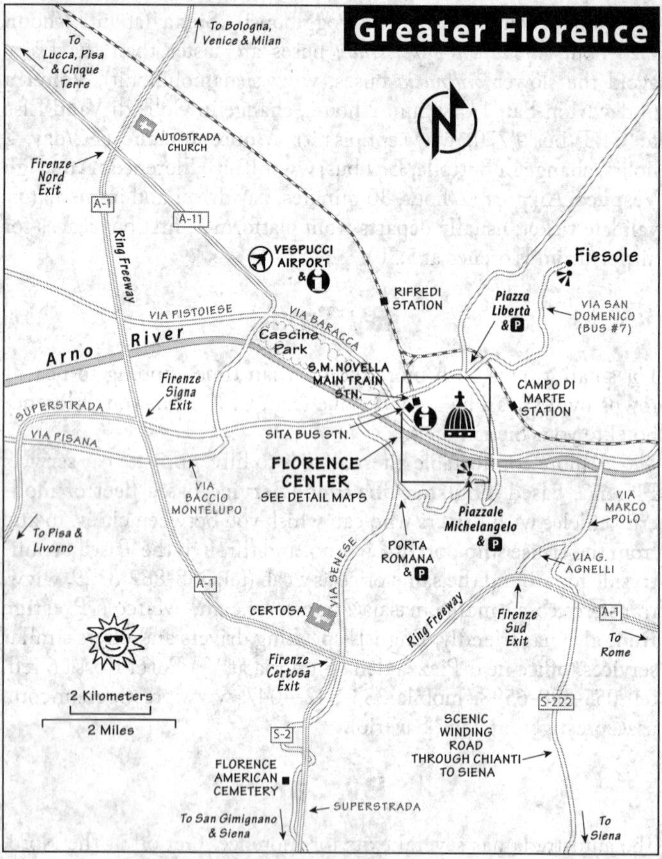

Italian and English)—the green light means it's currently OK to drive there, while the red light means, well...

If you have a reservation at a hotel within the ZTL area that has parking, ask them (in advance) if they can get you permission to enter town. Similarly, some parking garages within the ZTL area may be able to register you. But in general, it's risky to take that chance unless you've verified in advance that it's possible.

Another potentially expensive mistake when driving in Florence is using the lanes designated for buses only (usually marked with yellow stripes). Distracted tourists—trying to navigate in an unfamiliar city—routinely wind up driving in these lanes, get photographed, and are mailed a hefty ticket. Pay careful attention to signs.

Parking: The city center is ringed with big, efficient parking lots (signposted with the standard big *P*), each with taxi and bus service into the center. Check www.firenzeparcheggi.it for details on parking lots, availability, and prices. From the freeway, follow the signs to *Centro,* then *Stadio,* then *P.* I usually head for "Parcheggio del Parterre," just beyond Piazza della Libertà (€2/hour, €20/day, €70/week, open 24 hours daily, tel. 055-500-1994, 600 spots, automated, pay with cash or credit card, never fills up completely). To get into town, find the taxi stand at the elevator exit, or ride one of the minibuses that connect all of the major parking lots with the city center (see www.ataf.net for routes).

You can park for free along any suburban curb that feels safe; pick a place near a bus stop and take the bus into the city center from there. Check for signs that indicate parking restrictions—for example, a circle with a slash through it and "*dispari giovedi,* 0,00-06,00" means "don't park on Thursdays between midnight and six in the morning."

There is talk of closing the free parking lot at Piazzale Michelangelo (see page 69), but if it is open, don't park where the buses drop off passengers; park on the side of the piazza farthest from the view. To get from Piazzale Michelangelo to the center of town, take bus #12 or #13.

Car Rental: If you're picking up a rental car upon departure, don't struggle with driving into the center. Taxi with your luggage to the car-rental office, and head out from there. For more information on car rental and driving in Italy, see page 683. For tips on driving in Tuscany, see page 686.

By Plane

AMERIGO VESPUCCI AIRPORT

Also called Peretola Airport, Florence's compact, manageable airport is about five miles northwest of the city (open 5:00-23:00, no overnighting allowed, TI, airport code: FLR, airport info tel. 055-315-874, flight info tel. 055-306-1700—domestic only, www.aeroporto.firenze.it).

If you need a customs stamp for your VAT refund, you'll find the customs desk upstairs, facing the check-in area (follow *customs* signs); if you need to mail your paperwork after getting it stamped, look for the red mailbox at the small building that's straight ahead as you exit the airport.

Shuttle buses (to the far right as you exit the arrivals hall) connect the airport with Florence's bus station, 100 yards west of the train station on Via Santa Caterina da Siena (2/hour, 30 minutes, €6, buy ticket on board and validate immediately, daily 6:00-23:30). If you're changing to a different intercity bus in Florence (for instance, one bound for Siena), stay on the bus through the first stop (at the train station); it will continue on to the bus station nearby.

The official **taxi** companies have fixed rates for the 20- to 30-minute ride between the airport and downtown: €20 during the day (6:00-22:00), €23.30 at night, and €22 on Sunday. They may tack on €1 per bag, and €2 if you call for a cab rather than hailing one. Be sure to use an official taxi, marked with *Taxi/Comune di Firenze* and a red fleur-de-lis.

The airport's rental-car offices all share one big parking lot that's just a three-minute drive away. However, the streets around the airport (which is tucked behind a big elevated highway) are a dizzying maze, making it tricky to find the place to drop off your car. One option is to drive to the airport, wait for the shuttle bus to show up, then follow that bus to the lot.

For information on Pisa's **Galileo Galilei Airport,** see page 449.

By Cruise Ship

LIVORNO

If you're arriving in Tuscany by cruise ship, you'll disembark in the coastal town of Livorno (sometimes called "Leghorn" in English), located about 60 miles west of Florence. Around 900,000 travelers pass through Livorno's cruise ship ports each year.

Of the excursion options, **Florence** is the most time-consuming to reach (roughly two hours each way by public transit). You have three good options for getting into Florence: take the train; share a minibus taxi (arrange at the dock); or take a cruise-line excursion. **Pisa** is closer (about an hour each way), and—since Pisa is well-connected with **Lucca**—it's possible to combine those two cities into one long day. (If doing this, save Pisa until after lunch to avoid the cruise crowds that flock there in the morning, and be aware that most shops and restaurants in Lucca are closed Sun-Mon.) No matter where you go, if you're taking the train, keep in mind that it can take about 30 minutes just to get from Livorno's cruise port to the train station across town. Plan your day conservatively, as trains can be delayed.

Arrival at the Port: Livorno's port (at the western edge of town) is vast and sprawling, but most cruise ships dock in one of two places: Molo 75, at the Porto Mediceo; or at the adjacent Molo Capitaneria. At either pier, you'll find cruise-line excursion buses, a tiny TI desk, drivers hustling to fill their minibus taxis for trips into Florence, and a shuttle bus leaving every few minutes for Piazza del Municipio in the center of Livorno.

Tourist Information: The TI is inside the covered pedestrian mall just off Piazza del Municipio, a few steps from the port shuttle-bus stop (daily May-Oct 8:00-19:00, Nov-April 8:00-17:30, tel. 0586-894-236, www.costadeglietruschi.it). Public **WCs** are in City Hall, across the street from the TI on Piazza del Municipio.

Tours: The **TI** arranges local guides and has a free *Livorno* brochure with self-guided Livorno walks. They can also inform you about local tours, such as a boat trip around the canals of Livorno plus a visit to Pisa (€20). **Karin Kibby,** an Oregonian living in Livorno who leads Rick Steves tours, offers a morning "slice of Italian life" walk (includes Livorno's fantastic food market) and day trips from the cruise port throughout Tuscany. She'll work with you to find the best solution for your budget and interests (2-10 people, mobile 333-108-6348, karinkintuscany@yahoo.it).

CONNECTING LIVORNO AND FLORENCE, PISA, OR LUCCA

With a little patience, budget-minded travelers can use public transportation to go from Livorno to Florence, Pisa, or Lucca, and back again before the ship departs. Taxis to these places are very expensive, though if splitting the cost with a group, this can be a decent way to go.

By Public Transportation

To visit Florence, Pisa, or Lucca by public transit, follow this basic plan: Ride the cruise line's shuttle bus from the port to downtown Livorno; then ride a public bus to Livorno's train station; then take the train to wherever you're going.

Getting Between the Port and Downtown Livorno: Most cruise lines offer a **shuttle bus** to the center of Livorno, dropping you off at a bus stop near the TI on Piazza del Municipio (about €5-8 round-trip). You'll find plenty of transportation and tour deals being hawked here by a gaggle of small-time guides and tour operators eager to win your business.

Getting to Livorno Centrale Train Station: Livorno's city center clusters around two squares: Piazza del Municipio (TI, public WCs, shuttle-bus stop) and Piazza Grande (stop for buses #1 and #1R to train station). The squares are connected by a long, covered pedestrian mall (with the helpful TI inside).

Public **buses** #1 and #1R to the train station depart from the middle of Piazza Grande (in front of the cathedral). To reach Piazza Grande from the shuttle-bus stop on Piazza del Municipio, turn right out of the bus and walk two short blocks on Via Cogorano, or walk through the pedestrian mall (and visit the TI on the way). From here, the bus heads to Livorno Centrale Station, the end of the line (€1.20, €1.70 if bought from driver, 8/hour Mon-Sat, 4-6/hour Sun, 10 minutes). Before boarding, buy your bus ticket at a tobacco shop or newsstand; at the same place, you can also buy train tickets to Pisa, Lucca, or Florence (doing this now will help you save time and avoid lines at the train station).

Getting to Florence, Pisa, and Lucca: From Livorno Centrale Station, trains zip to Florence, Pisa, Lucca, and other points in Italy. If you're going to Pisa, note that it's usually listed as an intermediate station (for example, on the way to Firenze, Milano, or Torino) rather than the final destination. All Florence-bound trains stop in Pisa.

To Florence: Hourly, usually departs at :10 after the hour, arrive in Florence at :32 past the following hour—1 hour and 22 minutes total, €9 on a regional train. (Occasional departures are a few minutes shorter but require you to change trains at Pisa Centrale.)

To Pisa: 2-3/hour, 20 minutes, €2.50 on a regional train.

To Lucca: About hourly, 1-1.25 hours, transfer at Pisa Centrale, €5.10 on a regional train.

To Lucca and Pisa: If you want to visit Lucca and Pisa in one day, take the train to Lucca first. A handy bus connects Lucca's Piazzale Giuseppe Verdi to Pisa's Field of Miracles (€3, hourly Mon-Sat, fewer on Sun, 50 minutes).

Pisa Bus Alternative: If you want to go straight from downtown Livorno to Pisa, consider taking a bus. The Livorno TI arranges cheap and efficient shuttle buses for cruisers bound for the Leaning Tower. Cheaper still is the public bus labeled *PISA*, which connects downtown Livorno and Pisa hourly on the hour (€2.75, few buses Sat-Sun, 55 minutes, schedule posted at stop, buses have no number and vary in color). In Livorno, catch the *PISA* bus at the Largo Duomo stop behind the cathedral (which faces Piazza Grande; walk down the left side of the cathedral to find the stop by the CPT bus office). The bus leaves you about a block from Pisa's train station at Piazza Santo Antonio, across town from the Field of Miracles and Leaning Tower (see "Arrival in Pisa," page 413). Notice that the bus runs less frequently than the train, and weekend service is limited. It also takes more than twice as long as the train (which takes only 20 minutes)—but it saves you the trip from downtown Livorno to the train station.

By Taxi and Shared Minibus Excursion

Taxis wait at the dock to hustle up business as travelers disembark. While a private taxi is costly, enterprising drivers with eight-seat minibuses gather groups to split their €400 fee; €50/person is actually a great deal—you'll be driven one hour into Florence, dropped off near the center for four or five hours of free time, and then taken back to the port. Some groups cram in a stop at Pisa on the way back, which, while rushing a tour of Florence, is doable. If you have friends on board, this is a wonderful option worth considering and talking up before you arrive in Livorno.

Here are some ballpark round-trip fares for a four-seat car: **Pisa**—€120, **Pisa and Lucca**—€220, **Florence**—€320. Ask if wait time is included—if not, it can cost about €30/hour. In general, drivers at the port prefer to take passengers who will pay them for the whole day, so it can be difficult to get someone to take you just one-way (especially the long haul into Florence).

Taxis both at the port and in the city offer the same rates. Clarify the fare beforehand, even though by law the driver must have the meter on (the quoted price will usually be less than the meter). Don't pay for a round-trip excursion until your cabbie has returned you back to your ship...safe, sound, and on time.

By Cruise-Ship Excursion

Most cruise lines offer a "transportation-only" excursion from the ship to Florence. This includes a bus ride from the ship directly to a point in downtown Florence, free time to explore the city, then a bus ride back to your ship. This is extremely convenient but relatively expensive (around $100-125—which is about €75-95).

[illegible]

[illegible]

[illegible]

[illegible]

TUSCANY

Toscana

Tuscany
To Milan
To Venice
To Venice
Bologna
Adriatic Sea
Ravenna
To Milan
Apuan Alps
EMILIA-ROMAGNA
Imola
LIG.
La Spezia
QUARRIES
Carrara
Faenza
Cesena
CINQUE TERRE
A-12
Montecatini Terme
Pistoia
A-1
SAN MARINO
A-11
Lucca
Viareggio
Vespucci
Fiesole
LE MARCHE
Vinci
Ligurian Sea
Arno R.
Florence
To Urbino
Pisa
U.S. CEM.
Galileo
Empoli
S-222
Livorno
Poggibonsi
Sansepolcro
CHIANTI
San Gimignano
Arezzo
Volterra
Castellina
S-68
Saline
Monteriggione
Siena
S-326
Cortona
20 Kilometers
S-438
Camucia
20 Miles
TUSCANY
Ascano
Perugia
S-146
Pienza
Lake Trasimeno
Montalcino
Monte-pulciano
Assisi
Piombino
SANT' ANTIMO
UMBRIA
S-1
S-2
Portoferraio
Elba
A-1
Todi
Grosseto
Orvieto
MAREMMA
Lake Bolsena
Bagnoregio
Civita
Autostrada
Other Roads
Rail
Border of Tuscany
Border of Province
Viterbo
Monte Argentario
LAZIO
To Rome

SIENA

Siena was medieval Florence's archrival. And while Florence ultimately won the battle for political and economic superiority, Siena still competes for the tourists. Sure, Florence has the heavyweight sights. But Siena seems to be every Italy connoisseur's favorite town. In my office, whenever Siena is mentioned, someone exclaims, "Siena? I looove Siena!"

Once upon a time (about 1260-1348), Siena was a major banking and trade center, and a military power in a class with Florence, Venice, and Genoa. With a population of 60,000, it was even bigger than Paris. Situated on the north-south road to Rome (Via Francigena), Siena traded with all of Europe. Then, in 1348, the Black Death (bubonic plague) swept through Europe, hitting Siena and cutting the population by more than a third. Siena never recovered. In the 1550s, Florence, with the help of Philip II's Spanish army, conquered the flailing city-state, forever rendering Siena a nonthreatening backwater. Siena's loss became our sightseeing gain, as its political and economic irrelevance pickled the city in a purely medieval brine. Today, Siena's population is still 60,000.

Siena, situated atop three hills, qualifies as Italy's ultimate "hill town" (though it's much larger than its cousins covered in the Tuscan Hill Towns chapters). Its thriving historic center, with red-brick lanes cascading every which way, offers Italy's best medieval city experience. Most people do Siena, just 35 miles south of Florence, as a day trip, but it's best experienced at twilight. While Florence has the blockbuster museums, Siena has an easy-to-enjoy soul: Courtyards sport flower-decked wells, alleys dead-end at rooftop views, and the sky is a rich blue dome.

For those who dream of a Fiat-free Italy, Siena is a haven. Pedestrians rule in the old center of town, as the only drivers allowed are residents and cabbies. Sit at a café on the main square. Wander narrow streets lined with colorful flags and studded with iron rings to tether horses. Take time to savor the first European city to eliminate automobile traffic from its main square (1966) and then, just to be silly, wonder what would happen if they did it in your hometown.

PLANNING YOUR TIME

On a quick trip, consider spending two nights in Siena (or three nights with a whole-day side-trip into Florence). Whatever you do, be sure to enjoy a sleepy medieval evening in Siena. The next morning, you can see the city's major sights in half a day. Or consider using Siena as your jet-lag pillow. With its lazy small-town ambience, impressive but user-friendly sights, and easy connection by bus to Florence's airport (simply change at downtown Florence's bus station), this is a fine way to settle into Italian life.

Orientation to Siena

Siena lounges atop a hill, stretching its three legs out from Il Campo. This main square, the historic meeting point of Siena's neighborhoods, is pedestrian-only—and most of those pedestrians are students from the university.

Just about everything mentioned in this chapter is within a 15-minute walk of the square. Navigate by three major landmarks (Il Campo, Duomo, and Church of San Domenico), following the excellent system of street-corner signs. The typical visitor sticks to the Il Campo-San Domenico axis. Make it a point to stray from this main artery. Sienese streets go in anything but a straight line, so it's easy to get lost—but equally easy to get found. Don't be afraid to explore.

Siena itself is one big sight. Its individual sights come in two little clusters: the square (Civic Museum and City Tower) and the cathedral (Baptistery and Duomo Museum, with its surprise viewpoint). Check these sights off, and then you're free to wander.

TOURIST INFORMATION

The TI can be an exasperating place, but they may be able to answer a few questions (Mon-Sat 9:30-18:30, Sun 9:30-17:00, across from the Duomo at Piazza del Duomo at #1, tel. 0577-280-551, www.terresiena.it). They hand out a few pretty booklets (including the regional *Terre di Siena* guide) and a free map of Siena. The bookshop next to the information desk sells more detailed Siena maps

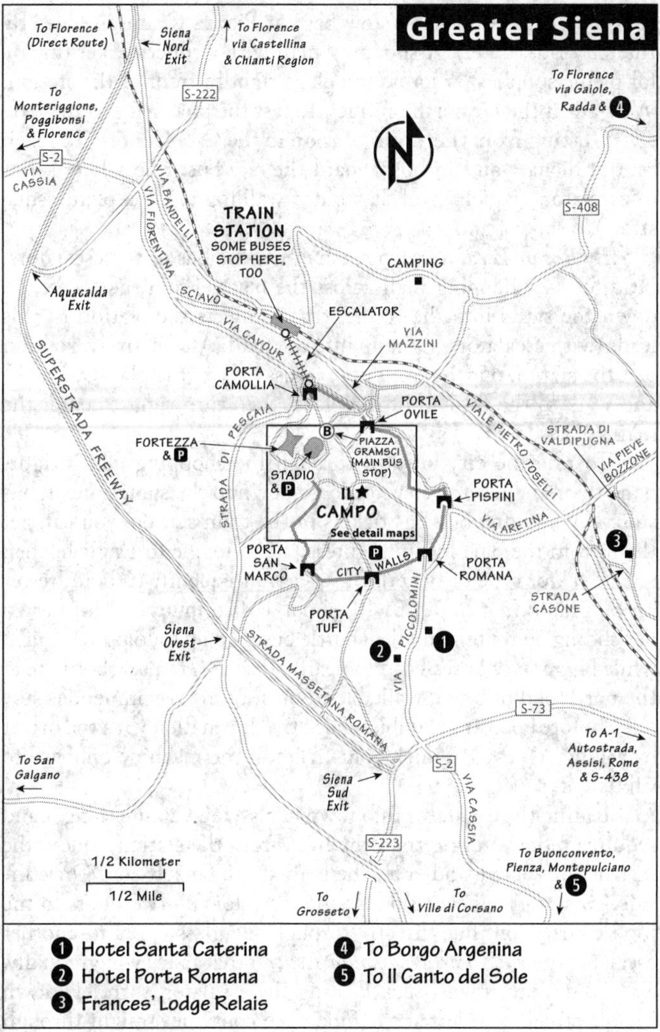

for €1. The TI organizes daily walking tours (described later, under "Tours in Siena").

ARRIVAL IN SIENA

By Train

The small train station, located at the base of the hill on the edge of town, has a bar/tobacco shop, a bus office (Mon-Fri 7:15-19:30, Sat 7:15-17:45, Sun 7:15-12:00 & 15:15-18:30, opens later in winter), and a newsstand (which sells local bus tickets and generally has no line—buy one now if you're taking the city bus into town), but no baggage check or lockers (stow bags at Piazza Gramsci—see "By Intercity Bus," later). A shopping mall with a supermarket (handy for picnic supplies) is across the plaza right in front of the station. WCs are at the far north on track 1, past the pharmacy to the left.

Getting from the Train Station to the City Center: To reach central Siena, you can hop aboard the city bus, ride a long series of escalators (which involves a bit of walking along a picturesque street), or take a taxi.

By Bus or Escalator: To reach either the bus or the escalators, head for the shopping mall across the plaza. From the tracks, go down the stairs into the tunnel that connects the platforms; this leads (with escalators) right up into the mall. Alternatively, you can exit the station out the front door, cross over to the plaza, turn left and walk to the far end of the plaza, then turn right to enter the mall's glass doors.

To ride the **city bus,** go through the shopping mall's right-hand door and use the elevator to go down to the subterranean bus stop. If you didn't buy bus tickets in the train station, you can get them from the blue machine (press "F" to toggle to English, then select "A" for type of ticket). Buses leave frequently (6/hour, fewer on Sun and after 22:00, €1.10, about a 10-minute ride into town depending on route). Smaller shuttle buses go up to Piazza del Sale, while bigger city buses head to nearby Piazza Gramsci (both are at the north end of town, walkable to most of my recommended hotels). Before boarding, double-check the destination with the driver by asking *"Centro?"* Punch your ticket in the machine onboard to validate it.

Riding the **escalator** into town takes a few minutes longer and requires more walking than the bus. From the station, follow the instructions above and enter the mall at the far-left end. Once inside, go straight ahead and ride the escalators up two floors to the food court. Continue directly through the glass doors to another escalator (marked *Porta Camollia/Centro*) that takes you gradually, up, up, up into town (free). Exiting the escalator, turn left down the big street, bear left at the fork, then continue straight through the town gate. From here, landmarks are well-signed (go up Via Camollia).

By Taxi: The taxi stand is to your right as you exit the train station, but as the city is chronically short on cabs, getting one here can take a while (about €10 to Il Campo, taxi tel. 0577-49222).

Getting to the Train Station from the City Center: If you're leaving Siena by train, you can ride a smaller shuttle bus from Piazza del Sale (which goes straight to the station), or catch an orange or red-and-silver city bus from Piazza Gramsci (which may take a more roundabout route). Multiple bus routes make this trip—look for *Ferrovia* or *Stazione* on schedules and marked on the bus. City buses drop off right in front of the station. Confirm with the driver that the bus is going to the *stazione* (staht-see-OH-nay); remember to purchase your ticket in advance from a tobacco shop or blue self-service machine, then validate it on board.

By Intercity Bus

Most buses arrive in Siena at Piazza Gramsci, a few blocks north of the city center. (Some buses only go to the train station; others go first to the train station, then continue to Piazza Gramsci—to find out, ask your driver, "pee-aht-sah GRAHM-chee?") The main bus companies are Sena/Baltour and Tiemme/Siena Mobilità (formerly called Tra-In). Day-trippers can store baggage in the Sottopassaggio la Lizza passageway underneath Piazza Gramsci at the Tiemme/Siena Mobilità office (€5.50/day, daily 7:00-19:00, carry-on-sized luggage no more than 33 pounds, no overnight storage). From Piazza Gramsci, it's an easy walk into the town center—just head in the opposite direction of the tree-filled park. For more on buses, see page 409.

By Car

Siena is not a good place to drive. Plan on parking in a big lot or garage and walking into town.

Drivers coming from the autostrada take the *Siena Ovest* exit and follow signs for *Centro,* then *Stadio* (stadium). The soccer-ball signs take you to the stadium lot (Parcheggio Stadio, €1.70/hour, pay when you leave) near Piazza Gramsci and the huge, bare-brick Church of San Domenico. The nearby Fortezza lot charges the same amount. Another good option is the underground Santa Caterina garage (you'll see signs on the way to the stadium lot, same price). From the garage, hike 150 yards uphill through a gate to an escalator on the right, which carries you up into the city. If you're staying in the south end of town, try the Il Campo lot, near Porta Tufi.

On parking spots, blue stripes mean pay and display; white stripes mean free parking. You can park for free in the lot west of the Fortezza; in white-striped spots behind the Hotel Villa Liberty (south of the Fortezza); and overnight in most city lots from 20:00 to 8:00. Watch for signs showing a street cleaner and a day of the week—that's when the street is closed to cars for cleaning.

Driving within Siena's city center is restricted to local cars and is policed by automatic cameras. If you drive or park anywhere marked *Zona Traffico Limitato (ZTL),* you'll likely have a hefty ticket waiting for you in the mail back home.

Technically, hotel customers are allowed to drop off bags at their hotel before finding a place to park overnight, but getting permission to do so isn't worth the trouble.

HELPFUL HINTS

Combo-Tickets: Siena always seems to be experimenting with different combo-tickets, but in general, only two are worth considering: the €12 Opa Si combo-ticket that includes the Duomo, Duomo Museum, Crypt, and Baptistery (a savings of at least €9 if see all of those sights, valid three days; sold only at ticket office just right of the Duomo, near Duomo Museum entrance), and the €13 combo-ticket covering the Civic Museum and City Tower (€3 savings, valid one day; sold only at ticket office in courtyard of City Hall—look for *Biglietteria*).

Wednesday Morning Market: The weekly market (clothes, knickknacks, and food) sprawls between the Fortezza and Piazza Gramsci along Viale Cesare Maccari and the adjacent Viale XXV Aprile. The fact that this is more local than touristy makes it, for some, even more interesting.

Internet Access: Cheap Phone Center is hidden in a small shopping mall near Il Campo (terminals-€2/hour, Wi-Fi-€1/hour; Mon-Thu and Sat 10:00-20:00, Fri 10:00-13:00 & 15:00-20:00, Sun 12:00-20:00; coming from Il Campo, go uphill past recommended Albergo Tre Donzelle, turn left at Via Cecco Angiolieri, after 20 yards look for #16).

Post Office: It's on Piazza Matteotti (Mon-Fri 8:15-19:00, Sat 8:15-13:30, closed Sun).

Bookstores: Libreria Senese sells books (including my guidebooks), newspapers, and magazines in English, with an emphasis on Italian-related topics (Mon-Sat 9:00-20:00, Sun 10:00-20:00, Via di Città 62, tel. 0577-280-845). The **Feltrinelli** bookstore at Banchi di Sopra 52 also sells books and magazines in English (Mon-Fri 9:00-19:45, Sat 9:30-20:00, closed Sun, tel. 0577-271-104; the bigger Feltrinelli branch farther down the street at #64 has no English books). See the map on page 362 for locations.

Laundry: Onda Blu is a modern, self-service launderette just 50 yards from Il Campo (about €6 wash and dry, daily 8:00-21:15, last load at 20:15, Via del Casato di Sotto 17—see map on page 362).

Travel Agency: Carroccio Viaggi, near recommended Rosticceria Vitti, sells train, plane, and some bus tickets. They charge a small fee, but this saves you a trip to the train station (Mon-Fri 9:00-12:30 & 13:30-19:00, Sat 9:30-12:00, closed Sun, Via Montanini 20, tel. 0577-226-964, www.carroccioviaggi.com, info@carroccioviaggi.com).

Wine Classes: The **Tuscan Wine School** gives two-hour classes in English on Italian wine and food. Midday classes (12:00) cover rotating topics: wines from all over Italy, olive-oil tasting, or a "Savor Siena" food tour that visits several vendors around town. Afternoon classes (16:00) focus on Tuscan wines, including five different samples. Rebecca and her fellow sommeliers keep things entertaining and offer classes for as few as two people (€40/person, 20 percent student discount to anyone with this book, classes offered Mon-Sat, closed Sun, reservations recommended—especially in peak season, Via di Stalloreggi 26, 30 yards from recommended Hotel Duomo, see map on page 362 for location, tel. 0577-221-704, mobile 333-722-9716, www.tuscanwineschool.com, info@tuscanwineschool.com). Their outlet store sells wine from local producers at cost (Mon-Sat 11:00-19:00, closed Sun).

Updates to This Book: For updates to this book, check www.ricksteves.com/update.

Tours in Siena

Tours by Roberto

Roberto Bechi specializes in off-the-beaten-path, ecologically friendly minibus tours of the surrounding countryside (up to eight passengers, convenient pickup at hotel). Roberto, your hardworking host, is married to an American (Patti) and, having run restaurants in Siena and the US, communicates well with Americans. His passions are Sienese culture, Tuscan history, and local cuisine. It's ideal to book well in advance, but you might be able to schedule a tour if you call the day before (seven different tours—explained on website, full-day tours-€90/person 4-hour off-season tours-€60/person, entry fees extra, assistant Carolina can schedule both city tours and alternative countryside excursions if Roberto is booked, Carolina's mobile 320-147-6590, Roberto's mobile 328-425-5648, www.toursbyroberto.com, toursbyroberto@gmail.com, multiday tours. If you book any tour with Roberto, he can advise you on other aspects of your trip.

Other Local Guides

Federica Olla, who leads walking tours of Siena, is a smart, youthful guide with a knack for creative teaching (€55/hour, mobile 338-133-9525, info@ollaeventi.com).

GSO Guides Co-op is a group of 10 young professional guides who offer good tours covering all of Tuscany and Umbria (€140/half-day, €260/full day, 10 percent discount for Rick Steves readers, www.guidesienaeoltre.com). Among them, charming Stefania Fabrizi specializes in Siena (mobile 338-640-7796, stefaniafabrizi@katamail.com; if unavailable call Silvia, mobile 338-611-0127).

Walking Tours

The TI offers walking tours of the old town. Guides usually conduct their walks in both English and Italian (€20, daily April-Nov

Siena at a Glance

▲▲▲**Il Campo** Best square in Italy. **Hours:** Always open. See page 359.

▲▲▲**Duomo** Art-packed cathedral with mosaic floors and statues by Michelangelo and Bernini. **Hours:** March-Oct Mon-Sat 10:30-19:00, Sun 13:30-18:00; Nov-Feb Mon-Sat 10:30-17:30, Sun 13:30-17:30. See page 367.

▲▲**Civic Museum** City museum in City Hall with Sienese frescoes, the *Effects of Good and Bad Government.* **Hours:** Daily mid-March-Oct 10:00-19:00, Nov-mid-March 10:00-18:00. See page 361.

▲▲**Duomo Museum** Siena's best museum, displaying cathedral art (including Duccio's *Maestà*) and offering sweeping Tuscan views. **Hours:** Daily March-Oct 10:30-19:00, Nov-Feb 10:30-17:30. See page 368.

▲**City Tower** 330-foot tower climb. **Hours:** Daily March-mid-Oct 10:00-19:00, mid-Oct-Feb 10:00-16:00. See page 361.

▲**Pinacoteca** Fine Sienese paintings. **Hours:** Tue-Sat 8:15-19:15, Sun-Mon 9:00-13:00. See page 365.

▲**Baptistery** Cave-like building with baptismal font decorated by Ghiberti and Donatello. **Hours:** Daily March-Oct 10:30-19:00, Nov-Feb 10:30-17:30. See page 368.

▲**Santa Maria della Scala** Museum with vibrant ceiling and wall frescoes depicting day-to-day life in a medieval hospital, much of the original *Fountain of Joy,* Byzantine reliquaries, and an Etruscan artifact exhibit. **Hours:** Daily March-Oct 10:30-18:30, Nov-Feb 10:30-16:00. See page 369.

Crypt Site of 12th-century church, housing some of Siena's oldest frescoes. **Hours:** Daily March-Oct 10:30-19:00, Nov-Feb 10:30-17:30. See page 368.

Church of San Domenico Huge brick church with St. Catherine's head and thumb. **Hours:** Daily 7:00-sunset. See page 370.

Sanctuary of St. Catherine Home of St. Catherine. **Hours:** Daily 9:00-18:00, Chapel of the Crucifixion closed 12:30-15:00. See page 371.

at 11:00, 2 hours, no interiors except for Duomo Mon-Sat and Crypt Sun, depart from TI, Piazza Duomo 1, tel. 0577-280-551).

Bus Tours

Somehow a company called My Tour has a lock on all hotel tour-promotion space. Every hotel has a rack of their brochures, which advertise a variety of five-hour big-bus tours into the countryside (€38, depart from Piazza Gramsci).

Sights in Siena

ON IL CAMPO, THE MAIN SQUARE

▲▲▲Il Campo

This square is the heart, both geographically and metaphorically, of Siena. It fans out from City Hall (Palazzo Pubblico) to create an amphitheater. It's the only town square I've ever seen where people stretch out as if at the beach. Il Campo's shining moment is the famous Palio horse races, which take place in summer (see sidebar on page 364).

Originally, this area was just a field *(campo)* located outside the former city walls. Bits of those original walls, which circled the Duomo (and curved against today's square), can be seen above the pharmacy (the black-and-white stones, to the right as you face City Hall). In the 1200s, with the advent of the Sienese Republic, the city expanded—once a small medieval town circling its cathedral, it became a larger, humanistic city gathered around its towering City Hall. In this newer and relatively secular age, the focus of power shifted from the bishop to the city council.

As the city expanded, Il Campo eventually became the historic junction of Siena's various competing *contrade* (neighborhood districts) and the old marketplace. The brick surface is divided into nine sections, representing the council of nine merchants and city bigwigs who ruled medieval Siena. The square and its buildings are the color of the soil upon which they stand—a color known to artists and Crayola users as "Burnt Sienna."

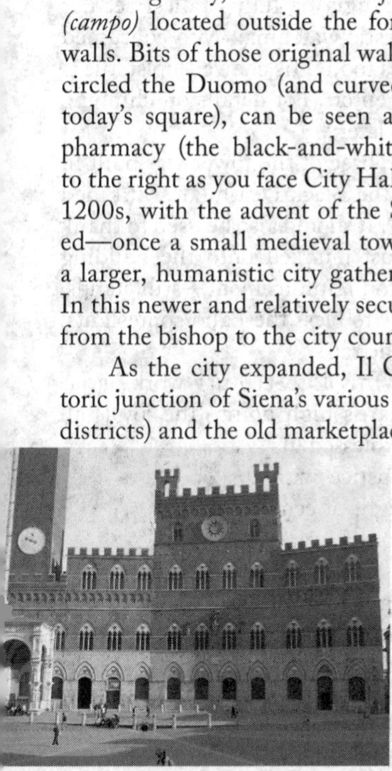

City Hall: This secular building, with its 330-foot

tower, dominates the square. In medieval Siena, this was the center of the city, and the whole focus of Il Campo still flows down to it.

The building's facade features the various symbols of the city. The **sun** hearkens back to St. Bernardino of Siena. Born on the day that St. Catherine of Siena died, he grew up here and went on to travel throughout Italy, giving spirited and humorous sermons that preached peace between warring political factions. His sermons often ended with reconciling parties exchanging a *bacio di pace* (kiss of peace). In Siena he would stand in front of the Palazzo and preach to crowds discreetly segregated by gender with a curtain down the middle. Bernardino personally designed the sun logo to attract crowds, and later he became the patron saint of advertising (and of Siena).

To either side of the sun logo, **she-wolf gargoyles** lean out and snarl, "Don't mess with Siena, Mister Pope!" This Ghibelline city prided itself on its political independence from the papacy; it embraced as a city symbol the pagan she-wolf who suckled Romulus and Remus (Remus' son was Siena's legendary founder). The black-and-white **shields** over the windows are another city symbol. Near ground level, the metal rings are for tying your horse, while the fixtures above once held flags.

The **City Tower** (Torre del Mangia) is Italy's tallest secular tower. It was named after a hedonistic watchman who consumed his earnings like a glutton consumes food. His chewed-up statue is in the courtyard, to the left as you enter. (For details on climbing the tower, see "City Tower" listing, later.)

The open **chapel** located at the base of the tower was built in 1348 as thanks to God for ending the Black Death (after it killed more than a third of the population). It should also be used to thank God that the top-heavy tower—just plunked onto the building with no extra foundation and no iron reinforcement—still stands. These days, the chapel is used solely to bless the Palio contestants, and the tower's bell only rings for the race.

Fountain of Joy (Fonte Gaia): This 15th-century work by Jacopo della Quercia marks the square's high point. The joy is all about how the Sienese Republic blessed its people with water. Notice Lady Justice with her scales (also holding a sword, right of center), overseeing the free distribution of water to all. Imagine residents gathering here in the 1400s to fill their jugs. The Fountain of Joy still reminds locals that life in Siena is good. Notice the pigeons politely waiting their turn to tightrope gingerly down slippery spouts to slurp a drink from wolves' snouts. The relief panel on

the left shows God creating Adam by helping him to his feet. It's said that this reclining Adam influenced Michelangelo when he painted his Sistine Chapel ceiling. This fountain is a copy—you can see most of the original fountain in an interesting exhibit at Siena's Santa Maria della Scala (described later).

To say that Siena and Florence have always been competitive is an understatement. In medieval times, a statue of Venus stood on Il Campo. After the plague hit Siena, the monks blamed the pagan statue. The people cut it to pieces and buried it along the walls of Florence.

▲▲Civic Museum (Museo Civico)

At the base of the tower is Siena's City Hall, the spot where secular government got its start in early Renaissance Europe. There you'll find city government still at work, along with a sampling of local art, including Siena's first fresco (with a groundbreaking down-to-earth depiction of the Madonna). While pricey, it's worth strolling through the dramatic halls to see fascinating frescoes and portraits extolling Siena's greats, saints, and the city-as-utopia.

Cost and Hours: €8, €13 combo-ticket with tower (ticket office is straight ahead as you enter City Hall courtyard—look for *Biglietteria*), daily mid-March-Oct 10:00-19:00, Nov-mid March 10:00-18:00, last entry 45 minutes before closing, info tel. 0577-292-223, www.comune.siena.it.

✪ See the Civic Museum Tour chapter.

▲City Tower (Torre del Mangia)

Siena gathers around its City Hall more than its church. Medieval Siena was a proud republic, and this tall tower is the exclamation point of its "declaration of independence." Its 300 steps get pretty skinny at the top, but the reward is one of Italy's best views.

Cost and Hours: €8, €13 combo-ticket with Civic Museum, daily March-mid-Oct 10:00-19:00, mid-Oct-Feb 10:00-16:00, last entry 45 minutes before closing, closed in rain, free and mandatory bag check.

Crowd Alert: Admission is limited to 50 people at a time, so be prepared for long lines or for tickets to be sold out. Wait at the bottom of the stairs for the green *Avanti* light. Try to avoid midday crowds (up to an hour wait at peak times).

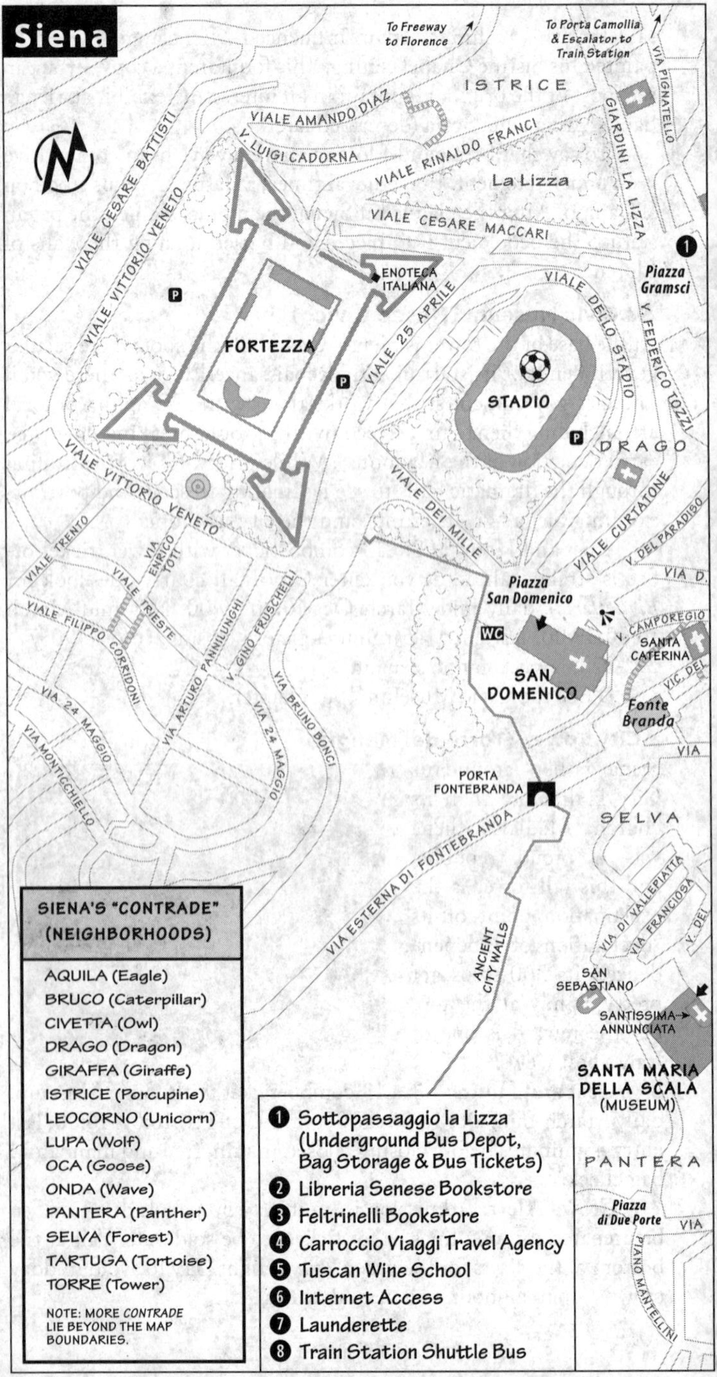
Siena
To Freeway to Florence
To Porta Camollia & Escalator to Train Station
ISTRICE
VIA PIGNATELLO
GIARDINI LA LIZZA
VIALE AMANDO DIAZ
V. LUIGI CADORNA
VIALE RINALDO FRANCI
La Lizza
VIALE CESARE MACCARI
VIALE CESARE BATTISTI
VIALE VITTORIO VENETO
ENOTECA ITALIANA
Piazza Gramsci
V. FEDERICO TOZZI
VIALE DELLO STADIO
VIALE 25 APRILE
FORTEZZA
STADIO
DRAGO
VIALE DEI MILLE
VIALE CURTATONE
V. DEL PARADISO
VIA D.
VIALE TRENTO
VIA ENRICO TOTI
VIALE TRIESTE
VIALE FILIPPO CORRIDONI
VIA ARTURO PANNILUNGHI
V. GINO FRUSCHELLI
VIA BRUNO BONCI
VIA 24 MAGGIO
VIA 24 MAGGIO
VIA MONTICCHIELLO
Piazza San Domenico
WC
SAN DOMENICO
V. CAMPOREGIO
SANTA CATERINA
VIC. DEL
Fonte Branda
VIA
PORTA FONTEBRANDA
SELVA
VIA ESTERNA DI FONTEBRANDA
ANCIENT CITY WALLS
VIA DI VALLEPIATTA
VIA FRANCIOSA
V. DEL
SAN SEBASTIANO
SANTISSIMA ANNUNCIATA
SANTA MARIA DELLA SCALA (MUSEUM)
PANTERA
Piazza di Due Porte
VIA
PIANO MANTELLINI
SIENA'S "CONTRADE" (NEIGHBORHOODS)
AQUILA (Eagle)
BRUCO (Caterpillar)
CIVETTA (Owl)
DRAGO (Dragon)
GIRAFFA (Giraffe)
ISTRICE (Porcupine)
LEOCORNO (Unicorn)
LUPA (Wolf)
OCA (Goose)
ONDA (Wave)
PANTERA (Panther)
SELVA (Forest)
TARTUGA (Tortoise)
TORRE (Tower)
NOTE: MORE CONTRADE LIE BEYOND THE MAP BOUNDARIES.
1 Sottopassaggio la Lizza (Underground Bus Depot, Bag Storage & Bus Tickets)
2 Libreria Senese Bookstore
3 Feltrinelli Bookstore
4 Carroccio Viaggi Travel Agency
5 Tuscan Wine School
6 Internet Access
7 Launderette
8 Train Station Shuttle Bus

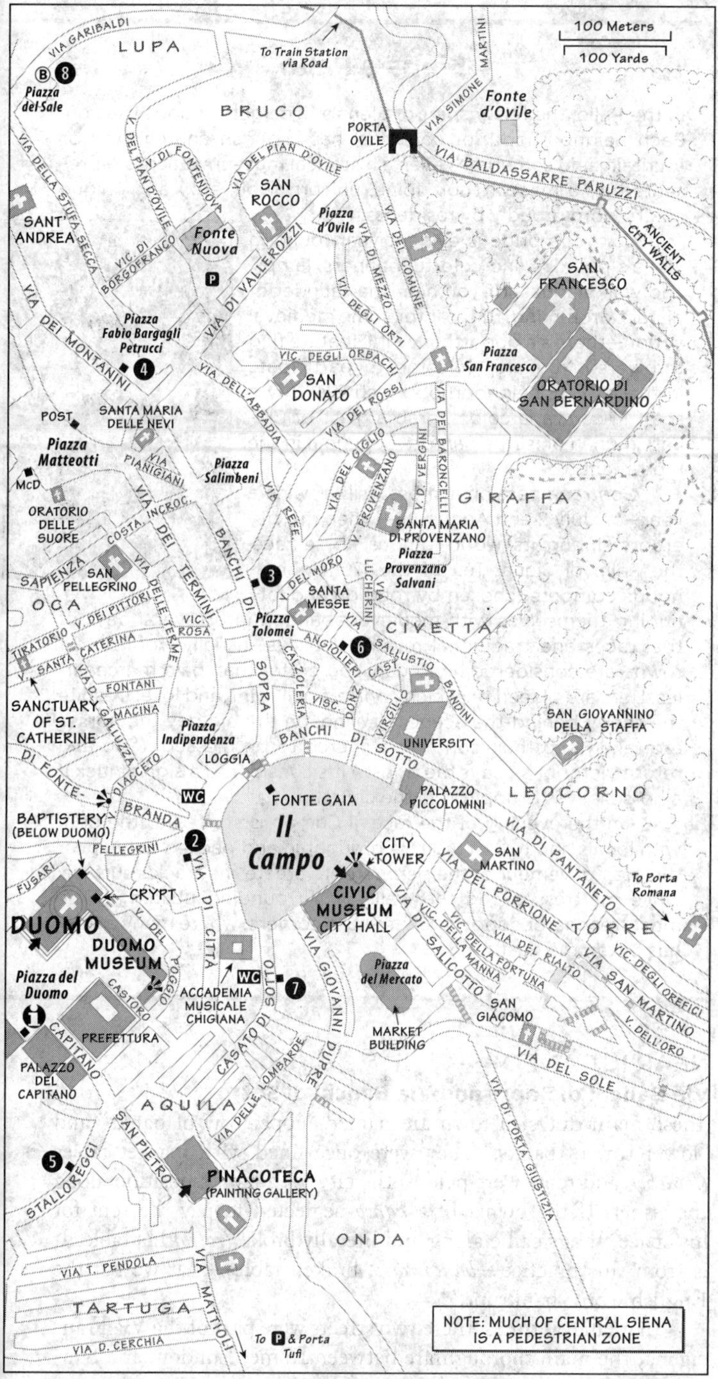
100 Meters
100 Yards
To Train Station via Road
LUPA
BRUCO
Piazza del Sale
PORTA OVILE
Fonte d'Ovile
VIA BALDASSARRE PARUZZI
ANCIENT CITY WALLS
SAN ROCCO
Piazza d'Ovile
SANT' ANDREA
Fonte Nuova
SAN FRANCESCO
Piazza San Francesco
ORATORIO DI SAN BERNARDINO
Piazza Fabio Bargagli Petrucci
SAN DONATO
POST
SANTA MARIA DELLE NEVI
Piazza Matteotti
Piazza Salimbeni
McD
ORATORIO DELLE SUORE
GIRAFFA
SANTA MARIA DI PROVENZANO
Piazza Provenzano Salvani
SAN PELLEGRINO
OCA
SANTA MESSE
Piazza Tolomei
CIVETTA
SANCTUARY OF ST. CATHERINE
SAN GIOVANNINO DELLA STAFFA
Piazza Indipendenza
UNIVERSITY
LOGGIA
FONTE GAIA
PALAZZO PICCOLOMINI
LEOCORNO
BAPTISTERY (BELOW DUOMO)
Il Campo
CITY TOWER
SAN MARTINO
To Porta Romana
CRYPT
CIVIC MUSEUM CITY HALL
DUOMO
DUOMO MUSEUM
TORRE
Piazza del Duomo
Piazza del Mercato
ACCADEMIA MUSICALE CHIGIANA
SAN GIACOMO
PREFETTURA
MARKET BUILDING
PALAZZO DEL CAPITANO
AQUILA
PINACOTECA (PAINTING GALLERY)
ONDA
TARTUGA
To & Porta Tufi
NOTE: MUCH OF CENTRAL SIENA IS A PEDESTRIAN ZONE

Siena's Palio

In the Palio, the feisty spirit of Siena's 17 neighborhoods lives on. Each neighborhood, or *contrada,* has a parish church, well or fountain, and sometimes even a historical museum. Each is represented by a mascot (porcupine, unicorn, wolf, etc.) and unique colors worn proudly by residents.

Contrada pride is evident year-round in Siena's parades and colorful banners, lamps, and wall plaques. (If you hear the thunder of distant drumming, run to it for some medieval action—there's a good chance it'll feature flag throwers.) You are welcome to participate in these lively neighborhood festivals. Buy a scarf in *contrada* colors, grab a glass of Chianti, munch on some *panforte,* and join in the merriment.

Contrada passion is most visible twice a year—on July 2 and August 16—when the city erupts during its world-famous horse race, the Palio di Siena. Ten of the 17 neighborhoods compete (chosen by rotation and lot), hurling themselves with medieval abandon into several days of trial races and traditional revelry. Jockeys—usually from out of town—are considered hired guns, no better than paid mercenaries. Bets are placed on which *contrada* will win...and lose. Despite the shady behind-the-scenes dealing, on the big day the horses are taken into their contrada's church to be blessed. ("Go and return victorious," says the priest.) It's considered a sign of luck if a horse leaves droppings in the church.

On the evening of the race, Il Campo is stuffed to the brim with locals and tourists. Dirt is brought in and packed down over the gray pavement of the perimeter to create the track's surface, while mattresses pad the walls of surrounding buildings. The most treacherous spots are the sharp corners, where many a rider has bitten the dust.

NEAR IL CAMPO

Via Banchi di Sopra and Via Banchi di Sotto

These main drags in town are named "upper row of banks" and "lower row of banks." They were once lined with market tables *(banchi),* and rents were paid to the city for a table's position along the street. If the owner of a *banco* neglected to pay the rent for his space, thugs came along and literally broke *(rotto)* his table. It is from this practice—*banco rotto,* broken table—that we get the English word "bankrupt."

In medieval times, these two streets were part of the Via Francigena, the main thoroughfare between Rome, London, and San-

Picture the scene: Ten snorting horses and their nervous riders line up near the pharmacy (on the west side of the square) to await the starting signal. Then they race like crazy while spectators wave the scarves of their neighborhoods. Every possible vantage point and perch is packed with people straining to see the action. One lap around the course is about a third of a mile (350 meters); three laps make a full circuit. In this literally no-holds-barred race—which lasts just over a minute—a horse can win even without its rider (jockeys perch precariously without saddles on the sweaty horses' backs, and often fall off).

When the winner crosses the line, 1/17th of Siena—the prevailing neighborhood—goes berserk. Winners receive a *palio* (banner), typically painted by a local artist and always featuring the Virgin Mary. But the true prizes are proving that your *contrada* is *numero uno,* and mocking your losing rivals.

All over town, sketches and posters depict the Palio. This is not some folkloric event—it's a real medieval moment. If you're packed onto the square with 60,000 people, all hungry for victory, you won't see much, but you'll feel it. Bleacher and balcony seats are expensive, but it's free to join the masses in the square. Be sure to go with an empty bladder as there are no WCs, and be prepared to surrender any sense of personal space.

While the actual Palio packs the city, you could side-trip in from Florence to see the horse-race trials—called *prove* (proh-vay)—on any of the three days before the main event (usually at 9:00 and after 19:00, free seats in bleachers). For more information, visit www.ilpalio.org.

tiago de Compostela in Spain. The medieval Sienese traded wool with passing travelers, which required money changers, which led to banks. As Siena was a secular town, local Christians were allowed to loan money and work as bankers. Today, strollers out each evening for their *passeggiata* fill Via Banchi di Sopra.

▲Pinacoteca

If you're into medieval art, you'll likely find this quiet, uncrowded, colorful museum delightful. The museum walks you through Siena's art chronologically, from the 12th through the 16th centuries, when a revolution in realism was percolating in Tuscany.

Cost and Hours: €4, Tue-Sat 8:15-19:15, Sun-Mon 9:00-

13:00, last entry 30 minutes before closing, free and mandatory bag check (must leave ID); photos without flash allowed for €1 fee—ask at ticket office. From Il Campo, walk out Via di Città and go left on Via San Pietro to #29; tel. 0577-281-161 or 0577-286-143, www.pinacotecanazionale.siena.it.

➲ **Self-Guided Tour:** In general, the collection lets you follow the evolution of painting styles from Byzantine to Gothic, then to International Gothic, and finally to Renaissance.

• *The core of the collection is on the second floor, in Rooms 1-19. To reach them, ascend two floors and go up a little landing to your right.*

Long after Florentine art went realistic, the Sienese embraced a timeless, otherworldly style glittering with lots of gold. But Sienese art features more than just paintings. In this city of proud craftsmen, the gilding and carpentry of the frames almost compete with the actual paintings. The exquisite attention to detail gives a glimpse into the wealth of the 13th and 14th centuries, Siena's Golden Age. As you walk through the museum, take time to trace the delicate features with your eyes. The woven silk and gold clothing you'll see was worn by the very people who once walked these halls, when this was a private mansion (appreciate the colonnaded courtyard).

Room 1 mostly features the pre-Duccio art world. (Duccio created the *Maestà* in the Duomo Museum, the Duomo's big stained-glass window, and a fresco in the Civic Museum.) Altarpieces emphasize the heavenly and otherworldly, rather than the human realism that Duccio helped to pioneer. (You may see a Duccio in here, as well.)

Rooms 2-4 contain a number of works by Duccio (and assistants), whose groundbreaking innovations are subtle to the layman's eyes: less gold-leaf background, fewer gold creases in robes, transparent garments, inlaid-marble thrones, and a more human Mary and Jesus. Notice that the Madonna-and-Bambino pose is eerily identical in each version.

In **Room 5** are works by Duccio's one-time assistant, Simone Martini, including his *St. Augustine of Siena.* The saint's life is set in pretty realistic Sienese streets, buildings, and landscapes. In each panel, the saint pops out at the oddest (difficult to draw) angles to save the day. (Simone Martini also did the *Maestà* and possibly the Guidoriccio frescoes in the Civic Museum.)

Room 7 includes religious works by the hometown Lorenzetti brothers (Ambrogio is best known for the secular masterpiece, the *Effects of Good and Bad Government,* in the Civic Museum). The rest of the rooms on this floor are a menagerie of gold-backed saints and Madonnas.

In **Room 12** are two famous small wooden panels: *Città sul Mare (City by the Sea)* and *Castello in Riva al Lago (Castle on the*

Lakeshore). These pieces, done by an early 14th-century Sienese painter (some scholars think it could be Sassetta), feature the strange, medieval landscape Cubism seen in the work of the contemporaneous *Guidoriccio da Fogliano* (in the Civic Museum). Notice the weird, melancholy light that captures the sense of the Dark Ages. These images are replicated on postcards found throughout the city.

• *Loop through the rest of this level, then descend one floor to view a minor collection of later art.*

In **Room 20,** suddenly the gold is gone—Madonna is set on Earth. See works by the painter/biographer Giorgio Vasari **(Room 22),** a stunning view out the window **(Room 26),** and several colorful rooms **(27-30)** dedicated to Domenico Beccafumi (1486-1551). Beccafumi designed many of the Duomo's inlaid pavement panels (including *Slaughter of the Innocents*), and his original cartoons are displayed in **Room 30.** With strong bodies, twisting poses, and dramatic gestures, Beccafumi's works epitomize the Mannerist style.

Room 31 has the sympathetic *Christ on the Column* by Sodoma (Giovanni Bazzi), and the long **Room 32** displays large-scale works by Sodoma, Beccafumi, and others. In **Room 33,** Bernardino Mei gives a Sienese take on the wrinkled saints and dark shadows of Caravaggio.

CATHEDRAL AREA

Each of the first four sights (Duomo, Duomo Museum, Crypt, and Baptistery) is covered by a separate ticket, or by the €12 Opa Si combo-ticket. If you're planning to visit only the Duomo and Duomo Museum, this ticket doesn't add up; but if you're curious about the Crypt and Baptistery, the combo-ticket lets you peek into those sights for just €1 more. Separate tickets and the Opa Si combo-ticket are sold only at the ticket office near the entrance to the Duomo Museum—to the right as you face the cathedral facade (no tickets sold at sight entrances).

▲▲▲Duomo

This 13th-century Gothic cathedral, with its six-story striped bell

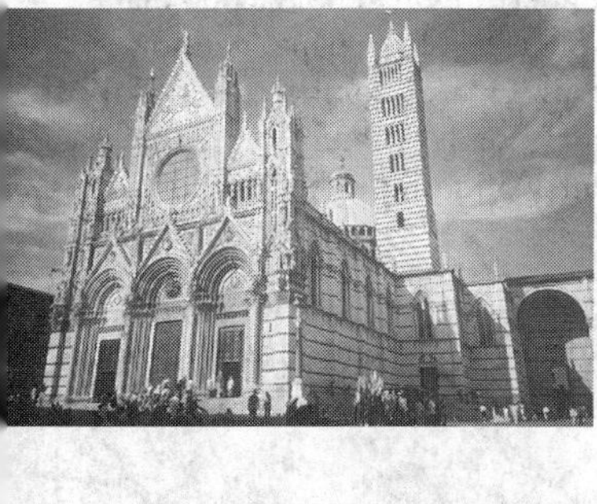

tower—Siena's ultimate tribute to the Virgin Mary—is heaped with statues, plastered with frescoes, and paved with art. Soak up the richly ornamented facade before venturing inside, where 1,000 years of popes keep watch from on high. The interior is a Renaissance riot of striped columns, remarkably intricate inlaid-marble floors, a Michelangelo statue, and evocative Bernini sculptures. The Piccolomini Library features a series of 15th-century frescoes chronicling the adventures of Siena's philanderer-turned-pope, Aeneas Piccolomini.

Cost and Hours: €4 includes cathedral and Piccolomini Library, covered by Opa Si combo-ticket, buy tickets near Duomo Museum entry; March-Oct Mon-Sat 10:30-19:00, Sun 13:30-18:00; Nov-Feb Mon-Sat 10:30-17:30, Sun 13:30-17:30; last entry 30 minutes before closing. Modest dress is required to enter, but paper ponchos are provided; guided cupola/roof tour and videoguide available; tel. 0577-286-300, www.operaduomo.siena.it.

✪ See the Siena Duomo Tour chapter.

▲▲Duomo Museum (Museo dell'Opera e Panorama)

Located in a corner of the Duomo's grand but unfinished extension (to the right as you face the main facade), Siena's most enjoyable museum was built to house the cathedral's art. The ground floor features the original Duccio stained-glass window that once hung over the high altar, along with an army of statues from the facade. Upstairs is Duccio's *Maestà* (*Enthroned Virgin,* 1311), one of the great pieces of medieval art. The flip side of the *Maestà* (displayed on the opposite wall) has 26 panels—the medieval equivalent of pages—showing scenes from the Passion of Christ. Finally, climb up to the Panorama dal Facciatone. From the first landing, take the skinny second spiral for Siena's surprise view.

Cost and Hours: €7, covered by Opa Si combo-ticket, buy tickets near Duomo Museum entry, daily March-Oct 10:30-19:00, Nov-Feb 10:30-17:30, last entry 30 minutes before closing, videoguide-€4 (€6/2 people), tel. 0577-286-300, www.operaduomo.siena.it.

✪ See the Siena Duomo Museum Tour chapter.

▲Baptistery

Siena is so hilly that there wasn't enough flat ground on which to build a big church. What to do? Build a big church anyway and prop up the overhanging edge with the Baptistery. This dark and quietly tucked-away cave of art is worth a look for its cool, tranquil bronze panels and angels by Ghiberti, Donatello, Jacopo della Quercia, and others that adorn the pedestal of the baptismal font.

Cost and Hours: €4, covered by Opa Si combo-ticket, buy tickets near Duomo Museum entry, daily March-Oct 10:30-19:00, Nov-Feb 10:30-17:30, last entry 30 minutes before closing, 10-minute videoguide-€2.

Crypt

The cathedral "crypt" is archaeologically important. The site of a small 12th-century Romanesque church, it was filled in with dirt a century after its creation to provide a foundation for the huge church that sits atop it today. Recently excavated, the several rediscovered frescoed rooms show off what are likely the oldest frescoes in town. Religious art exhibitions are sometimes held here.

Cost and Hours: €6, €8 during special exhibitions, covered by Opa Si combo-ticket, buy tickets near Duomo Museum entry, daily March-Oct 10:30-19:00, Nov-Feb 10:30-17:30, last entry 30 minutes before closing, entrance is halfway up the stairs between the Baptistery and Duomo Museum.

▲Santa Maria della Scala

This museum, opposite the Duomo entrance, was used as a hospital until the 1980s. Its labyrinthine 12th-century cellars—carved out of volcanic tuff and finished with brick—go down several floors and during medieval times were used to store supplies for the hospital upstairs. Today, the hospital and its cellars are filled with exhibits (well-described in English) and can be a welcome refuge from the hot streets. Stop in for a cool and quiet break in the air-conditioned lobby, which offers a fine bookshop (with TI next door) and big, comfy couches, all under great 15th-century timbers. The complex also houses a minimalist children's museum.

Cost and Hours: €10, daily March-Oct 10:30-18:30, Nov-Feb 10:30-16:00, last entry 30 minutes before closing, €5 guided tours sometimes available Fri at 11:00 or on request, tel. 0577-534-511, www.santamariadellascala.com.

➲ **Self-Guided Tour:** It's easy to get lost in this gigantic complex, so stay focused on the main attractions—the fancily frescoed Pellegrinaio Hall (ground floor), most of the original *Fountain of Joy* and some of the most ancient Byzantine reliquaries in existence (first basement), and the Etruscan collection in the Archaeological Museum (second basement), where the Sienese took refuge during WWII bombing. Just inside the complex (enter from the square) is the Church of the Santissima Annunziata.

• *From the entrance, walk down the lengthy hall to the long room with the colorful frescoes.*

The sumptuously frescoed walls of **Pellegrinaio Hall** show medieval Siena's innovative health care and social welfare system in action (c. 1442, wonderfully described in English). Starting in the 11th century, the hospital nursed the sick and cared for abandoned children, as is vividly portrayed in these frescoes. The good works paid off, as bequests and donations poured in, creating the wealth that's evident throughout this building.

• *Head down the stairs, then continue straight into the darkened rooms with pieces of Siena's landmark fountain—follow signs to* Fonte Gaia.

An engaging exhibit explains Jacopo della Quercia's early 15th-century ***Fountain of Joy*** *(Fonte Gaia)*—and displays the disassembled pieces of the original fountain itself. In the 19th century, after serious deterioration, the ornate fountain was dismantled and plaster casts were made. (From these casts, they formed the replica that graces Il Campo today.) Here you'll see the eroded original panels paired with their restored casts, along with the actual statues that once stood on the edges of the fountain.

• *To visit the reliquaries, retrace your steps and follow the signs for* Il Tesoro.

Many of these **Byzantine reliquaries** are made of gold, silver, and precious stones. Legend has it that some were owned by Helen, Constantine's mother. They were "donated" to the hospital shortly after the plague that decimated the city (and the rest of Europe), since the sale of reliquaries was forbidden.

• *Now, descend into the cavernous second basement.*

Under the groin vaults of the **Archaeological Museum,** you're alone with piles of ancient Etruscan stuff excavated from tombs dating centuries before Christ (displayed in a labyrinthine exhibit). Remember, the Etruscans dominated this part of Italy before the Roman Empire swept through—some historians think even Rome originated as an Etruscan town. A new section covering Siena's history is also on this floor.

SAN DOMENICO AREA

Church of San Domenico

This huge brick church is worth a quick look. The spacious, plain interior (except for the colorful flags of the city's 17 *contrade,* or neighborhoods) fits the austere philosophy of the Dominicans and invites meditation on the thoughts and deeds of St. Catherine. Walk up the steps in the rear to see paintings from her life. Halfway up the church on the right, find a metal bust of St. Catherine, a small case housing her thumb (on the left), and a glass box on the lowest shelf containing the chain she used to scourge herself. In the chapel (15 feet to the left) surrounded with candles, you'll see Catherine's actual head atop the altar. Through the door just beyond are the sacristy and the bookstore.

Cost and Hours: Free, daily 7:00-sunset, gift shop tel. 0577-286-848, www.basilicacateriniana.com. A WC (€0.50) is at the far end of the parking lot, to the right as you face the church entrance.

St. Catherine of Siena (1347-1380)

The youngest of 25 children born to a Sienese cloth dyer, Catherine began experiencing heavenly visions as a child. At 16 she became a member of the Dominican order, locking herself away for three years in a room in her family's house. She lived the life of an ascetic, which culminated in a vision wherein she married Christ. Catherine emerged from solitude to join her Dominican sisters, sharing her experiences, caring for the sick, and gathering both disciples and enemies. At age 23, she lapsed into a spiritual coma, waking with the heavenly command to spread her message to the world. She wrote essays and letters to kings, dukes, bishops, and popes, imploring them to find peace for a war-ravaged Italy. While visiting Pisa during Lent of 1375, she had a vision in which she received the stigmata, the wounds of Christ.

Still in her 20s, Catherine was invited to Avignon, France, where the pope had taken up residence. With her charm, sincerity, and reputation for holiness, she helped convince Pope Gregory XI to return the papacy to the city of Rome. Catherine also went to Rome, where she died young. She was canonized in the next generation (by a Sienese pope), and her relics were distributed to churches around Italy.

Because of her intervention in the papal schism, today Catherine is revered (along with St. Benedict) as the patron saint of Europe and remembered as a rare outspoken medieval woman still appreciated for her universal message: that this world is not a gift from our fathers, but a loan from our children.

Sanctuary of St. Catherine (Santuario di Santa Caterina)

Step into the cool and peaceful site of Catherine's home. Siena remembers its favorite hometown gal, a simple, unschooled, but mystically devout soul who, in the mid-1300s, helped convince the pope to return from France to Rome. Pilgrims have visited this place since 1464, and architects and artists have greatly embellished what was probably once a humble home (her family worked as wool dyers). You'll see paintings throughout showing scenes from her life.

Enter through the courtyard, and walk down the stairs at the far end. The church on your right contains the wooden crucifix upon which Catherine was meditating when she received the stigmata. Take a pew, gaze at it, and try to imagine the scene. Back outside, the oratory across the courtyard stands where the kitchen once was. Go down the stairs (left of the gift shop) to reach the saint's room. Catherine's bare cell is behind wrought-iron doors.

Cost and Hours: Free, daily 9:00-18:00, Chapel of the Crucifixion closed 12:30-15:00 but church is open, a few downhill blocks toward the center from San Domenico—follow signs to *Santuario di Santa Caterina*—at Costa di Sant'Antonio 6, tel. 0577-288-175.

Shopping in Siena

The main drag, Via Banchi di Sopra, is a cancan of fancy shops. Here are some things to look for:

Flags: For easy-to-pack souvenirs, get some of the large, colorful scarves/flags that depict the symbols of Siena's 17 different neighborhoods (such as the wolf, the turtle, or the snail). They're good for gifts or to decorate your home (sold in varying sizes at souvenir stands).

Sweets: All over town, Prodotti Tipici shops sell Sienese specialties. Siena's claim to caloric fame is its *panforte,* a rich, chewy concoction of nuts, honey, and candied fruits that impresses even fruitcake haters. There are a few varieties: *Margherita,* dusted in powdered sugar, is more fruity, while *panpepato* has a spicy, peppery crust. Locals prefer a chewy, white macaroon-and-almond cookie called *ricciarelli.*

SIENA DUOMO TOUR

The Duomo sits atop Siena's highest point, with one of the most extravagant facades in all of Europe. This ornate but surprisingly secular shrine to the Virgin Mary is stacked with colorful art inside and out, from inlaid-marble floors to stained-glass windows. Along with sculptures by Bernini and Michelangelo, the church features the Piccolomini Library, where a series of captivating frescoes by the Umbrian painter Pinturicchio tells the story of Aeneas Piccolomini, Siena's consummate Renaissance Man, who became Pope Pius II.

Orientation

Cost: €4 includes cathedral and Piccolomini Library, buy ticket at Duomo Museum entrance (facing the cathedral entry, the museum is 100 yards to the right, near the south transept). To add the Duomo Museum, Crypt, and Baptistery, consider the €12 Opa Si combo-ticket.

Check the line to get into the Duomo before buying tickets—if there's a long wait, you can pay an extra €1 for a (misnamed) "reservation" that lets you skip the line.

Hours: March-Oct Mon-Sat 10:30-19:00, Sun 13:30-18:00; Nov-Feb Mon-Sat 10:30-17:30, Sun 13:30-17:30; last entry 30 minutes before closing.

Dress Code: Modest dress is required, but stylish paper ponchos are provided for the inappropriately clothed.

Getting There: Just look up and head for the black-and-white-striped tower.

Information: Tel. 0577-286-300, www.operaduomo.siena.it. Inside the Duomo are €2 video terminals that give a history of the cathedral floor.

Tours: The Porta del Cielo ("Heaven's Gate") **guided tour** is popular—book well in advance for one in English. The 1.5-hour tour includes a 45-minute visit to the dome's cupola and roof for spectacular interior and exterior views. You'll climb 79 steps to see recently restored rooms near the top of the church (with impressive inlaid floors) and get a close-up look at the cupola, with its blue, star-decorated panels and 12 windows (representing the 12 apostles) by Ulisse De Matteis. You'll also walk briefly outside on the rooftop for a breath-taking view (not for those with a fear of heights). The second half of the tour takes you through the rest of the cathedral (which you could skip out on—particularly if you end up on an Italian-language tour).

Reservations are required at least 48 hours in advance, but ideally, book as soon as you know when you'll be in Siena. If you're in a pinch, ask about same-day reservations, as tours run every 45 minutes in high season. When you reserve, you'll be given a reference number, which you must show on arrival at the ticket office; they prefer payment by wire 10 days before the reserved tour (€25, tours run April-Jan; to book, call 0577-286-300 Mon-Fri 9:00-17:00). Given the tour's popularity, maybe more English tours will be added—or maybe not (check www.operaduomo.siena.it, opasiena@operalaboratori.com).

The **videoguide** (rent in central nave) is informative but extremely dry. I'd stick with the commentary in this chapter (for Duomo only: €6, €10/2 people; for Duomo plus Duomo Museum, Crypt, and Baptistery: €8, €14/2 people).

Length of This Tour: Allow one hour.

Photography: No flash permitted.

The Tour Begins

Exterior

Grab a spot on a stone bench opposite the entry to take in this architectural festival of green, white, pink, and gold. Like a medieval altarpiece, the facade is divided into sections, each frame filled with patriarchs and prophets, studded with roaring gargoyles, and topped with prickly pinnacles. Imagine pilgrims arriving at this church, its facade trumpeting the coming of Christ and the true path to salvation.

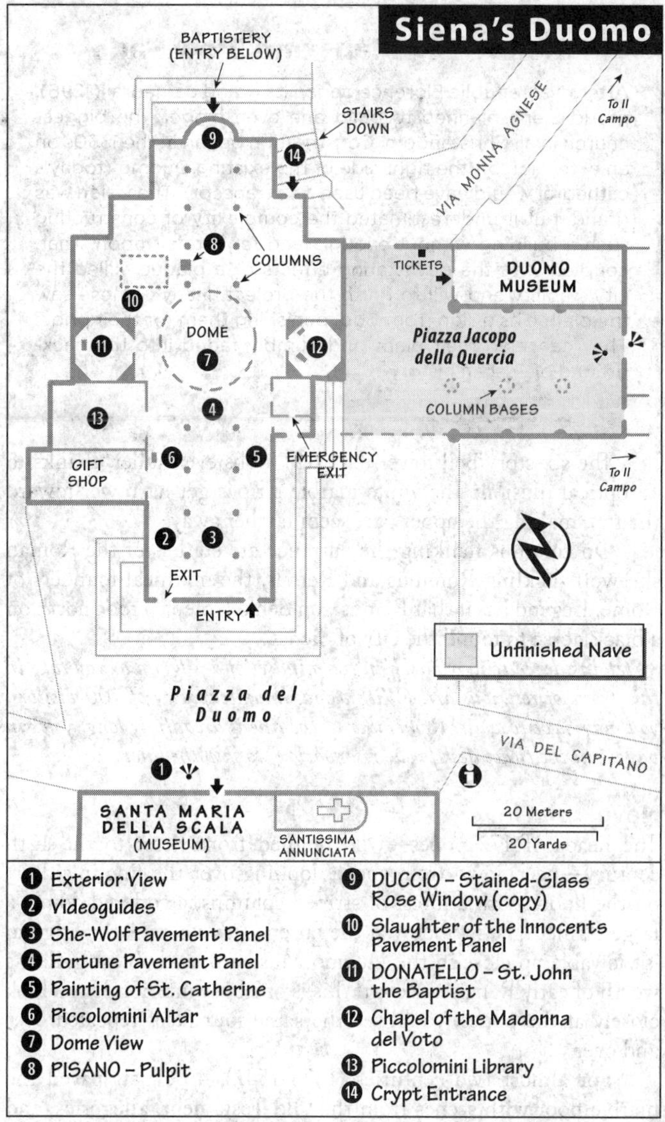

The current structure dates back to 1215, with the major decoration done during Siena's heyday (1250-1350). The lower story, by Giovanni Pisano (who worked from 1284 to 1297), features remnants of the fading Romanesque style (round arches over the doors), topped with the pointed arches of the new Gothic style that was seeping in from France. The upper half, in full-blown Gothic, was designed and built a century later.

Siena's Big Plans and Slow Fade

After rival republic Florence began its grand cathedral (1296), proud Siena planned to build one even bigger, the biggest church in all Christendom. Construction began in the 1330s on an extension off the right side of the existing Duomo (today's cathedral would have been used as a transept). The vision was grand, but it underestimated the complexity of constructing such a building without enough land for it to sit upon. That, coupled with the devastating effects of a plague, killed the city's ability and will to finish the project. Many Sienese saw the plague as a sign from God, punishing them for their pride. They canceled their plans and humbly faded into the background of Tuscan history.

The six-story bell tower (c. 1315) looks even taller, thanks to an optical illusion: The white marble stripes get narrower toward the top, making the upper part seem farther away.

On columns flanking the entrance are statues of the Roman she-wolf suckling Romulus and Remus, the mythical founders of Rome. Legend has it that Remus' son Senio ("Siena") rode north on a black horse to found the city of Siena.

• *Step inside, putting yourself in the mindset of a pilgrim as you take in this trove of religious art. (With a maximum capacity of 700 visitors, you may have to wait. Remember, if the line is dreadfully long, you can pay €1 at the ticket desk for a "reservation" to skip the line.)*

Nave

The heads of 172 popes—who reigned from Peter to the 12th century—peer down from above, looking over the fine inlaid art on the floor. With a forest of striped columns, a coffered dome, a large stained-glass window at the far end (it's a copy—the original is viewable up close in the Duomo Museum), and an art gallery's worth of early Renaissance art, this is one busy interior. If you look closely at the popes, you'll see the same four faces repeated over and over.

For almost two centuries (1373-1547), 40 artists paved the marble floor with scenes from the Old Testament, allegories, and intricate patterns.

The series starts near the entrance with historical allegories; the larger, more elaborate scenes surrounding the altar are mostly stories from the Old Testament. Many of the floor panels are roped off—and occasionally even covered—to prevent further wear and tear.

• *On the floor, find the second pavement panel from the entrance.*

She-Wolf Pavement Panel

Depicted as a she-wolf, the proud city of Siena is the center of the Italian universe, orbited by such lesser lights as Roma, Florentia (Florence), and Pisa. This is pretty secular stuff for such prime church real estate. Five yards to the left and right are panels with pre-Christian imagery—the ancient Greek prophetesses known as the sibyls. This church's mix of pre-Christian wisdom, secular humanism, and Christian piety gives an insight into the Sienese approach to religion.

• *The fifth pavement panel from the entrance is the...*

Fortune Panel

Lady Luck (lower right) parachutes down to earth, where she teeters back and forth on a ball and a tipsy boat. The lesson? Fortune is an unstable foundation for life. Truth seekers wind their way up the precarious path to the top, where Socrates accompanies Lady Wisdom. Having attained wisdom, the world's richest man ("Crates," upper right) realizes that money doesn't buy happiness, and he dumps his jewels out. They fall to earth, and the cycle of Fortune begins again.

On the right wall hangs a dim **painting of St. Catherine** (fourth from entrance). Siena's homegrown saint (see page 371) had a vision in which she mystically married Christ. Here's the wedding ceremony in heaven. Jesus places the ring on Catherine's finger as her future mother-in-law, Mary, looks on.

• *On the opposite wall is a marble altarpiece decorated with statues (next to a doorway leading to a shop, snacks, and WC).*

Piccolomini Altar

The Piccolomini Altar was designed for the tomb of the Sienese-born Pope Pius III (born Francesco Todeschini Piccolomini). It was commissioned when he was the cardinal of Siena, but because he later became a pope (see the fresco of his coronation with Pius wearing the golden robe—above and to the right of the Michelangelo statue), he was buried in the Vatican and this fancy tomb was never used. It's most interesting for its statues: one by Michelangelo and three by his students. Michelangelo was originally contracted to do 15 statues, but another sculptor had started the marble blocks, and Michelangelo's heart was never in the project. He personally finished only the figure of St. Paul (lower right, clearly more interesting than the bland, bored popes above him).

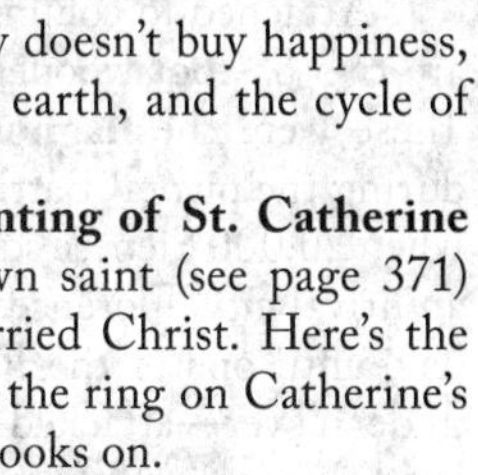

Paul has the look of Michelangelo's *Moses,* the broken-nosed self-portrait of the sculptor himself, and the relaxed hand of his *David.* It was the chance to sculpt *David* in Florence that convinced Michelangelo to abandon the Siena project.

• *Now grab a seat to study the...*

Dome and Surrounding Area

The dome sits on a 12-sided base, but its "coffered" ceiling is actually a painted illusion.

Get oriented to the array of sights by thinking of the church floor as a big 12-hour clock. You're the middle, and the altar is high noon: You'll find the *Slaughter of the Innocents* roped off on the floor at 10 o'clock, Pisano's pulpit between two pillars at 11 o'clock, a copy of Duccio's round stained-glass window at 12 o'clock, Bernini's chapel at 3 o'clock, the Piccolomini Altar at 7 o'clock, the Piccolomini Library at 8 o'clock, and a Donatello statue at 9 o'clock.

Attached to columns (easy to miss, at 7 o'clock and 5 o'clock) are two 65-foot wooden poles that are dear to any Sienese heart. These were the **flagpoles,** bearing the Florentine flag, captured during the pivotal Battle of Montaperti (1260, fought near Siena), when 20,000 Sienese squared off against 35,000 soldiers from their archrival city, Florence. The two armies battled back and forth all day, until one of the Florentine soldiers—actually, a Sienese spy under cover—attacked the Florentine standard-bearer from behind. Florence's flag fell to the ground, the army lost its bearings and confidence, and Siena seized the moment to counterattack and win. It was the city's finest hour, ushering in its 80-year Golden Age.

The church was intended to be much larger. Look into the right transept and mentally blow a hole in the wall. You'd be looking down the nave of the massive extension of the church—that is, if the original grandiose plan had been completed (see sidebar, page 376).

Pisano's Pulpit

The octagonal Carrara marble pulpit (1268) rests on the backs of lions, symbols of Christianity triumphant. Like the lions, the Church eats its catch (devouring paganism) and nurses its cubs. The seven relief panels tell the life of Christ in rich detail. The pulpit is the work of Nicola Pisano (c. 1220-1278), the "Giotto of sculpture," whose revival of classical forms (columns, sarcophagus-like relief panels) signaled the coming Renaissance. His son Giovanni (c. 1240-1319) carved many of the panels, mixing his dad's classicism and realism with the decorative detail and curvy lines of French Gothic—a style that would influence Donatello and the other Florentines.

The Crucifixion panel (facing the nave under the eagle) is proto-Renaissance. Christ's anatomy is realistic. Mary (bottom left) swoons into the arms of the other women, a very human outburst of emotion. And a Roman soldier (to the right, by Giovanni) turns to look back with an easy motion that breaks the stiff, frontal Gothic mold.

Look at the two panels facing the altar. It's Judgment Day, and Christ is flanked by the saved (on his right, almost hypnotized by the presence of their savior) and, on his left, the desperate damned.

If you visit Pisa, you'll see two similar Pisano pulpits there. (See pages 433 and 439 for more on the Pisanos and their pulpits.)

Duccio's Stained-Glass Rose Window

This is a copy of the original window, which was moved to the Duomo Museum a couple of years ago. The famous rose window was created in 1288 and dedicated to the Virgin Mary (read the complete description on page 385).

• *As you face the window, in the floor to the left (in the transept) is the...*

Slaughter of the Innocents Pavement Panel

Herod (left), sitting enthroned amid Renaissance arches, orders the massacre of all babies to prevent the coming of the promised Messiah. It's a chaotic scene of angry soldiers, grieving mothers, and dead babies, reminding locals that a republic ruled by a tyrant will always experience misery.

The work was designed by the Sienese Matteo di Giovanni (late 1400s) and inlaid with a colorful array of marble, including yellow marble, a Sienese specialty quarried nearby.

• *Step into the chapel just beyond the pavement panel (next to the Piccolomini Library) to see...*

Donatello's St. John the Baptist

The rugged saint in his famous rags stands in a quiet chapel. Donatello, the aging Florentine sculptor, whose style was now considered passé in Florence, came here to build bronze doors for the church (similar to Ghiberti's in Florence). He didn't complete the door project, but he did finish this bronze statue (1457). Notice the cherubs high above it, playfully dangling their feet.

• *Cross beneath the dome to find the Chigi Chapel, also known as the...*

Chapel of the *Madonna del Voto*

To understand why Bernini is considered the greatest Baroque sculptor, step into this sumptuous chapel (designed in the early 1660s for Fabio Chigi, a.k.a. Pope Alexander VII). Move up to the altar and look back at the **two Bernini statues:** Mary Magdalene in a state of spiritual ecstasy and St. Jerome playing the crucifix like a violinist lost in beautiful music. It's enough to make even a Lutheran light a candle.

The chapel is classic Baroque, combining colored marble, statues, stained glass, a dome, and golden angels holding an icon-like framed painting, creating a multimedia extravaganza that offers a glimpse of heaven.

That painting over the altar is the ***Madonna del Voto,*** a Madonna and Child adorned with a real crown of gold and jewels (painted by an unknown Italian master in the mid-13th century). In typical medieval fashion, the scene is set in the golden light of heaven. Mary has the almond eyes, long fingers, and golden folds in her robe that are found in orthodox icons of the time. Still, this Mary tilts her head and looks out sympathetically, ready to listen to the prayers of the faithful. This is the Mary to whom the Palio is dedicated, dear to the hearts of the Sienese.

For untold generations, the Sienese have prayed to the *Madonna del Voto* for help. In thanks, they give **offerings** of silver hearts and medallions, many of which hang now on the wall just to the left as you exit the chapel. On the other side of the chapel door is a glass display case that looks like a jewelry store's front window—with rings, necklaces, and other precious items given by thankful worshippers. Want to leave an offering yourself? Light a candle for a €0.50 donation.

• *Cross back to the other side of the church and head toward the main door. On the right, just before the big Piccolomini Altar we saw earlier, look for the door to the...*

Piccolomini Library

If crowds slow your way into this library, spend your waiting time reading ahead. Brilliantly frescoed, the library captures the exuberant, optimistic spirit of the 1400s, when humanism and the Renaissance were born. The never-restored frescoes look nearly as vivid now as the day they were finished 550 years ago. (With the bright window light, candles were unnecessary in this room—and didn't sully the art with soot.) The painter Pinturicchio (c. 1454-1513) was hired to celebrate the life of one of Siena's hometown boys—a man many call "the first humanist," Aeneas Piccolomini (1405-1464), who became Pope Pius II. Each of the 10 scenes is framed with an arch, as if Pinturicchio were opening a window onto the spacious 3-D world we inhabit. Begin with the episode to the right of the window, and let your eyes follow the frescoes clockwise to trace their progression:

1. Leaving for Basel: Twenty-seven-year-old Aeneas, riding a white horse and decked out in an outrageous hat, pauses to take

one last look back as he leaves Siena to charge off on the first of many adventures in his sometimes sunny, sometimes stormy life. Born poor but noble, he got all A's in his classics classes in Siena. Now, having soaked up all the secular knowledge available, he leaves home to crash a church council in Switzerland, where he would take sides against the pope.

2. Meeting James II of Scotland: Aeneas (with long brown hair) charmed King James and the well-dressed, educated, worldly crowd of Europe's courts. Among his many travels, he visited London (writing home about Westminster Abbey and St. Paul's), barely survived a storm at sea, negotiated peace between England and France, and fathered (at least) two illegitimate children.

3. Crowned Poet by Frederick III: Next we find Aeneas in Vienna, working as secretary to the German king. Aeneas kneels to ceremonially receive the laurel crown of a poet. Aeneas wrote love poetry, bawdy stories, and a play, and is best known for his candid autobiography. Everyone was talking about Aeneas—a writer, speaker, diplomat, and lover of the arts and pretty women, who was the very essence of the *uomo universale,* a.k.a. Renaissance Man.

4. Submitting to Pope Eugene IV: At age 40, after a serious illness, Aeneas changes his life. He journeys to Rome and kisses the pope's foot, apologizing for his heretical opposition. He repents for his wild youth and becomes a priest. (In his autobiography, he says it was time to change anyway, as women no longer aroused him...and he no longer attracted them.)

5. Introducing Frederick III and Eleanora: Quickly named Bishop of Siena, Aeneas (in white pointed bishop's hat) makes his hometown a romantic getaway for his friend Frederick and his fiancée. Notice the Duomo's bell tower in the distance and the city walls (upper left). Aeneas always seemed to be present at Europe's most important political, religious, and social events.

6. Made Cardinal: Kneeling before the pope, with shaved head and praying hands, Aeneas receives the flat red hat of a cardinal. In many of these panels, the artist Pinturicchio uses all the latest 3-D effects—floor tiles and carpets, distant landscapes, receding lines—to suck you into the scene. He tears down palace walls and lets us peek inside, into the day's centers of power.

7. Made Pope: In 1458, at age 53, Aeneas is elected to be Pope Pius II. Carried in triumph, he blesses the crowd. One of his first acts as pope is to declare as heresy the anti-pope doctrines he championed in his youth. (Pius II fans can visit his birthplace in Pienza, described in the Tuscan Hill Towns chapter.)

8. Proclaims a Crusade: He calls on all of Europe to liberate the Christian city of Constantinople, which had recently fallen (in 1453) to the Ottoman Turks. Europe is reluctant to follow his call, but Aeneas pushes the measure through.

9. Canonizes St. Catherine: From his papal throne, Aeneas looks down on the mortal remains of Catherine (clutching her symbol, the lily) and proclaims his fellow Sienese a saint. The well-dressed candle-holders in the foreground pose proudly.

10. Arrival in Ancona: Old and sick, the pope has to be carried everywhere on a litter because of rheumatic feet. He travels to Ancona, ready to board a ship to go fight the Turks. But only a handful of Venetian galleys arrive at the appointed time, the crusade peters out, and Aeneas, disheartened, dies. He wrote: "I do not deny my past. I have been a great wanderer, wandering away from the right path. But at least I know it, and hope the knowledge has not come too late."

Circle around a second time to appreciate the library's intricately decorated, illuminated music scores and a statue (a Roman

copy of a Greek original) of the Three Graces, who almost seem to dance to the beat. The oddly huge sheepskin sheets of music are from the days before individual hymnals—they had to be big so that many singers could read the music at the same time from a distance. If the musical notation looks off, that's because 15th-century Italians used a sliding C clef, not the fixed C and G clefs musicians know today. This clef marked middle C, and the melodies could be chanted in relation to it. Appreciate the fine painted decorations on the music—the gold-leaf highlights, the blue tones from newly discovered (and quite expensive) cobalt, and the miniature figures. All of this exquisite detail was lovingly crafted by Benedictine monks for the glory of God. Find your favorite—I like the blue, totally wild god of wind with the big hair (in the fourth case from the right of the window).

• *Exit the Duomo and make a U-turn to the left, walking alongside the church to Piazza Jacopo della Quercia.*

The Unfinished Church

The nave of the Duomo was supposed to be where the piazza is

today. Worshippers would have entered the church from the far end of the piazza through the unfinished wall. (Look way up at the highest part of the wall. That's the viewpoint accessible from inside the Duomo Museum.) Some of the nave's green-and-white-striped columns were built, but are now filled in with a brick wall. White stones in the pavement mark where a row of pillars would have been. Look through the unfinished entrance facade, note blue sky where the stained-glass windows would have been, and ponder the struggles, triumphs, and failures of the human spirit.

SIENA DUOMO MUSEUM TOUR

Museo dell'Opera del Duomo

Siena's most enjoyable museum was built to house the cathedral's art. Stand eye-to-eye with the saints and angels who once languished, unknown, in the church's upper reaches (where copies are found today). The museum's centerpiece—an altarpiece by Duccio—once stood in the center of the church. And the museum's high point is one of the loftiest in town, offering expansive views of the church and the city.

Orientation

Cost: €7, covered by Opa Si combo-ticket, buy tickets near Duomo Museum entry.

Hours: Daily March-Oct 10:30-19:00, Nov-Feb 10:30-17:30, last entry 30 minutes before closing.

Getting There: It's next to the Duomo, in the skeleton of the unfinished part of the church on the Il Campo side; look for the white banner.

Information: Tel. 0577-286-300, www.operaduomo.siena.it.

Tours: You can rent a tablet videoguide for €4 (€6/2 people; must leave ID). A pricier option adds the Duomo and other sights (€8, €14/2 people), but you have to pick it up and drop it off inside the cathedral (for details, see page 374).

Photography: Not allowed except from the viewpoint.

Length of This Tour: Allow one hour.

Starring: Duccio, the Virgin Mary, and the Tuscan view.

The Tour Begins

GROUND FLOOR

The ground floor houses the church's original statues, mainly from the facade and exterior. After descending a few steps (if you spot an exit sign, ignore it for now), turn your back on the hall of statues and wrought-iron gate.

• *You're now face-to-face with...*

Donatello's Madonna and Child

In this round, carved relief, a slender and tender Mary gazes down at her chubby-cheeked baby. The thick folds of her headdress stream down around her smooth face. Her sad eyes say that she knows the eventual fate of her son. Donatello creates the illusion of Mary's three-dimensional "lap" using only a few inches of depth cut into the creamy-rose stone. Move to the far right and look at Mary's face from an angle (try not to notice impish Jesus); think of the challenge involved in carving the illusion of such depth.

• *On the opposite side of the room is...*

Duccio's Stained-Glass Window

Until recently, this splendid original window was located above and behind the Duomo's altar. Now the church has a copy, and art lovers can enjoy a close-up look at this masterpiece. The rose window—20 feet across, made in 1288—is dedicated (like the church and the city itself) to the Virgin Mary. In the window's bottom panel, Mary (in blue) lies stretched across a red coffin while a crowd of mourners looks on. Miraculously, Mary was spared the pain of death (the Assumption, central panel); winged angels carry her up in a holy bubble to heaven (top panel), where Christ sets her on a throne beside him and crowns her.

The work was designed by Siena's most famous artist, Duccio di Buoninsegna (c. 1255-1319). Duccio combined elements from rigid Byzantine icons (Mary's almond-shaped bubble, called a *mandorla,* and the full-frontal saints that flank her) with a budding sense of 3-D realism (the throne turned at a three-quarter angle to simulate depth, with angels behind). Also notice how the angels in the central panel spread their wings out beyond the border of the window frame.

The Sienese army defeated Florence in the bloody battle of Montaperti, thanks, many believed, to the divine intervention of the Virgin. For the next 80 years of prosperity, Sienese artists cranked out countless Madonnas as a way of saying *grazie.* Bear in mind that the Duomo's main altar was originally dominated by Duccio's *Maestà,* a huge golden altarpiece of the Virgin in Majesty (which you'll see upstairs) that was bathed in the golden-blue light from this window.

• *Lining this main room are...*

Pisano's Statues

Giovanni Pisano spent a decade (c. 1285-1296) carving and orchestrating the decoration of the cathedral—saints, prophets, sibyls, animals, and the original she-wolf with Romulus and Remus. These life-size, robed saints stand in a relaxed *contrapposto,* with open mouths and expressive gestures. Their heads jut out—Pisano's way of making them more visible from below. Some turn and seem to converse with their neighbors, especially evident with Moses *(Mosè)* and the sister who raised him like a mother, Miriam (*Maria di Mosè,* on the left side of the room). The copies of these two stand on the right side of the church, where they appear to interact.

Down a few steps in Room 11 are the two lions that once looked down from the church's main entrance, and Pisano's 12 apostles, who originally lined the nave. (See old photos on the wall.) Tastes changed over the centuries, and the apostles were later moved up to the roof, where they eroded. Pisano's relaxed realism and expressive gestures were a major influence on later Florentine sculptors like Donatello.

• *Retrace your steps and go up to the...*

FIRST FLOOR

• *Head to the left, through a glass door into the darkened Room 6, for a private audience with Duccio's Madonna.*

Duccio—*Maestà* and Passion Panels, 1311

The panels in this room were once part of the Duomo's main altarpiece. Grab a seat and study one of the great pieces of medieval art. Although the former altarpiece was disassembled (and the frame was lost), most of the pieces are displayed here, with the front side (*Maestà,* with Mary and saints; pronounced my-STAH) at one end of the room and the back side (26 Passion panels) at the other.

Imagine these separate panels pieced together, set into their original gold, prickly, 15-by-15-foot wood frame and placed on the main altar in the Duomo. For two centuries it gave the congregation something to look at while the priests turned their backs at Communion time. The Christ Child stared back.

Maestà (Enthroned Virgin)

At the center of the front side sit the Virgin and Child, surrounded by angels and saints. Mary is a melancholy queen on an inlaid-marble throne. Young angels lean their elbows on the back of the throne and sigh. We see the throne head-on, unnaturally splayed open (a Byzantine style popular at the time in Siena). Mary is massive, twice the size of the saints around her, and she clearly stands out from the golden background. Unlike traditional full-frontal

Byzantine icons, she turns slightly sideways to touch her baby, who does not bless us.

The city of Siena is dedicated to this Lady, who backed the Sienese against Florence in the bloody battle of Montaperti in 1260. Here, she's triumphant, visited by Siena's four patron saints (kneeling in front), John the Baptist and other saints (the first choir row), more angels in a row (soprano section), and, chiming in from up in the balcony, James the Great and the 12 apostles.

The painting was revolutionary for the time in its sheer size and opulence, and in Duccio's budding realism, which broke standard conventions. Duccio, at the height of his powers, used every innovative arrow in his quiver. He replaced the standard gold-leaf background (symbolizing heaven) with a gold, intricately patterned curtain draped over the throne. Mary's blue robe opens to reveal her body, and the curve of her knee suggests real anatomy beneath the robe. Baby Jesus wears a delicately transparent garment. Their faces are modeled with light—a patchwork of bright flesh and shadowy valleys, as if lit from the left (a technique he likely learned from his contemporary Giotto during a visit to Florence).

Along the base of Mary's throne is an inscription (*"Mater sancta dei..."* or "Holy Mother of God...") asking Mary to bring peace to Siena *(Senis)* and long life to Duccio *(Ducio)*—quite a tribute in a time when painters were usually treated as anonymous craftsmen.

• *Look on the opposite wall to find scenes from...*

The Passion of Christ

The flip side of the altarpiece featured 26 smaller panels—the medieval equivalent of book pages—showing colorful scenes from the Passion of Christ.

The panels showcase the budding Tuscan style that united realism and storytelling. It doesn't take a Bible scholar to "read" these panels, left to right. Christ on a donkey (lower left) makes his triumphal entry into the city gate of Jerusalem (or is it Siena?). Next, he washes his disciples' feet in a realistic, three-dimensional room. But Duccio hasn't fully mastered perspective—in the Last Supper, we see Christ eye-to-eye, but view the table from above. Christ is arrested in Gethsemane, and so on, until the climactic Crucifixion. The Crucifixion is given the standard gold background, but the cross is set in a real-world location: on a terraced hillside, amid the crowd. Jesus' followers express human emotion rarely seen in earlier art.

The crowd scenes in the Passion panels aren't arranged in neat choir rows, but in more natural-looking groups. Duccio sets figures in motion, with individual faces expressing sorrow, anger, and agitation. Duccio's human realism would be taken to the next level by his Florentine counterpart Giotto, often called the proto-Renaissance painter.

Duccio and assistants (possibly including Simone Martini) spent three years on this massive altarpiece. It was a triumph, and at its dedication the satisfied Sienese marched it around the Campo and into the church in a public procession.

But by 1506, at the height of the Renaissance, Duccio's medieval altarpiece looked musty and old-fashioned, and was moved to a side altar. In 1771 it was disassembled and stored in the church offices (now the Duomo Museum). Today, scholars debate how to reassemble it accurately and hail it as a quantum leap in the evolution of art.

Room 9, to the left and behind the *Maestà*, contains wooden models of the Duomo's inlaid-marble floor and close-ups of the individual floor panels for easier inspection.

• *Return to the stairs and continue up. Take a right at the first landing. At the landing just before the top floor, turn right and walk past the rooms, going through the small doorway to the stairwell. If the line is all the way to the middle of the room, you're facing a 40-minute wait. Eventually you'll climb down the steps and then up about 60 claustrophobic spiral stairs to the first viewpoint. You can continue up another similar spiral staircase to reach the very top.*

PANORAMA DAL FACCIATONE

Standing on the wall from this high point in the city, you're rewarded with a stunning view of Siena...and an interesting perspective.

Look toward the Duomo and remember this: To outdo Florence, Siena had planned to enlarge this cathedral by turning it into a transept and constructing an enormous nave (see sidebar on page 376). You're standing on top of what would have been the new entrance facade (see map on page 362). Columns would have stood where you see the rows of white stones in the pavement below. Had the church been completed, you'd be looking straight down the nave toward the altar.

CIVIC MUSEUM TOUR

Museo Civico

Siena's City Hall (Palazzo Pubblico), still the seat of city government, symbolizes a republic independent from the pope and the Holy Roman Emperor. It also represents a rising secular society, one that appeared first in Tuscany and then spread throughout Europe in the Renaissance. City Hall also has a fine and manageable museum that displays a good sampling of Sienese art. Stroll through this civic center and let its fine day-in-the-life frescoes take you back to a time when this proud town understandably considered itself the vanguard of Western civilization.

Orientation

Cost: €8, €13 combo-ticket with tower, valid one day only.
Hours: Daily mid-March-Oct 10:00-19:00, Nov-mid-March 10:00-18:00, last entry 45 minutes before closing.
Getting There: As the focus of the main square, it's hard to miss. As you enter the City Hall courtyard, the ticket office is straight ahead—look for *Biglietteria*.
Information: Tel. 0577-292-223, www.comune.siena.it.
Length of This Tour: Allow one hour.
Photography: Not allowed.
Starring: Frescoes by Martini and Lorenzetti's *Effects of Good and Bad Government.*

The Tour Begins

• *Climb two flights of stairs (elevator on request—ask at ticket desk), pass through the gift shop, and on the left enter the...*

Siena's Civic Museum

1. Victor Emmanuel II at Battle of San Martino
2. Victor Emmanuel II Receives Politicians
3. Chapel
4. MARTINI – *Maestà*
5. MARTINI (?) – *Guidoriccio da Fogliano*
6. DUCCIO – *The Surrender of the Castle of Giuncarico*
7. St. Catherine & St. Bernardino Frescoes
8. LORENZETTI – *Good Government*
9. LORENZETTI – *Bad Government*

Sala del Risorgimento (Hall of Italian Unification)

This hall has dramatic scenes of the 19th-century unification of Italy (surrounded by statues that don't seem to care). In the paintings, see Victor Emmanuel II (left wall as you enter, on horseback with beard and pointy moustache), king of a small northern Italian province. His status as the only Italian-blooded provincial king made him a natural to become the first king of a united Italy. Here we see him at the **Battle of San Martino** (1859) while leading a united Italian nation against its Austrian oppressors. Beneath that, you'll see the coat he's wearing in the painting. Next (clockwise above the windows), the king's red-shirted troops cheer as he shakes hands with the dashing general Giuseppe Garibaldi. There was a concern that Garibaldi, the charismatic revolutionary who had won the south, might not submit to the king. In this scene, even as the king's white horse seems to honor Garibaldi, the revolutionary famously says, "I obey." Victorious, **the king receives politicians** (next painting), who bow and present the election results that made Italy united and democratic, with Victor Emmanuel II as a symbolic head. When he died in 1878 (see his funeral procession passing through Rome's Pantheon portico, filled with real portraits, on the far wall), Italy was well on the way to modern nationhood. The mythological grandeur on the ceiling seems designed to legitimize the Italian Republic, a latecomer to the European family of nations.

• *Pass through the hallway to the left, and walk through the Sala di Balia. In the next room, turn left to find the* ***chapel*** *where the city's governors and bureaucrats prayed. Continue into the large...*

Sala del Mappamondo (Hall of the World Map)

This room, where the Grand Council met, pumped up governors and citizens alike with its images of military victories and the blessings of Mary. On opposite ends of the room, you'll find two large frescoes. The beautiful ***Maestà*** (*Enthroned Virgin,* 1315), by Siena's great Simone Martini (c. 1280-1344), was the secular counterpart to Duccio's *Maestà* (then in the Duomo, now in the Duomo Museum). Mary sits on a throne under a red silk canopy, a model to Siena's city council of what a just ruler should be. Siena's black-and-white coat of arms is woven into both the canopy and the picture frame. Mary is surrounded by saints and angels, clearly echoing the *Maestà* of Simone's teacher, Duccio.

But this is a groundbreaking work. It's Siena's first fresco showing a Madonna not in a faraway, gold-leaf heaven, but under the blue sky of the real world that we inhabit. As Mary delicately holds Baby Jesus, her expressive face anticipates the sacrifice of her son. A scraggly John the Baptist connects viewers with the scene.

The canopy creates a 3-D stage, with saints in front of, behind, and underneath it. Some saints' faces are actually blocked by the support poles. These saints are not a generic conga-line of Byzantine icons, but a milling crowd of 30 individuals with expressive faces. Some look straight out, some are in profile, and some turn at that difficult-to-draw three-quarter angle, grabbing onto the canopy poles. And the Virgin's brooch is painted so well that it almost looks...uh, real.

With unbeatable Florence to its north, Siena expanded south. Facing the *Maestà* is the famous ***Equestrian Portrait of Guidoriccio da Fogliano*** (1330; long attributed to Simone Martini, but more recently art historians have debated its authorship). The year is MCCCXXVIII (1328), and Siena's renowned mercenary commander Guidoriccio da Fogliano rides across a barren landscape and surveys the imposing castle that his armies have just conquered. He has just successfully finished a six-month-long siege—see his camp on the right. This is one of Europe's first secular portraits. (Guido and his horse have the same tailor.)

On the same wall, just below the horse and rider, ***The Surrender of the Castle of Giuncarico,*** by Duccio (1314), shows a man in green about to hand over his sword to a representative of the Sienese republic (not pictured—the scene was obliterated when it was covered by a later fresco). In the background is the man's castle and village on a rocky outcrop. Duccio's *Surrender* apparently inspired the 3-D landscape of *Guidoriccio da Fogliano.*

Also in the room (among those painted between the arches) are frescoes of two saints with local connections, **St. Catherine** (see page 371) and **St. Bernardino** (1380-1444). Bernardino's charismatic sermons in Siena could hold a Campo crowd for several days. At sunset, he'd announce that he would begin speaking again at sunrise...and people would come back. He brought together sworn enemies to share a *bacio di pace*—kiss of peace.

• *Continue into the next room.*

Sala della Pace, a.k.a. Sala dei Nove (Hall of Peace/Hall of the Nine)

The Council of Nine, who ruled Siena from 1287 to 1355, met in this room. Looking down on the oligarchy during their meetings was a fascinating fresco series showing the *Effects of Good and Bad Government,* by Ambrogio Lorenzetti (1337-1340).

The short wall opposite the window features the ***Allegory of Good Government,*** which celebrates the Sienese social system: "Siena," the stately, bearded man on the throne, is flanked by the six virtues. The central virtue, Peace (Pax), lounges on a pile of discarded armor. Justice (in red on the left) is punishing and forgiving under the figure of wisdom. Justice holds a scale, with angels on either side, to execute her judgments. Wrongdoers (lower right) are rounded up by the authorities. At the foot of the stage, prominent Sienese citizens file by. Concordia (below the figure of Justice) makes society just and equal with the wooden plane on her lap. And the symbolic foundation of it all is the she-wolf with Romulus and Remus, recalling a myth meant to connect Siena's origins to the glory of ancient Rome (explained on page 376).

The allegory continues on the long wall with a well-preserved fresco depicting the effects of good government in town and country. Notice the whistle-while-you-work happiness of the utopian community ruled by the utopian government. The city and the countryside are exactly the same width (20 feet), an indication that they work together and need each other. Amid Siena's skyline (Duomo at upper left), young people dance to the beat of a tambourine, workers repair roofs, a professor teaches, and the conversation flows. The blessings of a good government extend even to the countryside, which feels safe and prosperous. Bringing stability and safety to the land outside the city walls was a big accomplishment in the 14th century. The fields are tilled, the Via Francigena is busy, and angels fly overhead.

Study this intimate and rare look at medieval commerce, and take in the details of the 14th-century cityscape. Notice, for instance, how today's exposed brick work, so "typical" of Siena, had then been stuccoed over and brightly painted. Notice also the pointy skyline, showing the city's proud towers before they were lopped off by the Florentines. The toppled towers ended up providing building material for the huge Fortezza—a repurposing that wasn't just practical but also psychological, serving as a reminder of the Florentine Medicis' success in keeping the Sienese down.

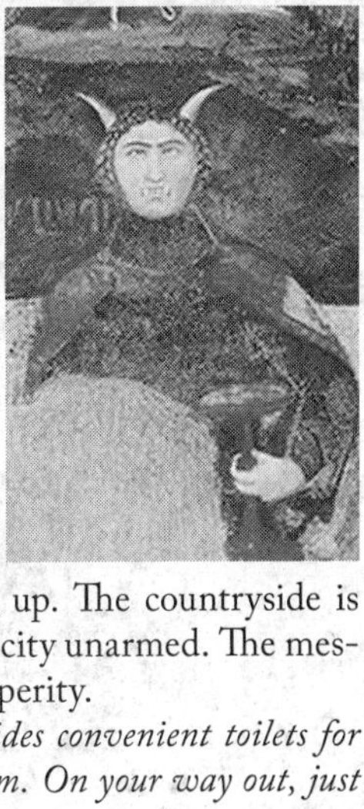

On the opposite long wall, in the ***Allegory of Bad Government*** (badly damaged), a horned, fanged, wine-drinking devil sets the vices loose ("Avarice," "Vainglory"). Rather than dancing in the streets, people are being arrested. Arsonists torch homes and fields, soldiers rape and pillage, crime is rampant, fields are barren, and frescoes get damaged. The only person still working is making weapons. Justice slumps at the devil's feet, bound, too depressed to look up. The countryside is dark and devastated, and no one leaves the city unarmed. The message: Without justice, there can be no prosperity.

• *An enlightened city government also provides convenient toilets for the public—which you'll find just off this room. On your way out, just before the Sala del Risorgimento, find the lo-o-o-o-ong stairs and head up for...*

A Grand View

Cap your visit by climbing up to the loggia for a sweeping view of the city and its surroundings. (For a less impressive version of this view, you could skip the stairs and simply peek behind the curtains in the Sala della Pace.)

SIENA SLEEPING, EATING & CONNECTIONS

Sleeping in Siena

Finding a room in Siena is tough during Easter (April 5 in 2015) or the Palio (July 2 and Aug 16). Many hotels won't take reservations until the end of May for the Palio, and even then they might require a four-night stay. While day-tripping tour groups turn the town into a Gothic amusement park in midsummer, Siena is basically yours in the evenings and off-season.

Part of Siena's charm is its lively, festive character—this means that all hotels can be plagued with noise, even (and sometimes especially) the hotels in the pedestrian-only zone. If tranquility is important for your sanity, ask for a room that's off the street, or consider staying at one of the recommended places outside the center. If your hotel doesn't provide breakfast, eat at a bar on Il Campo or near your hotel.

FANCY SLEEPS, SOUTHWEST OF IL CAMPO

These well-run places are a 10-minute walk from Il Campo.

$$$ Pensione Palazzo Ravizza is elegant and friendly, with 39 rooms and an aristocratic feel—fitting, as it was once the luxurious residence of a noble. Guests enjoy a peaceful garden set on a dramatic bluff, along with a Steinway in the upper lounge (Sb-€180, standard Db-€180, superior Db-€220, Tb-€255, family suites-€300, rates can vary, see website for room differences, rooms in back overlook countryside, air-con, elevator, guest computer, Wi-Fi, Via Piano dei Mantellini 34, tel. 0577-280-462, www.palazzoravizza.it, bureau@palazzoravizza.it). As parking is free and the hotel is easily walkable from the center, this is a particularly good value for drivers.

$$$ Hotel Duomo has 20 spacious and tidy but slightly dated

Sleep Code

(€1 = about $1.40, country code: 39)

Abbreviations
S = Single, **D** = Double/Twin, **T** = Triple, **Q** = Quad, **b** = bathroom, **s** = shower only

Price Rankings
$$$ Higher Priced—Most rooms €130 or more.
$$ Moderately Priced—Most rooms between €90-130.
$ Lower Priced—Most rooms €90 or less.

Unless otherwise noted, breakfast is included, credit cards are accepted, Wi-Fi is generally free, and English is spoken. Siena levies a hotel tax of €2 per person, per night, which must be paid in cash (not included in the rates I've quoted). Prices change; verify current rates online or by email. For the best prices, always book directly with the hotel.

rooms, a picnic-friendly roof terrace, and a bizarre floor plan (Sb-€105, Db-€130, Db suite-€180, Tb-€180, Qb-€230, elevator with some stairs, air-con, Wi-Fi, discounted parking-€20/day; follow Via di Città, which becomes Via di Stalloreggi, to #38; tel. 0577-289-088, www.hotelduomo.it, booking@hotelduomo.it, Alessandro). If you're arriving by train, take a taxi (€12) or ride bus #3 to the Porta Tufi stop, just a few minutes' walk from the hotel; you can also arrange to have Alessandro take you to/from the train station or airport (with this book: train station-€10, Florence's Vespucci Airport-€105, Pisa's Galilei Airport-€165; he'll also take you to nearby hill towns, e.g. Florence-€105 and Pisa-€165). If you're driving, go to Porta San Marco, turn right, and follow signs to the hotel—drop your bags, then park in the nearby Il Campo lot near Porta Tufi.

SIMPLE PLACES NEAR IL CAMPO

Most of these listings are forgettable but well-priced, and just a horse wreck away from one of Italy's most wonderful civic spaces.

$$ Piccolo Hotel Etruria, with 20 simple, recently redecorated rooms, is well-located and restful (S-€50, Sb-€60, Db-€100, Tb-€120-138, Qb-€145-166, higher rates are for peak-of-peak times, 10 percent discount with this book through 2015, optional breakfast-€6.50, air-con May-Oct only, elevator, Wi-Fi, at Via delle Donzelle 1-3, tel. 0577-288-088, www.hoteletruria.com, info@hoteletruria.com, friendly Conti family also run the Albergo Tre Donzelle, next door).

$ Albergo Tre Donzelle is a fine budget value with welcoming hosts and 20 plain but homey rooms. Although some of the showers have seen better days, these may be the cheapest rooms in the center. Il Campo, a block away, is your terrace (S-€38, D-€49, Db-€60, T-€70, Tb-€85, breakfast-€6.50, Wi-Fi in common areas; with your back to the tower, head away from Il Campo toward 2 o'clock to Via delle Donzelle 5; tel. 0577-270-390, www.tredonzelle.com, info@tredonzelle.com).

$ Hotel Cannon d'Oro, a few blocks up Via Banchi di Sopra, is a labyrinthine slumbermill renting 30 institutional, overpriced rooms (Sb-€71, Db-€90, Tb-€115, Qb-€136, these discounted prices good with this book through 2015, fans, Wi-Fi, a couple of blocks from the bus hub at Via dei Montanini 28, tel. 0577-44-321, www.cannondoro.com, info@cannondoro.com; Maurizio, Tommaso, Serge, and Rodrigo).

$ Casa Laura has eight clean, charming, well-maintained rooms, some of which have brick-and-beam ceilings (Db-€60, Db with air-con-€70, these prices through 2015 when you mention Rick Steves and book directly with hotel, Via Roma 3, about a 10-minute walk from Il Campo toward Porta Romana, tel. 0577-226-061, www.casalaurasiena.com, info@casalaurasiena.com).

B&BS IN THE OLD CENTER

$$ Antica Residenza Cicogna is a seven-room guesthouse with a homey elegance and an ideal location. It's warmly run by the young and charming Elisa and her friend Ilaria, who set out biscotti, *vin santo,* and tea all day for their guests. With artfully frescoed walls and ceilings, this is remarkably genteel for the price (Db-€98, suite Db-€120, third bed-€15, air-con, guest computer, Wi-Fi, Via delle Terme 76, tel. 0577-285-613, mobile 347-007-2888, www.anticaresidenzacicogna.it, info@anticaresidenzacicogna.it).

$$ Palazzo Masi B&B, run by Alizzardo and Daniela, is just below Il Campo. They rent six pleasant, spacious, antique-furnished rooms with shared common areas on the second and third floors of an old building. While a bit pricey, the fine location and warm welcome are appreciated (D-€70, Db-€110 with this book through 2015 when you book directly with hotel, cash only, breakfast-€8, Wi-Fi, discounted parking at nearby Il Campo lot-€25/24 hours; from City Hall, walk 50 yards down Via del Casato di Sotto to #29; mobile 349-600-9155, www.palazzomasi.com, info@palazzomasi.it). The place is sometimes unstaffed, so it's important to phone upon arrival.

$ B&B Alle Due Porte is a charming little establishment renting four big rooms with sweet furniture under big medieval beams. The shared breakfast room is delightful. The manager, Egisto, is a phone call and 10-minute scooter ride away (Db-€85,

Siena Hotels & Restaurants

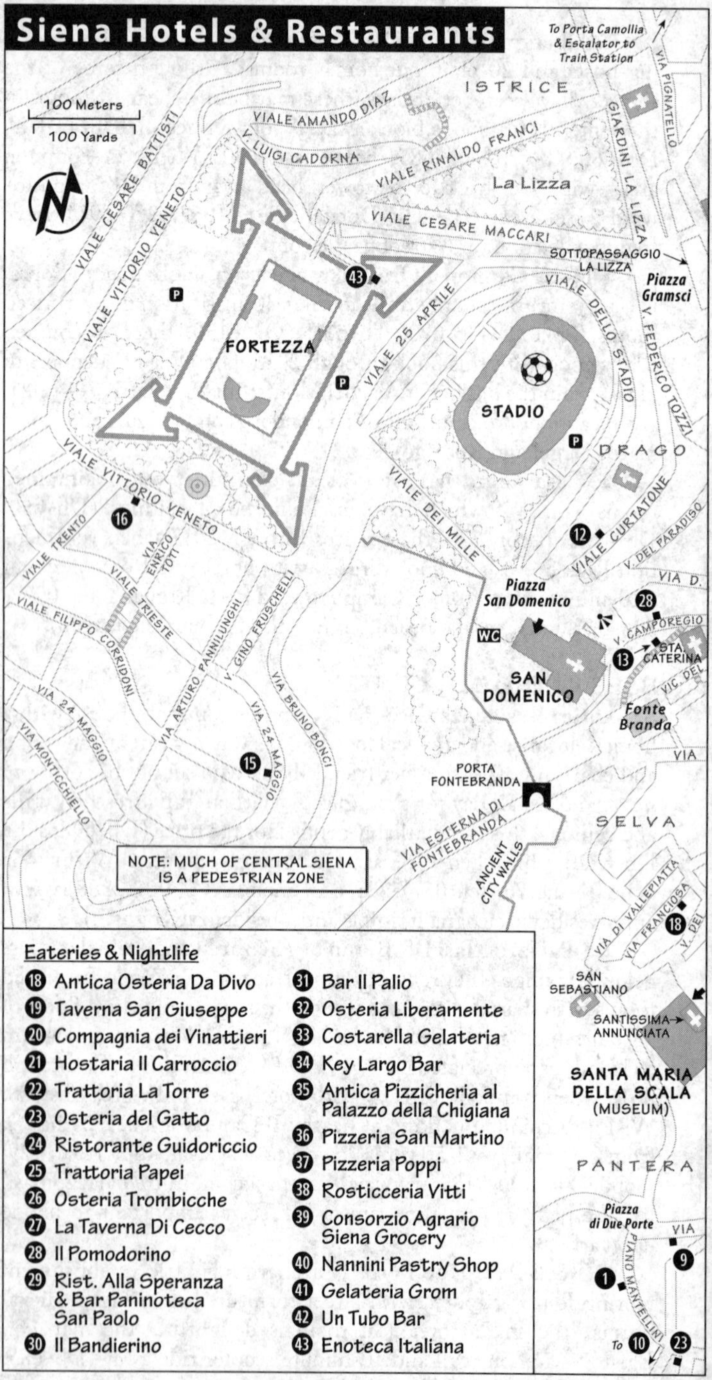

Eateries & Nightlife

- 18 Antica Osteria Da Divo
- 19 Taverna San Giuseppe
- 20 Compagnia dei Vinattieri
- 21 Hostaria Il Carroccio
- 22 Trattoria La Torre
- 23 Osteria del Gatto
- 24 Ristorante Guidoriccio
- 25 Trattoria Papei
- 26 Osteria Trombicche
- 27 La Taverna Di Cecco
- 28 Il Pomodorino
- 29 Rist. Alla Speranza & Bar Paninoteca San Paolo
- 30 Il Bandierino
- 31 Bar Il Palio
- 32 Osteria Liberamente
- 33 Costarella Gelateria
- 34 Key Largo Bar
- 35 Antica Pizzicheria al Palazzo della Chigiana
- 36 Pizzeria San Martino
- 37 Pizzeria Poppi
- 38 Rosticceria Vitti
- 39 Consorzio Agrario Siena Grocery
- 40 Nannini Pastry Shop
- 41 Gelateria Grom
- 42 Un Tubo Bar
- 43 Enoteca Italiana

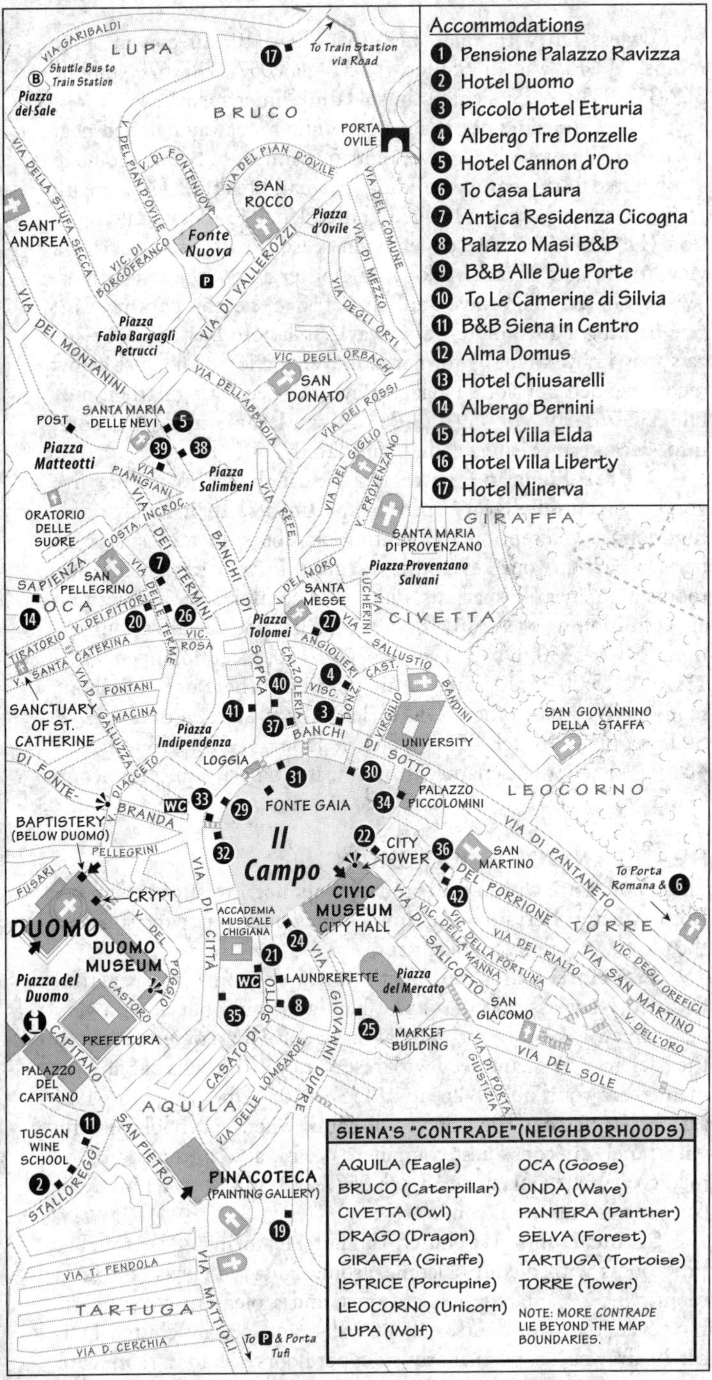
Accommodations
1 Pensione Palazzo Ravizza
2 Hotel Duomo
3 Piccolo Hotel Etruria
4 Albergo Tre Donzelle
5 Hotel Cannon d'Oro
6 To Casa Laura
7 Antica Residenza Cicogna
8 Palazzo Masi B&B
9 B&B Alle Due Porte
10 To Le Camerine di Silvia
11 B&B Siena in Centro
12 Alma Domus
13 Hotel Chiusarelli
14 Albergo Bernini
15 Hotel Villa Elda
16 Hotel Villa Liberty
17 Hotel Minerva
SIENA'S "CONTRADE" (NEIGHBORHOODS)
AQUILA (Eagle)
BRUCO (Caterpillar)
CIVETTA (Owl)
DRAGO (Dragon)
GIRAFFA (Giraffe)
ISTRICE (Porcupine)
LEOCORNO (Unicorn)
LUPA (Wolf)
OCA (Goose)
ONDA (Wave)
PANTERA (Panther)
SELVA (Forest)
TARTUGA (Tortoise)
TORRE (Tower)
NOTE: MORE CONTRADE LIE BEYOND THE MAP BOUNDARIES.
LUPA
BRUCO
GIRAFFA
CIVETTA
OCA
LEOCORNO
TORRE
AQUILA
TARTUGA
Shuttle Bus to Train Station
Piazza del Sale
To Train Station via Road
PORTA OVILE
SAN ROCCO
Piazza d'Ovile
SANT' ANDREA
Fonte Nuova
Piazza Fabio Bargagli Petrucci
SAN DONATO
POST
SANTA MARIA DELLE NEVI
Piazza Matteotti
Piazza Salimbeni
ORATORIO DELLE SUORE
SANTA MARIA DI PROVENZANO
Piazza Provenzano Salvani
SAN PELLEGRINO
SANTA MESSE
Piazza Tolomei
SANCTUARY OF ST. CATHERINE
Piazza Indipendenza
LOGGIA
UNIVERSITY
SAN GIOVANNINO DELLA STAFFA
FONTE GAIA
PALAZZO PICCOLOMINI
BAPTISTERY (BELOW DUOMO)
Il Campo
CITY TOWER
SAN MARTINO
To Porta Romana & 6
CRYPT
CIVIC MUSEUM CITY HALL
ACCADEMIA MUSICALE CHIGIANA
DUOMO
DUOMO MUSEUM
Piazza del Duomo
LAUNDRERETTE
Piazza del Mercato
SAN GIACOMO
PREFETTURA
MARKET BUILDING
PALAZZO DEL CAPITANO
TUSCAN WINE SCHOOL
PINACOTECA (PAINTING GALLERY)
To P & Porta Tufi
WC
VIA GARIBALDI
VIA DELLA STUFA SECCA
V. DEL PIAN D'OVILE
V. DI FONTENUOVA
VIA DEL PIAN D'OVILE
VIA DEL COMUNE
VIA DI MEZZO
VIA DEGLI ORTI
VIC. DI BORGOFRANCO
VIA DI VALLEROZZI
VIA DEI MONTANINI
VIC. DEGLI ORBACHI
VIA DELL'ABBADIA
VIA DEI ROSSI
VIA DEL GIGLIO
V. PROVENZANO
VIA PIANIGIANI
VIA REFE
BANCHI DI SOPRA
COSTA INCROC.
VIA DEI TERMINI
SAPIENZA
VIA DELLE TERME
V. DEI PITTORI
VIC. ROSA
V. DEL MORO
VIA LUCHERINI
VIA ANGIOLIERI
SALLUSTIO BANDINI
TIRATORIO
V. SANTA CATERINA
VIA D. GALLUZZA
FONTANI
MACINA
CALZOLERIA
VISC.
CAST.
V. DONZ.
BANCHI DI SOTTO
VIRGILIO
DI FONTE-
BRANDA
DIACCETO
PELLEGRINI
VIA DI CITTÀ
FUSARI
V. DEL POGGIO
CASTORO
CAPITANO
VIA DI PANTANETO
DEL PORRIONE
VIA DI SALICOTTO
VIC. DELLA MANNA
VIC. DELLA FORTUNA
VIA DEL RIALTO
VIA SAN MARTINO
VIC. DEGLI OREFICI
V. DELL'ORO
VIA GIOVANNI DUPRE
CASATO DI SOTTO
VIA DELLE LOMBARDE
VIA DI PORTA GIUSTIZIA
VIA DEL SOLE
STALLOREGGI
SAN PIETRO
VIA T. PENDOLA
VIA MATTIOLI
VIA D. CERCHIA

windowless Db with small bed-€65, Tb-€110, air-con in three rooms, Wi-Fi, Via di Stalloreggi 51, tel. 0577-287-670, mobile 368-352-3530, www.sienatur.it, soldatini@interfree.it).

$ Le Camerine di Silvia, a romantic hideaway perched near a sweeping, grassy olive grove, rents five simple but cozy rooms in a converted 16th-century building. A small breakfast terrace with fruit trees and a private hedged garden lends itself to contemplation (Db-€50-€80, rate depends on season, cash only, ask for a view room, add €5 for breakfast in cloister across the street, fans, Wi-Fi, shared microwave and small fridge, nearby parking-€12, free parking a 10-minute walk away, Via Ettore Bastianini 1—locals may know street by former name Via delle Scuole, just below recommended Pensione Palazzo Ravizza—see listing earlier, mobile 338-761-5052 or 339-123-7687, www.lecamerinedisilvia.com, info@lecamerinedisilvia.com, Conti family).

$ B&B Siena in Centro is a clearinghouse managing five good and centrally located private apartments. Their handy office functions as a reception area renting out about 15 rooms; stop by here to pick up your key and be escorted to your apartment. The rooms are generally spacious, quiet, and comfortable, but with no air-conditioning or Wi-Fi. Their website lets you visualize your options (Sb-€45-60, Db-€70-90, Tb-€90-120, reception open 9:00-13:30 & 15:00-19:00, later in high season, other times by phone request, Wi-Fi in office, OK to leave bags at reception, Via di Stalloreggi 14-16, tel. 0577-43041, mobile 331-281-0136 or 347-465-9753, www.bbsienaincentro.com, info@bbsienaincentro.com, Gioia or Michela).

NEAR SAN DOMENICO CHURCH

These hotels are within a 10-minute walk northwest of Il Campo. Both Albergo Bernini and Alma Domus offer fine panoramas of the old town for reasonable prices.

$$$ Hotel Chiusarelli, with 48 classy rooms in a beautiful frescoed Neoclassical villa, has a handy location but is on a very busy street. Expect traffic noise at night—ask for a quieter room in the back (can be guaranteed with reservation). The bells of San Domenico are your 7:00 wake-up call (Sb-€105, Db-€160, Tb-€190, ask for 10 percent Rick Steves discount when you book directly with hotel, air-con, guest computer, Wi-Fi, across from San Domenico at Viale Curtatone 15, tel. 0577-280-562, www.chiusarelli.com, info@chiusarelli.com).

$ Alma Domus is a church-run hotel featuring 28 spartan but tidy rooms with quaint balconies, some fantastic views (ask for a room *con vista*), stately public rooms, and a pleasant atmosphere. However, the thin doors, echoey halls, and nearby church bells can be drawbacks, particularly on upper floors; ask for a room with double-paned windows or bring earplugs. Consider upgrading to a superior room on the main floor for slightly more (Sb-€48, Db-€90, Tb-€120, air-con, elevator, guest computer, Wi-Fi; from San Domenico, walk downhill toward the view with the church on your right, turn left down Via Camporegio, make a U-turn down the brick steps to Via Camporegio 37; tel. 0577-44-177, www.hotelalmadomus.it, info@hotelalmadomus.it, Luigi).

$ Albergo Bernini makes you part of a Sienese family in a modest, clean home with 10 traditional rooms. Giovanni, charming wife Daniela, and their three daughters welcome you to their spectacular view terrace for breakfast and picnic lunches and dinners (S-€55, D-€65, Sb or small Db with view-€78, Db-€85, less in winter, optional breakfast-€5/small or €9/big, Wi-Fi, on the main Il Campo-San Domenico drag at Via della Sapienza 15, tel. 0577-289-047, www.albergobernini.com, hbernin@tin.it). If you're passing by, they're happy to give you a peek at their terrace if you show this book.

FARTHER FROM THE CENTER

These options, a 10- to 20-minute walk from the center, are great for drivers.

Near Porta Romana City Gate

These two fine spots are about 200 yards outside the Porta Romana (for locations, see the map on page 353). To get to downtown Siena from here, catch minibus line A uphill to Piazza al Mercato, just behind Il Campo (€1.10). To reach the bus and train stations, take bus #2 (which becomes #17 at Piazza del Sale; when arriving, catch #17 from the station). If driving, from the freeway, take the Siena Sud exit, continue in direction Romana, then at the first light turn left, following *Pta Romana/Centro* signs for about half a mile until you see the big city gate.

$$$ Hotel Santa Caterina is a three-star, 18th-century place renting 22 comfy rooms. It's professionally run with real attention to quality. While it's on a big city street, it has a delightful garden terrace with views over the countryside (Sb-€125, four small Db-€125, Db-€165, split-level Tb or Qb-€215, prices promised with this book through 2015, can be cheaper in low season, garden side is quieter, air-con, fridge in room, elevator, Wi-Fi, parking-€15/day—request when you reserve, Via E.S. Piccolomini 7, tel. 0577-221-105, www.hscsiena.it, info@hscsiena.it, Lorenza and her crew).

$$ Hotel Porta Romana is at the edge of town, off a busy road. Some of its 15 rooms face the open countryside (request one of these), and breakfast is served in the garden (Sb-€90, Db-€110, extra person-€20, 10 percent Rick Steves discount if you book direct and pay cash, air-con in most rooms, Wi-Fi, free parking, inviting sun terrace, outdoor hot tub open April-Oct at no extra charge with this book, Via E.S. Piccolomini 35, tel. 0577-42299, www.hotelportaromana.com, info@hotelportaromana.com, Marco and Evelia).

In the Posh Neighborhood South of the Fortress

These two places are in a villa-studded residential neighborhood across a gully from San Domenico Church. They're about 5-10 minutes farther than the listings under "Near San Domenico Church," earlier, but the extra walking gets you to a swankier address.

$$$ Hotel Villa Elda rents 11 bright and light rooms in a recently renovated villa. It's classy, stately, pricey, and run with a feminine charm (Db-€129-159, about €20 more for view, extra person-€30, air-con, no elevator, Wi-Fi, garden and view terrace, closed Nov-March, Viale Ventiquattro Maggio 10, tel. 0577-247-927, www.villaeldasiena.it, info@villaeldasiena.it).

$$$ Hotel Villa Liberty, across a busy street from the fortress, is a former private mansion. It has 17 big, bright, comfortable rooms and some road noise (Sb-€88, Db-€156, Tb-€196, €18 more for superior room, air-con, elevator, Wi-Fi, bar, courtyard, free and easy street parking, facing fortress at Viale Vittorio Veneto 11, tel. 0577-44-966, www.villaliberty.it, info@villaliberty.it).

Just Inside Porta Ovile, at the North End of Town

$$ Hotel Minerva is your big, professional, plain, efficient option. It's the most impersonal of my listings, with zero personality but predictable comfort. While its 56 rooms are boring, they don't hide any unpleasant surprises. It works best for those with cars—parking is reasonable (€12/day), and it's only a 10-minute walk from the action (Sb-€76, Db-€122, Tb-€168, bigger suites available at higher price, view room-€20 extra, air-con, elevator, guest computer, Wi-Fi, Via Garibaldi 72, tel. 0577-284-474, www.albergominerva.it, info@albergominerva.it).

East of Siena

$$$ Frances' Lodge Relais is a tranquil and delightfully managed farmhouse B&B a mile out of Siena. Each of its six rooms is bursting with character (all well-described on their website). Franca and Franco run this rustic-yet-elegant old place, which features a 19th-century orangery that's been made into a "better homes and palaces" living room, as well as a peaceful garden, eight acres of olive trees and vineyards, and great views of Siena and its countryside—even from the swimming pool (small Db-€170, Db-€190, Db suite-€220, Tb-€210-220, Tb suite-€280, Qb suite-€340, these prices promised to Rick Steves readers through 2015 if you book directly with hotel, possibly cheaper for longer stays, air-con, guest computer, Wi-Fi, free parking, Strada di Valdipugna 2—see map on page 353, tel. 0577-42379, mobile 337-671-608, www.franceslodge.it). To the center, it's a five-minute bus ride (€1.60, they'll call to arrange) plus a five-minute walk, or €10 by taxi. Consider having an al fresco dinner in the gazebo, complete with view (make your own picnic, or have your hosts assemble a very fancy one for €20/person).

OUTSIDE SIENA

The following accommodations are set in the lush, peaceful countryside surrounding Siena, and are best for those traveling by car (see map on page 353; for Il Canto also see map on page 518).

$$$ Borgo Argenina has seven rooms in a well-maintained, pricey splurge of a B&B. Run by helpful Elena Nappa, it's 20 minutes north of Siena by car in the Chianti region (Db-€170, beautiful gardens, Wi-Fi, mobile 345-353-7673, www.borgoargenina.it, info@borgoargenina.it).

$$ Il Canto del Sole is a restored 18th-century farmhouse turned family-friendly B&B located about six miles outside the Porta Romana city gate. Run by Laura, Luciano, and their son Marco, it features 10 bright and airy rooms, a saltwater swimming pool, a game room, and bike rentals. Their two apartments with original antique furnishings fit six to eight people (Db-€120, Tb-€140, extra bed-€30, apartment-€180-220, ask for Rick Steves discount, air-con, Wi-Fi, free parking, free pickup/drop-off from train/bus station, dinner cooked on request, Val di Villa Canina 1292, 53014 Loc. Cuna, tel. 0577-375-127, www.ilcantodelsole.com, info@ilcantodelsole.com).

Eating in Siena

Sienese restaurants are reasonable by Florentine and Venetian standards. You can enjoy ordering high on the menu here without going broke. For me, the best €5 you can spend in Siena is on a cocktail at Bar Il Palio, overlooking Il Campo. For pasta, a good option is *pici* (PEE-chee), a thick Sienese spaghetti that seems to be at the top of every menu.

FINE DINING IN THE OLD TOWN

For only a few euros more, these four places deliver a more upscale ambience and generally better food than my later recommendations.

Antica Osteria Da Divo is *the* place for a dressy and atmospheric €45 meal. The kitchen is creative, the ambience is flowery and candlelit, some of the seating fills old Etruscan tombs, and the food is fresh, delicate, and top-notch. While the cuisine is flamboyant and almost over-the-top, Chef Pino and his wife Susanna serve up my favorite splurge dinner in town. Pino is a fanatic for fresh ingredients, enjoys giving traditional dishes his creative spin, and is understandably proud of his desserts. The wine is good, too—you can order it by the glass (€4-7) if you ask (€10-12 pastas, €20-26 *secondi,* €3 cover, Wed-Mon 12:00-14:30 & 19:00-22:30, closed Tue, reservations smart; facing Baptistery door, take the far right street and walk one long curving block to Via Franciosa 29; tel. 0577-284-381, www.osteriadadivo.it). Those dining here with this book can finish with a complimentary biscotti and *vin santo* or coffee (upon request).

Taverna San Giuseppe offers modern Tuscan cuisine in a chic grotto atmosphere. While the vibe is high energy and casual, the food compares favorably with the slightly more upscale places listed here. The wine-and-cheese cellar in back is cut from an Etruscan tomb. Check the posters tacked around the entry for daily specials. Reserve or arrive early to get a table (€8-10 pastas, €15-20 *secondi,* Mon-Sat 12:00-14:30 & 19:00-22:00, closed Sun, air-con, 7-minute climb up street to the right of City Hall at Via Giovanni Dupre 132, tel. 0577-42-286, www.tavernasangiuseppe.it, Matteo).

Compagnia dei Vinattieri serves modern Tuscan dishes with a creative twist. In this elegantly unpretentious space, you can enjoy a quiet and romantic meal under graceful brick arches. The menu is small and accessible, and the young staff will help you match your meal with the right wine. Marco, the owner, is happy to take you down to the marvelous wine cellar (€9-10 pastas, €16-18 *secondi,* leave this book on the table for a complimentary *aperitivo,* daily 12:30-15:00 & 19:30-23:00, entries at Via dei Pittori 1 and Via delle Terme 79, tel. 0577-236-568, www.vinattieri.net).

Hostaria Il Carroccio, artsy and convivial, seats guests in a tight, sea-foam green dining room and serves elegantly presented, traditional "slow food" recipes with innovative flair at affordable prices (€8 pastas, €14-18 *secondi,* €30 tasting *menu*—minimum two people, cash only, reservations wise, Thu-Tue 12:30-15:00 & 19:30-22:00, closed Wed, Via del Casato di Sotto 32, tel. 0577-41-165, sweet Renata and Mauro).

TRADITIONAL AND RUSTIC PLACES IN THE OLD TOWN

Trattoria La Torre is a thriving, unfussy *casalinga* (home-cooking) eatery, popular for its homemade pasta, plates of which entice customers as they enter. The sound of its busy open kitchen adds to the conviviality. Ten tables are packed under one medieval brick arch. Service is brisk and casual, and despite its priceless position below the namesake tower, it feels more like a local hangout than a tourist trap (€8-9 pastas, €8-11 *secondi*, Fri-Wed 12:00-15:00 & 19:00-22:00, closed Thu, just steps below Il Campo at Via di Salicotto 7, tel. 0577-287-548, Lara Boccini).

Osteria del Gatto is a classic little hole-in-the-wall, thriving with townspeople and powered by a passion for serving good Sienese cuisine. Friendly Marco Coradeschi and his engaged staff cook and serve daily specials with attitude. As it's so small and popular, it can get loud. Reservations are recommended (€8 pastas, €8-10 *secondi*, Mon-Fri 12:30-15:00 & 19:30-22:00, Sat 19:30-22:00 only, closed Sun, 5-minute walk away from the center at Via San Marco 8, tel. 0577-287-133).

Ristorante Guidoriccio, just a few steps below Il Campo, feels warm and welcoming. You'll get smiling service from Ercole and Flora. While mostly filled with tourists, the place has charm—especially if you let gentle Ercole explore the menu with you and follow his suggestions (€9 pastas, €14-15 *secondi*, Mon-Sat 12:30-14:30 & 19:00-22:30, closed Sun, air-con, Via Giovanni Dupre 2, tel. 0577-44-350).

Trattoria Papei is a Sienese favorite, featuring a casual, rollicking family atmosphere and friendly servers dishing out generous portions of rib-stickin' Tuscan specialties and grilled meats. This big, sprawling place under brown tents in a parking lot is in all the guidebooks and often jammed—so call to reserve (€8 pastas, €9-13 *secondi*, daily 12:00-15:00 & 19:00-22:30, on the market square directly behind City Hall at Piazza del Mercato 6, tel. 0577-280-894; for 50 years Signora Giuliana has ruled her kitchen, Amedeo and Eduardo speak English).

Osteria Trombicche takes you back to another age—cheap and small, with tight indoor seating and two tiny outdoor tables from which to watch the street scene. Alessandro serves fast, hearty food to a local crowd. For strong, traditional flavors, try tripe on Thursdays and salted dried cod on Fridays (€7 *ribollita*—bean-and-vegetable soup, €6 *panzanella*—bread salad with tomato and basil, €8-10 mixed-vegetable antipasto plates, hand-cut prosciutto, Mon-Sat 11:00-15:00 & 18:00-22:00, Sun 11:30-17:00, Via delle Terme 66, tel. 0577-288-089).

La Taverna Di Cecco is a simple, comfortable little eatery on an uncrowded back lane where earnest Luca and Gianni serve tasty salads and Sienese specialties made with fresh ingredients by an Italian grandmother (€10-12 pastas, €12-16 *secondi*, daily 12:00-16:00 & 19:00-24:00, Via Cecco Angiolieri 19, tel. 0577-288-518).

Il Pomodorino is a lively restaurant with a great view of the Duomo from its outdoor terrace. Tasty €8 pizzas pair well with a beer from their wide selection. The more intimate interior has Italian proverbs on the walls (daily April-Oct 12:30-late, Nov-March

17:00-late, a few steps from the recommended Alma Domus hotel at Via Camporegio 13, tel. 0577-286-811, mobile 345-026-5865).

PLACES ON IL CAMPO

If you choose to eat on perhaps the finest town square in Italy, you'll pay a premium, meet waiters who don't need to hustle, and get mediocre food. And yet I recommend it. The clamshell-shaped square is lined with venerable cafés, bars, restaurants, and pizzerias.

To experience Il Campo without paying for a full meal, consider having drinks or breakfast on the square. Some bars serve food. And if your hotel doesn't include breakfast or if you'd like something more memorable, Il Campo has plenty of options. A cappuccino and a *cornetto* (croissant) run about €5-6.

Dining and Drinks on the Square

Ristorante Alla Speranza has perhaps the best view in all of Italy. If you're looking to eat reasonably on Il Campo, this is your place (€9-11 pastas and pizzas, €17-18 *secondi,* €3 cover, daily 9:00-late, tel. 0577-280-190, www.allasperanza.it). It's smart to reserve the view table of your choice online or by phone—or simply stop by while you're sightseeing in the square.

Il Bandierino is another decent option with an angled view of City Hall (€9-10 salads, €11-12 pizzas, €14-15 pastas; no cover but a 20 percent service fee, daily 11:00-23:00, tel. 0577-282-217, Tony).

Bar Il Palio is the best bar on Il Campo for a pre- or post-dinner drink: It has straightforward prices, no cover, decent waiters, and a fantastic perspective out over the square.

Dynamic little **Osteria Liberamente** has a trendy vibe and is popular with young people (fine wine by the glass, €7 cocktails with good tapas, daily 9:00-late, Pino).

Drinks or Snacks from Balconies Overlooking Il Campo

Three places have skinny balconies with benches overlooking the main square for their customers. Sipping a coffee or nibbling a pastry here while marveling at the Il Campo scene is one of my favorite things to do in Europe. And it's very cheap. Survey these three places from Il Campo (with your back to the tower, they are at 10 o'clock, high noon, and 3 o'clock, respectively).

The little **Costarella Gelateria,** on the corner of Via di Città and Costa dei Barbieri, has good drinks and light snacks, such as cute little €3.50 sandwiches, though the gelato tastes artificial (daily 8:00-late, Via di Città 33). While the restaurant is for regular service, you're welcome to take anything from the bar out to the simple benches for a slight surcharge (just walk through the "table

Nightlife in Siena

Evenings are a wonderful time to be out and about in Siena, after the tour groups have left for the day.

Join the evening *passeggiata* (peak strolling time is 19:00) along Via Banchi di Sopra with gelato in hand. I like **Gelateria Grom,** which serves "Gelato like it used to be." Its seasonal flavors *(gusti del mese)* and all-natural ingredients make it a popular stop for any Sienese in need of something cool and sweet to lick while strolling (a little pricier than the competition, daily 11:00-24:00, Banchi di Sopra 13).

A fun trend in Siena is the *aperitivo*. All over town, you'll find bars attracting an early evening crowd by serving a free buffet of food with the purchase of a drink. For many, this can be a light dinner for the cost of a drink. Or consider starting or ending a meal with a drink or dessert on Il Campo. For suggestions, see "Places on Il Campo."

Un Tubo is a chic little bar tucked away in a mysterious alley just five minutes from Il Campo. It's perched on top of Etruscan caves, which are open to visitors and serve as a cellar for their many international wines. The scene—mainly local artsy types—is sometimes accompanied by live music or a DJ playing lounge music (Tue-Sat 19:00-late, closed Sun, light snacks available, Via del Luparello 2; from Il Campo, head down Via Porrione and turn right on Via del Luparello, just after San Martino church; tel. 0577-271-312). Giandomenico speaks English and will make you feel welcome.

Enoteca Italiana is a good wine bar in a cellar in the Fortezza, funded in part by the government to promote Italian wine production. They have about 15 different bottles open on any given day, and they offer tastings for €3-10. To get there, enter the Fortezza via the bridge, cross the running track, and—after passing a tree—go left down a ramp (Mon-Tue 12:00-19:30, Wed-Sat 12:00-24:00, closed Sun, snacks served when the bar's pricey restaurant is between mealtimes, outside terrace, tel. 0577-228-843).

service only" section upstairs) and eat with a grand view overlooking Il Campo.

Bar Paninoteca San Paolo has a youthful pub ambience and a row of stools overlooking the square. It serves big €7 salads and 50 kinds of €4 sandwiches, hot and cold—not authentic Italian, but quick and filling (order and pay at the counter, food served daily 12:00-2:00 in the morning, live music on Fri night, on Vicolo di San Paolo, tel. 0577-226-622).

Key Largo Bar has two long, second-story benches in the corner offering a wonderful secret perch. Buy your drink or snack at the bar (no cover and no extra charge to sit on balcony), climb upstairs, and slide the ancient bar to open the door. Enjoy stretching out, and try to imagine how, during the Palio, three layers of spectators cram into this space—note the iron railing used to plaster the top row of sardines up against the wall. Suddenly you're picturing Palio ponies zipping wildly around the corner (€4 cocktails, Sun-Thu 7:00-24:00, Fri-Sat 8:30-late, on the corner of Via Rinaldini). If you can't get a seat on the outdoor benches, skip the nondescript interior.

EATING CHEAPLY IN THE CENTER

Antica Pizzicheria al Palazzo della Chigiana (look for the sign reading *Pizzicheria de Miccoli*) may be the official name, but I bet locals just call it Antonio's. For most of his life, frenzied Antonio has carved salami and cheese for the neighborhood. Most of the day, a hungry line spills onto the street as people wait for their €4-5 sandwiches—meat and cheese sold by weight—with a good €10 bottle of Chianti (Italian law dictates that he must sell you a bottle of wine—cheap and good—and lend you the glasses). Even if you don't eat here, you could pop in to inhale the commotion or peruse Antonio's gifty traditional edibles (Mon-Sat 8:00-20:00, Sun 10:00-18:00, Via di Città 93-95, tel. 0577-289-164).

Pizza: Budget eaters look for *pizza al taglio* shops, scattered throughout Siena, selling pizza by the slice. One good bet, **San Martino,** a couple of blocks behind Il Campo, is a local-feeling spot with €2-3 slices and sandwiches (Mon-Fri 10:00-21:00, Sat 11:00-21:00, closed Sun, Via del Porrione 64). **Pizzeria Poppi,** near the recommended Hotel Etruria, is a funky stop filled with locals. With very few menu options, the choice is easy. Grab a *ciaccino ripieno* (stuffed "white" pizza—no tomatoes) and use Il Campo as a dining room (€1-2/slice, Mon-Fri 10:00-15:00 & 16:30-20:30, Sat 10:30-15:00 & 16:30-21:00, closed Sun, Via Banchi di Sotto 25—look for a white-and-blue *Pizzeria* sign at the corner of Via di Calzoneria).

Rosticcerie: For cheap take-out food, look for a *rosticceria* (explained on page 650). One affordable yet forgettable central option that feels at least partly untouristed is **Rosticceria Vitti,** near Piazza Gramsci's bus terminus (point to what you want in the glass case, figure €5 for a light meal, Sun-Fri 9:00-21:30, until 16:00 off-season, closed Sat, Via dei Montanini 14/16, tel. 0577-289-291).

Supermarket: You won't find many cheap grocery shops in the touristy center of Siena. But one handy (if fancy) option is **Consorzio Agrario Siena.** Ask them to make you up a *panino.* As this place specializes in artisanal Tuscan foods, both the quality and prices are high (Mon-Sat 8:00-20:30, Sun 9:30-20:00, a block off Piazza Matteotti, toward Il Campo at Via Pianigiani 5).

DESSERTS AND TREATS

For a special dessert or a sweet treat any time of day, stop by **Nannini**—considered the top-end pastry shop and *the* place to go for quality local specialties (Mon-Sat 7:30-21:00, Sun 8:00-24:00, *aperitivo* happy hour 18:00 until closing, Banchi di Sopra 24). Across the street is the wonderful **Gelateria Grom** (see "Nightlife in Siena" sidebar)—but you have my permission to sample every *gelateria* in town to pick your own favorite.

Siena Connections

Siena has sparse train connections but is a great hub for buses to the hill towns, though frequency drops on Sundays and holidays. For most, Florence is the gateway to Siena. Even if you are a rail-pass user, connect these two cities by bus—it's faster than the train, and Siena's bus station is more convenient and central than its train station. (Note: Many travelers mistake old signs for a former bus company, Tra-In, as signs for trains or the train station. Those buses have nothing to do with the railway.)

BY TRAIN

Siena's train station is at the edge of town. For details on getting between the town center and the station, see page 353.

From Siena by Train to: Florence (direct trains hourly, 1.5-2 hours; bus is better), **Pisa** (2/hour, 1.75 hours, change at Empoli), **Assisi** (10/day, 3.25-4.25 hours, most involve 2 changes, bus is faster), **Rome** (1-2/hour, 3-3.5 hours, change in Florence or Chiusi), **Orvieto** (12/day, 2.5 hours, change in Chiusi). For more information, visit www.trenitalia.com.

BY BUS

The main bus companies are **Tiemme/Siena Mobilità** (formerly called Tra-In; mostly handles buses to regional destinations, tel. 0577-204-111, www.sienamobilita.it) and **Sena/Baltour** (for long-distance connections, tel. 0861-199-1900, www.baltour.it). On schedules, the fastest buses are marked *rapida*. I'd stick with these. Most buses depart Siena from Piazza Gramsci; others leave from the train station (confirm when you buy your ticket).

Tiemme/Siena Mobilità Buses to: Florence (roughly 2/hour, 1.25-hour *rapida/via superstrada* buses are faster than the train, avoid the 2-hour *ordinaria* buses unless you have time to enjoy the beautiful scenery en route; if there are lines at bus-ticket office, tickets also available at tobacco shops/*tabacchi*; generally leaves from Piazza Gramsci as well as train station), **San Gimignano** (8/day direct, on Sun must change in Poggibonsi, 1.25 hours, leaves from Piazza Gramsci), **Volterra** (4/day Mon-Sat, no buses on Sun,

2 hours, change in Colle di Val d'Elsa, leaves from Piazza Gramsci), **Montepulciano** (6-8/day, none on Sun, 1.25 hours, leaves from train station), **Pienza** (6/day, none on Sun, 1.5 hours, leaves from train station), **Montalcino** (6/day Mon-Sat, 4/day Sun, 1.25 hours, leaves from train station or Piazza del Sale), and **Pisa's Galileo Galilei Airport** (3/day, 1.75 hours, one direct, two via Poggibonsi).

Sena/Baltour Buses to: Rome (9-10/day, 3 hours, from Piazza Gramsci, arrives at Rome's Tiburtina station on Metro line B with easy connections to the central Termini train station), **Naples** (2/day, 6.5 hours, one at 17:00 and an overnight bus that departs at 23:59), **Milan** (6/day, 4 hours, departs from Piazza Gramsci, arrives at Milan's Cadorna Station with Metro access and direct trains to Malpensa Airport), or **Assisi** (daily at 17:30, 1.75 hours, departs from Siena train station, arrives at Assisi Santa Maria degli Angeli; from there it's a 10-minute taxi/bus ride uphill to city center).

To reach the town center of **Pisa,** the train is better (described earlier).

Tickets and Information: You can buy tickets in the underground passageway (called Sottopassaggio la Lizza) beneath Piazza Gramsci—look for stairwells in front of NH Excelsior Hotel. The larger office (marked *Siena Mobilità*) handles Tiemme/Siena Mobilità buses (Mon-Fri 6:30-19:30, Sat-Sun 7:00-19:30). The smaller one is for Sena/Baltour buses (Mon-Sat 8:30-19:45; on Sun, when the Sena/Baltour bus ticket office is closed, buy tickets next door at Tiemme/Siena Mobilità office; Sena/Baltour office also has a desk selling *Eurolines* tickets for bus connections to other countries). Tiemme/Siena Mobilità is cash-only; Sena/Baltour accepts credit cards. You can also get tickets for both Tiemme/Siena Mobilità buses and Sena/Baltour buses at the train station (look for bus-ticket kiosk just inside main door—see page 353 for hours). If necessary, you can buy tickets from the driver, but it costs €3-5 extra.

Services: Sottopassaggio la Lizza also has luggage storage (see page 355 for details), posted bus schedules and WCs (€0.50).

PISA

In A.D. 1200, Pisa's power peaked. For nearly three centuries (1000-1300), Pisa had rivaled Venice and Genoa as a sea-trading power, exchanging European goods for luxury items in Muslim lands. As a port near the mouth of the Arno River (six miles from the coast—when the wind blows in a certain direction, you can still smell the sea), the city enjoyed easy access to the Mediterranean, plus the protection of sitting a bit upstream. The Romans made it a naval base, and by medieval times the city was a major player.

Pisa's 150-foot galleys cruised the Mediterranean, gaining control of the sea, establishing outposts on the islands of Corsica, Sardinia, and Sicily, and trading with other Europeans, Muslims, and Byzantine Christians as far south as North Africa and as far east as Syria. European Crusaders hired Pisan boats to carry them and their supplies as they headed off to conquer the Muslim-held Holy Land. The Pisan "Republic" prided itself on its independence from both popes and emperors. The city used its sea-trading wealth to build the grand monuments of the Field of Miracles, including the now-famous Leaning Tower.

The Pisans fancied themselves the natural heirs of the Roman Empire, and they peppered Roman engineering—and actual ancient fragments—into their distinct architectural style: Pisan Romanesque. In many of Pisa's buildings and decoration from these glory days, you can see the earliest inklings of the coming Renaissance—centuries before it took hold in earnest in Florence.

But the Pisan fleet was routed in battle by Genoa (1284, at Meloria, off Livorno), and their overseas outposts were taken away. Then the port silted up, and Pisa was left high and dry, with only its Field of Miracles and its university keeping it on the map. In 1406, it fell under the auspices of its former rival, the Medici family of Florence. Cosimo de' Medici, like so many bigwigs before him, favored Pisa for its mild climate (thanks to that sea breeze) and distance from his enemies. He built palaces here and raised a mighty army. But—as a backwater of Florence—Pisa lacked the opportunities to flourish in its own right, and entered a period of steady decline.

Today's Pisa is a thriving mid-size city with some fine Renaissance architecture (as well as some gloomy, post-WWII flourishes). It's known for two things: its fine university and its remarkable Field of Miracles. That means it's thronged with both students and tourists.

Pisa's three important sights—the Duomo, Baptistery, and the Tower—float regally on the best lawn in Italy. The style throughout is Pisa's very own Pisan Romanesque. Even as the church was being built, Piazza del Duomo was nicknamed the "Campo dei Miracoli," or Field of Miracles, for the grandness of the undertaking.

The Tower recently underwent a decade of restoration and topple-prevention. To ascend, you must get your ticket and book a time at least a few hours in advance (for details, see page 425).

PLANNING YOUR TIME

For most visitors, Pisa is a touristy quickie—seeing the Tower, visiting the square, and wandering through the church are 90 percent of their Pisan thrills. But it's a shame to skip the rest of the city. Considering Pisa's historic importance and the wonderful ambience created by its rich architectural heritage and vibrant student population, the city deserves a half-day visit. For many, the lack of tourists outside the Field of Miracles is both a surprise and a relief.

If you want to climb the Tower, go straight to the ticket office upon your arrival to snag an appointment—usually for a couple of hours later, especially in summer (for directions to the Field of Miracles, see "Arrival in Pisa," later). You can also buy a ticket and book a time in advance online (no sooner than 20 days but at least one day beforehand) at www.opapisa.it. If you'll be seeing both the town and the Field of Miracles, plan on a six-hour stop. If just blitzing the Field of Miracles, three hours is the minimum. Spending the night lets you savor a youthful Italian city scene.

If you're connecting between Pisa and Lucca, note that a handy bus runs hourly (less frequently on Sun) between the Field of Miracles and Lucca, saving time and hassle (see page 449).

Orientation to Pisa

The city of Pisa is manageable, with just 100,000 people, but its 45,000 students keep it lively, especially at night. The city is framed on the north by the Field of Miracles (Leaning Tower) and on the south by Pisa Centrale train station. The Arno River flows east to west, bisecting the city. Walking from Pisa Centrale directly to the Tower takes about 30 minutes (but allow up to an hour if you take my self-guided walk). The two main streets for tourists and shoppers are Via Santa Maria (running south from the Tower) and Corso Italia/Borgo Stretto (running north from the station).

TOURIST INFORMATION

The TI is about 200 yards from Pisa Centrale train station—exit and walk straight up the left side of the street to the big, circular Piazza Vittorio Emanuele II. The TI is on the left at #13 (Mon-Fri 10:00-13:00 & 14:00-16:00, Sat-Sun 10:00-13:00, tel. 050-42291, www.pisaunicaterra.it). There's also a TI at the airport, in the arrivals hall (daily 9:00-21:30, tel. 050-502-518).

ARRIVAL IN PISA

By Train

Most trains (and visitors) arrive at Pisa Centrale train station, about a mile south of the Tower and Field of Miracles. A few trains, particularly those from Lucca, also stop at the smaller Pisa San Rossore Station, a dreary but manageable four-block walk from the Tower (not all trains stop here, but if yours does, hop off).

Pisa Centrale: This station has a baggage-check desk—look for *deposito bagagli* (€4/bag for 12 hours, daily 6:00-21:00). With the tracks to your back, it's to the right at the far end of platform 1, just after the police station.

To get from this station to the Field of Miracles, you can **walk** (get free map from TI, 30 minutes direct, one hour if you follow my self-guided walk), take a **taxi** (€10-15, tel. 050-541-600, taxi stand at station), or go by **bus.** At all bus stops in Pisa, be cautious of pickpockets, who take advantage of crowds to operate.

Bus **LAM Rossa** ("Red," also marked *L/R*) stops across the street from the train station, in front of the NH Cavalieri Hotel. Buy a €1.20 bus ticket from the tobacco/magazine kiosk in the train station's main hall or at any tobacco shop (€2 on board; ticket good for 70 minutes, round-trip permitted; bus departs at least every 10

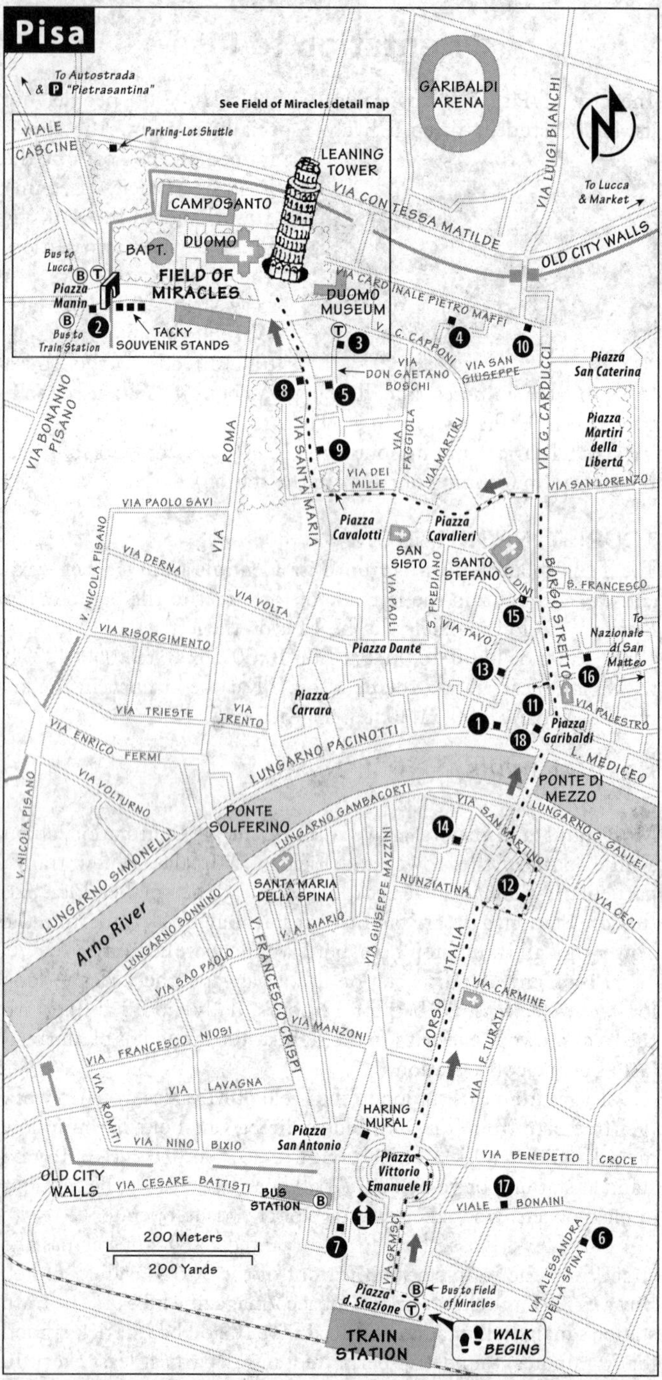

Pisa
To Autostrada & P "Pietrasantina"
See Field of Miracles detail map
GARIBALDI ARENA
VIALE CASCINE
Parking-Lot Shuttle
LEANING TOWER
CAMPOSANTO
VIA CONTESSA MATILDE
BAPT.
DUOMO
FIELD OF MIRACLES
Bus to Lucca
Piazza Manin
Bus to Train Station
TACKY SOUVENIR STANDS
DUOMO MUSEUM
VIA CARDINALE PIETRO MAFFI
V. C. CAPPONI
VIA DON GAETANO BOSCHI
VIA SAN GIUSEPPE
VIA LUIGI BIANCHI
To Lucca & Market
OLD CITY WALLS
Piazza San Caterina
Piazza Martiri della Libertá
VIA G. CARDUCCI
VIA SAN LORENZO
VIA BONANNO PISANO
ROMA
VIA SANTA MARIA
VIA FAGGIOLA
VIA MARTIRI
VIA DEI MILLE
VIA PAOLO SAVI
VIA
Piazza Cavalotti
Piazza Cavalieri
SAN SISTO
SANTO STEFANO
U. DINI
BORGO STRETTO
S. FRANCESCO
V. NICOLA PISANO
VIA DERNA
VIA VOLTA
VIA PAOLI
S. FREDIANO
VIA TAVO
To Nazionale di San Matteo
VIA RISORGIMENTO
Piazza Dante
Piazza Carrara
VIA TRIESTE
VIA TRENTO
VIA PALESTRO
Piazza Garibaldi
VIA ENRICO FERMI
LUNGARNO PACINOTTI
L. MEDICEO
PONTE DI MEZZO
VIA VOLTURNO
PONTE SOLFERINO
LUNGARNO GAMBACORTI
VIA SAN MARTINO
LUNGARNO G. GALILEI
V. NICOLA PISANO
LUNGARNO SIMONELLI
SANTA MARIA DELLA SPINA
VIA GIUSEPPE MAZZINI
NUNZIATINA
VIA CECI
Arno River
LUNGARNO SONNINO
V. A. MARIO
V. FRANCESCO CRISPI
CORSO ITALIA
VIA SAO PAOLO
VIA CARMINE
VIA MANZONI
VIA FRANCESCO NIOSI
VIA F. TURATI
VIA LAVAGNA
VIA ROMITI
HARING MURAL
VIA NINO BIXIO
Piazza San Antonio
Piazza Vittorio Emanuele II
VIA BENEDETTO CROCE
OLD CITY WALLS
VIA CESARE BATTISTI
BUS STATION
VIALE BONAINI
VIA ALESSANDRA DELLA SPINA
200 Meters
200 Yards
VIA GRAMSCI
Piazza d. Stazione
Bus to Field of Miracles
TRAIN STATION
WALK BEGINS

Pisa Key

1. Hotel Royal Victoria, Caffè dell'Ussero & De' Coltelli Gelato
2. Hotel Pisa Tower
3. Hotel Villa Kinzica
4. Casa San Tommaso
5. Pensione Helvetia
6. Hotel Alessandro della Spina
7. Hotel Milano
8. Paninoteca il Canguro
9. Panetteria Antiche Tradizioni
10. Pizzeria al Bagno di Nerone
11. La Vineria di Piazza & Produce Market
12. Pane e Vino
13. Antica Trattoria il Campano
14. Ristorante Bagus
15. Il Montino Pizzeria
16. Orzo Bruno Brewpub
17. Da Michele
18. La Bottega del Gelato

minutes, runs until 20:30, 15-minute trip). Before getting on the bus, confirm that it is indeed going to "Campo dei Miracoli." The bus lets you off at Piazza Manin, in front of the gate to the Field of Miracles (at the stop called "Torre").

To return to the train station from the Tower, catch bus LAM Rossa in front of the BNL bank, across the street from where you got off (again, confirm the destination—"Stazione Centrale," staht-see-OH-nay chen-TRAH-lay). You'll also find a taxi stand 30 yards from the Tower (at Bar Duomo).

Pisa San Rossore: From this train station to the Field of Miracles, it's just a four-block walk (10 minutes). Take the underground walkway to Piazza Fancelli, and turn left onto Via Andrea Pisano. Continue for about 150 yards, and you'll see the Tower ahead of you, a few minutes away.

By Car

Driving in the city center is risky, as Pisa has several restricted areas that are monitored by camera (you could get a ticket by mail). Instead, it's best to leave your car at the big Pietrasantina parking lot, designed for tour buses (which pay to park) and tourists with cars (who park for free). From there, you can walk to the Field of Miracles or hop on a shuttle bus.

To reach the parking lot, exit the autostrada at *Pisa Nord* and follow signs to *Pisa* (on the left), then *Bus Parking*. The parking lot has a cafeteria, WC, and a bus stop for the orange shuttle *(navetta)* that goes back and forth between the lot and the Largo Cocco Griffi bus stop, just behind the walls of the Field of Miracles (€1 ticket covers round-trip, runs about every 10 minutes). If you'd rather not wait for the bus, the walk to the Tower takes about 15 minutes. Or, to follow my self-guided walk through Pisa to the Field of Miracles, take bus LAM Rossa to Pisa Centrale train station (€1.20 at parking-lot cafeteria, €2 on board; also stops near the Tower at Piazza Manin en route).

By Plane

For details on Pisa's Galileo Galilei Airport, see page 449.

HELPFUL HINTS

Markets: An open-air produce market attracts picnickers to Piazza delle Vettovaglie, one block north of the Arno River near Ponte di Mezzo, and nearby Piazza Sant'Uomobuono (Mon-Sat 7:00-18:00, main section closes at 13:00, closed Sun). A street market—with more practical goods than food—bustles on Wednesday and Saturday mornings between Via del Brennero and Via Paparrelli (8:00-13:00, just outside of wall, about 6 blocks east of the Tower).

Festivals: June is a big month in Pisa, when some hotels raise their rates. The first half of June has many events, culminating in a celebration for Pisa's patron saint (June 16-17). The last week in June is the Gioco del Ponte ("Game of the Bridge") festival, where burly residents of the city's four districts meet on the bridge for a game of tug-of-war with a big carriage.

Local Guides: Dottore Vincenzo Riolo is a great guide for Pisa and the surrounding area (€140/3 hours, mobile 338-211-2939, www.pisatour.it, info@pisatour.it). **Martina Manfredi** happily guides visitors through the Field of Miracles, but particularly enjoys helping them discover Pisa's other charms, from hidden gardens and piazzas to cuisine to artisans (€140/3 hours, €250/6 hours, mobile 328-898-2927, www.tuscanyatheart.it, info@tuscanyatheart.it).

Tours: The TI coordinates with local guides to offer walking tours most days. There's usually a tour in English on Sundays at 10:30 (€12), but others are likely offered; check with the TI for the latest.

Updates to This Book: For updates to this book, check www.ricksteves.com/update.

Pisa Walk

FROM PISA CENTRALE TRAIN STATION TO THE TOWER

A leisurely one-hour stroll from the station to the Tower is a great way to get acquainted with the more subtle virtues of this fine city. Because the hordes who descend daily on the Tower rarely bother with the rest of the town, you'll find most of Pisa to be delightfully untouristy—a student-filled, classy, Old World town with an Arno-scape much like its upstream rival, Florence.

• *From Pisa Centrale train station, walk north up Viale Antonio Gramsci to the circular square called...*

Piazza Vittorio Emanuele II

The Allies considered Pisa to be strategically important in World War II, and both the train station and its main bridge were targeted for bombing. Forty percent of this district was destroyed. The piazza has been recently rebuilt, and now this generous public space with grass and benches is actually a lid for an underground parking lot. The TI is on this piazza, in the arcade to the left. The circular pink building in the middle of the square, on the right, is La Bottega del Parco, a shop that sells Tuscan products that originated within or near the San Rossore natural park—cheese, salami, spices, oils, sauces, and so on (daily 9:30-20:30, tel. 050-086-8019).

At the top of the square, on the left (by the Credito Artigiano bank), find the little mini-piazza with a colorful bar/café that faces a mural, called *Tuttomondo (Whole Wide World),* painted by American artist **Keith Haring** in 1989. Haring (who died of AIDS in 1990) brought New York City graffiti into the mainstream. This painting is a celebration of diversity, chaos, and the liveliness of our world, vibrating with energy.

• *Head back to the big square and walk up Pisa's main drag, Corso Italia, toward the river.*

Corso Italia

As you leave Piazza Vittorio Emanuele II, look to the right (on the wall of the bar on the corner, under the gallery) to see the circa-1960 wall map of Pisa with a steam train. You'll also see plenty of youthful fashions, as kids are out making the scene here. Be on guard for pickpockets—too young to arrest, they can only be kicked out of town. Pushed out of their former happy hunting grounds, the Field of Miracles, they now work the crowds here, often dressed as tourists.

Follow the pedestrianized Corso Italia straight north for several blocks. This is Pisa's main shopping street for locals, not tourists. For a peek at off-the-beaten-track Pisa, after #45, on the right, watch for the little covered lane called Via San Bernardo. Follow it to pop out at the very local-feeling **Piazza Chiara Gambacorti.** Neighbors sit on the benches or at café tables and chat, while budding soccer stars practice their kicks at the far end. The recommended Pane e Vino is a fine place to grab a sandwich or takeaway pasta.

Locals call this square by another name, Piazza della Pera. To find out why, exit the square at the top-right corner (the opposite corner from where you entered) and go one block along the yellow wall. At the first intersection, watch for the knee-high, onion-shaped chunk of stone on your right. Dubbed **La Pera** ("The Pear"), it once topped an Etruscan tomb—a striking reminder of the layers of history underfoot in Pisa.

Turn left at the stone (on Via San Martino) and walk one block back to Corso Italia. You'll run into a gorgeous **loggia.** Like much of the city, this was built under Medici (Florentine) rule—and it resembles the markets you'll still find in Florence. But remember that before Florence ruled Pisa, this city was an independent and strong maritime republic. This area was a marshland until the 11th century, and in the Middle Ages it was a crossroads of merchants from faraway lands: smelly, polluted, and a commotion of activity.

• *Turn right at the loggia and cross to the middle of the bridge.*

Ponte di Mezzo

This modern bridge, constructed on the same site where the Romans built one, marks the center of Pisa. In the Middle Ages, this bridge (like Florence's Ponte Vecchio) was lined with shops. It's been destroyed several times by floods...and in 1943 by British and American bombers. Enjoy the view from the center of the bridge of the elegant mansions that line the riverbank, recalling Pisa's days of trading glory—the cityscape feels a bit like Venice's Grand Canal. Back when the loggia area was stinky and crowded, nobles preferred to live in stately residences along the river.

Looking to the right, notice the red-brick building (the former silk merchants' quarters) that looks like it's about to slide into the river. Pisa sits on shifting delta sand, making construction tricky. The entire town leans. Using innovative arches above ground and below, architects didn't stop the leaning—but they have made buildings that wobble without being threatened.

• *Cross the bridge to...*

Piazza Garibaldi

This square is named for the charismatic leader of the Risorgimento, the unification movement that led to Italian independence in 1870. Knowing Pisa was strongly nationalist, a wounded Garibaldi came here to be nursed back to health; many Pisans died in the national struggle.

For a gelato break, stop by **La Bottega del Gelato,** right on this square and most Pisans' sentimental favorite. Or, for a fresh take on the same old gelato, head about 100 yards downstream (to the left as you come off the bridge) to **De' Coltelli** (at #23), which scoops up organic, artisanal gelato with unusual and vibrant flavors...some of the best I've had. Just beyond that, in the slouching red building (at #28), step into **Caffè dell'Ussero.** This venerable café has long been a hangout of both politicians...and the students bent on overthrowing them. Browse its time-warp interior, lined with portraits and documents from the struggle for Italian independence (Sun-Fri 7:00-21:00, closed Sat).

• *Back on Piazza Garibaldi, continue north up the elegantly arcaded street called...*

Borgo Stretto

Welcome to Pisa's other main shopping street. On the right, the Church of St. Michael, with its fine Pisan Romanesque facade, still sports some 16th-century graffiti. I'll bet you can see some modern graffiti across the street. Students have been pushing their causes here—or simply defacing things—for five centuries.

From here, look farther up the street and notice how it undulates like a flowing river. In the sixth century B.C., Pisa was born when two parallel rivers were connected by canals. This street echoes the flow of one of those canals. An 11th-century landslide rerouted the second river, destroying ancient Pisa, and the entire city had to regenerate.

• *Just past the church, detour left onto Via delle Colonne, and walk one block down to...*

Piazza delle Vettovaglie

Pisa's historic market square, Piazza delle Vettovaglie, is lively day and night. Its Renaissance loggia has hosted the fish and vegetable market for generations. The stalls are set up in this piazza during the morning (Mon-Sat 7:00-13:00, closed Sun) and stay open later in the neighboring piazza to the west (Piazza Sant'Uomobuono, Mon-Sat 7:00-18:00, closed Sun). You could cobble together a picnic from the sandwich shops and fruit-and-veggie stalls ringing these squares.

• *Return to Borgo Stretto and continue north another 100 yards, passing an ugly bomb site on the right, with its horrible 1960s reconstruction (Largo Ciro Menotti). Then take the second left on nondescript Via Ulisse Dini (immediately at the arcade's end, just before the pharmacy). This leads to Pisa's historic core, Piazza dei Cavalieri.*

Piazza dei Cavalieri

With its old clock and colorfully decorated palace, this piazza was once the seat of the independent Republic of Pisa's government. Around 1500, Florence conquered Pisa and made this square the training place for the knights of its navy. The statue of Cosimo I de'

PISA

Medici shows the Florentine who ruled Pisa in the 16th century. With a foot on a dolphin, he reminded all who passed that the Florentine navy controlled the sea—at least a little of it. The frescoes on the exterior of the square's buildings, though damaged by salty sea air and years of neglect, reflect Pisa's fading glory under the Medici.

With Napoleon, this complex of grand buildings became part of the University of Pisa. The university is one of Europe's oldest, with roots in a law school that dates back as far as the 11th century. In the mid-16th century, the city was a hotbed of controversy, as spacey professors like Galileo Galilei studied the solar system—with results that challenged the Church's powerful doctrine. Galileo's legacy lives on, as the U of P is most highly regarded for its scientific faculties, especially engineering and medicine. The blind tenor Andrea Bocelli attended law school in Pisa before embarking on his well-known musical career.

From here, take Via Corsica (to the left of the clock). The humble **Church of San Sisto,** ahead on the left (side entrance on Via Corsica), is worth a quick look. With simple bricks, assorted reused columns, heavy walls, and few windows, this was the typical Romanesque style that predated the more lavish Pisan Romanesque style of the Field of Miracles structures.

Follow Via Corsica as it turns into Via dei Mille, then turn right on Via Santa Maria, which leads north (and grab a quick bite at the recommended Panetteria Antiche Tradizioni, on the right, or Paninoteca il Canguro, on the left). You'll pass through increasingly touristy claptrap, directly to the Field of Miracles and the Tower.

Sights in Pisa

AT THE FIELD OF MIRACLES

▲▲▲Leaning Tower

A 15-foot lean from the vertical makes the Tower one of Europe's most recognizable images. You can see it for free—it's always viewable—or you can pay to climb nearly 300 stairs to the top.

Cost and Hours: €18, kids under eight not allowed, daily April-Sept 8:00-20:00 (until 22:00 mid-June-Aug), Oct 9:00-19:00, Nov-Feb 10:00-17:00, March 9:00-18:00, ticket office opens 30 minutes early, last entry 30 minutes before closing, timed entry, reservations recommended, www.opapisa.it.

✪ See the Leaning Tower Tour chapter.

▲▲Duomo (Cathedral)

This gargantuan Pisan Romanesque church has a Pisano pulpit, modest dress code, and no baggage check.

Field of Miracles Tickets

Pisa has a combo-ticket scheme designed to get you into its neglected secondary sights: the Baptistery, Camposanto Cemetery, Duomo Museum, and Museum of the Sinopias (fresco pattern museum). For €5, you get your choice of one of these sights; for two of these sights, the cost is €7; and for the works, you pay €9 (credit cards accepted except AmEx). No matter which ticket you get, you have to pay an additional €18 if you want to climb the Tower. Entry into the Duomo is free, but you need a free voucher (or you can show your combo-ticket).

You can get the Duomo voucher (good for up to two people) and any of these tickets from either ticket office on the Field of Miracles: One is behind the Leaning Tower and the other is at the Museum of the Sinopias (near the Baptistery, almost suffocated by souvenir stands). Both ticket offices have big, yellow, triangle-shaped signs. You can buy tickets in advance online at www.opapisa.it (no sooner than 20 days but at least one day ahead of your visit; the free voucher for the Duomo is not available online).

So, which ticket to buy? This depends on your time and level of interest. The shortest visit doesn't cost a dime: Ogle the Tower and other buildings, and enter the Duomo (with the best interior). With a bit more time, the interiors of the Baptistery and Camposanto Cemetery are well worth paying for and easy to appreciate. The two museums—Duomo Museum and Museum of the Sinopias—are "extra credit" for those fascinated by the artistic details of the other sights; for most travelers, they're skippable.

And what about entering the Tower? Is it worth that hefty price tag—and the likelihood of having to wait to enter? It's a minor thrill to clomp up those twisty stairs, and the view from the top is enjoyable. But Pisa isn't a particularly scenic city, and it's a lot of expense and hassle for a view. Unless climbing the Tower is what you came to do, I consider ascending it optional. The real thrill comes from seeing it from the outside.

Cost and Hours: Free, pick up a voucher—for a maximum of two people—at either ticket office; you cannot get this voucher in advance online; daily April-Sept 10:00-20:00, Oct 10:00-19:00, Nov-Feb 10:00-13:00 & 14:00-17:00, March 10:00-18:00, last entry 30 minutes before closing.

✪ See the Pisa Duomo Tour chapter.

▲▲▲Field of Miracles (Campo dei Miracoli)

Scattered across a golf-course-green lawn are five grand buildings: the cathedral (or Duomo), its bell tower (the Leaning Tower), the

Baptistery, the hospital (today's Museum of the Sinopias), and the Camposanto Cemetery. The buildings are constructed from similar materials—bright white marble—and have comparable decoration. Each has a simple ground floor and rows of delicate columns and arches that form open-air arcades, giving the Campo a pleasant visual unity.

The style is called Pisan Romanesque. Unlike traditional Romanesque, with its heavy fortress-like feel—thick walls, barrel arches, few windows—Pisan Romanesque is light and elegant. At ground level, most of the structures have simple half-columns and arches. On the upper levels, you'll see a little of everything—tight rows of thin columns; pointed Gothic gables and prickly spires; Byzantine mosaics and horseshoe arches; and geometric designs (such as diamonds) and striped, colored marbles inspired by mosques in Muslim lands.

Architecturally, the Campo is unique and exotic. Theologically, the Campo's buildings mark the main events of every Pisan's life: christened in the Baptistery, married in the Duomo, honored in ceremonies at the Tower, healed in the hospital, and buried in the Camposanto Cemetery.

Lining this field of artistic pearls is a gauntlet of Europe's tackiest souvenir stands, as well as dozens of people who have simultaneously had the same bright idea: posing for a photo as though they're propping up the Leaning Tower. Although the smooth green carpet looks like the ideal picnic spot—and many people are doing just that—officially, lounging on this lawn can result in a €25 fine.

The next four sights—the Baptistery, Camposanto Cemetery, Museum of the Sinopias, and Duomo Museum—are covered in more detail within the ✪ Field of Miracles Tour chapter.

▲Baptistery

The round Baptistery, located in front of the Duomo, has superb acoustics and another fine Pisano pulpit.

Cost and Hours: €5, but most visitors buy one of the various combo-tickets to save money (see sidebar on page 421), daily April-Sept 8:00-20:00, Oct 9:00-19:00, Nov-Feb 10:00-17:00, March 9:00-18:00, last entry 30 minutes before closing.

Camposanto Cemetery

Lined with faint frescoes, this centuries-old cemetery on the north side of the Campo is famous for its "Holy Land" dirt, reputedly brought here from the Middle East in the 12th century. Artillery fire during World War II set the lead roof ablaze, greatly damaging the building and its frescoes (same cost and hours as Baptistery).

Museum of the Sinopias (Museo delle Sinopie)

Across from the Baptistery, housed in a 13th-century hospital (with its entrance nearly obscured by souvenir stands), this museum displays some of the original preliminary sketches (sinopias) that lay beneath the frescoed walls of the Camposanto Cemetery—the drawings were recovered after a WWII fire severely damaged the frescoes themselves. This museum comes with two free, short, introductory videos that you can watch even without a ticket. Good students might want to come here first for this orientation (same cost and hours as Baptistery).

Duomo Museum (Museo dell'Opera del Duomo)

Located behind the Leaning Tower, the Duomo Museum (likely closed for renovation through 2016) is big on Pisan art, displaying treasures of the cathedral, paintings, silverware, and sculptures (from the 12th to 14th centuries, particularly by the Pisano dynasty), as well as ancient Egyptian, Etruscan, and Roman artifacts (when open, same cost and hours as Baptistery, Piazza Arcivescovado 18).

ELSEWHERE IN PISA

City Walls

Plans are being made to open the city walls that run behind the Field of Miracles to visitors, but details are constantly in flux. If you see people up on the walls, ask around about how to do it: The view from atop the walls offers a different angle on the great buildings.

Museo Nazionale di San Matteo

In a former convent on the river, this art museum displays 12th- to 15th-century sculptures, illuminated manuscripts, and paintings on wood by pre- and early-Renaissance masters Martini, Masaccio, and others. It's a fine collection—especially its painted wood crucifixes—and gives you a chance to see Pisan innovation in 11th- to 13th-century art, before Florence took the lead.

Cost and Hours: €5, Tue-Sat 8:30-19:00, Sun 8:30-13:00, closed Mon, near Piazza San Paolo at Lungarno Mediceo, a 5-minute walk upriver (east) from the main bridge, tel. 050-541-865.

LEANING TOWER TOUR

You've seen it in TV ads, in movies, and on posters, key chains, and souvenir dishes—now it's time to see it in the flesh. And, the funny thing is, it's one iconic image that really looks like its famous reproductions.

The off-kilter Tower parallels Pisa's history. It was started in the late 12th century, when Pisa was at its peak: one of the world's richest, most powerful, and most sophisticated cities. Pisans had built their huge cathedral to reflect their city's superpower status, and the cathedral's bell tower—the Leaning Tower—was the perfect complement. But as Pisa's power declined, the Tower reclined, and ever since, both have required a great deal of effort to prop up. However, after a 10-year renovation, the Tower's been stabilized. You can admire it in all its cockeyed glory and even climb up for a commanding view.

Orientation

Cost: Free to look, €18 to go inside and climb to the top (see age restrictions in "Reservations to Climb the Tower," below).

Hours: Always viewable from the outside. It's open to climb daily April-Sept 8:00-20:00 (until 22:00 mid-June-Aug), Oct 9:00-19:00, Nov-Feb 10:00-17:00, March 9:00-18:00, ticket office opens 30 minutes early, last entry 30 minutes before closing.

Reservations to Climb the Tower: Entry to the tower is by a timed ticket good for a 30-minute visit. Every 15 minutes, 45 people can clamber up the 294 tilting steps to the top. Children under age eight are not allowed to go up. Children ages 8-12 must be accompanied by—and hold hands at all times with—an adult. Teenagers (under 19) must also be accompanied by an adult.

Reserve your timed entry in person at either ticket office

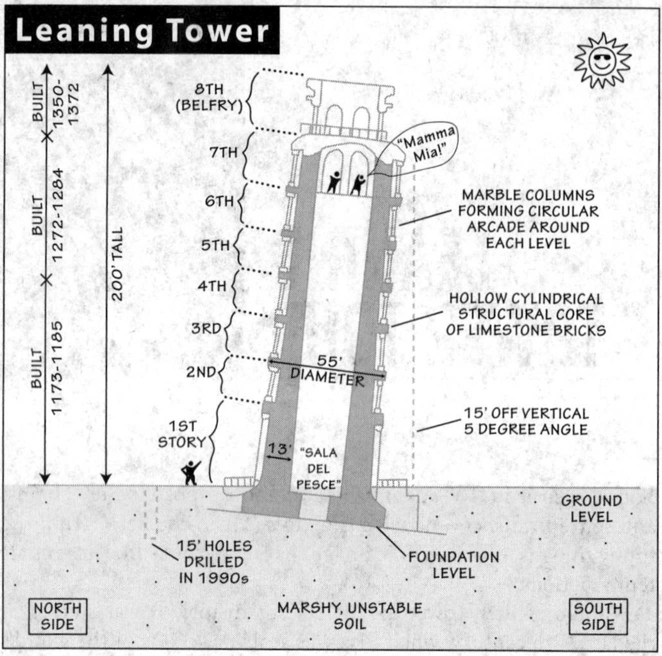

(see below), or choose your entry time and buy your ticket online at www.opapisa.it.

Online bookings are accepted no earlier than 20 days and no later than one day in advance. Print out the voucher and bring it to the Tower 15 minutes before your entry time.

To reserve in person, go to the **ticket office,** behind the Tower on the left (in the yellow building), or to the Museum of the Sinopias ticket office, hidden behind the souvenir stalls. In summer, for same-day entry, you'll likely need to wait two or three hours before going up (see the rest of the monuments and grab lunch while waiting). It's busiest between 12:00 and 15:00; the wait is usually much shorter at the beginning or end of the day.

At the Tower: Even though this is technically a "guided" visit, the "guide" is a museum guard who makes sure you don't stay past your scheduled time. For your 30-minute time slot, figure about a 5-minute presentation at the start, 10 minutes to climb, and 10 to descend. This leaves about five minutes for vertigo at the top.

Getting There: From Pisa Centrale train station, you can walk (30 minutes), take a taxi (€10-15), or catch bus LAM Rossa (at least every 10 minutes, runs until 20:30, 15 minutes); see page 413 for details.

Remember, if your train stops at the smaller Pisa San Rossore Station, get off there and you're only about four blocks from the Tower (head for the Baptistery's dome following Via Andrea Pisano).

If you're traveling by car, see "Arrival in Pisa: By Car," on page 415.

Baggage Check: You can't take any bags up the Tower, but day-bag-size lockers are available at the ticket office—show your Tower ticket to check your bag. You may check your bag 10 minutes before your reservation time and must pick it up immediately after your Tower visit.

Caution: The railings are skinny, the steps are slanted, and rain makes the marble slippery—all in all, it's more dizzying than you might expect. Anyone with balance issues of any sort should think twice before ascending.

Starring: The Tower's frilly Pisan Romanesque look and its famous lean.

The Tour Begins

• *If you're going inside, you may have to wait around for a few minutes at the base of the Tower—the perfect opportunity to read this. If you're not ascending, almost all of this tour is just as interesting from down below.*

Yep, There It Is

Rising up alongside the cathedral, the Tower is nearly 200 feet tall and 55 feet wide, weighing 14,000 tons and currently leaning at a five-degree angle (15 feet off the vertical axis). It started to lean almost immediately after construction began (it would take two centuries to finish the structure). Count the eight stories—a simple base, six stories of columns (forming arcades), and a belfry on top. The inner structural core is a hollow cylinder built of limestone bricks, faced with white marble brought here by barge from San Giuliano, northeast of the city. The thin columns of the open-air arcades make the heavy Tower seem light and graceful.

The Building of the Tower

The Tower was built over two centuries by at least three different architects. You can see how each successive architect tried to cor-

LEANING TOWER

rect the leaning problem—once halfway up (after the fourth story), once at the belfry on the top.

The first stones were laid in 1173, probably under the direction of the architect Bonanno Pisano (who also designed the Duomo's bronze back door). Five years later, just as the base and the first arcade were finished, someone said, "Is it just me, or does that look crooked?" The heavy Tower—resting on a very shallow 13-foot foundation—was obviously sinking on the south side into the marshy, multilayered, unstable soil. (Actually, all of the Campo's buildings tilt somewhat.) The builders carried on anyway, until they'd finished four stories (the base, plus three arcade floors). Then, construction suddenly halted—no one knows why—and for a century the Tower sat half-finished and visibly leaning.

Around 1272, the next architect continued, trying to correct the problem by angling the next three stories backward, in the opposite direction of the lean. The project then again sat mysteriously idle for nearly another century. Finally, Tommaso Pisano put the belfry on the top (c. 1350-1372), also kinking it backward.

Man Versus Gravity

After the Tower's completion, several attempts were made to stop its slow-motion fall. The architect/artist/writer Giorgio Vasari reinforced the base in 1550, and it actually worked. But in 1838, well-intentioned engineers pumped out groundwater, destabilizing the Tower and causing it to increase its lean at a rate of a millimeter per year.

It got so bad that in 1990 the Tower was closed for repairs, and $30 million was spent trying to stabilize it. Engineers dried the soil with steam pipes, anchored the Tower to the ground with steel cables, and buried 600 tons of lead on the north side as a counterweight (not visible)—all with little success. The breakthrough came when they drilled 15-foot-long holes in the ground on the north side and sucked out 60 tons of soil, allowing the Tower to sink on the north side and straighten out its lean by about six inches.

As well as gravity, erosion threatens the Tower. Since its construction, 135 of the Tower's 180 marble columns have had to be replaced. Stone decay, deposits of lime and calcium phosphate, accumulations of dirt and moss, cracking from the stress of the lean—all of these are factors in its decline.

Thanks to the Tower's lean, there are special trouble spots. The lower south side (which is protected from cleansing rain and wind) is a magnet for dirty airborne particles, while the stone on the upper areas has more decay (from eroding rain and wind).

The Tower, now stabilized, has been cleaned as well. Cracks have been filled, and accumulations removed with carefully formulated atomized water sprays and poultices of various solvents.

Galileo and Gravity

The Leaning Tower figures prominently in scientific lore. Legend has it that the scientific pioneer Galileo Galilei dropped objects off the Tower in attempts to understand gravity. Galileo (1564-1642) was born in Pisa, grew up here on Via Giuseppe Giusti (where the family home still stands, adorned with a humble plaque), and taught math at the university. Galileo is said to have climbed the Tower and dropped two balls: one heavy and metal, the other a lighter wooden ball. Which object hit the ground first? The heavier object, of course—but through further reasoning and experimentation, Galileo figured out that the lighter object fell more slowly only because of air resistance. In doing so, he shattered the conventional wisdom, established by Aristotle, that heavier objects accelerate faster. We don't know whether Galileo actually dropped those orbs from this Tower, but we do know he tested this theory of gravity by rolling balls of different weights down ramps, which would have been easier to time (see page 261). These experiments led to Isaac Newton's formulation of the laws of gravity. Moreover, by forging theories through rigorous testing, rather than through reasoning alone (as Aristotle had), Galileo helped re-envision science itself.

All the work to shore up, straighten, and clean the Tower has probably turned the clock back a few centuries. In fact, art historians figure the Tower leans today as much as it did when Galileo reputedly conducted his gravity experiment here 400 years ago.

• *Wait's over? Great. It's time to head inside.*

Visiting the Tower

First, an attendant takes you into the room at the bottom of the tower (known as the *Sala del Pesce* for the Christian fish symbol on the wall) and offers a short explanation of the Tower's construction and history. Gape up through the hollow Tower to the oculus at the top, and marvel at the acoustics. Also check out the heavy metal braces stretching up to the top.

Then you'll wind your way up the outside along a spiraling ramp, climbing 294 stairs. At the top, you'll have fine views over the Duomo and the rest of the Field of Miracles, as well as over the rooftops of Pisa (admittedly, not the most striking city).

PISA DUOMO TOUR

The huge Pisan Romanesque cathedral, with its carved pulpit by Giovanni Pisano, is artistically more important than its more famous bell tower. Budget some sightseeing time for the church's artistic and historic treasures.

Orientation

Cost: Free; you can enter using any of the combo-tickets (see sidebar on page 421) or pick up a free voucher (valid for up to two people) at one of the ticket offices nearby.

Hours: Daily April-Sept 10:00-20:00, Oct 10:00-19:00, Nov-Feb 10:00-13:00 & 14:00-17:00, March 10:00-18:00, last entry 30 minutes before closing.

Crowd-Beating Tips: Because the Duomo is the only free interior at the Field of Miracles, it's on every tour itinerary. Local authorities plan to start monitoring the number of visitors allowed inside, which could mean you'll have to wait in line at busy times. Remember, the sights are most crowded between 12:00 and 15:00; ideally, try to see the Duomo before or after that window.

Dress Code: Shorts are OK as long as they're not too short, and shoulders should be covered (although it's not really enforced).

Audioguides: Don't let the sparkle of the new coin-operated "phone guides" tempt you. These €2 machines still use narration from a bygone era.

Length of This Tour: Allow one hour.

Baggage: Big backpacks are not allowed, nor is storage provided. If you have a day bag, carry it.

Starring: Pisano's pulpit, Galileo's lamp, and the remains of a saint.

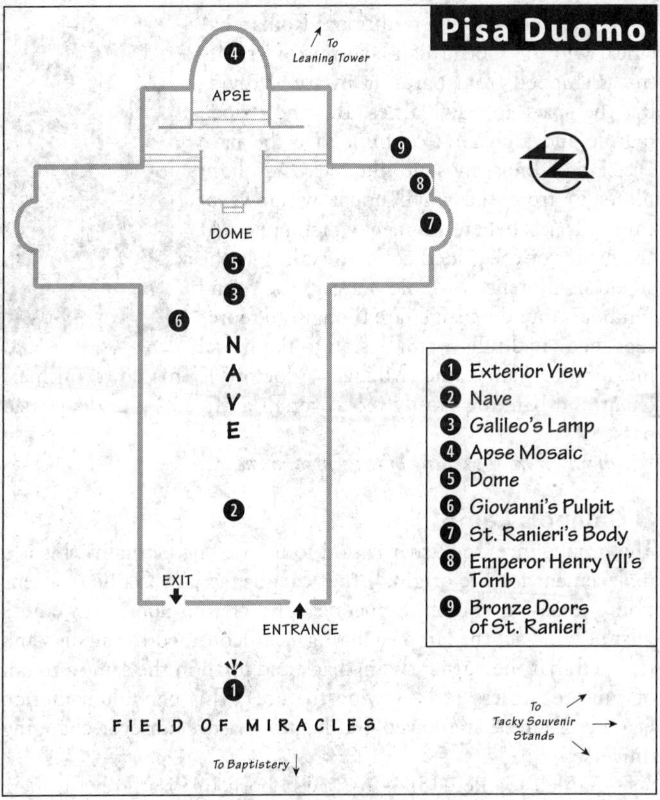

The Tour Begins

❶ Exterior

The Duomo is the centerpiece of the Field of Miracles' complex of religious buildings. Begun in 1063, it was financed by a galley-load of booty ransacked that year from the Muslim-held capital of Palermo, Sicily. The architect Buschetto created the Pisan Romanesque style that set the tone for the Baptistery and Tower. Five decades later (1118), the architect Rainaldo added the impressive main-entrance facade (which also leans out about a foot).

The lower half of the church is simple Romanesque, with blind arches. The upper half has four rows of columns that form arcades. Stripes of black-and-white marble, mosaics, stone inlay, and even recycled Roman tombstones complete the decoration.

• *Enter the church at the facade, opposite the Baptistery.*

❷ Nave

The 320-foot nave was the longest in Christendom when it was

built. It's modeled on a traditional Roman basilica, with 68 Corinthian columns of granite (most shipped from Sardinia in 1063) dividing the space into five aisles. But the striped marble and arches-on-columns give the nave an exotic, almost mosque-like feel. Dim light filters in from the small upper windows of the galleries, where women worshipped. At the center of the gilded coffered ceiling is the shield of Florence's Medici family; the round symbols around its edges are thought to represent medicinal pills—an allusion to the literal meaning of their name (Medici = "doctors"). This powerful merchant and banking family took over Pisa after its glory days had passed.

• *Hanging from the ceiling of the central nave is...*

❸ Galileo's Lamp

The bronze incense burner is said to be the one (actually, this is a replacement for the original) that caught teenage Galileo's attention one day in church. Someone left a church door open, and a gust of wind set the lamp swinging. Galileo timed the swings and realized that the burner swung back and forth in the same amount of time regardless of how wide the arc. (This pendulum motion was a constant that allowed Galileo to measure our ever-changing universe.)

Galileo Galilei (1564-1642) was born in Pisa, grew up here on Via Giuseppe Giusti, and taught math at the university (1584-1591). Legend says he dropped things off the Tower to time their falls, fascinated by gravity (see sidebar on page 429).

• *High up in the apse (behind the altar) is the...*

❹ Apse Mosaic

The mosaic (c. 1300, partly done by the great artist Cimabue) shows Christ as the Ruler of All (Pantocrator) between Mary and St. John the Evangelist. The Pantocrator image of Christ is standard fare among Eastern Orthodox Christians—that is, the "Byzantine" people who were Pisa's partners in trade.

As King of the Universe, Christ sits on a throne, facing directly out, with penetrating eyes. Only Christ can wear this style of halo, divided with a cross. In his left hand is a Bible open to the verse *"Ego Lux Sum Mundi"*—"I am the light of the world." While his feet crush the devil in serpent form, Christ blesses us with his right hand. His fingers form the Greek letters *chi* and *rho,* the first two letters of "Christos." The thumb (almost) touches the fingers, symbolizing how Christ unites both his divinity and his humanity.

❺ Dome

Look up into the dome—the heavens open, and rings of saints and angels spiral up to a hazy God. Beneath the dome is an inlaid-marble, Cosmati-style mosaic floor. The modern (and therefore controversial) marble altar and pulpit were carved by a Florentine artist in 2002.

• *Next to Galileo's Lamp, you'll find...*

❻ Giovanni's Pulpit (1301-1311)

The 15-foot-tall, octagonal pulpit by Giovanni Pisano (c. 1240-1319) is the last, biggest, and most complex of the four pulpits created by the Pisano father-and-son team. Giovanni's father, Nicola, started the family tradition four decades earlier, carving the pulpit in the Baptistery. Giovanni grew up working side-by-side with his dad on numerous projects. Now on his own, he crams everything he's learned into his crowning achievement.

Giovanni left no stone uncarved in his pursuit of beauty. Four hundred intricately sculpted figures smother the pulpit, blurring the architectural outlines. In addition, the relief panels are actually curved, making it look less like an octagon than a circle. The creamy-white Carrara marble has the look and feel of carved French ivories, which the Pisanos loved. Originally, this and the other pulpits were frosted with paint, gilding, and colored pastes.

At the base, lions roar and crouch over their prey, symbolizing how Christ (the lion) triumphs over Satan (the horse, as in the Four Horsemen of the Apocalypse).

Four of the pulpit's support "columns" are statues. The central "column" features three graceful ladies representing Faith, Hope, and Charity, the three pillars of Christianity. They in turn stand on the sturdy base of knowledge, representing the liberal arts taught at the U. of Pisa. Another column is Hercules, standing *contrapposto,* nude, holding his club and lion skin. Nearby, Lady Church suckles the babies of the Old and New Testaments, while at her feet are the Four Virtues, including Justice (with her scales), Moderation (modestly covering her nakedness), Courage (holding a lion), and Wisdom (with a horn of plenty).

Around the top of the pulpit, Christ's life unfolds in a series of panels saturated with carvings. The panels tilt out from the top, so the viewer below has a better look, and they're bordered on top with a heavy cornice as a backdrop. Since the panels are curved and unframed, you "read" Christ's life less like a nine-frame comic strip and more like a continuous scroll.

The story unfolds from left to right, beginning at the back near the stairs:

1. Story of Elizabeth and Zechariah: John the Baptist's parents.

2. Nativity: Mary lounges across a bed, unfazed by labor and delivery. Her pose is clearly inspired by carved Roman sarcophagi (which you can see in the Camposanto Cemetery), showing the dearly departed relaxing for eternity atop their coffins. Mary and the babe are surrounded by angels (above) and shepherds (right).

3. Adoration of the Magi: The Wise Men ride in with horses and camels.

4. Presentation in the Temple: On the left side, Joseph and Mary hold Baby Jesus between them. On the right side of the panel, Giovanni adds the next scene in the story, when the nuclear family gets on a donkey and escapes into Egypt.

5. Massacre of the Innocents: Herod (at the top) turns and gestures dramatically, ordering the slaughter of all babies. A mother (bottom left corner) grabs her head in despair. Giovanni uses thick lips and big noses to let the faces speak the full range of human emotions. The soldiers in the tangled chaos are almost freestanding.

6. Kiss of Judas: Jesus is betrayed by a kiss (left side).

7. Crucifixion: An emaciated Christ is mourned by his followers, who turn every which way. A Roman horseman (bottom right corner) rides directly away from us—an example of Renaissance "foreshortening" a century before its time.

8. and 9. Last Judgment: Christ sits in the center, the dead rise from their graves, and he sends the good to heaven (left) and the bad to hell (right).

Giovanni was a better pure sculptor than his father. Armed with more sophisticated chisels, he could cut even deeper into the marble, freeing heads from the stone backdrop, creating almost freestanding, 3-D figures. Where Nicola shows figures either facing forward or in profile, Giovanni mastered the difficult three-quarters angle.

If the pulpit seems a bit cluttered and asymmetrical, blame Mussolini. Originally, Giovanni built the pulpit standing on the right side of the altar (the traditional location). But after a massive fire in 1595 (when the roof burned), the pulpit was disassembled and stored away for three centuries. In 1926, they pulled it out of storage, reassembled it on this spot...and ended up with pieces left over (now in other museums), leading scholars to debate the authenticity of the current look.

• *Find the following two sights in the right (south) transept, near the back of the church. First, at the end of the transept, you'll see...*

❼ St. Ranieri's Body

In a glass-lined casket on the altar, Pisa's patron saint lies mummified, encased in silver at his head and feet, with his hair shirt covering his body. The silver, mask-like face dates from 2000 and is as realistic as possible—derived from an FBI-style computer scan of Ranieri's skull.

Ranieri Scuggeri (1117-1161) was born into the city of Pisa at its peak, when the Field of Miracles was a construction zone. (Ranieri was one year old when this Duomo was consecrated in thanks for Pisa's lucrative victory over the Muslim Saracens.) The son of a rich sea-trader, Ranieri chose the life of a hard-partying, popular, touring musician. Backstage one night, he met a mysterious stranger who changed his life. Ranieri was inspired to take his musical instrument and set it on fire, while opening his arms to the heavens (à la Jimi Hendrix). He returned to his father's shipping business and amassed a fortune. Then, one day, he smelled something funky—his own money. He gave it all away, joined a monastery, and put on a hair shirt.

The former wandering troubadour, traveling salesman, and pilgrimaging monk finally settled down in his hometown of Pisa. He devoured the Bible, then used his showmanship to wow audiences here—in the Duomo—when he took the stage atop the pulpit to deliver spirited sermons.

Ranieri, honored in grand style on June 16 and 17, is cause for Pisa's biggest local event—the Luminara—celebrated along the Arno with tens of thousands of candles lining the buildings and floating on the river. The next day, rowing teams play a game of capture-the-flag, racing to a boat in the Arno and shimmying up a long rope to claim the prize.

• *Look on the wall to the left to find...*

❽ Emperor Henry VII's Tomb

Pause at the tomb of Holy Roman Emperor Henry VII, whose untimely death plunged Pisa into its centuries-long decline. Henry lies sleeping, arms folded, his head turned to the side, resting on a soft pillow.

This German king (c. 1275-1313) invaded Italy and was welcomed by Pisans as a nonpartisan leader who could bring peace to Italy's warring Guelphs and Ghibellines. In 1312, he was crowned emperor by the pope in Rome. He returned to his base in Pisa and was preparing to polish off the last opposition when he caught a fever (or was poisoned by a priest)...and died. Ghibelline Pisa was suddenly at the mercy of Guelph rivals such as rising Florence, and the city never recovered.

• *Exit the church and walk around to its back end (facing the Tower), where you'll find (under a canopy) the...*

❾ Bronze Doors of St. Ranieri (Porta San Ranieri)

Designed by Bonanno Pisano (c. 1186)—who is thought by some historians to have been the Tower's first architect—the doors have 24 different panels that show Christ's story using the same simple, skinny figures found in Byzantine icons. (The doors are actually copies; the originals are housed—but not always on display—in the Duomo Museum.)

The story begins in the lower right panel ("Magis"), as the three Wise Men ride up a hill, heading toward...the panel to the left, where tiny Baby Jesus lies in a manger while angels and shepherds look down from above. Above the manger scene, King Herod ("Erodi") sits under a canopy (in Pisan Romanesque style) and orders a soldier to raise his sword to kill all potential Messiahs. The terrified mother pulls her hair out. In the panel to the right, John the Baptist stands under a swaying palm and baptizes the adult Jesus, who wears the rippling River Jordan like a blanket.

Cast using the lost-wax technique, these doors were an inspiration for Lorenzo Ghiberti's bronze doors in Florence.

PISA DUOMO

FIELD OF MIRACLES TOUR

Campo dei Miracoli

Imagine arriving in Pisa as a sailor in the 12th century when the Arno came to just outside the walls surrounding this square, the church here was one of the biggest in the world, and this ensemble in gleaming white marble was the most impressive space in Christendom. Calling it the Field of Miracles (Campo dei Miracoli) would not have been hyperbole.

The Leaning Tower nearly steals the show from the massive cathedral, which muscles out the other sights. But don't neglect the rest of the Field of Miracles: the Baptistery, Camposanto Cemetery, Museum of the Sinopias, and the Duomo Museum.

Orientation

Cost: €9 combo-ticket includes all the sights, plus the Duomo (credit cards accepted except AmEx; see sidebar on page 421 for run-down on various combo-tickets).

Hours: All of the sights on this tour share the same schedule: daily April-Sept 8:00-20:00, Oct 9:00-19:00, Nov-Feb 10:00-17:00, March 9:00-18:00, last entry 30 minutes before closing. Note that the Duomo Museum will likely be closed for renovation through 2016.

Getting There: The Baptistery is located in front of the Duomo's facade. The Camposanto Cemetery is behind the church on the north side of the Field of Miracles. The Museum of the Sinopias is hidden behind souvenir stands, across the street from the Baptistery entrance. The Duomo Museum is housed behind the Tower.

Length of This Tour: Allow two hours.

The Tour Begins

BAPTISTERY

Pisa's Baptistery is Italy's biggest. It's interesting for its pulpit and interior ambience, and especially great for its acoustics.

Exterior

The building is 180 feet tall—John the Baptist on top is almost eye-to-eye with the tourists looking out from the nearly 200-foot Leaning Tower. Notice that the Baptistery leans nearly six feet to the north (the Tower leans 15 feet to the south). The building (begun in 1153) is modeled on the circular-domed Church of the Holy Sepulchre in Jerusalem, seen by Pisan Crusaders who occupied Jerusalem in 1099.

From the outside, you see three distinct sections, which reflect the changing tastes of the years spent building it: simple Romanesque blind arches at the base (1153), ornate Gothic spires and pointed arches in the middle (1250), and a Renaissance dome (15th century). The roofing looks mismatched but was intentionally designed with red clay tiles on the seaward side and lead tiles (more prestigious but prone to corrosion) on the sheltered east side. The statues of the midsection are by Nicola Pisano (c. 1220-1278, Giovanni's father), who sculpted the pulpit inside.

Interior

Inside, it's simple, spacious, and baptized with light. Tall arches atop thin columns once again echo the Campo's architectural theme of arches above blank spaces. The columns encircle just a few pieces of religious furniture.

In the center sits the beautiful marble **octagonal font** (1246). A statue of the first Baptist, John the Baptist, stretches out his hand and says, "Welcome to my Baptistery." The font contains plenty of space for baptizing adults by immersion (the medieval custom), plus four wells for dunking babies.

Baptismal fonts—where sinners symbolically die and are reborn—are traditionally octagons. The shape suggests a cross (symbolizing Christ's death), and the eight sides represent the eighth day of Christ's ordeal, when he was resurrected. The font's sides,

carved with inlaid multicolored marble, feature circle-in-a-square patterns, indicating the interlocking of heaven and earth. The circles are studded with interesting faces, both human and animal. Behind the font, the altar features similar inlaid-marble work.

Nicola Pisano's Pulpit

Is this the world's first Renaissance sculpture? It's the first authenticated (signed) work by the "Giotto of sculpture," working in what came to be called the Renaissance style. The freestanding sculpture has classical columns, realistic people and animals, and 3-D effects in the carved panels.

The 15-foot-tall, hexagonal pulpit is by Nicola Pisano, and is the earliest (1260) and simplest of the four pulpits by the Pisano father-and-son team. Nicola, born in southern Italy, settled in Pisa, where he found steady work. Ten-year-old Giovanni learned the art of pulpit-making here at the feet of his father.

The speaker's platform stands on columns that rest on the backs of animals, representing Christianity's triumph over paganism. The white Carrara-marble panels are framed by dark rose-colored marble, making a pleasant contrast. Originally, this and the other pulpits were touched up with paint, gilding, and colored pastes.

The relief panels, with scenes from the life of Christ, are more readable than the Duomo pulpit. They show bigger, simpler figures in dark marble "frames." Read left to right, starting from the back:

1. Nativity: Mary reclines across a bed like a Roman matron, a pose inspired by Roman sarcophagi, which had been found around Pisa in Nicola's day (on display in the Camposanto Cemetery, described later).

2. Adoration of the Magi: The Three Kings kneel before Baby Jesus in simple profile; but notice the strong 3-D of the horses' heads coming straight out of the panel. Just below and to the left of this relief, note the small statue of Hercules. Many art historians consider this the first Renaissance carving. Sculpted in 1260—200 years before Michelangelo—it's a nude depiction of a pagan character, with a realistic body standing in a believable *contrapposto* pose. This was clearly inspired by carvings found on ancient sarcophagi.

3. Presentation in the Temple: It lacks the star of the scene, the Christ Child, who got broken off, but on the panel's right side, a powerful, bearded man in a voluminous robe epitomizes Nicola's solemn classical style.

4. Crucifixion: Everyone faces either straight out or in profile; the Roman in front actually has to look back over his shoulder to razz Jesus.

5. Last Judgment: Christ reigns over crowded, barely controlled chaos. The pulpit's lectern is an eagle clutching its prey, echoing the "triumph of Christianity" theme of the base.

Acoustics

Make a sound in here and it echoes for a good 10 seconds. A priest standing at the baptismal font (or a security guard today) can sing three tones within those 10 seconds—"Ave Maria"—and make a chord, singing haunting harmonies with himself. This medieval form of digital delay is due to the 250-foot-wide dome. Recent computer analysis suggests that the 15th-century architects who built the dome intended this building to function not just as a Baptistery, but also as a musical instrument. A security guard sings every half-hour, starting when the doors open in the morning.

Climb 75 steps to the interior gallery (midway up) for an impressive view back down on the baptismal font.

CAMPOSANTO CEMETERY

The cemetery is enclosed within the long white building (1278-1465) that borders the Field of Miracles on the north. This site has been a cemetery since at least the 12th century. Highlights are the building's cloistered interior courtyard, some ancient sarcophagi, and the large 14th-century fresco, *The Triumph of Death.*

Courtyard

The delightful open-air courtyard is surrounded by an arcade with intricately carved tracery in the arches. The courtyard's grass grows on special dirt (said to turn a body into bones in a single day) shipped here by returning Crusaders from Jerusalem's Mount Calvary, where Christ was crucified.

The arcade floor is paved with the **coats of arms** of some 600 dearly departed Pisans. In death all are equal—the most humble peasant (or tourist) can walk upon these VIP tombstones. Today much of the marble flooring is scarred, the result of lead melting from the roof during WWII bombing.

Displayed in the arcade are dozens of ancient Roman **sarcophagi.** These coffins, which originally held dead Romans, were reused by medieval big shots. In anticipation of death, a wealthy Pisan would shop around, choose a good sarcophagus, and chip his message into it. When he died, his marble box was placed with the others around the exterior of the cathedral. Great sculptors such as Nicola and Giovanni Pisano passed them daily, gaining inspiration.

Circle the courtyard clockwise, noticing **traces of fresco** on the bare-brick walls. (We'll see some reconstructed frescoes later.) The huge **chains** on the west wall once stretched across the mouth of Pisa's harbor as a defense. Then Genoa attacked, broke the chains, carried them off as a war trophy, and gave them to Pisa's archrival Florence. After unification, they were returned to Pisa as a token of friendship.

Straight ahead is the cemetery's oldest object, an ochre-colored Greek tombstone. This **stele,** dating from the time of Alexander the Great (fourth century B.C.), shows a woman (seated) who's just given birth. A maid (standing) shows the baby while the mother gazes on adoringly.

In the floor 10 yards away, by the corner of the courtyard, is a **pavement slab** dedicated to an American artist, Deane Keller. After serving in Italy during World War II as one of the "Monuments Men," he helped rebuild the Camposanto Cemetery and restore its frescoes.

On the wall in the corner, what looks like a big, faded **bull's-**

eye is the politically correct 14th-century view of the universe—everything held by Christ, with the earth clearly in the center.

World War II Photos

At the back of the courtyard—opposite where you entered—step through the door to see photos of the bombed-out Camposanto. You might also catch a 15-minute video that highlights the cemetery's reconstruction (seating limited). By the summer of 1944, Allied troops had secured much of southern Italy and pushed Nazi forces to the north bank of the Arno. German Field Marshal Kesselring dug in at Pisa, surrounded by the US Army's 91st Infantry. Germans and Americans lobbed artillery shells at each other. (The Americans even considered blowing up the Leaning Tower—the "Tiltin' Hilton" was suspected to be the German lookout point.) Most of the Field of Miracles was miraculously unscathed, but the Camposanto took a direct hit from a Yankee incendiary grenade. It melted the lead-covered arcade roof and peeled historic frescoes from the walls—one of the many tragic art losses of World War II. The Americans liberated the city on September 2 and rebuilt the Camposanto.

Some of the much-damaged frescoes are displayed in this big hall. (After careful restoration, these are now slowly and steadily being returned to their original spots on the walls of the Camposanto.)

The Triumph of Death

This 1,000-square-foot fresco (on the left wall, c. 1340, by an unknown 14th-century master) captures late-medieval Europe's concern with death—predating but still accurately depicting Pisa's mood in the wake of the bubonic plague (1348), which killed one in three Pisans. Well-dressed ladies and gents (left half of the painting) are riding gaily through the countryside when they come across three coffins with corpses (bottom left). Confronted with death, they each react differently—a woman puts her hand thoughtfully to her chin, a man holds his nose against the stench, while a horse leans in for a better whiff. Above them, a monk scours the Bible for the meaning of death. Mr. Death, a winged demon with a scythe, stands to the right of center and eyes his future victims.

In the right half of the painting, young people gather in a garden (bottom right) to play music (symbolizing earthly pleasure), oblivious to the death around them. Winged demons swoop down from above to pluck souls from a pile of corpses, while winged angels fight them for the souls. The action continues in the next fresco (the room's far wall), where Jesus and Mary judge the dead at the Last Judgment. The wicked are led away to hell (the right side of the fresco) to be tortured by a horned Satan. Grim stuff, but appropriate for the Camposanto's permanent residents—and to anyone alive who needed a reminder of the fleeting and corruptive nature of wealth and worldly pleasures.

As you leave the fresco room, look left to see a third-century A.D. **Roman sarcophagus** carved with mythological scenes.

Back Outside

Stepping back into the piazza, consider how this richly artistic but utilitarian square fit into the big picture of life. The ensemble around you includes the Baptistery, the cathedral, the bell tower, the hospital (present-day Museum of the Sinopias), and the Christian cemetery you just visited. The Jewish cemetery is adjacent but just outside the walls. Pisa, a pragmatic port town, needed the money and business connections of the Jews and treated them relatively well for the age. Unlike in Rome or Venice, there was no Jewish ghetto here in the Middle Ages.

MUSEUM OF THE SINOPIAS (MUSEO DELLE SINOPIE)

Housed in a 13th-century hospital, this museum features the preparatory sketches (sinopias) for the Camposanto's WWII-damaged frescoes. If you loved *The Triumph of Death* and others in the Camposanto, or if you're interested in fresco technique, this museum is worthwhile. If not, you'll wonder why you're here.

Whether or not you pay to go in, you can watch two free videos in the entry lobby that serve to orient you to the square: a seven-minute, 3-D computer tour of the complex and a 15-minute story of the Tower, its tilt, and its fix.

Just past the ticket-taker, you'll see the multiringed, earth-centric, Ptolemaic universe of the *Theological Cosmography*. Continue to your right to find a faint *Crucifixion* and scenes from the Old Testament. At the end of the long hall, climb the stairs to the next floor to find (near the end of the right wall) the red-tinted sinopias for *The Triumph of Death* and the *Last Judgment* and *Hell*.

Sinopias are sketches made in red paint directly on the wall, designed to guide the making of the final colored fresco. The master always did the sinopia himself. It was a way for him (and for those who paid for the work) to see exactly how the scene would look in its designated spot. If it wasn't quite right, the master changed a detail here and there. Next, assistants made a "cartoon" by tracing the sinopia onto large sheets of paper *(cartone)*. Then the sinopia was plastered over. To put the drawing back on the wall, assistants perforated the drawing on the cartoon, hung the cartoon over the wall, and dabbed it with a powdered bag of charcoal. This process printed dotted lines onto the newly plastered wall, re-creating the cartoon. While the plaster was still wet, the master and his team quickly filled in the color and details, producing the final frescoes (now on display at the Camposanto). These sinopias—never meant to be seen—were uncovered by the bombing and restoration of the Camposanto and brought here.

DUOMO MUSEUM (MUSEO DELL'OPERA DEL DUOMO)

Near the Tower is the entrance to the Duomo Museum, which houses many of the original statues and much of the artwork that once adorned the Campo's buildings (where copies stand today), notably the statues by Nicola and Giovanni Pisano. The museum will likely be closed for restoration through sometime in 2016. But if it's open, here's some of what you'll see.

The museum has several large-scale wooden models of the Duomo, Baptistery, and Tower, as well as the Duomo's original 12th-century bronze doors of St. Ranieri, with scenes from the life of Jesus, done by Bonanno Pisano. Farther in, you can stand face-to-face with the Pisanos' very human busts, which once ringed the outside of the Baptistery. Giovanni Pisano's stone *Madonna del Colloquio* solemnly exchanges gazes with Baby Jesus in her arms. The most charming piece is Giovanni's small, carved-ivory *Madonna and Child.* Mary leans back gracefully to admire Baby Jesus, her pose matching the original shape of what she's carved from—an elephant's tusk.

You'll see a mythical sculpted hippogriff (a medieval jackalope) and other oddities brought back from the Holy Land by Pisan Crusaders. The church treasury is here as well, with vestments, chalices, and bishops' staves.

On the next floor up, you'll see the fine inlaid woodwork that once graced the choir stalls of the sacristy, as well as illuminated manuscripts. The collection of antiquities includes Etruscan funerary urns with reclining people—the inspiration for the Roman sarcophagi that inspired the Pisanos. Beyond the ancient sculptures are beautiful small-scale copies of the Camposanto frescoes, painted in the 1830s. There's also a scene that shows the building's appearance before it was bombed.

The museum's grassy interior courtyard has a two-story, tourist-free view of the Tower, Duomo, and Baptistery.

PISA SLEEPING, EATING & CONNECTIONS

Sleeping in Pisa

Pisa is an easy side-trip from Florence or Lucca, either of which is a more all-around pleasant place to stay. But there's more to Pisa than the Tower, and if you want time to experience it, consider a night here. To locate these hotels, see the map on page 414.

NORTH OF THE RIVER, NEAR THE TOWER

$$$ Hotel Royal Victoria, a classy place along the Arno River, claims to be the oldest hotel in Italy; while a hotel has stood here since around 1100, this version has been run by the Piegaja family since 1837. With 44 creaky, historical rooms filled with antiques, it's ideal for romantics who missed out on the Grand Tour. The location, dead-center between the Tower and Pisa Centrale train station, is the most atmospheric of my listings (S-€55, D-€80, standard Db-€120, "traditional" Db-€155, suite-€200, family rooms, breakfast-€5, 10 percent discount with this book if you book directly with the hotel, check website for special deals, half-price off-season, air-con on request, elevator, Wi-Fi, parking garage-€20/day, bike rental, lush communal terrace, Lungarno Pacinotti 12, tel. 050-940-111, www.royalvictoria.it, mail@royalvictoria.it).

$$ Hotel Pisa Tower overlooks the tacky-souvenir-stand square just outside the gate to the Field of Miracles, along a busy street. But the location couldn't be handier to the big sights, and the 12 rooms are crisp, modern, and romantically decorated. Their annex—a long block away—has 13 similar rooms at the same prices (Db-€80, prices very flexible, no breakfast, air-con, Wi-Fi, Piazza Daniele Manin 9, tel. 050-5200700, www.hotelpisatower.com, info@hotelpisatower.com).

$$ Hotel Villa Kinzica has 30 tired, worn rooms with high

Sleep Code

(€1 = about $1.40, country code: 39)

Abbreviations

S = Single, **D** = Double/Twin, **T** = Triple, **Q** = Quad, **b** = bathroom, **s** = shower only

Price Rankings

$$$ **Higher Priced**—Most rooms €135 or more.

$$ **Moderately Priced**—Most rooms between €80-135.

$ **Lower Priced**—Most rooms €80 or less.

Unless otherwise noted, credit cards are accepted, breakfast is included, Wi-Fi is generally free, and English is spoken. Pisa, like many towns in Italy, levies a hotel tax of €1-2 per person, per night, which is not usually included in the rates I've quoted. Prices change; verify current rates online or by email. For the best prices, always book directly with the hotel.

ceilings—and a prime location just steps from the Field of Miracles; ask for a room with a view of the Tower, ideally #42 (Sb-€70, Db-€89, Tb-€109, Qb-€119, better prices off-season, air-con, elevator, guest computer, Wi-Fi, Piazza Arcivescovado 2, tel. 050-560-419, www.hotelvillakinzica.com, info@hotelvillakinzica.com).

$ Casa San Tommaso has 22 fresh but classic-feeling, homey rooms in a big house on a quiet back lane about a five-minute walk from the Tower (Sb-€58, Db-€68, no breakfast, air-con, Wi-Fi, Via San Tommaso 13, tel. 050-830-782, www.casasantommaso.it, santommaso@paimturismo.it).

$ Pensione Helvetia is a no-frills, homey, clean, and quiet inn just 100 yards from the Tower. Its 29 economical rooms are spread over four floors (no elevator); the lower your room number, the lower your altitude (S-€45, Sb-€54, D-€54, Db-€60, Tb-€75, no breakfast but small lounge with vending machines, ceiling fans, guest computer, Wi-Fi, Via Don G. Boschi 31, tel. 050-553-084, www.pensionehelvetiapisa.com, helvetiapisatravel@gmail.com, Maria, Sandra, and Micaele).

SOUTH OF THE RIVER, NEAR THE TRAIN STATION

This zone is far less atmospheric than the zone near the Tower—with a lot of concrete and congestion. Stay here only if you value the convenience of proximity to the station.

$$$ Hotel Alessandro della Spina, in a nondescript neighborhood near Pisa Centrale train station, has 16 elegant and colorful rooms, each named after a flower (Sb-€140, Db-€180, discounts off-season and online, air-con, guest computer, Wi-Fi, parking-€10/day; head straight out from the train station, turn right on Viale F. Bonaini, and then take the third right on Via Alessandro della Spina—the hotel is on your left at #5; tel. 050-502-777, www.hoteldellaspina.it, info@hoteldellaspina.it).

$ Hotel Milano, near Pisa Centrale train station, is run with youthful enthusiasm. Barbara and Francisco offer 10 simple, clean rooms (D-€50, Db-€65, 10 percent discount for Rick Steves readers if you book directly with the hotel, no breakfast, Wi-Fi, air-con, Via Mascagni 14, tel. 050-23-162, www.hotelmilano.pisa.it, hotelmilano.pisa@gmail.com).

Eating in Pisa

A QUICK LUNCH CLOSE TO THE TOWER

Particularly for day-trippers, a quick lunch may be all you need here. Fortunately, several good options are tucked between the many interchangeable snack stands.

At **Paninoteca il Canguro,** Fabio makes warm, hearty sandwiches to order. Check the chalkboard for seasonal specials, such as *porchetta* (€3-5 sandwiches, €7 pastas, same prices to eat in or take out, daily 9:00-24:00, may be closed Sun in winter, Via Santa Maria 151, tel. 050-561-942).

Panetteria Antiche Tradizioni—not to be confused with another *panetteria* across the street—is a sandwich/bread shop with complete fixings for a picnic. Build your own sandwich with homemade bread or focaccia, then choose fruit from the counter, fresh pastries from the window, and cold drinks or wine to round out your meal. If you prefer, you can sit in the air-conditioned back room or out on the streetside terrace for no extra charge (€3-5 sandwiches, daily 8:00-20:00, Via Santa Maria 66, tel. 050-561-1857).

Pizzeria al Bagno di Nerone is a local favorite and particularly popular with students. Belly up to the bar and grab a slice to go, or sit in their small dining room for a whole pie. Try the €3 *cecina,* a crepe-like garbanzo-bean cake (€5-8 pizzas, Wed-Mon 12:00-14:30 & 18:00-22:30, closed Tue, a 5-minute walk from the Tower at Largo Carlo Fedeli 26, tel. 050-551-085). Don't mistake this for the similarly named *gelateria* a bit closer to the Tower.

REAL MEALS DEEPER IN THE TOWN CENTER

Make no mistake: Pisa is in Tuscany. And if you want to sample some famously delicious Tuscan cuisine, these restaurants make it easy. All are within about a 10- to 15-minute walk from the Tower, near the river, and several are within a few steps of the old Renaissance-style market loggia, Piazza delle Vettovaglie (described on page 419).

La Vineria di Piazza is a quintessential little Tuscan trattoria tucked under the arcades of Piazza delle Vettovaglie. The chalkboard menu lists today's choices: a few *antipasti*, a few *primi* (homemade pastas and soups), and a few *secondi*. This place feels sophisticated, but without pretense. Sit in the elegantly simple interior or out at long tables facing the market. Most days, they serve lunch only (€8-9 pastas, €9-14 *secondi,* Sun-Thu 12:30-15:00, Fri-Sat 12:30-15:00 & 19:30-23:00, Piazza delle Vettovaglie 14, tel. 050-382-0433).

Pane e Vino is a delightful *pizzicheria/enoteca/spuntineria* (grocery/wine bar/place to eat) overlooking the very local-feeling Piazza Chiara Gambacorti, just south of the river. Step inside to review the display case, with a few carefully selected, seasonal Tuscan dishes (homemade pastas, soups, and *secondi*) prepared each day. They can also whip you up a sandwich with your choice of top-quality local ingredients. You can sit at one of the few tables tucked in the back, out on the square, or take your food to go—all for the same price (€3-5 sandwiches, €8-10 meals, vegetarian options, Tue-Sat 12:30-15:00 & 18:00-23:30, open Sun for dinner in summer and for lunch in winter, closed Mon, Piazza Chiara Gambacorti 7, mobile 347-531-4312).

Antica Trattoria il Campano, just off the market square, has a typically Tuscan menu and a candlelit, stay-awhile atmosphere. Their €30 tasting menus include wine and generous portions of local specialties. The ground floor, surrounded by wine bottles, is cozier, while the upstairs—with high wood-beam ceilings—is classier (€8-9 pastas, €15-16 *secondi,* €15 fixed-price lunches, Fri-Tue 12:30-15:00 & 19:30-22:45, Thu 19:30-22:45, closed Wed, reservations smart, Via Cavalca 19, tel. 050-580-585, Giovanna).

Ristorante Bagus, tucked in a gloomy square just off the river, attempts trendy twists on typical Tuscan fare in a modern setting (€9-10 pastas, €14-18 *secondi,* €30 fixed-price meal, Mon-Fri 12:30-14:30 & 19:30-23:00, Sat 19:30-23:00 only, closed Sun; heading south on Corso Italia, turn right on Via Nunziata and take your first right after Piazza Griletti to Piazza dei Facchini 13; tel. 050-26196).

Pizza: **Il Montino** is every local's favorite for tasty, no-frills pizza. Tucked behind a church in a grubby corner deep in the old center, it has a loyal following—particularly among students. Enjoy full pies in the old-school interior or out on the alley, or get a slice to go (€6-8 pizzas, Mon-Sat 11:30-15:00 & 17:30-22:30, Vicolo del Monte 1, tel. 050-598-695).

Lively Beer Hall: **Orzo Bruno**—*il birrifico artigiano* ("the artisan brewpub")—is the place to go to relive your student days. This lively, rollicking brewpub is filled with Pisans of all ages enjoying the five different microbrews and simple menu of sandwiches and salads (€5-8 pub grub, nightly 19:00-24:00, Via Case Dipinte 6, tel. 050-578-802).

NEAR THE TRAIN STATION

Da Michele is a handy choice if you are sleeping near the train station. A family-run, basic affair, the home-cooking is tasty and reasonably priced, and the place stays open late. The tiramisù is a classic (€6-8 pastas, €7-11 *secondi*, daily 12:00-15:00 & 18:00-23:00, sometimes closed Wed, a 3-minute walk from recommended Hotel Alessandro della Spina heading toward the station at Viale Bonaini 96, tel. 050-24128).

Pisa Connections

Pisa has good connections by train, bus, or car. The busy airport is practically downtown.

Side-Tripping to Lucca: Pisa and Lucca are well-connected by train and by bus (both options are about €3), making a half-day side-trip from one town to the other particularly easy. The **train** takes about half as long as the bus (about 25-30 minutes compared with 50 minutes)—but getting to the train station is more time-consuming, so it's a toss-up. If you're heading directly to Lucca from the Leaning Tower, you can catch the train at San Rossore Station, a gloomy 10-minute walk from the Tower (the station area is a maze of tunnels; leave yourself enough time to find the ticket machines and make it to the platform).

A handy **bus** connects the Field of Miracles with Lucca's Piazzale Giuseppe Verdi in about 50 minutes (Mon-Sat hourly, fewer on Sun, buy ticket on bus; in Pisa, wait at the Vai Bus signpost, immediately outside the wall behind the Baptistery on the right). You can also catch this bus at Pisa's airport, Pisa Centrale train station, or around the corner from Pisa's TI.

From Pisa Centrale Station by Train to: Florence (2-3/hour, 45-75 minutes), **Livorno** (2-3/hour, 20 minutes), **Rome** (2/hour, many change in Florence, 3-4 hours), **La Spezia,** gateway to Cinque Terre (about hourly, 1-1.5 hours), **Siena** (2/hour, 1.75 hours, change at Empoli), **Lucca** (1-2/hour, 25-30 minutes; also see bus option, earlier). Even the fastest trains stop in Pisa, so you might change trains here whether you plan to stop or not.

By Car: The drive between Pisa and Florence is that rare case where the non-autostrada highway (free, more direct, and at least as fast) is a better deal than the autostrada.

By Plane: Pisa's handy **Galileo Galilei Airport**—which is just two miles from the train station ("So close you can walk," locals brag)—handles both international and domestic flights (airport code: PSA, tel. 050-849-300, www.pisa-airport.com). Two different buses zip you into central Pisa: a shuttle bus designed for train travelers, which drops you off just behind Pisa Centrale train station (€1.30, runs every 10 minutes; someday this may be replaced by a tram); and public bus LAM Rossa, which stops first at the station and then continues to the Leaning Tower (every 10 minutes, €1.20 ticket at kiosk, €2 on board). If you're heading for the station, either bus will do; if you're making a beeline for the Field of Miracles, take LAM Rossa. A taxi into town costs €10-15.

Pisa's airport is handy for other towns as well: The bus to **Lucca** (described above) originates at the airport. To reach **Florence**—or other destinations in Italy—take the shuttle bus to Pisa Centrale train station and connect from there (allow about 1.5 hours total). Two companies also run buses from the airport directly to Florence's Santa Maria Novella train station in about 1.5 hours: Terravision (€6, about hourly, www.terravision.eu) and Autostradale (€7.50, typically coordinated with Ryanair flights, online discounts, www.autostradale.it).

LUCCA

Surrounded by well-preserved ramparts, layered with history, alternately quaint and urbane, Lucca charms its visitors. The city is a paradox. Though it hasn't been involved in a war since 1430, it is Italy's most impressive fortress city, encircled by a perfectly intact wall. Most cities tear down their walls to make way for modern traffic, but Lucca's effectively keeps out both traffic and, it seems, the stress of the modern world. Locals are very protective of their wall, which they enjoy like a community roof garden.

Lucca, known for being Europe's leading producer of toilet paper and tissue (with a monopoly on the special machinery that makes it), is nothing to sneeze at. However, the town has no single monumental sight to attract tourists—it's simply a uniquely human and undamaged, never-bombed city. Romanesque churches seem to be around every corner, as do fun-loving and shady piazzas filled with soccer-playing children.

Locals say Lucca is like a cake with a cherry filling in the middle...every slice is equally good. Despite Lucca's charm, few tourists seem to put it on their maps, and it remains a city for the Lucchesi (loo-KAY-zee).

PLANNING YOUR TIME

Low-impact Lucca has no must-see sights, but its pleasant ambience, ample churches, and pristine piazzas reward any time you've got. With the better part of a day, stroll through the town center, dipping into the sights that interest you. Once you've had your fill, rent a bike and do a few spins around the ramparts (or do the loop in slow motion, by foot) before dinner.

Orientation to Lucca

Lucca (population 87,000) is big enough to be engaging but small enough to be manageable. Everything of interest to a visitor is within the 2.5-mile-long city wall; it takes just 15-20 minutes to walk from one end of the old town to the other. The train station sits just south of the wall (near the cathedral), and the bus stop from Pisa is just inside the western tip. My self-guided walk traces the main thoroughfares through town; venturing beyond these streets, you realize Lucca is bigger than it first seems, but its back streets are very sleepy. While the core of the town is based on an old Roman grid street plan, the surrounding areas—especially near the circular footprint of the amphitheater—are less intuitive. This, combined with tall houses and a lack of consistent signage, makes Lucca easy to get lost in. Use a map to find your way back to landmarks.

TOURIST INFORMATION

Lucca has two TIs. The very helpful main TI, on **Piazzale Giuseppe Verdi,** offers city information and a no-fee room-booking service (daily April-Sept 9:00-19:00, Oct-March 9:00-17:00, futuristic WC-€0.60, baggage storage—see "Helpful Hints," later, tel. 0583-583-150, www.luccaitinera.it).

The second TI, which may be useful for drivers, is west of town on Via Luporini (between Via Parri and Via delle Città Gemelle), at the tourist-bus checkpoint and near parking (April-Sept 9:00-17:00, closed Oct-March, tel. 0583-583-462).

ARRIVAL IN LUCCA

By Train: There is no baggage check at the train station, but you can leave luggage at Tourist Center Lucca (near the station) or at the main TI on Piazzale Guiseppe Verdi (see "Helpful Hints" for specifics on both).

To reach the city center from the train station, walk toward the walls and head left, to the entry at Porta San Pietro. Or, if you don't mind steps, go straight ahead and follow the path through the moat-like park to go up and over the wall. Taxis may be waiting out front; otherwise, try calling 025-353 (ignore any recorded message—just wait for a live operator); a ride from the station to Piazza dell'Anfiteatro costs about €10.

By Bus: Buses from Pisa, Viareggio, and nearby villages arrive inside the walls at Piazzale Giuseppe Verdi, where the main TI is located.

By Car: The key for drivers: Don't try to drive within the walls. Much of the center of Lucca is designated a "ZTL" (limited traffic zone), which could cost you a €90 fine. The old town is ringed by parking lots (with two just inside the walls, both usually full).

An easy option is to park near the tour-bus lot and second TI, not far from the southwest wall. As you leave the autostrada, follow signs for *Bus Turistico Checkpoint*, which will lead you to parking lots on Via Luporini—one is for buses, but the other has free and paid parking for cars. White lines denote free parking, and blue lines are paid parking (daily 8:00-20:00, €1-1.50/hour, pay at automated kiosks). Avoid the yellow lines—these spots are for locals only. From here it's about a five-minute walk to Porta Sant'Anna.

Parking is always free in Piazzale Don Franco, a five-minute walk north of the city walls. If you must park inside the city walls, try just inside Porta Santa Maria (€1.50/hour). Or consider parking outside the gates near the train station or on the boulevard surrounding the city (meter rates vary; also about €1/hour). Overnight parking (20:00-8:00) on city streets and in city lots is usually free. Check with your hotelier to be sure.

HELPFUL HINTS

Shops and Museums Alert: Shops close most of Sunday and Monday mornings. Many museums are closed on Monday as well.

Markets: Lucca's atmospheric markets are worth visiting. Every third weekend of the month (whenever the third Sun falls), one of the largest **antique markets** in Italy sprawls in the blocks between Piazza Antelminelli and Piazza San Giovanni (8:00-19:00). The last weekend of the month, local artisans sell **arts and crafts** around town, mainly near the cathedral (also 8:00-19:00). At the **general market,** held Wednesdays and Saturdays, you'll find produce and household goods (8:30-13:00, from Porta Elisa to Porta San Jacopo on Via dei Bacchettoni).

Concerts: San Giovanni Church hosts one-hour concerts featuring a pianist and singers performing highlights from hometown composer Giacomo Puccini (€20 at the door, €18 advance purchase at TI and some hotels, daily April-Oct at 19:00, Nov-March check schedule and location at www.puccinielasualucca.com).

Festival: On September 13 and 14, the city celebrates Volto Santo ("Holy Face"), with a procession of the treasured local crucifix and a fair in Piazza Antelminelli.

Internet Access: Cafés around town have free Wi-Fi with a purchase. If you need a terminal, head for **Betty Blue,** a wine

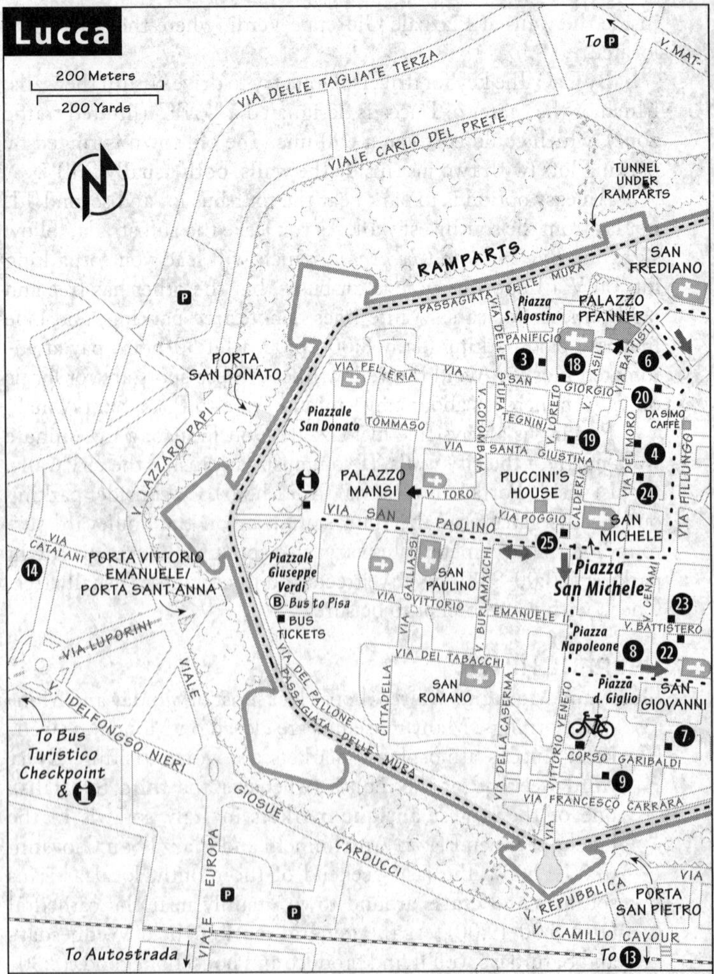

Accommodations

1. A Palazzo Busdraghi
2. La Romea B&B
3. La Locanda Sant'Agostino
4. La Bohème B&B
5. Hotel la Luna
6. Alla Dimora Lucense
7. Albergo San Martino
8. Alla Dimora Lucense
9. Le Violette B&B
10. Ostello San Frediano
11. To Hotel San Marco
12. Hotel Rex
13. To Hotel Moderno
14. La Mimosa B&B
15. Sogni d'Oro Guest House

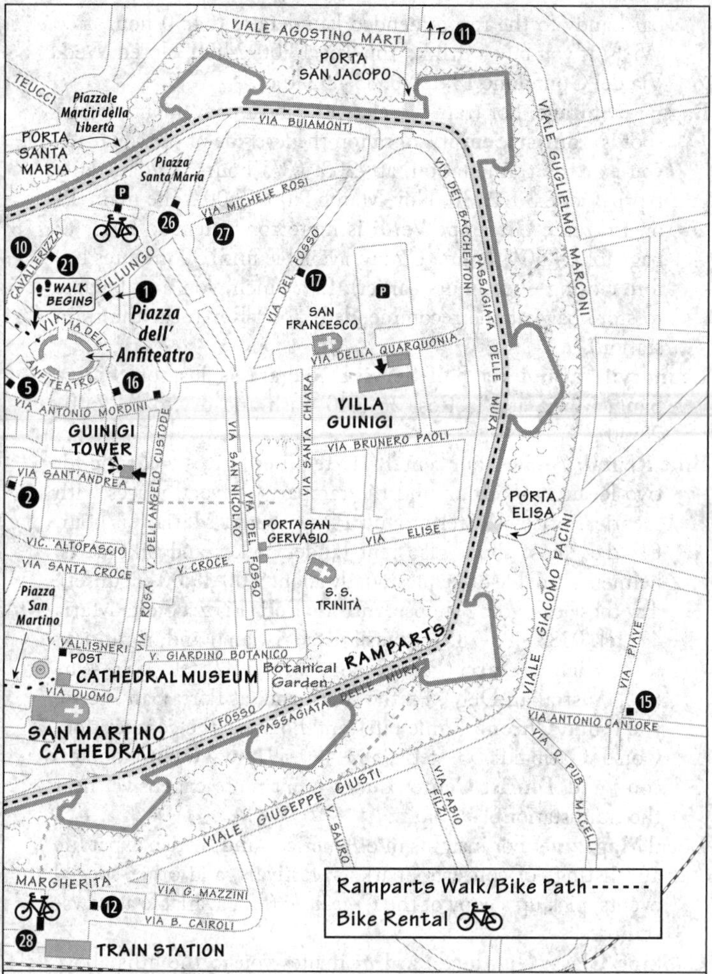

Eateries & Other

- 16 Canuleia Trattoria
- 17 Port Ellen Clan
- 18 Vecchia Trattoria Buralli
- 19 Trattoria da Leo
- 20 Osteria Via San Giorgio
- 21 Bella 'Mbriana Pizzeria
- 22 Il Cuore Enogastronomia/Rist.
- 23 Il Cuore Bistrot
- 24 Pizzeria da Felice
- 25 De' Coltelli Gelateria
- 26 Betty Blue (Internet Access)
- 27 Launderette
- 28 Tourist Center Lucca (Bag Storage, Bikes)

bar handy to the recommended launderette (€4.50/hour, free Wi-Fi if you buy a drink, Thu-Tue 13:00-24:00, closed Wed, Via del Gonfalone 18, tel. 0583-492-166).

Baggage Storage: For train travelers, the most convenient storage spot is **Tourist Center Lucca** (on the left side of the square as you exit the train station, at #203, €3/3 hours, €5/day, daily April-Oct 8:30-19:30, Nov-March 9:00-18:00). The main TI on **Piazzale Giuseppe Verdi** is more convenient to buses (2 bags for €4.50/5 hours, €7/day, available until 30 minutes before closing—see hours earlier). In a pinch, you may be able to store bags at the recommended Hotel Rex (near the train station).

Laundry: Lavanderia Self-Service Niagara is just off Piazza Santa Maria at Via Rosi 26 (€10 wash and dry, daily 7:00-23:00).

Bike Rental: A one-hour rental (ID required) gives you time for two leisurely loops around the ramparts. Several places with identical prices cluster around Piazza Santa Maria (€3/hour, €15/day, most shops also rent tandem bikes and bike carts, helmets available on request, daily about 9:00-19:00 or sunset). Try these easygoing shops: **Antonio Poli** (Piazza Santa Maria 42, tel. 0583-493-787, enthusiastic Cristiana) and, right next to it, **Cicli Bizzarri** (Piazza Santa Maria 32, tel. 0583-496-682, Australian Dely). At the south end, at Porta San Pietro, you'll find **Chronò** (same rates and hours as the competition, Corso Garibaldi 93, tel. 0583-490-591, www.chronobikes.com) and **Tourist Center Lucca** (a bit more expensive, near the train station).

Local Magazine: For insights into American and British expat life and listings of concerts, markets, festivals, and other special events, pick up a copy of the *Grapevine* (€2), available at newsstands.

Cooking Class: Gianluca Pardini invites you to the hills above Lucca to learn to make Tuscan fare. You prepare and then eat a four-course meal. Depending on how many others attend, the price ranges from €50 (a steal) to a whopping €125 per person. This is great for groups of four or more (€14 cab ride from town, 3-hour lesson plus time to dine, includes wine, reserve at least 2 days in advance, Via di San Viticchio 414, tel. 0583-378-071, mobile 347-678-7447, www.italiancuisine.it, info@italiancuisine.it).

Language School: LIS (Lucca Italian School) offers a variety of immersive one- and two-week Italian language classes, with options including cultural activities, cooking classes, and nature walks. They can arrange lodging ranging from homestays to B&Bs and apartments (Via Sant'Anna 14, see website for prices and course details, book online and mention Rick Steves for a 10 percent discount, tel. 0583-311-051, www.luccaitalianschool.com, info@luccaitalianschool.com).

Tours in Lucca

Walking Tours

The TI offers two-hour guided city walks in English and Italian, departing from the office on Piazzale Giuseppe Verdi (€10, daily at 14:00, tel. 0583-583-150).

Local Guide

Gabriele Calabrese knows and shares his hometown well (€120/3 hours, by foot or bike, mobile 347-788-0667, www.turislucca.com, turislucca@turislucca.com).

Lucca Walk

Visitors quickly discover that there's not much to actually "do" in Lucca, beyond biking its walls, dipping into a few churches, and considering some mediocre museums. But this sane and sleepy town is ideal for strolling and browsing. This hour-long walk (not counting time at the sights) connects Lucca's main points of interest by way of its most entertaining streets. A visit to Lucca has no single, logical starting point (since the bus stop, train station, and parking lots are in different corners of town), so I've started this walk right in the heart of things, at Lucca's main square.

Piazza dell'Anfiteatro

The architectural ghost of a Roman amphitheater can be felt in the delightful Piazza dell'Anfiteatro. With the fall of Rome, the theater (which seated 10,000 and sat just outside the rectangular city walls) was gradually cannibalized for its stones and inhabited by people living in a mishmash of huts. The huts were cleared away at the end of the 19th century to better show off the town's illustrious past. Today, the square is a circle of touristy shops, mediocre restaurants, and inviting al fresco cafés.

(For a cheap seat on the square, buy a gelato at Gelateria Anfiteatro, at #18, and nurse it at one of their tables.) The modern street level is nine feet above the original arena floor. The only bits of surviving Roman stonework are a few arches on the northern exterior (at Via Fillungo 42 and on Via dell'Anfiteatro).

The History of Lucca

Lucca began as a Roman settlement. In fact, the grid layout of the streets (and the shadow of an amphitheater) survives from Roman times. Trace the rectangular Roman wall—indicated by today's streets—on the map. As in typical Roman towns, two main roads quartered the fortified town, crossing at what was the forum (main market and religious/political center)—today's Piazza San Michele. The amphitheater sat just outside the original Roman walls.

Christianity came here early; it's said that the first bishop of Lucca was a disciple of St. Peter. While churches were built here as early as the fourth century, the majority of Lucca's elegant Romanesque churches date from about the 12th century.

Feisty Lucca, though never a real power, enjoyed a long period of independence (maintained by clever diplomacy). Aside from 30 years of being ruled from Pisa in the 14th century, Lucca was basically an independent city-state until Napoleon came to town.

In the Middle Ages, wealthy Lucca's economy was built on the silk industry, dominated by the Guinigi (gwee-NEE-jee) family. Paolo Guinigi (1372-1432)—whose name you'll see everywhere around town—was the Lord of Lucca for the first three decades of the 15th century, during which time he spurred the town's growth and development. Without silk, Lucca would have been just another sleepy Italian town. By 1500, the town had 3,000 silk looms employing 25,000 workers. Banking was also big. Many pilgrims stopped here on their way to the Holy Land, deposited their money for safety...and never returned to pick it up.

In its heyday, Lucca packed 160 towers—one on nearly every corner—and 70 churches within its walls. Each tower was the home of a wealthy merchant family. Towers were many stories tall, with single rooms stacked atop each other: ground-floor shop, upstairs living room, and top-floor fire-safe kitchen, all connected by exterior wooden staircases. The rooftop was generally a vegetable garden, with trees providing shade. Later, the wealthy city folk moved into the countryside, trading away life in their city palazzos to establish farm estates complete with fancy villas. (You can visit some of these villas today—the TI has a brochure—but they're convenient only for drivers and are generally not worth the cost of admission.)

In 1799, Napoleon stormed into Italy and took a liking to Lucca. He liked it so much that he gave it to his sister (who ruled 1805-1814). After Napoleon was toppled, Europe's ruling powers gave Lucca to Maria Luisa, the daughter of the king of Spain. Duchess Maria Luisa (who ruled 1817-1824) was partially responsible for turning the city's imposing (but no longer particularly useful) fortified wall into a fine city park that is much enjoyed today. Her statue stands on Piazza Napoleone, near Palazzo Ducale.

• *There are four exits from this square. Take the one between #16 and #17, toward the* Baralla *sign. Turn left down the little alley. You'll soon pass the tempting Pizzicheria La Grotta* salumi *shop on the left, then turn left onto the busy shopping street, Via Fillungo. After a block, you'll reach a little square on the right, which leads to the beautiful mosaic-slathered facade of the...*

Church of San Frediano

This impressive church was built in 1112 by the pope to counter Lucca's bishop and his spiffy cathedral. Lucca was the first Mediterranean stop on the pilgrim route from northern Europe, and the pope wanted to remind pilgrims that the action, the glory, and the papacy awaited them in Rome. Therefore, he had the church made "Roman-esque." The pure marble facade frames an early Christian Roman-style mosaic of Christ with his 12 apostles.

Cost and Hours: Free, Mon-Sat 8:30-12:00 & 15:00-17:30, Sun 9:00-11:30 & 15:00-17:30, Piazza San Frediano, tel. 0583-493-627.

Visiting the Church: Step inside and you're struck by the sight of 40 powerful (if recycled) ancient Roman columns. The message: Lucca may be impressive, but the finale of your pilgrimage—in Rome—is worth the hike.

Inside, there's a notable piece of art in each corner: At rear right is the 12th-century baptistery, with some interesting Church propaganda showing the story of Moses (the evil Egyptians are played by Holy Roman Empire troops). In the chapel just to the left as you face the baptistery is St. Zita's actual body, put there in 1278. Two more exquisite pieces of wooden art are in chapels on either side of the nave; in both chapels, the art sits along the back wall, facing the front of the church. First, on the left side (high on the back wall, facing the stone-carved altar), is a particularly serene Virgin Mary, depicted at the moment she gets the news that she'll bring the Messiah into the world (carved and painted by Lucchesi artist Matteo Civitali, c. 1460). Across the nave, in the corresponding chapel on the right side, is a painting on wood of the *Assumption of the Virgin* (c. 1510), with Doubting Thomas receiving Mary's red belt as she ascends so he'll doubt no more. The pinball-machine composition serves as a virtual catalog of the fine silk material produced in Lucca—a major industry in the 16th century.

• *Leaving the church, head straight back through the little square, and turn right onto...*

Via Fillungo

The street to stroll, this main pedestrian drag connects the town's two busiest squares: Piazza dell'Anfiteatro (which we just left) and Piazza San Michele. Along the way, you'll get a taste of Lucca's rich past, including several elegant, century-old storefronts. Many of the original storefront paintings, reliefs, and mosaics survive—even if today's shopkeeper sells something entirely different.

Head down the street. After a block, on the left, you'll pass Piazza degli Scapellini, with market stalls and another entrance into Piazza dell'Anfiteatro.

Between #104 and #102, notice the snazzy Old World **shopping gallery,** with glass canopies in the Liberty Style (Italy's version of Art Nouveau).

You'll see symptoms of Italy's burgeoning obsession with **craft beers** at #92 (on the left), a hole-in-the-wall bottle shop selling a wide array of microbrews.

Farther down, on the right at #97, is a classic old **jewelry store** (marked *Carli*), with a rare storefront that has kept its T-shaped arrangement (when closed, you see a wooden T, and during open hours it unfolds with a fine old-time display). This design dates from when the merchant sold his goods in front, did his work in the back, and lived upstairs.

Di Simo Caffè, at #58 (but currently closed), has long been the hangout of Lucca's artistic and intellectual elite. Composer and hometown boy Giacomo Puccini tapped his foot while sipping coffee here.

A surviving five-story **tower house** is at #67 (on the right, after Via Buia). At one time, nearly every corner sported its own tower (see the sidebar). The stubby stones that still stick out once supported wooden staircases (there were no interior connections between floors). So many towers cast shadows over this part of town that this cross-street is called "Dark Street" (Via Buia). Look left down Via San Andrea for a peek at the town's tallest tower, Guinigi, in the distance—with its characteristic oak trees sprouting from the top. You can pay to climb up for the view or drop into a fine little city history museum for free at the base of the tower (see "More Sights in Lucca," later).

At #45 and #43 (on the right), you'll see two more good examples of tower houses. Across the street, on the left, the **Clock Tower** (Torre delle Ore) has a hand-wound Swiss clock that clanged four times an hour since 1754...until it died for good a few years back (€4 to climb the 207 wooden steps to see the view and the non-functioning mechanism, €6 combo-ticket includes Guinigi Tower, daily April-Oct 9:30-18:30, Nov-March 9:30-17:30, last entry 20 minutes before closing, corner of Via Fillungo and Via del'Arancio).

The intersection of Via Fillungo and Via Roma/Via Santa Croce (the street jogs a bit to the right here) marks the center of town, where the two original Roman roads crossed. The big building you're facing—with the heavy grates on the windows and the benches built into its stony facade—is the **In Mondadori bookstore.** While the interior is worth a peek (for its speckled mosaic floors, columns, and stained-glass skylight), the benches out front are even more interesting—they're the town hangout, where old-timers sit to swap gossip.

• *Turn right down Via Roma, and you'll pop out at...*

Piazza San Michele

This square has been the center of town since Roman times, when it was the forum. It's dominated by the **Church of San Michele.** Circle around to the church's main door. Towering above the fancy Pisan Romanesque facade, the archangel Michael stands ready to flap his wings—which he was known to do on special occasions.

The square is surrounded by an architectural hodgepodge. The circa-1495 loggia (to the right as you face the church) was the first Renaissance building in town. There's a late 19th-century interior in Buccellato Taddeucci, a 130-year-old pastry shop (#34, next to the church tower). The left section of the BNL bank (#5, facing the church facade) sports an Art Nouveau facade that celebrates both Amerigo Vespucci and Cristoforo Colombo.

Perhaps you've noticed that the statues of big shots that decorate many an Italian piazza are mostly absent from Lucca's squares. That's because unlike Venice, Florence, and Milan—which were dominated by a few powerful dynasties—Lucca was traditionally run by an oligarchy of a hundred leading families, with no one central figure to commemorate in stone. But after Italian unification, when leaders were fond of saying, "We have created Italy...now we need to create Italians," stirring statues of national heroes popped up everywhere—even in Lucca. The statue on Piazza San Michele is a two-bit local guy, dredged up centuries after his death because he favored strong central government.

Look back at the church facade, which also has an element of patriotism—designed to give roots and legitimacy to Italian statehood. Perched above many of the columns are the faces of heroes in the Italian independence and unification movement: Victor Emmanuel II (above the short red column on the right, second level up), the Count of Cavour (next to Victor, above the column with black zigzags), and Giuseppe Mazzini.

• *From here, take a little detour down...*

Via San Paolino

This bustling street—which eventually goes all the way to Piazzale Guiseppe Verdi, with the TI and bus stop to Pisa—is another fine shopping drag. Along here, a wide variety of storefronts cater not just to tourists but also to locals. Appliance and electronics stores are mixed in with gifty Tuscan specialties boutiques. You'll also pass—after just a half-block, on the right—the best gelato in town (the recommended De' Coltelli, at #10).

One block down this street, in the little square called **Piazza Citadella** (on the right), a statue of Giacomo Puccini (1858-1924) sits genteelly on a chair, holding court. The great composer was born in the house down the little alley over his left shoulder (now the well-presented Puccini's House museum, worth a visit for music lovers—see "More Sights in Lucca," later). The ticket office for the museum—on the left side of the square, in front of Puccini—is also a well-stocked gift shop with all manner of Puccini-bilia.

Puccini had deep roots in Lucca. His musical family had served as choirmasters for the San Martino Cathedral for five generations. As a young man, Giacomo sang in the cathedral choir, served as the substitute organist, and attended the church school. Even when he left for Milan to pursue his opera career, he kept a villa near Lucca. The citizens of Lucca can be rightfully proud of their native son: Puccini is easily the most popular opera composer today, and his *La Boheme, Madame Butterfly, Tosca,* and a half-dozen other works are regularly performed across the globe. His style, known as *verismo* (realism), is highly accessible and dramatic, making his works seem more like sung plays than merely a string of arias.

• *Feel free to browse your way as far down this street as you like, but eventually return to Piazza San Michele to continue the walk to the cathedral. Facing the church facade, turn right and go down Via Vittorio Veneto (with the loggia on your left) to the vast, café-lined Piazza Napoleone—named for the French despot who was the first outsider to take over Lucca. Cut diagonally through this square, and continue to the little adjacent square with the statue. Continue straight, along the big orange building, up Via del Duomo. After a block, you'll see...*

San Giovanni Church

This first cathedral of Lucca is interesting only for its archaeological finds. The entire floor of the 12th-century church has been excavated in recent decades, revealing layers of Roman houses, ancient hot tubs that date back to the time of Christ, early churches, and theological graffiti. Sporadic English translations help you understand what you're looking at. As you climb under the church's present-day floor and wander the lanes of Roman Lucca, remember that the entire city sits on similar ruins. Climb the 190 steps of the church's campanile (bell tower) for a panoramic view.

Cost and Hours: €4, €7 combo-ticket includes cathedral and Cathedral Museum; mid-March-Oct daily 10:00-18:00; Nov-mid-March Sat-Sun 10:00-17:00, closed Mon-Fri; audioguide-€1; see concert info on page 453.

• *Continuing past San Giovanni, you'll be face-to-face with...*

▲San Martino Cathedral

This cathedral, begun in the 11th century, is an entertaining mix of architectural and artistic styles. It's also home to the exquisite 15th-century tomb of Ilaria del Carretto, who married into the wealthy Guinigi family.

Cost and Hours: €3, €7 combo-ticket includes Cathedral Museum and San Giovanni Church; Mon-Fri 9:30-18:00, Sat 9:30-18:45; Sun 9:00-10:15 & 11:30-18:00; Piazza San Martino.

Visiting the Cathedral: The cathedral's elaborate Pisan Romanesque **facade** features Christian teaching scenes, animals, and candy-cane-striped columns.

The horseback figure (over the two right arches) is St. Martin, a Roman military officer from Hungary who, by offering his cloak to a beggar, more fully understood the beauty of Christian compassion. (The impressive original, a fine example of Romanesque sculpture, hides from pollution just inside, to the right of the main entrance.) Each of the columns on the facade is unique. Notice how the facade is asymmetrical: The 11th-century bell tower was already in place when the rest of the cathedral was built, so the builders cheated on the right side to make it fit the space. Over the right portal (as if leaning against the older tower), the architect Guideo from Como holds a document declaring that he finished the facade in 1204. On the right (at eye level on the pilaster), a labyrinth is set into the wall. The maze relates the struggle and challenge our souls face in finding salvation. (French pilgrims on their way to Rome could relate to this, as it's the same pattern they knew from the floor of the church at Chartres.) The Latin plaque just left of the main door is where money changers and spice traders met to seal deals (on the doorstep of the church—to underscore the reliability of their promises). Notice the date: *An Dni MCXI* (A.D. 1111).

Buy a ticket and go inside. The **interior**—bigger than it seems from outside—features brightly frescoed Gothic arches, Renaissance paintings, and stained glass from the 19th century.

On the left side of the nave, a small, elaborate, birdcage-like temple contains the wooden crucifix—much revered by locals—called **Volto Santo.** It's said to have been sculpted by Nicodemus in Jerusalem and set afloat in an unmanned boat that landed on the coast of Tuscany, from where wild oxen miraculously carried it to Lucca in 782. The sculpture (which is actually 12th-century Byzantine-style) has quite a jewelry collection, which you can see in the Cathedral Museum (described next).

On the right side of the nave, the sacristy houses the enchantingly beautiful **memorial tomb of Ilaria del Carretto** by Jacopo della Quercia (1407). Pick up a handy English description (on the right as you enter). This young bride of silk baron Paolo Guinigi is decked out in the latest, most expensive fashions, with the requisite little dog (symbolizing her loyalty) curled up at her feet in eternal sleep. She's so realistic that the statue was nicknamed "Sleeping Beauty." Her nose is partially worn off because of a long-standing tradition of lonely young ladies rubbing it for luck in finding a boyfriend.

• There's one more sight to consider, but it's extra credit—worthwhile only if you want to dig deeper into the history of the cathedral. As you face the cathedral facade, on the little square to the left is the entrance to the...

Cathedral Museum (Museo della Cattedrale)

This beautifully presented museum houses original paintings, sculptures, and vestments from the cathedral and other Lucca churches. Pass through a room with illuminated manuscripts on your way to the ticket desk, then follow the one-way route up and down through the collection. The first room displays jewelry made to dress up the Volto Santo crucifix (described earlier), including gigantic gilded silver shoes. Upstairs, notice the fine red brocaded silk—a reminder that this precious fabric is what brought riches and power to the city. You'll also see church paintings and sculptures, silver ecclesiastical gear, and a big cutaway model of the cathedral. The exhibits in this museum have basic labels and are meaningful only with the slow-talking €1 audioguide—if you're not in the mood to listen, skip the place altogether.

Cost and Hours: €4, €7 combo-ticket includes cathedral and San Giovanni Church; mid-March-Oct daily 10:00-18:00; Nov-mid-March Mon-Fri 10:00-14:00, Sat 10:00-18:00, Sun 10:00-17:00; to the left of the cathedral as you're facing it, Piazza Antelminelli, tel. 0583-490-530, www.museocattedralelucca.it.

• Our walk is finished. From here, it's just a short stroll south to the city wall—and a bike-rental office, if you want to take a spin. Otherwise, simply explore the city...lose yourself in Lucca.

More Sights in Lucca

▲▲BIKE THE RAMPARTS

Lucca's most remarkable feature, its Renaissance wall, is also its most enjoyable attraction—especially when circled on a rental bike.

Stretching for 2.5 miles, this is an ideal place to come for an overview of the city by foot or bike.

Lucca has had a protective wall for 2,000 years. You can read three walls into today's map: the first rectangular Roman wall, the later medieval wall (nearly the size of today's), and the 16th-century Renaissance ramparts that still survive.

With the advent of cannons, thin medieval walls were suddenly vulnerable. A new design—the same one that stands today—was state-of-the-art when it was built (1550-1650). Much of the old medieval wall (look for the old stones) was incorporated into the Renaissance wall (with uniform bricks). The new wall was squat: a 100-foot-wide mound of dirt faced with bricks, engineered to absorb a cannonball pummeling. The townspeople cleared a wide no-man's-land around the town, exposing any attackers from a distance. Eleven heart-shaped bastions (now inviting picnic areas) were designed to minimize exposure to cannonballs and to maximize defense capabilities. The ramparts were armed with 130 cannons.

The town invested a third of its income for more than a century to construct the wall, and—since it kept away the Florentines and nasty Pisans—it was considered a fine investment. In fact, nobody ever bothered to try to attack the wall. Locals say that the only time it actually defended the city was during an 1812 flood of the Serchio River, when the gates were sandbagged and the ramparts kept out the high water.

Today, the ramparts seem made-to-order for a leisurely bike ride (wonderfully smooth 20-30-minute pedal, depending on how fast you go and how crowded the wall-top park is). You can rent bikes cheaply and easily from one of several bike-rental places in town (listed earlier, under "Helpful Hints"). There are also several handy places to get up on the wall. Note that the best people-watching—and slowest pedaling—is during *passeggiata* time, just before dinner, when it seems that all of Lucca is doing slow laps around the wall.

OTHER MUSEUMS

Lucca has several small museums that stir local pride, but they're pretty dull on a pan-European (or even pan-Italian) scale. Visit the following sights only if you have time to burn and/or a special interest (with the exception of the MUST Museum, which is free and offers a nice introduction to the city).

Guinigi Tower (Torre Guinigi)

Many Tuscan towns have towers, but none is quite like the Guinigi family's. Up 227 steps is a small garden with fragrant trees, surrounded by fine views over the city's rooftops. On your way up, you'll pass colorful illustrations of historical Lucca—with its many towers—then huff up twisty metal stairs through the hollow brick tower. From the top, orient yourself to the town. Lucca sits in a flat valley ringed by protective hills, so it's easy to see how the town managed to stay independent through so much of its history, despite its lack of a strategic hilltop position. From up here, pick out landmarks: the circular form of Piazza dell'Anfiteatro to the north, with the mosaic facade of the Church of San Frediano nearby; to the left (east), the open top of the Clock Tower, marking the Roman grid-planned streets of the oldest part of town; and to the south, the big, marble facade of San Martino Cathedral.

Cost and Hours: €4, €6 combo-ticket includes Clock Tower and botanical garden, daily April-May 9:30-18:30, June-Sept 9:30-19:30, March and Oct 9:30-17:30, Nov-Feb 9:30-16:30, Via Sant'Andrea 41.

▲MUST Museum

This modest, free museum—its initials stand for Memoria Urbana, Società e Territorio (Urban, Societal, and Territorial Memory)—does a fine job of introducing visitors to Lucca's charms: its Roman heritage, sturdy walls, musical connections, and so on. Find the easy-to-miss entrance around the corner from the Guinigi Tower (inside the same building). On the first floor is an extensive wooden model of the town (helpful for getting your bearings) and video screens showing virtual re-creations of Roman Lucca. One thought-provoking exhibit shows a life-size cross-section of what lies underfoot in Lucca, illustrating the layers of history that have made the city what it is today. A quick spin through these exhibits is a good way to kick off your wanderings through town.

Cost and Hours: Free, Tue-Sun 10:00-18:00, closed Mon, enter around the corner from the Guinigi Tower entrance, on Via Guinigi.

Puccini's House

This modern, well-presented museum fills the home where Giacomo Puccini grew up. It's well worth a visit for opera enthusiasts...

but mostly lost on anybody else. Buy your ticket at the shop/office on the square, then buzz the door to be let in. You'll tour the composer's birthplace—including the room where he was born—and see lots of artifacts (including the Steinway piano where he did much of his composing, personal belongings, and pull-out drawers with original compositions and manuscripts). An elaborate costume from one of his works is on display, and if you ask, the attendant can accompany you for a peek in the garret (storage room up above the house), where a stage set from *La Bohème* evokes the composer's greatest work.

Cost and Hours: €7; April-Oct Wed-Mon 10:00-18:00, Nov-March Wed-Mon 11:00-17:00, closed Tue year-round; Corte San Lorenzo 9, tel. 0583-584-028, www.puccinimuseum.it.

Palazzo Pfanner

Garden enthusiasts (and anyone needing a break from churches) will enjoy this 18th-century palace built for a rich Swiss expat who came to Lucca to open a brewery. A visit has two parts: the residence and the garden. Up the stairs is the palace's lived-in interior, with Baroque furniture, elaborate frescoes, and a centuries-old kitchen. Those in the medical profession may be interested in the display of early-20th-century medical equipment and books. (Pfanner's son became a renowned doctor, and treated everyone from vagrants to Giacomo Puccini on the building's ground floor.) The second part is the restful garden, with manicured lawns, rows of dynamic statues, potted citrus trees, and gurgling fountains, tucked up against Lucca's imposing wall. While far from the finest garden in Italy, it's a nice escape from the crowds and heat of the city.

Cost and Hours: Garden or residence-€4.50 apiece, €6 for both, April-Oct daily 10:00-18:00, closed Nov-March, Via degli Asili 33, tel. 0583-954-029, www.palazzopfanner.it.

Villa Guinigi

Built by Paolo Guinigi in 1413, the family villa is now a well-presented but empty-feeling museum displaying a lot of "also-ran" art and artifacts that are meaningful to the Lucchesi, but generally not to outsiders. The exhibit starts with an archaeological section—Etruscan, Ligurian (a local pagan tribe), Roman. Upstairs, you proceed chronologically through the Middle Ages, with lots of church art and altars, and the Renaissance. Highlights include a precious crucifix by Berlinghiero Berlinghieri (who also created the fine mosaic facade at the Church of San Frediano), two terra-cotta *Madonna-and-Bambino* sculptures attributed to Donatello, fine inlaid-wood panels from San Martino Cathedral, several works by the locally famous Lucchese sculptor Matteo Civitali, a *Sacra Conversazione* by Fra Bartolomeo, and a fine triptych by the multitalented Giorgio Vasari. In Vasari's vibrant altar painting, Adam and

Eve clutch the tree of knowledge, while the devil (a snake with a woman's head) twists up the trunk toward the sky, flanked by biblical big shots (David, Solomon, Moses, and John the Baptist). But Mary floats triumphant on top, with one foot keeping down the devil's head. The collection wraps up with the Counter-Reformation and Neoclassicism (with works by more locally beloved artists, Paolo Guidotti and Pompeo Batoni). While art lovers may find a few gems embedded here, others can skip it.

Cost and Hours: €4, €6.50 combo-ticket includes Palazzo Mansi, Tue-Sat 8:30-19:30, may be open Sun—check website, closed Mon, may have to wait in high season for an attendant to accompany you, Via della Quarquonia, tel. 0583-496-033, www.luccamuseinazionali.it.

Palazzo Mansi

Minor paintings by Tintoretto, Pontormo, Veronese, and others vie for attention, but the palace itself—a sumptuously furnished and decorated 17th-century confection—steals the show. This is your chance to appreciate the wealth of Lucca's silk merchants. You'll gape through several grand halls of both public and private apartments. In one wing, every surface is slathered in bubbly Baroque scenes; in another, each room is completely draped in tapestries, leading to one of the most impressive two-story canopy beds I've seen. Since all visitors must be accompanied by an attendant, during high season you may have to wait a bit for your chance to enter.

Cost and Hours: €4, €6.50 combo-ticket includes Villa Guinigi, generally Tue-Sat 8:30-19:30, may be open Sun—check website, closed Mon, no photos, request English booklet at ticket desk, Via Galli Tassi 43, tel. 0583-55-570, www.luccamuseinazionali.it.

Sleeping in Lucca

FANCY LITTLE BOUTIQUE B&BS WITHIN THE WALLS

$$$ A Palazzo Busdraghi has seven comfortable, pastel-colored rooms with modern baths (some with Jacuzzi-style tubs) in a tastefully converted 13th-century palace tucked inside a creaky old courtyard. Sweet Marta hustles to keep guests happy, and bakes tasty cakes for breakfast. It's very conveniently located right on busy Via Fillungo, but can be noisy on weekends—bring earplugs (Sb-€120, Db-€150-170 depending on size, junior suite-€180, extra bed-€20, cheaper prices off-season, air-con, Wi-Fi, parking-€15, Via Fillungo 170, tel. 0583-950-856, www.apalazzobusdraghi.it, info@apalazzobusdraghi.it).

$$$ La Romea B&B, in an air-conditioned, restored, 14th-century palazzo near Guinigi Tower, feels like a royal splurge. Its four posh rooms and one suite are lavishly decorated in handsome colors and surround a big, plush lounge with stately Venetian-style floors (Db-€100-135 depending on season, big junior suite-€160, extra bed-€20-25; 10 percent discount when you book directly with the hotel, show this book, and pay cash; Wi-Fi; from the train station, take Via Fillungo, turn right on Via Sant'Andrea, then take the second right to Vicolo delle Ventaglie 2; tel. 0583-464-175, www.laromea.com, info@laromea.com, Giulio and wife Gaia).

$$$ La Locanda Sant'Agostino has three romantic, bright, and palatial rooms. The vine-draped terrace, beautiful breakfast spread, and quaint views invite you to relax (Db-€160, extra bed-€20, air-con, guest computer, Wi-Fi, from Via Fillungo take Via San Giorgio to Piazza Sant'Agostino 3, best to reserve by email, tel. 0583-443-100, mobile 347-989-9069, www.locandasantagostino.it, info@locandasantagostino.it).

$$ La Bohème B&B has a cozy yet elegant ambience, offering six large rooms, each painted with a different color scheme. Chandeliers, 1920s-vintage tile floors, and tasteful antiques add to the charm (Db-€125, less off-season, 10 percent discount with this book if you pay cash and book directly with hotel, air-con, Wi-Fi, Via del Moro 2, tel. 0583-462-404, www.boheme.it, info@boheme.it, Sara).

SLEEPING MORE FORGETTABLY WITHIN THE WALLS

$$ Hotel la Luna, run by the Barbieri family, has 29 rooms in a great location, right in the heart of the city. Updated rooms are split between two adjacent buildings just off the main shopping street. The annex has an elevator, but I prefer the rooms in the main building, which are larger and classier, with old wood-beam ceilings (Sb-€90, Db-€125, suite-€190, these prices for Rick Steves readers who book directly with hotel, air-con, guest computer, Wi-Fi, parking-€20/day, Via Fillungo at Corte Compagni 12, tel. 0583-493-634, www.hotellaluna.com, info@hotellaluna.com).

$$ Alla Dimora Lucense's seven newer rooms are bright, modern, clean, and peaceful, with all the comforts. Enjoy their relaxing, sunny interior courtyard (Db-€125, suite for 2-4 people-€150-200; 5 percent discount if you pay cash, book directly with hotel, and show this book; air-con, Wi-Fi, half a block from Via Fillungo at Via Fontana 19, tel. 0583-495-722, www.dimoralucense.it, info@dimoralucense.it).

$$ Albergo San Martino is conveniently located for train travelers: It's just inside the wall, about a block from the cathedral, but also close to the station. They have rooms in three different buildings. The 12 art-adorned rooms in the main hotel—with a cozy lounge and nice curbside breakfast terrace—are long in the

Sleep Code

(€1 = about $1.40, country code: 39)

Abbreviations
S = Single, **D** = Double/Twin, **T** = Triple, **Q** = Quad, **b** = bathroom, **s** = shower only

Price Rankings
$$$ Higher Priced—Most rooms €135 or more.
$$ Moderately Priced—Most rooms between €80-135.
$ Lower Priced—Most rooms €80 or less.

Unless otherwise noted, credit cards are accepted, English is spoken, breakfast is included (but usually optional), and Wi-Fi is generally free. Many towns in Italy levy a hotel tax of about €2 per person, per night (usually not included in the rates I've quoted). Prices change; verify current rates online or by email. For the best prices, always book directly with the hotel.

tooth and not a great value (Db-€120, €30 more for bigger and newer "superior" rooms). The six rooms in the annex are newer and more affordable (Db-€90-100). And the nine good-value rooms in their sister Hotel Diana are fresh, minimalist, and retro-style at an affordable price (Db-€90—but these rooms only don't include breakfast; all rooms: air-con, Wi-Fi, parking-€15, reception at Via della Dogana 9, tel. 0583-469-181, www.albergosanmartino.it, info@albergosanmartino.it).

$$ Hotel Universo, renting 55 rooms right on Piazza Napoleone and facing the theater and Palazzo Ducale, is a 19th-century town fixture. While it clearly was once elegant, now it's old and tired, with a big Old World lounge and soft prices ("comfort" Db-€100, "superior" Db with updated bath for €20 more, air-con in most rooms, elevator, Piazza del Giglio 1, tel. 0583-493-678, www.universolucca.com, info@universolucca.com).

$ At **Le Violette B&B,** cheerful American Elizabeth will settle you into one of her six homey rooms near the train station inside Porta San Pietro (S-€40, D-€60, Db-€75, extra bed-€15, air-con in some rooms, Wi-Fi, communal kitchen, €5 to use washer and dryer, Via della Polveriera 6, tel. 0583-493-594, bbleviolette@gmail.com).

$ Ostello San Frediano, in a central, sprawling ex-convent with a peaceful garden, is a cut above the average hostel, though it's still filled mainly with a young crowd. Its 29 rooms are bright and modern, and some have fun lofts (€20 beds in 6- to 8-person dorms, 140 beds, Db-€68, Tb-€82, Qb-€105, nice two-story family rooms, prices include sheets, €2 extra/night for non-members, breakfast extra, no curfew, lockers, elevator, Wi-Fi, cheap restaurant, free parking, Via della Cavallerizza 12, tel. 0583-469-957, www.ostellolucca.it, info@ostellolucca.it).

OUTSIDE THE WALLS

$$$ Hotel San Marco, a seven-minute walk outside the Porta Santa Maria, is a postmodern place decorated à la Stanley Kubrick. Its 42 rooms are sleek, with all the comforts (Sb-€95, Db-€140, extra bed-€10, includes nice breakfast spread on terrace, air-con, Wi-Fi, elevator, pool, bikes-€7/half-day, free parking, taxi from station-€13, Via San Marco 368, tel. 0583-495-010, www.hotelsanmarcolucca.com, info@hotelsanmarcolucca.com).

$$ Hotel Rex rents 25 rooms in a practical contemporary building on the train station square. While in the modern world, you're just 200 yards away from the old town and get more space for your money (Db-€80-100, ask for best Rick Steves price, includes breakfast buffet, air-con, elevator, Wi-Fi, small gift when you show this book, free loaner bikes for guests, free parking, a few steps from the train station at Piazza Ricasoli 19, tel. 0583-955-443, www.hotelrexlucca.com, info@hotelrexlucca.com).

$$ Hotel Moderno is indeed modern, with 12 rooms tastefully decorated in shades of white. Although it backs up to the train tracks, the rooms are quiet (Sb-€70, Db-€90, air-con, pay Wi-Fi, Via Vincenzo Civitali 38—turn left out of train station and go over bridge across tracks, tel. 0583-55-840, www.albergomodernolucca.com, info@albergomodernolucca.com).

$ La Mimosa B&B has five cozy rooms a 10-minute walk west of Porta Sant'Anna. Most practical if you're arriving or leaving Lucca by bus, this trendy little house is run by the Zichi cousins, Giuseppe and Stefano, and decorated with modern paintings. It's located on a main road, but double-paned windows reduce traffic noise (Sb-€50, Db-€80, Qb-€120, cheaper prices off-season, air-con, Wi-Fi, free street parking nearby, Via Pisana 66; leave Piazzale Giuseppe Verdi through Porta Sant'Anna, swing right, then cross road, walk straight down Via Catalani, and take second road on the left; tel. 0583-583-121, www.bblamimosa.it, info@bblamimosa.it).

$ Sogni d'Oro Guesthouse ("Dreams of Gold"), run by Davide, is a handy budget option for drivers, with five basic rooms and a cheery communal kitchen (grocery store next door). It's a 10-minute walk from the train station and a five-minute walk from the city walls (D-€50, Db-€65, Q-€70, 10 percent discount with cash; free ride to and from station with advance notice—then call when your train arrives in Lucca; from the station, head straight out to Viale Regina Margherita and turn right, follow the main boulevard as it turns into Viale Giuseppe Giusti, at the curve turn right onto Via Antonio Cantore to #169; tel. 0583-467-768, mobile 329-582-5062, www.bbsognidoro.com, info@bbsognidoro.com).

Eating in Lucca

Canuleia Trattoria is run by enthusiastic Matteo and Eleonora, who make everything fresh in their small kitchen. You can eat tasty Tuscan cuisine in a dressy little dining room or outside on the garden courtyard. As this place is justifiably popular—and well worth reserving ahead—call to book for dinner (€9-10 pastas, €16-18 *secondi,* Tue-Sun 12:00-14:30 & 19:00-22:00, closed Mon, Via Canuleia 14, tel. 0583-467-470).

Port Ellen Clan is an unusual concept in traditional Lucca—a combination restaurant, wine bar, and whisky bar (featuring more than 150 types of whisky) in a trendy modern setting. Though the cuisine is purely Italian with a modern twist, the theme is creative and original, with a Scottish flair (€9-11 pastas, €15-18 *secondi,* Wed-Fri 12:30-15:00 & 19:30-24:00, Sat-Sun 12:30-15:00 only, closed Mon-Tue, Via del Fosso 120, tel. 0583-493-952 or 329-245-2762, www.portellenclan.com).

Vecchia Trattoria Buralli, on quiet Piazza Sant'Agostino, is a good bet for traditional cooking and juicy steaks, with bright-pastel indoor and piazza seating (€7-9 pastas, €8-12 *secondi,* €12 fixed-price lunches, €20-30 fixed-price dinners, Thu-Tue 12:00-14:45 & 19:00-22:30, closed Wed, Piazza Sant'Agostino 10, tel. 0583-950-611).

Trattoria da Leo packs in chatty locals for typical, cheap home-cooking in a hash-slingin' Mel's-diner atmosphere. This place is a high-energy winner...you know it's going to be good as soon as you step in. Sit in the rollicking interior, or out on an atmospheric tight lane. Arrive early or reserve in advance (€7-8 pastas, €10-12 *secondi,* daily 12:00-15:00 & 19:30-22:30, cash only, leave Piazza San Salvatore on Via Asili and take the first left to Via Tegrimi 1, tel. 0583-492-236).

Osteria Via San Giorgio, where Daniela cooks and her brother Piero serves, is a cheery family eatery that satisfies both fish-lovers and meat-lovers (€10-12 pastas, €13-18 *secondi,* daily 12:00-16:00 & 19:00-23:00, Via San Giorgio 26, tel. 0583-953-233).

Bella 'Mbriana Pizzeria focuses on doing one thing very well: turning out piping-hot, wood-fired pizzas to happy locals in a no-frills, welcoming, wood-paneled dining room. Order and pay at the counter, take a number, and they'll call you when your pizza's ready. Consider takeout to munch on the nearby walls (€6-7 pizzas, Wed-Mon 11:30-14:30 & 18:30-23:00, closed Tue, to the right as you face the Church of San Frediano, Via della Cavallerizza 29, tel. 0583-495-565).

Specialties in Lucca

Lucca has some tasty specialties worth seeking out. *Ceci* (CHEH-chee), also called *cecina* (cheh-CHEE-nah), makes an ideal cheap snack any time of day. This garbanzo-bean crepe is sold in pizza shops and is best accompanied by a nip of red wine. *Farro,* a grain (spelt) dating back to ancient Roman cuisine, shows up in restaurants in soups or as a creamy rice-like dish *(risotto di farro). Tordelli,* the Lucchesi version of *tortelli,* is homemade ravioli. It's traditionally stuffed with meat and served with more meat sauce, but chefs creatively pair cheeses and vegetables, too, *Lardo di Colonnata* is *salumi* made with cured lard and rosemary, sliced thin, and served as an antipasto.

Meat, not fish, is the star at most restaurants, especially steak, which is listed on menus as *filetto di manzo* (filet), *tagliata di manzo* (thin slices of grilled tenderloin), or the king of steaks, *bistecca alla fiorentina.* Order *al sangue* (rare), *medio* (medium rare), *cotto* (medium), or *ben cotto* (well). Anything more than *al sangue* is considered a travesty for steak connoisseurs. *Ravellino* is a thin cut of beef that's deep-fried, then pan-fried again later to heat it up.

Note that steaks (as well as fish) are often sold by weight, noted on menus as *s.q.* (according to quantity ordered) or *l'etto* (cost per 100 grams—250 grams is about an 8-ounce steak).

For something sweet, bakeries sell *buccellato,* bread dotted with raisins, lightly flavored with anise, and often shaped like a wreath. It's sold only in large sizes, but luckily it stays good for a few days (and it also pairs well with *vin santo*—fortified Tuscan dessert wine). An old proverb says, "Coming to Lucca without eating the *buccellato* is like not having come at all." *Buon appetito!*

LUCCA

Il Cuore Enogastronomia/Ristorante includes a delicatessen and restaurant. For a fancy picnic, drop in the deli for ready-to-eat lasagna, saucy meatballs, grilled and roasted vegetables, vegetable soufflés, Tuscan bean soup, fruit salads, and more, sold by weight and dished up in disposable trays to go. Ask them to heat your order *(riscaldare),* then picnic on nearby Piazza Napoleone. Or you can eat in their small "restaurant" (a few tables tucked in the back) for the same price. For curious traveling foodies on a budget who want to eat right there, they can assemble a €10 "degustation plate"—just point to what you want from among the array of tasty treats under the glass (Tue-Sun 9:30-19:30, closed Mon, Via del Battistero 2, tel. 0583-493-196, Cristina).

Il Cuore Bistrot, located across the way, is a trendy find for wine-tasting or a meal on a piazza. Try the €8 *aperitivo* (available

18:00-20:00), which includes a glass of wine and a plate of cheese, *salumi*, and snacks, or feast on fresh pastas and other high-quality dishes from their lunch and dinner menus (Wed-Sun 12:00-22:00 with limited menu 15:00-19:30, Tue 12:00-15:00, closed Mon, Via del Battistero, tel. 0583-493-196).

Pizzeria da Felice is a little mom-and-pop hole-in-the-wall serving *cecina* (garbanzo-bean crepes) and slices of freshly baked pizza to throngs of snackers. Grab an *etto* of *cecina* and a short glass of wine for €2.50. From fall through spring (Sept-early April), they're known for their roasted chestnuts with ricotta (Mon-Sat 10:00-20:30, closed Sun and 3 weeks in Aug, Via Buia 12, tel. 0583-494-986).

Gelato: Just off Piazza San Michele, **De' Coltelli** has some of my favorite gelato in Italy. Like its sister shop in Pisa, this *gelateria* uses organic ingredients to pull out delicious—and often unique—flavors (Via San Paolino 10).

Lucca Connections

From Lucca by Train to: Florence (2/hour, about 1.5 hours), **Pisa** (roughly 1-2/hour, 25-30 minutes; if going directly to Leaning Tower, hop off at Pisa San Rossore station—for more on this connection, see page 449), **Livorno** (about hourly, 1-1.25 hours, transfer at Pisa Centrale, €5.10), **Milan** (2/hour except Sun, 4-5 hours, transfer in Florence), **Rome** (1/hour except Sun, 3-4 hours, change in Florence).

From Lucca by Bus to Pisa: Direct buses from Lucca's Piazzale Giuseppe Verdi drop you right at the Leaning Tower (Mon-Sat hourly, fewer on Sun, 50 minutes, also stops at Pisa's airport, €3). Even with a car, I'd opt for this much faster and cheaper option. For more on day-tripping to Pisa, see page 449.

TUSCAN HILL TOWNS

Tuscany is rich in history, and proud locals will remind you that their ancestors, the Etruscans, were thriving long before anyone had heard of Julius Caesar. The region offers a blissful mix of scenic beauty and rich history...and a taste of the rustic Italian good life.

Many of the hill towns—so emblematic of Tuscany—trace their roots to Etruscan times (well before ancient Rome). Others date from the fall of Rome, when barbarian invasions chased lowland townsfolk to the hills, where they built fortified communities. The Middle Ages were formative times for many cities, when warring factions divided towns between those loyal to the pope (Guelphs) and to the Holy Roman Emperor (Ghibellines). Cities developed monumental defensive walls and built great towers. Then, the Black Death swept through Tuscany in 1348 and devastated the region. The plague, plus the increasing dominance of Florence, turned many bustling cities into docile backwaters. Ironically, what was bad news in the 14th century is good news today: The hill towns enjoy a tourist-fueled affluence and retain a unique, medieval charm.

Tuscan towns are best enjoyed by adapting to the pace of the countryside. So, slow...down...and savor the delights that this region offers. Spend the night if you can, as many hill towns are mobbed by day-trippers from Florence and Siena.

But how in Dante's name does a traveler choose from Italy's hundreds of hill towns? I've covered some of my favorites in the next three chapters. The one(s) you visit will depend on your interests, time, and mode of transportation.

For me, **Volterra**—with its rustic vitality—is a clear winner, and its out-of-the-way location keeps it from being trampled by tourist crowds. Multitowered **San Gimignano** is a classic, but because it's such an easy hill town to visit (about 1.5 hours by bus

from Florence), peak-season crowds can overwhelm its charms. The village of **Monteriggioni** has a tiny, perfectly preserved ring fort, worth a quick stop between San Gimignano and Siena.

Wine aficionados head for **Montalcino** and **Montepulciano** (my favorite of the two towns)—each a happy gauntlet of wine shops and art galleries. Fans of architecture and urban design appreciate **Pienza**'s well-planned streets and squares. All three towns are covered in the Heart of Tuscany chapter, which also includes driving routes tying together the sights, villages, *agriturismi*, and wineries in the countryside.

Finally, those enamored by Frances Mayes' memoir, *Under the Tuscan Sun*, make the pilgrimage to touristy but down-to-earth **Cortona.**

One of the greatest Tuscan treats—the food—varies wildly depending on where you are. The areas around Florence and Siena are famed for serving hearty "farmer food," but as you move west, dishes become lighter, based more on seafood and grains. Each town proudly boasts local specialties—ask for the *specialità della città*. Wine is good throughout Tuscany, with pleasing selections for both amateurs and connoisseurs (see page 656.)

VOLTERRA AND SAN GIMIGNANO

This fine duo of hill towns—perhaps Italy's most underrated and most overrated, respectively—sit just a half-hour drive apart in the middle of the triangle formed by three major destinations: Florence, Siena, and Pisa. Volterra and San Gimignano are both worth a brief visit, but either one also works well as a home-base for the region. (To choose between them, see "Planning Your Time," later.)

San Gimignano is the region's glamour girl, getting all of the fawning attention from passing tour buses. And a quick stroll through its core, in the shadows of its 14 surviving medieval towers, is a goose-pimply delight. But once you've seen it, you've seen it...and that's when you head for Volterra.

Volterra isn't as eye-catching as San Gimignano, but has an unmistakable authenticity and a surprising depth, richly rewarding travelers adventurous enough to break out of the San Gimignano rut. With its many engaging museums, Volterra offers the best sightseeing of all of Italy's small hill towns.

And to round things out with a look at a well-preserved hilltop fort—with a San Gimignano-style touristy patina—consider stopping off for a quick visit to Monteriggioni, perched above the highway south to Siena.

GETTING THERE

These towns work best for drivers, who can easily reach both of them in one go. Volterra is farther off the main Florence-Siena road, but it's on the main road connecting that corridor to the coast, and closer to Pisa and Lucca.

If you're relying on public transportation, both towns are reachable—to a point. Visiting either one by bus from Florence or Siena requires a longer-than-it-should-be trek with a transfer in a gloomy valley town (Colle di Val d'Elsa for Volterra, Poggibonsi

Volterra & San Gimignano Area

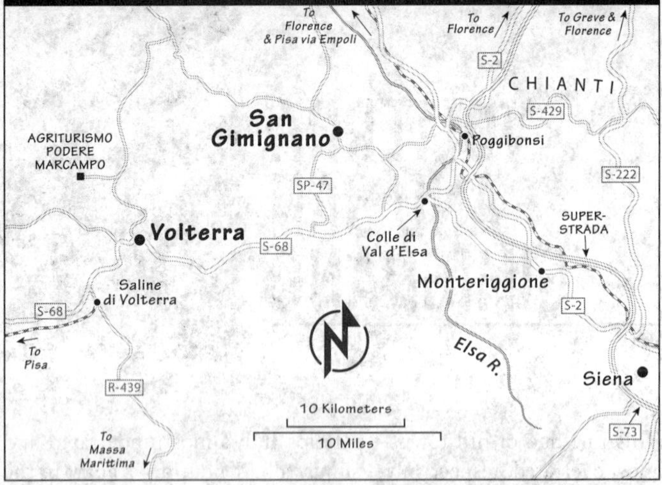

for San Gimignano; see each town's "Connections" section for details). San Gimignano is better-connected, but Volterra merits the additional effort. Note that while these towns are only about a 30-minute drive apart, they're poorly connected to each other by public transit (requiring an infrequent two-hour connection).

PLANNING YOUR TIME

Volterra and San Gimignano are a handy yin-and-yang duo. Ideally, you'll overnight in one town, and visit the other either as a side-trip or en route. There are pros and cons to overnighting in either town: Sleeping in Volterra lets you really settle into a charming, real-feeling burg with good restaurants, but forces you to visit San Gimignano when it's busiest (during the day). Sleeping in San Gimignano lets you enjoy that gorgeous town when it's relatively quiet, but some visitors find it *too* quiet—less interesting to linger in than Volterra. Ultimately I'd aim to sleep in Volterra, and try to visit San Gimignano as early or late in the day as is practical (to mitigate crowds there).

Volterra

Encircled by impressive walls and topped with a grand fortress, Volterra perches high above the rich farmland surrounding it. More than 2,000 years ago, Volterra was one of the most important Etruscan cities, and much larger than we see today. Greek-trained Etruscan artists worked here, leaving a significant stash of art, particularly funerary urns. Eventually Volterra was absorbed into the Roman Empire, and for centuries it was an independent city-state. Volterra fought bitterly against the Florentines, but like many Tuscan towns, it lost in the end and was given a fortress atop the city to "protect" its citizens.

Unlike other famous towns in Tuscany, Volterra feels neither cutesy nor touristy...but real, vibrant, and almost oblivious to the allure of the tourist dollar. Millennia past its prime, Volterra seems to have settled into a well-worn groove; locals are resistant to change. At a recent town meeting about whether to run high-speed Internet cable to the town, a local grumbled, "The Etruscans didn't need it—why do we?" This stubbornness helps make Volterra a refreshing change of pace from its more commercial neighbors. It also boasts some interesting sights for a small town, from a remarkably intact ancient Roman theater, to a finely decorated Pisan Romanesque cathedral, to an excellent museum of Etruscan artifacts. All in all, Volterra is my favorite small town in Tuscany.

Orientation to Volterra

Compact and walkable, Volterra (pop. 11,000) stretches out from the pleasant Piazza dei Priori to the old city gates. Be ready for lots of steep walking; while the main square and main drag are fairly level, nearly everything else involves a lot of up or down.

TOURIST INFORMATION

The helpful TI is on the main square, at Piazza dei Priori 19 (daily 9:30-13:00 & 14:00-18:00, tel. 0588-87257, www.volterratur.it). The TI's excellent €5 audioguide narrates 20 stops (2-for-1 discount on audioguides with this book).

ARRIVAL IN VOLTERRA

By Public Transport: Buses stop at Piazza Martiri della Libertà in the town center. Train travelers can reach the town with a short bus ride (see "Volterra Connections," later.)

By Car: Don't attempt to drive into the town center—a "ZTL" limited-traffic zone marked with a red circle—or you'll get a huge fine. Instead, use one of the numbered parking lots that ring the town walls. The easiest (and most expensive) choice—always open to visitors—is P1, the underground garage at Piazza Martiri della Libertà (€1.50/hour, €11/24 hours); parking here, you'll pop out right in the heart of town. Less expensive and farther out are P4, the handy but small (and often full) lot near the Roman Theater and Porta Fiorentina gate; and the unnumbered bus parking lot (below the road to San Gimignano). Also behind town, lot P3 is free, but requires a steep climb from the Porta di Docciola gate up into town. For a longer but more gradual climb from this lot, you can walk along the road around to Porta Fiorentina. Other lots—and possibly even some of these—are designated for residents only, but this is constantly in flux (due to frequent landslides and local politics). Before you park anywhere but P1, look for signs or ask locals to ensure it's OK.

HELPFUL HINTS

Market Day: The market is on Saturday morning near the Roman Theater (8:00-13:00, at parking lot P5; in winter, it's right on Piazza dei Priori). The TI hands out a list of other market days in the area.

Festivals: Volterra's Medieval Festival takes place on the third and fourth Sundays of August. Fall is a popular time for food festivals—check with the TI for dates and events planned.

Internet Access: Several cafés around town offer free Wi-Fi to customers. If you need a terminal, head for **Enjoy Café Internet Point,** right by the main bus stop (€3/hour, free Wi-Fi with purchase, daily 6:30-24:00, Piazza dei Martiri 3, tel. 0588-80530).

Laundry: The handy self-service **Lavanderia Azzurra** is just off the main square (€4 wash, €4 dry, change machine, daily 7:00-23:00, Via Roma 7, tel. 0588-80030).

Tours in Volterra

▲▲Guided Volterra Walk

Annie Adair (also listed individually, next) and her colleagues offer a great one-hour, English-only introductory walking tour of Volterra for €10. The walk touches on Volterra's Etruscan, Roman, and medieval history, as well as the contemporary cultural scene (daily April-July and Sept-Oct, rain or shine—Thu-Tue at 18:00, Wed at 12:30; meet in front of alabaster shop on Piazza Martiri della Libertà, no need to reserve—just show up, they need a minimum of 3 people, or €30—to make the tour go, www.volterrawalkingtour.com or www.tuscantour.com, info@volterrawalkingtour.com). There's no better way to spend €10 and one hour in this city.

Local Guide

American **Annie Adair** is an excellent guide for private, in-depth tours of Volterra (€60/hour, minimum 2 hours). Her husband Francesco, a sommelier, leads a one-hour "Wine Tasting 101" crash course in sampling Tuscan wines, held at a local wine bar (€50 per group plus cost of wine). Annie and Francesco also organize

Chianti and other regional wine tours and even Tuscan weddings for Americans (tel. 0588-086-201, mobile 347-143-5004, www.tuscantour.com, info@tuscantour.com).

Sights in Volterra

I've arranged these sights as a handy little town walk, connected by directions on foot. Not all the sights will interest everyone, so skim the listings to decide which detours appeal to you.

• *Begin your visit of town at the Etruscan Arch. To find it, go all the way down to the bottom of Via Porta all'Arco (you'll find the top of this street between Piazza Martiri della Libertà, with the town bus stop, and the main square, Piazza dei Priori).*

▲Etruscan Arch (Porta all'Arco)

Volterra's most famous sight is its Etruscan arch, built of massive, volcanic tuff stones in the fourth century B.C. (for more information on tuff, see the sidebar on page 486). Volterra's original wall was four miles around—twice the size of the wall that encircles it today. With 25,000 people, Volterra was a key trading center and one of 12 leading towns in the confederation of *Etruria Propria*. The three seriously eroded heads, dating from the first century B.C., show what happens when you leave something outside for 2,000 years. The newer stones are part of the 13th-century city wall, which incorporated parts of the much older Etruscan wall.

A plaque just outside remembers June 30, 1944. That night, Nazi forces were planning to blow up the arch to slow the Allied advance. To save their treasured landmark, Volterrans ripped up the stones that pave Via Porta all'Arco and plugged the gate, managing to convince the Nazi commander that there was no need to blow up the arch. Today, all the stones are back in their places, and like silent heroes, they welcome you through the oldest standing Etruscan gate into Volterra. Locals claim this as the only surviving round arch of the Etruscan age; most experts believe this is where the Romans got the idea for using a keystone in their arches.

• *Go through the arch and head up Via Porta all'Arco, which I like to call...*

"Artisan Lane" (Via Porta all'Arco)

This steep and atmospheric strip is lined with interesting shops featuring the work of artisans and producers. Because of its alabaster heritage, Volterra attracted craftsmen and artists, who brought

Volterra

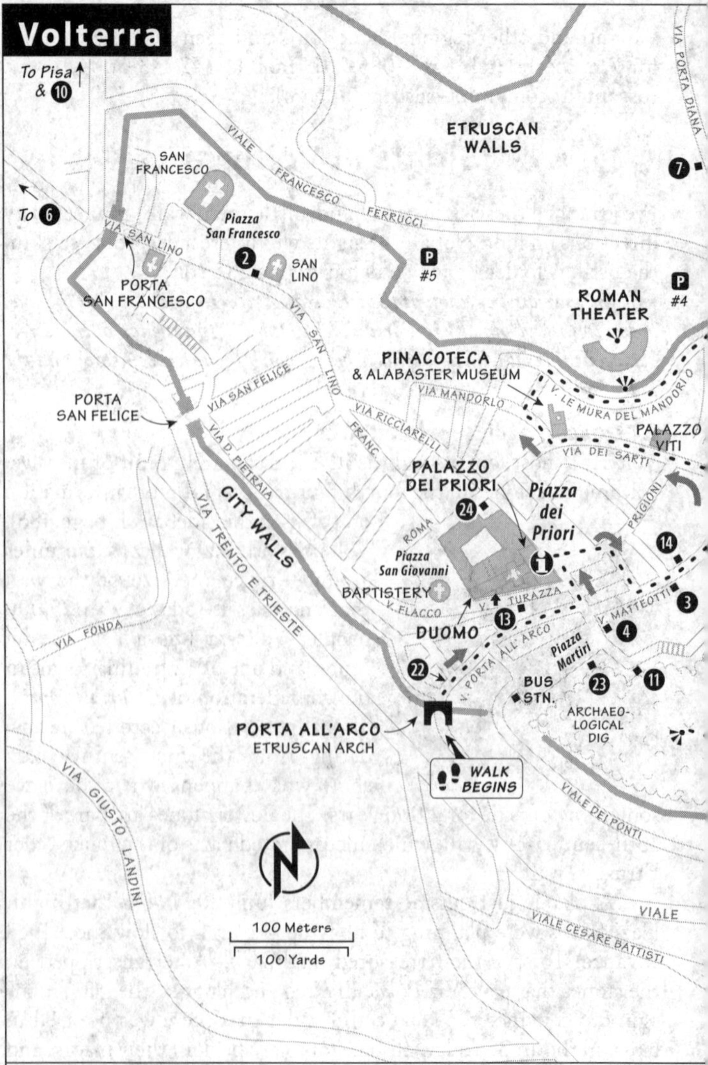

Accommodations

1. Hotel La Locanda
2. Hotel San Lino
3. Albergo Etruria
4. Albergo Nazionale
5. To Park Hotel Le Fonti
6. To Albergo Villa Nencini & Old Etruscan Wall
7. La Primavera B&B
8. Seminario Vescovile Sant'Andrea
9. To Chiosco delle Monache Hostel, Hotel Foresteria &Trattoria da Badò
10. To Podere Marcampo

Eateries

11. Ristorante Enoteca del Duca
12. La Carabaccia

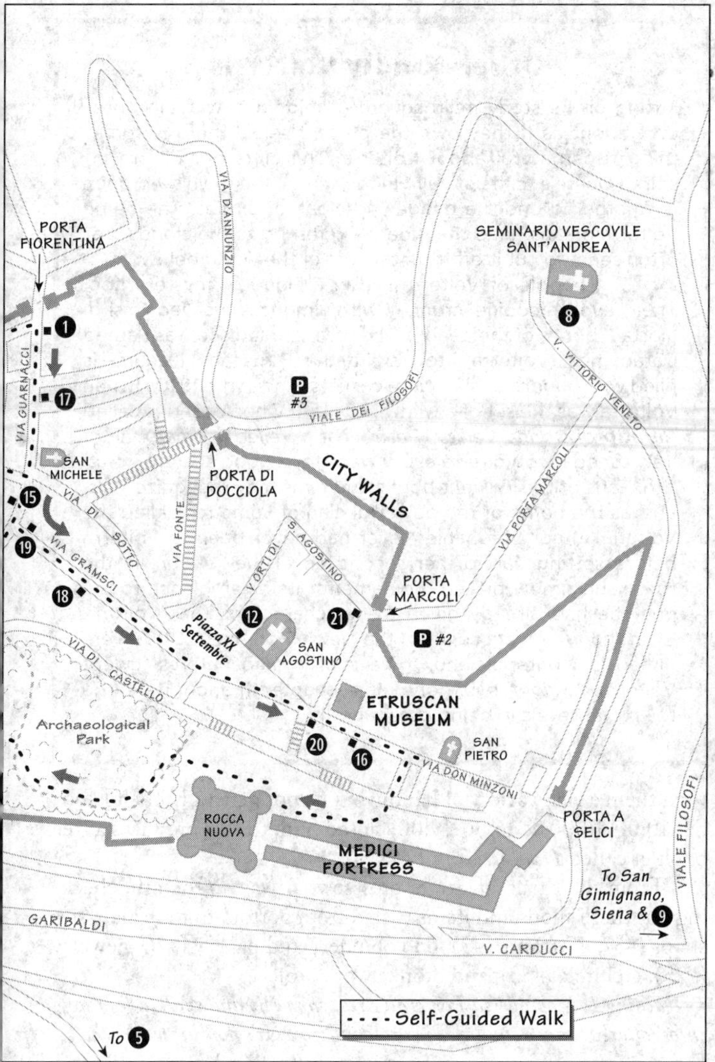

13 Ristorante il Sacco Fiorentino
14 La Vecchia Lira
15 Don Beta Trattoria
16 La Vena di Vino Wine Bar
17 Ombra della Sera & Pizzeria Tavernetta
18 Despar Market
19 L'Isola di Gusto Gelato

Other

20 Alab'Arte Alabaster Showroom
21 Alab'Arte Alabaster Workshop
22 "Artisan Lane"
23 Internet Café
24 Launderette

Otherworldly Volterra

Sitting on its stony main square at midnight, watching bats dart about as if they own the place, I sense there is something supernatural about Volterra. The cliffs of Volterra inspired Dante's "cliffs of hell." In the winter, the town's vibrancy is smothered under a deadening cloak of clouds. The name Volterra means "land that floats"—referring to the clouds that often seem to cut it off from the rest of the world below.

The people of Volterra live in a cloud of mystery, too. Their favorite cookie, crunchy with almonds, is called Ossi di Morta ("bones of the dead"). The town's first disco was named Catacombs. Volterra's top sight—the Etruscan Museum—is filled with hundreds of ancient caskets. And in the 1970s, when Volterra was the set of a wildly popular TV horror series called *Ritratto di Donna Velata (Portrait of a Veiled Woman),* all of Italy tuned in to Volterra every week for a good scare.

Fans of the *Twilight* books and films may recognize Volterra as the home of the powerful clan of vampires called the Volturi. Author Stephanie Meyer had never been to Volterra before setting part of her second novel, *New Moon,* in the town; she simply picked the name for its resemblance to the one she had already given to her characters, the "Volturi." Even though most scenes in the *New Moon* film (2009) were filmed in Montepulciano, a wave of *Twilight* interest swept Volterra. *Twilight* is just one more chapter in a long tale of a town that revels in being otherworldly.

with them a rich variety of handiwork (shops generally open Mon-Sat 10:00-13:00 & 16:00-19:00, closed Sun; the TI produces a free booklet called *Handicraft in Volterra*).

From the Etruscan Arch, browse your way up the hill, checking out these shops and items (listed from bottom to top): alabaster shops (#57, #50, and #45); book bindery and papery (#26); jewelry (#25); etchings (#23); and bronze work (#6).

• *Reaching the top of Via Porta all'Arco, turn left and walk a few steps into Volterra's main square, Piazza dei Priori. It's dominated by the...*

Palazzo dei Priori

Volterra's City Hall (c. 1209) claims to be the oldest of any Tuscan city-state. It clearly inspired the more famous Palazzo Vecchio in Florence. Town halls like this are emblematic of an era when city-states were powerful. They were architectural exclamation points declaring that, around here, no pope or emperor called the shots. Towns such as Volterra were truly city-states—proudly independent and relatively democratic. They had their own armies, taxes, and even weights and measures. Notice the horizontal "cane" cut into the City Hall wall (right of the door). For a thousand years, this square hosted a market, and the "cane" was the local yardstick. You can pay to see the council chambers, and to climb to the top of the bell tower.

Cost and Hours: €1.50 for council chambers, €2 tower climb, mid-March-Oct daily 10:30-17:30, Nov-mid-March Sat-Sun only 10:00-16:30.

Visiting the Palazzo: When not in use for meetings or weddings, the building's historic **High Council Hall**—fine arches lavishly frescoed and lit with fun dragon lamps, as they have been for centuries of town meetings—is open to visitors. The adjacent Sala della Giunta is a simpler, smaller meeting room with bare stone walls.

The adventurous can continue up to the top of the **tower** (159 steps total from the front door). Partway up, you'll find a modest exhibit about the history of the town, including a model of Volterra in the late 13th century (looking much as it does today) and a wooden cutaway model of the tower itself. Then you'll huff up a tight, winding, metal staircase to a small platform with panoramic views of the city and surrounding countryside. They don't let visitors go up on the hour or half-hour, when the eardrum-piercing bell clangs.

• *Facing the City Hall, notice the black-and-white-striped wall to the right (set back from the square). The door in that wall leads into Volterra's...*

Duomo

This church is not as elaborate as its cousin in Pisa, but the simple 13th-century facade and the interior (rebuilt in the late 16th century), with its central nave flanked by monolithic stone columns, are beautiful examples of the Pisan Romanesque style.

Cost and Hours: Free, daily 8:00-12:30 & 15:00-18:00, Nov-March until 17:00, closed Fri 15:00-16:00 while the cleaners religiously perform their duties.

Visiting the Church: Enter through the door off Piazza dei Priori (technically the back door), and take a moment to let your eyes adjust to this dark, Romanesque space. (If you come through the main door around on Piazza San Giovanni, do this tour in reverse.) The interior was decorated mostly in the late 16th century, during Florentine rule under the Medici family. Their coat of arms, with its distinctive balls (called *palle,* representing the "pills" of the Medici—or "Medics"), is repeated multiple times throughout the building.

Head down into the nave to face the main altar. Up the stairs just to the right is a dreamy, painted and gilded-wood ***Deposition*** (Jesus being taken down from the cross), restored to its original

Italy Is Made of Tuff Stuff

Tuff (*tufo* in Italian) is a light-colored volcanic rock that is common in Italy. A part of Tuscany is even called the "Tuff Area." The seven hills of Rome are made of tuff, and quarried blocks of this stone can be seen in the Colosseum, Pantheon, and Castel Sant'Angelo. Just outside of Rome, the catacombs were carved from tuff. Sorrento rises above the sea on a tuff outcrop. Orvieto, Civita di Bagnoregio (pictured), and many other hill towns perch on bluffs of tuff.

Italy's early inhabitants, including the Etruscans and Romans, carved caves, tunnels, burial niches, and even roads out of tuff. Blocks of this rock were quarried to make houses and walls. Tuff is soft and easy to carve when it's first exposed to air, but hardens later, which makes it a good building stone.

Italy's tuff-producing volcanoes resulted from a lot of tectonic-plate bumping and grinding. This violent geologic history is reflected in Italy's volcanoes, like Vesuvius and Etna, and earthquakes such as the 2009 quake in the L'Aquila area northeast of Rome.

Tuff is actually just a big hardened pile of old volcanic ash. When volcanoes hold magma that contains a lot of water, they erupt explosively (think heat + water = steam = POW!). The exploded rock material gets blasted out as hot volcanic ash, which settles on the surrounding landscape, piles up, and over time welds together into the rock called tuff.

So when you're visiting an area in Italy of ancient caves or catacombs built out of this material, you'll know that at least once (and maybe more) upon a time, it was a site of a lot of volcanic activity.

form. Carved in 1228, a generation before Giotto, it shows emotion and motion way ahead of its time (€1 buys some light).

The glowing **windows** in the transept and behind the altar are sheets of alabaster. These, along with the recorded Gregorian chants, add to the church's wonderful ambience.

The 12th-century marble **pulpit,** partway down the nave, is also beautifully carved. In the relief panel of the Last Supper, all the apostles are together except Judas, who's under the table with the evil dragon (his name is the only one not carved into the relief).

Just past the pulpit on the right (at the Rosary Chapel), check out the ***Annunciation*** by Fra Bartolomeo (who was a student of Fra Angelico and painted this in 1497). Bartolomeo delicately gives worshippers a way to see Mary "conceived by the Holy Spirit." Note the vibrant colors, exaggerated perspective, and Mary's *contrapposto* pose—all attributes of the Renaissance.

At the end of the nave, the large **chapel** to the right of the doors has painted terra-cotta statue groups of the Nativity and the Adoration of the Magi, thought to be the work of master ceramists Luca and Andrea della Robbia. Luca is credited with inventing the glazing formula that makes his inventive sculptures shine even in poorly lit interiors. At the end of the chapel, ponder a statue with an unusual but poignant theme: Mary, *Mater Dolorosa* ("mother in pain"), literally pierced by swords as she suffers the agony of seeing her crucified son's body.

To see a classically Pisan space, step outside the door into Piazza San Giovanni. A common arrangement in the Middle Ages—when Pisa, not Florence, was the big regional influence here—was for the church to face the baptistery (you couldn't enter the church until you were baptized)...and for the hospital to face the cemetery (now the site of the local ambulance corps). These buildings all overlooked a single square. That's how it is in Pisa, and that's how it is here. Step into the baptistery and look up into the vast, empty space—plenty of room for the Holy Spirit.

• *Exit the cathedral out the back door—the way you entered—and into today's main square, Piazza dei Priori. Face the City Hall, and go down the street to the left; after one short block, you're standing at the head (on the left) of...*

▲Via Matteotti

The town's main drag, named after the popular Socialist leader Giacomo Matteotti (killed by the Fascists in 1924), provides a good cultural scavenger hunt.

At **#1,** on the left, is a typical Italian bank security door. (Step in and say, "Beam me up, Scotty.") Back outside, stand at the corner, and look up and all around. Find the medieval griffin torch holder—symbol of Volterra, looking down Via Matteotti—and imagine it holding a lit torch. The pharmacy sports the symbol of its medieval guild. Across the street from the bank, **#2** is the base of what was a San Gimignano-style fortified Tuscan tower. Look up and imagine heavy beams cantilevered out, supporting extra wooden rooms and balconies crowding out over the street. Throughout Tuscany, today's stark and stony old building fronts once supported a tangle of wooden extensions.

As you head down Via Matteotti, notice how the doors show centuries of refitting work. Doors that once led to these extra rooms are now partially bricked up to make windows. Contemplate urban density in the 14th century, before the plague thinned out the population. Be careful: There's a wild boar (a local delicacy) at **#10.**

At **#12,** on the right, notice the line of doorbells: This typical palace, once the home of a single rich family, is now occupied by many middle-class families. After the social revolution in the 18th century and the rise of the middle class, former palaces were condominium-ized. Even so, like in *Dr. Zhivago,* the original family still lives here. Apartment #1 is the home of Count Guidi.

On the right at **#16,** pop in to the alabaster showroom. Alabaster, mined nearby, has long been a big industry here. Volterra alabaster—softer and more porous than marble—was sliced thin to serve as windows for Italy's medieval churches.

At **#19,** the recommended La Vecchia Lira is a lively cafeteria. The Bar L'Incontro across the street is a favorite for pastries; in the summer, they sell homemade gelato, while in the winter they make chocolates.

Across the way, up Vicolo delle Prigioni, is a fun bakery (Panificio Rosetti). They're happy to sell small quantities if you want to try the local *cantuccini* (almond biscotti) or another treat (closed 14:00-17:30, Sat after 14:00, and all day Sun).

Continue to the end of the block. At **#51,** on the left, a bit of Etruscan wall is artfully used to display more alabaster art. And #56A is the alabaster art gallery of Paolo Sabatini, who specializes in unique, contemporary sculptures.

Locals gather early each evening at Osteria dei Poeti (at **#57**) for some of the best cocktails in town—served with free munchies. The cinema is across the street. Movies in Italy are rarely in *versione originale*; Italians are used to getting their movies dubbed into Italian. To bring some culture to this little town, they also show live broadcasts of operas and concerts (advertised in the window).

At **#66,** another Tuscan tower marks the end of the street. This noble house has a ground floor with no interior access to the safe upper floors. Rope ladders were used to get upstairs. The tiny door was wide enough to let in your skinny friends...but definitely not anyone wearing armor and carrying big weapons.

Across the little square stands the ancient Church of St. Michael. After long years of barbarian chaos, the Lombards moved in from the north and asserted law and order in places like Volterra. That generally included building a Christian church on the old Roman forum to symbolically claim and tame the center of town. (Locals still call this San Michele in Foro—"in the forum.") The church standing here today is Romanesque, dating from the 12th century. Around the right side, find the crude little guy and the smiling octopus under its eaves—they've been making faces at the passing crowds for 800 years.

• *Three more sights—Palazzo Viti (fancy old palace), the Pinacoteca (gallery of gilded altarpieces), and the Alabaster Museum (within the Pinacoteca building)—are a short stroll down Via dei Sarti: From the end of Via Matteotti, turn left. If you want to skip straight down to the Roman Theater, just head straight from the end of Via Matteotti onto Via Guarnacci, then turn left when you get to the Porta Fiorentina gate. To head directly to Volterra's top sight, the Etruscan Museum, just turn around, walk a block back up Via Matteotti, turn left on Via Gramsci, and follow it all the way through Piazza XX Settembre up Via Don Minzoni to the museum.*

▲Palazzo Viti

Go behind the rustic, heavy stone walls of the city and see how the nobility lived (in this case, rich from 19th-century alabaster wealth). One of the finest private residential buildings in Italy, with 12 rooms open to the public, Palazzo Viti feels remarkably lived in—because it is. You'll also find Signora Viti herself selling admission tickets. It's no wonder this time warp is so popular with Italian movie directors. Remember, you're helping keep a noble family in leotards.

Cost and Hours: €5, April-Oct daily 10:00-13:00 & 14:30-18:30, closed Nov-March, Via dei Sarti 41, tel. 0588-84047, www.palazzoviti.it.

Visiting the Palazzo: The elegant interior is compact and well-described by the loaner English descriptions. You'll climb up a stately staircase, buy your ticket, and head into the grand ballroom. From here, you'll tour the blue-hued dining room (with slice-of-life Chinese scenes painted on rice paper); the salon of battles (with warfare paintings on the walls); and the long hall of temporary exhibits. Looping back, you'll see the porcelain hall (decorated with priceless plates) and the inviting library (notice the delicate lamp with a finely carved alabaster lampshade). The Brachettone Salon is named for the local artist responsible for the small sketch of near-nudes hanging just left of the door into the next room. Bracchettone (from *brache,* "pants") is the artistic nickname for Volterra-born Daniele Ricciarelli, who owns the dubious distinction of having painted all of those wispy loincloths over the genitalia of Michelangelo's figures in the Sistine Chapel. (In this drawing, notice a similar aversion to showing the full monty...though everything but is fair game.) In the red room, portraits of the Viti boys face each other (hanging next to the doors). Your visit ends with bedrooms and a dressing room, making it easy to imagine how the other half lived...and, from November through March, presumably still does.

• *A block past Palazzo Viti, also on Via dei Sarti, is the...*

Pinacoteca and Alabaster Museum

The Pinacoteca fills a 15th-century palace with fine paintings that feel more Florentine than Sienese—a reminder of whose domain this town was in. You'll see roomfuls of gilded altarpieces and saintly statues, as well as a trio of striking High Renaissance altar paintings by Signorelli, Fiorentino, and Ghirlandaio. While this isn't worth the entry price, if you're visiting the Etruscan Museum, the combo-ticket gets you in here for just €2 extra.

Cost and Hours: €8, €10 combo-ticket includes Etruscan Museum, daily mid-March-Oct 9:00-19:00, Nov-mid-March 10:00-16:00, Via dei Sarti 1, no photos permitted, tel. 0588-87580.

Visiting the Museum: Begin with the **Pinacoteca,** and head upstairs to the first floor. If you go left, you'll circle all the way around and save the best for last—but to cut to the chase, turn right at the landing and go directly into the best room (#11), with Luca Signorelli's beautifully lit *Annunciation* (1491), an example of classic High Renaissance (from the town cathedral), and (to the right) *Deposition from the Cross* (1521), the groundbreaking Mannerist work by Rosso Fiorentino (note the elongated bodies and harsh emotional lighting and colors). In the adjacent room (#10), see Ghirlandaio's *Christ in Glory* (1492). The two devout-looking kneeling women are actually pagan, pre-Christian Etruscan demigoddesses, Attinea and Greciniana, but the church identified them as obscure saints to make the painting acceptable. Rather than attempt to get locals to stop venerating them (as their images were all over town), the church simply sainted them. Upstairs, the second floor has three more rooms of similar art—huge frescoes and oil-on-wood paintings.

Back on the main floor, head through the fine, tranquil, cloister-like courtyard—with the remains of its original well—and enter the **Alabaster Museum.** With alabaster sculptures spread over three floors, the museum contains examples from Etruscan times until the present—but lacks English descriptions. The top floor displays stone-working tools and offers fine views. Etruscan pieces are on the middle floor, and modern sculptures—including an intriguing alabaster fried egg—are on the lower floor.

• *Exiting the museum, turn right, then right again down the Passo del Gualduccio passage into the parking-lot square; at the end of this square, turn right and walk along the wall, with fine views of the...*

Roman Theater

Built in the first century B.C., this well-preserved theater has good acoustics. Because a fine aerial view is available from the city wall promenade, you may find it unnecessary to pay admission to enter. Belly up to the 13th-century wall and look down. The wall that you're standing on divided the theater from the town center...so, naturally, the theater became the town dump. Over time, the theater was forgotten—covered in the garbage of Volterra. Luckily, it was rediscovered in the 1950s, by an administrator (and armchair historian) at the local mental hospital. Since they couldn't secure government funding for the dig, the theater was first excavated by mental patients who found the activity therapeutic.

The stage wall was standard Roman design—with three levels from which actors would appear: one level for mortals, one for heroes, and the top one for gods. Parts of two levels still stand. Gods leaped out onto the third level for the last time around the third century A.D., which is when the town began to use the theater stones to build fancy baths instead. You can see the remains of the baths behind the theater, including the round sauna with brick supports that raise the heated floor.

From the vantage point on the city wall promenade, you can trace Volterra's vast Etruscan wall. Find the church in the distance, on the left, and notice the stones just below. They are from the Etruscan wall that followed the ridge into the valley and defined Volterra in the fourth century B.C.

Cost and Hours: €3.50, but you can view the theater free from Via Lungo le Mure; the entrance is near the little parking lot just outside Porta Fiorentina—you can see the entry to the right as you survey the theater from above; mid-March-Oct daily 10:30-17:30, Nov-mid-March Sat-Sun only 10:00-16:00, may be closed in bad weather.

• *From the Roman Theater, make your way back to Via Matteotti (follow Via Guarnacci straight up from Porta Fiorentina). A block down Via Matteotti, you can't miss the wide, pedestrianized shopping street called Via Gramsci. Follow this up to Piazza XX Settembre, walk through that leafy square, and continue uphill on Via Don Minzoni. Watch on your left for the...*

▲▲Etruscan Museum (Museo Etrusco Guarnacci)

Filled top to bottom with rare Etruscan artifacts, this museum—even with few English explanations and its dusty, almost neglectful, old-school style—makes it easy to appreciate how advanced this pre-Roman culture was.

Cost and Hours: €8, €10 combo-ticket includes the Pinacoteca and Alabaster Museum; daily mid-March-Oct 9:00-19:00, Nov-mid-March 10:00-16:00; ask at the ticket window for mildly interesting English pamphlet, audioguide-€3, Via Don Minzoni 15, tel. 0588-86347, www.comune.volterra.pi.it/english.

Visiting the Museum: The museum's three floors feel dusty and disorganized. As there are scarcely any English explanations, consider the serious but interesting audioguide; the information below hits the highlights.

Ground Floor: The collection starts with a small gathering of pre-Etruscan Villanovian artifacts (c. 1500 B.C., to the left as you enter), but one of its highlights is straight ahead, sprawling through several rooms: a seemingly endless collection of Etruscan **funerary urns** (dating from the seventh to the first century B.C.). Designed to contain the ashes of cremated loved ones, each urn is tenderly carved with a unique scene, offering a peek into the still-mysterious Etruscan society. Etruscan urns have two parts: The casket on the bottom contained the remains (with elaborately carved panels), while the lid was decorated with a sculpture of the departed.

First pay attention to the people on top. While contemporaries of the Greeks, the Etruscans were more libertine. Their religion was less demanding, and their women were a respected part of both the social and public spheres. Women and men alike are depicted lounging on Etruscan urns. While they seem to be just hanging out, the lounging dead were actually offering the gods a banquet—in order to gain their favor in the transition to the next life. The banquet—where Etruscans really did lounge like this in front of a table—was the epitome of their social structure. But the outcome of this particular banquet had eternal consequences. The dearly departed are often depicted holding scrolls, blank wax tablets (symbolizing blank new lives in the next world), and containers that would generally be used at banquets, including libation cups for offering wine to the gods. The women in particular are finely dressed, sometimes holding a pomegranate (symbolizing fertility) or a mirror. Look at the faces, and imagine the lives they lived and the loved ones they left behind.

Now tune into the reliefs carved into the fronts of the caskets. The motifs vary widely, from floral patterns to mystical animals (such as a Starbucks-like mermaid) to parades of magistrates. Most show journeys on horseback—appropriate for someone leaving this world and entering the next. The most evocative scenes show the fabled horseback-and-carriage ride to the underworld, where the dead are greeted by Charon, an underworld demon, with his hammer and pointy ears.

While the finer urns are carved of alabaster, most are made of limestone. Originally they were colorfully painted. Many lids are mismatched—casualties of reckless 18th- and 19th-century archaeological digs.

First Floor: Upstairs, you'll enter a room with a circular mosaic in the floor (a Roman original, found in Volterra and transplanted here). Turn left into a series of green rooms—the best presented (and most important) of the museum.

The first room, Sala XIV, collects scenes of Ulysses carved into the fronts of caskets. Turn left and head into Sala XV, with the museum's prize piece. Fans of Alberto Giacometti will be amazed at how the tall, skinny figure called ***The Evening Shadow*** (*L'Ombra della Sera,* third century B.C.) looks just like the modern Swiss sculptor's work—but is 2,500 years older. This is an exceptional example of the *ex-voto* bronze statues that the Etruscans created in thanks to the gods. With his supremely lanky frame, distinctive wavy hairdo, and inscrutable Mona Lisa smirk, this Etruscan lad captures the illusion of a shadow stretching long late in the day. Admire the sheer artistry of the statue; with its right foot shifted slightly forward, it even hints at the *contrapposto* pose that would become common in this same region during the Renaissance, two millennia later.

Continue circling clockwise, through Sala XVI (alabaster urns with more Greek myths), Sala XVII (ex-voto water-bearer statues, kraters—vases with handles, and bronze hand mirrors), and Sala XVIII (exquisite golden jewelry that would still be fashionable today). Sala XIX shows off the museum's other top piece, the ***Urn of the Spouses*** (*Urna degli Sposi,* first century B.C.). It's unique for various reasons, including its material (it's in terra-cotta—a relatively rare material for these funerary urns) and its depiction of two people rather than one. Looking at this elderly couple, it's easy to imagine the long life they spent together and their desire to pass eternity lounging with each other at a banquet for the gods.

The rest of this floor has a battle helmet ominously dented at the left temple; black glazed pottery; thousands of Etruscan, Greek, and Roman coins; and many more bronze ex-votos and jewelry.

Top Floor: From the top of the stairs, turn right, then immediately right again to find a re-created grave site, with several neatly aligned urns and artifacts that would have been buried with the deceased. Some of these were funeral dowries (called *corredo*) that the dead would pack along. You'll see artifacts such as mirrors, coins, hardware for vases, votive statues, pots, pans, and jewelry. On the landing are fragments from Volterra's acropolis—a site now occupied by the Medici Fortress. The rest of this floor shows even more burial urns, pottery, and ex-votos.

• *After your visit, duck across the street to the alabaster showroom and the wine bar (both described next).*

Under the Etruscan Sun
(c. 900 B.C.–A.D. 1)

Around 550 B.C.—just before the Golden Age of Greece—the Etruscan people of central Italy had their own Golden Age. Though their origins are mysterious, their mix of Greek-style art with Roman-style customs helped lay a civilized foundation for the rise of the Roman Empire. As you travel through Italy—particularly in Tuscany (from "Etruscan"), you'll find traces of this long-lost people.

Etruscan tombs and artifacts are still being discovered, often by farmers in the countryside. Museums in Volterra and Cortona house fine collections of urns, pottery, and devotional figures. You can visit several domed tombs outside Cortona.

The Etruscans first appeared in the ninth century B.C., when a number of cities sprouted up in sparsely populated Tuscany and Umbria, including today's hill towns of Cortona, Chiusi, and Volterra. Possibly immigrants from Turkey, but more likely local farmers who moved to the city, they became traders and craftsmen, and welcomed new ideas from Greece.

More technologically advanced than their neighbors, the Etruscans mined metal, exporting it around the Mediterranean, both as crude ingots and as some of the finest-crafted jewelry in the known world. They drained and irrigated large tracts of land, creating the fertile farmland of central Italy's breadbasket. With their disciplined army, warships, merchant vessels, and (from the Greek perspective) pirate galleys, they ruled central Italy and the major ports along the Tyrrhenian Sea. For nearly two centuries (c. 700-500 B.C.), much of Italy lived a Golden Age of peace and prosperity under the Etruscan sun.

Judging from the frescoes and many luxury items that have survived, the Etruscans enjoyed the good life: They look healthy and vibrant as they play flutes, dance with birds, or play party games. Etruscan artists celebrated individual people, showing their wrinkles, crooked noses, silly smiles, and funny haircuts.

Thousands of surviving ceramic plates and cups attest to the importance of food. Men and women ate together, propped on their elbows on dining couches, surrounded by colorful decor. According to contemporary accounts, the Etruscans, even their slaves, were Europe's best-dressed people. The banqueters were entertained with music and dancing, and served by elegant and well-treated slaves.

Scholars today have deciphered the Etruscans' Greek-style alphabet and some individual words, but they have yet to fully crack the code. Much of what we know of the Etruscans comes from their tombs. The tomb was a home in the hereafter, complete with all of the deceased's belongings. The sarcophagus might have a statue on the lid of the deceased at a banquet—lying across a dining couch, spooning with his wife, smiles on their

faces, living the good life for all eternity.

Seven decades of wars with the Greeks (545-474 B.C.) disrupted their trade routes and drained the Etruscan League, just as a new Mediterranean power was emerging: Rome. In 509 B.C., the Romans overthrew their Etruscan king, and Rome expanded, capturing Etruscan cities one by one (the last in 264 B.C.). Etruscan resisters were killed, the survivors intermarried with Romans, and their kids grew up speaking Latin. By Julius Caesar's time, the only remnants of Etruscan culture were its priests, who became Rome's professional soothsayers. Interestingly, the Etruscan prophets had foreseen their own demise, having predicted that Etruscan civilization would last 10 centuries.

But Etruscan culture lived on in Roman religion (pantheon of gods, household gods, and divination rituals), art (realism), lifestyle (the banquet), and in a taste for Greek styles—the mix that became our "Western civilization."

▲Alabaster Workshop

Alab'Arte offers a fun peek into the art of alabaster. Their showroom is across from the Etruscan Museum, but to find their powdery workshop, go a block downhill, in front of Porta Marcoli, where you can watch Roberto Chiti and Giorgio Finazzo at work. They are delighted to share their art with visitors. (Everything—including Roberto and Giorgio—is covered in a fine white dust.) Lighting shows off the translucent quality of the stone and the expertise of these artists. This is not a touristy guided visit, but something far more special: the chance to see busy artisans practicing their craft. For more such artisans in action, visit "Artisan Lane" (Via Porta all'Arco) described earlier, or ask the TI for their list of the town's many workshops open to the public.

Cost and Hours: Free, showroom—daily 9:30-13:00 & 15:00-19:00, Via Don Minzoni 18; workshop—March-Oct Mon-Sat 9:30-12:30 & 15:00-19:00, closed Sun, usually closed Nov-Feb—call ahead, Via Orti Sant'Agostino 28; tel. 0588-87968, www.alabarte.com.

▲La Vena di Vino (Wine-Tasting with Bruno and Lucio)

La Vena di Vino, also just across from the Etruscan Museum, is a fun *enoteca* where two guys who have devoted themselves to the wonders of wine share it with a fun-loving passion. Each day Bruno and Lucio open six or eight bottles, serve your choice by the glass, pair it with characteristic munchies, and offer fine music (guitars available for patrons) and an unusual decor (the place is strewn with bras). Hang out here with the local characters. This is your chance to try the Super Tuscan wine—a creative mix of international grapes grown in Tuscany. According to Bruno, the Brunello (€7/glass) is just right with wild boar, and the Super Tuscan (€6-7) is perfect for meditation. Food is served all day, including some microwaved hot dishes or a plate of meats and cheeses. Although Volterra is famously quiet late at night, this place is full of action. Downstairs is a rustic cellar that doubles on weekend nights as a sort of disco.

Cost and Hours: Pay per glass, open Wed-Mon 11:30-24:00, closed Tue—but may be open Tue in summer, 3- to 5-glass wine tastings, shipping options available, Via Don Minzoni 30, tel. 0588-81491, www.lavenadivino.com.

• *Volterra's final sight is perched atop the hill just above the wine bar. Climb up one of the lanes nearby, then walk (to the right) along the formidable wall to find the park.*

Medici Fortress and Archaeological Park

The Parco Archeologico marks what was the acropolis of Volterra from 1500 B.C. until A.D. 1472, when Florence conquered the pesky city and burned its political and historic center, turning it into a grassy commons and building the adjacent Medici Fortezza. The old fortress—a symbol of Florentine dominance—now keeps people in rather than out. It's a maximum-security prison housing only about 150 special prisoners. (When you're driving from San Gimignano to Volterra, you pass another big, modern prison—almost surreal in the midst of all the Tuscan wonder.) Authorities prefer to keep organized crime figures locked up far away from their family ties in Sicily.

The park sprawling next to the fortress (toward the town center) is a rare, grassy meadow at the top of a rustic hill town—a favorite place for locals to relax and picnic on a sunny day. Nearby are the remains of the acropolis (€3.50 to enter, ticket also includes the Roman Theater), but these can be viewed through the fence for free.

Cost and Hours: Free to enter park, open until 20:00 in peak of summer, progressively shorter hours off-season, until 17:00 in winter.

Countryside Strolls

All the sights listed above are in a tight little zone of the old town, about a 10-minute walk from each other. But if you have time for a stroll, Volterra—perched on a ridge overlooking pristine Tuscan hills—has countryside galore to explore. Get some advice from the TI.

One popular walk is to head to the west end of town, out Porta San Francesco, into a workaday area (dubbed "Borghi," literally "neighborhoods") that sees few tourists. Continuing downhill (past the Church of San Giusto), you'll come to a cliff with a stretch of the original fourth-century B.C. Etruscan wall. Peering over the cliff from here, you can see that Volterra sits upon orange sandy topsoil packed onto clay cliffs, called Le Balze. At various points in its history, the town has been threatened by landslides, and parts of its hilltop have simply disappeared. The big church you see in the distance was abandoned in the late 1800s for fear that it would be swallowed up by the land. The distinctive cliffs surrounding Volterra are called *calanchi* (similar to the French *calanques* that slash the Mediterranean coast).

Sleeping in Volterra

Predictably for a small town, Volterra's accommodations are limited, and all have their quirks—but there are plenty of places offering a good night's sleep at a fair price. While it's convenient to stay inside the old town, the lodgings that are a short walk away are generally a bit cheaper (and easier for drivers). But keep in mind that all of the "outside the old town" places involve not just walking, but steep walking.

INSIDE VOLTERRA'S OLD TOWN

$$$ Hotel La Locanda feels stately and old-fashioned. This well-located place (just inside Porta Fiorentina, near the Roman Theater and parking lot) rents 18 decent rooms with flowery decor and modern comforts (Db-€104, less off-season, 10 percent Rick Steves discount, air-con, elevator, Wi-Fi, Via Guarnacci 24/28, tel. 0588-81547, www.hotel-lalocanda.com, staff@hotel-lalocanda.com, Stefania and Irina).

$$$ Hotel San Lino fills a former convent with 32 modern, nondescript rooms at the sleepy lower end of town—close to the Porta San Francisco gate, and about a five-minute uphill walk to the main drag. Although it's within the town walls, it doesn't feel like it: The hotel has a fine swimming pool and view terrace, and is the only in-town option that's convenient for drivers, who can park at the on-site garage for €11 (Db-€109, "superior" room adds slightly newer furnishings for €10 more—not worth it, air-con, elevator, Wi-Fi, Via San Lino 26, tel. 0588-85250, www.hotelsanlino.net, info@hotelsanlino.com).

$$ Albergo Etruria, on Volterra's main drag, rents 21 fresh, modern, and spacious rooms within an ancient stone structure. They have a welcoming TV lounge and a peaceful rooftop garden (Sb-€75, Db-€95, Tb-€115, 10 percent discount with cash and this book when you book direct, fans, spotty Wi-Fi, Via Matteotti 32, tel. 0588-87377, www.albergoetruria.it, info@albergoetruria.it, Lisa and Giuseppina are fine hosts).

$$ Albergo Nazionale, with 38 big and aging rooms, is simple, a little musty, short on smiles, popular with school groups, and steps from the bus stop. It's a nicely located last resort if you have your heart set on sleeping in the old town (Sb-€65, Db-€88, Tb-€105, 10 percent discount with cash and this book if you book directly with the hotel, reception closes at midnight, elevator, Wi-Fi, Via dei Marchesi 11, tel. 0588-86284, fax 0588-84097, www.hotelnazionale-volterra.it, info@hotelnazionale-volterra.it).

Sleep Code

(€1 = about $1.40, country code: 39)

Abbreviations
S = Single, **D** = Double/Twin, **T** = Triple, **Q** = Quad, **b** = bathroom, **s** = shower only

Price Rankings
$$$ Higher Priced—Most rooms €100 or more.
$$ Moderately Priced—Most rooms between €70-100.
$ Lower Priced—Most rooms €70 or less.

Unless otherwise noted, credit cards are accepted, breakfast is included (but usually optional), Wi-Fi is generally free, and English is spoken. Many towns in Italy levy a hotel tax of about €2 per person, per night (usually not included in the rates I've quoted). Prices change; verify current rates online or by email. For the best prices, always book directly with the hotel.

JUST OUTSIDE THE OLD TOWN

These accommodations are within a 5- to 20-minute walk of the city walls.

$$$ Park Hotel Le Fonti, a dull and steep 10-minute walk downhill from Porta all'Arco, can't decide whether it's a business hotel or a resort. The spacious, imposing building feels old and stately, and has 64 modern, comfortable rooms, many with views. While generally overpriced (the management knows it's the only hotel of its kind in Volterra), it can be a good value if you manage to snag a deal. In addition to the swimming pool, guests can use a small spa with sauna, hot tub, and an intriguing "emotional shower" (Db-€89-165, average is about Db-€129 but prices vary wildly with the season, identical "superior" room adds a view for €20 extra, "deluxe" room with terrace costs €30 extra, elevator, Wi-Fi in lobby, on-site restaurant, wine bar, free parking, Via di Fontecorrenti 2, tel. 0588-85219, www.parkhotellefonti.com, info@parkhotellefonti.com).

$$ Albergo Villa Nencini, a steep 15-minute walk below town, is older-feeling and listlessly run, with 36 cheaply furnished rooms. But a few rooms have terraces, and many have views. Guests also enjoy the large pool and free parking (Sb-€67, Db-€88, Tb-€115, 10 percent discount with cash and this book, air-con, pay Wi-Fi, Borgo Santo Stefano 55, tel. 0588-86386, www.villanencini.it, info@villanencini.it, Nencini family).

$ La Primavera B&B feels like a British B&B transplanted to Tuscany. It's a great value just a few minutes' walk outside Porta Fiorentina (near the Roman Theater). Silvia rents five charming, neat-as-a-pin rooms that share a cutesy-country lounge. The house is along a fairly busy road, but set back in a pleasant courtyard. With free parking and the shortest walk (among my out-of-town listings) to the old town, this is a handy option for drivers (Sb-€50, Db-€75, Tb-€100, Wi-Fi, free parking, Via Porta Diana 15, tel. 0588-87295, mobile 328-865-0390, www.affittacamere-laprimavera.com, info@affittacamere-laprimavera.com).

$ Chiosco delle Monache, Volterra's youth hostel, fills a wing of the restored Convent of San Girolamo with 68 beds in 23 rooms. It's modern, spacious, and very institutional, with lots of services and a tranquil cloister to wander. However, it's about a 20-minute hike out of town, in a boring area near deserted hospital buildings (bed in 6-bed dorm-€18, breakfast extra, lockers; Db-€69, includes breakfast; reception closed 13:00-15:00 and after 22:00, elevator, Wi-Fi, free parking, kids' playroom, Via dell Teatro 4, look for hospital sign from main Volterra-San Gimignano road, tel. 0588-86613, www.ostellovolterra.it, chioscomonache@gmail.com). Nearby and run by the same organization, **$ Hotel Foresteria** has 35 big, utilitarian, new-feeling rooms with decent prices but the same location woes as the hostel; it's worth considering for budget travelers, families, and drivers—and ideal for someone who's all three (Sb-€58, Db-€82, Tb-€103, Qb-€122, includes breakfast, air-con, elevator, Wi-Fi, restaurant, free parking, Borgo San Lazzaro, tel. 0588-80050, www.foresteriavolterra.it, info@foresteriavolterra.it).

$ Seminario Vescovile Sant'Andrea is your cheap and monastic option. This place has been training priests for more than 500 years. Today, the remaining eight priests still train students, but when classes are over, their 40 rooms—separated by vast and holy halls in an echoing old mansion—are rented very cheaply. Look for the 15th-century Ascension ceramic by Andrea della Robbia, tucked away in a corner upstairs, and ask to see the abandoned, circa-1400 church (S-€20, Sb-€25, D-€40, Db-€50, T-€60, Tb-€75, no breakfast, closed Oct-March, elevator, closes at 24:00, groups welcome, free parking, 10-minute walk from Etruscan Museum, Viale Vittorio Veneto 2, tel. 0588-86028, seminariosantandre@gmail.com; Sergio and Sergio—*due Sergi*).

NEAR VOLTERRA

$$ Podere Marcampo is a newer *agriturismo* about 2.5 miles outside Volterra on the road to Pisa. Run by Genuino (owner of the recommended Ristorante Enoteca del Duca), his wife Ivana, and their English-speaking daughter Claudia, this peaceful spot has three well-appointed rooms and three apartments, plus a swimming pool with panoramic views. Genuino produces his award-winning Merlot on site and offers €20 wine-tastings with cheese and homemade salami. Cooking classes at their restaurant in town are also available (Db-€94, Db apartment-€118/€145 depending on size, Qb apartment-€195, more expensive mid-July-Aug, includes breakfast with this book, air-con, Wi-Fi, free self-service laundry, free parking, tel. 0588-85393, Claudia's mobile 328-174-4605, www.agriturismo-marcampo.com, info@agriturismo-marcampo.com).

Eating in Volterra

Menus feature a Volterran take on regional dishes. *Zuppa alla Volterrana* is a fresh vegetable-and-bread soup, similar to *ribollita* (except that it isn't made from leftovers). *Torta di ceci,* also known as *cecina,* is a savory-pancake-like dish made with garbanzo beans. Those with more adventurous palates dive into *trippa* (tripe; comes in a bowl like stew), the traditional breakfast of the alabaster carvers. *Fegatelli* are meatballs made with liver.

Ristorante Enoteca del Duca, with a locally respected chef named Genuino, serves well-presented and creative Tuscan cuisine. You can dine under a medieval arch with walls lined with wine bottles, in a sedate, high-ceilinged dining room (with an Etruscan statuette at each table), on a nice little patio out back, or in their little *enoteca* (wine cellar). It's a good place for truffles, and has a friendly staff and a fine wine list (which includes Genuino's own merlot, plus several much pricier options—choose carefully). The spacious seating, dressy clientele, and calm atmosphere make this a good choice for a romantic splurge (€42 food-sampler fixed-price meal, €10-15 pastas, €15-22 *secondi,* Wed-Mon 12:30-15:00 & 19:30-22:00, closed Tue, near City Hall at Via di Castello 2, tel. 0588-81510, www.enoteca-delduca-ristorante.it).

La Carabaccia is unique: not "Italian home cooking," but *real* Italian home cooking. No, seriously. This simple, family-run trattoria—which feels like a local family invited you over for dinner—serves classic Tuscan comfort food that's rarely seen on restaurant menus. They serve only two pastas and two *secondi* on any given night (listed on the chalkboard by the door). Committed to tradition, on Fridays they serve only fish. They also whip up €3-4 take-away sandwiches at the deli up front (€7-9 pastas and *secondi,* Tue-Sun 12:30-14:30 & 19:30-22:00, closed Mon, Piazza XX Settembre 4, tel. 0588-86239).

Ristorante il Sacco Fiorentino is a local favorite for traditional cuisine and seasonal seafood specials (€8-10 pastas, €11-15 *secondi,* Thu-Tue 12:00-15:00 & 19:00-22:00, closed Wed, Via Giusto Turazza 13, tel. 0588-88537).

Trattoria da Badò, a 10-minute hike out of town (along the main road toward San Gimignano, near the turn-off for the old hospital), is every local's favorite for its *tipica cucina Volterrana*. Giacomo and family offer a rustic atmosphere and serve food with no pretense—"the way you wish your mamma cooks." Reserve before you go, as it's often full (€10-12 pastas, €13 *secondi,* Thu-Tue 12:30-14:30 & 19:30-22:00, closed Wed, Borgo San Lazzero 9, tel. 0577-80402, www.trattoriadabado.com).

La Vecchia Lira, bright and cheery, is a classy self-serve eatery that's a hit with locals as a quick and cheap lunch spot by day (with €5-10 meals), and a fancier restaurant at night (€9-10 pastas, €13-16 *secondi;* Fri-Wed 11:30-14:30 & 19:00-22:30, closed Thu, Via Matteotti 19, tel. 0588-86180, Lamberto and Massimo).

Don Beta is a family-run trattoria on the main drag, popular with travelers for its flashy location, long menu, and reasonable prices. Mirko supervises the lively young team as they whisk out steaming plates of pasta and homemade desserts (€7-10 pastas, €12-18 *secondi,* daily 12:00-14:30 & 19:00-23:00, reservations smart, Via Matteotti 39, tel. 0588-86730, www.donbeta.it).

La Vena di Vino is an *enoteca* serving up simple and traditional dishes and the best of Tuscan wine in a fun atmosphere. As their hot dishes are microwaved (there's no real kitchen), come here more for the wine and ambience than for the food (€8-12 meals, closed Tue, Via Don Minzoni 30, tel. 0588-81491). For more details, read the description on page 496.

Pizzerias: **Ombra della Sera** dishes out what local kids consider the best pizza in town. At €6-9 a pop, their pizzas make for a cheap date (Tue-Sun 12:00-15:00 & 19:00-22:00, closed Mon, Via Guarnacci 16, don't confuse this with their second, pricier location on Via Gramsci; tel. 0588-85274). **Pizzeria Tavernetta,** next door, is more romantic, with delightful indoor and on-the-street seating. Its romantically frescoed dining room upstairs is the classiest I've seen in a pizzeria (€5-8 pizzas, Wed-Mon 12:00-15:00 & 18:30-22:30, closed Tue, Via Guarnacci 14, tel. 0588-88155).

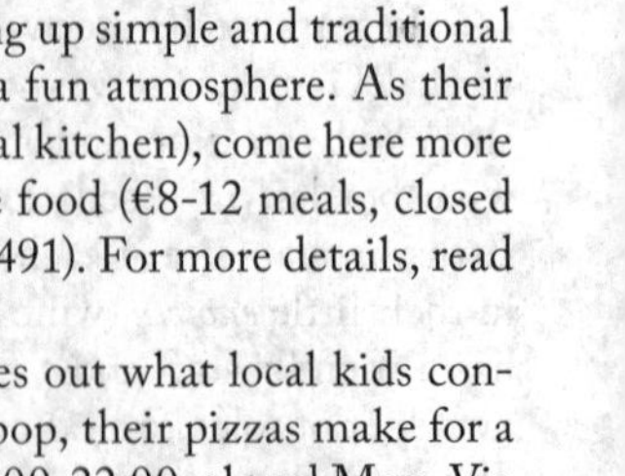

Picnic: You can assemble a picnic at the few *alimentari* around town (try Despar Market at Via Gramsci 12, Mon-Sat 7:30-13:00 & 16:00-20:00, Sun 8:30-13:00) and eat in the breezy Archaeological Park.

Gelato: Of the many ice-cream stands in the center, I've found **L'Isola di Gusto** to be reliably high quality (daily 11:00-late, Via Gramsci 3).

Volterra Connections

In Volterra, buses come and go from Piazza Martiri della Libertà (buy tickets at the tobacco shop right on the piazza; if it's closed, purchase on board for small extra charge). Most connections—except to Pisa—are with the C.P.T. bus company (www.cpt.pisa.it) through Colle di Val d'Elsa ("koh-leh" for short), a workaday town in the valley (4/day Mon-Sat, 1/day Sun, 50 minutes). The nearest train station is in Saline di Volterra, a 15-minute bus ride away (7/day, 2/day Sun); however, trains from Saline run only to the coast, not to the major bus destinations listed here.

From Volterra by Bus to: Florence (4/day Mon-Sat, 1/day Sun, 2 hours, change in Colle di Val d'Elsa), **Siena** (4/day Mon-Sat, no buses on Sun, 2 hours, change in Colle di Val d'Elsa), **San Gimignano** (4/day Mon-Sat, 1/day Sun, 2 hours, change in Colle di Val d'Elsa, one connection also requires change in Poggibonsi), **Pisa** (9/day, 2 hours, change in Pontedera).

San Gimignano

The epitome of a Tuscan hill town, with 14 medieval towers still standing (out of an original 72), San Gimignano (sahn jee-meen-YAH-noh) is a perfectly preserved tourist trap. There are no important interiors to sightsee, and the town is packed with crass commercialism. The locals seem spoiled by the easy money of tourism, and most of the rustic is faux. But San Gimignano is so easy to reach and so visually striking that it remains a good stop, especially if you can sidestep some of the hordes. The town is an ideal place to go against the touristic flow—arrive late in the day, enjoy it at twilight, then take off in the morning before the deluge begins. (Or if you're day-tripping from Volterra, try to visit San Gimignano early or late.)

In the 13th century—back in the days of Romeo and Juliet—feuding noble families ran the hill towns. They'd periodically battle things out from the protection of their respective family towers. Pointy skylines, like San Gimignano's, were the norm in medieval Tuscany.

San Gimignano's cuisine is mostly what you might find in Siena—typical Tuscan home cooking. *Cinghiale* (cheeng-GAH-lay, boar) is served in almost every way: stews, soups, cutlets, and, my favorite, salami. Most shops will give you a sample before you commit to buying. The area is well known for producing some of the best saffron in Italy (collected from the purple flowers of *Crocus sativus*); you'll find the spice for sale in shops (it's fairly expensive) and as a flavoring in meals at finer restaurants. Although Tuscany is normally a red-wine region, the most famous Tuscan white wine comes from here: the inexpensive, light, and fruity Vernaccia di San Gimignano. Look for the green "DOCG" label around the neck for the best quality (see "Wines Labels and Lingo" on page 656).

Orientation to San Gimignano

While the basic ▲▲▲ sight here is the town of San Gimignano itself (pop. 7,000), there are a few worthwhile stops. From the town gate, head straight up the traffic-free town's cobbled main drag to Piazza della Cisterna (with its 13th-century well). The town sights cluster around the adjoining Piazza del Duomo.

TOURIST INFORMATION

The helpful TI is in the old center on Piazza del Duomo (daily March-Oct 10:00-13:00 & 15:00-19:00, Nov-Feb 10:00-13:00 & 14:00-18:00, free maps, sells bus tickets, books rooms, handles VAT refunds, tel. 0577-940-008, www.sangimignano.com). They also offer a two-hour minibus tour to a countryside winery (€20, April-Oct Tue and Thu at 17:00, book one day in advance).

ARRIVAL IN SAN GIMIGNANO

The **bus** stops at the main town gate, Porta San Giovanni. There's no baggage storage anywhere in town (day-trippers can store bags in Siena, Florence, etc.).

You can't **drive** within the walled town; the "ZTL" limited-traffic zone (marked by a red circle) indicates that you'll get socked with a big fine if you carelessly cross the line. Three numbered pay lots are a short walk outside the walls: The handiest is Parcheggio Montemaggio (P2), at the bottom of town near the bus stop, just outside Porta San Giovanni (€2/hour, €20/day). Least expensive is the lot below the roundabout and Co-op supermarket, called Parcheggio Giubileo (P1; €1.50/hour, €6/day), but it comes with a steeper hike into town. And at the north end of town, by Porta San Jacopo, is Parcheggio Bagnaia (P3/P4, €2/hour, €15/day). Note that some lots—including the one directly in front of the Co-op and the one just outside Porta San Matteo—are designated for locals and have a one-hour limit for tourists.

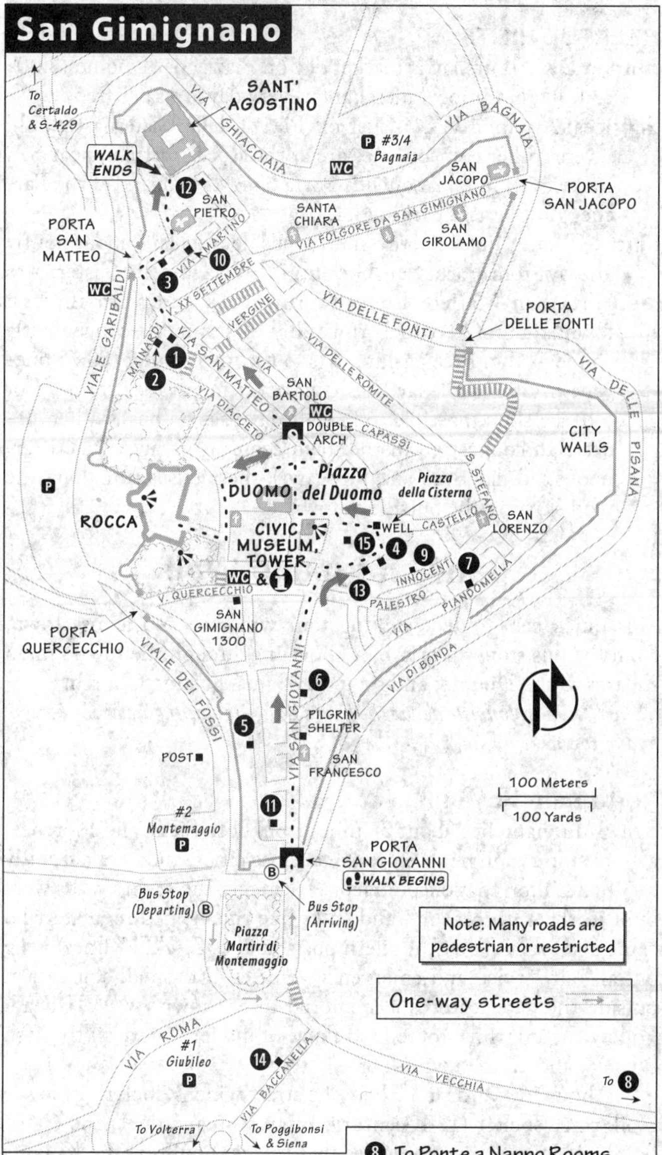

1. Hotel l'Antico Pozzo
2. Le Undici Lune
3. Locanda il Pino
4. Hotel la Cisterna
5. Palazzo al Torrione
6. Tobacco Shop (Torrione Keys)
7. Le Vecchie Mura Camere & Ristorante
8. To Ponte a Nappo Rooms
9. Dulcis in Fundo Ristorante
10. Cum Quibus Ristorante
11. Trattoria Chiribiri
12. Locanda di Sant'Agostino
13. diVinorum Wine Bar
14. Co-op Supermarket
15. Gelateria Dondoli

HELPFUL HINTS

Market Day: Thursday is market day on Piazza del Duomo (8:00-13:00), but for local merchants, every day is a sales frenzy.

Services: A public **WC** is just off Piazza della Cisterna (€0.50); several other coin-op ones are at the Rocca fortress, near San Bartolo church, just outside Porta San Matteo, and at the Parcheggio Bagnaia parking lot.

Shuttle Bus: A little electric shuttle bus does its laps about hourly all day from Porta San Giovanni to Piazza della Cisterna to Porta San Matteo. Route #1 runs back and forth through town; route #2—which runs only in summer—conveniently connects the three parking lots to the town center (€0.75 one-way, €1.50 for all-day pass, buy ticket in advance from TI or tobacco shop, possible to buy all-day pass on bus). When pedestrian congestion in the town center is greatest (Sat afternoons, all day Sun, and July-Aug), these buses run along the road skirting the outside of town.

San Gimignano Walk

This quick self-guided walking tour will take you across town, from the bus stop at Porta San Giovanni through the town's main squares to the Duomo, and on to the Sant'Agostino Church.

• *Start, as most tourists do, at the Porta San Giovanni gate at the bottom end of town.*

Porta San Giovanni

San Gimignano lies about 25 miles from both Siena and Florence, a good stop for pilgrims en route to those cities, and on a naturally fortified hilltop that encouraged settlement. The town's walls were built in the 13th century, and gates like this helped regulate who came and went. Today, modern posts (and stiff "ZTL" fines) keep out all but service and emergency vehicles. The small square just outside the gate features a memorial to the town's WWII dead. Follow the pilgrims' route (and flood of modern tourists) through the gate and up the main drag.

About 100 yards up, where the street widens, look right to see a pilgrims' shelter (12th-century, Pisan Romanesque). The eight-pointed Maltese cross indicates that this was built by the Knights of Malta, whose early mission (before they became a military unit) was to provide hospitality for pilgrims. It was one of 11 such shelters in town. Today, only the wall of this shelter remains.

• *Carry on past all manner of touristy rip-off shops, up to the town's central Piazza della Cisterna. Sit on the steps of the well.*

Piazza della Cisterna

The piazza is named for the cistern that is served by the old well standing in the center of this square. A clever system of pipes drained rainwater from the nearby rooftops into the underground cistern. This square has been the center of the town since the ninth century. Turn in a slow circle and observe the commotion of rustic-yet-proud facades crowding in a tight huddle around the well. Imagine this square in pilgrimage times, lined by inns and taverns for the town's guests. Now finger the grooves in the lip of the well and imagine generations of maids and children fetching water. Each Thursday, the square fills with a market—as it has for more than a thousand years.

• *Notice San Gimignano's famous towers.*

The Towers

Of the original 72 towers, only 14 survive. Before effective city walls were developed, rich people fortified their own homes with these towers: They provided a handy refuge when ruffians and rival city-states were sacking the town. If under attack, tower owners would set fire to the external wooden staircase, leaving the sole entrance unreachable a story up; inside, fleeing nobles pulled up behind them the ladders that connected each level, leaving invaders no way to reach the stronghold at the tower's top. These towers became a standard part of medieval skylines. Even after town walls were built, the towers continued to rise—now to fortify noble families feuding within a town (Montague and Capulet-style).

In the 14th century, San Gimignano's good times turned very bad. In the year 1300, about 13,000 people lived within the walls. Then in 1348, a six-month plague decimated the population, leaving the once-mighty town with barely 4,000 survivors. Once fiercely independent, now crushed and demoralized, San Gimignano came under Florence's control and was forced to tear down its towers. (The Banca CR Firenze building occupies the remains of one such toppled tower.) And, to add insult to injury, Florence redirected the vital trade route away from San Gimignano. The town never recovered, and poverty left it in a 14th-century architectural time warp. That well-preserved cityscape, ironically, is responsible for the town's prosperity today.

• *From the well, walk 30 yards uphill to the adjoining square with the cathedral.*

Piazza del Duomo

The square faces the former cathedral. The twin towers to the right are 10th century, among the first in town. The stubby tower opposite the church is typical of a merchant's tower: main door on ground floor, warehouse upstairs, holes to hold beams that once supported wooden balconies and exterior staircases, heavy stone on the first floor, cheaper and lighter brick for upper stories.

• *On the piazza are the Civic Museum and Tower, worth checking out. You'll also see the...*

Duomo (or Collegiata)

Inside San Gimignano's Romanesque cathedral, Sienese Gothic art (14th century) lines the nave with parallel themes—Old Testament on the left and New Testament on the right. (For example, from back to front: Creation facing the Annunciation, the birth of Adam facing the Nativity, and—farther forward—the suffering of Job opposite the suffering of Jesus.) This is a classic use of art to teach. Study the fine Creation series (along the left side). Many scenes are portrayed with a local 14th-century "slice of life" setting, to help lay townspeople relate to Jesus—in the same way that many white Christians are more comfortable thinking of Jesus as Caucasian (€4, €6 combo-ticket includes mediocre Religious Art Museum—skip it, admission includes dry audioguide; April-Oct Mon-Fri 10:00-19:30, Sat 10:00-17:30, Sun 12:30-19:00; shorter hours off-season; last entry 20 minutes before closing, buy ticket and enter from the courtyard around the left side).

• *From the church, hike uphill (passing the church on your left) following signs to* Rocca e Parco di Montestaffoli. *Keep walking until you enter a peaceful hilltop park and olive grove within the shell of a 14th-century fortress.*

Hilltop Views at the Rocca

On the far side, 33 steps take you to the top of a little tower (free) for the best views of San Gimignano's skyline; the far end of town and the Sant'Agostino Church (where this walk ends); and a commanding 360-degree view of the Tuscan countryside. San Gimignano is surrounded by olives, grapes, cypress trees, and—in the Middle Ages—lots of wild dangers. Back then, farmers lived inside the walls and were thankful for the protection.

• *Return to the bottom of Piazza del Duomo, turn left, and continue your walk, cutting under the double arch (from the town's first wall). In around 1200, this defined the end of town. The* ***Church of San Bartolo*** *stood just outside the wall (on the right). The Maltese cross over the door indicates that it likely served as a hostel for pilgrims. As you continue down Via San Matteo, notice that the crowds have dropped by at least half. Enjoy the breathing room as you pass a fascinating array of stone facades from the 13th and 14th centuries—now a happy cancan of wine shops and galleries. Reaching the gateway at the end of town, follow signs to the right to reach...*

Sant'Agostino Church

This tranquil church, at the far end of town (built by the Augustinians who arrived in 1260), has fewer crowds and more soul. Behind the altar, a lovely fresco cycle by Benozzo Gozzoli (who painted the exquisite Chapel of the Magi in the Medici-Riccardi Palace in Florence) tells of the life of St. Augustine, a North African monk who preached simplicity. The kind, English-speaking friars (from Britain and the US) are happy to tell you about their church and way of life, and also have Mass in English on Sundays at 11:00. Pace the peaceful cloister before heading back into the tourist mobs (free, €0.50 lights the frescoes; April-Oct daily 7:00-12:00 & 15:00-19:00; shorter hours off-season). Their fine little shop, with books on the church and its art, is worth a look.

Sights in San Gimignano

▲Civic Museum and Tower (Musei Civici and Torre Grossa)

This small, entertaining museum, consisting of just three unfurnished rooms, is inside City Hall (Palazzo Comunale). The main reason to visit is to scale the tower, which offers sweeping views over San Gimignano and the countryside.

Cost and Hours: €6 includes museum and tower, €7.50 when there's a special exhibit; daily April-Sept 9:30-19:00, Oct-March 11:00-17:30, Piazza del Duomo, tel. 0577-990-312, www.sangimignanomusei.it.

Visiting the Museum: You'll enter the complex through a delightful stony courtyard (to the left as you face the Duomo). Climb up to the loggia to buy your ticket.

The main room (across from the ticket desk), called the **Sala di Consiglio** (a.k.a. Dante Hall), is covered in festive frescoes, including the *Maestà* by Lippo Memmi. This virtual copy of Simone

Martini's *Maestà* in Siena proves that Memmi didn't have quite the same talent as his famous brother-in-law.

Upstairs, the **Pinacoteca** displays a classy little painting collection of mostly altarpieces. The highlight is a 1422 altarpiece by Taddeo di Bartolo honoring St. Gimignano (far end of last room). You can see the saint, with the town—bristling with towers—in his hands, surrounded by events from his life.

Before going back downstairs, be sure to stop by the **Mayor's Room** (Camera del Podestà, across the stairwell from the Pinacoteca). Frescoed in 1310 by Memmo di Filippuccio, it offers an intimate and candid peek into the 14th century. The theme: profane love. As you enter, look to the left corner where a young man is ready to experience the world. He hits his parents up for a bag of money and is free. On the opposite wall (above the window), you'll see a series of bad decisions: Almost immediately he's entrapped by two prostitutes, who lead him into a tent where he loses his money, is turned out, and is beaten. Above the door, from left to right, you see a parade of better choices: marriage, the cradle of love, the bride led to the groom's house, and newlyweds bathing together and retiring happily to their bed.

The highlight for most visitors is a chance to climb the **Tower** (Torre Grossa, entrance halfway down the stairs from the Pinacoteca). The city's tallest tower, 200 feet and 218 steps up, rewards those who climb it with a commanding view. See if you can count the town's 14 towers (yes, that includes the stubby little one just below this tower). It's a sturdy, modern staircase most of the way, but the last stretch is a steep, ladder-like climb.

San Gimignano 1300

This small but interesting attraction, in an old church on a quiet street a block over from the main square, is a trip back in time: a painstakingly rendered 1:100 scale clay model of San Gimignano at the turn of the 14th century. You can see the 72 original "tower houses," and marvel at how unchanged the street plan remains today. You'll peek into cross-sections of buildings, view scenes of medieval life both within and outside the city walls, and watch a video about the making of the model.

Cost and Hours: Free; April-Oct daily 10:00-18:00; Nov-March Mon-Fri 10:00-17:00, Sat-Sun until 18:00; Via Costarella 3, mobile 327-439-5165, www.sangimignano1300.com.

Sleeping in San Gimignano

Although the town is a zoo during the daytime, locals outnumber tourists when evening comes, and San Gimignano becomes mellow and enjoyable. Drivers can unload near their hotels, then park outside the walls in recommended lots. Hotel websites provide instructions.

NEAR PORTA SAN MATTEO, AT THE QUIET END OF TOWN

If arriving by bus, save a crosstown walk to these by asking for the Porta San Matteo stop (rather than the main stop near Porta San Giovanni). Drivers can park at the less-crowded Bagnaia lots (P3 and P4), and walk around to Porta San Matteo.

$$$ Hotel l'Antico Pozzo is an elegantly restored, 15th-century townhouse with 18 tranquil, comfortable rooms, a peaceful interior courtyard terrace, and an elite air (Sb-€95, small Db-€119, standard Db-€139, big Db-€180, air-con, elevator, Wi-Fi, Via San Matteo 87, tel. 0577-942-014, www.anticopozzo.com, info@anticopozzo.com; Emanuele, Elisabetta, and Mariangela).

$$ Le Undici Lune ("The 11 Moons"), with three rooms and an apartment in a tight but characteristic circa-1300 townhouse with steep stairs at the tranquil end of town, has been tastefully decorated with modern flair by Gabriele. While there's no air-conditioning, the building was designed as a storehouse for food, so it's naturally cool (Db-€85, apartment-€100, book directly with hotel for these prices, Wi-Fi, Via Mainardi 9, mobile 389-236-8174, www.leundicilune.com, leundicilune@gmail.com).

$ Locanda il Pino has just seven rooms and a big living room. It's dank but clean and quiet. Run by English-speaking Elena and her family, it sits above their elegant restaurant at the quiet end of town, just inside Porta San Matteo (Db-€55, no breakfast, no air-con, Wi-Fi in lobby, Via Cellolese 4, tel. 0577-940-415, locanda@ristoranteilpino.it).

NEAR THE MAIN SQUARE, AT THE BUSY END OF TOWN

$$$ Hotel la Cisterna, right on Piazza della Cisterna, feels old and stately, with 48 aging rooms, some with panoramic view terraces—a scene from the film *Tea with Mussolini* was filmed from one (Sb-€78, Db-€100, Db with view-€125, Db with view terrace—€140, 10 percent discount with this book when you book direct, air-con, elevator, Wi-Fi, good restaurant with great view, closed Jan-Feb, Piazza della Cisterna 23, tel. 0577-940-328, www.hotelcisterna.it, info@hotelcisterna.it, Alessio).

$$ Palazzo al Torrione, on an untrampled side street just inside Porta San Giovanni, is quiet and handy, and generally better than most hotels (even though they don't have a full-time reception). Their 10 modern rooms are spacious and tastefully appointed (Db-€90, terrace Db-€110, Tb-€100, terrace Tb-€120, Qb-€120-130, 10 percent discount with this book when you book directly with hotel, breakfast-€7, Wi-Fi in communal kitchen, parking-€6/day, inside and left of gate at Via Berignano 76; operated from tobacco shop 2 blocks away, on the main drag at Via San Giovanni 59; tel. 0577-940-480, mobile 338-938-1656, www.palazzoaltorrione.com, palazzoaltorrione@palazzoaltorrione.com, Vanna and Francesco).

$ Le Vecchie Mura Camere offers three good rooms above their recommended restaurant along a rustic lane, clinging just below the main square (Db-€65, no breakfast, air-con, Wi-Fi, Via Piandornella 15, tel. 0577-940-270, www.vecchiemura.it, info@vecchiemura.it, Bagnai family).

IN THE COUNTRYSIDE, WITH A STUNNING VIEW OF SAN GIMIGNANO

$$$ Ponte a Nappo, run by enterprising Carla Rossi (who doesn't speak English) and her sons Francesco and Andrea (who do), has seven comfortable rooms and two apartments in a kid-friendly farmhouse. Located a long half-mile below town (best for drivers, but doable for hardy walkers), this place has killer views of the multi-towered city and the rolling hills all around. A picnic dinner lounging on their comfy garden furniture as the sun sets is good Tuscan living (Db-€100-130, 2-to-6 person apartment-€130-250, price depends on season and length of stay, for best price book directly by email or phone and mention Rick Steves—or use promo code "RickSteves" on their website, air-con in hot weather only, Wi-Fi, free parking, pool, lunch and dinner sometimes available for guests, 15-minute walk or 5-minute drive from Porta San Giovanni—if you're arriving by bus they'll pick you up, tel. 0577-907-282, mobile 349-882-1565, www.accommodation-sangimignano.com, info@rossicarla.it). About 100 yards below the monument square at Porta San Giovanni, find Via Vecchia (not left or right, but down a tiny road) and follow it down a gravel road for five minutes by car. They also rent a dozen or so rooms and apartments in town (Db-€60-110, cheap Wi-Fi, each room is described on their website).

Eating in San Gimignano

My first two listings cling to quiet, rustic lanes overlooking the Tuscan hills (yet just a few steps off the main street); the rest are buried deep in the old center.

Dulcis in Fundo Ristorante, small and family-run, proudly serves modest portions of "revisited" Tuscan cuisine (with a modern twist and gourmet presentation) in a jazzy ambience. This enlightened place, whose menu identifies the sources of their ingredients, offers lots of vegetarian options and gladly caters to gluten-free diets—rare in Tuscany (€10-12 pastas, €13-17 *secondi,* meals served 12:30-14:30 & 19:15-21:45, closed Wed, Vicolo degli Innocenti 21, tel. 0577-941-919, Roberto and Cristina).

Le Vecchie Mura Ristorante has good and fast service, great prices, tasty if unexceptional home cooking, and the ultimate view. It's romantic indoors or out. They have a dressy, modern interior where you can dine with a view of the busy stainless-steel kitchen under rustic vaults, but the main reason to come is for the incredible cliffside garden terrace. Cliffside tables are worth reserving in advance by calling or dropping by: Ask for "front view" (€8-11 pastas, €12-15 *secondi,* open only for dinner from 18:00, last order at 22:00, closed Tue, Via Piandornella 15, tel. 0577-940-270, Bagnai family).

Cum Quibus ("In Company"), tucked away near Porta San Matteo, has a smallish dining room with soft music, beamed ceilings, modern touches, and a sophisticated vibe; it also offers al fresco tables in its interior patio in summer. Lorenzo and Simona produce tasty Tuscan cuisine, fresh truffle specialties, and artistic desserts (€10 pastas, €14-19 *secondi,* truffle dishes more expensive, Wed-Mon 12:30-14:30 & 19:00-22:00, closed Tue, reservations advised, Via San Martino 17, tel. 0577-943-199, www.cumquibus.it).

Trattoria Chiribiri, just inside Porta San Giovanni on the left, serves homemade pastas and desserts at remarkably fair prices. While its petite size and tight seating make it hot in the summer, it's a good budget option—and as such, it's in all the guidebooks (€7-8 pastas, €8-11 *secondi,* daily 11:00-23:00, Piazza della Madonna 1, tel. 0577-941-948, Maria and Maurizio).

Locanda di Sant'Agostino spills out onto the peaceful square, facing Sant'Agostino Church. It's cheap and cheery, serving lunch and dinner daily—big portions of basic food in a restful setting. Dripping with wheat stalks and atmosphere on the inside, there's shady on-the-square seating outside (€8-12 pizzas, pastas, and *bruschette;* €9-15 *secondi,* daily 11:00-23:00, closed Tue off-season, closed Jan-Feb, Piazza Sant'Agostino 15, tel. 0577-943-141, Genziana and sons).

***Enoteca:* diVinorum,** a cool wine bar with a small entrance right on Piazza Cisterna, has a contemporary cellar atmosphere and—best of all—a row of tables out back overlooking rolling Tuscan hills (just downhill and toward the main drag from Dulcis in Fundo, recommended above; at mealtimes, you'll have to order food to sit at the outdoor tables). They have local wines by the glass

(€3-5) as well as snacks that can make a light meal. The food is nothing special; this place is all about the tranquil view and good wine (€10-15 *antipasti* plates, €7-8 *bruschette* and warm plates, daily 11:00-21:30, shorter hours off-season, Piazza Cisterna 30 or Via degli Innocenti 5, tel. 0577-907-192, Matteo).

Picnics: The big, modern **Co-op supermarket** sells all you need for a nice spread (Mon-Sat 8:30-20:00, Sun 8:30-12:30 except closed Sun Nov-March, at parking lot below Porta San Giovanni). Or browse the little shops guarded by boar heads within the town walls; they sell pricey boar meat *(cinghiale)*. Pick up 100 grams (about a quarter pound) of boar, cheese, bread, and wine and enjoy a picnic in the garden at the Rocca or the park outside Porta San Giovanni.

Gelato: To cap the evening and sweeten your late-night city stroll, stop by **Gelateria Dondoli** on Piazza della Cisterna (at #4). Gelato-maker Sergio was a member of the Italian team that won the official Gelato World Cup—and his gelato really is a cut above (tel. 0577-942-244, Dondoli family).

San Gimignano Connections

Bus tickets are sold at the bar just inside the town gate or at the TI. Many connections require a change at Poggibonsi (poh-jee-BOHN-see), which is also the nearest train station.

From San Gimignano by Bus to: Florence (hourly, less on Sun, 1.5-2 hours, change in Poggibonsi), **Siena** (8/day direct, on Sun must change in Poggibonsi, 1.25 hours), **Volterra** (4/day Mon-Sat; 1/day Sun—in the late afternoon and usually crowded—with no return to San Gimignano; 2 hours, change in Colle di Val d'Elsa, one connection also requires change in Poggibonsi). Note that the bus connection to Volterra is four times as long as the drive; if you're desperate to get there faster, you can pay about €70 for a taxi.

By Car: San Gimignano is an easy 45-minute drive from Florence (take the A-1 exit marked *Firenze Certosa,* then a right past tollbooth following *Siena per 4 corsie* sign; exit the freeway at Poggibonsi). From San Gimignano, it's a scenic and windy half-hour drive to Volterra.

Near San Gimignano: Monteriggioni

The perfectly preserved ring fort of Monteriggioni (mohn-teh-rih-jee-OH-nee) proudly caps its hill high above the main highway, running from the Volterra/San Gimignano area south to Siena. Although it's a mostly empty shell today—and a tourist-bus magnet on par with San Gimignano—it's worth a quick stop if you're ready for a stretch-your-legs break. Visitors enjoy its tidy square and climbing parts of its walls. Unless you linger over a meal, Monteriggioni works best as a half-hour to hour-long stop.

Monteriggioni's stout fortifications vividly illustrate two major historical trends in medieval Tuscany: Siena built the fortress around 1213 to protect its lands from the threatening expansion of its rival city-state, Florence. But Monteriggioni also protected religious pilgrims treading the Via Francigena route from northern Europe to Rome (who were, not coincidentally, a major source of Sienese wealth). Dante wrote poetically about Monteriggioni's might in his *Divine Comedy*. It was finally surrendered to the Medici in 1554, becoming part of Florence and remaining in remarkably good repair.

Today, Monteriggioni feels like a historical theme park. English information plaques posted around the village explain its history. Entering its main gate (Porta Romana), you emerge onto its pleasant piazza, ringed with souvenir shops and al fresco eateries. On the right side of the square, tucked back in a little courtyard, is the **TI** and **Armor Museum,** with historical exhibits and models of the fortress, an explanation of siege warfare, and modern recreations of weapons and armor that you can try on (museum-€3, combo-ticket with walls-€4, €1 audioguide explains museum and walls, TI/museum open daily 9:30-13:30 & 14:00-19:30, shorter hours Nov-March, Piazza Roma 23, tel. 0577-304-834, www.monteriggioniturismo.it).

If you poke into the little courtyard beyond the TI, you'll find a **pilgrim's *ospitalità*,** a rustic refuge offering basic accommodations for present-day pilgrims following the Via Francigena. Like the more famous Camino de Santiago across northern Spain, this medieval pilgrim route is again in vogue—as, for the first time in centuries, people are walking its entire length, through Tuscan splendor to Rome. (For more on the Via Francigena, see page 544.)

The other main sight in Monteriggioni is the town's impressively intact **walls.** The blocky, angular towers—designed to shed incoming arrows—indicate the walls were built before the advent of cannons (when round towers became the norm). From Roman times through the Middle Ages, towers like these were built 50 yards apart—the distance an arrow could fly with accuracy. While the walls are about a third of a mile around, you can ascend them only for a stroll on two short stretches: above the town's main Porta Romana entrance gate, and at the opposite end, near the Porta

Fiorentina gate. The same ticket—sold at the entry points, or at the TI—covers both sections (€2, or €4 combo-ticket with Armor Museum, same hours as TI/museum). Once up top, appreciate the strategic location, with 360-degree views over Tuscan hills. The busy highway below follows the route of the Via Cassia, the Roman-built road that connects Rome to Florence and points north, making it popular among ancient traders, medieval pilgrims...and contemporary tourists.

Getting There: Monteriggioni is well-signed and only a mile off the main SR-2 highway, just north of Siena. You can try parking in the lot at the top of the hill, below the main gate (€2/hour); but if that's full, you may be forced to park at the large gravel lot closer to the base of the hill instead (€1.50/hour).

THE HEART OF TUSCANY

Montepulciano • Pienza and the Val d'Orcia • Montalcino and the Brunello Wine Country • Crete Senesi

If your Tuscan dreams feature vibrant neon-green fields rolling to infinity, punctuated by snaking cypress-lined driveways; humble but beautiful (and steep) hill towns; and world-class wines to make a connoisseur weep, set your sights on the heart of the region.

An hour south of Siena, this slice of splendor—which seems to specialize in views and wine—is a highlight, particularly for drivers. With an astonishing diversity of towns, villages, abbeys, wineries, countryside restaurants and accommodations, all set within jaw-dropping scenery, this sub-region of Tuscany is the best place to abandon your itinerary and just slow down.

Even though the area's towns sometimes seem little more than a rack upon which to hang the vine-draped hills, each one has its own endearing personality. The biggest and most interesting, Montepulciano, boasts a medieval cityscape wearing a Renaissance coat, wine cellars that plunge deep down into the cliffs it sits upon, and a classic town square. Pienza is a sure-of-itself planned Renaissance town that once gave the world a pope. And mellow Montalcino is (even more than most towns around here) all about its wine: Brunello di Montalcino.

Outside of these three centers are some smaller, often offbeat attractions that engage visitors with surprising variety and depth: the sumptuously (and idiosyncratically) decorated Abbey of Santo Oliveto Maggiore, one of Tuscany's top undiscovered art treasures; the historic spa town of Bagno Vignoni, whose main piazza is filled with a naturally fed hot-water pool; the perfectly manicured gardens of La Foce; and—just to the north, a bit closer to Siena—the more rugged, moonscape-beautiful scenery of the hilly Crete Senesi. And at the core of this region is the stunning landscape of the Val d'Orcia, with its famous tree-lined lanes and hill-capping farmhouses.

This area also enjoys a rich history: During the Middle Ages, the Via Francigena pilgrimage route ran from northern Italy—and northern Europe—right through here to Rome, blessing it with a series of stout fortresses (including Rocca d'Orcia) and welcoming pilgrim churches (including Sant'Antimo Abbey, where monks still worship God each evening with a Gregorian chant).

Don't be overly focused on ticking off a list of sights here. This region's attractions—while substantial—are best seen as an excuse for a countryside drive, and I've narrated four separate but overlapping self-guided loop drives to help you connect the very best.

Along the way, shutterbugs can collect gorgeous images; for a list of quintessential panoramas, see the "Top Tuscan Views" sidebar on page 548. Standing at the edge of a rolling field, filling your viewfinder with a solitary circle of cypress trees stretching up toward a wide azure sky, you can only think one word: Tuscany.

PLANNING YOUR TIME

This region richly rewards whatever time you're willing to give it. At a minimum, you can do part or all of one of my loop drives on your way between destinations to the north (Siena, Florence) and to the south (Rome). As this compact region is hemmed in by Italy's two main north-south thoroughfares—the A-1 expressway and the scenic SR-2 highway—even those with a few hours to spare can get an enticing taste. But ideally, spend at least one night (or many more if you enjoy wine and views). Many travelers enjoy home-basing here for a week, not only to see the many attractions listed in this chapter, but also to use this area as a springboard for visits to Siena and Cortona; even Volterra, San Gimignano, and Florence are realistic as long side-trips.

Choosing a Home Base: Montepulciano is the most all-around engaging town, and works well for travelers with or without a car. With its easy access to the vineyards, Montalcino makes sense for wine pilgrims. For drivers who'd like to home-base in the scenic countryside, I've listed several *agriturismi* and other rural accommodations throughout this chapter, including a few that are strategically located near Pienza.

GETTING AROUND THE HEART OF TUSCANY

By Car: This area is ideal by car, and I've designed this chapter primarily with drivers in mind. You'll find four complementary self-guided driving tours, carefully planned to link the best stops with the most scenic route. Each of the four is a self-contained loop, but they also overlap, making it easy to combine parts (or all) of several routes. When planning your time in this area, carefully study the map on page 519 to figure out the most efficient way to link as many loops (or partial loops) as possible, depending on where you're coming from, headed to, and staying in the area.

A quick overview: The **"Best of Tuscany" loop** (page 550) is the top overall choice, as it links the two most charming large towns of the area (Montepulciano and Pienza) with the area's best scenery, and its most offbeat and intriguing villages and countryside sights. Wine lovers will enjoy the **"Brunello Wine Country" loop** (page 571), which combines the area's most accessible wineries with nearby attractions. The two other loops are "extra credit" for those wanting to explore areas even farther off the beaten path: The **"Toscana Minore" loop** (page 553) focuses on well-kept, off-the-beaten-path villages tucked just a few minutes' drive from the more famous places, and the **Crete Senesi loop** (page 589) is the most scenic back-roads alternative to the already very scenic SR-2 highway south from Siena, and includes the art-packed Abbey of Monte Oliveto Maggiore.

Most of the driving tours include at least a short stretch on gravel roads, but in each case, I've provided a (typically longer and/

or less scenic) alternative for those who prefer to stick to pavement. Driving in this area, navigate by town names, and equip yourself with a good map and/or mapping app on your smartphone or tablet: Many of the attractions I've described are on tiny back lanes, marked only with easy-to-miss, low-profile signs from the main roads. Even road names can differ between maps and local signage. Expect to backtrack periodically to find your turnoff. I've given distances in kilometers to match up with your rental car's odometer.

Even many of the small towns in this area are designated as "ZTL" (limited-traffic zone)—off-limits to non-local traffic. While tiny village ZTLs aren't monitored by cameras (as in big cities), you can still be ticketed if you're found crossing that line. When parking, remember that white lines indicate free parking (sometimes time-limited—look for explanatory signs); blue lines indicate paid parking (pay at the station, then display the ticket on your windshield); and yellow lines are only for locals.

By Public Transportation: While you can reach many of this chapter's sights by public transportation (mostly buses), connections are slow, infrequent, and often require a transfer. Taxis can help connect the dots more efficiently. Montepulciano is the best home base for those without a car. See the map on page 519 for an overview.

TOURS IN TUSCANY

A good local guide can help you take full advantage of everything this area has to offer. **Roberto Bechi,** based in Asciano near Siena, capably tells this region's story (see listing on page 357). **Antonella Piredda,** who lives in the village of Montisi (just north of Pienza) is smart, well-organized, and enjoyably opinionated (€60/hour, 3-hour minimum, €350/all day, she can join you in your car or hire a driver for extra, mobile 347-456-5150, anto@antonellapiredda.com, www.antonellapiredda.com). Antonella also offers a beautiful apartment for rent in Montisi (www.casaparva.com).

Montepulciano

Curving its way along a ridge, Montepulciano (mohn-teh-pull-chee-AH-noh) delights visitors with *vino,* views, and—perhaps more than any other town in this area—a sense of being a real, bustling community rather than just a tourist depot.

Alternately under Sienese and Florentine rule, the city still retains its medieval *contrade* (districts), each with a mascot and flag. The neighborhoods compete the last Sunday of August in the Bravio delle Botti, where teams of men push large wine casks uphill from Piazza Marzocco to Piazza Grande, all hoping to win a banner and bragging rights. The entire last week of August is a festival: Each *contrada* arranges musical entertainment and serves food at outdoor eateries along with generous tastings of the local *vino*.

The city is a collage of architectural styles, but the elegant San Biagio Church, at the base of the hill, is its best Renaissance building. Most visitors ignore the architecture and focus more on the city's other creative accomplishment, the tasty Vino Nobile di Montepulciano red wine.

Montepulciano is a good jumping-off point for my "Best of Tuscany" self-guided driving tour, described on page 550.

Orientation to Montepulciano

Commercial action in Montepulciano centers in the lower town, mostly along Via di Gracciano nel Corso (nicknamed "Corso"). This stretch begins at the town gate called Porta al Prato (near the TI, bus station, and some parking) and winds slowly up, up, up through town—narrated by my self-guided walk. Strolling here, you'll find eateries, gift shops, and tourist traps. The back streets are worth exploring. The main square, at the top of town (up a steep switchback lane from Corso), is Piazza Grande. Standing proudly above all the touristy sales energy, it has a noble, Florentine feel.

TOURIST INFORMATION

The helpful TI is just outside the Porta al Prato city gate, directly underneath the small tree-lined parking lot. It offers a free town map, books hotels and rooms for no fee, sells train tickets (€1 fee), has an Internet terminal (€3.50/hour), and can book one of the town's few taxis (Mon-Sat 9:30-12:30 & 15:00-18:00, Sun 9:30-12:30, daily until 20:00 in July-Aug, Piazza Don Minzoni, tel. 0578-757-341, www.prolocomontepulciano.it, info@prolocomontepulciano.it).

The office on the main square that looks like a TI is actually a privately run "Strada del Vino" (Wine Road) agency. They don't have city info, but they do provide wine-road maps, organize **wine tours** in the city, and lead minibus winery tours farther afield. They also offer other tours (olive oil, cheese, and slow food), cooking classes, and more, depending on season and demand (Mon-Fri 10:00-13:00 & 15:00-18:00, likely open Sat-Sun in summer, Piazza Grande 7, tel. 0578-717-484, www.stradavinonobile.it).

ARRIVAL IN MONTEPULCIANO

Well-signed pay-and-display **parking** lots ring the city center (marked with blue lines, usually €1.30/hour). But there are also a lot of free spaces mixed in (marked with white lines)—look around before you park.

If you want to start your visit by following my self-guided walk (up the length of the Corso to the main square), park at the north end of town, near the Porta al Prato gate. Around here, the handiest lots are P1 (in front of the TI, with some free spaces) and the un-numbered lot just above, directly in front of the stone gate. If these are full, try lots P2, P3 (with a 1-hour limit), or P4. Lot P5 is near the bus station (ride up to the gate on the elevator described below).

Alternatively, to get to the main square quickly, make a beeline to the lots up at the top end of town: Follow signs for *centro storico, duomo,* and *Piazza Grande,* and use the *Fortezza* or *San Donato* lots (flanking the fortress).

Avoid the "ZTL" no-traffic zone (marked with a red circle), and don't park on yellow lines (which are for locals only). If you're sleeping in town, your hotelier can give you a permit to park within the walls; be sure to get very specific instructions.

Buses leave passengers at the station on Piazza Nenni, down a steep hill from the Porta al Prato gate. From the station, cross the street and head inside the modern orange-brick structure burrowed into the hillside, where there's an elevator. Ride to level 1, walk straight ahead down the corridor (following signs for *centro storico*), and ride another elevator to level 1. You'll pop out at the Poggiofanti Gardens; walk to the end of this park and hook left to find the gate. From here, it's a 15-minute walk uphill along the Corso, the bustling main drag, to the main square, Piazza Grande (following my self-guided walk, described later). Alternatively, you can wait for the orange shuttle bus that takes you all the way up to Piazza Grande (2/hour, €1.10, buy tickets at bars or tobacco shops); it's a good strategy to take the bus up and walk back down. There's a bus stop just before the TI, beside a gray metal canopy over a hotel-booking booth.

HELPFUL HINTS

Market Day: It's on Thursday morning (8:00-13:00), near the bus station.

Services: There's no official **baggage storage** in town, but the TI might let you leave bags with them if they have space (€2). Public **WCs** are located at the TI, to the left of Palazzo Comunale, and at the Sant'Agostino Church.

Laundry: An elegant self-service launderette is at Via del Paolino

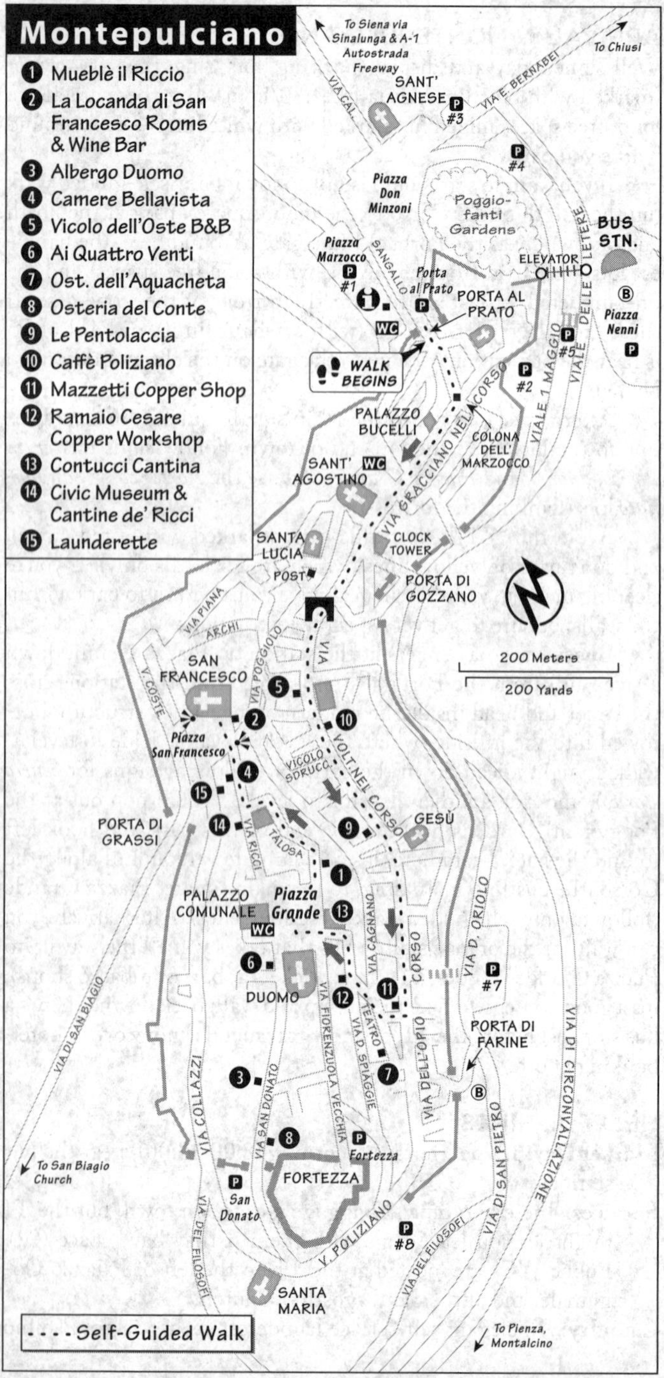
Montepulciano
1 Mueblè il Riccio
2 La Locanda di San Francesco Rooms & Wine Bar
3 Albergo Duomo
4 Camere Bellavista
5 Vicolo dell'Oste B&B
6 Ai Quattro Venti
7 Ost. dell'Aquacheta
8 Osteria del Conte
9 Le Pentolaccia
10 Caffè Poliziano
11 Mazzetti Copper Shop
12 Ramaio Cesare Copper Workshop
13 Contucci Cantina
14 Civic Museum & Cantine de' Ricci
15 Launderette
To Siena via Sinalunga & A-1 Autostrada Freeway
To Chiusi
VIA E. BERNABEI
VIA CAL.
SANT' AGNESE
#3
#4
Piazza Don Minzoni
Poggio-fanti Gardens
BUS STN.
Piazza Marzocco
#1
SANGALLO
Porta al Prato
ELEVATOR
VIALE DELLE LETERE
PORTA AL PRATO
Piazza Nenni
WC
WALK BEGINS
#5
#2
VIALE 1 MAGGIO
PALAZZO BUCELLI
VIA GRACCIANO NEL CORSO
COLONA DELL' MARZOCCO
SANT' AGOSTINO
SANTA LUCIA
CLOCK TOWER
POST
PORTA DI GOZZANO
VIA PIANA
ARCHI
VIA POGGIOLO
VIA
200 Meters
200 Yards
SAN FRANCESCO
V. COSTE
Piazza San Francesco
VICOLO SDRUCC.
VOLT. NEL CORSO
PORTA DI GRASSI
VIA RICCI
TALOSA
GESÙ
PALAZZO COMUNALE
Piazza Grande
VIA CAGNANO
CORSO
VIA D. ORIOLO
#7
DUOMO
VIA DI SAN BIAGIO
VIA FIORENZUOLA VECCHIA
TEATRO
VIA D. SPIAGGIE
VIA DELL'OPIO
PORTA DI FARINE
VIA DI CIRCONVALLAZIONE
VIA COLLAZZI
VIA SAN DONATO
Fortezza
FORTEZZA
VIA DI SAN PIETRO
To San Biagio Church
San Donato
VIA DEL FILOSOFI
V. POLIZIANO
#8
VIA DEL FILOSOFI
SANTA MARIA
Self-Guided Walk
To Pienza, Montalcino

2, just around the corner from the recommended Camere Bellavista (€4 wash, €4 dry, daily 8:00-22:00, tel. 0578-717-544).

Taxis: Two taxi drivers operate in Montepulciano. Call 330-732-723 for short trips within town (€10 for rides up or down hill); to reach other towns, call 348-702-4124 (www.strollingintuscany.com).

Montepulciano Walk

This two-part walk traces the spine of the town, from its main entrance up to its hilltop seat of power. Part 1 begins at Porta al Prato (where you'll enter if arriving at the bus station, parking at certain lots, or visiting the TI). Note that this part of the walk is uphill; if you'd rather skip straight to the more level part of town, ride the twice-hourly shuttle bus up, or park at one of the lots near the Fortezza. In that case, you can still do Part 1, backwards, on the way down.

PART 1: UP THE CORSO

This guided stroll takes you up through Montepulciano's commercial (and touristic) gamut, which curls ever so gradually from the bottom of town to the top. While the street is lined mostly with gift shops, you'll pass a few relics of an earlier, less commercial age.

Begin in front of the imposing Porta al Prato, one of the many stout city gates that once fortified this highly strategic town. Facing the gate, find the sign for the Porta di Bacco ***"passaggio segreto"*** on the left. While Montepulciano did have secret passages tunneled through the rock beneath it for coming and going in case of siege, this particular passage—right next to the city's front door—was probably no *segreto*...though it works great for selling salami.

Walk directly below the entrance to the **Porta al Prato,** and look up to see the slot where the portcullis (heavily fortified gate) could slide down to seal things off. Notice that there are two gates, enabling defenders to trap would-be invaders in a no-man's land where they could be doused with hot tar (sticky and painful). Besides having a drop-down portcullis, each gate also had a hinged door—effectively putting four barriers between the town and its enemies.

Pass through the gate and head a block uphill to reach the **Colonna del Marzocco.** This column, topped with a lion holding the Medici shield, is a reminder that Montepulciano existed under the auspices of Florence—but only for part of its history. Originally the column was crowned by a she-wolf suckling human twins, the civic symbol of Siena. At a strategic crossroads of mighty regional powers (Florence, Siena, and the papal states), Montepulciano often switched allegiances—and this column became a flagpole where the overlords du jour could tout their influence.

The column is also the starting point for Montepulciano's masochistic tradition, the **Bravio delle Botti,** held on the last Sunday of August, in which each local *contrada* (fiercely competitive neighborhood, like Siena's) selects its two stoutest young men to roll a 180-pound barrel up the hill through town. If the vertical climb through town wears you out, be glad you're only toting a camera.

A few steps up, on the right (at #91), is one of the many fine noble palaces that front Montepulciano's main strip. The town is fortunate to be graced with so many bold and noble *palazzos*—Florentine nobility favored Montepulciano as a breezy and relaxed place for a secondary residence. Grand as this palace is, with its stylized lion heads, it's small potatoes—the higher you go in Montepulciano, the closer you are to the town center...and the fancier the mansions.

Farther up on the right, at #75 (Palazzo Bucelli), take a moment to examine the **Etruscan and Roman fragments** embedded in the wall (left here by a 19th-century antiques dealer). You can quickly distinguish which pieces came from the Romans and those belonging to the earlier Etruscans by the differences in their alphabets: The "backwards" Etruscan letters (they read from right to left) look more similar to Greek than to the more recent Roman letters. Many of the fragments show a circle flanked by a pair of inward-facing semicircular designs. The circle represents the libation cup used for drinking at an Etruscan banquet. Banquets were at the center of Etruscan social life, and burial urns depict lounging nobles presenting a feast for the gods.

At the top of the block on the right, pass by the Church of Sant'Agostino. Huff up a few more steps, then take a breather to look back and see the **clock tower** in the middle of the street. The bell ringer at the top takes the form of the character Pulcinella, one of the wild and carefree revelers familiar from Italy's comedy theater *(commedia dell'arte)*.

Continuing up, at the *alimentari* on the right (at #23), notice the classic old sign advertising milk, butter, margarine, and olive and canola oil. Keep on going (imagine pushing a barrel now), and bear right with the street under another sturdy **gateway**—indicating that this city grew in concentric circles. Passing through the gate and facing the loggia (with the Florentine Medici seal—a shield with balls), turn left and keep on going.

As you huff and puff, notice (on your right, and later on both sides) the steep, narrow, often covered lanes called ***vicolo*** ("little street"). You're getting a peek at the higgledy-piggledy medieval Montepulciano. Only when the rationality of Renaissance aesthetics took hold was the main street realigned, becoming symmetrical and pretty. Beneath its fancy suit, though, Montepulciano remains a rugged Gothic city.

On the left, watch for the hulking former palace (I told you they'd get bigger) that's now home to Banca Etruria. "Etruria"—a name you'll see everywhere around here—is a term for the Etruscan territory of today's Tuscany.

Just after is a fine spot for a coffee break (on the left, at #27): **Caffè Poliziano,** the town's most venerable watering hole (from 1868). Step inside to soak in the genteel atmosphere, with a busy espresso machine, loaner newspapers on long sticks, and a little terrace with spectacular views (open long hours daily; it also has free Wi-Fi). It's named for a famous Montepulciano-born 15th-century poet who was a protégé of Lorenzo the Magnificent de Medici and tutored his two sons. So important is he to civic pride that townspeople are nicknamed *poliziani*.

A bit farther up and on the right, notice the precipitous Vicolo dello Sdrucciolo—literally "slippery lane." Any *vicolo* on the right can be used as a steep shortcut to the upper part of town, while those on the left generally lead to fine views. Many of these side lanes are spanned by brick arches, allowing the centuries-old buildings to lean on each other for support rather than toppling over—a fitting metaphor for the tight-knit communities that vitalize Italian small towns.

Soon the street levels out—enjoy this nice, lazy, easy stretch. Near the end, on the right (at #64), look for the **Mazzetti** copper shop, crammed full of both decorative and practical items. Because of copper's unmatched heat conductivity, it's a favored material in premium kitchens. The production of hand-hammered copper vessels like these is a dying art; in this shop, you can see works by Cesare, who makes them in his workshop just up the street.

To get there, go up the covered lane just after the copper shop (Vicolo Benci, on the right). You'll emerge partway up the steep street just below the main square. Turn right and head uphill steeply; at #4 (on the left), marked *Ramaio,* is Cesare's workshop and museum (for details on him, see page 530). Steeply uphill, on the right just before reaching the square, Cesare's buddy Adamo loves to introduce travelers to Montepulciano's fine wines at the Contucci Cantina (described on page 530). Visit Cesare and Adamo now, or head up to the square for Part 2 of this walk before coming back down later.

Either way, Montepulciano's main square is just ahead. You made it!

PART 2: PIAZZA GRANDE AND NEARBY

This pleasant, lively piazza is surrounded by a grab bag of architectural sights. If the medieval **Palazzo Comunale,** or town hall, reminds you of Palazzo Vecchio in Florence, it's because Florence dominated Montepulciano in the 15th and 16th centuries. The crenellations along the roof were never intended to hide soldiers—they're just meant to symbolize power. But the big, square central tower makes it clear that the city is keeping an eye out in all directions.

Take a moment to survey the square, where the town's four great powers stare each other down. Face the Palazzo Comunale, and keep turning to the right to see: the one-time building of the courts, behind the well (Palazzo del Capitano); the noble Palazzo Tarugi, a Renaissance-arcaded confection; and the aristocratic Palazzo Contucci, with its 16th-century Renaissance facade. (The Contucci family still lives in their palace, producing and selling their own wine.) Continuing your spin, you see the unfinished Duomo looking glumly on, wishing the city hadn't run out of money for its facade. (Its interior, described later under "Sights and Experiences in Montepulciano," looks much better.)

A cistern system fed by rainwater draining from the roofs of surrounding palaces supplied the fine **well** in the corner. Check out its 19th-century pulleys, the grills to keep animals from contaminating the water supply, and the Medici coat of arms (with lions symbolizing the political power of Florence, and the little white "pills" representing the family of "medics").

Climbing the town hall's **tower** rewards you with a windy but commanding view from the terrace below the clock. Go into the Palazzo Comunale, head up the stairs to your left, and pay on the second floor. You can pay to go just as far as the terrace, at the base of the tower (€2.50, 71 stairs), or pay more to go all the way to the top, twisting up extremely narrow brick steps past the antiquated bell-ringing mechanism (€5, 76 additional stairs). If you don't mind the claustrophobic climb, it's worth paying extra to reach the very top, where you enjoy commanding views of the region—all the way to Pienza (look just to the right of San Biagio Church; tower open daily 10:00-13:00 & 14:00-18:00, often closed in winter).

The street to the left as you face the tower leads to the **Fortezza,** or fortress. While you might expect the town to be huddled protectively around its fortress, in Montepulciano's case, it's built on a distant ledge at the very edge of town. That's because this fort wasn't meant to protect the townspeople, but to safeguard its rulers by keeping an eye on those townspeople.

Detour to the Church of San Francesco and Views: From the main square, it's a short, mostly level walk to a fine viewpoint. You could head down the wide street to the right as you face the tower. But for a more interesting look at Montepulciano behind its pretty Renaissance facades, go instead up the narrow lane between the two Renaissance palaces in the corner of the square (Via Talosa). Within just a few steps, you'll be surrounded not by tidy columns and triangles, but by a mishmash of brick and stone. Pause at the Mueblè il Riccio B&B (with a fine courtyard—peek inside) and look high up across the street to see how centuries of structures have been stitched together, sometimes gracelessly.

Follow along this lane as it bends left, and eventually you'll pop out just below the main square, facing the recommended Cantine de' Ricci wine cellar (described later). Turn right and head down toward the church. At #21 (on the left), look for a red-and-gold shield, over a door, with the name *Talosa*. This marks the home of one of Montepulciano's *contrade*, or neighborhoods; birth and death announcements for the *contrada* are posted on the board next to the door.

Soon you'll come to a viewpoint (on the right) that illustrates Montepulciano's highly strategic position. The ancient town sitting on this high ridge was surrounded by powerful forces—everything you see in this direction was part of the Papal States, ruled from Rome. In the distance is Lake Trasimeno, once a notorious swampland that made it even harder to invade this town.

Continue a few steps farther to the big parking lot in front of the church. Head out to the terrace for a totally different view: the rolling hills that belonged to Siena. And keep in mind that Montepulciano itself belonged to Florence. For the first half of the 16th century, those three formidable powers—Florence, Siena, and Rome (the papacy)—vied to control this small area. Take in the view of Montepulciano's most impressive church, San Biagio—well worth a visit for drivers or hikers (described later).

From here, you can head back up to the main square, or drop into the recommended Cantine de' Ricci to spelunk its wine cellars.

Sights and Experiences in Montepulciano

These are listed in the order you'll reach them on the self-guided walk, above. For me, Montepulciano's best "experiences" are personal: dropping in on either Adamo, the winemaker at Contucci Cantina, or Cesare, the coppersmith at Ramaio Cesare. Either one will greet you with a torrent of cheerful Italian; just smile and nod, pick up what you can from gestures, and appreciate this rare opportunity to meet a true local character. If you're visiting one of the wine cellars, read the sidebar on page 558.

▲▲Contucci Cantina

Montepulciano's most popular attraction isn't made of stone...it's the famous wine, Vino Nobile. This robust red can be tasted in any of the cantinas lining Via Ricci and Via di Gracciano nel Corso, but the cantina in the basement of Palazzo Contucci is both historic and fun. Skip the palace's formal wine-tasting showroom facing the square, and instead head down the lane on the right to the actual cellars, where you'll meet lively Adamo (ah-DAH-moh), who has been making wine since 1953 and welcomes tourists into his cellar. While at the palace, you may meet Andrea Contucci, whose family has lived here since the 11th century. He loves to share his family's products with the public. Adamo and Signor Contucci usually have a dozen bottles open, and when it's busy, other members of their staff are likely to speak English.

After sipping a little wine with Adamo, explore the palace basement, with its 13th-century vaults. Originally part of the town's wall, these chambers have been filled since the 1500s with huge barrels of wine. Dozens of barrels of Croatian, Italian, and French oak (1,000-2,500 liters each) cradle the wine through a two-year in-the-barrel aging process, while the wine picks up the personality of the wood. After about 35 years, an exhausted barrel has nothing left to offer its wine, so it's retired. Adamo explains that the French oak gives the wine "pure elegance," the Croatian is more masculine, and the Italian oak is a marriage of the two. Each barrel is labeled with the size in liters, the year the wine was barreled, and the percentage of alcohol (determined by how much sun shone in that year). "Nobile"-grade wine needs a minimum of 13 percent alcohol.

Cost and Hours: Free drop-in tasting, daily 9:30-12:30 & 14:30-19:00, Piazza Grande 13, tel. 0578-757-006, www.contucci.it.

▲Ramaio Cesare

Cesare (CHEH-zah-ray) the coppersmith is an institution in Montepulciano, carrying on his father's and grandfather's trade by hammering into existence an immense selection of copper objects in his cavernous workshop. Though his English is limited, he's happy to show you photos of his work—including the copper top of the Duomo in Siena and the piece he designed and personally delivered to Pope Benedict. Peruse his tools: a giant Road Runner-style anvil, wooden hammers, and stencils dating from 1857 that have been passed down from his grandfather and father. Next door, he has assembled a fine museum with items he and his relatives have made, as well as pieces from his personal collection. Cesare is evangelical about copper, and if he's not too busy, he'll create personalized mementoes for visitors—he loves meeting people from around the world who appreciate his handiwork (as his brimming photo album demonstrates). Cesare's justifiable pride in his vocation evokes the hardworking, highly skilled craft guilds that once dominated small-town Italy's commercial and civic life.

Cost and Hours: Demonstration and museum are free; Cesare is generally in his workshop Mon-Sat 8:00-12:30 & 14:30-18:30, closed Sun, Piazzetta del Teatro 4, tel. 0578-758-753, www.rameria.com. Cesare's shop *(negozio)* is on the main drag, just downhill at Corso #64—look for Rameria Mazzetti, open long hours daily.

Duomo

This church's unfinished facade—rough stonework left waiting for the final marble veneer—is not that unusual. Many Tuscan churches were built just to the point where they had a functional interior, and then, for various practical reasons, the facades were left unfinished. But step inside and you'll be rewarded with some fine art. A beautiful blue-and-white, glazed-terra-cotta *Altar of the Lilies* by Andrea della Robbia is behind the baptismal font (on the left as you enter). The high altar, with a top like a pine forest, features a luminous, early-Renaissance Assumption triptych by the Sienese artist Taddeo di Bartolo. Showing Mary in her dreamy eternal sleep as she ascends to be crowned by Jesus, it illustrates how Siena clung to the Gothic aesthetic—elaborate gold leaf and lacy pointed arches—to show heavenly grandeur at the expense of realism.

Cost and Hours: Free, daily 9:00-13:00 & 15:00-18:30.

▲Cantine de' Ricci

The most impressive wine cellars in Montepulciano sit below the Palazzo Ricci, just a few steps off the main square (toward the Church of San Francesco). Enter through the unassuming door and find your way down a spiral staircase—with rounded steps designed to go easy on fragile noble feet, and lined with rings held in place by finely crafted tiny wrought-iron goat heads. You'll wind up in the dramatic cellars, with gigantic barrels under even more gigantic vaults—several stories high. As you go deeper and deeper into the cellars, high up, natural stone seems to take over the brick. At the deepest point, you can peer into the atmospheric Etruscan cave, where a warren of corridors spins off from a filled-in well. Finally you wind up in the shop, where you're welcome to taste two or three wines for free—or, if you show them this book, they'll offer you the free wines along with some light food.

Cost and Hours: Free tasting, €7-8 bottles, affordable shipping, daily 10:30-19:00, next to Palazzo Ricci, look for signs either for *Cantine de' Ricci* or *Cantine del Redi*—its former name, tel. 0578-757-166, www.dericci.it.

Civic Museum (Museo Civico)

Eclectic and surprisingly modern, but small and ultimately forgettable, this museum collects bits and pieces of local history with virtually no English explanation. The ground floor and cellar hold ancient artifacts and vases, including some Etruscan items. The next two floors are the pinacoteca (art gallery), of which the highlight is the first-floor room filled with colorful Andrea della Robbia ceramic altarpieces. You'll find a similar della Robbia altarpiece in situ, in the Duomo, for free.

Cost and Hours: €5, Tue-Sun 10:00-13:00 & 15:00-18:00, closed Mon, Via Ricci 10, tel. 0578-717-300.

JUST OUTSIDE MONTEPULCIANO

San Biagio Church

At the base of Montepulciano's hill, down a picturesque driveway lined with cypresses, this church—designed by Antonio da Sangallo the Elder and built of locally quarried travertine—is Renaissance perfection. The proportions of the Greek cross floor plan give the building a pleasing rhythmic quality. Bramante, who designed St. Peter's at the Vatican in 1516, was inspired by this dome. The lone tower was supposed to have a twin, but it was never built. The soaring interior, with a high dome and lantern, creates a fine Renaissance space. Walk around the building to study the freestanding towers, and consider a picnic or snooze on the grass in back. The street called Via di San Biagio, leading from the church up into town, makes for an enjoyable, if challenging, walk.

Cost and Hours: Likely €2, generally daily 8:30-18:30.

Sleeping in Montepulciano

$$$ Mueblè il Riccio ("The Hedgehog") is medieval-elegant, with 10 modern and spotless rooms, an awesome roof terrace, and friendly owners. Five are new "superior" rooms with grand views across the Tuscan valleys (Sb-€80, Db-€100, view Db-€110, superior Db-€150, superior Db with balcony-€180, Tb-€116, superior Tb-€180, superior Qb-€200, breakfast-€8, air-con, guest computer and Wi-Fi, limited free parking—request when you reserve, a block below the main square at Via Talosa 21, tel. 0578-757-713, www.ilriccio.net, info@ilriccio.net, Gió and Ivana speak English).

Sleep Code

(€1 = about $1.40, country code: 39)

Abbreviations

S = Single, **D** = Double/Twin, **T** = Triple, **Q** = Quad, **b** = bathroom, **s** = shower only

Price Rankings

$$$ Higher Priced—Most rooms €100 or more.
$$ Moderately Priced—Most rooms between €70-100.
$ Lower Priced—Most rooms €70 or less.

Unless otherwise noted, credit cards are accepted, breakfast is included (but usually optional), Wi-Fi is generally free, and English is spoken. Many towns in Italy levy a hotel tax of about €2 per person, per night (generally not included in the rates I've quoted). Prices change; verify current rates online or by email. For the best prices, always book directly with the hotel.

Gió and his son Iacopo give tours of the countryside (€50/hour) in one of their classic Italian cars; for details, see their website. Ivana makes wonderful breakfast tarts.

$$$ La Locanda di San Francesco is pricey but luxurious, with four stylish rooms over a classy wine bar at the quiet top end of town (standard Db-€185, superior Db-€205, suite-€225, these are nonrefundable prices—pay €20 more for "flexible" rates, closed Nov-Easter, air-con, guest computer and Wi-Fi, free parking nearby, Piazza San Francesco 5, tel. 0578-758-725, www.locandasanfrancesco.it, info@locandasanfrancesco.it, Cinzia and Lucca).

$$ Albergo Duomo is big, modern, and nondescript, with 13 rooms (with small bathrooms) and a comfortable lounge downstairs. With a handy location just a few steps from the main square, it's at the very top of town, with free parking nearby (Sb-€60, small Db-€80, standard Db-€100, Tb-€120, family deals, elevator, air-con in some rooms for €5 extra, Wi-Fi, loaner laptops, Via di San Donato 14, tel. 0578-757-473, www.albergoduomo.it, albergoduomo@libero.it, Elisa and Saverio).

$$ Camere Bellavista has 10 charming, tidy rooms. True to its name, each room has a fine view—though some are better than others. Room 6 has a view terrace worth reserving (Db-€80, terrace Db-€100, cash only, optional €3-10 breakfast at a bar in the piazza, lots of stairs with no elevator, Wi-Fi, Via Ricci 25, no reception—call before arriving or ring bell, mobile 347-823-2314, www.camerebellavista.it, bellavista@bccmp.com, Gabriella speaks only a smidgen of English).

$$ Vicolo dell'Oste B&B, just off the main drag halfway up through town, has five modern rooms with fully outfitted kitchenettes (Db-€95-100, Tb-€130, Qb-€140, includes breakfast at nearby café, Wi-Fi, on Via dell'Oste 1—an alley leading right off the main drag just after Caffè Poliziano and opposite the *farmacia* at #47, tel. 0578-758-393, www.vicolodelloste.it, info@vicolodelloste.it, Luisa and Giuseppe).

Countryside Options near Montepulciano: If you'd rather be in the countryside, consider the options listed under "Sleeping in the Val d'Orcia," later. All are within a 5- to 15-minute drive of Montepulciano.

Eating in Montepulciano

These places are all open for lunch (about 12:30-14:30) and again for dinner (about 19:30-22:00). I've noted closed days.

Ai Quattro Venti is fresh, flavorful, fun, and right on Piazza Grande, with a simple dining room and outdoor tables right on the square. It distinguishes itself by offering reasonable portions of tasty, unfussy Tuscan food in an unpretentious setting. Try their very own organic olive oil and wine (€8-9 pastas, €9-10 *secondi*, closed Thu, next to City Hall on Piazza Grande, tel. 0578-717-231, Chiara).

Osteria dell'Aquacheta is a carnivore's dream come true, famous among locals for its excellent beef steaks. Its long, narrow room is jammed with shared tables and tight seating, with an open fire in back and a big hunk of red beef lying on the counter like a corpse on a gurney. Chiara serves while Giulio, with a pen tucked into his ponytail, whacks off slabs with a cleaver, confirms the weight and price with the diner, and tosses the meat on the grill—seven minutes per side. Steaks are sold by weight (€3/100 grams, or *etto,* one kilo is about the smallest they serve, two can split it for €30). They also serve hearty €6-8 pastas and salads and a fine house wine. In the tradition of old trattorias, they serve one glass, which you use alternately for wine and water (€8-10 nonsteak *secondi,* closed Tue, Via del Teatro 22, tel. 0578-758-443 or 0578-717-086).

Osteria del Conte, an attractive but humble family-run bistro, offers a €30 *menù del Conte*—a four-course dinner of local specialties including wine—as well as à la carte options and cooking like mom's. While the interior is very simple, they also have outdoor tables on a stony street at the edge of the historic center (€7-8 pastas, €9-15 *secondi,* closed Wed, Via San Donato 19, tel. 0578-756-062).

Le Pentolaccia is a small, family-run restaurant at the upper, relatively untouristy end of the main drag. With both indoor and outdoor seating, they make tasty traditional Tuscan dishes as well as daily fish specials. Cristiana serves, and husband-and-wife team Jacobo and Alessia stir up a storm in the kitchen (€8-10 pastas, €8-15 *secondi,* closed Thu, Corso 86, tel. 0578-757-582).

Wine Bar: **La Locanda di San Francesco,** with a fine terrace at the tranquil top of town—in front of the namesake church and its spectacular view terrace—is a fine place to nurse a glass of local wine in elegant surroundings (€4-9 glasses; also €7-10 pastas, salads, and soups; €9 daily specials, no afternoon closure, closed Mon and Nov-Easter, Piazza San Francesco 5, tel. 0578-758-725).

Near Montepulciano, in Monticchiello: If you'd enjoy getting out of town for dinner—but not *too* far—consider the 15-minute drive to the smaller, picturesque hill town of Monticchiello, where you can dine at the excellent **La Porta** restaurant, with its fine view terrace, or at the modern-feeling **La Cantina** (both described on page 546). To get to Monticchiello directly from Montepulciano, first take the road toward Pienza; then, shortly after passing the road to San Biagio Church (on the right), watch on the left for the Albergo San Biagio. Turn off and take the road that runs up past the left side of this big hotel, and follow it all the way to Monticchiello. This is a rough (partly gravel), middle-of-nowhere drive.

Montepulciano Connections

Schedule information and bus tickets are available at the TI. All buses leave from Piazza Pietro Nenni. The bus station seems to double as the town hangout, with a lively bar and locals chatting inside. In fact, there's no real ticket window—you'll buy your tickets at the bar. Check www.sienamobilita.it for schedules.

From Montepulciano by Bus to: Florence (1-2/day, 2 hours, change in Bettolle, LFI bus, www.lfi.it), **Siena** (6-8/day, none on Sun, 1.25 hours), **Pienza** (8/day, 30 minutes), **Montalcino** (3-4/day Mon-Sat, none Sun, change in Torrenieri, 1-1.25 hours total). There are hourly bus connections to **Chiusi,** a town on the main Florence-Rome rail line (50 minutes); Chiusi is a much better bet than the distant Montepulciano station (5 miles away), which is served only by milk-run trains, but it is handy on Sundays if you want to go to Siena. Buses connect Montepulciano's bus station and its train station (3/day, none on Sun).

As the **Montalcino** connection is problematic by public transportation, consider asking at the TI for a taxi (also see contact numbers under "Helpful Hints," earlier). Although expensive (about

€70), taking a taxi could make sense for two or more people. For drivers, it's a straight shot on S-146 (through Pienza, great scenery, and several classic Tuscan views) to Montalcino; for a more scenic route see my "Best of Tuscany" loop drive (page 550). **Cortona** is another awkward public-transit connection, involving a bus to Chiusi, then a 30-minute train ride to the Camuccia-Cortona train station, four miles below town with poorly timed bus connections to Cortona itself. Consider taking a taxi (about €60).

Pienza and the Val d'Orcia

The heart and soul of this part of Tuscany are the rolling farm fields near the valley of the Orcia River—called the Val d'Orcia (val DOR-chah). Tucked between Montepulciano to the east and the Montalcino hills to the west, the Val d'Orcia boasts some of the best scenery in Italy. The Renaissance town of Pienza is the area's centerpiece, with the spa town of Bagno Vignoni, the hill-capping fortified towns of Monticchiello and Rocca d'Orcia, and countryside sights such as the elegant La Foce Gardens rounding out the Val d'Orcia's appeal. As this is also one of Italy's most rewarding areas to explore by car, I've outlined two self-guided driving tour loops: A "Best of Tuscany" route that hits just the highlights, and a "Toscana Minore" loop focusing on the lesser-known villages north of Pienza.

Pienza

Set on a crest and surrounded by green, rolling hills, the small town of Pienza packs a lot of Renaissance punch. In the 1400s, locally born Pope Pius II of the Piccolomini family decided to remodel his birthplace into a city fit for a pope, in the style that was all the rage: Renaissance. Propelled by papal clout, the town of Corsignano was transformed—in only five years' time—into a jewel of Renaissance architecture. It was renamed Pienza, after Pope Pius. The plan was to remodel the entire town, but work ended in 1464 when both the pope and his architect, Bernardo Rossellino, died. Their vision—what you see today—was completed a century later.

Pienza's architectural focal point is its main square, Piazza Pio II, surrounded by the Duomo and the pope's family residence,

Palazzo Piccolomini. While Piazza Pio II is Pienza's pride and joy, the entire town—a mix of old stonework, potted plants, and grand views—is fun to explore, especially with a camera or sketchpad in hand. You can walk every lane in the tiny town in a few minutes. While it offers fine views of the surrounding countryside, Pienza is situated on a relatively flat plateau rather than the steep pinnacle of more dramatic towns like Montepulciano and Montalcino. (This is a plus for visitors with limited mobility, who find basically level Pienza much easier to explore than most hill towns.)

Tidy, tranquil, and tame, Pienza feels like the idealized Renaissance burg it was designed to be. But along with that civic pride comes more than its share of pretense. (I guess constantly being reminded of your "Renaissance perfection" by architecture snobs tends to stoke the ego.) And, cute as the town is, it's far from undiscovered; tourists flood Pienza in peak season, and boutiques selling gifty packages of pecorino cheese and local wine greatly outnumber authentic local shops. Restaurants here are—in general—more expensive and less reliably good than alternatives in the nearby countryside. For these reasons, Pienza is made to order as a stretch-your-legs break to enjoy the setting, and perhaps tour the palace, but it's not ideal for lingering overnight (though for some excellent countryside options just outside of town, see page 555).

Nearly every shop sells the town's specialty: pecorino, a pungent sheep's cheese that sometimes contains other ingredients, such as truffles or cayenne peppers. Look on menus for warm pecorino *(al forno* or *alla griglia),* often topped with honey or pears and served with bread. Along with a glass of local wine, this just might lead you to a new understanding of *la dolce vita.*

Orientation to Pienza

Tourist Information: The TI is 10 yards up the street from Piazza Pio II, inside the Diocesan Museum (Wed-Mon 10:30-13:30 & 14:30-18:00, closed Tue, Sat-Sun only in Nov-March, Corso il Rossellino 30, tel. 0578-749-905). Ignore the kiosk just outside the gate, labeled *Informaturista,* which is a private travel agency.

Arrival in Pienza: If **driving,** read signs carefully—some parking spots are reserved for locals, others require the use of a cardboard clock, and others are pay-and-display. Parking is tight, so if you don't see anything quickly, head for the large lot at Piazza del Mercato near Largo Roma outside the old town: As you approach town and reach the "ZTL" cul-de-sac (marked with a red circle) surrounding the park right in front of the town gate, head up the left side of town and look for the turnoff on the left for parking (€1.50/hour, closed Fri morning during market).

Pope Pius II

Pope Pius II (born Enea Silvio Bartolomeo Piccolomini, 1405-1464) was a fascinating man. Born into one of the most powerful families in Siena, he had an illustrious career as a diplomat, traveled far and wide (and fathered two illegitimate children, in Switzerland and Scotland), and gained a reputation for his erotic writings *(The Tale of Two Lovers).* Upon donning the frock, Piccolomini went from ordination to the papacy in just 11 years—a stunning pace spurred, no doubt, by his esteemed genealogy. Owing to his educated and worldly upbringing, upon ascending to the papacy Piccolomini chose a name that was not religious, but literary: the ancient poet Virgil first used the term "pious" to describe his hero, Aeneus. One of the most enlightened popes of his time, Pius embraced the burgeoning Renaissance and set out to remake his hometown in pure Renaissance style. Pius was also the first prominent figure known to have suggested the notion of a united Europe, with a common heritage and shared goals (at that time, facing off against the invading Ottomans).

Buses drop you just a couple of blocks directly in front of the town's main entrance.

Helpful Hints: Market day is Friday morning at Piazza del Mercato, just outside the town walls. A public **WC,** marked *gabinetti pubblici,* is on the right as you face the town gate from outside, on Piazza Dante Alighieri (down the lane next to the faux TI).

Sights in Pienza

I've connected the town's main sights with walking directions, which can serve as a handy little orientation to the town. You could do this stroll in 30 minutes, but entering some of the sights could extend your visit to half a day.

• *Begin in the little park just in front of the town (near the main roundabout and bus stop), called Piazza Dante Alighieri. Facing the town, go through the big, ornamental gateway on the right (which was destroyed in World War II, and rebuilt in 1955) and head up the main street...*

Corso Rossellino

This main drag—named for Bernardo Rossellino (1409-1464), the Renaissance architect who redesigned Pienza according to Pius' orders—is jammed with touristy boutiques. While you won't find great values, these shops are (like Pienza) cute and convenient. At the end of the second block on the left, at #21, step into the **Marusco e Maria** cheese-and-salami shop. Take a deep whiff and survey the racks of pecorino cheese, made from sheep's milk. For €3 per person, Fabio can give you a quick taste of three types of pecorino: *fresco* (young, soft, and mild), *medio* (medium), and *stagionato* (hard, crumbly, and pungent). Consider stocking up at one of these shops for a pricey but memorable picnic. *Finocchiona* is salami with fennel seeds. This was first popularized by wine traders, because fennel seeds make wine taste better. To this day, Italians use the word *infinocchiare* ("fennel-ize") to mean "to trick."

Farther along, watch for the **Church of San Francesco** on the right. Step inside for a glimpse of the gloomy Middle Ages, which inspired Pius in all the wrong ways when it came time to build his church—he wanted the exact opposite of this atmosphere. Also peek into the adjacent, tranquil cloister.

• *Continuing one more block, you'll pop out at Pienza's showcase square...*

▲Piazza Pio II

While Pienza's main piazza is relatively small, and at first seems visually underwhelming, architecture highbrows consider it one of Italy's most interesting squares for its elegance and artistic unity. The piazza and surrounding buildings were all designed by Rossellino to form an "outdoor room." Everything is perfectly planned and plotted.

Do a clockwise spin to check out the buildings that face the square, starting with the **Duomo** (which we'll enter soon). High up on the facade is one of many examples you'll spot around town of the Piccolomini family crest: five half-moons, advertising the number of crusades that his family funded. To the right of the Duomo is the **Piccolomini family palace,** now a tourable museum (described later). Notice that the grid lines in the square's pavement continue all the way up the sides of this building, creating a Renaissance cube. Looking farther right, you'll see **City Hall** (Palazzo Comunale), with a Renaissance facade and a fine loggia (to match the square) but a 13th-century bell tower that's shorter than the church's tower. (That's unusual here in civic-minded Tuscany, where municipal towers usually trumpet the importance of the town over the Church.)

Looking up the lane to the left of City Hall, notice the cantilevered upper floors of the characteristic old houses—a reminder that, while Pienza appears Renaissance on the surface, much of that sheen was added later to fit Pius' vision. Looking farther right, see the last building, the **Bishop's Palace** (now housing the TI and the Diocesan Museum, described later), also called the Borgia Palace. Pius invited prominent cardinals to occupy the real estate in his custom-built town. The Borgia clan, who built this palace, produced one of the most controversial popes of that age, Alexander VI, who ascended to the papacy a few decades after Pius II. The Borgia were notorious for their shrewd manipulation of power politics. Our word "nepotism"—which comes from the Italian *nipote* (nephew)—dates from this era, when a pope would pull strings to ensure his relatives would succeed him. Finally, between the Bishop's Palace and the Duomo, a lane leads to the best **view terrace** in town.

• *Now take the time to tour whichever of the square's attractions interest you (listed next).*

Duomo

The cathedral's classic, symmetrical Renaissance facade (1462) dominates Piazza Pio II. The interior, bathed in light, is an illuminating encapsulation of Pius II's architectural philosophy.

Cost and Hours: Free, generally daily 7:00-13:00 & 14:30-19:00.

Visiting the Church: Step inside...and into the light. Pius envisioned this church as an antidote of sorts to dark, claustrophobic medieval churches, like the one we saw earlier. Instead, this was to be a "house of glass," representing the cultural enlightenment that came with the Renaissance. This concept clashed with the architect's plans for the building, but Pius insisted on his way—creating this unusual (and unstable) space. Although an east-west footprint would have better suited this location, Pius demanded that the nave's tall Gothic windows face south (to capture maximum light). Atop the columns, notice the short extenders. Pius was into astronomy: He had the cathedral made tall enough so that on the spring equinox, the shadow cast by the facade would just reach the pavement grid line defining the far end of the square.

All of this caused structural problems. As you walk to the end of the church, notice the cracks in the apse walls, and get seasick behind the main altar. The church's cliff-hanging position bathes the interior in light, but also makes it feel as if the building could break in half if you jumped up and down.

The church decoration is also a bit unusual. Instead of the colorful frescoes you'd expect, the church has clean, white walls to reflect the light. Windows feature the crescent-moons crest of Pius II, and Sienese Gothic altarpieces and painted arches round out the decor.

▲Palazzo Piccolomini

The home of Pius II and the Piccolomini family (until 1962) can only be visited on an escorted audioguide tour (about 30 minutes total).

You can peek inside the door for free to check out the well-preserved, painted courtyard. In Renaissance times, most buildings were covered with elaborate paintings like these.

Cost and Hours: €7, Tue-Sun 10:00-13:00 & 14:00-18:30, first tour departs at 10:30, last tour at 18:00, closed Mon, Piazza Pio II 2, tel. 0578-748-392, www.palazzopiccolominipienza.it.

Visiting the Palazzo: You'll see six rooms (dining room, armory, bedroom, library, and so on), three galleries (art-strewn hallways), and the panoramic loggia before being allowed to linger in the beautiful hanging gardens.

The palace's drab interiors, faded paintings, coffered ceilings, and scuffed furniture have a mothballed elegance that makes historians wish they'd seen it in its heyday, when this small-town palace once hosted a big-name player in European politics. The audioguide dryly identifies each item in each room.

While the palace is not quite the interesting slice of 15th-century aristocratic life that it could be (I'd like to know more about the pope's toilet), this is still the best small-town palace experience I've found in Tuscany (it famously starred as the Capulets' home in Franco Zeffirelli's 1968 Academy Award-winning *Romeo and Juliet*).

Diocesan Museum (Museo Diocesano)

This measly collection of religious paintings, ecclesiastical gear, altarpieces, and old giant hymnals from local churches fills one room of the cardinal's Renaissance palace. The art is provincial Sienese, displayed in chronological order from the 12th through 17th centuries (but with no English information).

Cost and Hours: €4.50, same hours as TI—where you'll buy the ticket, Corso il Rossellino 30.

View Terrace

As you face the church, the upper lane leading left brings you to the panoramic promenade. Views from the terrace include the Tuscan countryside and, in the distance, Monte Amiata, the largest mountain in southern Tuscany. You can exit the viewpoint down the first alley, Via del'Amore—the original Lover's Lane—which leads back to the main drag.

The Rest of the Town

After your brief orientation stroll, you can explore your choice of flower-lined back lanes. Work your way to the back-left corner of town, where—along **Via delle Case Nuove**—you'll find a charming row of homes with staggered doorways. These "new houses" (as the street's name means) were built by the pope to house the poor.

Just to the left (as you face these houses) is Pienza's "destination" *gelateria:* **Buon Gusto** is run by Nicola, who focuses on quality ingredients and intense flavors. He makes just a few batches each morning (typically ready by around 13:30—just in time for after lunch), and once they're gone, they're gone. He also does fresh pressed juices, smoothies, and jams designed to complement local cheeses and other flavors (Tue-Sun 11:00-20:00, until 22:00 in summer, closed Mon, Via delle Case Nuove 26, mobile 335-704-9165).

Just Outside Pienza

A short drive or a long walk from Pienza, you can step into one of this region's many well-preserved Romanesque churches.

Corsignano Parish Church (Pieve di Corsignano)

This classic Romanesque parish church *(pieve)*—a reminder of a much earlier, rougher, simpler time (before Pope Pius II)—sits on the slope just below Pienza.

Getting There: On foot from Pienza, it's a steep 10-minute downhill walk, then a 15-minute uphill return hike (as you exit Pienza into the main park, look to your left for the *pieve di Corsignano* signs, leading downhill). For details on driving to this church, see "Leg #3" of my "Best of Tuscany" drive on page 552.

Visiting the Church: The round, eighth-century watchtower guards a 12th-century church, whose facade is carved with unusual iconography from an age when the pagan roots of early Christianity were vivid and unmistakable. The church is decorated not with saints and angels, but with nature: leaves and mysterious creatures. Carved in the stone lintel immediately above the front door, find the mermaid-like creature holding the two halves of her split tail. Locals enjoy the (quite plausible) idea that Starbucks appropriated its logo from this common pagan symbol. She's flanked by other figures fighting off demons, including (on the left) a snake that represents the sins of humanity. The mermaid tails and wavy water-like lines suggest the springs that spout near here.

Head around the right side of the church, and check out the carving above the side doorway: the three Wise Men walking to the Nativity. Examining the rest of the exterior, notice the monsters at the tops of the pillars—a suggestion that the world is a very dangerous place, but here you'll find safety.

If the church is open, step inside and let your eyes adjust to the very low light. This gloomy, cave-like, somber interior—with three parallel naves—is a far cry from later, brighter styles. Near the entrance on the right, look for the font that was used to baptize the man who would grow up to be Pope Pius II.

Pienza Connections

Bus tickets are sold at the bar/café (marked *Il Caffè,* closed Tue) just outside Pienza's town gate (or pay a little extra and buy tickets from the driver). Buses leave from a few blocks up the street, directly in front of the town entrance. Montepulciano is the nearest transportation hub to other points.

From Pienza by Bus to: Siena (6/day, none on Sun, 1.5 hours), **Montepulciano** (8/day, 30 minutes), **Montalcino** (3-4/day Mon-Sat, none Sun, change in Torrenieri, 45-60 minutes total).

Route Tips for Drivers: My self-guided "Best of Tuscany" loop drive links Pienza to Montepulciano and sights in between, while my "Toscana Minore" loop drive focuses on the less-discovered area just to the north of Pienza.

Val d'Orcia Countryside Sights and Drives

In this section, I've listed the main sights in the Val d'Orcia from east to west. Then I've suggested two self-guided driving routes to connect them (and other worthwhile stops).

Sights in the Val d'Orcia

▲▲La Foce Gardens

One of the finest gardens in Tuscany, La Foce (lah FOH-cheh) caps a hill with geometrical Italian gardens and rugged English gardens that flow seamlessly into the Tuscan countryside. A visit here comes with tales of an English-born, Italian-bred aristocrat—Iris Origo—who left her mark on this area, and wrote evocatively about her time here. The gardens can be visited only with a guided tour, and only three days each week (Wed, Sat, Sun). But a trip here comes with some grand scenery and is worth a pilgrimage for garden lovers.

Cost and Hours: €10; 50-minute tours offered mid-March-early Nov Wed at 15:00, 16:00, 17:00, and 18:00, Sat-Sun at 11:30, 15:00, and 16:30; no tours in winter, confirm tour time and reserve in advance, tel. 0578-69101, www.lafoce.com.

Getting There: La Foce sits in the hills above the busy town of Chianciano Terme. To avoid driving through Chianciano (heavy traffic, poor signage), consider a more scenic route through the

The Via Francigena

Many of the sights in this region—and others in this book (including Siena, Lucca, and San Gimignano)—line up along the route of the Via Francigena (VEE-ah frahn-CHEE-jeh-nah). During the Middle Ages, when devout Christians undertook a once-in-a-lifetime pilgrimage to Rome, this route was heavily trod by the footsore faithful flowing from northern Italy and northern Europe (hence the name, "Road of the Franks"—referring to the Germanic tribes who lived in present-day Germany and France). While there were many variations and feeder paths, the Via Francigena followed more or less the route of today's SR-2 highway, from Florence to Siena, then through the Val d'Orcia south to Rome. Without even realizing it, many modern-day tourists follow this millennium-old route as they travel through this part of Italy.

The first documented pilgrimages along here took place around A.D. 725, and the trend continued for many centuries. In 990, Archbishop Sigeric of Canterbury undertook the entire 1,100-mile round-trip from England. Upon his return, he documented tips for fellow pilgrims about where to sleep, where to eat, what to see, and how to pack light in a carry-on-the-plane-size rucksack...arguably the world's first travel guidebook.

The history of Tuscany is inextricably tied to the Via Francigena. During those oh-so-Dark Ages, a long journey was treacherous, rife with opportunity for illness, injury, and being robbed or murdered. Pilgrim traffic represented a huge injection of wealth into communities along the Via Francigena, and fortresses popped up—or were repurposed—to keep the route safe. Abbeys and churches were built to cater to the masses. And many shrewd communities leveraged the passing pilgrim trade into enormous prosperity; for example, Siena boomed both as a financial center and a trading outpost for Via Francigena pilgrims.

Like the recently-in-vogue Camino de Santiago in northern Spain, this medieval pilgrim route—forgotten for centuries—has recently enjoyed a renewed interest. Though the numbers are still small—and the path lacks the well-orchestrated conveniences of the Camino de Santiago—a handful of modern-day pilgrims are, once again, walking through Tuscany south to Rome.

countryside from Montalcino (described at the start of my "Best of Tuscany" driving tour on page 551).

Background: In 1924, the British aristocrat Iris Cutting—who had grown up amidst wealth and privilege at Villa Medici in Fiesole, overlooking Florence—married Antonio Origo, the son of the marquis of the Val d'Orcia. They took over a dilapidated country home high in the hills above Chianciano Terme and set about converting it into a luxurious estate of manor homes and gardens, importing British landscape architect Cecil Pinsent to bring their vision to life. The Origo clan also revived the Renaissance ideal of landowners helping the local peasants, and built a school and other institutions for the public good. During World War II, the Origos took in refugee children and hid partisans (all recounted in Iris Origo's memoir, *War in Val d'Orcia*). Iris' daughters, Benedetta ("blessed") and Donata ("given"), still own and manage the property today.

Visiting the Garden: From the entrance, your tour guide leads you first into the tidy Renaissance garden nearest the main house, with angular hedges, wisteria-draped walls, and potted citrus trees on pedestals. As you move away from the house, notice that the garden's style changes to a more rugged, English-style design—providing a bridge between the tidy villa and the pristine Tuscan wilderness all around. (In a sense, the Origo family itself is also a successful hybrid of Italian and English.) From the garden, you'll have a perfect view of a classic Tuscan road—a cypress-lined lane zigzagging up an adjacent hill. If this road seems a little too perfect, that's because it is: It was built by the grandfather of Antonio Origo, who had a similar appreciation for aesthetics, and made sure even a utilitarian road was beautiful. He based the road's design on scenes in Renaissance-era frescoes in Florence's Medici-Riccardi Palace.

Eating and Sleeping near La Foce: Near the gardens, the Origo family runs a memorably charming restaurant and a remote, restful B&B. The roadside restaurant **Dopolavoro La Foce** ("After Work") was literally the after-work hangout for local farmers. Today its country-chic interior feels trendy, but with a respect for local tradition, and the garden terrace out back is a chirpy delight. The parking lot across the busy road offers one of the best views of that perfect Tuscan road (€4-5 *panini*-like *bico* sandwiches, €8-12 pastas, €10-13 *secondi,* Tue-Sun 8:00-23:00, closed Mon, Strada della Vittoria 90, tel. 0578-754-025).

$$$ The family's **B&B Palazzolo La Foce** lets you sleep aristocratically in a small villa just below the gardens. Its four colorful rooms share a welcoming kitchen/lounge with a giant fireplace, and an outdoor swimming pool with glorious Tuscan views. All of the rooms bask in fine panoramas, and two rooms share a bathroom (D-€120, Db-€140, no air-con but breezy, Wi-Fi, Strada della Vittoria 61—but check in at gardens' main entrance to get specific directions to your room, tel. 0578-69101, www.lafoce.com, info@lafoce.com). They also rent more expensive villas (described on their website).

▲Monticchiello

This 200-person fortified village clings to the high ground in the countryside just south of Pienza and Montepulciano. As it's not along a main road, it feels more remote (for route tips on getting there from Pienza, see page 553; from Montepulciano, see page 535). While not quite "undiscovered," Monticchiello is relatively untrampled, and feels like a real place where you can get in touch with authentic Tuscan village life. It's also a fine place for a meal.

Ignore the flat, modern lower town, and head up to the circular, fortified upper town huddled against the hillside. Hike up through the main gate (passing the recommended La Porta restaurant on your left) and just explore. The town is dominated by the late-13th-century Church of Sts. Leonardo and Christopher. Tucked in a square nearby is Piazza del Teatro ("Theater Square"), where townspeople periodically enact a summer al fresco theatrical show—called Teatro Povero ("Theater of the Poor")—about the town's past and present (www.teatropovero.it). Continuing up through town, you'll find a large park sprawling at the base of a leaning tower, which keeps watch over valley views.

Eating in Monticchiello: Just inside the town's gate is **La Porta,** where warm and classy Daria pleases diners either indoors or out with traditional Tuscan dishes presented with flair. Sophisticated but not snobby, La Porta is particularly enjoyable for its idyllic little terrace, which comes with grand Tuscan views—reserve ahead (€9-14 pastas, €12-18 *secondi*; seatings at 12:30, 14:00, 19:30, and 21:30; closed Thu in Oct-March, Via del Piano 1, tel. 0578-755-163, www.osterialaporta.it). If La Porta is closed or you want a bit more contemporary preparation in a modern atmosphere, continue 50 yards up into town and turn right to find **La Cantina,** run by daughter Deborah (€9-10 pastas, €10-14 *secondi,* Tue-Thu 12:30-15:00 & 19:30-22:00, closed Wed, Via San Luigi 3, tel. 0578-755-280).

▲Bagno Vignoni

Thanks to the unique geology of this part of Tuscany (see sidebar on page 578), several natural hot springs bubble up between the wineries and hill towns. And the town of Bagno Vignoni (BAHN-yoh veen-YOH-nee)—with a quirky history, a pleasant-to-stroll street plan punctuated with steamy canals, and various places to take a dip—is the most accessible and enjoyable to explore. If you'd like to recuperate from your sightseeing and wine-tasting by soaking in the thermal baths, bring your swimsuit.

Getting There: Bagno Vignoni is well-signed, just off the main SR-2 highway linking Siena to Rome (3 miles south of San Quirico d'Orcia). Park in the lot by the big roundabout (€1/hour) and walk into town, taking the left fork (in front of Hotel Le Terme).

Bagno Vignoni Town Walk: Emerging into the main square, walk under the covered loggia and look out over the aptly named **Piazza delle Sorgenti** ("Square of the Sources"), filled with a vast pool. Natural spring water bubbles up at the far end at temperatures around 125 degrees Fahrenheit. Known since Roman times, these hot springs were harnessed for their medicinal properties in the Middle Ages, when footsore pilgrims could stop for a refreshing, soothing soak midway through their long walk from northern Europe to Rome along the Via Francigena. St. Catherine of Siena also came here to convalesce, but—in true ascetic style—threw herself into the hottest part of the spring as a form of self-flagellation. (Under the loggia, notice the little chapel to St. Catherine, with pottery vases decorated with her symbolic goose.) Other Tuscan big shots—from Lorenzo the Magnificent (the Medici paterfamilias) to Pope Pius II (who remade Pienza in his own image)—also came here seeking cures for arthritis and other ailments.

You're not allowed to wade or swim in this pool today, but an easy stroll through town shows you other facets of these healing waters. Facing the pool, turn left, walk to the end of the loggia, then turn left again down Via delle Sorgenti (passing the recommended Il Loggiato restaurant, then Piazza del Moretto and the recommended Osteria del Leone restaurant). Listen for the water that gushes under your feet, as it leaves the pool and heads for its big plunge over the cliff. Continuing straight, notice the stairs (on your right) down to Hotel Posta Marcucci, with the **Piscina Val di Sole**—the most accessible place in town for a dip (details later).

But continuing straight ahead for now, you'll emerge at an open zone with the cliff-capping **ruins** of medieval mills and cisterns that once made full use of Bagno Vignoni's main resource. Here you'll also have a chance to dip your toes or fingers into streams of now-tepid water. At the canals' end, the water plunges down into the gorge carved by the Orcia River. Looking deep into the valley, notice the pond with white mud, where locals enjoy going for a free soak. Then peek into the giant basin at the edge of the cliff, where thick mineral deposits indicate where natural showers once poured—back when this was a bathing complex. Dominating your view of the adjacent hillside is **Rocca d'Orcia,** a heavily fortified near-ghost-town that's just a short drive away (described later).

Taking the Waters: The modern **Piscina Val di Sole** bath complex, inside Hotel Posta Marcucci, is simple but sophisticated—a serene spot to soak. After changing into your swimsuit,

Top Tuscan Views

Tuscany is a land of splendid vistas, and many of the best—and most famous—viewpoints are in or near the Val d'Orcia. Shutterbugs who want to make their own custom calendar of iconic Tuscan scenes (rolling fields, cypress trees, serpentine driveways) should make a point to squeeze as many of these viewpoints as possible into their itineraries.

Circle of Cypresses (Rondò): This ring of cypress trees stands dramatically alone on a gently sloping hillside of brilliant green crops (in springtime). Originally built as a shelter for shepherds or famers caught out in the elements, today it's one of Tuscany's top photo ops. You'll find it along the main SR-2 road north of San Quirico d'Orcia (about 4 kilometers north of the main San Quirico exit; it's just 1 kilometer south of the Montalcino exit, and 2 kilometers south of the Torrenieri exit). Pullouts on both sides of the road—next to a long bridge—can get crowded. Avid photographers walk partway across the bridge for fine views back on the Rondò, and similar rolling-fields views face the opposite side of the bridge, as well.

Cypress-Lined Driveways: You'll find dozens upon dozens of cypress-lined driveways in your Tuscan travels. But two in this area are classics. The first is the perfectly twisty road near **La Foce** gardens; the most accessible and unobstructed view is from the parking lot across the street from the recommended Dopolavoro La Foce restaurant (see page 545)—but if you're touring the gardens, the views from inside are even better. Another ideal serpentine driveway crests a hill adjacent to **Monticchiello** (you'll get a nice view of it on the main road from Pienza).

Chapel and Trees: The super-scenic road between San Quirico d'Orcia and Pienza (SP-146) has several fine viewpoints,

HEART OF TUSCANY

you'll immerse yourself in water (ranging from 90 to 109 degrees Fahrenheit) and take in soaring views of Rocca d'Orcia across the valley (€15, €5 towel rental with €10 deposit, April-Sept Fri-Wed 9:30-13:00 & 14:00-18:00, Oct-March Fri-Wed 10:00-17:00, closed Thu year-round, last entry one hour before closing, tel. 0577-887-112, www.piscinavaldisole.it).

Eating in Bagno Vignoni: **Osteria del Leone,** on the cheery

but the best-known is the tidy little **chapel** (Cappella della Madonna di Vitaleta) on a ridge, flanked by pudgy cypress trees.

Keep an eye out for this view (it's pretty distant) on the south side of the road, about two kilometers north of San Quirico d'Orcia (near Agriturismo Poderino). On the same road, closer to Pienza, is a classic **"farmhouse with trees"** tableau (north side of road, just a kilometer outside of Pienza).

Farmhouse with Twisty Driveway: Another timeless scene is easy to spot if you're visiting Pienza: From anywhere along the panoramic terrace, just gaze off to the south, to the rolling hills of the Val d'Orcia. In the foreground, you'll see a perfect little farmhouse with a meandering driveway (Agriturismo Podere Terrapille). If this looks familiar, it's because you've seen it before: It was Russell Crowe's dreamy home-sweet-home in *Gladiator.*

Abbey in Pasture and Olive Grove: The Sant'Antimo Abbey, which is well worth a visit and described on page 569, sits in a

picturesque meadow. An adjacent cypress tree towers toward the heavens, seemingly in a contest with the church's bell tower to see who will get there first. Views of the abbey from the road above, or from the abbey to the surrounding landscape, are equally thrilling.

Honorable Mention—Winery Views: Several wineries—clinging to the high ground to pull the maximum sweetness out of their vines—have spectacular territorial views overlooking rolling vineyards, with other landmarks lingering on the horizon. Two of the best are **Altesino** (10 kilometers north of Montalcino, on the road to Buonconvento, with great views of Montalcino) and **Mastrojanni** (11 kilometers south of Montalcino, on a ridge high above Sant'Antimo Abbey). Both are described on pages 567-568, and incorporated in the Montalcino driving loop.

little *piazzetta* just behind the loggia, is the town's class act, with charming tables out on the square. Inside it's dull and modern, with a fine interior garden (€8-12 pastas, €10-18 *secondi*, closed Mon, Via dei Mulini 3, tel. 0577-887-300, www.osteriadelleone.it). For something a bit more affordable and casual, drop by the nearby **Il Loggiato,** with stony indoor seating or outdoor tables

(€6-7 *crostini* and polenta dishes, closed Thu, Via delle Sorgenti 36, tel. 0577-888-973).

Rocca d'Orcia

The looming fortress of Rocca d'Orcia (ROH-kah DOR-chah) perches high above the main SR-2 highway from Siena to Rome. Likely inhabited and fortified since Etruscan times, this strategic hilltop was a seat of great regional power in the 12th century, crowned by a fortress called Tentennano. During this time, Rocca d'Orcia was one of a chain of forts that watched over pilgrims walking the Via Francigena to Rome. Supposedly, St. Catherine of Siena miraculously learned to read and write overnight while staying here. Today the **Rocca di Tentennano** fortress feels abandoned, and is a very steep hike up from the parking lots that cling below its base (€3 entry; June-Sept daily 10:00-13:00 & 16:00-19:00; Sat-Sun only in May; March-April and Oct Sat-Sun 10:00-16:00, closed Mon-Fri; shorter hours off-season, mobile 333-986-0788, www.parcodellavaldorcia.com). The pleasant village of Rocca d'Orcia, just below the castle, is a sleepy and stony spot to stroll, but there's not much to see. The village focuses on its stone cistern, which marks the center of the main square, the aptly named Piazza della Cisterna. The bigger town just behind Rocca, Castiglione d'Orcia, also has a fortified hilltop town center.

Eating in Rocca d'Orcia: **La Cisterna nel Borgo** sits on Rocca's main square, facing the town's namesake cistern. Marta and Fede serve up deliciously executed dishes in a classic setting (€9-10 pastas, €11-13 *secondi,* cash only, closed Mon, Borgo Mestro 37, tel. 0577-887-280, www.cisternanelborgo.com).

"BEST OF TUSCANY" DRIVING TOUR

If you have just one day to connect the ultimate Tuscan towns and views, this is the loop I'd stitch together. While the rockier wine country farther west and north has its fans, the appeal here is exactly the opposite: Most of this journey is through velvety, gentle, rolling hillsides generously draped with vivid-green crops in the springtime, and a parched moonscape in the late summer and fall. This almost otherworldly smoothness constitutes many travelers' notions of Tuscan perfection.

If you're in a rush and don't linger in any of the towns, you could do this drive (just for the views) in a couple of hours. To hit the sights, explore the towns, and linger over a meal or a glass of wine, you could split this up over several days. If you're in the region for a longer stay, this is a great loop to do early in your visit, to get your bearings. I've started and ended the clockwise loop in Montepulciano, but you could just as easily start and end in Pienza (or anywhere else along the way). If gardens are your thing, try to do this loop when La Foce Gardens are open (Wed, Sat, or Sun), and time your drive to join one of their guided tours (see page 543). To make it easier to mix and match over several days, I've divided the directions into four legs.

Note that the first stretch of this loop includes some steep gravel roads, which help spare you a lot of traffic. But if that makes you uncomfortable, you could instead take the longer (and poorly signed) route farther south, via the congested, sprawling mess of **Chianciano Terme.**

Leg #1: Montepulciano to La Foce

Before leaving Montepulciano, consider dropping by the showpiece Renaissance **San Biagio Church,** which sits at the base of the town (watch for its long, level, tree-lined driveway exactly where you leave Montepulciano and head toward Pienza—see page 532). Once you're done there, drive south, at first following signs to *Chianciano Terme* and *Chiusi*. Just one kilometer south of Montepulciano, watch on the right for the turnoff to *Castelluccio* and *Monticchiello*. Zip along this scenic back road for five kilometers. You'll pass the turnoff for Monticchiello on your right, but carry on straight ahead, as the road continues uphill and becomes gravel. Grinding your way up, you'll enjoy views on the right of the jagged cliffs called *calanchi* and begin to get your first glimpse of the famous twisty road above La Foce Gardens. You'll pass around the front door of an old country estate (just stick with the road as it curves), and pop out at the T-intersection in front of the entrance to the recommended **La Foce Gardens** (from this intersection, parking and reception is just to the left—look for *Loc. La Foce;* for details, see page 543. To skip the gardens and continue with the loop, turn right at this T-intersection, toward *Siena/Roma/Cassia.*

Leg #2: La Foce to Bagno Vignoni

From La Foce, head downhill toward *Siena* and *Roma*. After a few hundred yards, watch on the left for the big gravel parking lot of the recommended **Dopolavoro La Foce** restaurant (the restaurant itself is across the street). From this lot, you have a fine view of one of *the* iconic cypress-lined driveways of Tuscany (see "Top Tuscan Views" sidebar on page 548).

Continue downhill along this road for about five kilometers, through pristine farm fields, until you reach a major intersection, where you'll turn right toward *Pienza* and *Siena* (on SP-53). Immersed in spectacular scenery, you'll twist between giant cypresses for about 10 kilometers. This road parallels the region's namesake Orcia River ("Val d'Orcia" means "Orcia River Valley"). Take a moment to simply appreciate your surroundings. The famous Chianti region to the north and the Brunello region (near Montalcino) to the west are a short drive away; in those places, the rocky soil is perfect for grapes. But here, instead of rocks, you're surrounded by clay hills—once the floor of a prehistoric sea—that are ideal for cereal crops. Grains alternate every few years with a crop of fava beans, which help reintroduce nitrogen to the soil. It seems that every grassy hilltop is capped with a family farmhouse. Partway along this road, you'll pass a turnoff (on the right) for Pienza, which you're welcome to take if you're in a hurry to cut the loop short (just 8 scenic kilometers). But there's so much more to see; I'd rather carry on.

The tower looming on the hill ahead of you is Rocca d'Orcia (which you can visit as an optional detour—see later). Nearing the end of the road, you'll pass (on the left) the front door of an old farmhouse with oddly formidable, crenellated towers, like a little castle in the field. This is **Spedaletto Castle,** built during the 12th century as a hospice for pilgrims walking the Via Francigena to Rome. Today it serves essentially the same purpose, as an *agriturismo* called La Grancia ("The Granary").

When you reach the T-intersection with the main S-2 highway, turn left (toward *Roma*), then immediately take the exit for **Bagno Vignoni.** To explore this fascinating medieval spa town—with its main square filled with a thermal-spring-fed pool dating back centuries—see page 546. (To see the empty fortress at **Rocca d'Orcia**—and its views—you can overshoot Bagno Vignoni by just 1 kilometer and turn to page 550.)

Leg #3: Bagno Vignoni to Pienza

When you're ready to move on, head north on SR-2 (toward *San Quirico d'Orcia* and *Siena*). After just four kilometers, in San Quirico d'Orcia, turn off onto the SP-146 road to Pienza, also marked for *Chiusi, Chianciano Terme,* and *Montepulciano.* (Or, if you're collecting views and don't mind backtracking a bit, carry on past San Quirico straight—toward *Siena*—for four kilometers and pull over next to the circle of cypress trees in a field called the **Rondò**—described in the "Top Tuscan Views" sidebar on page 548. After seeing it, return to San Quirico, then head toward Pienza.) Along the San Quirico-Pienza road—one of the region's most scenic—you'll enjoy grand views in both directions, including two more quintessential Tuscan scenes: the **Chapel of Madonna di Vitaleta** (after 2 kilometers, on the right); and a classic **farmhouse-with-trees,** just before Pienza (about 9 kilometers after San Quirico, on the left;

both described on page 548). Finally you'll pull into **Pienza,** where you can park and tour the town using the information on page 537.

Leg #4: Pienza to Montepulciano (via Monticchiello)

If you're in a hurry or losing sunlight, just hop back on the main SP-146 road—it's a 12-kilometer straight-shot back to Montepulciano (enjoying some pullouts with fine views of the town on the left). But I prefer this longer, even more scenic route, via the fortified village of Monticchiello.

From the traffic circle at the entry to Pienza's town center, instead of heading for Montepulciano, follow the road that runs along the left side of town (marked *Amiata* and *Monticchiello*—as you face Pienza, you'll continue straight when the main road bends left). This road loops around behind and below the far end of the village, where you can consider a brief detour to see Pienza's oldest church: Turn off on the right at the brown sign for *Pieve di Corsigiano* and drive just a few hundred yards to **Corsignano Parish Church** (described on page 542).

Continuing on the main road past that turnoff, you'll drop steeply down into the valley, feeling as if you're sinking into a lavish painting. Your view is dominated by **Monte Amiata,** the tallest mountain in Tuscany. This looming behemoth blocks bad weather, creating a mild microclimate that makes the Val d'Orcia a particularly pleasant place to farm...or to vacation. Meanwhile, don't forget to savor the similarly stellar views of Pienza in your rearview mirror. After five kilometers, watch on the left for the turnoff to *Monticchiello* (brown sign). From here, carry on for four kilometers—watching on the left for fine views of Pienza, and for another classic "twisty cypress-lined road" view (see the sidebar on page 548)—to the pleasant town of **Monticchiello.** This town, with an excellent recommended restaurant (La Porta) and a compact, fortified townscape worth exploring, is a good place to stretch your legs (and described on page 546).

From Monticchiello, there are two routes back to Montepulciano: For the shorter route (6 kilometers), partly on gravel roads, drive all the way to the base of the Monticchiello old town, then turn right. For the longer route (10 kilometers), which stays on paved roads but loops back the way our loop started, turn off for *Montepulciano* at the main intersection, in the flat part of town that's lower down.

"TOSCANA MINORE" DRIVING TOUR

This quick and easy loop connects a series of charming, relatively untouristy villages with scenic rural roads. I call this region "Toscana Minore"—which means, loosely, "lesser-known" or "underrated Tuscany." While the charms of these towns are subtle compared to the biggies, people who truly want to get off the beaten path—and prize ambience and local charm—find this area rewarding. I've narrated it in a clockwise order, starting and ending in Pienza, but you can do it in reverse just as easily, and begin or end wherever you like.

From **Pienza,** head west on the main road (SP-146) to San Quirico d'Orcia (passing two great views—the classic farmhouse and the chapel with trees—described in the sidebar on page 548). In San Quirico, hop onto the main SR-2 highway heading north, toward Siena. After four kilometers (just before the bridge), you'll reach the pullout for the **Rondò** viewpoint (also described on page 548). Soon after, take the Torrenieri exit, and follow signs nine kilometers to **San Giovanni d'Asso** (described later, on page 576). Consider a truffle lunch or a stroll through the modern Bosco della Ragnaia park. From San Giovanni, follow *Montisi* signs six kilometers through the countryside, passing terra-cotta showrooms. In the 1300s, Siena (which controlled this area) switched its favored building material from stone to brick—a resource it had in abundance, thanks to these clay hills. Hovering on the right is the Abbey of Sant'Anna in Camprena, which you'll be circling all the way back to Pienza.

When you reach **Montisi,** park your car and walk up into town, following brown *centro storico* signs. This endearing little village of only 400 residents has four *contrade* (very competitive rival districts, as in Siena). As you hike steeply up through the almond-shaped old town, watch for flags indicating the *contrade* of *castello* (castle), *torre* (tower), *piazza* (square), and *San Martino.* Pass through the minuscule piazza (big enough for just two cars), then proceed up to the top of town, with a harpsichord academy and Church of Santa Maria Assunta.

Returning to your car, head back the way you came to find the turnoff for *Castelmuzio,* three kilometers away. For a glimpse at an extremely old church, just as you're approaching Castelmuzio, you could turn off on the right, following brown signs for *Pieve di Santo Stefano a Cennano* and *Strada della Pieve.* You'll drive through an olive grove to what's likely the oldest church in Tuscany: **Santo Stefano a Cennano,** with three apses, dating from 1285. In the dimly lit Romanesque interior, the only light leaks in through extremely narrow slits.

Back on the main road, continue to **Castelmuzio**—more tightly packed and even more scenic than Montisi. Parking your car, walk up into the knot-shaped old town, following the charming tree-lined main street to the panoramic terrace at the far end, with stunning views southeast over the region. From here, you can survey Montepulciano, Pienza, and the Abbey of Sant'Anna in Camprena. The olive groves at your feet are some of the best in

Italy: This area—Montisi, Trequanda, and Petroio—forms an area called the "Golden Triangle" for its high-quality olive oil.

When you're ready to continue, you could carry on another three kilometers to the village of **Petroio,** known as a terra-cotta-making center. But as the views and townscape in Petroio don't quite match those in Montisi and Castelmuzio—and you'll have to backtrack here anyway to complete our loop—I'd give it a pass.

From Castelmuzio, heading at first toward Petroio, watch for the hard right turn to Pienza (with brown signs for *Sant'Anna in Camprena*). After about three kilometers on this road, watch for the turnoff on the right to the **Abbey of Sant'Anna in Camprena.** Fans of *The English Patient* are charmed by this abbey, where much of that movie was filmed (you'll recognize the courtyard and the big window that opens out onto huge Tuscan views). It also offers a peek at the vivid, often quirky Renaissance frescoes of Il Sodoma, who also frescoed the cloister at the Abbey of Monte Oliveto Maggiore (described on page 578). Erratic hours make a visit here challenging, but if you're a fan of the film, you could stop by to see if it's open (www.camprena.it).

The road that passes the Abbey of Sant'Anna in Camprena carries on, through thick woods, until it deposits you on the main Pienza-San Quirico Road back where we began—just a few hundred feet outside of **Pienza.**

Sleeping in the Val d'Orcia

While I wouldn't hang my hat in sleepy Pienza itself, some fine countryside options sit just outside town. The first two are immersed in Tuscan splendor, midway between Montepulciano and Montalcino (on the main road from Pienza toward Montalcino, about 2.5 miles outside of Pienza); the third, La Bruciata, is on the other side of Pienza, in the direction of Montepulciano.

$$$ Agriturismo Cretaiole, ideally situated in pristine farmland just outside Pienza, is perfect for those who want to settle in for a week and fully experience Tuscany. This family-friendly farm welcomes visitors for weeklong stays (generally Sat-Sat) in six comfortable apartments. One of my favorite *agriturismo* experiences in Italy, Cretaiole is warmly run by reformed city-slicker Isabella, who came here on vacation and fell in love with country-boy Carlo. Now Carlo and his father, Luciano, tend to the farm, while Isabella and her helper Carlotta pride themselves on personally assisting guests in finding exactly the Tuscan experience they're

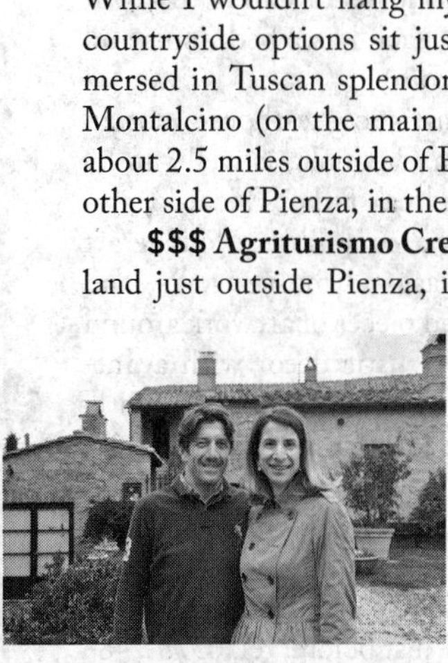

dreaming of. More than just a place to stay, Cretaiole is a remarkably rich cultural education; Isabella has thoughtfully planned an extensive slate of optional activities (each one for a reasonable extra charge). These can include pasta-making and olive-oil tasting classes, family-style Tuscan dinners, winery tours, truffle hunts and grape and olive harvesting (in season), artisan studio visits, Siena side-trips, watercolor classes, and more. All of these activities make Cretaiole feel like an idyllic summer camp for grown-ups. While you could just let momentum overtake you here—not a bad plan, given the grand views from the manicured lawn—those wanting to delve more deeply into Tuscany should opt for the fairly priced "Dolce Vita Stay" package (Db-€860/week, small Db apartment-€1,050/week, large Db apartment-€1,350/week, same apartment for a family of up to four-€1,550/week, larger apartments available, these prices promised with this book in 2015; weeklong stays preferred but shorter stays possible when it's slow—Db-€130/night, 3-night minimum, you can only book one month ahead; fewer activities and lower prices mid-Nov-mid-March, no air-con or swimming pool—for philosophical reasons, Wi-Fi, loaner bikes, loaner mobile phones, Isabella's mobile 338-740-9245, Carlotta's mobile 338-835-1614, tel. 0578-748-083, www.cretaiole.it, info@cretaiole.it). The same family runs two properties in the atmospheric medieval village of Castelmuzio, five miles north of Pienza (both with access to activities at the main *agriturismo*): **Le Casine di Castello** is a townhouse with two units (same prices as Cretaiole), while the more upscale **Casa Moricciani** is a swanky villa with dreamy views, plush interiors, and loads of extras (€3,250/week upstairs, €4,250/week downstairs, each has 2 bedrooms and 2 bathrooms; www.buongiornotoscana.com).

$$$ Fonte Bertusi, a classy and artistic guesthouse (not an *agriturismo*) nearly across the road from Cretaiole, is well-run by young couple Manuela and Andrea, Andrea's father Edoardo, and their attention-starved cats. They have a cozy library/lounge/art gallery that hosts installations and occasional music events, and they've scattered vivid, whimsical bits and pieces of artwork around the complex. The eight apartments mix rustic decor with avant-garde creations; it's a bit pricey, but the setting is sublime (nightly rate: 1-bedroom apartment-€130, 2-bedroom apartment-€260, includes breakfast; weekly rate: €750-1,150, €50 extra per person for breakfast all week; Wi-Fi, laundry service, swimming pool, grand view terrace, communal BBQ and outdoor kitchen, just outside Pienza toward San Quirico d'Orcia on the right—don't confuse it with the turnoff for "Il Fonte" just before, tel. 0578-748-077, Manuela's mobile 339-655-5648, www.fontebertusi.it, info@fontebertusi.it).

$$$ La Bruciata is a family-friendly *agriturismo* charmingly tucked in remote-feeling countryside just a five-minute drive outside of Montepulciano (on the way to Pienza). Can-do Laura and her family produce wine and olive oil, and rent seven tasteful, modern rooms split among four apartments (for 2-6 people each). In the summer (June-Aug), they prefer one-week stays, but shorter visits are possible at other times (Db-€100-120 depending on size, air-con for extra charge, Wi-Fi, farm-fresh meals and cooking classes for extra charge, Via del Termine 9, tel. 0578-757-704, mobile 339-781-5106, www.agriturismolabruciata.it, info@agriturismolabruciata.it). Leaving Montepulciano toward Pienza, turn off on the left for *Poggiano,* then carefully track red *La Bruciata* signs (using gravel roads).

Montalcino and the Brunello Wine Country

On a hill overlooking vineyards and valleys, Montalcino—famous for its delicious and pricey Brunello di Montalcino red wines—is a must for wine lovers. It's a pleasant, low-impact town with a fine ambience and a smattering of classy shopping, but little sightseeing. Everyone touring this area seems to be relaxed and in an easy groove...as if enjoying a little wine buzz.

In the Middle Ages, Montalcino (mohn-tahl-CHEE-noh) was considered Siena's biggest ally. Originally aligned with Florence, the town switched sides after the Sienese beat up Florence in the Battle of Montaperti in 1260. The Sienese persuaded the Montalcinesi to join their side by forcing them to collect corpses and sleep one night in the bloody, Florentine-strewn battlefield. Later, the Montalcinesi took in Sienese refugees. To this day, in gratitude for their support, the Sienese invite the Montalcinesi to lead the parade that kicks off Siena's Palio celebrations.

Montalcino prospered under Siena, but like its ally, it waned after the Medici family took control of the region. The village became a humble place. Then, in the late 19th century, the Biondi Santi family created a fine, dark red wine, calling it "the brunette" (Brunello). Today's affluence is due to the town's much-sought-after wine. (For more on this wine, see the "Wines in the Region" sidebar, next page).

If you're not a wine lover, you may find Montalcino a bit too focused on *vino,* but one sip of Brunello makes even wine skeptics

Wines in the Region

This region has two well-respected red wines, each centered on a specific town: Montepulciano is known for its Vino Nobile, while Montalcino is famous for its Brunello. In each wine, the predominant grape is a clone of sangiovese (Tuscany's main red wine grape)—but the specific qualities of each vintage can vary dramatically, based on the unique microclimate where the grape is grown, the specific blend of grapes (when blends are allowed), and how the wine is aged.

Vino Nobile di Montepulciano ("noble wine of Montepulciano") is a high-quality dry ruby red, made mostly with the Prugnolo Gentile variety of sangiovese (70 percent), plus other varieties like Mammolo (30 percent). Aged two years (or three for a *riserva*), one year of which must be in oak casks, it's more full-bodied than a typical Chianti and less tannic than a Brunello. It pairs well with meat, especially roasted lamb with rosemary, rabbit or boar ragù over pasta, grilled portobello mushrooms, and local cheeses like pecorino. Several large wineries produce and age their Vino Nobile in the sprawling cellars beneath the town of Montepulciano. Two of these—Contucci Cantina and Cantine de' Ricci—are fun and easy to tour (see "Sights and Experiences in Montepulciano" on page 529). The oldest red wine in Tuscany, Vino Nobile has been produced since the late 1500s. Don't mistake this wine for lesser-quality wines from the Le Marche or Abruzzo regions that use a grape confusingly named Montepulciano.

Brunello di Montalcino ("the little brown one of Montalcino"—named for the color of the grapes before harvest) is even more highly regarded and ranks among Italy's finest and most expensive wines. Made from 100 percent Sangiovese Grosso (a.k.a. Brunello) grapes, it's smooth, dry, and aged for a minimum of two years in wood casks, plus an additional four months in the bottle. *Riserva* wines are aged an additional year. Brunello is designed to cellar for 10 years or longer—but who can wait? It pairs well with the local cuisine, including the dishes mentioned above, but the perfect match is the fine Chianina beef. *Buon appetito!*

First created by the Biondi Santi clan in the late 19th century, this wine quickly achieved a sterling reputation, and became Italy's first DOCG (highest-quality) wine in 1980. Today, there are around 240 mostly small producers of Brunello in the Montalcino region; I've recommended just a few, which I find fun and accessible, and tied them together with the self-guided driving loop on page 571. A simpler option (that avoids having the taster be behind the wheel) is to sample a few different wines at one of the good wine bars in the town center of Montalcino (see page 564). You'll also see Rosso di Montalcino (a younger version of Brunello), which is aged for one year. This "poor man's Brunello" is very good, at half the price. Note that in lesser-quality years only Rosso di Montalcino is produced.

Montalcino's climate is drier and warmer than Chianti or Montepulciano. Diverse soils and slopes create many microclimates that affect the wine. Locals explain that, due to overall temperature increases resulting from climate change, wineries on the higher ground reap benefits from slightly cooler temperatures, as grapes like hot days and cool nights. Elevation is a bonus for wine-loving tourists, who enjoy stellar views while sampling the best wines.

Touring a winery, you'll see that many winemakers age Brunello in giant oak casks rather than smaller barrels. This means that less liquid is in contact with the wood surface, so the wine picks up less of the harsh wood (tannic) taste and vanilla-like flavors, while still absorbing the desired leathery and peppery notes. You'll also notice glass jars (an invention of Leonardo da Vinci) poking up from the tops of those casks, which allow expansion of the liquid during fermentation, and—by providing a small overflow reservoir—ensure that the wine reaches the very top of the cask to avoid excessive contact with the air. Before placing the wine in casks, modern wineries ferment it in temperature-controlled cement or stainless steel tanks, which are easier to maintain than wood, and preserve a more fruity bouquet.

Strolling through vineyards, you may notice "sentinel" roses at the ends of some of the rows of vines. These aren't just decorative; because disease affects roses before grapes, historically the flowers acted as a canary in a coal mine, giving vintners advance notice if a phylloxera epidemic was imminent. Today the roses can warn of mildew. But disease isn't the only pest: Locals say that wild boars make the best winemakers—they wait to raid the vineyards until the grapes are perfectly sweet. At that magic moment, it becomes a race between the boars and their fellow, human harvesters. But humans have the last laugh or bite—boar is found on many Tuscan menus and the perfect accompaniment is the local wines!

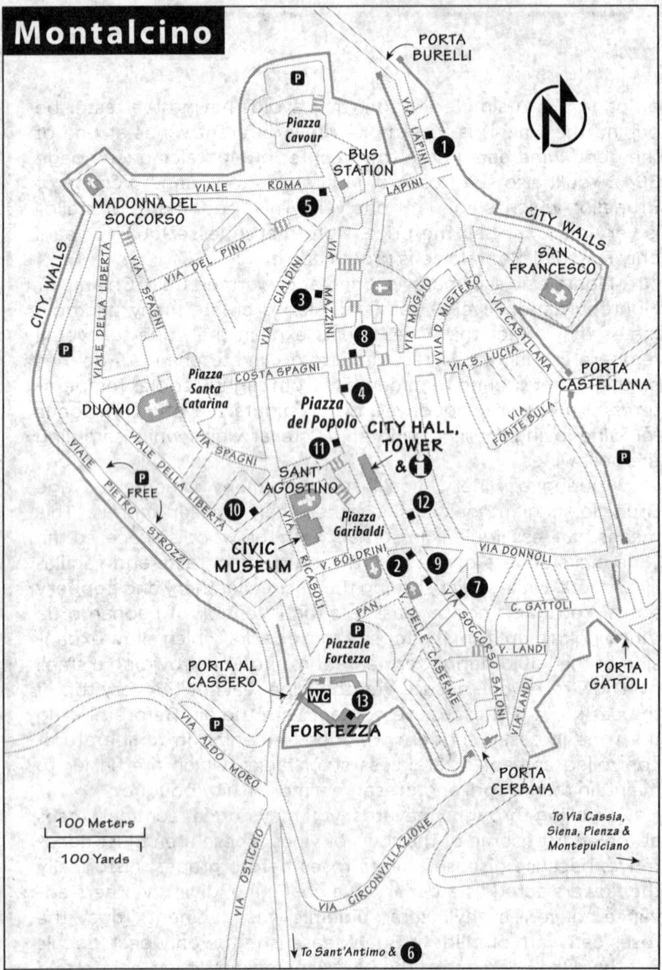

1. Hotel Dei Capitani
2. Palazzina Cesira
3. B&B da Idolina
4. Affittacamere Mariuccia
5. Albergo Giardino
6. To La Crociona Agriturismo
7. Re di Macchia Ristorante
8. Taverna il Grappolo Blu
9. Ristorante-Pizzeria San Giorgio
10. Co-op Supermarket
11. Caffè Fiaschetteria Italiana
12. Enoteca di Piazza
13. Enoteca la Fortezza di Montalcino

believe that Bacchus was onto something. Those with a sweet tooth will enjoy crunching the Ossi di Morto ("bones of the dead") cookies popular in Tuscany.

Montalcino also provides a handy springboard for exploring the surrounding wine region—with a more varied landscape than the Val d'Orcia near Montepulciano and Pienza. "Montalcino" literally means "Mountain of Holm Oaks"—and sure enough, its surrounding hills are generously forested. For a self-guided driving tour connecting some of the most enjoyable wineries and views, see page 571.

Orientation to Montalcino

Sitting atop a hill amidst a sea of vineyards, Montalcino is surrounded by walls and dominated by the Fortezza (a.k.a. "La Rocca"). From here, roads lead down into the two main squares: Piazza Garibaldi and Piazza del Popolo.

Tourist Information: The helpful TI, just off Piazza Garibaldi in City Hall, can find you a room for no fee. They sell bus tickets; can call ahead to book a visit at a countryside winery (€1/person service fee); and have information on taxis to nearby towns, abbeys, and monasteries (daily 10:00-13:00 & 14:00-17:50, tel. 0577-849-331, www.prolocomontalcino.com).

Arrival in Montalcino: Drivers coming in for a short visit should drive around the old gate under the fortress, take the first right (follow signs to *Fortezza;* it looks almost forbidden), and grab a spot in the pay lot at the fortress (€1.50/hour, free 20:00-8:00). If you miss this lot—or if it's full—follow the town's western wall toward the Madonna del Soccorso church and a long pay lot with the same prices. Otherwise, park for free a short walk away.

The **bus** station is on Piazza Cavour, about 300 yards from the town center. From here, simply follow Via Mazzini straight up into town. While Montalcino has no official baggage storage, a few shops are willing to hold onto one or two bags on a short-term basis; ask at the TI for details.

Helpful Hints: Market day is Friday (7:00-13:00) on Viale della Libertà (near the Fortezza).

Sights in Montalcino

Fortezza

This 14th-century fort, built under Sienese rule, is now little more than an empty shell. You're welcome to enter the big, open courtyard (with WCs out the far end), or just enjoy a picnic in the park surrounding the fort, but if you want climb the ramparts for a panoramic view, you'll have to pay. Most people visit the fortress for its wine bar (see page 565).

Cost and Hours: €4 for rampart walk—buy ticket and enter in the wine bar, €6 combo-ticket includes Montalcino Museums (sold only at museum), daily 9:00-20:00, until 18:00 Nov-March, last entry 30 minutes before closing.

Piazza del Popolo

All roads in tiny Montalcino seem to lead to the main square, Piazza del Popolo ("People's Square").

Since 1888, the recommended **Caffè Fiaschetteria Italiana** has been *the* elegant place to enjoy a drink. Its founder, inspired by Caffè Florian in Venice, brought fine coffee to this humble town of woodcutters.

City Hall was the fortified seat of government. It's decorated by the coats of arms of judges who, in the interest of fairness, were from outside of town. Like Siena, Montalcino was a republic in the Middle Ages. When Florentines took Siena in 1555, Siena's ruling class retreated here and held out for four more years. The Medici coat of arms (with the six pills), which supersedes all the others, is a reminder that in 1559 Florence finally took Montalcino.

The one-handed **clock** was the norm until 200 years ago. For five centuries the arcaded **loggia** hosted the town market. And, of course, it's fun to simply observe the *passeggiata*—these days mostly a parade of tourists here for the wine.

Montalcino Museums (Musei di Montalcino)

While it's technically three museums in one (archaeology, medieval art, and modern art), and it's surprisingly big and modern for this little town, Montalcino's lone museum ranks only as a decent bad-weather activity. The archaeology collection, filling the cellar, includes interesting artifacts from the area dating back as far as—gulp—200,000 B.C. With good English explanations, this section also displays a mannequin dressed as an Etruscan soldier and a model of the city walls in early Roman times. The ground, first, and second floors hold the medieval and modern art collections, with an emphasis on Gothic sacred art (with works from Montalcino's heyday, the 13th to 16th centuries). Most of the art was created by local artists. The ground floor is best, with a large collection of crucifixes and the museum's highlights, a glazed-terra-cotta altarpiece and statue of St. Sebastian, both by Andrea della Robbia.

Cost and Hours: €4.50, €6 combo-ticket includes rampart walk at Fortezza, daily 10:00-13:00 & 14:00-17:50, Via Ricasoli 31, to the right of Sant'Agostino Church, tel. 0577-846-014.

Sleeping in Montalcino

$$$ Hotel Dei Capitani, at the end of town near the bus station, has plush public spaces, an inviting pool, and a cliffside terrace offering plenty of reasons for lounging. About half of the 29 rooms come with vast Tuscan views for the same price (request a view room when you reserve), the nonview rooms are bigger, and everyone has access to the terrace (Db-€138 in 2015 when you book directly with the hotel and mention this book, extra bed-€40, air-con, elevator, guest computer and Wi-Fi, limited free parking—first come, first served, Via Lapini 6, tel. 0577-847-227, www.deicapitani.it, info@deicapitani.it).

$$ Palazzina Cesira, right in the heart of the old town, is a gem renting five spacious and tastefully decorated rooms in a fine 13th-century residence with a palatial lounge and a pleasant garden. You'll enjoy a refined and tranquil ambience, a nice breakfast (with eggs), and the chance to get to know Lucilla and her American husband Roberto, who are generous with local advice (Db-€105, suites-€125, cash only, 2-night minimum, 3-night minimum on holiday weekends, air-con, guest computer and Wi-Fi, free off-street parking, Via Soccorso Saloni 2, tel. 0577-846-055, www.montalcinoitaly.com, p.cesira@tin.it).

$$ B&B da Idolina has four good, mid-range rooms above a wine shop on the main street (Db-€75, includes basic breakfast in shared kitchen, Wi-Fi, check-in available 14:00-20:00—call if arriving later, Via Mazzini 65, mobile 333-771-2102, www.poggiorubino.it, camereidolina@poggiorubino.it, Alessandro).

$ Affittacamere Mariuccia has three small, colorful, good-value, Ikea-chic rooms on the main drag over a heaven-scented bakery (Sb-€40, Db-€60, air-con, Wi-Fi, check in across the street at Enoteca Pierangioli before 20:00 or let them know arrival time, Piazza del Popolo 16, rooms at #28, tel. 0577-849-113, mobile 347-365-5364, www.affittacameremariuccia.it, enotecapierangioli@hotmail.com, Alessandro and Stefania speak English).

$ Albergo Giardino, old and basic, has nine big simple rooms, no public spaces, and a convenient location near the bus station (Db-€55-60, 10 percent discount with this book outside May and Sept, no breakfast, free Wi-Fi, Piazza Cavour 4, tel. 0577-848-257, mobile 338-684-3163, albergoilgiardino@virgilio.it; Roberto and dad Mario).

NEAR MONTALCINO

$$ La Crociona, an *agriturismo* farm and working vineyard, rents seven fully equipped apartments with dated furnishings. Fiorella Vannoni and Roberto and Barbara Nannetti offer cooking classes and tastes of the Brunello wine grown and bottled on the premises

(Db-€95, or €65 in Oct-mid-May; Qb-€130, or €95 in Oct-mid-May; lower weekly rates, reception open 10:00-12:00 & 15:00-18:00, metered gas heating, laundry service-€8/load, covered pool, hot tub, fitness room, La Croce 15, tel. 0577-847-133, www.lacrociona.com, info@lacrociona.com). The farm is two miles south of Montalcino on the road to the Sant'Antimo Abbey; don't turn off at the first entrance to the village of La Croce—wait for the second one, following directions to Tenuta Crocedimezzo e Crociona. For location, see the map on page 519. A good restaurant is next door.

Eating in Montalcino

RESTAURANTS

Re di Macchia is an invitingly intimate restaurant where Antonio serves up the Tuscan fare Roberta cooks. Look for their seasonal menu and Montalcino-only wine list. Try the €25 fixed-price meal, and for €17 more, have it paired with local wines carefully selected to accompany each dish (€10 pastas, €16 *secondi,* Fri-Wed 12:00-14:00 & 19:00-21:00, closed Thu, reservations strongly recommended, Via Soccorso Saloni 21, tel. 0577-846-116).

Taverna il Grappolo Blu is unpretentious, friendly, and serious about its wine, serving local specialties and vegetarian options to an enthusiastic crowd (€8-9 pastas, €9-14 *secondi,* Sat-Thu 12:00-15:00 & 19:00-22:00, closed Fri, reservations smart, near the main square, a few steps off Via Mazzini at Scale di Via Moglio 1, tel. 0577-847-150, Luciano, www.grappoloblu.it).

Ristorante-Pizzeria San Giorgio is a homey trattoria/pizzeria with kitschy decor and reasonable prices. It's a reliable choice for a simple meal (€5-6 pizzas, €8 pastas, €8-13 *secondi,* daily 12:00-15:30 & 19:00-23:00, Via Soccorso Saloni 10, tel. 0577-848-507, Mara).

Picnic: Gather ingredients at the **Co-op supermarket** on Via Sant'Agostino (Mon-Sat 8:30-13:00 & 16:00-20:00, closed Sun, just off Via Ricasoli in front of Sant'Agostino Church), then enjoy your feast up at the Madonna del Soccorso Church, with vast territorial views.

Wine Bars: Note that two of the places listed under "Wine Bars *(Enoteche)*" also serve light food.

WINE BARS *(ENOTECHE)*

There are two basic approaches for sampling Montalcino's wines: at an *enoteca* in town, or at a countryside winery. Serious wine connoisseurs will enjoy a day of winery-hopping, sipping the wines right where they were created; I've listed fine wineries on page 566, and a recommended driving loop on page 571. But if you're short on time (or don't have a designated driver—penalties here are harsh for driving under the influence), or want to try more than one producer's wines, you might prefer to simply visit a wine bar in town, where you can comfortably taste a variety of vintages before safely stumbling back to your hotel.

Caffè Fiaschetteria Italiana, a classic, venerable café/wine bar, was founded by Ferruccio Biondi Santi, the creator of the famous Brunello wine. The wine library in the back of the café boasts many local choices. A meeting place since 1888, this grand café also serves light lunches and espresso to tourists and locals alike (€6-13 Brunellos by the glass, €3-5 light snacks, €8-12 plates; same prices inside, outside, or in back room; daily 7:30-23:00, Wi-Fi, Piazza del Popolo 6, tel. 0577-849-043). And if it's coffee you need, this place—with its classic 1961 espresso machine—is considered the best in town.

Enoteca di Piazza is one of a chain of wine shops with a system of mechanical dispensers. A "drink card" (like a debit card) keeps track of the samples you take, for which you'll pay from €1 to €9 for each 50-milliliter taste of the 100 different wines, including some whites—rare in this town. The only nibbles are saltine-type crackers. They hope you'll buy a bottle of the samples you like, and are happy to educate you in English. (Rule of thumb: A bottle costs about 10 times the cost of the sample. If you buy a bottle, the sample of that wine is free.) While the place feels a little formulaic, it can be fun—the wine is great, and the staff is casual and helpful (daily 9:00-20:00, near Piazza del Popolo at Via Matteotti 43, tel. 0577-848-104, www.enotecadipiazza.com). Confusingly, there are three similarly named places in this same area—this tasting room is a block below the main square.

Enoteca la Fortezza di Montalcino offers a chance to taste top-end wines by the glass, each with an English explanation. While the prices are a bit higher than most other *enoteche* in town, the medieval setting inside Montalcino's fort is a hit for most visitors. Spoil yourself with Brunello in the cozy *enoteca* or at an outdoor table (€13 for 3 tastings, or €22 for 3 "top-end" tastings; €10-18 two-person sampler plates of cheeses, *salumi*, honeys, and olive oil; daily 9:00-20:00, closes at 18:00 Nov-March, inside the Fortezza, tel. 0577-849-211, www.enotecalafortezza.com, info@enotecalafortezza.com).

Montalcino Connections

Montalcino is poorly connected to just about everywhere except Siena—making it a good day trip if Siena is your base—but other connections are generally workable. Montalcino's bus station is on Piazza Cavour, within the town walls. Bus tickets are sold at the bar on Piazza Cavour, at the TI, and at some tobacco shops, but not on board (except for the bus to Sant'Antimo). Check schedules at the TI, at the bus station, or at www.sienamobilita.it. The nearest train station is a 20-minute bus ride away, in Buonconvento (bus runs nearly hourly, €2.05).

From Montalcino by Bus: The handiest direct bus is to **Siena** (6/day Mon-Sat, 4/day Sun, 1.25 hours). To reach **Pienza** or **Montepulciano,** ride the bus to Torrenieri (3-4/day Mon-Sat, none on Sun, 20 minutes), where you'll switch to line #114 for the rest of the way (from Torrenieri: 25 minutes to Pienza; 45 minutes to Montepulciano). A local bus runs to **Sant'Antimo** (3/day Mon-Fri, 2/day Sat, none on Sun, 15 minutes, buy tickets on board). Anyone going to **Florence** by bus changes in Siena; since the bus arrives at Siena's train station, it's handier to go the rest of the way to Florence by train. Alternatively, you could take the bus to Buonconvento (described earlier), and catch the train from there to Florence.

Route Tips for Drivers: My self-guided "Brunello Wine Country" loop drive begins at Montalcino's doorstep (see page 571). The town is also a short trip from my loop drives of the "Best of Tuscany" area (page 550) and the Crete Senesi (page 589).

Sights and Wineries near Montalcino

For this rugged, fun-to-explore area, I've recommended several excellent wineries; described a historic abbey that's worth a visit, particularly if you want to experience a traditional Gregorian Mass; and outlined a self-guided driving route that links these sights.

WINERIES NEAR MONTALCINO

The surrounding countryside is littered with wineries, some of which offer tastings. A few require an appointment, but many are happy to serve a glass to potential buyers and show them around. The Montalcino TI can give you a list of more than 150 regional wineries and will call ahead for you (€1/person service fee). Or check with the vintners' consortium (tel. 0577-848-246, www.consorziobrunellodimontalcino.it, info@consorziobrunellodimontalcino.it).

If you lack a car (or don't want to drive), you can take a tour on the **Brunello Wine Bus,** which laces together a variety of wineries (€25, mid-June-Oct Tue, Thu, and Sat, departs at 9:00, returns at 20:00, tel. 0577-846-021, www.lecameredibacco.com, info@lecameredibacco.com).

The local wine-tasting culture is nothing like the Napa Valley scene—you typically can't just show up and expect to taste a few sips. If you're serious about tasting, make a reservation in advance for a tour and guided tasting (an in-depth visit that usually lasts about an hour). I've highlighted a few places that are a bit more flexible, but even at these, there's a fairly narrow window during which drop-ins are welcome, so keep a close eye on those hours.

If you're paying for a wine tasting, you aren't obligated to buy. But if a winery is doing a small tasting just for you, they're hoping you'll buy a bottle or two. Italian vintners understand that North Americans can't take much wine with them, and they don't expect to make a big sale, but they do hope you'll look for their wines in the US. Some shops and wineries can arrange shipping.

Le Potazzine

This endearingly small, friendly, family-run winery, about a five-minute drive south of Montalcino, is operated by gregarious Gigliola and her assistant, Michele. The name is a type of small bird that also means "Little Girls," in honor of Gigliola's daughters. It's best to call or email ahead to schedule a one-hour tour and tasting (€15, includes 3 tastes). But on most afternoons (Tue-Sun) you can drop by between 12:00 and 15:30 for a quicker, more casual taste without the full tour (€10-36 bottles, Loc. Le Prata 262, tel. 0577-846-168, www.lepotazzine.it, tenuta@lepotazzine.it).

Mastrojanni

Perched high above the Sant'Antimo Abbey, this winery hits a nice balance: Run by three brothers from Rome, it's owned by the big Illy coffee company. This big, glitzy winery overlooks vast vineyards and spectacular views, yet doesn't feel as corporate or soulless as some of the bigger players. You can call ahead to arrange a full tour and tasting (€10). Or, for a more casual experience, stop by any weekday afternoon (Mon-Fri 13:00-15:00) for a tasting and a brief tour (€17-36 bottles, Podere Loreto e San Pio, tel. 0577-835-681, www.mastrojanni.com). To reach it, head up into the town of Castelnuovo dell'Abate (just above Sant'Antimo Abbey), bear left at the Bassomondo restaurant, and continue along the gravel road up, up, up (enjoying vineyard and abbey views) to the end.

Ciacci Piccolomini d'Aragona

Easier to remember by just its first name (think Chachi from *Happy Days*), this offers a great combination of a well-respected, family-run vineyard that's big enough to offer a drop-in-anytime tasting room. Situated down a back lane on the way from Sant'Antimo Abbey to the "La Sesta" gravel road, Ciacci has a classy tasting room/*enoteca* and an outdoor view terrace. Belly up to the wine bar for two or three free tastes, or order a more formal tasting of top-quality wines for €10-25, which includes a tour of the cellar (reserve ahead for full tasting; for a casual taste just drop by Mon-

Fri 9:00-19:00, Sat-Sun 10:30-18:30, tel. 0577-835-616, www.ciaccipiccolomini.com, info@ciaccipiccolomini.com).

Altesino

Elegant and aloof, Altesino owns perhaps the most stunning location of all, just off the back road connecting Montalcino north to Buonconvento. You'll twist up on cypress-lined gravel lanes to this perch, which looks out over an expanse of vineyards with Montalcino hovering on the horizon. While you can try just dropping in, to be assured of a tasting it's better to call ahead (€12.50-35 tastings, generally daily 8:30-13:00 & 14:30-17:00, Loc. Altesino 54, tel. 0577-806-208, www.altesino.it, info@altesino.it).

Santa Giulia

On the outskirts of Torrenieri, this may be the quintessential family-run winery, with an emphasis on quality over quantity. For that reason, you'll have to reserve ahead for a tasting here, but it's worth the hassle. Flatter, a bit less scenic, and much more rustic (with a working-farm feel rather than a swanky tasting room) than the others listed here, this is a Back Door experience. They also produce excellent olive oil and top-notch prosciutto and salami (€15 for tasting and tour, €12-27 bottles, Loc. San Giulia 48, tel. 0577-834-270, www.santagiuliamontalcino.it, info@santagiuliamontalcino.it). It's tricky to find: From Torrenieri's main intersection, follow the brown *Via Francigena* signs. After crossing the train tracks and a bridge, watch on the left to follow signs for *Sasso di Sole*, then *Sta. Chiara*; you'll take gravel roads through farm fields to the winery.

WINE-RELATED SIGHTS AND TOWNS NEAR MONTALCINO

Museum of the Montalcino Community and of Brunello (Museo della Comunità di Montalcino e del Brunello)

Serious wine connoisseurs scouring the Montalcino wine-growing area may want to fit in a visit to this dry but thorough museum. (Those with a purely hedonistic interest in wine may find this a good way to sober up before moving on to the next vineyard.) The first part focuses on the agricultural history of the region, with lots of old tools, clothes, and other illustrations of the humble local economy before the age of winemaking—back when forestry and carpentry were the dominant occupation of this mostly wooded area. The second half delves deeply into the age after Clemente Santi (1795-1885) introduced sangiovese grapes to the area; his grandson, Ferruccio Biondi Santi, used those grapes to create Brunello. You'll see exhibits on the Biondi Santi gang and other pioneers, as well as a detailed survey of the most prestigious Brunello producers. On summer Saturdays, they have tastings of Brunello and local foods (€10, call or email for details).

Cost and Hours: €5, Mon-Sat 10:00-13:00 & 14:30-18:00, Sun by appointment only, Loc. Podernovi 170, just past crossroads village of La Croce, tel. 0577-849-546, mobile 348-333-9829, www.museobrunello.it, Maurizio and Paolo.

Getting There: From Montalcino, head south toward Sant'Antimo. After passing through the tiny crossroads of La Croce, watch for signs on the left for *Podernuovi*; once on this small road, you'll pass the winery on your right, then keep going straight to the museum (watch for red *Museo del Brunello* signs).

Sant'Angelo in Colle

This nondescript hill town, about 5.5 miles south of Montalcino, is worth visiting only if you'd like a meal (and some high-altitude views) while wine-tasting in the area. Twist up to the top of the hill and park by the square; both restaurants are just steps away. **Trattoria Il Leccio** is the pricier option, with a cozy stone interior and seating out on the square (€10-12 pastas, €16-18 *secondi,* closed Wed, Costa Castellare 1/3, tel. 0577-844-175, www.trattoriailleccio.it). **Il Pozzo** sits just a few steps below the square, serving affordable homemade pasta dishes in a pleasant interior with big windows overlooking the hillsides (€9-10 pastas, €8-12 *secondi,* closed Tue, tel. 0577-844-015, www.trattoriailpozzo.com).

▲Sant'Antimo Abbey

Set amidst postcard-perfect olive groves and pastures ringed by cypress-prickled hills just south of Montalcino, this Romanesque abbey—adorned with mysterious, pagan-seeming carvings—is one of the region's most rewarding to visit. It also offers an opportunity to listen to a traditional Gregorian-chanted Mass in a fitting space.

Cost and Hours: Free, open to tourists Mon-Sat 10:15-12:30 & 15:00-18:30, Sun 9:15-10:45 & 15:00-18:00, closed to tourists during frequent services, open to worshippers daily 6:00-21:00, www.antimo.it.

Gregorian Chants: Each evening (Mon-Sat at 19:00, Sun at 18:30), the monks celebrate vespers with a Gregorian chanted service; their melodious reverence echoes profoundly through this space's fine acoustics. Confirm the schedule online or by phone before planning your day around it. This is a church service, not a concert; for some, a little chanting goes a long way.

Getting There: From Montalcino, **drivers** should head south toward Castelnuovo dell'Abate ("New Castle of the Abbot"). Keep an eye out for the abbey—below you in the fields—as you approach. Large pay parking lots are just a short walk from the abbey. A **bus** runs from Montalcino (see "Montalcino Connections," earlier).

Background: Legends suggest that Sant'Antimo was founded by Charlemagne, who passed through here around the year 781, following the Via Francigena on his way back north from Rome. His army, suffering from illness, convalesced near here, and in appreciation Charlemagne presented the local religious community with relics of St. Anthimus (Sant'Antimo). Most of its current structure dates from the 11th and 12th centuries, when Sant'Antimo Abbey became a highly important center both for local aristocrats and for pilgrims walking the Via Francigena. But after Pope Pius II moved the diocese from Montalcino to Pienza in 1462, the abbey sat neglected for centuries, even becoming a stable for a while. Finally, starting in the late 19th century, it was restored, and in 1992 a small number of Augustinian monks moved in, reconnecting Sant'Antimo with its medieval importance.

Visiting the Abbey: Before going inside, circle around the building to see its faded but evocative decorations. At the back end of the church is the Charlemagne-era round apse. Circling back around the right side toward the entrance, examine the carvings at the tops of the pillars under the roofline. Each one is different: geometrical patterns, heads of monsters (suggesting that the world outside is unsafe, but this church provides shelter), and more pagan symbols. The stout rectangular bell tower is echoed by a strategically planted cypress tree. On the back side of the tower, look up to find the sphinx, the small Madonna and Bambino, and the four evangelists.

Circle back around to the main entrance. Ignore the modern doors and notice the faint outline of the four original arches; at its peak, this church had two doors—an entrance and an exit—to handle the massive number of Via Francigena pilgrims who passed through. Just to the right, peek into the tranquil garden that fills the ruins of the original cloister.

Step inside the church and let your eyes adjust to the low light. While Romanesque, the church stretches as far as it can to the heavens—suggesting the need for a new architectural style (Gothic would soon come along to help churches reach greater heights). Looking up, see the windows to a gallery that once kept the female worshippers separate from the men. Walk up the nave, noticing that the carved capital of each pillar is different. (The second one on the right side—Daniel and the lions—is a favorite. On one side, a fearless Daniel prays despite being surrounded by lions; on the other side, those lions attack his enemies.) Reaching the front of the church and walking around the apse, notice that part of the altar platform is made of giant chunks of translucent alabaster, a prized material that suggests the importance of this holy space. The many small chapels around the apse are another French architectural feature that made its way to Sant'Antimo. These chapels—and the overall height of the building—suggest a French influence...which seems fitting, here along the Via Francigena.

THE BRUNELLO WINE COUNTRY DRIVING TOUR

This region is famous for its wine, and the rocky hillsides immediately surrounding Montalcino produce some of the best wine in Italy: Brunello di Montalcino (and the less pricey, nearly-as-good Rosso di Montalcino). While the other driving tours in this chapter focus on rolling hillsides, this route takes you through a more wooded and jagged terrain, where sangiovese grapes struggle for survival on their way to becoming fine wine. Ideal for wine lovers, this loop drive focuses on connecting worth-a-linger towns and remote rural wineries where you can have the opportunity to sample the prized local product. It also takes you past some worthwhile non-wine sights: a secluded abbey in a valley, a cliff-topping abandoned castle, and a unique spa town with a giant thermal pool dominating its main square.

For a primer on wine-tasting in this area, see page 566.

This driving loop assumes you're coming from Siena or other points north (through the town of Buonconvento on the SR-2 highway). From elsewhere, simply skip the first stretch and begin in Montalcino, looping south through the hills from there. Be aware that this loop contains the most challenging driving of the tours in this chapter, with narrow and twisty roads. The most difficult stretch is a leg on the super-scenic gravel road called "La Sesta"; I've suggested an alternative for drivers preferring to skip it.

Buonconvento to Montalcino

Coming south on the SR-2 highway, about 28 kilometers south of Siena (following signs toward *Buonconvento* and *Roma*), you'll pass through the small fortified valley town of **Buonconvento.** While sleepy, this village (described on page 575) is worth a quick visit to see its stout old fortifications. Continuing south (toward *Roma*) from Buonconvento, at the outskirts of town (just after the Co-op supermarket), watch for the turnoff on the right to *Montalcino.*

Once on this Montalcino road, after just another kilometer or so, you'll see signs on the left for the **Altesino** winery, which perches high on the hill (described on page 568). While they prefer reservations, you can try dropping in during their opening times. Even if they're not taking visitors, the views from their perch—across vineyards all the way to Montalcino—are breathtaking. Head up this gravel road and behind the big building, following brown-and-yellow *Altesino* signs to their dramatic cypress-lined driveway.

When finished at Altesino, backtrack to the main road and continue south about 9 more kilometers to the town of Montalcino. Enjoy the crescendoing views. **Montalcino**—your next stop—looms on the horizon. Once there, turn to page 560 to tour the town.

Montalcino to Sant'Antimo Abbey

The rocky hillsides south of Montalcino have a high concentration of wineries. The roads branch off in a V—southwest, to Sant'Angelo in Colle; and southeast, to Sant'Antimo Abbey and Castelnuovo dell'Abate—giving you two options for reaching our next stop. (If you're basing in Montalcino, you can also combine these options to create a pleasant little wine-tasting loop.) You'll make your choice at the main roundabout directly below the old town of Montalcino (which circles around a modern mosaic statue that's unpopular with many locals).

Option 1—"Scenic Route" via Sant'Angelo in Colle and La Sesta: This slightly longer route branches off to the southwest before "cutting the corner" on the rugged gravel road called "La Sesta." Leaving Montalcino, follow signs up to *Grosseto* and *S. Angelo*. This road will take you all the way to Sant'Angelo in Colle (9 kilometers south), but if you're looking for a wine-tasting, head to one of my favorite small family wineries in the region—**Le Potazzine** (see page 567), which offers drop-in tastings on some afternoons. It's an easy detour from this road: Watch for the turnoff on the right for *Camigliano* and *Tavernelle* (onto SP-103), then carefully track *Le Potazzine* signs through the countryside (bear right at the fork, then watch for their driveway on the left).

Leaving Le Potazzine, head back to the main road and continue south toward **Sant'Angelo in Colle.** Just one kilometer before that town (worth visiting only for its restaurants, if you're ready for a meal—see page 569), watch carefully on the left for *Strada Sesta* signs, indicating the small turn-off onto the gravel road called **"La Sesta"** ("The Sixth"). This dramatic road—about seven rugged kilometers that feel like double that—may test your axles, but it comes with spectacular views. Near the end of this road, on the right, watch carefully for the snazzy **Ciacci Piccolomini d'Aragona** winery. This is effectively the only one in the area with a Napa Valley-style "drop in anytime you like for a taste" approach... just head to the wine bar inside and ask for a pour (for details, see page 567).

From Ciacci, it's another two kilometers to the **Sant'Antimo Abbey:** you'll curl up on a gravel road around the bottom of the town of Castelnuovo dell'Abate, then watch for the abbey below you in a field. Park in the large lot and head inside to step back to the Romanesque period (abbey described on page 569). Note: If you'd like to visit the **Museum of Brunello** (explained in "Option 2," below), you'll have to backtrack about six kilometers back up the main road toward Montalcino to find the turnoff.

Option 2—Brunello Museum and Direct to Sant'Antimo: To cut the corner—and avoid the gravel roads—simply follow signs from Montalcino's main roundabout downhill, toward *Castelnuovo dell'Abate* (also marked with a brown sign for *Sant'Antimo*). About four kilometers south of Montalcino, just past the tiny crossroads village of La Croce, watch on the left for the turnoff to *Fattoria dei Barbi* and *Podernuovi*; this road leads up to the **Museum of the Montalcino Community and of Brunello,** with interesting exhibits about the history of the region and of Brunello winemaking (described on page 568; watch for red *Museo del Brunello* signs).

Back on the main road, it's another five kilometers south to Castelnuovo dell'Abate; approaching town, watch for the sharp, downhill turnoff on the right to **Sant'Antimo Abbey,** which sits picturesquely in the valley below you. If you're taking this route and want to visit the classy and accessible **Ciacci Piccolomini d'Aragona** winery described earlier, under "Option 1," it's a short drive on gravel roads from the abbey (follow *Sant'Angelo in Colle* signs for about two kilometers, and watch for the winery on your left).

Sant'Antimo to Rocca d'Orcia and Bagno Vignoni

The Sant'Antimo Abbey sits in farm fields below the town of Castelnuovo dell'Abate ("New Castle of the Abbot"). There's not much to see in the town itself, but on the hill above there is another excellent winery that's worth a visit for its vintages and views: **Mastrojanni** (see page 567). Before continuing on our loop, consider checking it out: First, coming up the hill from the abbey, you'll pop out facing the Bassomondo restaurant. Head up the road around the left side of the restaurant, then keep going, as the road turns to gravel and climbs up, up, and up along the ridge. You'll enjoy spectacular views back down over the pasture and olive groves surrounding Sant'Antimo. After 2.5 stunning kilometers, at the end of the road, you'll run into Mastrojanni.

After your visit there, head back down to the main road at Castelnuovo dell'Abate. If you've had enough driving (and/or enough wine), it's easy to cut this loop short by taking the main road back up to Montalcino. But for a scenic continuation that traverses some twisty mountain roads on its way to a pair of fortified towns and a historic spa town, stick with me: From the main road in front of Castelnuovo dell'Abate, head south on the uphill road, following signs for *Seggiano* (brown) and *Castiglione d'Orcia* (blue).

This twisty road—with few worthwhile stops, but ample scenery—twists 19 kilometers over the mountains to the main valley road.

Leaving Castelnuovo, you'll crest a hill, then pass the dramatic **Castello di Velona,** a medieval castle-turned-luxury hotel. Locals explain that Silvio Berlusconi (Italy's repeatedly disgraced former prime minister) considered buying this property a few years back. But when he came to Montalcino—in the famously liberal region of Tuscany—locals threw rocks at the conservative politician. The road drops down steeply to the valley village of Monte Amiata, where you'll cross the train tracks, then the Orcia River, then wind your way back up the other side. From here, just enjoy the remote scenery as you follow signs: At the T-intersection with the twisty road, turn left, toward *Castiglione d'Orcia*. You'll pass through the hamlet of Poggio Rosa, and then, at the next T-intersection, bear left again, for *Siena*, *San Quirico d'Orcia*, and *Castiglione d'Orcia*.

In about four kilometers, you'll reach **Castiglione d'Orcia,** with a fortified hilltop old town; just past that, you'll see the dramatic tower of **Rocca d'Orcia** (described on page 550; the easiest way to reach the top of Rocca is to drive through the town of Castiglione, and then—on the twisty road past Castiglione heading down toward the main valley road—watch for turnoff on the left for *Rocca d'Orcia*; drive up that road, park, and hike the rest of the way up into town and to the castle).

About three kilometers farther along, you'll reach the intersection with the main SR-2 Siena-to-Rome highway, where we started our loop. Head north (toward Siena), then immediately turn off (on the left) for **Bagno Vignoni,** a fascinating old thermal spa town (to explore this town, see page 546).

Back on SR-2, you can head north (toward Siena) to reach **San Quirico d'Orcia.** At this crossroads town, you can turn off for **Pienza** (10 kilometers from San Quirico) and **Montepulciano** (24 kilometers from San Quirico; this road passes some of the "Top Tuscan Views" described on page 548, and ties in with the loop drive on page 550). Or you can continue straight, to pass the dramatic **Rondò** viewpoint (described under "Top Tuscan Views") on your way to the turnoff for **Montalcino** (13 kilometers from San Quirico) or all the way back to Buonconvento and Siena.

Towns Between Siena and the Val d'Orcia

These crossroads towns—which you're likely to pass through on your way between Siena and the other towns and sights listed in this chapter—are mentioned in this chapter's self-guided driving tours. While neither is worth going out of your way just to visit, both are worth considering for a stretch-your-legs rest stop or a meal to break up a busy day of driving.

BUONCONVENTO

This valley-crossroads town—an important refueling stop for weary pilgrims on the Via Francigena—has a name that literally means "happy meeting place." Today it's humble but handy, with a large chunk of surviving town wall and some fine restaurants. While its museums are modest, it's an easy and accessible fortified town to explore.

Park in the big parking lot between the main road and the town wall. As you face that wall, loop around the right side. First you'll pass the entrance to the **Sharecropping Museum** (Museo della Mezzadria), a well-presented, endearing, but challenging-to-appreciate (limited English) exhibit about the simple agrarian lifestyle that predominated here well into the 20th century. You'll see lots of actual old tools and clothes, and walk into re-created interiors of traditional farmhouses (same cost and hours as TI/Sacred Art Museum, later).

Continuing around the far end of town, you'll eventually reach the 13th-century **main gate** of Buonconvento, called Porta Senese (for the city it faces). Step inside the 17th-century doors and explore the tight lanes immediately on either side. This was the double-decker **guard path** (originally there was another gallery overhead), allowing town defenders to keep a close watch on approaching enemies. Old houses lean up against the wall, like flying buttresses. Notice the slits—wide on the inside, but tapering to a very narrow opening—which allowed archers maximum range of motion but minimum exposure to enemy fire. On the side of town closest to the parking lot is a small green belt—an area used as a garden, which came in handy as a source of food in times of siege.

Head back to the main gate, then continue straight ahead down the main drag (Via Soccini) toward the tower of the **town hall** (on the left). The building's facade is embedded with coats of arms—some dating to the 15th century—of the various regional aristocrats who served two-year terms here as the town judge. Next door is the Sacred Art Museum (with pieces from the 14th-19th centuries), which also houses the **TI** (€5 apiece for either sharecropping or art museum, €8 for both, museums and TI open Wed-Sun 10:30-13:30 & 15:00-19:00, closed Mon-Tue, tel. 0577-165-8634).

Farther along the street, you'll pass the recommended Ristorante da Mario, after which the lane opens up into the town's main square. A left turn here takes you back out to the parking lot where you started.

Eating in Buonconvento: **Ristorante da Mario** is a favorite recommendation for a cozy, unpretentious trattoria with outdoor tables right along the main pedestrian street (€7 pastas, €9-12 *secondi,* closed Sat, Via Soccini 60, tel. 0577-806-157).

SAN GIOVANNI D'ASSO

This one-street village perches proudly on its steep throne of clay, which rises majestically straight up from the plains. There's not much to see in the town itself, which is known mostly as a center for the local truffle-gatherers. The big, blocky castle houses the town square and the small **Truffle Museum,** which tries hard, with lots of kid-oriented, marginally successful interactive exhibits (€4, Wed-Sun 10:30-13:30 & 15:00-19:00, closed Mon-Tue, Oct-March Sat-Sun only, Piazza Gramsci 1, tel. 0577-803-268). If you want a real truffle experience, your best bet is to splurge on a meal (see recommendation below).

On the hillside behind San Giovanni d'Asso is an interesting public garden that may be worth exploring for those interested in artistic modern landscaping. The **Bosco della Ragnaia** was built by 20th-century American landscape architect Sheppard Craige, who created a variety of terrains to explore: wooded areas, a natural amphitheater of cypress trees and hedges, and lots of sculptures—including panels embedded in the ground engraved with thought-provoking messages. The intention is to provide a place for a contemplative stroll through nature (free, daily dawn to dusk, www.laragnaia.com). To find the park, drive through San Giovanni d'Asso following *Asciano* signs; it's on your left, on your way out of town.

Eating in San Giovanni d'Asso: For a splurge truffle meal, head to the well-regarded **La Locanda del Castello,** burrowed into the stout castle wall just next to the Truffle Museum. The chef is a transplant from northern Italy, who brings a slightly different approach—and, of course, an emphasis on local truffles—to his cuisine. Choose between indoor seating, under arches; outside, overlooking the workaday main square; or on the garden terrace in back. Reservations are recommended at this chichi spot (€30 truffle dishes, closed Tue, Piazza Vittorio Emanuele II 4, tel. 0577-802-939, www.lalocandadelcastello.com).

The Crete Senesi

Between Siena and the trio of towns described earlier (Montepulciano, Pienza, Montalcino), the hilly area known as the "Sienese Clay Hills" is full of colorful fields and curvy, scenic roads. The Crete Senesi (KRAY-teh seh-NAY-zee) begins at Siena's doorstep and tumbles south through eye-pleasing scenery. You'll see an endless parade of classic Tuscan scenes: rolling hills topped with medieval towns, olive groves, rustic stone farmhouses, and a skyline punctuated with cypress trees.

During the spring, the fields are painted in yellow and green with fava beans and broom, dotted by red poppies on the fringes. Sunflowers decorate the area during June and July, and expanses of windblown grass fill the landscape for much of the early spring and summer.

Sights in the Crete Senesi

I've listed several villages and sights in this area, followed by a self-guided driving tour that you can use to link them together.

Asciano

This quaint, non-touristy, but not-quite charming village offers a medieval town center, a smattering of churches and museums, and a rare look at everyday Tuscan living. While there's not much to see here, it can be a convenient spot for lunch. If you're in town on Saturday, gather a picnic at the outdoor market (Via Amendola, 8:00-13:00). Or stop by **La Mencia,** an unpretentious, local-feeling restaurant on the main street, with an inviting garden terrace out back and not a tourist in sight (€6-8 pizzas, €9 pastas, €14-16 *secondi,* closed Mon, Corso Matteotti 85, tel. 0577-718-227).

Chiusure

The charming, neatly preserved, and scenically situated stone village of Chiusure (kyew-ZOO-reh) is a fine stop for those seeking "untouristy Tuscany." This steep town offers no sights, but grand views and a real-world village atmosphere. Park at the entrance to town, then follow signs as you walk up a steep driveway to the *casa di riposo* (the castle-turned-nursing home)/*Gesù Redentore* for a fine viewpoint over the Crete Senesi, including views of jagged *calanchi* cliffs and the Abbey of Monte Oliveto Maggiore (described next). On a clear day, you can see all the way to Siena. After getting your

The Beauty of Tuscany's Geology (and Vice Versa)

While North Americans have romanticized notions of the "Tuscan" landscape, there's a surprisingly wide variety of land forms in the region. Never having been crushed by a glacier, Tuscany is anything but flat. The hills and mountains scattered around the area are made up of different substances, each of which is ideal for very different types of cultivation.

The Chianti region (between Florence and Siena) is rough and rocky, with an inhospitable soil that challenges grape vines to survive while coaxing them to produce excellent wine grapes.

Farther south, the soil switches from rock to clay, silt, and sand. The region called the Crete Senesi is literally translated as the "Sienese Clay Hills"—a perfect description of the landscape. Seen from a breezy viewpoint, it's easy to imagine that these clay hills were once at the bottom of the sea floor. The soil here is the yin to Chianti's yang: not ideal for wine, but perfect for truffles and for vast fields of cereal crops such as wheat, sun-yellow rapeseed (for canola oil), and periodically fava beans (to add nitrogen to the soil). In the spring and summer, the Crete Senesi is blanketed with brightly colorful crops and flowers. But by the fall, after the harvest, it's a brown and dusty desolate wasteland punctuated with pointy cypress trees—still picturesque, but in a surface-of-the-moon way. Within the Crete Senesi, you can distinguish two types of hills shaped by erosion: smooth, rounded *biancane* and pointy, jagged *calanchi.*

The sharecropping system—an almost feudal economic

fill of views, follow the lone, twisty street steeply downhill into the village of just 85 people, enjoying the solitude. You'll arrive at Chiusure's general store/*tabacchi*/sometimes-restaurant (closed Wed), where you can grab a €3-4 sandwich to munch back up at the viewpoint. Continuing to loop around (and bearing right after the square), you'll wind up back at the main road and parking lot.

▲▲▲Abbey of Monte Oliveto Maggiore

This basilica features perhaps the best in-situ art you'll find in rural Tuscany. It stars an astonishingly detailed inlaid choir, and a cloister frescoed with vivid, detail-and-symbolism-packed, sometimes outlandish scenes by Renaissance masters Il Sodoma and Luca Signorelli. These frescoes are a good example of art that's underwhelming at first glance, but becomes captivating once you understand the symbolism and the stories behind it.

model, where a few super-elite aristocrats owned all of the arable farmland and rented it out to serf-like peasant farmers—flourished here until soon after the birth of the Italian Republic in 1948. This prompted a population shift, as many Tuscans moved north, to more lucrative industrial jobs in Turin, Milan, and other cities. The land they vacated became dirt-cheap, and investors—many from Sardinia—moved in, bringing their own sheep and recipe for the pecorino cheese that abounds here. To this day, many people in this area have Sardinian surnames (which often end in -u).

The area around Montepulciano and Montalcino is more varied, with rocky protuberances breaking up the undulating clay hills (and providing a suitable home for wine grapes). Even farther south is the Val d'Orcia, the valley of the Orcia River. This area is similar to the Crete Senesi, but has fewer rocks and jagged *calanchi.* Montepulciano sits in a unique position between the Val d'Orcia and another, much flatter valley, the Val di Chiana, through which Italy's main north-south expressway runs.

You'll see many hot springs in this part of Tuscany, as well as town names with the word Terme (for "spa" or "hot spring") or Bagno ("bath"). These generally occur where clay meets rock: Water moving through the clay encounters a barrier and gets trapped. Aside from hot water, another byproduct of this change in landscapes is travertine, explaining the quarries you may see in or near spa towns.

Cost and Hours: Free, modest dress required, daily 9:15-12:00 & 15:15-18:00, Nov-March until 17:00, Gregorian chanting Mon-Sat at 18:15, Sun at 11:00, call to confirm, tel. 0577-707-611, www.monteolivetomaggiore.it.

Arrival at the Abbey: The abbey is well-signed both from the SR-2 highway (turn off at Buonconvento) and from the scenic S-451 road through the Crete Senesi. Park at the lot across from the fortress at the top of the monastery complex (€1/hour, pay at meter near restaurant before returning to car). From the parking lot, it's a steep but pleasant 10-minute wooded walk down to the monastery: Head across the drawbridge and through the fortress (noticing the fine ceramic della Robbia sculptures over the doors of Mary and St. Benedict), pass the restaurant, then exit the other side and continue down the hill. A huge, somewhat artistically jarring statue of Bernardo Tolomei stands in the courtyard before the church. From here, the shop and WCs are to the left; to reach the church entrance, circle around the right side.

Background: In the 14th century, Bernardo Tolomei (1272-

1348), the middle son of a wealthy Sienese silver-mining family, decided to become a hermit monk and moved to the hillsides south of Siena. One day he had a vision of a glorious staircase leading dramatically up into the heavens. He decided that he was to build a church on that very spot, and founded the Olivetan order (a branch of the Benedictines, named for the Holy Mount of Olives). His original, humble church has since been turned into a brick monastery complex with a beautiful Baroque church interior and a Renaissance-frescoed cloister. (The order is still thriving, and Tolomei was made a saint in 2009.) The order spared no expense in decorating their main church, importing the great artists of the day: Fra Giovanni da Verona, one of the most talented inlaid-wood artists who ever lived, and the talented fresco artists Luca Signorelli and Il Sodoma. While all of the art is gorgeous, the stories surrounding Il Sodoma—from his possible sexual orientation (see sidebar) to his ongoing conflicts with the people who sponsored this work—make this sight even more entertaining.

➲ **Self-Guided Tour:** Your visit has two parts: The church interior (with its amazing choir) and the adjacent, fresco-slathered cloister.

• *From the entrance, head into the cloister (ignoring the frescoes for now): Jog left and loop around the corridor, following* church *signs. Turn left at the end of the hall into the church. You'll enter near the right transept; once inside, head for the main nave, filled with...*

Fra Giovanni da Verona's Choir: This spectacularly detailed masterpiece is made entirely of inlaid wood—no paint or other foreign flourishes were used to enhance the remarkable detail and optical illusions. Fra Giovanni (1457-1525), from the city of Verona, used this painstaking method to achieve a mastery of three dimensions that eluded many of his contemporaries working in far more forgiving media. Even more astonishing, this was completed in just two years (1503-1505). While often overshadowed by his contemporaries who worked in sculpture, paint, or frescoes, Fra Giovanni is often deservedly called the "Michelangelo of Wood." Have several €1 coins ready to illuminate the work; it's worth several coins to linger on the details.

Start with the **left panel** (with your back to the main altar) and work clockwise: You'll see a self-portrait of Fra Giovanni, then 3-D shutters that are left partway open, allowing contrast between very different qualities of light. The 3-D square is followed by a set of not two, but four shutters—as if upping the technical complexity of the first set. The fifth panel shows Siena's Palazzo Civico. While it's unusual for church art to depict an important civic (and secular) structure, in this case it honors monks who had gone to Siena to help during a plague, and lost their lives there. The next panel shows more shutters, decorated with a wafer for the Eucha-

Il Sodoma (1477-1549)

Giovanni Antonio Bazzi was as irreverent as he was talented, a free spirit in every sense: He filled his house with exotic animals, he dressed in garish colors, and he was known to sing dirty little ditties to himself while he worked. During the time that he painted this cloister, the monks gave him the nickname Il Mattaccio ("the Madman").

A few years later, his contemporary Giorgio Vasari—an artist, academic, and vocal critic—gave him a different nickname, which stuck: Il Sodoma. Vasari wasn't a fan of Bazzi, and in those very primitive times, a homophobic slur ("The Sodomite") was one of the most withering insults possible. Ever iconoclastic, the artist embraced the nickname, and today it's how history remembers him.

But was Sodoma actually gay? Scholars are divided. Some art critics point to details in the frescoes that suggest a proclivity for the male form, or even suggestions of gay relationships between his figures. Others suggest that Sodoma was just being his usual, provocative self, adhering to an artistic style and documenting events he observed. (I've pointed a few of these out—along with a few by Signorelli, for comparison—so you can make up your own mind.) As with other were-they-or-weren't-they greats throughout history—from Michelangelo to Shakespeare to Abraham Lincoln—it's impossible to know for sure.

rist (symbolizing the sacrifice of Jesus). The seventh panel depicts a woodpecker, with this monastery on the right side. Notice that the terrain is accurate—showing the jagged *calanchi* cliffs—but is missing the familiar cypress-lined roads, which weren't added until the 18th century to reduce erosion. The next panel is another four-shutter composition. Examine the potted flower (representing fertility), were each petal is different. The ninth panel shows a utopian, geometrically flawless depiction of the artist's hometown of Verona. (Soon after this was created, Pienza's main square would be remodeled in a similar style.) Finally, in the 10th panel, get lost in the perfectly executed, three-dimensional details of a scene with four shutters and two gutters, all sticking out at different angles. Notice the individual strings of the guitar, and the crumpled piece of sheet music with actual notes.

Cross over to the **right side** and start working your way back toward the front of the church, starting with the panel showing the skull—a common symbol for Adam, often shown at the base of Jesus' cross (reminding us that Jesus died because of the original sin of Adam). Next is the arena of Verona (evoking the classical period that provided a foundation for the Renaissance), then tambourines that allow Fra Giovanni to experiment with the play of light. Next is another view of this monastery, followed by another four-shutter composition. In the top part, the universe rests on two books (the Old and New Testaments); below that are the guild symbols of the monks (axe, compass, and so on) wrapped in a ribbon. This side finishes with another idealized Verona view; symbols of pharmacists and alchemists; another perfect town; earth on top and the universe below, circling it; and another self-portrait. Before moving on, pause and say your thanks to this brilliant artist.

• *Before heading to the cloister, check out a few more features worthy of note.*

The Rest of the Church: In the side chapel to the rear of the main altar, find the medieval **crucifix** that clashes with its Baroque surroundings. Supposedly, this crucifix would periodically—and miraculously—speak to Bernardo Tolomei. Notice that Jesus' eyes appear to be closed...until you move to the far left. Behind the crucifix is a painting of Tolomei talking to Jesus.

At the chapel to the right of the altar, examine the huge **stand** for illuminated manuscripts. This was created by Fra Raffaelle, a student of Fra Giovanni. Sitting smugly at the base of the stand is a cat—an important symbol at this monastery (we'll see more of them in the cloister decorations). A cat is vigilant, and is also loyal—not to a person, but to a house (just as monks must be loyal to the house of God).

• *Now head into the...*

Great Cloister: Pause in the alcove between the church door and the main part of the cloister to ponder the big personalities—and clashes between them—that brought about the art you're about to see. In 1419, the abbot of this monastery commissioned the famous artist Luca Signorelli to decorate the cloister with scenes from the life of St. Benedict. But Signorelli completed only a handful of frescoes before he got an even better gig decorating a chapel in the cathedral of Orvieto. Scholars suspect that Signorelli anticipated that he'd never finish this composition: He didn't start Benedict's life at the beginning, but in the middle—in the part of the cloister that enjoyed the most light, where Signorelli could work faster (and therefore finish more scenes—and make more money—before taking off). Several years after Signorelli left, the abbot commissioned another artist: Il Sodoma. To test him before entrusting the cloister to him, the abbot had him paint the **panel** to

the right of the door into the church, with Benedict giving books to the Olivetan monks. It was a hit, and Sodoma was hired.

A temperamental artist, Sodoma liked to work at his own pace. But after his frustrating experience with Signorelli, the abbot was short on patience, and nudged Sodoma to work faster and faster (while not always paying him on time). You'll see passive-aggressive—and sometimes simply aggressive—signs of the troubled relationship between Sodoma and the abbot throughout the cloister.

We'll head clockwise around the cloister. As we move from scene to scene, keep track of the two parallel narratives: the primary story traces events from the life of St. Benedict (based on the sixth-century accounts of St. Gregory). But the subtext is the hostility between Sodoma and the abbot. And as an overlay upon all of that, this series of frescoes also offers remarkable insight into both monastic and pilgrim life at the cusp of the Renaissance. Gothic art was for the glory of God. But Renaissance art—including these frescoes—are designed for a viewer: in this case, pilgrims walking the Via Francigena. This art tells a story and serves an agenda: recruitment.

• *Head into the cloister and begin with the first panel, on your left.*

1. During the fifth century, Benedict (in the blue tunic and orange sash) leaves his hometown and heads for Rome. He leans back on his horse toward his mother, suggesting his reluctance to set out on this journey. In the little townscape on the far-right horizon, notice the body of a man hanging on the gallows—suggesting the barbarism of the time. In the lower left, amidst the hubbub of activity surrounding Benedict, notice the young girl (his sister) with the dog pulling on her leg—Sodoma seems to be saying that the abbot is pestering him. Just above and to the right, in the middle ground, notice the two donkeys that share six legs. It seems unlikely that the detail-oriented Sodoma would make a mistake; here he seems to be saying to the abbot, "Working too fast causes mistakes."

2. On the right side of this rounded panel, we see Benedict leaving the theology school in Rome, which he has concluded is corrupt.

3. On the left, Benedict performs his first miracle: fixing a broken panel (before and after, on the ground in front of him). Sodoma has included a self-portrait in this scene, dead-center, with his pet badger and sarcastic smirk.

4. Benedict seeks a mentor (Romano) to help him become a hermit. He leaves his civilian clothes on the ground, taking on the white robe and beard of the monastic lifestyle, where individuality is irrelevant. By covering their bodies, monks are symbolically returning to the Garden of Eden (which is also represented by the green courtyard this cloister surrounds).

5. A shaved-headed Benedict goes into the wilderness to fast. As he can't be seen by other people during this time, Romano must lower food to him with a basket on a rope. The devil spins in—Tasmanian-style—from the left to throw a rock and break the bell on the food basket, so Benedict won't know it's chow time. The small snake peeking out from behind the rock just to the right represents both temptation and paganism.

6. It's Easter—the lamb is on the table (left of window). Inspired by a vision of Christ (see the figure at the far right, looking up toward a mysterious voice), a local priest brings some of the feast to Benedict, who realizes that it will be through community with others—not as a hermit—that he will find his calling.

7. Benedict begins his mission, converting shepherds, enumerating the points he's making on his fingers. (Notice the sheepdog at the far-right. Why do dogs wear spiked collars? Because wolves would go after the sheepdogs first—clamping down on their necks—before going after the sheep.) The two men whispering and giggling in the middle of this scene have been interpreted as "gay" and flirtatious, suggesting Sodoma's own sexual orientation.

8. After being tempted by fantasies of a woman (at the top, with horns and a see-through negligee, being chased away by the Archangel Michael), Benedict tries to regain his self-control by stripping and throwing himself into a patch of poison ivy.

9. Impressed by his devotion, monks come to Benedict and ask him to become their leader.

10. Benedict accepts their offer and comes up with an extremely strict set of rules. Regretting their decision, the monks try to kill him with poisoned wine (left side). But miraculously, the glass shatters in the poisoner's hand. (The man with the long nose, holding the glass, is an unflattering caricature of the abbot.) On the right, notice the watchful cat—a symbol of vigilance against the forces of sin and temptation.

11. The last panel before the corner shows that Benedict was also an architect, building 12 monasteries in his life.

12. The first panel on the next wall is one of Sodoma's masterpieces. Benedict meets the two young boys who will eventually carry on his mission after his death: Placido (on his right) and Mauro (on his left). Sodoma has sprinkled some portraits of his contemporaries and competitors through this fresco: On the left, with the red-and-gold cloak, is Leonardo da Vinci. The bearded jokester playing peekaboo over Leo's right shoulder is Michelangelo. The long-haired gentleman to the right of Benedict is Lo-

renzo the Magnificent. And the somewhat effeminate gent showing us his derriere is Raphael. (If this pose is unflattering, perhaps it's because Raphael had to scrape some Sodoma frescoes off the wall inside the Vatican before creating his own works there.) And there's one more portrait: Sodoma was working on this fresco when the monks first discovered his long-nosed portrait of the abbot (as the poisoner) a few frescoes back. They informed Sodoma that his predecessor, Signorelli, had been a much nicer person. So Sodoma added Signorelli—with a sarcastic saint's halo—between Benedict and Lorenzo the Magnificent.

13. The devil possesses a monk, leading him away from the monastery. Benedict catches up to him and beats the hell out of him—literally (right)—while the devil escapes (top). In the small scene in the middle ground of the right side, we see the monk being forgiven in the chapel.

14. Eight monks who live on a mountain are tired of hauling up their own water, so they come to Benedict to ask for divine intervention. He instructs them where to find a spring. The ghostly outlines of a tree and birds showing through were an unintentional mistake: Sodoma decided to paint over some frescoes he didn't like, but didn't wait for them to dry—causing this double exposure (and the palm tree in the next scene).

15. A monk loses the head of his shovel in a lake, but Benedict sticks the handle in to miraculously reattach it. The distant scene on the right, with the naked men wrestling, is quite unusual for church art (and has been taken as another indication of Sodoma's sexuality).

16. Benedict's main disciples, Placido and Mauro, are now teenagers. Placido is drowning, and Benedict—inspired by a divine vision—sends Mauro to walk across the water and save him.

17. In this fresco—hard to see, as it's partly blocked by a doorway—an unscrupulous servant who's supposed to deliver two jars of wine to Benedict hides one of them in a bush for himself. But Benedict knows, and tells the servant to be careful when he opens it. On the right, we see that the jug now contains a dangerous serpent.

• *Phew. That's a lot of frescoes. We're about halfway through. Let's take a break by ducking into the little side courtyard.*

Entering this **courtyard,** turn left and look to the far end of the hall to see a ghostly monk walking this way. Oops, it's not a monk—it's another Sodoma fresco, this one a well-executed practical joke.

Head into the **refectory**—the grand dining hall where monks, in Sodoma's day and today, gathered for meals. Monks ringed the outside of the long table, not facing each other—eating in silence, without distraction. (It's no coincidence that sign language was originally invented by monks.) On the wall at the far end are the faint remains of a faded Signorelli fresco. In the hall just outside the refectory, notice the big, yellow-marble trough, where monks washed their hands before eating. Along the back of the basin, look for the very faded carving of a scale, a reminder to eat—and live—in moderation.

• *Head back out into the main cloister to resume our tour.*

18. The monastery's custodian, Florenzo (top left), is overcome with jealousy—and the devil—so he gives poisoned bread to a servant to bring to Benedict. On the right, Benedict throws the bread on the ground for a crow. Nearby sits another ever-vigilant cat.

19. In this racy-for-church scene, Florenzo (still under the devil's influence) opens the monastery gate to let prostitutes in. Sodoma's salacious sensibilities come through boldly here. Notice the two ladies dancing, with their fingers intertwined (on the right)—one of them sticking her index finger into a hole formed by the other's hand. Subtle. In the lower right is another scandalously charged detail: A prostitute with a dark-skinned daughter. Even the animals in the scene are symbolic: The fluffy dog is a prostitute, while the hardworking donkey is a monk.

20. The first fresco of the next wing is the only one in the cloister *not* by Sodoma or Signorelli. It shows Placido and Mauro (wearing cowboy boots and spurs) receiving their mission from Benedict.

Now begins the stretch of frescoes by **Signorelli**—remember, he chose to start on the most light-filled (read: easiest) part of the cloister. Pay attention to the differences between the two artists: Signorelli is more of an anatomist (like Michelangelo), while Sodoma is less literal, gravitating to a figurative lyricism—like Botticelli. For example, compare the hands of Sodoma's prostitutes with the veiny, muscled monk's hand in Signorelli's first fresco.

21. Fed up with his failing to do in Benedict, the devil decides to kill Florenzo by collapsing the room he's in. In the upper right, in a scene resembling modern cartoons, devils carry off Florenzo's screaming soul while they beat him.

22. Benedict goes to Monte Cassino—then deep in the pagan and barbarian wilds—for an important mission. On arrival, his monks pull graven images down from the temple (right), while the faint and ghostly devil escapes at the top. On the left, monks convert pagan worshippers. The hourglass carries a not-so-subtle symbolism: It's time to convert.

23. The devil is busy tormenting the monks: In the center, he sits on a rock, making it impossible to move—until Benedict (far left) makes the sign of the cross. In the upper right, the devil sets a fire that the monks must scramble to extinguish. And in the upper left, the monks bury a false idol.

24. The devil kills a monk who's building a church (upper

left)—but other monks bring him to Benedict (lower left), who revives him (lower right). Sodoma wasn't the only artist who reveled in details that bring out the inner five-year-old: notice the devil's fiery flatulence.

25. Two monks disobey the rules and eat in a restaurant in the company of fair maidens (left side). Returning to the monastery (tiny scene on right side), they lie about where they've been—so Benedict shames them by telling them exactly what they ordered. Like Sodoma earlier, Signorelli uses the fluffy dog (lower right) to suggest prostitution. Position yourself close to the wall and walk back and forth, noticing that the table moves with you—an impressive optical illusion.

26. A youth (in blue) aspiring to become a monk—who's supposed to be fasting—bumps into a friend on the road (on the right, horns and legless pants), and they decide to eat after all (upper left). In the main scene (lower left), the monk returns home and is admonished by Benedict.

27. The Ostrogoths' leader sends a stand-in (center, in armor) to pretend he wants to be converted. The monks sense the trick, and go to find the real guy (the half-moon at the top represents the "mysterious East").

28. Benedict meets with and converts the real Ostrogoth leader. Notice the fine details on the faces of the soldiers. These two are the final scenes by Signorelli.

29. Sodoma returns, with bright colors and exacting details (see the horse's face). In the upper right, the monastery in Monte Cassino is destroyed—just as Benedict had prophesied.

30. In the first panel on the final wall of the cloister, the monks have dinner. One sneaky fellow (far right) steals his neighbor's bread. This thief looks suspiciously like the accountant who was responsible for paying Sodoma. Sodoma got tired of hearing how amazing Signorelli's moving-table illusion was (back in #25)—so he topped it. You can actually see the objects on Sodoma's table more clearly the farther away you stand: Head back up the hallway you just came down, then walk slowly toward the table. When you reach it, turn right with the hall...and just keep your eyes on that table. The table stretches and shimmies, highlighting different details with each step.

31. Two monks dream of Benedict showing off a new monastery (left)—so they build it (right). The monk holding the plumb

line is Fra Giovanni da Verona, who created the remarkable inlaid choir inside the church.

32. At a funeral, a nun has a vision that the two deceased people had sinned and would not be admitted to heaven. In the tiny scene on the far-right, Benedict intervenes. In the church scene, the dark, brooding figure in the black cloak on the front-right side is Dante Alighieri.

33. The corpse of a deceased monk surfaces from its grave each night, because he had sinned by lying to Benedict. They place a communion host on top of the body, symbolizing the hope for rebirth, and his remains find peace. This is a powerful and chilling message to pilgrims: God, and his Church on earth, controls both your life and your afterlife.

34. A monk (on the right) leaves the monastery with the devil. But he returns and begs forgiveness from Benedict (scene on the left). The monk's face radiates devotion—Sodoma has brilliantly captured his emotion. The message: Outside of the monastery is a dangerous place, where the devil will hijack your faith.

35. A farmer is captured by soldiers (right, middle ground). They demand all of his money, and he says Benedict has it. They bring him to Benedict (left), and miraculously, the rope binding him becomes untied. The terrified soldiers agree that they'll go easier in the future.

The right side of this final scene is Sodoma's final kiss-off to the abbot: A horse's rear end is very prominent (symbolism obvious). Look at the house up above the horse, to the tiny upper-floor window where a shirt hangs in the breeze. During this time, people would have seven shirts: six for workdays, and a seventh for Sunday, when they could rest (and do laundry). With this detail, Sodoma is saying to the abbot: "You made me work on Sunday—made me sweat through my seventh shirt. You horse's ass!"

Murlo

Perched high on a hill, surrounded by olive groves and overlooking the sprawl of the adjacent town of Vescovato, Murlo has very old roots. The foundations here date back to Etruscan times, and recent genetic tests found two local residents who still have Etruscan DNA. Park your car and hike up through the main gate into the heart of town. While the Etruscans had a settlement here, the current fortifications were added by a bishop in the 13th century. His palace—at the very center of town—now hosts an Etruscan Museum. In its lobby you can see its prized possession, a 3,000-year-old bust wearing a floppy-brimmed "cowboy" hat (museum closed Mon-Tue). The smaller building attached by a walkway was the residence of servants who waited on the bishop. Farther in the village center is a large square—look for the cistern in the center, with its big pendulum. Continuing to the far end, you'll find your way to the opposite gate from the one you entered. This two-gate design was typical of fortified towns—no matter which direction your enemy approached from, you'd have an escape hatch.

Eating in Murlo: **Il Libridinoso** is an appealingly unpretentious eatery that clings to Murlo's hilltop, with a glassed-in terrace offering steep, sweeping views over the valley (€8-9 pastas and *secondi,* closed Mon, Via delle Carceri 13, tel. 0577-046-541).

THE CRETE SENESI DRIVING TOUR

This driving loop is designed for someone home-basing in Siena seeking an accessible look at the Crete Senesi's dramatic scenery, plus visits to some less-trampled hill towns and the undisputed artistic treasure of this part of Tuscany, the Abbey of Monte Oliveto Maggiore.

"Part 1" takes you south from Siena to Buonconvento, where you'll meet the main S-2 highway. From here, you can continue south to Montalcino (my Montalcino winery driving loop, outlined earlier, begins at Buonconvento), or to Pienza or Montepulciano. Or continue with "Part 2," which loops you back up to Siena on some even-less-traveled roads.

Part 1: Siena to Buonconvento

While this journey could be a 25-kilometer straight shot south on the SR-2 highway, I'll outline an even more scenic back-roads route. Begin by leaving Siena, heading east on E-78 (following green *Roma/A1* signs toward the expressway). After just three kilometers, take the Taverne d'Arbia exit (marked for *Presciano, Vico d'Arbia, Arba, Asciano,* and a brown sign for *Crete Senesi*). Once off the expressway, carefully track *Asciano* signs, which will put you on road S-438—also called the **Via Lauretana.** Just sit back and enjoy the scenery; it's about 18 kilometers to Asciano, through stunning and very desolate-feeling landscape. You'll come across plenty of turnouts for panoramic photo opportunities on this road, as well as a few roadside picnic areas and several good accommodations (see "Sleeping in the Crete Senesi," later). Eventually you'll drop down into the village of **Asciano,** with a humble but historic townscape and a good lunch restaurant (for details, see page 577).

At Asciano's main roundabout, follow signs for *Chiusure* and *Monte Oliveto Maggiore.* This puts you on S-451, which winds through beautiful hills for about eight kilometers to our next two stops. What you do next depends on the time: If the abbey is closed for its mid-day break, you might as well first drop into the pleasant village of **Chiusure**—a charming, steep, relatively untouristy town that's a fun place to explore or grab lunch (for details, see page 577; at the roundabout just before Monte Oliveto Maggiore, take the left turn, marked for S. *Giovanni d'Asso, Pienza,* and—in brown—*Chiusure*).

Once you're done at Chiusure—or if the abbey is open anyway—head for the **Abbey of Monte Oliveto Maggiore,** with a remarkable inlaid-wood choir and a fascinating fresco cycle of the life of St. Benedict, painted by Renaissance masters Il Sodoma and Luca Signorelli (for details—including a self-guided tour of the art—see page 578).

Leaving Chiusure, you have a couple of options. To link up with my "Toscana Minore" driving tour, continue past Chiusure and follow signs south about six kilometers south to **San Giovanni d'Asso** (described on page 576). After visiting that town, you can head through the area I call "Toscana Minore" to Pienza or Montepulciano (see driving route on page 553).

To link to "Part 2" of this loop—or to tie in with "The Brunello Wine Country" driving tour—carry on past the abbey on S-451, following *Buonconvento* and *Roma* signs. This takes you (in about 9 kilometers) to **Buonconvento,** another fine village with some good eating options (see page 575). From Buonconvento, you can head south to pick up my Montalcino driving loop (see page 571); continue south to San Quirico d'Orcia, where you can branch off to Pienza and Montalcino (and join my "Best of Tuscany" driving loop—see page 550); head straight back up to Siena on SR-2; or, if you have ample time to spare and are enjoying all of this off-the-beaten-path scenery, continue with...

Part 2: Scenic Return Route from Buonconvento to Siena

This very off-the-beaten-path route (partly on gravel roads) takes you through less-traveled areas and ends with a gorgeous approach to Siena. From the main parking lot next to Buonconvento's old town, head just a few short blocks south (toward *Roma*), and watch for the easy-to-miss turnoff on the right to *Murlo.* Drive 12 kilometers through beautiful countryside until you reach **Murlo** (for more on this hamlet—including lunch options—see page 588). Leaving Murlo, continue to Vescovado (the adjacent town), where you'll follow signs to *Grosetto.* Watch on the right for the turnoff to *Radi*—on a gravel road—and then on the left for *Ville di Corsano.* As you approach and go through **Ville di Corsano,** you'll start to notice sumptuous country-estate villas, built by aristocrats who wanted a grand view of Siena. In the village, turn right toward *Siena,* and head on into town, enjoying the ever-closer views of the looming city.

Sleeping in the Crete Senesi

If pastoral landscapes and easy access to varied towns are your goals, you can't do much better than sleeping in the Crete Senesi. These countryside options sit between Siena, Montepulciano, Pienza, and Montalcino (a 15- to 45-minute drive from any of them). These options line up on (or just off) the scenic roads (S-438 and S-451) south of Siena; I've listed them from north to south.

$$ Podere Casalciccia, run by recommended local guide Roberto Bechi (see page 357) and his American wife Patti, is a spacious, very remote-feeling modern home perched on a ridge immersed in 360 degrees of gorgeous Crete Senesi scenery (about 15 minutes south of Siena). In all five rooms, each window offers a vista nearly indistinguishable from a stunning Tuscan-countryside painting. The name—which goes back centuries—means "house of drought," and they've designed their entirely "green" house to be self-sufficient, with a zero-carbon footprint (Db-€80, extra bed-€15, these prices for Rick Steves readers, includes self-service breakfast, 2-night minimum, Wi-Fi, Patti's mobile 328-727-3186, Roberto's mobile 328-425-5648, www.casalciccia.com). It's just off road S-438: Turn down the rough gravel road next to the sign for *Fontanelle*, and follow it straight ahead for about five minutes.

$ Casanova Agriturismo is for people who *really* want to stay on an authentic, working farm surrounded by spectacular scenery. This rustic place comes with tractors, plenty of farm smells and noises, and a barn full of priceless Chianina cows. If the five simple rooms and two apartments take a back seat to the farm workings, the lodgings are accordingly inexpensive, and you'll appreciate the results of their hard work when you dig into one of their excellent farm-fresh dinners (€25/person, available only some nights—ask when you reserve). German Wiebke (who speaks great English and runs the accommodations), her Tuscan husband Bartolo (who works the fields), his mama Paola (who cooks), and the rest of the Conte clan make this a true *agriturismo* experience (Db-€70, apartment-€85 for 2 and €10 per additional person up to 4, breakfast-€8, book directly with hotel for best prices, Wi-Fi, swimming pool, just outside Asciano on road S-451 toward Chiusure, tel. 0577-718-324, mobile 346-792-0859, www.agriturismo-casanova.it, info@agriturismo-casanova.it).

$$ Agriturismo il Molinello ("Little Mill") rents three rooms and six apartments (two built over a medieval mill) on the grounds of a working farm with organic produce, olives, and a truffle patch. Hardworking Alessandro and Elisa share their organic produce and offer weekly wine and olive-oil tastings for a minimum of four people; they also lead bike tours or wine tours on request. From late May through September, they give free guided tours of Siena on Tuesday afternoons. More rustic than romantic, and lacking the dramatic views of some other places, this is a nice mix of farm and style. With children, friendly dogs, toys, and a swimming pool, it's ideal for families (Db-€50-80, Qb-€70-100, apartment for up to 8-€160-200 depending on season and number of people, optional organic breakfast-€9.50, one-week stay required July-Aug, discounts and no minimum stay off-season, Wi-Fi, mountain- and road bike rentals, biking maps, between Asciano and the village of Serre di Rapolano—on the road toward Rapolano, 30 minutes southeast of Siena, tel. 0577-704-791, mobile 335-692-5720, www.molinello.com, info@molinello.com).

CORTONA

Cortona blankets a 1,700-foot hill surrounded by dramatic Tuscan and Umbrian views. Frances Mayes' book *Under the Tuscan Sun* placed this town in the touristic limelight, just as Peter Mayle's books popularized the Luberon region in France. But long before Mayes ever published a book, Cortona was popular with Romantics and considered one of the classic Tuscan hill towns. Although it's unquestionably touristy, unlike San Gimignano, Cortona maintains a rustic and gritty personality—even with its long history of foreigners who, enamored with its Tuscan charm, made this their adopted home.

The city began as one of the largest Etruscan settlements, the remains of which can be seen at the base of the city walls, as well as in the nearby tombs. It grew to its present size in the 13th to 16th centuries, when it was a colorful and crowded city, eventually allied with Florence. The farmland that fills almost every view from the city was marshy and uninhabitable until about 200 years ago, when it was drained and turned into some of Tuscany's most fertile land.

Art lovers know Cortona as the home of Renaissance painter Luca Signorelli, Baroque master Pietro da Cortona (Berretini), and the 20th-century Futurist artist Gino Severini. The city's museums and churches reveal many of the works of these native sons.

Orientation to Cortona

Most of the main sights, shops, and restaurants cluster around the level streets on the Piazza Garibaldi-Piazza del Duomo axis, but Cortona will have you huffing and puffing up some steep hills. From Piazza Garibaldi, it's a level five-minute walk down bustling shop-lined Via Nazionale to Piazza della Repubblica, the heart of the town, which is dominated by City Hall (Palazzo del Comune).

From this square, a two-minute stroll leads you past the TI, the interesting Etruscan Museum, and the theater to Piazza del Duomo, where you'll find the recommended Diocesan Museum. These sights are along the more-or-less level spine that runs through the bottom of town; from here, Cortona sprawls upward. Steep streets, many of them stepped, go from Piazza della Repubblica up to the San Niccolò and Santa Margherita churches and the Medici Fortress (a 30-minute climb from Piazza della Repubblica). In this residential area, you'll see fewer tourists and get a better sense of the "real" Cortona.

In the flat valley below Cortona sprawls the modern, workaday town of Camucia (kah-moo-CHEE-ah), with the train station and other services (such as launderettes) that you won't find in the hill town itself.

TOURIST INFORMATION

To reach the TI, head to Piazza Signorelli, then walk through the courtyard of the Etruscan Museum and up a short flight of steps, at the back (Mon-Fri 9:00-13:00 & 15:15-18:00, Sat 9:00-13:00, closed Sun, tel. 0575-637-223 or 0575-637-276, www.turismo.provincia.arezzo.it).

ARRIVAL IN CORTONA

Cortona is challenging but doable by public transportation. There are few intercity buses, so your best bet for reaching the town is by train (then bus or taxi) or by car.

By Train: Most trains arrive at the unstaffed **Camucia station,** in the valley four miles below Cortona. Sporadic local buses connect the train station and Piazza Garibaldi in Cortona in about 10 minutes. (If you choose to walk, it's a long, steep climb, and there are no sidewalks.) From the station, walk out the front door and look left to find the bus shelter (with schedules posted). Unfortunately, buses depart only about once per hour—and only twice daily on Sundays—and the schedule is not well-coordinated with train times (purchase €1.60 ticket from driver; you want a bus marked for Cortona rather than the opposite direction, Terontola). On the schedule, departures marked with *S* do not run during school vacations; those marked with *N* run only during school vacations. Buses usually drop off at Piazza Garibaldi, but may stop instead at Piazza del Mercato (just outside the city walls near Porta Santa Maria), requiring a 10-minute uphill walk to Piazza Signorelli (for the TI and the Etruscan Museum).

You could also consider taking a taxi into town (€10, call for Dejan and his eight-seater cab, mobile 348-402-3501—Dejan arranges day trips and airport transfers as well, see "Local Guides," later; or you can ask your hotel to arrange a taxi).

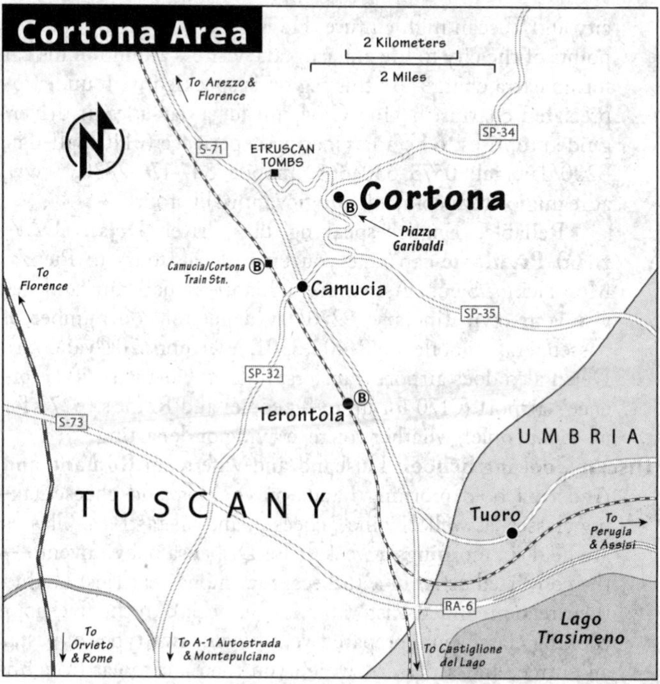

The high-speed trains that link Rome, Florence, and Assisi nearly hourly arrive at **Terontola,** 10 miles away from Cortona (€2, 30 minutes by bus to Cortona's Piazza Garibaldi, runs about hourly, check schedule at bus stop).

By Car: You'll find several lots ringing the walls; some are free (white lines), others require payment (blue lines), and still others are for local residents only (yellow lines), so check signs carefully. Your best bet is the large, free lot on Viale Cesare Battisti, just after the big Santo Spirito Church. From here, a series of stairs and escalators take you steeply up to Piazza Garibaldi. Piazza Garibaldi itself may have a handful of pay spots available (marked by blue lines, pay & display, free 20:00-8:00). The small town is actually very long, and it can be smart to drive to the top for sightseeing up there (free parking at Santa Margherita Basilica).

CORTONA

HELPFUL HINTS

Market Day: The market is on Saturday on Piazza Signorelli (from early morning until about 14:00).

Services: The town has **no baggage storage,** so try asking nicely at a hotel to leave your bag there. The best public **WC** is located in Piazza del Duomo, under Santa Margherita's statue.

Local Guides: Giovanni Adreani exudes energy and a love of his city and Tuscan high culture. He is great at bringing the fine points of the city to life and can take visitors around in his car for no extra charge. As this region is speckled with underappreciated charms, having Giovanni for a day as your driver/guide promises to be a fascinating experience (€110/half-day, €200/day, tel. 0575-630-665, mobile 347-176-2830, www.adreanigiovanni.com, adreanigiovanni@libero.it).

Reliable, English-speaking taxi driver **Dejan** (DAY-zhan) **Prvulovic** can take you on full-day tours to Pienza, Montalcino, Siena, Assisi, and Chianti—email him and devise your own itinerary (€270/day depending on number of passengers, mobile 348-402-3501, dejanprvi70@yahoo.it). Dejan also does airport transfers, linking Cortona with Florence's airport (€170 for up to 8 people) and Rome's (€270 for up to 8 people), whether you're arriving or departing.

Tuscan Cooking School: Husband-and-wife team **Romano and Agostina** hold morning hands-on cooking and cheesemaking classes, as well as wine-, cheese-, and oil-tastings. Classes are held six mornings a week at La Dispensa del Convento—the converted cellar of a 16th-century monastery (just behind their recommended Ristorante La Bucaccia). In the five-hour cooking class, you'll prepare two *antipasti,* two types of pasta, an entrée, and a dessert, which you then get to eat (roughly €90/person, price includes wine, 5 percent discount if you show this book, classes start at 9:30). A three-hour version starts at 11:00 (€70/person; book at least a month or two in advance, personalized classes available). Or stop by for Italian snack tastings with Romano's homemade cheeses and cold meats (16:30-23:00, €10 includes a free glass of wine if you show this book; Vicolo Cattani 1, tel. 0575-630-584, www.labucaccia.it, info@labucaccia.it).

Cortona Walk

This introductory walking tour will take you from Piazza Garibaldi and up the main strip to the town center, its piazzas, and the Duomo. (If your bus drops off at Piazza del Mercato, see the map on page 598 to locate Piazza Garibaldi.)

• *Start at the bus stop in...*

Piazza Garibaldi

Many visits start and finish in this square, thanks to its bus stop. While the piazza, bulging out from the town fortifications like a big turret, looks like part of an old rampart, it's really a souvenir of those early French and English Romantics—the ones who first created the notion of a dreamy, idyllic Tuscany. During the Napoleonic Age, the French built this balcony (and the scenic little park behind the adjacent San Domenico Church) simply to enjoy a commanding view of the Tuscan countryside.

With Umbria about a mile away, Cortona marks the end of Tuscany. This is a major cultural divide, as Cortona was the last town in Charlemagne's empire and the last under Medici rule. Umbria, just to the south, was papal territory for centuries. These deep-seated cultural disparities were a great challenge for the visionaries who unified the fractured region to create the modern nation of Italy during the 1860s. An obelisk in the center of this square honors one of the heroes of the struggle for Italian unification—the brilliant revolutionary general, Giuseppe Garibaldi.

Enjoy the commanding view from here. Assisi is just over the ridge on the left. Lake Trasimeno peeks from behind the hill, looking quite normal today. But, according to legend, it was blood-red after Hannibal defeated the Romans here in 217 B.C., when 15,000 died in the battle. The only sizable town you can see, on the right, is Montepulciano. Cortona is still defined by its Etruscan walls—remnants of these walls, with stones laid 2,500 years ago, stretch from here in both directions.

Frances Mayes put Cortona on the map for many Americans with her book (and later movie) *Under the Tuscan Sun.* The book describes her real-life experience buying, fixing up, and living in a run-down villa in Cortona with her husband, Ed. The movie romanticized the story, turning Frances into a single, recently divorced writer who restores the villa and her peace of mind. Mayes' villa isn't "under the Tuscan sun" very often; it's named "Bramasole"—literally, "craving sun." On the wrong side of the hill, it's in the shade after 15:00. She and her husband still live there part of each year and are respected members of their adopted community (outside the walls, behind the hill on the left—a 20-minute walk away; ask at the TI for directions if you'd like to see it up close).

• *From this square, head into town along...*

Via Nazionale

The only level road in town, locals have nicknamed Via Nazionale the *ruga piana* (flat wrinkle). This is the main commercial street in this town of 2,500, and it's been that way for a long time. Every shop seems to have a medieval cellar or an Etruscan well. Notice the crumbling sandstone door frames. The entire town is constructed from this grainy, eroding rock.

• *Via Nazionale leads to...*

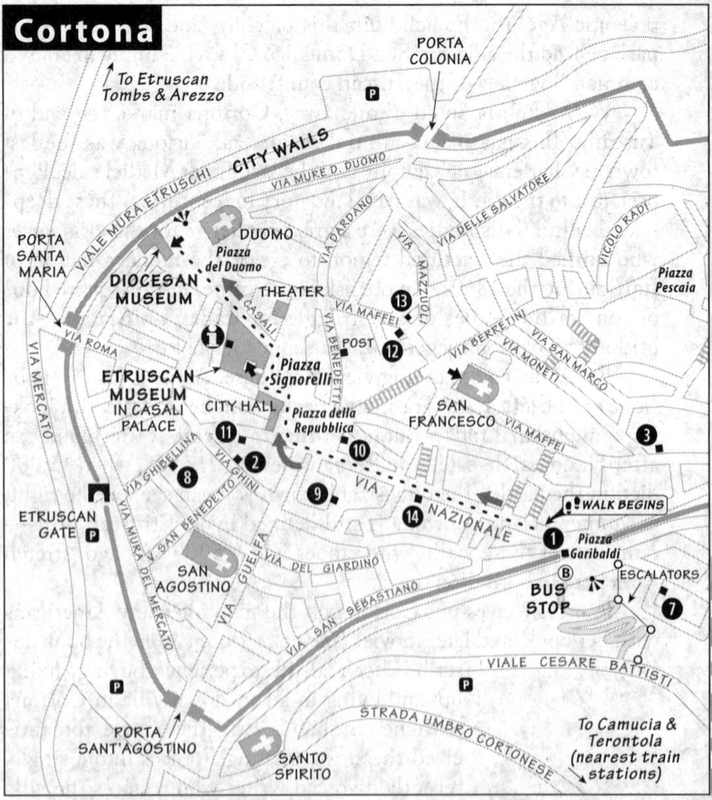

Piazza della Repubblica

City Hall faces Cortona's main square. Note how the building is a clever hodgepodge of twin medieval towers, with a bell tower added to connect them, and a grand staircase to lend some gravitas. Notice also the fine wood balconies on the left. In the Middle Ages, wooden extensions like these were common features on the region's stone buildings. These balconies (not original, but rebuilt in the 19th century) would have fit right into the medieval cityscape. These days, you usually see only the holes that once supported the long-gone wooden beams.

This spot has been the town center since Etruscan times. Four centuries before Christ, an important street led from here up to the hill-capping temple. Later, the square became the Roman forum. Opposite City Hall is the handy, recommended Despar Market Molesini, good for cheap sandwiches. Above that is the loggia—once a fish market, now the recommended Ristorante La Loggetta.

• *The second half of the square, to the right of City Hall, is...*

Piazza Signorelli

Dominated by Casali Palace, this square was the headquarters of the Florentine captains who used to control the city. Peek into the palace entrance (under the MAEC sign) for a look at the coats of arms. Every six months, Florence would send a new captain to Cortona, who would help establish his rule by inserting his family coat of arms into the palace's wall. These date from the 15th to the 17th century, and were once painted with bright colors. Cortona's fine Etruscan Museum (described later, under "Sights in Cortona") is in the Casali Palace courtyard, which is lined with many more of these family coats of arms. The inviting Caffè del Teatro fills the loggia of the theater that is named for the town's most famous artist, Luca Signorelli.

• *Head down the street, just to the right of the museum, to...*

Piazza del Duomo

Here you'll find the Diocesan Museum (listed later, under "Sights in Cortona"), cathedral, and (closer to the top of the square) a statue of Santa Margherita. The cathedral's facade, though recently renovated, still seems a little underwhelming and tucked away. Cortona so loves its hometown saint, Margherita, that it put the energy it would otherwise have invested in its cathedral into the Santa Margherita Basilica, at the top of the hill (at the other end of town—not visible from here). Margherita was a 13th-century rich girl who took good care of the poor and was an early follower of St. Francis and St. Clare. Many locals believe that Margherita protected Cortona from WWII bombs.

The Piazza del Duomo terrace comes with a commanding view of the Tuscan countryside. Notice the town cemetery in the foreground. If you were standing here before the time of Napoleon, you'd be surrounded by tombstones. But Cortona's graveyards—like other urban graveyards throughout Napoleon's realm—were cleaned out in the early 1800s to reclaim land and improve hygiene.

• *Next, enter the...*

Duomo

The Cortona cathedral is not, strictly speaking, a cathedral, because it no longer has a bishop. The white-and-gray Florentine Renaissance-style interior is mucked up with lots of Baroque chapels filling once-spacious side niches. In the rear (on the right) is an altar cluttered with relics. Technically, any Catholic altar, in order to be consecrated, needs a relic embedded in it. Gently lift up the tablecloth (go ahead—the priest here doesn't mind), and you'll see a little marble patch that holds a bit of a saint (daily in summer 7:30-18:30, daily in winter 8:00-12:30 & 15:00-17:30, closed during Mass).

• *From here, you can visit the nearby Diocesan Museum, or head back toward Piazza della Repubblica to visit the Etruscan Museum in Piazza Signorelli (both listed next) or to get a bite to eat (see "Eating in Cortona," later).*

Sights in Cortona

▲Etruscan Museum (Museo dell'Accademia Etrusca e della Città di Cortona)

Located in the 13th-century Casali Palace and called MAEC for short, this fine gallery (established in 1727) is one of the first dedicated to artifacts from the Etruscan civilization. (In the logo, notice the E is backwards—in homage to the Etruscan alphabet.) This sprawling collection is nicely installed on four big floors with plenty of English information. The bottom two floors (underground) are officially the "Museum of the Etruscan and Roman City of Cortona." You'll see an exhibit on the Roman settlement and take a virtual tour of the Etruscan "Il Sodo" tombs (in the nearby countryside). The Cortona Tablet (*Tabula Cortonensis,* second century B.C.), a 200-word contract inscribed in bronze, contains dozens of Etruscan words archaeologists had never seen before its discovery in 1992. Along with lots of gold and jewelry, you'll find a seventh-century B.C. grater (for some *very* aged Parmesan cheese). The top two floors, called the "Accademia," display an even more eclectic collection, including more Etruscania, Egyptian artifacts, fine Roman mosaics, and a room dedicated to 20th-century abstract works by Severini, all lovingly described in English. A highlight is the magnificent fourth-century B.C. bronze oil lamp chandelier with 16 spouts. On the top floor, peek into the classic old library of the Etruscan Academy, founded in 1727 to promote an understanding of the city through the study of archaeology.

Cost and Hours: €12, €13 combo-ticket includes Diocesan Museum; April-Oct daily 10:00-19:00; Nov-March Tue-Sun 10:00-17:00, closed Mon; Casali Palace on Piazza Signorelli, tel. 0575-637-235, www.cortonamaec.org.

▲Diocesan Museum (Museo Diocesano)

This small collection contains some very choice artworks from the town's many churches, including works by Fra Angelico and Pietro Lorenzetti, and masterpieces by hometown hero and Renaissance master Luca Signorelli.

Cost and Hours: €5, €13 combo-ticket includes Etruscan Museum, helpful audioguide-€3; April-Oct daily 10:00-19:00; Nov-March Tue-Sun 10:00-17:00, closed Mon; Piazza del Duomo 1, tel. 0575-62-830.

Visiting the Museum: From the entrance, head straight into the Signorelli Room (Sala 4). Signorelli was a generation ahead of Michelangelo and, with his passion for painting ideas, was an inspiration for the younger artist (for more on Signorelli, visit the San Niccolò Church, described later). Take a slow stroll past his very colorful canvases, mostly relocated here from local churches. Among the most striking is *Lamentation over the Dead Christ* (*Compianto sul Cristo Morto,* 1502). Everything in Signorelli's painting has a meaning: The skull of Adam sits under the sacrifice of Jesus; the hammer represents the Passion (the Crucifixion leading to the Resurrection); the lake is blood; and so on. I don't understand all the medieval symbolism, but it is intense.

Then cut across the top of the stairwell into Sala 3, which was once the nave of the Gesù Church (look up at the beautiful wood-carved ceiling). In Fra Angelico's sumptuous *Annunciation* (c. 1430), Mary says "Yes," consenting to bear God's son. The angel's words are top and bottom, while Mary's answer is upside down (logically, since it's directed to God, who would be reading while looking down from heaven). Notice how the house sits on a pillow of flowers...the new Eden. The old Eden, featuring the expulsion of Adam and Eve from Paradise, is in the upper left. The bottom edge of the painting comes with comic strip-like narration of scenes from Mary's life. On the wall to the right, the crucifix (by Pietro Lorenzetti, c. 1325) is striking in its severity. Notice the gripping realism—even the tendons in Jesus' arms are pulled tight.

Now head back to the stairwell, which is lined with colorful Stations of the Cross scenes by another local but much later artist, the 20th-century's Gino Severini. These are actually "cartoons," models used to create permanent pieces for the approach up to the Santa Margherita Basilica. Downstairs, the lower refectory (Sala 6) has a vault with beautiful frescoes (1545) designed by Giorgio Vasari. Back up near the entrance, another staircase leads down to an important but dull collection of vestments and ecclesiastical gear.

San Francesco Church

Established by St. Francis' best friend, Brother Elias, this church dates from the 13th century. The wooden beams of the ceiling are original. While the place was redecorated in the Baroque age, some of the original frescoes that once wallpapered the church peek through the whitewash in the second chapel on the left. Francis fans visit for its precious Franciscan relics. To the left of the altar, you'll find one of Francis' tunics, his pillow (inside a fancy cover), and his gospel book. Notice how the entire high altar seems designed to frame its precious relic—a piece of the cross Elias brought back from his visit to the patriarch in Constantinople. You're welcome to climb the altar for a close-up look. In the humble choir area behind the main altar is Elias' very simple tomb (just a stone slab in the middle of the floor—on a nearby slab, see the *Frate Elia da Cortona* plaque).

Cost and Hours: Free, daily 9:00-17:30, often until 19:00 in summer; Mass on Sun at 10:00, Mon-Sat at 17:30.

San Niccolò Church

Although this tiny church is rarely open, Signorelli enthusiasts may want to make the pilgrimage—a steep 10-minute walk above the San Francesco Church. While it's not worth going out of the way for (the picturesque neighborhood surrounding it is, for many, more interesting), it's an easy detour if you're hiking up to Santa Margherita. The highlight of this humble church is an altarpiece painted on both sides by Signorelli; it's usually pulled halfway open so you can see both sides.

Cost and Hours: €1 donation, check with TI before making the trip to make sure it's open.

Santa Margherita Basilica

From San Niccolò Church, another steep path leads uphill 10 minutes to this basilica, which houses the remains of Margherita, the town's favorite saint. The red-and-white-striped interior boasts some colorfully painted vaults. Santa Margherita, an unwed mother from Montepulciano, found her calling with the Franciscans in Cortona, tending to the sick and poor. The well-preserved and remarkably emotional 13th-century crucifix on the right is the cross that, according to legend, talked to Margherita.

Cost and Hours: Free, daily 9:00-19:00 except closed Mon morning, may close for lunch, tel. 0575-603-116.

Nearby: Need more altitude and expansive views? Continuing uphill five more minutes takes you to **Medici Fortezza Girifalco,** which is likely closed for renovation (check with TI; if open, likely €3, may host special exhibits). Italian rocker Jovanotti, who lives in a villa beyond San Niccolò Church, financed repairs to one of the four bastions and has his own recording studio inside the fortress. The views are stunning, stretching all the way to distant Lago Trasimeno.

Etruscan Tombs near Cortona

Guided tours to the tombs (called *melone* for their melon-like shape), in the locality of Sodo, are complicated to arrange. But the excavation site and bits of the ruins are easy to visit and can be seen even from outside the fence. A caretaker sometimes opens the gates, allowing you a closer inspection (8:30-13:30). It's a couple of miles northwest of Cortona just off the Arezzo road (R-71), at the foot of the Cortona hill; ask anyone for "Il Sodo."

Sleeping in Cortona

INSIDE THE OLD TOWN

$$$ Hotel San Luca, perched on the side of a cliff, has 54 impersonal business-class rooms, half with stunning views of Lago Trasimeno. While the hotel feels tired and the rooms have seen better days, it's friendly and conveniently located, right on Piazza Garibaldi at the entrance to the Old Town (Sb-€70, Db-€100, Tb-€130, request a view room when you reserve for no extra charge, popular with Americans and groups, air-con, elevator, Wi-Fi, Piazza Garibaldi 2, tel. 0575-630-460, www.sanlucacortona.com, info@sanlucacortona.com). If driving, you might find a spot at the small public parking lot at the hotel; otherwise you can park at the big lot down below and ride the escalator up.

$$ Dolce Maria B&B is located in a 16th-century building with high-beamed ceilings. The six rooms are good-value, luminous, and spacious, with tasteful period furnishings and modern

Sleep Code

(€1 = about $1.40, country code: 39)

Abbreviations

S = Single, **D** = Double/Twin, **T** = Triple, **Q** = Quad, **b** = bathroom, **s** = shower only

Price Rankings

$$$ Higher Priced—Most rooms €100 or more.
$$ Moderately Priced—Most rooms between €70-100.
$ Lower Priced—Most rooms €70 or less.

Unless otherwise noted, credit cards are accepted, breakfast is included (but usually optional), English is spoken, and Wi-Fi is generally free. Many towns in Italy levy a hotel tax of about €2 per person, per night (usually not included in the rates I've quoted). Prices change; verify current rates online or by email. For the best prices, always book directly with the hotel.

bathrooms. The B&B is run by warm and efficient Paola, who also runs the Antico Pozzo restaurant next door—the two businesses share a patio (Db-€80-100, air-con, Wi-Fi, Via Ghini 12, tel. 0575-601-577, www.cortonastorica.com, info@cortonastorica.com).

$ San Marco Hostel, at the top of town, is housed in a remodeled 13th-century palace (bunk in 4- to 6-bed dorm-€19, in 2-bed room-€25, includes breakfast, lunch or dinner-€11; from Piazza Garibaldi head up steep Via Santa Margherita, then turn left to find Via Maffei 57; tel. 0575-601-392, mobile 335-315-987, www.cortonahostel.com, ostellocortona@libero.it, Sergio).

OUTSIDE THE OLD TOWN

These accommodations line up along the road that angles downhill from Piazza Garibaldi, within a 10-minute (uphill) walk to the entrance to the Old Town. Drivers may find these handier than the places in town.

$$$ Hotel Villa Marsili is a comfortable splurge just below town. It was originally a 15th-century church, then an elegant 18th-century home. Its 26 rooms and public areas have been recently redecorated and restored, and come with lots of thoughtful little touches. Guests can enjoy an evening aperitif with free snacks on the panoramic terrace (19:00-20:00) as well as a sweet goodnight treat after dinner. In general, the higher up the room, the fancier the decor and the higher the price. Diane Lane slept in one of the suites while filming *Under the Tuscan Sun* (Sb-€110, small standard Db-€150, superior Db-€180, deluxe Db-€230,

Db suite-€350, extra bed-€25/child or €50/adult, Jacuzzi in deluxe room and suites, air-con, elevator, guest computer and Wi-Fi, free street parking nearby—first come, first served, otherwise €12, Viale Cesare Battisti 13, tel. 0575-605-252, fax 0575-605-618, www.villamarsili.net, info@villamarsili.net, Marina).

$ Casa Betania, a big, wistful convent with an inviting view terrace, rents 28 fine rooms (mostly twin beds) for the best price in town. While it's primarily for "thoughtful travelers," anyone looking for a peaceful place to call home will feel welcome in this pilgrims' resort. Marco, a big-city lawyer escaping from the rat race, has taken over this place and turned it into an impressive retreat facility, with conference rooms, a chapel, wine cellar, cooking classes, and more (S-€32, D-€44, Db-€48, Tb-€66, extra bed-€20, breakfast-€4, Wi-Fi, free parking, about a third of a mile out of town, a few minutes' walk below Piazza Garibaldi and through iron gates on the right at Via Gino Severini 50, tel. 0575-630-423, www.casaperferiebetania.com, info@casaperferiebetania.com).

$ Villa Santa Margherita, run by the Serve di Maria Riparatrici sisters, rents 22 nicely renovated rooms in a smaller and more traditional-feeling convent just up the street from Casa Betania (Sb-€50, Db-€70, Tb-€90, Qb-€102, elevator, Wi-Fi-€1/day, free parking, Viale Cesare Battisti 17, tel. 0575-630-336, fax 0575-630-549, www.santamargherita.smr.it, info@villasm.it or comunitacortona@smr.it).

$ Casa Kita, renting five slightly quirky rooms, is a homey place just below Piazza Garibaldi with fine views from its terrace. You'll really feel like you're staying in someone's home, but the prices are good (Db-€65, Wi-Fi, 100 yards below Piazza Garibaldi at Vicolo degli Orti 7, tel. 389-557-9893, www.casakita.com, info@casakita.com, Lorenzini family).

Eating in Cortona

Ristorante La Bucaccia is a family-run eatery set in a rustic medieval wine cellar. It's dressy and romantic. Taking an evangelical pride in their Chianina beef dishes and homemade pastas, Romano hosts and his wife Agostina cooks. Reservations are required for dinner—and worth making (€9-10 pastas, €12-15 *secondi,* daily 12:30-15:30 & 19:00-23:00 except closed Mon in winter, show this book for a 5 percent discount and a small free appetizer, Via Ghibellina 17, tel. 0575-606-039, www.labucaccia.it). They also run the Tuscan cooking school next door (see "Helpful Hints," earlier).

Trattoria la Grotta, just off Piazza della Repubblica, is a traditional place serving daily specials to an enthusiastic clientele under grotto-like vaults (€7-9 pastas, €7-20 *secondi,* good wine by the glass, Wed-Mon 12:00-14:30 & 19:00-22:00, closed Tue, Piazza Baldelli 3, tel. 0575-630-271).

Locanda al Pozzo Antico offers an affordable menu of Tuscan fare, with a focus on fresh, quality produce, and local olive oil. Eat in a classy, minimalist dining room or tucked away in a tranquil secret courtyard. Paola is a charming hostess; ask about her cooking classes (€9-13 pastas, €10-16 *secondi,* Fri-Wed 12:30-14:30 & 19:30-22:00, closed Thu, Via Ghini 12, tel. 0575-62091 or 0575-601-577; Paola, husband Franco, and son Gianni).

Ristorante La Loggetta serves up big portions of well-presented Tuscan cuisine on the loggia overlooking Piazza della Repubblica. While they have fine indoor seating under stone vaults, I'd eat here for the chance to gaze at the square over a meal (€8-10 pastas, €8-15 *secondi,* Thu-Tue 12:30-15:00 & 19:30-23:00, closed Wed, Piazza Pescheria 3, tel. 0575-630-575).

Fufluns Tavern Pizzeria (that's the Etruscan name for Dionysus) is remarkably unpretentious considering its location in the town center. It's popular with locals for its good, inexpensive Tuscan cooking and stone-and-beam-cozy interior (€5-7 pizza and €6-10 pastas plus big salads, good house wine, Wed-Mon 12:15-14:30 & 19:15-22:30, closed Tue, a block below Piazza della Repubblica at Via Ghibellina 3, tel. 0575-604-140).

Osteria del Teatro tries very hard to create a romantic Old World atmosphere, and does it well. Chef and owner Emiliano serves nicely presented and tasty Italian and local cuisine (taking creative liberties with traditions). There's good outdoor seating, too. It feels upscale and a bit self-important (€8-9 pastas, €11-16 *secondi,* Thu-Tue 12:30-14:30 & 19:30-22:00, closed Wed, 2 blocks uphill from the main square at Via Maffei 2—look for the gnomes on the steps, tel. 0575-630-556, www.osteria-del-teatro.it). They also own the bright little restaurant just opposite, **Fiaschetteria Fett'unta,** which has traditional light snacks and sandwiches.

Enoteca la Saletta, dark and classy with a nice, mellow vibe, is good for fine wine and a light meal. You can sit inside surrounded by wine bottles or outside to people-watch on the town's main drag (€3-5 sandwiches and pizzas, €7-12 pastas and *secondi,* daily 7:30-24:00, meals served 12:00-22:00, closed Wed in winter, Wi-Fi, Via Nazionale 26, tel. 0575-603-366).

Picnic: On the main square, the chic little **Despar Market Enoteca Molesini** makes tasty sandwiches, served with a smile (see list on counter and order by number, or invent your own), and sells whatever else you might want for a picnic (Mon-Sat 9:00-13:00 & 16:00-20:00, Sun 10:00-13:30 & 15:00-19:30, Piazza della Repubblica 3). Munch your picnic across the square on the steps of City Hall or just past Piazza Garibaldi in the public gardens behind San Domenico Church.

Cortona Connections

Cortona has good train connections with the rest of Italy through its Camucia-Cortona station. The station is usually unstaffed, but it has two ticket machines: One is in front as you enter the station, and one is outside on platform 1. They take credit cards and cash (change is given). When purchasing, choose the British flag for English, and then follow the clear instructions, delivered with a charming Italian accent. After buying your ticket, immediately validate it in one of the green boxes next to the ticket machine in the main station or on platforms 1 and 3.

To get to the train station at the foot of the hill, take a €10 taxi or hop the €1.20 bus (see "Arrival in Cortona," earlier; runs only about once hourly; buy tickets at a newsstand or tobacco shop, or buy from driver for €1.60). Be sure to confirm with the TI whether these buses leave from Piazza Garibaldi or Piazza del Mercato, outside Porta Santa Maria. Some buses take you only as far as the newsstand that's 200 yards in front of the station.

From Camucia-Cortona by Train to: Rome (6/day direct, 2.5 hours, 4 more with change), **Florence** (hourly, 1.5 hours), **Assisi** (hourly, 1.5 hours), **Montepulciano** (9/day, 1-2 hours, change in Chiusi; because few buses serve Montepulciano's town center from its distant train station, it's better to go by train to Chiusi, then by hourly 40-minute bus to Montepulciano, or easier still to take a taxi for about €60), **Chiusi** (hourly, 25 minutes).

From Terontola by Train: Most trains stop at the Camucia-Cortona train station, but nearly hourly high-speed trains to/from **Rome, Florence, and Assisi** stop at Terontola, 10 miles away (buses go about hourly to Terontola, leaves from Piazza Garibaldi, 30 minutes, €2, check the schedule at the bus stop or pick up printed bus schedule from the TI).

FLORENTINE & TUSCAN HISTORY

This chapter kicks off with an analysis of how Renaissance Florence—that town, in that place, at that moment in history—became the cultural capital of all Europe. Then you'll find a rundown of Florence and Tuscany's history, divided into major historical periods. For each era, I've given a brief overview; then a more specific timeline; and finally, a list of sights you can see during your travels that bring that period to life.

Renaissance Florence: Cradle of the Modern World

There was just something dynamic about the Florentines. Pope Boniface VIII said there were five elements: earth, air, fire, water... and Florentines. For 200 years, starting in the early 1300s, their city was a cultural hub.

Florence's contributions to Western culture are immense: the revival of the arts, humanism, and science after centuries of medieval superstition and oppression; the seeds of democracy; the modern Italian language (which grew out of the popular Florentine dialect); the art of Botticelli, Leonardo, and Michelangelo; the writings of Machiavelli, Boccaccio, and Dante; and the explorations of Amerigo Vespucci, who gave his name to a newly discovered continent. Florentines considered themselves descendants of the highly cultured people of the Roman Empire. But Florence, even in its Golden Age, was always a mixture of lustiness and refinement. The streets were filled with tough-talking, hardened, illiterate merchants who strode about singing verses from Dante's *Divine Comedy.*

Florentine culture came from money, and that money came from the wool trade, silk factories, and banking. The city had a large middle class and strong guilds (trade associations for skilled craftsmen). Success was a matter of civic pride, and Florentines showed that pride in the mountains of money they spent to rebuild and beautify the city.

Technically, Florence was a republic, ruled by elected citizens rather than nobility. While there was some opportunity for upward mobility among the middle class, most power was in the hands of a few wealthy banking families. The most powerful was the Medici family. The Medici bank had branches in 10 European cities, including London, Geneva, Bruges (Belgium), and Lyon (France). The pope kept his checking account in the Rome branch. The Florentine florin was the monetary standard of the continent.

Florence dominated Italy economically and culturally, but not militarily. The independent Italian city-states squabbled and remained scattered until the nationalist movement four centuries later. (When someone suggested to the Renaissance Florentine Niccolò Machiavelli that the Italian city-states might unite against their common enemy, France, he wrote back, "Don't make me laugh.")

Lorenzo de' Medici (1449-1492), inheritor of the family's wealth and power, and his grandfather Cosimo's love of art, was a central figure of the Golden Age. He was young (20 when he took power), athletic, and intelligent, in addition to being a poet, horseman, musician, and leader. He wrote love songs and humorous ditties to be performed loudly and badly at carnival time. His marathon drinking bouts and illicit love affairs were legendary. He learned Greek and Latin and read the classics, yet his great passion was hunting. He was the original Renaissance Man—a man of knowledge and action, a patron of the arts, a scholar and a man of the world. He was Lorenzo the Magnificent.

Lorenzo epitomized the Florentine spirit of optimism. Born on New Year's Day and raised in the lap of luxury (Donatello's *David* stood in the family courtyard) by loving parents, he grew up feeling that there was nothing he couldn't do. Florentines saw themselves as part of a "new age," a great undertaking of discovery and progress in man's history. They boasted that within the city walls, there were more "nobly gifted souls than the world has seen in the entire thousand years before." These people invented the term "Dark Ages" for the era that preceded theirs.

Lorenzo surrounded himself with Florence's best and brightest. They created an informal "Platonic Academy," based on that of ancient Greece, to meet over a glass of wine under the stars at the Medici villa and discuss literature, art, music, and politics—witty conversation was considered an art in itself.

Their neo-Platonic philosophy stressed the goodness of man and the created world; they believed in a common truth behind all religion. The Academy was more than just an excuse to go out with the guys: The members were convinced that their discussions were changing the world and improving their souls.

Sandro Botticelli (1445-1510) was a member of the Platonic Academy. He painted scenes from the classical myths that the group read, weaving contemporary figures and events into the ancient subjects. He gloried in the nude body, which he considered God's greatest creation.

Artists such as Botticelli thrived on the patronage of wealthy individuals, government, the Church, and guilds. Botticelli commanded as much as 100 florins for one work, enough to live on for a year in high style, which he did for many years. In Botticelli's art we see the lightness, gaiety, and optimism of Lorenzo's court.

Another of Lorenzo's protégés was the young **Michelangelo Buonarroti** (1475-1564). Impressed with his work, Lorenzo took the poor, unlearned 13-year-old boy into the Medici household and treated him like a son.

Michelangelo's playmates were the Medici children, later to become Popes Leo X and Clement VII, who would give him important commissions. For all the encouragement, education, and contacts Michelangelo received, his most important gift from Lorenzo was simply a place at the dinner table, where he could absorb the words of the great men of the time and their love of art for art's sake.

Even with all the art and philosophy of the Renaissance, violence, disease, and warfare were still present in medieval proportions. For the lower classes, life was as harsh as it had always been. Many artists and scholars wore swords and daggers as part of everyday dress. This was the time of the ruthless tactics of the Borgias (known for murdering their political enemies) and of other families battling for power. Lorenzo himself barely escaped assassination in the cathedral during Easter Mass; his brother died in the attack.

The center of the Renaissance gradually shifted to Rome, but its artists were mostly Florentine. In the 15th century, the Holy City of Rome was a dirty, decaying, crime-infested place. Then a series of popes, including Lorenzo's son and nephew, launched a building and beautification campaign. They used fat commissions (and outright orders) to lure Michelangelo, Raphael, and others to Rome. The Florentine Renaissance headed south.

Two Millennia of Eras

550 B.C.-A.D. 1000: Etruscans, Romans, and "Barbarians"

In prehistoric times, much of what we today call "Tuscany" was part of the Etruscan Empire. This mysterious early civilization

built hilltop forts (such as at Fiesole), traded metals with other Mediterranean peoples (including the Golden Age Greeks), established agriculture in central Italy, and buried their dead in distinctive sculpted caskets that show the deceased lounging at an eternal banquet. Having lived their day in the sun, the Etruscans faded as Rome rose. (For more on the Etruscans, see page 494.)

The Romans abandoned the fortified hilltop settlement of Fiesole, seeking better access to water. In 59 B.C., Julius Caesar founded Florentia (meaning "flowering" or "flourishing") at an easy-to-cross point on the Arno River. (That original settlement's typical, rectangular grid plan—aligned by compass points, rather than the river—is still plainly evident in maps of today's city.) From then on, it's the usual Rome story—military outpost, thriving provincial capital, conversion to Christianity, overrun by barbarians—except Florence never really fell. Proud medieval Florentines traced their roots back to civilized Rome, and the city remained a Tuscan commercial center during the Dark Ages.

Many of Tuscany's medieval hill towns also date from this era. They were either founded by the Etruscans (who—more concerned about safety than the trade-and-transportation-minded Romans—appreciated a sky-high location); or built after the fall of Rome and the encroachment of barbarians, when terrified locals fled to protective enclaves huddled near hilltop forts. Some of those forts were constructed to protect the Via Francigena, the pilgrimage route from northern Europe to Rome, which passed through the heart of today's Tuscany (for more on the Via Francigena, see page 544).

Timeline

c. 550 B.C.	Etruscans settle in Fiesole, overlooking the Arno River Valley (and today's Florence).
59 B.C.	Julius Caesar establishes Florentia.
c. A.D. 200	Thriving Roman city, pop. 10,000.
c. 350	In the wake of Constantine's legalization of Christianity, Bishop (and Saint) Zenobius builds a church where the Duomo stands today.
450	Rome falls. Ostrogoths from the east, Byzantines from modern-day Turkey, and Germanic barbarians sweep through in waves. But Florence survives as a small trading town.
800	Charlemagne's Franks sweep through; he becomes the first Holy Roman Emperor. Florence is part

HISTORY

of the Empire for the next 300 years, and is the regional capital.

990 Archbishop Sigeric of Canterbury travels to Rome along the Via Francigena pilgrimage road, writing history's first "guidebook."

Sights

- Etruscan fragments, Florence's Duomo Museum (closed through late 2015)
- Etruscan wall in cellar of Church of San Francesco, and artifacts in Archeological Area, Fiesole
- Etruscan gate, museum, and other artifacts in Volterra
- Etruscan museums in several other towns (Cortona, Chiusi, Chianciano Terme, and many others)
- Florence's Piazza della Repubblica (the old Forum)

1000-1400: Pisa's Peak, Florence's Medieval Rise, and Political Squabbles

Through the Middle Ages, Florence hummed along as a regional trading power. The maritime republic of Pisa (at the mouth of the Arno River) traded with the Far East, funneling some of its wealth into the construction of a glorious ensemble of buildings in the "Pisan Romanesque" style: The Field of Miracles, marked by a bell tower that began to lean before it had even been completed.

While Pisa was busy building, Florentine woolen cloth manufacture, trade, banking, and money lending made urban merchants—organized into guilds—more powerful than rural, feudal nobles. Around the same time, Florence's fierce rival, Siena, was also on the rise. Unlike Florence, Siena sat right along the bustling Via Francigena pilgrim route, which kept it wealthy. In all of these thriving merchant towns, aristocratic families erected tall, fortified tower houses, showing off their wealth and might (San Gimignano had 72).

In the 1200s, Florence was wracked by ongoing power struggles between the pope-supporting Guelphs and the emperor-loyal Ghibellines (see sidebar). Even so, through shrewd diplomacy and military might, Florence gradually vanquished and absorbed its rivals. As part of a budding democracy with civic pride, Florence's guilds and merchants financed major construction projects (some begun in the late 1200s). But Florence's population of 90,000 suddenly was cut nearly in half by the Black Death (bubonic plague)

Guelphs vs. Ghibellines

In medieval times, Italy was divided between two competing political factions, characterized by these differences:

	Guelphs	Ghibellines
Leader	Pope	Emperor
Constituency	Middle-class merchants and craftsmen	Aristocrats of feudal order
Economics	Urban (new economy)	Rural (traditional economy)
Politics	Independence of city-states under local Italian leaders	Unification of small states under traditional dukes and kings

Their conflict had more to do with power than ideology. (It wasn't what you believed, but with whom you were allied.) The names could mean something different depending on the particular place and time.

of 1348. Recovery was slowed by more plagues, bank failures, and political rivalries. But eventually a new leading family emerged: the Medici.

Timeline

c. 1050 Baptistery built, likely on site of ancient Roman temple.

1100 Matilda, Countess of Tuscany, allies with the pope and rises against the German-based Holy Roman Empire, gaining independence for Florence.

1173 A wealthy Pisa begins building its (soon-to-be-) Leaning Tower, part of its Field of Miracles.

1200 Pisa's power peaks, while Florence is steadily on the rise.

1215 Power struggles erupt among nobles (Ghibellines), rich merchants and craftsmen (Guelphs), and laborers. The different factions seek support from outsiders—Guelphs ally with pope, Ghibellines with emperor. In general, Ghibellines dominate in first half of 1200s.

1222-1235 Florentine armies defeat Pisa, Siena, and Pistoia. Florence is the dominant city-state in Tuscany, heading a rich, commercial marketplace.

1252 Gold florin minted, one of Europe's strongest currencies.

1266 Merchants and craftsmen (Guelphs) organize into guilds, oust nobles and establish the *primo popolo,* the first "rule by the people."

1284 Following a devastating naval defeat (against Genoa), Pisa becomes a backwater of Florence.

1293 Guelphs solidify rule by the rich middle class, establishing a constitution that forbids nobles and laborers from holding office. The Ghibellines are gone, but bitter political infighting continues, with Florence divided between Black and White Guelphs.

1296 Construction begins on the Duomo. Santa Croce and Santa Maria Novella are also being built.

1302 The poet Dante, a prominent White Guelph, is exiled. Traveling around Europe and Italy, he writes his epic poem, *The Divine Comedy.*

1347 Florence's population is 90,000, making it one of Europe's biggest cities.

1348 Population nearly halved after the horrific Black Death (bubonic plague). Bank failures and ongoing political squabbles make recovery more difficult.

1378 The Ciompi revolt, led by wool-factory workers, is suppressed by rich merchant families. The guilds (craftsmen unions) lose power as a few wealthy families rise—the Strozzi, Ricci, Alberti, and... Medici.

Sights

- Baptistery
- Roman fragments (Duomo Museum, closed through late 2015)
- Pisa's Field of Miracles (Duomo, Baptistery, Cemetery, and Leaning Tower)
- San Gimignano's 14 surviving tower houses
- Bargello (it was built as the City Hall)
- Palazzo Vecchio
- Orsanmichele Church
- Baptistery interior mosaics
- Duomo and Campanile (original decorations in Duomo Museum)
- Santa Croce, Santa Maria Novella, and Giotto's bell-tower design (Campanile) and his paintings in Uffizi

1400s: The Quattrocento: A Prosperous Renaissance City Under Medici Princes

While 1500 marks Europe's Renaissance, in Florence—where the whole revival of classical culture got its start—the Renaissance began and ended in the 1400s (the Quattrocento). The Medici, a rich textile-and-banking family whose wealth gave them political leverage around Europe, ruled the most prosperous city in Italy, appeasing the masses with philanthropy and public art. For more on this era, see "Renaissance Florence: Cradle of the Modern World," at the start of this chapter.

Timeline

1401 Baptistery door competition energizes an already civic-minded city.

1406 Florence, by conquering Pisa, gains a port and becomes a sea-trading power.

1421 Giovanni de' Medici, a shrewd businessman, expands the Medici family business from textiles into banking.

1434 Cosimo the Elder (Giovanni's son) returns triumphant from exile to rule Florence. Outwardly, he honors the Florentine constitution, but, in fact, he uses his great wealth to rule as a tyrant, buying popularity with lavish patronage of public art.

1436 Dedication of the Duomo, topped by Brunelleschi's dome.

1440 Battle of Anghiari—Florence defeats Milan.

c. 1440 Donatello's *David*.

1458 Cosimo the Elder creates a rubber-stamp Council of the Hundred.

1464 Cosimo the Elder's son, Piero the Gouty, rules stiffly but ably.

1469 Lorenzo the Magnificent, Cosimo the Elder's grandson, rules over the most powerful city in Italy. He is a popular politician but a so-so businessman.

1492 Lorenzo dies. Many Medici banks go bankrupt. Lorenzo's son, Piero the Unfortunate, faces an invasion force from France and appears to side with the foreigners.

1494 Reviled for being morally, financially, and politically bankrupt, the Medici family is exiled. In the political vacuum, the monk Girolamo Savonarola appears as a voice of moral authority. He reestablishes the Florentine constitution.

1498 Savonarola is hanged and burned on Piazza della Signoria by political enemies and a citizenry tired of his morally strict rule. The constitution-driven republic continues.

Sights

- Brunelleschi's Duomo dome and Pazzi Chapel
- Donatello's statues in Bargello, Duomo Museum, and on Orsanmichele exterior
- Ghiberti's two bronze doors on Baptistery (originals in Duomo Museum)
- Botticelli's paintings in Uffizi
- The Uffizi, tracing painting's history from medieval to Michelangelo
- The Bargello, tracing sculpture's history
- Masaccio's frescoes in Santa Maria Novella and Brancacci Chapel
- Fra Angelico paintings (and Savonarola history) in San Marco Museum

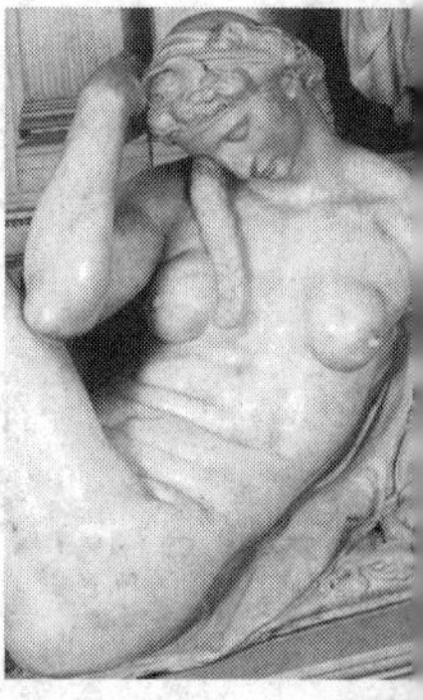

1500-1800: Decline, Medici Dukes, Renaissance Goes South

Bankrupt, the antidemocratic Medici were exiled to Rome, where they married into royalty and returned—backed by foreign powers—as even less democratic nobles. The "Renaissance spirit" moved elsewhere, taking Michelangelo, Leonardo, and Raphael with it. In succeeding centuries, the Medici dukes ruled an economically and politically declining city, but still financed art.

Timeline

1501 Michelangelo begins sculpting *David*.

1512 The Medici family, having established a power base in Rome, returns to take political power as tyrants, backed by the pope and the Spanish army of Holy Roman Emperor Charles V.

1513 Lorenzo the Magnificent's son, Giovanni, becomes Pope Leo X.

1523 Lorenzo's nephew, Giulio de' Medici, becomes Pope Clement VII.

1527 Renegade, unpaid, mercenary troops loot Rome. In the political chaos that follows, Florentines drive the Medici from Florence, re-establishing a republic.

1530 After a yearlong siege, Pope Clement VII and Charles V retake Florence, abolishing the republic and reinstalling Medici rulers.

1533 The Medici marry off Catherine de' Medici to the future King Henry II of France.

1537 Cosimo I, a Medici descended from Cosimo the Elder's brother, is made Duke of Florence. He and his wife, Eleonora of Toledo, rule as tyrannical nobles but beautify the city with the Uffizi, a renovated Palazzo Vecchio, and a rebuilt Pitti Palace.

1574 Francesco I becomes duke, soon to be followed by various Ferdinandos and Cosimos. Florence is now a minor player in world affairs, a small dukedom with a stagnant economy.

1587 The medieval facade of the Duomo is torn down. It remains bare brick for the next 200 years while different proposals are debated.

1600 Maria de' Medici marries Henry IV to become queen of France.

1610-1633 Galileo, backed by the Medici family, works in Florence.

1737 Gian Gastone, the last of the Medici line, dies. Florence is ruled by Austrian Habsburg nobles.

Sights

- Michelangelo's Florentine works—*David,* Medici Chapels, and Laurentian Medici Library
- Pitti Palace and Boboli Gardens (the later Medici palace)
- Later paintings (Uffizi) and statues (Bargello)
- Destruction of the original Duomo facade (Duomo Museum)
- Medici Chapels—pompous tombs of (mostly) later Medici

Typical Church Architecture

History comes to life when you visit a centuries-old church. Even if you wouldn't know your apse from a hole in the ground, learning a few simple terms will enrich your experience. Note that not every church has every feature, and that a "cathedral" isn't a type of church architecture, but rather a designation for a church that's a governing center for a local bishop.

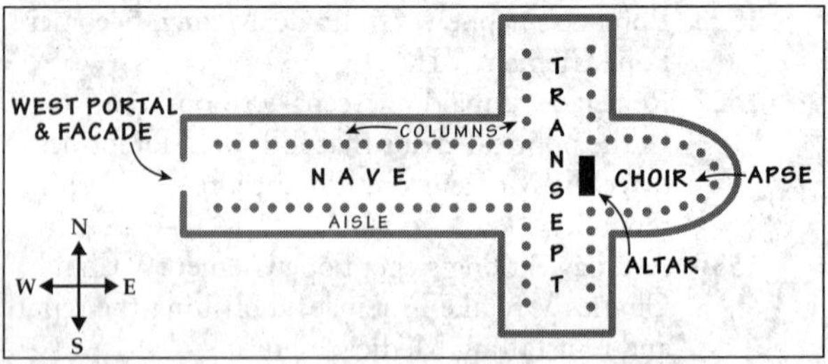

Aisles: The long, generally low-ceilinged arcades that flank the nave.

Altar: The raised area with a ceremonial table (often adorned with candles or a crucifix), where the priest prepares and serves the bread and wine for Communion.

Apse: The space beyond the altar, generally bordered with small chapels.

Barrel Vault: A continuous round-arched ceiling that resembles an extended upside-down U.

Choir: A cozy area, often screened off, located within the church nave and near the high altar, where services are sung in a more intimate setting.

Cloister: Covered hallways bordering a square or rectangular open-air courtyard, traditionally where monks and nuns got fresh air.

Facade: The exterior surface of the church's main (west) entrance, generally highly decorated.

Groin Vault: An arched ceiling formed where two equal barrel vaults meet at right angles. Less common usage: term for a medieval jock strap.

Narthex: The area (portico or foyer) between the main entry and the nave.

Nave: The long, central section of the church (running west to east, from the entrance to the altar) where the congregation sits or stands through the service.

Transept: In a traditional cross-shaped floor plan, the transept is one of the two parts forming the "arms" of the cross. The transepts run north-south, perpendicularly crossing the east-west nave.

West Portal: The main entry to the church (on the west end, opposite the main altar).

HISTORY

- Ponte Vecchio cleaned up for jewelry shops
- Baroque interiors of many older churches
- Galileo's fingers, telescopes, and experiments in the Galileo Science Museum

1800s to Today: Italian Unification, Uncontrolled Urbanization, Urban Renewal

After years of rule by Austrian nobles, Florence peacefully booted out the *Ausländer*s and joined the Italian unification movement. It even served briefly as modern Italy's capital (1865-1870). The city enjoyed an artistic revival of both medieval (Neo-Gothic) and Renaissance (Neoclassical) styles.

In the 20th century, population growth, rapid industrialization, WWII destruction, and the 20-foot-high flood of 1966 made Florence a chaotic, noisy, dirty, traffic-choked city. In the last 30 years, however, the tourist zone has been cleaned and cleared, museums revamped, hours extended, and the people have become accustomed to welcoming foreign visitors. Now if they could just do something about those Vespas....

Timeline

1799 Napoleon "liberates" the city, briefly establishing a pseudo-democracy with his sister as duchess.

1814 Napoleon falls, and the city returns to Austrian rule, under a distant descendant of the Medici family.

1848 Florentine citizens join an uprising all over Italy against foreign rule. The Risorgimento (unification movement) is on.

1860 Florence joins the kingdom of Victor Emmanuel II, forming the nucleus of united, democratic, modern Italy.

1865 Florence is made Italy's capital.

1870 Rome is liberated from papal forces and becomes the de facto capital of a unified Italy (officially in 1871).

1944 Under Nazi occupation as the Allies close in, all the Arno bridges except Ponte Vecchio are blown up.

1966 A disastrous flood, up to nearly 20 feet high, covers the city's buildings and art treasures in mud. The city is a cultural, economic, and touristic mess.

An international effort of volunteer "mud angels" slowly brings these treasures back into view.

1993 The Mafia tries to strike terror with a bomb that destroys a section of the Uffizi, but the museum and the city recover. With a thriving university, plentiful cafés, and sparkling clean museums, Florence is a model cultural destination.

2009 The area around the Duomo is declared traffic-free. As in Renaissance times, Florence proves itself to be a trendsetter for other cities.

2015 Florence's idealistic, visionary, and controversial mayor, Matteo Renzi, becomes prime minister of Italy.

2015 You visit Florence, the art capital of Europe.

Sights

- Duomo's current Neo-Gothic facade
- Piazza della Repubblica (commemorating unification), with its fine 19th-century cafés
- The upscale designer boutiques on Via de' Calzaiuoli, Via degli Strozzi, and Via de' Tornabuoni
- Ever-growing pedestrian zones in the city center—around the Duomo, along Via de' Calzaiuoli and Via de' Tornabuoni, and more

For more on Florentine and Tuscan history, consider *Europe 101: History and Art for the Traveler,* written by Rick Steves and Gene Openshaw (available at www.ricksteves.com).

PRACTICALITIES

Contents

This chapter covers the practical skills of European travel: how to get tourist information, pay for purchases, sightsee efficiently, find good-value accommodations, eat affordably but well, use technology wisely, and get between destinations smoothly. To study ahead and round out your knowledge, check out "Resources" for a summary of recommended books and films.

Tourist Information

The Italian national tourist offices **in the US** are a wealth of information. Before your trip, scan their website (www.italia.it) or contact the nearest branch to briefly describe your trip and request information. You can download many brochures free of charge or call to order a free, general Italy guide. If you have a specific problem, they're a good source of sympathy.

In New York: Tel. 212/245-5618, newyork@enit.it

In Chicago: Tel. 312/644-0996, chicago@enit.it

In Los Angeles: Tel. 310/820-1898, losangeles@enit.it

In Italy, your best first stop in every town is generally the tourist information office (abbreviated **TI** in this book); for TIs in Florence, see page 19 (www.firenzeturismo.it). TIs are good places to get a city map, advice on public transportation (including bus and train schedules), walking tours, special events, and nightlife. Many TIs have information on the entire country or at least the region, so try to pick up maps for destinations you'll be visiting later in your trip. While Italian TIs are about half as helpful as those in other countries, their information is twice as important. Prepare a list of questions and a proposed plan to double-check.

Be wary of the travel agencies or special information services that masquerade as TIs but serve fancy hotels and tour companies. They're in the business of selling things you don't need.

Travel Tips

Emergency and Medical Help: In Italy, dial 113 for English-speaking police help. To summon an ambulance, call 118. If you get sick, do as the locals do and go to a pharmacist for advice. Or ask at your hotel for help—they'll know the nearest medical and emergency services. For English-speaking doctors in Florence, see page 23.

Theft or Loss: To replace a passport, you'll need to go in person to a US embassy or consulate (see page 695). If your credit and debit cards disappear, cancel and replace them (see "Damage Control for Lost Cards" on page 627). File a police report, either on the spot or within a day or two; you'll need it to submit an insurance claim for lost or stolen rail passes or travel gear, and it can help with replacing your passport or credit and debit cards. For more information, see www.ricksteves.com/help. Precautionary measures can minimize the effects of loss—back up your digital photos and other files frequently.

Time Zones: Italy, like most of continental Europe, is generally six/nine hours ahead of the East/West Coasts of the US. The exceptions are the beginning and end of Daylight Saving Time: Europe "springs forward" the last Sunday in March (two weeks after most of North America), and "falls back" the last Sunday in October (one week before North America). For a handy online converter, try www.timeanddate.com/worldclock.

Business Hours: Traditionally, Italy uses the siesta plan. People generally work from 9:00 to 13:00 and from 15:30 to 19:00, Monday through Saturday. But many businesses have adopted the government's recommended 8:00 to 14:00 workday, although in tourist areas, shops are open longer. Still, expect small towns and villages to be more or less shut tight during the midafternoon.

Stores are usually closed on Sunday, and often on Monday. Many Florence shops close for a couple of weeks around August 15. Banking hours are generally Monday through Friday from 8:30 to 13:30 and 15:30 to 16:30, but can vary wildly.

Saturdays are virtually weekdays, with earlier closing hours. Sundays have the same pros and cons as they do for travelers in the US: Sightseeing attractions are generally open, while shops and banks are closed; public transportation options are fewer (for example, no bus service to or from the smaller hill towns), and there's no rush hour. Rowdy evenings are rare on Sundays.

Watt's Up? Europe's electrical system is 220 volts, instead of North America's 110 volts. Most newer electronics (such as laptops, battery chargers, and hair dryers) convert automatically, so you won't need a converter, but you will need an adapter plug with two round prongs, sold inexpensively at travel stores in the US. Avoid bringing older appliances that don't automatically convert voltage; instead, buy a cheap replacement in Europe.

Discounts: Discounts are not listed in this book. However, many sights offer discounts for youths (up to age 18), students (with proper identification cards, www.isic.org), families, seniors (loosely defined as retirees or those willing to call themselves seniors), and groups of 10 or more. Always ask. Italy's national museums generally offer free admission to children under 18, but some discounts are available only for citizens of the European Union (EU).

Online Translation Tip: You can use Google's Chrome browser (available free at www.google.com/chrome) to instantly translate websites. With one click, the page appears in (very rough) English translation. You can also paste the URL of the site into the translation window at www.google.com/translate.

Money

This section offers advice on how to pay for purchases on your trip (including getting cash from ATMs and paying with plastic), dealing with lost or stolen cards, VAT (sales tax) refunds, and tipping.

WHAT TO BRING

Bring both a credit card and a debit card. You'll use the debit card at cash machines (ATMs) to withdraw local cash for most purchases, and the credit card to pay for larger items. Some travelers carry a third card as a backup, in case one gets demagnetized or eaten by a temperamental machine.

For an emergency stash, bring several hundred dollars in hard cash in $20 bills. If you have to exchange the bills, go to a bank; avoid using currency-exchange booths because of their lousy rates and/or outrageous fees.

Affordable Tuscany

Here are some ideas to help stretch your travel dollars:

Sightseeing

- Many of Florence's sights and activities are free. There is no charge for entry to the Duomo, Orsanmichele Church, Santo Spirito Church, and San Miniato Church. It's free to visit the leather school at Santa Croce Church and the perfumery near the Church of Santa Maria Novella. The three markets (Centrale for produce, San Lorenzo and Nuovo for goods) are fun to browse through.
- Free public spaces include the Uffizi and Palazzo Vecchio courtyards; the art-filled loggia on Piazza della Signoria; and Piazzale Michelangelo, with glorious views over Florence. A walk across the picturesque Ponte Vecchio costs nothing at all—unless you succumb to temptation at one of the many shops along the way. A stroll anywhere in Florence with a gelato in hand is an inexpensive treat.
- Remember you can download lots of free information from Rick Steves Audio Europe; see page 9.

Hotels

- Choose hotels that offer a Rick Steves discount.
- Offer to pay cash to get the lowest rate.

Dining

- Don't order too much at restaurants. Servings are often big—and splittable. While restaurants frown on a couple splitting just one dish, if you and your travel partner order a selection of dishes and enjoy them family-style, you can sample several different things, save some euros, and still have room for gelato. Sharing a €8 pizza makes for a cheap meal.

- Takeaway sandwich shops and food carts abound in Florence's old center, making it easy to grab a €3-4 lunch to enjoy on a picturesque piazza. Or order takeout from delicatessens. Many shops have ready-to-eat entrées and side dishes, and will heat them up and send you on your way with plastic cutlery and napkins. Find a scenic picnic spot and enjoy your feast, having paid just a fraction of what you'd pay to eat in a restaurant.

Exchange Rate

1 euro (€) = about $1.40

To convert prices in euros to dollars, add about 40 percent: €20 = about $28; €50 = about $70. (Check www.oanda.com for the latest exchange rates.) Just like the dollar, one euro is broken down into 100 cents. You'll find coins ranging from €0.01 to €2, and bills ranging from €5 to €500.

CASH

Cash is just as desirable in Europe as it is at home. Small businesses (mom-and-pop cafés, shops, etc.) prefer that you pay your bills with cash. Some vendors will charge you extra for using a credit card, and some won't take credit cards at all. Cash is the best—and sometimes only—way to pay for bus fare, taxis, sights, and local guides.

Throughout Europe, ATMs are the standard way for travelers to get cash. To withdraw money from an ATM (known as a *bancomat*), you'll need a debit card (ideally with a Visa or MasterCard logo for maximum usability), plus a PIN code. Know your PIN code in numbers; there are only numbers—no letters—on European keypads. For increased security, shield the keypad when entering your PIN code, and don't use an ATM if anything on the front of the machine looks loose or damaged (a sign that someone may have attached a skimming device to capture account information). Try to withdraw large sums of money to reduce the number of per-transaction bank fees you'll pay.

Whenever possible, use ATMs located outside banks—a thief is less likely to target a cash machine near surveillance cameras, and if your card is munched by a machine, you can go inside for help. Stay away from independent ATMs such as Travelex, Euronet, Moneybox, Cardpoint, and Cashzone, which charge huge commissions, have terrible exchange rates, and may try to trick users with "dynamic currency conversion" (described at the end of "Credit and Debit Cards," next).

Although you can use a credit card for an ATM transaction, it only makes sense in an emergency, because it's considered a cash advance (borrowed at a high interest rate) rather than a withdrawal.

While traveling, if you want to monitor your accounts online to detect any unauthorized transactions, be sure to use a secure connection (see page 670).

Pickpockets target tourists. To safeguard your cash, wear a money belt—a pouch with a strap that you buckle around your waist like a belt and tuck under your clothes. Keep your cash, credit cards, and passport secure in your money belt, and carry only a day's spending money in your front pocket.

CREDIT AND DEBIT CARDS

For purchases, Visa and MasterCard are more commonly accepted than American Express. Just like at home, credit or debit cards work easily at larger hotels, restaurants, and shops. I typically use my debit card to withdraw cash to pay for most purchases. I use my credit card only in a few specific situations: to book hotel reservations by phone, to cover major expenses (such as car rentals, plane tickets, and long hotel stays), and to pay for things near the end of my trip (to avoid another visit to the ATM). While you could use a debit card to make most large purchases, using a credit card offers a greater degree of fraud protection (because debit cards draw funds directly from your account).

Ask Your Credit- or Debit-Card Company: Before your trip, contact the company that issued your debit or credit cards.

• Confirm your **card will work overseas,** and alert them that you'll be using it in Europe; otherwise, they may deny transactions if they perceive unusual spending patterns.

• Ask for the specifics on transaction **fees.** When you use your credit or debit card—either for purchases or ATM withdrawals—you'll typically be charged additional "international transaction" fees of up to 3 percent (1 percent is normal) plus $5 per transaction. If your card's fees are too high, consider getting a card just for your trip: Capital One (www.capitalone.com) and most credit unions have low-to-no international fees.

• If you plan to withdraw cash from ATMs, confirm your daily **withdrawal limit,** and if necessary, ask your bank to adjust it. Some travelers prefer a high limit that allows them to take out more cash at each ATM stop (saving on transaction fees), while others prefer to set a lower limit in case their card is stolen. Note that foreign banks also set maximum withdrawal amounts for their ATMs.

• Get your bank's emergency **phone number** in the US (but not its 800 number, which isn't accessible from overseas) to call collect if you have a problem.

• Ask for your credit card's **PIN** in case you need to make an emergency cash withdrawal or encounter Europe's "chip and PIN" system; the bank won't tell you your PIN over the phone, so allow time for it to be mailed to you.

Chip and PIN: Europeans are increasingly using chip-and-PIN cards, which are embedded with an electronic security chip (in addition to the magnetic stripe found on American-style cards). To make a purchase with a chip-and-PIN card, the cardholder inserts the card into a slot in the payment machine, then enters a PIN (like using a debit card in the US) while the card stays in the slot.

The chip inside the card authorizes the transaction; the cardholder doesn't sign a receipt. Your American-style card might not work at payment machines using this system, such as those at train and subway stations, toll roads, parking garages, luggage lockers, bike-rental kiosks, and self-serve gas pumps.

If you have problems using your American card in a chip-and-PIN machine, here are some suggestions: For either a debit card or a credit card, try entering that card's PIN when prompted. (Note that your credit-card PIN may not be the same as your debit-card PIN; you'll need to ask your bank for your credit-card PIN.) If your cards still don't work, look for a machine that takes cash, seek out a clerk who might be able to process the transaction manually, or ask a local if you can pay them cash to run the transaction on their card.

And don't panic. Many travelers who use only magnetic-stripe cards don't run into problems. Still, it pays to carry plenty of euros; remember, you can always use an ATM to withdraw cash with your magnetic-stripe debit card.

If you're still concerned, you can apply for a chip card in the US (though I think it's overkill). One option is the no-annual-fee GlobeTrek Visa, offered by Andrews Federal Credit Union in Maryland (open to all US residents; see www.andrewsfcu.org). In the future, chip cards should become standard issue in the US: Visa and MasterCard have asked US banks and merchants to use chip-based cards by late 2015.

Dynamic Currency Conversion: If merchants offer to convert your purchase price into dollars (called dynamic currency conversion, or DCC), refuse this "service." You'll pay even more in fees for the expensive convenience of seeing your charge in dollars. Independent ATMs (such as Travelex and Moneybox) may try to confuse customers by presenting DCC in misleading terms. If an ATM offers to "lock in" or "guarantee" your conversion rate, choose "proceed without conversion." Other prompts might state, "You can be charged in dollars: Press YES for dollars, NO for euros." Always choose the local currency in these situations.

Damage Control for Lost Cards

If you lose your credit, debit, or ATM card, you can stop people from using your card by reporting the loss immediately to the respective global customer-assistance centers. Call these 24-hour US numbers collect: Visa (tel. 303/967-1096), MasterCard (tel. 636/722-7111), and American Express (tel. 623/492-8427). In Italy, to make a collect call to the US, dial 800-172-444 (press zero or stay on the line for an English-speaking operator). European toll-free numbers (listed by country) can also be found at the websites for Visa and MasterCard.

Providing the following information allows for a quicker cancellation of your missing card: full card number, whether you are the primary or secondary cardholder, the cardholder's name exactly as printed on the card, billing address, home phone number, circumstances of the loss or theft, and identification verification (your birth date, your mother's maiden name, or your Social Security number—memorize this, don't carry a copy). If you are the secondary cardholder, you'll also need to provide the primary cardholder's identification-verification details. You can generally receive a temporary card within two or three business days in Europe (see www.ricksteves.com/help for more).

If you report your loss within two days, you typically won't be responsible for any unauthorized transactions on your account, although many banks charge a liability fee of $50.

TIPPING

Tipping in Italy isn't as automatic and generous as it is in the US. For special service, tips are appreciated, but not expected. As in the US, the proper amount depends on your resources, tipping philosophy, and the circumstances, but some general guidelines apply.

Restaurants: In Italy, a service charge *(servizio)* is usually built into your bill, so the total you pay already includes a basic tip. It's up to you whether to tip beyond this. For details on restaurant tipping, see page 643.

Taxis: To tip the cabbie, round up. For a typical ride, round up your fare a bit (for instance, if the fare is €4.50, pay €5). If the cabbie hauls your bags and zips you to the airport to help you catch your flight, you might want to toss in a little more. But if you feel like you're being driven in circles or otherwise ripped off, skip the tip.

Services: In general, if someone in the service industry does a super job for you, a small tip of a euro or two is appropriate...but not required. If you're not sure whether (or how much) to tip for a service, ask your hotelier or the TI.

GETTING A VAT REFUND

Wrapped into the purchase price of your Italian souvenirs is a Value-Added Tax (VAT) of about 22 percent. You're entitled to get most of that tax back if you purchase more than €155 (about $200) worth of goods at a store that participates in the VAT-refund scheme. Typically, you must ring up the minimum at a single retailer—you can't add up your purchases from various shops to reach the required amount.

Getting your refund is usually straightforward and, if you buy a substantial amount of souvenirs, well worth the hassle. If you're lucky, the merchant will subtract the tax when you make your purchase. (This is more likely to occur if the store ships the goods to your home.) Otherwise, you'll need to:

Get the paperwork. Have the merchant completely fill out the necessary refund document. You'll have to present your passport. Get the paperwork done before you leave the store to ensure you'll have everything you need (including your original sales receipt).

Get your stamp at the border or airport. Process your VAT document at your last stop in the European Union (such as at the airport) with the customs agent who deals with VAT refunds. Before checking in for your flight, find the local customs office, and be prepared to stand in line. Keep your purchases readily available for viewing by the customs agent (ideally in your carry-on bag—don't make the mistake of checking the bag with your purchases before you've seen the agent). You're not supposed to use your purchased goods before you leave. If you show up at customs wearing your new leather shoes, officials might look the other way—or deny you a refund.

Collect your refund. You'll need to return your stamped document to the retailer or its representative. Many merchants work with a service, such as Global Blue or Premier Tax Free, that has offices at major airports, ports, or border crossings (either before or after security, probably strategically located near a duty-free shop). These services, which extract a 4 percent fee, can refund your money immediately in cash or credit your card (within two billing cycles). If the retailer handles VAT refunds directly, it's up to you to contact the merchant for your refund. You can mail the documents from home, or more quickly, from your point of departure (using an envelope you've prepared in advance or one that's been provided by the merchant). You'll then have to wait—it can take months.

CUSTOMS FOR AMERICAN SHOPPERS

You are allowed to take home $800 worth of items per person duty-free, once every 30 days. You can also bring in duty-free a liter of alcohol. As for food, you can take home many processed and packaged foods: vacuum-packed cheeses, dried herbs, jams, baked goods, candy, chocolate, oil, vinegar, mustard, and honey. Fresh fruits and vegetables and most meats are not allowed. However, canned meat is allowed if it doesn't contain any beef, veal, lamb, or mutton. Any liquid-containing foods must be packed in checked luggage, a potential recipe for disaster. To check customs rules and duty rates, visit http://help.cbp.gov.

Sightseeing

Sightseeing can be hard work. Use these tips to make your visits to Florence and Tuscany's finest sights meaningful, fun, efficient, and painless.

PLAN AHEAD

Set up an itinerary that allows you to fit in all your must-see sights. For a one-stop look at opening hours in Florence, see "Florence at a Glance" on page 36 (also see "Daily Reminder" on page 26). You'll find "Siena at a Glance" on page 358. Most sights keep stable hours, but you can easily confirm the latest by checking with the TI or visiting museum websites.

For Florence, make reservations for the Uffizi and Accademia (see page 38) or plan to get a Firenze Card (see page 34).

Don't put off visiting a must-see sight—you never know when a place will close unexpectedly for a holiday, strike, or restoration. Many museums are closed or have reduced hours at least a few days a year, especially on holidays such as Labor Day (May 1), Christmas, and New Year's. A list of holidays is on page 696; check museum websites for possible closures during your trip. In summer, some sights may stay open late. Off-season, many museums have shorter hours.

Going at the right time helps avoid crowds. This book offers tips on the best times to see specific sights. Try visiting popular sights very early or very late. Evening visits are usually peaceful, with fewer crowds.

Study up. To get the most out of the self-guided tours and sight descriptions in this book, read them before you visit.

AT SIGHTS

Here's what you can typically expect:

Entering: Be warned that you may not be allowed to enter if you arrive 30 to 60 minutes before closing time. And guards start ushering people out well before the actual closing time, so don't save the best for last.

Some important sights have a security check, where you must open your bag or send it through a metal detector. Some sights require you to check daypacks and coats. (If you'd rather not check your daypack, try carrying it tucked under your arm like a purse as you enter.)

Photography: If the museum's photo policy isn't clearly posted, ask a guard. Generally, taking photos without a flash or tripod is allowed. Some sights ban photos altogether.

Temporary Exhibits: Museums may show special exhibits in addition to their permanent collection. Some exhibits are included in the entry price, while others come at an extra cost (which you may have to pay even if you don't want to see the exhibit).

Expect Changes: Artwork can be on tour, on loan, out sick, or shifted at the whim of the curator. To adapt, pick up a floor plan as you enter, and ask the museum staff if you can't find a particular item. Say the title or artist's name, or point to the photograph in this book and ask, *"Dov'è?"* (doh-VEH, meaning "Where is?").

Audioguides: Many sights rent audioguides, which generally offer excellent recorded descriptions of the art in English (about $7). Bring along your own earbuds to enjoy better sound and avoid holding the device to your ear. To save money, bring a Y-jack and share one audioguide with your travel partner. I've produced free downloadable audio tours of Florence's major sights; see page 9.

It helps to know the terms. Art historians and Italians refer to the great Florentine centuries by dropping a thousand years. The Trecento (300s), Quattrocento (400s), and Cinquecento (500s) were the 1300s, 1400s, and 1500s. In Italian museums, art is dated with *sec* for *secolo* (century, often indicated with Roman numerals), A.C. (*avanti Cristo,* or B.C.), and D.C. (*dopo Cristo,* or A.D.). O.K.?

Services: Important sights may have an on-site café or cafeteria (usually a good place to rejuvenate during a long visit). The WCs at sights are free and generally clean.

Before Leaving: At the gift shop, scan the postcard rack or thumb through a guidebook to be sure that you haven't overlooked something that you'd like to see.

Every sight or museum offers more than what is covered in this book. Use the information in this book as an introduction—not the final word.

FIND RELIGION

Churches offer some amazing art (usually free), a cool respite from heat, and a welcome seat.

A modest dress code (no bare shoulders or shorts for anyone, even kids) is enforced at larger churches, but is often overlooked elsewhere. If you're caught by surprise, you can improvise, using maps to cover your shoulders and a jacket for your knees. A few major churches let you borrow or buy disposable ponchos to cover up in a pinch. (I wear a super-lightweight pair of long pants rather than shorts for my hot and muggy big-city Italian sightseeing.)

Some churches have coin-operated audioboxes that describe the art and history; just set the dial on English, put in your coins, and listen. Coin boxes near a piece of art illuminate the art (and present a better photo opportunity). I pop in a coin whenever I can. It improves my experience, is a favor to other visitors trying to appreciate a great piece of art in the dark, and is a little contribution to that church and its work. Whenever possible, let there be light.

Sleeping

I favor hotels and restaurants that are handy to your sightseeing activities. Nearly all of my recommended accommodations are located in city or town centers, within minutes of the great sights. (To stay in the countryside, try *agriturismo* farmhouses; for more information on these rural B&Bs, see page 639.)

A major feature of this book is its extensive listing of good-value rooms. I like places that are clean, central, relatively quiet at night, reasonably priced, friendly, small enough to have a hands-on owner and stable staff, run with a respect for Italian traditions, and not listed in other guidebooks. (In Florence and Tuscany, for me, six out of these eight criteria means it's a keeper.) I'm more impressed by a convenient location and a fun-loving philosophy than flat-screen TVs and a pricey laundry service.

Book your accommodations well in advance if you'll be traveling during busy times. See page 696 for a list of major holidays and festivals in Tuscany; for tips on making reservations, see page 636.

Some people make reservations as they travel, calling hotels a few days to a week before their arrival. If you'd rather travel without any reservations at all, you'll have greater success snaring rooms if you arrive at your destination early in the day. If you anticipate crowds (weekends are worst) on the day you want to check in, call hotels at about 9:00 or 10:00, when the receptionist knows who'll be checking out and which rooms will be available. If you encounter a language barrier, ask the fluent receptionist at your current hotel to call for you.

RATES AND DEALS

I've described my recommended accommodations using a Sleep Code (see sidebar). Prices listed are for one-night stays in peak season, and assume you're booking directly with the hotel (not through an online hotel-booking engine or TI). Booking services extract a commission from the hotel, which logically closes the door on special deals. Book direct.

While most taxes are included in the price, a variable city tax of €1-4/person per night is often added to hotel bills (and is not included in the prices in this book).

My recommended hotels each have a website (often with a built-in booking form) and an email address; you can expect a response in English within a day (and often sooner).

If you're on a budget, it's smart to email several hotels to ask for their best price. Comparison-shop and make your choice. This is especially helpful when dealing with the larger hotels that use "dynamic pricing," a computer-generated system that predicts the demand for particular days and sets prices accordingly: High-de-

Sleep Code

(€1 = about $1.40, country code: 39)

Price Rankings

To help you easily sort through my listings, I've divided the accommodations into three categories based on the price for a double room with bath during high season:

$$$ Higher Priced
$$ Moderately Priced
$ Lower Priced

I always rate hostels as $, whether or not they have double rooms, because they have the cheapest beds in town. Prices can change without notice; verify the hotel's current rates online or by email. For the best prices, always book directly with the hotel.

Abbreviations

To pack maximum information into minimum space, I use the following code to describe accommodations in this book. Prices listed are per room, not per person. When a price range is given for a type of room (such as double rooms listing for €100-150), it means the price fluctuates with the season, size of room, or length of stay; expect to pay the upper end for peak-season stays.

- **S** = Single room (or price for one person in a double).
- **D** = Double or twin room. "Double beds" can be two twins sheeted together and are usually big enough for nonromantic couples.
- **T** = Triple (generally a double bed with a single).
- **Q** = Quad (usually two double beds; adding an extra child's bed to a T is usually cheaper).
- **b** = Private bathroom with toilet and shower or tub.
- **s** = Private shower or tub only (the toilet is down the hall).

According to this code, a couple staying at a "Db-€140" hotel would pay a total of €140 (about $196) for a double room with a private bathroom. Unless otherwise noted, breakfast is included, hotel staff speak basic English, credit cards are accepted, and Wi-Fi is free. If a city adds a room tax, it generally isn't included in the rates I list.

mand days will often be more than double the price of low-demand days. This makes it impossible for a guidebook to list anything more accurate than a wide range of prices. I regret this trend. While you can assume that hotels listed in this book are good, it's very difficult to say which ones are the better value unless you email to confirm the price.

As you look over the listings, you'll notice that some accommodations promise special prices to Rick Steves readers. To get these rates, you must book directly with the hotel (that is, not through a booking site like TripAdvisor or Booking.com), mention this book when you reserve, and then show the book upon arrival. Rick Steves discounts apply to readers with ebooks as well as printed books. Because we trust hotels to honor this, please let me know if you don't receive a listed discount. Note, though, that discounts understandably may not be applied to promotional rates.

In general, prices can soften if you do any of the following: offer to pay cash, stay at least three nights, or mention this book. You can also try asking for a cheaper room or a discount, or offer to skip breakfast.

If you can handle waiting until the last minute to snare a spot, fancy hotels put empty rooms on an aggressive push list, offering great prices. Check hotel websites or sites such as www.booking.com, www.expedia.com, or www.venere.com starting two or three weeks before your arrival date. Before you bite, check to see if rates are lower than the prices in this book.

TYPES OF ACCOMMODATIONS

Hotels

In Florence, you can snare a stark, clean, and comfortable double with breakfast and a private bath for about €100. You get near-elegance in peak season for €170.

Solo travelers find that the cost of a *camera singola* is often only 25 percent less than a *camera doppia*. Three or four people can save money by requesting one big room. (If a Db is €110, a Qb would be about €150.) Most listed hotels have rooms for any size party from one to five people. If there's room for an extra cot, they'll cram it in for you (charging you around €25).

You'll save €30/night if you book a room with the shower down the hall. Generally rooms with a bath or shower also have a toilet and a bidet (which Italians use for quick sponge baths). The cord that dangles over the tub or shower is not a clothesline. You pull it when you've fallen and can't get up.

Double beds are called *matrimoniale,* even though hotels aren't interested in your marital status. Twins are *due letti singoli.* Convents offer cheap accommodation but only *letti singoli.*

When you check in, the receptionist will normally ask for your passport and keep it for anywhere from a couple of minutes to a couple of hours. Hotels are legally required to register each guest with the police. Relax. Americans are notorious for making this chore more difficult than it needs to be.

Hotels and B&Bs are sometimes located on the higher floors of a multipurpose building with a secured door. In that case, look

Chill Out

All but the cheapest hotels have air-conditioning. Because Europeans are generally careful with energy use, you'll find government-enforced limits on air-conditioning and heating. There's a one-month period each spring and fall when neither is allowed. Air-conditioning sometimes costs an extra per-day charge, is worth seeking out in summer (though it may be on only at certain times of the day), and is rarely available from fall through spring. Conveniently, many business-class hotels drop their prices in July and August, just when the air-conditioned comfort they offer is most important.

Most hotel rooms with air-conditioners come with a control stick (like a TV remote) that generally has the same symbols and features: fan icon (click to toggle through wind power, from light to gale-force); louver icon (choose steady airflow or waves); snowflake and sunshine icons (cold air or heat, depending on season); clock ("O" setting: run x hours before turning off; "I" setting: wait x hours to start); and the temperature control (21 degrees Celsius is comfortable).

for your hotel's name on the buttons by the main entrance. When you ring the bell, you'll be buzzed in.

Assume that breakfast is included in the prices I've listed, unless otherwise noted. If breakfast is included but optional, you may want to skip it. While convenient, it's usually expensive—€5-8 per person for a simple continental buffet with ham, cheese, yogurt, and unlimited *caffè latte*. A picnic in your room followed by a coffee at the corner café can be cheaper.

More pillows and blankets are usually in the closet or available on request. In Italy, towels and linen aren't always replaced every day. Hang your towel up to dry. Some hotels use lightweight "waffle," or very thin, tablecloth-type towels; these take less water and electricity to launder and are preferred by many Italians.

Most hotel rooms have a TV, telephone, and free Wi-Fi (although in old buildings with thick walls, the Wi-Fi signal doesn't always make it to the rooms; sometimes it's only available in the lobby). Sometimes there's a guest computer with Internet access in the lobby. Simpler places rarely have a room phone, but often have free Wi-Fi. Pricier hotels usually come with elevators, air-conditioning, and a small stocked fridge called a *frigo bar* (FREE-goh bar; pay for what you use). Hotel elevators, while becoming more common, are often very small—pack light, or you may need to send your bags up one at a time.

If you're arriving early in the morning, your room probably won't be ready. You can drop your bag safely at the hotel and dive right into sightseeing.

Making Hotel Reservations

Reserve your rooms several weeks in advance—or as soon as you've pinned down your travel dates—particularly if you'll be traveling during peak times. Note that some national holidays jam things up and merit your making reservations far in advance (see "Holidays and Festivals" on page 696).

Requesting a Reservation: It's easiest to book your room through the hotel's website. (For the best rates, always use the hotel's official site and not a booking agency's site.) If there's no reservation form, or for complicated requests, send an email (see below for a sample request). Most recommended hotels take reservations in English.

The hotelier wants to know:

- the number and type of rooms you need
- the number of nights you'll stay
- your date of arrival (use the European style for writing dates: day/month/year)
- your date of departure
- any special needs (such as bathroom in the room or down the hall, cheapest room, twin beds vs. double bed, and so on)

Mention any discounts—for Rick Steves readers or otherwise—when you make the reservation.

Confirming a Reservation: Most places will request a credit-card number to hold your room. If they don't have a secure online reservation form—look for the *https*—you can email it (I do), but it's safer to share that confidential info via a phone call or two emails (splitting your number between them).

Canceling a Reservation: If you must cancel, it's courteous—and smart—to do so with as much notice as possible, especially

Hoteliers can be a great help and source of advice. Most know their cities well, and can assist you with everything from public transit and airport connections to finding a good restaurant or the nearest launderette.

Even at the best places, mechanical breakdowns occur: Air-conditioning malfunctions, sinks leak, hot water turns cold, and toilets gurgle and smell. Report your concerns clearly and calmly at the front desk. For more complicated problems, don't expect instant results.

If you suspect night noise will be a problem (if, for instance, your room is over a nightclub), ask for a quieter room in the back or on an upper floor. To guard against theft in your room, keep valuables out of sight. Some rooms come with a safe, and other hotels have safes at the front desk. I've never bothered using one.

Checkout can pose problems if surprise charges pop up on your bill. If you settle your bill the afternoon before you leave,

From: rick@ricksteves.com
Sent: Today
To: info@hotelcentral.com
Subject: Reservation request for 19-22 July

Dear Hotel Central,

I would like to reserve a room for 2 people for 3 nights, arriving 19 July and departing 22 July. If possible, I would like a quiet room with a double bed and a bathroom inside the room.

Please let me know if you have a room available and the price.

Thank you!
Rick Steves

for smaller family-run places. Be warned that cancellation policies can be strict; read the fine print or ask about these before you book. Internet deals may require prepayment, with no refunds for cancellations.

Reconfirming a Reservation: Always call to reconfirm your room reservation a few days in advance. For smaller hotels and B&Bs, I call again on my day of arrival to tell my host what time I expect to get there (especially important if arriving late—after 17:00).

Phoning: For tips on how to call hotels overseas, see page 660.

you'll have time to discuss and address any points of contention (before 19:00, when the night shift usually arrives).

Above all, keep a positive attitude. Remember, you're on vacation. If your hotel is a disappointment, spend more time out enjoying the city you came to see.

Hostels

You'll pay about €20 per bed to stay at a hostel. Travelers of any age are welcome if they don't mind dorm-style accommodations and meeting other travelers. Most hostels offer kitchen facilities, Internet access, Wi-Fi, and a self-service laundry. Nowadays, concerned about bedbugs, hostels are likely to provide all bedding, including sheets. Family and private rooms may be available on request.

Independent hostels tend to be easygoing, colorful, and informal (no membership required); www.hostelworld.com is the standard way backpackers search and book hostels these days, but also try www.hostelz.com, www.hostels.com, and www.backpackers.it.

Official hostels are part of Hostelling International (HI) and share an online booking site (www.hihostels.com). HI hostels typically require that you either have a membership card or pay extra per night.

Private Rooms and Apartments

In small towns, there are often few hotels to choose from, but an abundance of *affitta camere,* or rental rooms. This can be anything from a set of keys and a basic bed to a cozy B&B with your own Tuscan grandmother. In Italy, even luxury B&Bs can suffer from absentee management—the proprietors often live off-site (or even in another town) and may be around only when they are expecting guests, so clearly communicate your arrival time. After checking in, be sure you have your host's telephone number in case you need to reach them.

Local TIs can give you a list of possibilities (or try the free Ciao Italia Bed & Breakfast, which books B&Bs and hostels in Rome, Florence, and Venice; www.ciaoitalia-bb.com—site sometimes "under maintenance"). These rooms are usually a good budget option, but since they vary in quality, shop around to find the best value. It's always OK to ask to see the room before you commit.

Whether you're in a city or the countryside, renting an apartment, house, or villa can be a fun and cost-effective way to delve into Europe. Apartment rentals, a great value for families or multiple couples traveling together, are also listed at TIs and are common in small towns. Websites such as HomeAway.com and its sister sites VRBO and GreatRentals let you correspond directly with European property owners or managers. Rentals are generally by the week, with prices starting around €100 per day. A bigger place for a group of four to five rents for around €200. Apartments generally offer a couple of bedrooms, a sitting area, and a teensy *cucinetta* (kitchenette), usually stocked with dishes and flatware. After you check in, you're basically on your own. While you won't have a doorman to carry your bags or a maid to clean your room each day, you will get an inside peek at an Italian home, and you can save lots of money—especially if you take advantage of the cooking facilities—with no loss of comfort.

Another option is **Cross-Pollinate.com,** an online booking agency representing B&Bs and apartments in a handful of European cities, including Florence. Search their website for a listing you like, then submit your reservation online. If the place is available, you'll be charged a small deposit and emailed the location and check-in details. Policies vary from owner to owner, but in most cases you'll pay the balance on arrival in cash. Minimum stays vary from one to three nights (US tel. 800-270-1190, Italy tel. 06-9936-9799, www.cross-pollinate.com, info@cross-pollinate.com).

Airbnb.com and Roomorama makes it reasonably easy to find a place to sleep in someone's home. Beds range from air-mattress-in-living-room basic to plush-B&B-suite posh. If you want a place to sleep that's free, Couchsurfing.org is a vagabond's alternative to Airbnb. It lists millions of outgoing members, who host fellow "surfers" in their homes.

Agriturismo

Agriturismo (agricultural tourism), or rural B&Bs, began in the 1980s as a way to allow small farmers in the countryside to survive in a modern economy where, like in the US, so many have been run out of business by giant agricultural corporations. By renting rooms to travelers, farmers receive generous tax breaks that allow them to remain on their land and continue to produce food. A peaceful home base for exploring the region, these rural Italian B&Bs are ideal for those traveling by car—especially families.

It's wise to book several months in advance for high season (late April-mid-Oct). July and August are jammed with Italians and other European vacationers; in spring and fall, it's mostly Americans. Weeklong stays (typically Saturday to Saturday) are preferred at busy times, but shorter stays are possible off-season. To sleep cheaper, avoid peak season. In the winter, you might be charged extra for heat, so confirm the price ahead of time. Payment policies vary, but generally a 25 percent deposit is required (lost if you cancel), and the balance is due one month before arrival.

As the name implies, *agriturismi* are in the countryside, although some are located on the outskirts of a large town or city. Most are family-run. *Agriturismi* vary dramatically in quality—some properties are rustic, while others are downright luxurious, offering amenities such as swimming pools and riding stables. The rooms are usually clean and comfortable. Breakfast is often included, and *mezza pensione* (half-pension, which in this case means a home-cooked dinner) might be built into the price whether you want it or not. Most places serve tasty homegrown food; some are vegetarian or organic, others are gourmet. Kitchenettes are often available to cook up your own feast.

To qualify officially as an *agriturismo,* the farm must still generate more money from its farm activities, thereby ensuring that the

Tips for Enjoying an *Agriturismo* Farmhouse Stay

- To sleep cheap, avoid peak season. Rental prices follow the old rule of supply and demand. Prices that are sky-high in summer can drop dramatically in early spring and late fall.
- Make sure your trip fits their requirements. Many properties rent on a traditional Saturday-to-Saturday time period. You might be unable to rent for a different or shorter time, especially during peak season.
- If you want amenities, be willing to pay more. A swimming pool can add substantially to the cost, but at the height of summer, could be worth every extra euro, particularly if you're bringing kids.
- Consider renting a rural apartment rather than an entire villa or farmhouse. Often the owners have renovated an original rambling farmhouse or medieval estate into a series of well-constructed apartments with private kitchens, bathrooms, living areas, and outdoor terraces. They usually share a common pool.

- You will need private transportation, such as a rental car, to fully enjoy—or even reach—your accommodations.
- To make the most of your time, ask an expert—the owner—for suggestions on restaurants, sights, and activities. Make sure you know how to operate the appliances.
- Slow down. One of the joys of staying for at least a week in one location is you can develop a true *dolce far niente* (sweetness of doing nothing) attitude. If it rains, grab a book from the in-house library and curl up on the sofa.
- While your time in the countryside may not be action-packed, staying put in one spot leaves you open to the unexpected pleasures that come when you just let the days unwind without a plan.

land is worked and preserved. Some farmhouse B&Bs aren't working farms, but are still fine places to stay. Some travelers who are enticed by romanticized dreams of *agriturismi* are turned off when they arrive to actual farm smells and sounds. These folks would be more comfortable with a countryside B&B or villa that offers a bit more upscale comfort. In this book, I've listed both types of rural accommodations; if you want the real thing, make sure the owners call their place an *agriturismo*.

In addition to my listings—which I've included in the "Sleeping" sections for the towns that they're nearest to—local TIs can

The Good and Bad of Online Reviews

User-generated travel review websites—such as TripAdvisor, Booking.com, and Yelp—have quickly become a huge player in the travel industry. These sites give you access to actual reports—good and bad—from travelers who have experienced the hotel, restaurant, tour, or attraction.

My hotelier friends in Europe are in awe of these sites' influence. Small hoteliers who want to stay in business have no choice but to work with review sites—which often charge fees for good placement or photos, and tack on commissions if users book through the site instead of directly with the hotel.

While these sites work hard to weed out bogus users, my hunch is that a significant percentage of reviews are posted by friends or enemies of the business being reviewed. I've even seen hotels "bribe" guests (for example, offer a free breakfast) in exchange for a positive review. Also, review sites can become an echo chamber, with one or two flashy businesses camped out atop the ratings, while better, more affordable, and more authentic alternatives sit ignored farther down the list. (For example, I find review sites' restaurant recommendations skew to very touristy, obvious options.)

Remember that a user-generated review is based on the experience of one person. That person likely stayed at one hotel and ate at a few restaurants, and doesn't have much of a basis for comparison. A guidebook is the work of a trained researcher who has exhaustively visited many alternatives to assess their relative value. I recently checked out some top-rated TripAdvisor listings in various towns; when stacked up against their competitors, some are gems, while just as many are duds.

Both types of information have their place, and in many ways, they're complementary. If a hotel or restaurant is well-reviewed in a guidebook or two, and also gets good ratings on one of these sites, it's likely a winner.

give you a list of places in their area. For a sampling, visit www.agriturismoitaly.it or search online for *agriturismo*. One booking agency among many is Farm Holidays in Tuscany (closed Sat-Sun, tel. 0564-417-418, www.byfarmholidays.com, info@byfarmholidays.com).

Eating

The Italians are masters of the art of fine living. That means eating long and well. Lengthy, multicourse meals and endless hours sitting in outdoor cafés are the norm. Americans eat on their way to an evening event and complain if the check is slow in coming. For Italians, the meal is an end in itself, and only rude waiters rush you. When you want the bill, mime-scribble on your raised palm or request it: *"Il conto, per favore."* You may have to ask for it more than once. If you're in a hurry, request the check when you receive the last item you've ordered.

A highlight of your Italian adventure will be Tuscany's cafés, cuisine, and wines. Trust me: This is sightseeing for your palate. Even if you liked dorm food and are sleeping in cheap hotels, your taste buds will relish an occasional first-class splurge. You can eat well without going broke. But be careful: You're just as likely to blow a small fortune on a disappointing meal as you are to dine wonderfully for €25. Your euros typically will go much farther, and will net you far better food, in smaller Tuscan towns than in Florence.

In general, Italians eat meals a bit later than we do. At 7:00 or 8:00 in the morning, they have a light breakfast (coffee—usually cappuccino or espresso—and a pastry, often standing up at a café). Lunch (between 13:00 and 15:00) is traditionally the largest meal of the day. Then they eat a late, light dinner (around 20:00-21:30, or maybe earlier in winter). To bridge the gap, people drop into a bar in the late afternoon for a *spuntino* (snack) and aperitif.

Most restaurant kitchens close between their lunch and dinner service. Good restaurants don't reopen for dinner before 19:00. Small restaurants with a full slate of reservations for 20:30 or 21:00 often will accommodate walk-in diners willing to eat a quick, early meal, but you aren't expected to linger.

BREAKFAST

Italian breakfasts, like Italian bath towels, are small: The basic, traditional version is coffee and a roll with butter and marmalade. These days, many places also have juice, yogurt, maybe cereal, possibly cold cuts and sliced cheese, and sometimes eggs (typically hard-boiled; scrambled or fried eggs are rare). Small budget hotels may leave a basic breakfast in a fridge in your room (stale croissant, roll, jam, yogurt, coffee). In general, the pricier the hotel, the bigger the breakfast.

The strong coffee at breakfast is often mixed about half-and-half with heated milk. At your hotel, refills are usually free. The delicious red orange juice *(spremuta di arance rossa)* is made from Sicilian blood oranges.

If you want to skip your hotel breakfast, consider browsing for a morning picnic at a local open-air market. Or do as the Italians do: Stop into a bar or café to drink a cappuccino and munch a *cornetto* (croissant) while standing at the bar. While the *cornetto* is the most common pastry, you'll find a range of *pasticcini* (pastries, sometimes called *dolci*—"sweets"). Look for *otto* ("8"-shaped pastry, often filled with custard, jam, or chocolate), *sfoglia* (can be

Eating with the Seasons

Italian cooks love to serve you fresh produce and seafood at its tastiest. If you must have porcini mushrooms outside of October and November, they'll be dried. To get the freshest veggies at a fine restaurant, request *"Il piatto di verdure della stagione, per favore"* ("A plate of seasonal vegetables, please").

Here are a few examples of what's fresh when:

April-May:	Squid, green beans, asparagus, artichokes, and zucchini flowers
April-May and Sept-Oct:	Black truffles
May-June:	Asparagus, zucchini, cantaloupe, and strawberries
May-Aug:	Eggplant
Oct-Nov:	Mushrooms and white truffles
Fresh year-round:	Clams and meats

fruit-filled, like a turnover), or *ciambella* (doughnut filled with custard or chocolate)—or ask about local specialties.

ITALIAN RESTAURANTS

While *ristorante* is self-explanatory, you'll also see other types of Italian eateries: A *trattoria* and an *osteria* (which can be more casual) are generally family-owned places serving home-cooked meals, often at moderate prices. A *locanda* is an inn, a *cantina* is a wine cellar, and a *birreria* is a brewpub. *Pizzerie, rosticcerie* (delis), *enoteche* (wine bars), and other alternatives are explained later.

When restaurant-hunting, choose places filled with locals, not places with big neon signs boasting "We Speak English and Accept Credit Cards." Restaurants parked on famous squares generally serve bad food at high prices to tourists. Venturing even a block or two off the main drag leads to higher-quality food for less than half the price of the tourist-oriented places. Locals eat better at lower-rent locales. Family-run places operate without hired help and can offer cheaper meals.

Cover and Tipping

Before you sit down, look at a menu to see what extra charges a restaurant tacks on. Two different items are routinely factored into your bill: the *coperto* and the *servizio.*

The ***coperto*** (cover charge), sometimes called *pane e coperto* (bread and cover), offsets the overhead expenses from the basket of bread on your table to the electricity running the dishwasher. It's not negotiable, even if you don't eat the bread. Think of it as covering the cost of using the table for as long as you like. (Italians like to linger.) Most restaurants add the *coperto* onto your bill as a flat fee (€1-3.50 per person; the amount should be clearly noted on the menu).

The ***servizio*** (service charge) of about 10 percent pays for the waitstaff. At most legitimate eateries, the words *servizio incluso* are written on the menu and/or the receipt—indicating that the listed prices already include the fee. You can add on a tip, if you choose, by including €1-2 for each person in your party. While Italians don't think about tips in terms of percentages—and many don't tip at all—this extra amount usually comes out to about 5 percent (10 percent is excessive for all but the very best service).

A few trendy restaurants don't include the service in the menu prices—but will automatically tack on a 10 percent *servizio* charge to your bill. If a menu reads *servizio 10%,* the listed prices don't include the fee; it will be added onto your bill for you (so you don't need to calculate it yourself and pay it separately). Rarely, you'll see the words *servizio non incluso* on the menu or bill; in this case, you're expected to add a tip of about 10 percent.

Most Italian restaurants have a cover charge, and include service in the menu prices (i.e., *servizio incluso*). A few have just a service charge. Places with *both* a cover and a tacked-on service charge are best avoided—that's a clue that a restaurant is counting on a nonlocal clientele who can't gauge value. In recent years some (especially less formal) cafés and restaurants with table service have stopped charging these fees, though they have probably raised their prices to compensate. Self-service restaurants never have a cover or service charge.

Courses: Antipasto, *Primo*, and *Secondo*

A full Italian meal consists of several courses:

Antipasto (usually €5-10): An appetizer such as bruschetta, grilled veggies, deep-fried tasties, thin-sliced meat (such as prosciutto or carpaccio), or a plate of olives, cold cuts, and cheeses. A plate of *antipasti misti* ("mixed"—an assortment) could make a light meal in itself.

Primo piatto (usually €7-15): A "first dish" generally consisting of pasta, rice, or soup. If you think of pasta when you think of Italy, you can dine well here without ever going beyond the *primo.*

Secondo piatto (usually €10-25): A "second dish," equivalent to our main course, of meat or fish/seafood. Italians freely admit the *secondo* is the least interesting part of their cuisine.

A vegetable side dish *(contorno)* may come with the *secondo* but more often must be ordered separately (€5-6).

The euros can add up in a hurry, and for most travelers, a complete meal with all three courses (plus *contorni,* dessert, and wine) is simply too much food. To avoid overeating (and to stretch your budget), share dishes. A good rule of thumb is for each person to order any two courses. For example, a couple can order and share one antipasto, one *primo*, one *secondo*, and one dessert; or two *antipasti* and two *primi*; or whatever combination appeals. Some restaurants serve a *piatta unica,* with smaller portions of each course on one dish (for instance, a meat, starch, and vegetable).

Another good option is sharing an array of *antipasti;* you can order several specific dishes, or at restaurants that have self-serve *antipasti* buffets, you can choose from a variety of cooked appetizers spread out like a salad bar. You pay per plate, not by weight; a typical serving costs about €8 (generally Italians don't treat buffets as all-you-can-eat, but take a one-time moderate serving; watch others and imitate).

To maximize the experience and flavors, small groups can mix *antipasti* and *primi piatti* family-style (skipping *secondi*). If you do this right (e.g., under-ordering because courses are often bigger than necessary), you can eat well in better places for less than the cost of a tourist *menù* in a cheap place.

Ordering Tips

Seafood and steak may be sold by weight (priced by the kilo—1,000 grams, or just over two pounds; or by the *etto*—100 grams). The abbreviation *s.q. (secondo quantità)* means an item is priced "according to quantity." Unless the menu indicates a fillet *(filetto),* fish is usually served whole, with the head and tail. However, you can always ask your waiter to select a small fish for you. Sometimes, especially for steak, restaurants require a minimum order of four or five *etti* (which diners can share). Make sure you're really clear on the price before ordering.

Some special dishes come in larger quantities meant to be shared by two people. The shorthand way of showing this on a menu is "X2" (for two), but the price listed generally indicates the cost per person.

In a traditional restaurant, if you order a pasta dish and a side salad—but no main course—the waiter will bring the salad after the pasta (Italians prefer it this way, believing that it enhances digestion). If you want the salad with your pasta, specify *insieme* (een-see-YEH-meh, "together"). At eateries more accustomed to tourists, you may be asked when you want the salad.

Because pasta and bread are both starches, Italians consider them redundant. If you order only a pasta dish, bread may not come with it; you can request it, but you may be charged extra. On the other hand, if you order a vegetable antipasto or a meat *secondo*, bread is often provided to balance the ingredients.

At places with counter service—such as at a bar or a freeway rest-stop diner—you'll order and pay at the *cassa* (cashier). Take your receipt over to the counter to claim your food.

Fixed-Price Meals

You can save by getting a fixed-priced meal, which is frequently exempt from cover and service charges. Avoid the cheapest ones (often called a *menù turistico*), which tend to be bland and heavy, pairing a very basic pasta with reheated schnitzel and roast meats. Look instead for a genuine *menù del giorno* (menu of the day), which offers diners a choice of appetizer, main course, and dessert. It's worth paying a little more for an inventive fixed-price meal that shows off the chef's creativity.

While fixed-price meals can be easy and convenient, galloping gourmets order à la carte with the help of a menu translator. (The *Rick Steves' Italian Phrase Book & Dictionary* has a menu decoder with plenty of useful phrases.) When going to an especially good restaurant with an approachable staff, I like to find out what they're eager to serve, or I'll simply say, *"Mi faccia felice"* (Make me happy) and set a price limit.

BUDGET EATING

Italy offers many budget options for hungry travelers, but beware of cheap eateries that sport big color photos of pizza and piles of different pastas. They have no kitchens and simply microwave disgusting prepackaged food.

Self-service cafeterias offer the basics without add-on charges. Those on a hard-core budget equip their room with a pantry stocked at the market (fruits and veggies are remarkably cheap) or pick up a sandwich or *döner kebab* (rotisserie meat wrapped in pita bread), then dine in at picnic prices. Bars and cafés, described later, are another good place to grab a meal on the go.

Pizzerias

Pizza is cheap and readily available. Stop by a pizza shop for standup or takeout pizza (*pizza al taglio* means "by the slice"). Some shops sell individual slices of round, Naples-style pizza, while others feature *pizza rustica*—thick pizza baked in a large rectangular pan and sold by weight. If you simply ask for a piece, you may wind up with a gigantic slab and be charged top euro. Instead, clearly indicate how much you want: 100 grams, or *un etto,* is a hot and cheap snack; 200 grams, or *due etti,* makes a light meal. Or show the size with your hands—*tanto così* (TAHN-toh koh-ZEE) means "this much."

Key pizza vocabulary: *capricciosa* (literally the "chef's caprice," generally prosciutto, mushrooms, olives, and artichokes), *funghi* (mushrooms), *marinara* (tomato sauce, oregano, garlic, no cheese), *napoletana* (mozzarella, anchovies, and tomato sauce), *vegetariana* or *ortolana* ("greengrocer-style," with vegetables), *quattro formaggi* (four different cheeses), and *quattro stagioni* (different toppings on each of the four quarters, for those who can't choose just one menu item). If you ask for pepperoni on your pizza, you'll get *peperoni* (green or red peppers, not sausage); request *diavola* or *salsiccia piccante* instead (the closest thing in Italy to American pepperoni). Kids like the bland *margherita* (tomato sauce, mozzarella, and basil—the red, white, and green of the Italian flag). *Pizza bianca* (or *pizza ciaccina*) is "white" pizza, with no tomatoes.

Bars/Cafés

Italian "bars" are not taverns, but inexpensive cafés. These neighborhood hangouts serve coffee, mini-pizzas, premade sandwiches, and drinks from the cooler. Many dish up plates of fried cheese and vegetables from under the glass counter, ready to reheat. This budget choice is the Italian equivalent of English pub grub.

Food: For quick meals, bars usually have trays of cheap, premade sandwiches (*panini,* on a baguette; *piadini,* on flatbread; or *tramezzini,* on crustless white bread)—some are delightful grilled. (Others have too much mayo.) To save time for sightseeing and room for dinner, stop by a bar for a light lunch, such as a ham-and-cheese sandwich (called *toast*); have it grilled twice if you want it really hot. To get food "to go," say, "*da portar via*" (for the road). Many bars are small—if you can't find a table, you'll need to stand up or find a ledge to sit on outside. Most charge extra for table service (see next). All bars have a WC *(toilette, bagno)* in the back, and customers—and the discreet public—can use it.

Prices and Paying: You'll notice a two- or three-tiered pricing system. Drinking a cup of coffee while standing at the bar is cheaper than drinking it at an indoor table (you'll pay still more at an outdoor table). Many places have a *lista dei prezzi* (price list) with two columns—*al bar* and *al tavolo* (table)—posted somewhere

Pasta, Pasta!

Italy is famous for its cuisine, but above all, it's known for pasta. Each of the more than 600 varieties of Italian pasta has a reason for being—usually as the perfect platform for highlighting the sauce, meat, or regional ingredients of a particular dish. While we think of pasta as a main dish, in Italy it's considered a *primo piatto*—first course. Italian pasta falls into two broad categories: long and short.

Long pasta *(pasta lunga)* is long enough to twist around a fork. Aside from the universally familiar spaghetti, you'll find *capellini* (thin "little hairs"), *vermicelli* (slightly thicker "little worms"), and long, hollow *bucatini.* Flattened versions of *pasta lunga* include *linguine* (narrow "little tongues"), *fettuccine* (wider "small ribbons"), *tagliatelle* (even wider), and *pappardelle* (very wide, best with meat sauces).

Short pasta *(pasta corta)* can be speared or scooped with a fork. The most common *pasta corta* are short tubes, such as *penne, rigatoni, ziti, manicotti,* and *cannelloni;* they come either *lisce* (smooth) or *rigate* (grooved—better to catch and cling to sauce). Many short pastas are named for their unique shapes: *conchiglie* (shells), *farfalle* (butterflies), *cavatappi* (corkscrews), *ditali* (thimbles), *gomiti* ("elbow" macaroni), *lumache* (snails), *marziani* (spirals resembling "Martian" antennae), and even *strozzapreti* (priest stranglers)...to name just a few.

The short pastas are almost always made fresh and often are designed to be filled *(ripieni).* Aside from the familiar ravioli and tortellini, this category includes *gnocchi* (shell-shaped, hand-rolled dumplings usually made from potatoes), *tortelli* (C-shaped, stuffed ravioli), and *agnolotti* or *mezzelune* (stuffed pasta shaped like "priest's hats" or "half-moons").

Most types of pasta can come in slight variations: If it's a bit thicker, *-one* is added to the end; if it's a bit thinner, *-ine, -ette,* or *-elle* is added. *Tortellini* are smaller *tortelli,* while *tortelloni* are bigger.

by the bar or cash register. If you're on a budget, don't sit down without first checking out the financial consequences. Ask, "Same price if I sit or stand?" by saying, *"Costa uguale al tavolo o al banco?"* (KOH-stah oo-GWAH-lay ahl TAH-voh-loh oh ahl BAHN-koh). Throughout Italy, you can get cheap coffee at the bar of any establishment, no matter how fancy, and pay the same low, government-regulated price (generally less than a euro if you stand).

If the bar isn't busy, you can probably just order and pay when you leave. Otherwise: 1) Decide what you want; 2) find out the price by checking the price list on the wall, the prices posted near the food, or by asking the barista; 3) pay the cashier; and 4) give the

As for what to put on that pasta, the options are almost as endless as the shapes. The following terms are usually preceded by *alla* (in the style of) or *in* (in):

aglio e olio: garlic and olive oil
alfredo: butter, cream, and parmesan
amatriciana: pork cheek, pecorino cheese, and tomato
arrabbiata: "angry," spicy tomato sauce with chili peppers
bolognese: meat and tomato sauce
boscaiola: mushrooms and sausage
burro e salvia: butter and sage
cacio e pepe: parmigiano cheese and ground pepper
carbonara: bacon, egg, cheese, and pepper
carrettiera: spicy and garlicky, with olive oil and little tomatoes
diavola: "devil-style," spicy hot
frutti di mare: seafood
funghi: mushrooms
genovese: pesto (basil ground with parmigiano cheese, garlic, pine nuts, and olive oil)
gricia: cured pork and pecorino romano cheese
marinara: usually tomato, often with garlic and onions, but can be a seafood sauce ("sailor's style")
norma: tomato, eggplant, and ricotta cheese
pajata (or ***pagliata***): calf intestines
pescatora: seafood ("fisherman-style")
pomodoro: tomato only
puttanesca: "harlot-style" tomato sauce with anchovies, olives, and capers
ragù: meaty tomato sauce
scoglio: mussels, clams, and tomatoes
sorrentina: "Sorrento-style," with tomatoes, basil, and mozzarella (usually over gnocchi)
sugo di lepre: rich sauce made of wild hare
tartufi (or ***tartufate***): truffles
umbria: sauce of anchovies, garlic, tomatoes, and truffles
vongole: clams and spices

receipt to the barista (whose clean fingers handle no dirty euros) and tell him or her what you want.

For more on drinking, see "Beverages," later.

Ethnic Food

A good bet for a cheap, hot meal is a *döner kebab.* Look for little hole-in-the-wall kebab shops, where you can get a hearty, meaty takeaway dinner wrapped in pita bread for €3.50. Pay an extra euro to super-size it, and it'll feed two. Asian restaurants, although not as common as in northern Europe and usually serving only Chinese dishes, can also be a good value.

Rosticcerie

For a fast and cheap lunch, find an Italian variation on the corner deli: a *rosticceria* (specializing in roasted meats and accompanying *antipasti*). For a healthy light meal, ask for a mixed plate of vegetables with a hunk of mozzarella (*piatto misto di verdure con mozzarella;* pee-AH-toh MEE-stoh dee vehr-DOO-ray). Don't be limited by what's displayed. If you'd like a salad with a slice of cantaloupe and a hunk of cheese, they'll whip that up for you in a snap. Belly up to the bar and, with a pointing finger, you can assemble a fine meal. If something's a mystery, ask for *un assaggio* (oon ah-SAH-joh) to get a little taste. To have your choices warmed up, ask for them to be heated (*scaldare;* skahl-DAH-ray).

Wine Bars

Wine bars *(enoteche)* are a popular, fast option for lunch. Surrounded by the office crowd, you can get a fancy salad, a plate of meats and cheeses, and a glass of fine wine (see blackboards for the day's selection and price per glass—and go for the top end). A good *enoteca* aims to impress visitors with its wine, and will generally choose excellent-quality ingredients for the simple dishes it offers with the wine (though the prices add up—be careful with your ordering to keep this a budget choice).

Aperitivo Buffets

The Italian term *aperitivo* means a pre-dinner drink (specific drinks described later), but it's also used to describe their version of what we might call "happy hour": a light buffet that many bars serve to customers during the pre-dinner hours (typically around 19:00-21:00). The drink itself may not be cheap (typically €8-15), but bars lay out an enticing array of meats, cheeses, grilled vegetables, and other *antipasti*-type dishes, and you're welcome to nibble to your heart's content while you nurse your drink. Though it's intended as an appetizer course before heading out for a full dinner, light eaters could discreetly turn this into a small meal. If this interests you, drop by a few bars around this time of day to scope out their buffets before choosing.

Groceries and Delis

Another budget option is to drop by an *alimentari* (neighborhood grocery) or *salumeria* (delicatessen) to pick up some cold cuts, cheeses, and other supplies for a picnic. Some *salumerie,* and any *paninoteca* or *foccaceria* (sandwich shop), can make you a sandwich to order. Just point to what you want, and they'll stuff it into a *panino* (baguette); if you want it heated, remember the word *scaldare* (skahl-DAH-ray).

To get a sampler plate of cold cuts and cheeses in a restaurant, ask for *affettato misto* (mixed cold cuts), *antipasto misto* (cold cuts, cheeses, and marinated vegetables), or—in Tuscany—*tagliere* (a sampler "board"). If ordering an assortment, some unscrupulous shops may try to pad the bill by pushing their most expensive ingredients. Be clear on what you want: *un tagliere da* [fill in price] *euro, per favore* (a sampler board—tahl-yee-eh-ray—for ___ euros, please).

Salumi ("salted" meats), also called *affettati* ("cut" meats), are an Italian staple. While most American cold cuts are cooked, in Italy they're far more commonly cured by air-drying, salting, and smoking. (Don't worry; these so-called "raw" meats are safe to eat and very flavorful.)

The two most familiar types of *salumi* are *salame* and prosciutto. ***Salame*** is an air-dried, sometimes spicy sausage that comes in many varieties, including *finocchiona* (with fennel seeds), *salame piccante* (spicy hot, similar to pepperoni), and *salame di Sant'Olcese* (what we'd call "Genoa salami"). When Italians say ***prosciutto,*** they usually mean *prosciutto crudo*—the "raw" ham that air-cures on the hock and is then thinly sliced. Produced mainly in the north of Italy, prosciutto can be either *dolce* (sweet) or *salato* (salty). Purists say the best is *prosciutto di Parma.*

Other *salumi* may be less familiar. Air-cured pork variations include *culatello* (prosciutto made with only the finest cuts of meat), *capocollo* (or *coppa*; peppery pork shoulder), *speck* (smoked pork shoulder), *guanciale* (tender pork cheek), and *lonzino* (cured pork loin). *Pancetta*—which can be eaten raw or added to cooked dishes—is salt-cured, peppery pork belly meat (similar to bacon). *Mortadella,* a finely ground pork loaf, is similar to our baloney, and *bresaola* is air-cured beef. But look out for *testa in cassetta* (headcheese—organs in aspic) and *sopressata* (in other parts of Italy, this is a spicy salame—but in Tuscany, it's often headcheese).

As for ***formaggio*** (cheese), you're probably already familiar with several Italian favorites: *asiago* (hard cow cheese that comes either *mezzano*—young, firm, and creamy; or *stravecchio*—aged, pungent, and granular); *fontina* (semi-hard, nutty, Gruyère-style mountain cheese); *gorgonzola* (pungent, blue-veined cheese, either *dolce*—creamy, or *stagionato*—aged and hard); *mascarpone* (sweet, buttery, spreadable dessert cheese); *parmigiano-reggiano* (hard, crumbly, sharp, aged cow cheese with more nuanced flavor than American "parmesan"; *grana padano* is a less expensive variation); *pecorino* (either *fresco*—fresh, soft, and mild; or *stagionato*—aged and sharp, sometimes called *pecorino romano*); *provolone* (rich, firm, aged cow cheese), *ricotta* (soft, airy cheese made by "recooking" leftover whey), and, of course, mozzarella. The best mozzarella is *mozzarella di bufala,* made from the milk of water buffaloes; other variations include *burrata* (a creamy mozzarella) and *scamorza* (similar to mozzarella, but often smoked).

Picnic Tips

Picnicking saves lots of euros and is a great way to sample regional specialties. A typical picnic for two might be fresh rolls, 100 grams (*un etto*, EH-toh, plural *etti*, EH-tee—about a quarter pound) of cheese, 100 grams of meat (sometimes ordered by the slice—*fetta*—or piece—*pezzi;* for two people, I might get *cinque pezzi*—five pieces—of prosciutto). Add two tomatoes, three carrots, two apples, yogurt, and a liter box of juice. Total cost: about €10.

In the process of assembling your meal, you get to deal with the Italians in the market scene. For a colorful experience, gather your ingredients in the morning at a produce market (Florence's main one is the Mercato Centrale, near the Church of San Lorenzo); you'll probably need to hit several market stalls to put together a complete meal (note that many stalls close in the early afternoon). While it's fun to visit the small specialty shops, an *alimentari* is your one-stop corner grocery store (most will slice and stuff your sandwich for you if you buy the ingredients there). The rare *supermercato* (look for the Conad, Despar, and Co-op chains) gives you more efficiency with less color for less cost. At busier supermarkets you'll need to take a number for deli service.

Juice lovers can get a liter of O.J. for the price of a Coke or coffee. Look for "100% *succo*" (juice) on the label—or be surprised by something diluted and sugary sweet. Hang on to the half-liter mineral-water bottles (sold everywhere for about €1). Buy juice in cheap liter boxes, then drink some and store the extra in your water bottle. (I refill my water bottle with tap water—*acqua del rubinetto.*)

Picnics can be an adventure in high cuisine. Be daring. Try the fresh mozzarella, *presto* pesto, shriveled olives, and any UFOs the locals are excited about. If ordering *antipasti* (such as grilled or marinated veggies) at a deli counter, you can ask for *una porzione* in a plastic takeaway container *(contenitore)*. Use gestures to show exactly how much you want. The word *basta* (BAH-stah)—"enough"—works as a question or as a statement.

Shopkeepers are happy to sell small quantities of produce, but it's customary to let the merchant choose for you. Say *"per oggi"* (pehr OH-jee; "for today") and he or she will grab you something ready to eat. To avoid being overcharged, know the cost per kilo and study the weighing procedure as if you're doing the arithmetic.

GELATO

Gelato is an edible art form—and it's one souvenir that can't break and won't clutter your luggage. While American ice cream is made with cream and has a high butterfat content, Italian gelato is made

with milk. It's also churned more slowly, making it denser. Connoisseurs believe that because gelato has less air and less fat (which coats the mouth and blocks the taste buds), it's more flavorful than American-style ice cream.

Stop by a *gelateria* and survey your options. A key to gelato appreciation is sampling liberally and choosing flavors that go well together. Ask, as Italians do, for *"Un assaggio, per favore?"* (A taste, please?; oon ah-SAH-joh pehr fah-VOH-ray) and *"Quali gusti stanno bene insieme?"* (What flavors go well together?; KWAH-lee GOO-stee STAH-noh BEH-nay een-see-EH-may).

Most *gelaterie* clearly display prices and sizes. In the textbook *gelateria* scam, the tourist orders two or three flavors—and the clerk selects a fancy, expensive chocolate-coated waffle cone, piles it high with huge scoops, and cheerfully charges the tourist €10. To avoid rip-offs, point to the price or say what you want: *"Una coppetta da tre euro"* (OO-nah ko-PEH-tah dah tray eh-OO-roh; a €3 cup).

Not all *gelaterie* are created equal. The best ones display signs reading *artiginale, nostra produzione,* or *produzione propia,* meaning the gelato is made on the premises. Seasonal flavors are also a good sign. Gelato stored in covered metal tins (rather than white plastic) is more likely to be homemade. Gelato aficionados avoid colors that don't appear in nature; for fewer chemicals and real flavor, go for mellow hues.

Gourmet gelato shops are popping up all over Italy, selling expensive, exotic flavors. A chain called Grom is comparable to Ben & Jerry's in the US. But even regular shops offer many fun flavors.

Most *gelaterie* label each tub with the flavor (in Italian and, often, in English) and, sometimes, a little picture to help identify it. Aside from the typical *crema* (vanilla), *cioccolato* (chocolate), and *fragola* (strawberry), here are a few flavors worth trying: After Eight (chocolate and mint), *bacio* (chocolate hazelnut, named for Italy's popular "kiss" candies), *croccantino* ("crunchy," with toasted peanut bits), *cassata* (with dried fruits), *fior di latte* (sweet milk), *macedonia* (mixed fruits), *riso* (with actual bits of rice mixed in), *malaga* (similar to rum raisin), *tartufo* (super chocolate), *zabaione* (named for the egg yolk and Marsala wine dessert), *zuppa inglese* (sponge cake, custard, chocolate, and cream), and the popular *stracciatella* (vanilla with chocolate chips). Flavors named Snickers, Lion, and Bounty resemble their namesake candy bars.

Gelato variations or alternatives include *sorbetto* (sorbet—made with fruit, but no milk or eggs); *granita* or *grattachecca* (a cup of slushy ice with flavored syrup); and *cremolata* (a gelato-*granita* float).

BEVERAGES

Italian bars serve great drinks—hot, cold, sweet, caffeinated, or alcoholic. Chilled bottled water, still *(naturale)* or carbonated *(frizzante),* is sold cheap in stores. Coffee and wine—two Italian specialties—are covered in greater depth later.

Juice: *Spremuta* means freshly squeezed, as far as *succo* (fruit juice) is concerned (order *una spremuta*—don't confuse it with *spumante*, sparkling wine). It's usually orange juice *(arancia),* and from February through April it's almost always made from blood oranges *(arance rosse).*

Beer: While Italy is traditionally considered wine country, in recent years there's been a huge and passionate growth in the production of craft beer *(birra artigianale).* Even in small towns, you'll see microbreweries slinging their own brews. You'll also find local brews (Peroni and Moretti), as well as imports such as Heineken. Beer on tap is *alla spina*. Get it *piccola* (33 cl, 11 oz), *media* (50 cl, about a pint), or *grande* (a liter). Italians drink mainly lager beers. A *lattina* (lah-TEE-nah) is a can and a *bottiglia* (boh-TEEL-yah) is a bottle.

Cocktails and Spirits: Italians appreciate both *aperitivi* (palate-stimulating cocktails) and *digestivi* (after-dinner drinks designed to aid digestion). Popular ***aperitivo*** options include Campari (dark-colored bitters with herbs and orange peel), Americano (vermouth with bitters, brandy, and lemon peel), Cynar (bitters flavored with artichoke), and Punt e Mes (sweet red vermouth and red wine). Widely used vermouth brands include Cinzano and Martini. ***Digestivo*** choices are usually either a strong herbal bitters or something sweet. Many restaurants have their own secret recipe for a bittersweet herbal brew called *amaro*; popular commercial brands are Fernet Branca and Montenegro. If your tastes run sweeter, try *amaretto* (almond-flavored liqueur), Frangelico (hazelnut liqueur), *limoncello* (lemon liqueur), *nocino* (dark, sweet walnut liqueur), and *sambuca* (syrupy, anise-flavored liqueur; *con moscha* adds "flies"—three coffee beans). *Grappa* is a brandy distilled from grape skins and stems; *stravecchio* is an aged, mellower variation.

Coffee and Other Hot Drinks

The espresso-based style of coffee so popular in the US was born in Italy. If you ask for *"un caffè,"* you'll get a shot of espresso in a little cup—the closest thing to American-style drip coffee is a *caffè americano.* Most Italian coffee drinks begin with espresso, to which is added varying amounts of hot water and/or steamed or foamed milk. Milky drinks, like cappuccino or *caffè latte,* are served to locals before noon and to tourists any time of day (to an Italian, cappuccino is a morning drink; they believe having milk after a big meal or anything with tomato sauce impairs digestion). If they add any milk after lunch, it's just a splash, in a *macchiato* (mah-kee-AH-toh). Italians like their coffee only warm—to get it very hot, request *"Molto caldo, per favore"* (MOHL-toh KAHL-doh pehr fah-VOH-ray). Any coffee drink is available decaffeinated—ask for it *decaffeinato:* deh-kah-feh-ee-NAH-toh.

Experiment with a few of the options:

- ***Cappuccino:*** Espresso with foamed milk on top
- ***Caffè latte:*** Espresso mixed with hot milk, no foam, in a tall glass (ordering just a "latte" gets you only milk)
- ***Caffè macchiato:*** Espresso "marked" with just a splash of milk, in a small cup
- ***Latte macchiato:*** Layers of hot milk and foam, "marked" by an espresso shot, in a tall glass
- ***Caffè corto/lungo:*** Concentrated espresso diluted with a tiny bit of hot water, in a small cup
- ***Caffè americano:*** Espresso diluted with even more hot water, in a larger cup
- ***Caffè corretto:*** Espresso "corrected" with a shot of liqueur (normally grappa, amaro, or Sambuca)
- ***Marocchino:*** "Moroccan" coffee with espresso, foamed milk, and cocoa powder; the similar *mocaccino* has chocolate instead of cocoa
- ***Caffè freddo:*** Sweet and iced espresso
- ***Cappuccino freddo:*** Iced cappuccino
- ***Caffè hag:*** Instant decaf

Notice that there's a big difference between *caffè macchiato* and *latte macchiato*. If you order simply a "*macchiato*," you'll probably get the coffee version...and have to get your milk fix elsewhere.

More Hot Drinks: *Cioccolato* is hot chocolate. *Tè* is hot tea. *Tè freddo* (iced tea) is usually from a can—sweetened and flavored with lemon or peach.

Wine

The ancient Greeks who colonized Italy more than 2,000 years ago called it Oenotria—land of the grape. Centuries later, Galileo wrote, "Wine is light held together by water." Wine *(vino)* is certainly a part of the Italian culinary trinity—grape, olive, and wheat. (I'd add gelato, too.) Ideal conditions for grapes (warm climate, well-draining soil, and an abundance of hillsides) make the Italian peninsula a paradise for grape growers, winemakers, and wine drinkers. Italy makes and consumes more wine per capita than any other country. For regional wines produced in Tuscany, see "Top Local Wines," later.

Describing Wine in Italian

dry	*secco*	SEH-koh
sweet	*dolce*	DOHL-chay
earthy	*terroso*	teh-ROH-zoh
tannic	*tannico*	TAH-nee-koh
young	*giovane*	JOH-vah-nay
mature	*maturo*	mah-TOO-roh
sparkling	*spumante / frizzante*	spoo-MAHN-tay / freed-ZAHN-tay
fruity	*fruttato*	froo-TAH-toh
full-bodied	*corposo / pieno*	kor-POH-zoh / pee-EH-noh
elegant	*elegante*	eh-leh-GAHN-tay

To order a glass (*bicchiere;* bee-kee-EH-ree) of red *(rosso)* or white *(bianco)* wine, say, "*Un bicchiere di vino rosso/bianco.*" *Corposo* means full-bodied. House wine *(vino della casa)* comes in a carafe; choose from a quarter-liter pitcher (8.5 oz, *un quarto*), half-liter pitcher (17 oz, *un mezzo*), or one-liter pitcher (34 oz, *un litro*).

Wine Labels and Lingo

Even if you're clueless about wine, the information on an Italian wine label can help you choose something decent. Terms you may see on the bottle include *classico* (from a defined, select area), *annata* (year of harvest), *vendemmia* (harvest), and *imbottigliato dal produttore all'origine* (bottled by producers). To figure out what you like—and what suits your pocketbook—visit an *enoteca* (wine bar) and sample wines side-by-side.

In general, Italy designates its wines by one of four official categories:

Vino da Tavola (VDT) is table wine, the lowest grade, made from grapes grown anywhere in Italy. It's inexpensive, but Italy's wines are so good that, for many people, a basic *vino da tavola* is just fine with a meal. Many restaurants, even modest ones, take pride in their house wine *(vino della casa)*, bottling their own or working with wineries.

Denominazione di Origine Controllata (DOC) meets national standards for high-quality wine. Made from grapes grown in a defined area, it's usually quite affordable and can be surprisingly good. Hundreds of wines have earned the DOC designation. In

Tuscany, for example, many such wines come from the Chianti region, located between Florence and Siena.

Denominazione di Origine Controllata e Guarantita (DOCG), the highest grade, meets national standards for the highest-quality wine (made with grapes from a defined area whose quality is "guaranteed"). These wines can be identified by the pink or green label on the neck...and the scary price tag on the shelf. Only a limited number of wines in Italy can be called DOCG. They're generally a good bet if you want a quality wine, but you don't know anything else about the winemaker. (*Riserva* indicates a DOC or DOCG wine matured for a longer, more specific time.)

Indicazione Geographica Tipica (IGT) is a broad group of wines that range from basic to some of Italy's best. These wines don't follow the strict "recipe" required for DOC or DOCG status, but give local vintners creative license. This category includes the Super Tuscans—wines made from a mix of international grapes (such as cabernet sauvignon) grown in Tuscany and aged in small oak barrels for only two years. The result is a lively full-bodied wine that dances all over your head...and is worth the steep price for aficionados.

Florentine and Tuscan Cuisine

While many restaurants in Florence and Tuscany serve your basic Italian fare—pasta and pizza, veal cutlets, and mixed salad—you can find a few specialties without looking too hard. In general, the cuisine of this region is hearty, simple farmers' food: grilled meats, high-quality seasonal vegetables, fresh herbs, prized olive oil, and rustic bread. By the way, there's nothing wrong with your *pane alla toscana* (Tuscan bread)—it's supposed to taste like that. Tuscan bread is unsalted (from the days when salt's preservative powers made it more valuable than gold) and nearly flavorless. Tuscans turn it into a basic appetizer by drenching it in olive oil and sprinkling it with salt.

Here are some typical foods you'll encounter throughout Tuscany:

ANTIPASTI

Bruschetta: Toasted bread brushed with olive oil and rubbed with garlic, topped with chopped tomato, mushrooms, or whatever else sounds good.

Crostini: Small toasted bread rounds topped with meat or vegetable pastes. *Alla toscana* generally means with chicken liver paste.

Panzanella: A simple summer salad, made of day-old bread with chopped tomatoes, onion, and basil, tossed in a light vinaigrette.

Pecorino cheese: Fresh *(fresco)* or aged *(stagionato)*, from ewe's milk.

Porcini mushrooms: Harvested in the fall and used in pasta and soups.

Salumi: Cold cuts, usually air- or salt-dried pork. Some popular kinds are prosciutto (air-cured ham hock), *pancetta* (cured pork belly), *lardo* (cured pork lard) and *finocchiona* (fennel salami). For a list of other *salumi*, see page 651.

Tagliere: A wooden platter with a sampling of cold cuts.

PRIMO PIATTO

Pappardelle al sugo di lepre: A long, broad noodle served with a rich sauce made from wild hare.

Pici al ragù: A fat, spaghetti-like hand-rolled pasta served with a meat-tomato sauce.

Ribollita: "Reboiled" soup, traditionally made with leftovers including white beans *(fagioli)*, seasonal vegetables, and olive oil, with layers of day-old Tuscan bread slices.

Zuppa alla volterrana: "Volterra-style" soup, similar to *ribollita* but with fresh bread.

Pappa al pomodoro: Thick stew of tomatoes, olive oil, and bread.

Carabaccia: Onion soup.

SECONDO PIATTO

Arrosto misto: An assortment of roasted meats, sometimes served on a skewer *(spiedino)*.

Bistecca alla fiorentina: A thick T-bone steak, generally grilled very rare and lightly seasoned. (The best—and most expensive—is from the white Chianina breed of cattle you'll see grazing throughout Tuscany.) This dish is often sold by weight (per *etto*, or 100 grams).

Cinghiale: Wild boar, served grilled or in soups, stews, and pasta. It is also made into many varieties of sausage and salami.

Fegatelli: Liver meatballs.

Game birds: Squab *(piccione)*, pheasant *(fagiano)*, and guinea hen *(faraona)* are popular.

Trippa alla fiorentina: Tripe (intestines) and vegetables sautéed in a tomato sauce, sometimes baked with parmesan cheese. *Trippa* (and the similar *lampredotto*) are also popular in sandwiches; see page 290.

...alla fiorentina* or *alla toscana: Anything cooked in the "Florentine" or "Tuscan" style. Usually these phrases describe a rustic preparation highlighting local products, but in practice they can mean almost anything.

DOLCI

Gelato: The Florentines claim they invented Italian-style ice cream. Many think they serve some of the world's best. Rather than order dessert in a restaurant, I like to stroll with a cup or cone of gelato from a popular *gelateria.* For more on gelato, see 652, and for tips on enjoying it here, see page 302.

Cantucci: Florentines love to end a meal by dipping this crunchy almond cookie in Vin Santo (literally "holy wine"), a sweet, golden dessert wine.

Panforte: Dense, dark, clove-and-cinnamon-spiced cake from Siena. Panforte makes a good, enduring gift.

TOP LOCAL WINES

The region of Tuscany produces some of the most famous and tastiest wines in Italy. Many Tuscan wines are made with sangiovese ("blood of Jupiter") grapes. But the characteristics of the soil, temperature, and exposure make each wine unique to its area. Even if you don't often drink wine, try some here.

Brunello di Montalcino: One of Italy's top reds, this full-bodied wine comes from the slopes of Montalcino, south of Siena. Smooth and dry, it's aged at least four years in wood and pairs well with hearty, meaty food.

Rosso di Montalcino: This cheaper, younger "baby Brunello," also made in Montalcino, lacks Brunello's depth of flavor and complexity—but it's still a great wine at a bargain price.

Chianti: This hearty red from the Chianti region (20 miles south of Florence) is world famous. Varieties range from cheap, acidic basket-bottles of table wine (called *fiaschi*) to the hearty Chianti Classico.

Vino Nobile di Montepulciano: This high-quality, ruby red, dry wine pairs well with meat, especially chicken.

Super Tuscans: This newer breed of Italian wine blends traditional grapes with locally grown non-Italian grapes (such as cabernet or merlot).

Vernaccia di San Gimignano: This medium-dry white is a decent choice and goes well with pasta and salad. Trebbiano and vermentino are two other local white grapes.

Vin Santo: Sweet and syrupy, this "holy" dessert wine is often served with a cookie for dipping.

Communicating

"How can I stay connected in Europe?"—by phone and Internet—may be the most common question I hear from travelers. You have three basic options:

1. "Roam" with your US smartphone. This is the easiest option, but likely the most expensive. It works best for people who won't be making very many calls, and who value the convenience of sticking with what's familiar (and their own phone number). In recent years, as data roaming fees have dropped and free Wi-Fi has become easier to find, the majority of travelers are finding this to be the best all-around option.

2. Use an unlocked mobile phone with European SIM cards. This is a much more affordable option if you'll be making lots of calls, since it gives you 24/7 access to cheap European rates. Although remarkably cheap, this option does require a willingness to grapple with the technology and do a bit of shopping around for the right phone and card. Savvy travelers who routinely use SIM cards swear by them.

3. Use public phones and get online at your hotel or at Internet cafés. These options can work in a pinch, particularly for travelers who simply don't want to hassle with the technology, or want to be (mostly) untethered from their home life while on the road.

Each of these options is explained in greater detail in the following pages. Mixing and matching works well. For example, I routinely bring along my smartphone for Internet chores and Skyping on Wi-Fi, but also carry an unlocked phone and buy cheap SIM cards for affordable calls on the go.

For an even more in-depth explanation of this complicated topic, see www.ricksteves.com/phoning.

HOW TO DIAL

Many Americans are intimidated by dialing European phone numbers. You needn't be. It's simple, once you break the code.

Dialing Within Italy

The following instructions apply whether you're dialing from an Italian mobile phone or a landline (such as a pay phone or your hotel-room phone). If you're roaming with a US phone number, follow the "Dialing Internationally" directions described later.

Italy has a direct-dial phone system (no area codes). To call anywhere within Italy, just dial the number. For example, the number of one of my recommended Florence hotels is 055-289-592. That's the number you dial whether you're calling it from Florence's train station or from Milan.

Hurdling the Language Barrier

Many Italians—especially those in the tourist trade and in big cities such as Florence—speak English. Still, you'll get better treatment if you learn and use Italian pleasantries. In smaller, non-touristy towns, Italian is the norm. Italians have an endearing habit of talking to you even if they know you don't speak their language—and yet, thanks to gestures and thoughtfully simplified words, it somehow works. Don't stop them to tell them you don't understand every word—just go along for the ride. For a list of survival phrases, see page 703.

Note that Italian is pronounced much like English, with a few exceptions, such as: *c* followed by *e* or *i* is pronounced ch (to ask, *"Per centro?"*—To the center?—you say, pehr CHEHN-troh). In Italian, *ch* is pronounced like the hard c in Chianti (*chiesa*—church—is pronounced kee-AY-zah). Give it your best shot. Italians appreciate your efforts.

Italy's land lines start with 0 and mobile lines start with 3. The country's toll-free lines begin with 80. These 80 numbers—called *freephone* or *numero verde* (green number)—can be dialed free from any phone without using a phone card. Note that you can't call Italy's toll-free numbers from the US, nor can you count on reaching American toll-free numbers from Italy. Any Italian phone number that starts with 8 but isn't followed by a 0 is a toll call, generally costing €0.10-0.50 per minute.

Dialing Internationally to or from Italy

Always start with the **international access code**—011 if you're calling from the US or Canada, 00 from anywhere in Europe. If you're dialing from a mobile phone, simply insert a + instead (by holding the 0 key).

• Dial the **country code** of the country you're calling (39 for Italy, or 1 for the US or Canada).

• Then dial the **local number.** Note that in most European countries, you have to drop the zero at the beginning of the local number—but in Italy, you dial it. The European calling chart lists specifics per country.

Calling from the US to Italy: To call the Florence hotel from the US, dial 011 (US access code), 39 (Italy's country code), then 055-289-592.

Calling from any European country to the US: To call my office in Edmonds, Washington, from anywhere in Europe, I dial 00 (Europe's access code), 1 (US country code), 425 (Edmonds' area code), and 771-8303.

More Dialing Tips

The chart on page 664 shows how to dial per country. For online instructions, see www.countrycallingcodes.com or www.howtocallabroad.com.

Remember, if you're using a mobile phone, dial as if you're in that phone's country of origin. So, when roaming with your US phone number in Italy, dial as if you're calling from the US. But if you're using a European SIM card, dial as you would from that European country.

Note that calls to a European mobile phone are substantially more expensive than calls to a fixed line. Off-hour calls are generally cheaper.

In Italy, phone numbers can have varying lengths. For instance, a hotel might have a seven-digit phone number and an eight-digit fax number.

For tips on communicating over the phone with someone who speaks another language, see sidebar on previous page.

USING YOUR AMERICAN SMARTPHONE IN EUROPE

Even in this age of email, texting, and near-universal Internet access, smart travelers still use the telephone. I call TIs to smooth out sightseeing plans, hotels to get driving directions, museums to confirm tour schedules, restaurants to check open hours or to book a table, and so on.

Most people enjoy the convenience of bringing their own smartphone. Horror stories about sky-high roaming fees are dated and exaggerated, and major service providers work hard to avoid surprising you with an exorbitant bill. With a little planning, you can use your phone—for voice calls, messaging, and Internet access—without breaking the bank.

Start by figuring out whether your phone works in Europe. Most phones purchased through AT&T and T-Mobile (which use the same technology as Europe) work abroad, while only some phones from Verizon or Sprint do—check your operating manual (look for "tri-band," "quad-band," or "GSM"). If you're not sure, ask your service provider.

Types of Roaming

"Roaming" with your phone—that is, using it outside of its home region, such as in Europe—generally comes with extra charges, whether you're making voice calls, sending texts, or reading your email. The fees listed here are for the three major American providers—Verizon, AT&T, and T-Mobile; Sprint's roaming rates tend to be much higher. But policies change fast, so get the latest details before your trip. For example, as of mid-2014, T-Mobile waived voice, texting, and data roaming fees for some plans.

Voice calls are the most expensive. Most providers charge from $1.29 to $1.99 per minute to make or receive calls in Europe. (As you cross each border, you'll typically get a text message explaining the rates in the new country.) If you plan to make multiple calls, look into a global calling plan to lower the per-minute cost, or buy a package of minutes at a discounted price (such as 30 minutes for $30). Note that you'll be charged for incoming calls whether or not you answer them; to save money ask your friends to stay in contact by texting, and to call you only in case of an emergency.

Text messaging costs 20 to 50 cents per text. To cut that cost, you could sign up for an international messaging plan (for example, $10 for 100 texts). Or consider apps that let you text for free (iMessage for Apple, Google Talk for Android, or WhatsApp for any device); however, these require you to use Wi-Fi or data roaming. Be aware that Europeans use the term "SMS" ("short message service") to describe text messaging.

Data roaming means accessing an Internet signal that's carried over the cellular telephone network. Prices have dropped dramatically in recent years, making this an affordable way to bridge gaps between Wi-Fi hotspots. You'll pay far less if you set up an international data roaming plan. Most providers charge $25-30 for 100-120 megabytes of data. That's plenty for basic Internet tasks—100 megabytes lets you view 100 websites or send/receive 1,000 text-based emails, but you'll burn through that amount quickly by streaming videos or music. If your data use exceeds your plan amount, most providers will automatically kick in an additional 100- or 120-megabyte block for the same price. (For more on Wi-Fi versus data roaming—including strategies for conserving your data—see "Using Wi-Fi and Data Roaming," later.)

Setting Up (or Disabling) International Service

With most service providers, international roaming (voice, text, and data) is disabled on your account unless you call to activate it. Before your trip, call your provider (or navigate their website), and cover the following topics:

- Confirm that your phone will work in Europe.
- Verify global roaming rates for voice calls, text messaging, and data roaming.
- Tell them which of those services you'd like to activate.
- Consider any add-on plans to bring down the cost of international calls, texts, or data roaming.

When you get home from Europe, be sure to cancel any add-on plans that you activated for your trip.

Some people would rather use their smartphone exclusively on Wi-Fi, and not worry about either voice or data charges. If that's you, call your provider to be sure that international roaming

European Calling Chart

Just smile and dial, using this key:
AC = Area Code, LN = Local Number.

European Country	Calling long distance within ...	Calling from the US or Canada to ...	Calling from a European country to ...
Austria	AC + LN	011 + 43 + AC (without initial zero) + LN	00 + 43 + AC (without initial zero) + LN
Belgium	LN	011 + 32 + LN (without initial zero)	00 + 32 + LN (without initial zero)
Bosnia-Herzegovina	AC + LN	011 + 387 + AC (without initial zero) + LN	00 + 387 + AC (without initial zero) + LN
Croatia	AC + LN	011 + 385 + AC (without initial zero) + LN	00 + 385 + AC (without initial zero) + LN
Czech Republic	LN	011 + 420 + LN	00 + 420 + LN
Denmark	LN	011 + 45 + LN	00 + 45 + LN
Estonia	LN	011 + 372 + LN	00 + 372 + LN
Finland	AC + LN	011 + 358 + AC (without initial zero) + LN	999 (or other 900 number) + 358 + AC (without initial zero) + LN
France	LN	011 + 33 + LN (without initial zero)	00 + 33 + LN (without initial zero)
Germany	AC + LN	011 + 49 + AC (without initial zero) + LN	00 + 49 + AC (without initial zero) + LN
Gibraltar	LN	011 + 350 + LN	00 + 350 + LN
Great Britain & N. Ireland	AC + LN	011 + 44 + AC (without initial zero) + LN	00 + 44 + AC (without initial zero) + LN
Greece	LN	011 + 30 + LN	00 + 30 + LN
Hungary	06 + AC + LN	011 + 36 + AC + LN	00 + 36 + AC + LN
Ireland	AC + LN	011 + 353 + AC (without initial zero) + LN	00 + 353 + AC (without initial zero) + LN
Italy	LN	011 + 39 + LN	00 + 39 + LN

European Country	Calling long distance within...	Calling from the US or Canada to...	Calling from a European country to...
Latvia	LN	011 + 371 + LN	00 + 371 + LN
Montenegro	AC + LN	011 + 382 + AC (without initial zero) + LN	00 + 382 + AC (without initial zero) + LN
Morocco	LN	011 + 212 + LN (without initial zero)	00 + 212 + LN (without initial zero)
Netherlands	AC + LN	011 + 31 + AC (without initial zero) + LN	00 + 31 + AC (without initial zero) + LN
Norway	LN	011 + 47 + LN	00 + 47 + LN
Poland	LN	011 + 48 + LN	00 + 48 + LN
Portugal	LN	011 + 351 + LN	00 + 351 + LN
Russia	8 + AC + LN	011 + 7 + AC + LN	00 + 7 + AC + LN
Slovakia	AC + LN	011 + 421 + AC (without initial zero) + LN	00 + 421 + AC (without initial zero) + LN
Slovenia	AC + LN	011 + 386 + AC (without initial zero) + LN	00 + 386 + AC (without initial zero) + LN
Spain	LN	011 + 34 + LN	00 + 34 + LN
Sweden	AC + LN	011 + 46 + AC (without initial zero) + LN	00 + 46 + AC (without initial zero) + LN
Switzerland	LN	011 + 41 + LN (without initial zero)	00 + 41 + LN (without initial zero)
Turkey	AC (if there's no initial zero, add one) + LN	011 + 90 + AC (without initial zero) + LN	00 + 90 + AC (without initial zero) + LN

- The instructions above apply whether you're calling to or from a European landline or mobile phone.
- If calling from any mobile phone, you can replace the international access code with "+" (press and hold 0 to insert it).
- The international access code is 011 if you're calling from the US or Canada.
- To call the US or Canada from Europe, dial 00, then 1 (country code for US and Canada), then the area code and number. In short, 00 + 1 + AC + LN = Hi, Mom!

options are deactivated on your account. To be double-sure, put your phone in "airplane mode," then turn your Wi-Fi back on.

Using Wi-Fi and Data Roaming

A good approach is to use free Wi-Fi wherever possible, and fill in the gaps with data roaming.

Wi-Fi (sometimes called "WLAN")—Internet access through a wireless router—is readily available throughout Europe. But just like at home, the quality of the signal may vary. Be patient, and don't get your hopes up. At accommodations, access is often free, but you may have to pay a fee, especially at expensive hotels. At hotels with thick stone walls, the Wi-Fi router in the lobby may not reach every room. If Wi-Fi is important to you, ask about it when you book—and be specific ("in the rooms?"). Get the password and network name at the front desk when you check in.

When you're out and about, your best bet for finding free Wi-Fi is often at a café. They'll usually tell you the password if you buy something. Or you can stroll down a café-lined street, smartphone in hand, checking for unsecured networks every few steps until you find one that works. Some towns have free public Wi-Fi in highly trafficked parks or piazzas. You may have to register before using it, or get a password at the TI.

Data roaming—that is, accessing the Internet through the cellular network—is handy when you can't find usable Wi-Fi. Because you'll pay by the megabyte (explained earlier), it's best to limit how much data you use. Save bandwidth-gobbling tasks like Skyping, watching videos, or downloading apps or emails with large attachments until you're on Wi-Fi. Switch your phone's email settings from "push" to "fetch." This means that you can choose to "fetch" (download) your messages when you're on Wi-Fi rather than having them continuously "pushed" to your device. And be aware of apps—such as news, weather, and sports tickers—that automatically update. Check your phone's settings to be sure that none of your apps are set to "use cellular data."

I like the safeguard of manually turning off data roaming on my phone whenever I'm not actively using it. To turn off data and voice roaming, look in your phone's menu—try checking under "cellular" or "network," or ask your service provider how to do it. If you need to get online but can't find Wi-Fi, simply turn on data roaming long enough for the task at hand, then turn it off again.

Figure out how to keep track of how much data you've used (in your phone's menu, look for "cellular data usage"; you may have to reset the counter at the start of your trip). Some companies automatically send you a text message warning if you approach or exceed your limit.

There's yet another option: If you're traveling with an unlocked

Internet Calling

To make totally free voice and video calls over the Internet, all you need are a smartphone, tablet, or laptop; a strong Wi-Fi signal; and an account with one of the major Internet calling providers: Skype (www.skype.com), FaceTime (preloaded on most Apple devices), or Google+ Hangouts (www.google.com/hangouts). If the Wi-Fi signal isn't strong enough for video, try sticking with an audio-only call. Or...wait for your next hotel. Many Internet calling programs also work for making calls from your computer to telephones worldwide for a very reasonable fee—generally just a few cents per minute (you'll have to buy some credit before you make your first call).

smartphone (explained later), you can buy a SIM card that also includes data; this can be far, far cheaper than data roaming through your home provider.

USING EUROPEAN SIM CARDS

Using your American phone in Europe is easy, but it's not always cheap. And unreliable Wi-Fi can make keeping in touch frustrating. If you're reasonably technology-savvy, and would like to have the option of making lots of affordable calls, it's worth getting comfortable with European SIM cards.

Here's the basic idea: First you need an unlocked phone that works in Europe. Then, in Europe, shop around for a SIM card—the little data chip that inserts into your phone—to equip it with a European number. Turn on the phone, and bingo! You've got a European phone number (and access to cheaper European rates).

Getting an Unlocked Phone

Your basic options are getting your existing phone unlocked, or buying a phone (either at home or in Europe).

Some phones are electronically "locked" so that you can't switch SIM cards (keeping you tied to your original service provider). But it's possible to "unlock" your phone—allowing you to replace the original SIM card. An unlocked phone is versatile; not only does it work with any European provider, but many US providers now offer no-contract, prepaid (or "pay-as-you-go") alternatives that work with SIM technology.

You may already have an old, unused mobile phone in a drawer somewhere. Call your service provider and ask if they'll send you the unlock code. Otherwise, you can buy one: Search an online shopping site for an "unlocked quad-band phone," or buy one at a mobile-phone shop in Europe. Either way, a basic model typically costs $40 or less.

Buying and Using SIM Cards

Once you have an unlocked phone, you'll need to buy a SIM card—a small, fingernail-size chip that stores your phone number and other information. (A smaller variation called "micro-SIM" or "nano-SIM" cards—used in most iPhones—are less widely available.)

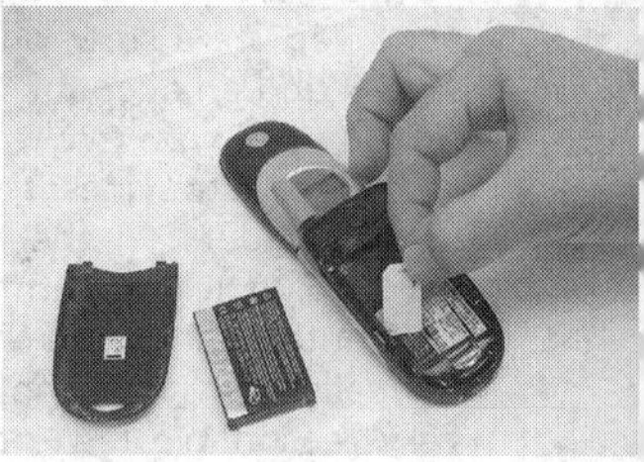

SIM cards are sold at mobile-phone shops, department-store electronics counters, and newsstands for $5-10, and usually include about that much prepaid calling credit (making the card itself virtually free). Because SIM cards are prepaid, there's no contract and no commitment; I routinely buy one even if I'm in a country for only a few days.

However, an increasing number of countries—including Italy—require you to register the SIM card with your passport (an antiterrorism measure). This takes only a few minutes longer: The shop clerk will ask you to fill out a form, then submit it to the service provider. Sometimes you can register your own SIM card online. Either way, an hour or two after submitting the information, you'll get a text welcoming you to that network. In Italy, the major mobile phone providers are Wind, TIM, Vodafone, and 3 ("Tre"). The vendor will make a copy of your passport to register the SIM card with the service provider.

When using a SIM card in its home country, it's free to receive calls and texts, and it's cheap to make calls—domestic calls average 20 cents per minute. You can also use SIM cards to call the US—sometimes very affordably (Lebara and Lycamobile, which operate in multiple European countries, let you call a US number for less than 10 cents a minute). Rates are higher if you're roaming in another country. But if you bought the SIM card within the European Union, roaming fees are capped no matter where you travel throughout the EU (about 25 cents/minute to make calls, 7 cents/minute to receive calls, and 8 cents for a text message).

While you can buy SIM cards just about anywhere, I like to seek out a mobile-phone shop, where an English-speaking clerk can help explain my options, get my SIM card inserted and set up, and show me how to use it. When you buy your SIM card, ask about rates for domestic and international calls and texting, and about roaming fees. Also find out how to check your credit balance (usually you'll key in a few digits and hit "Send"). You can top up your credit at any newsstand, tobacco shop, mobile-phone shop, or many other businesses (look for the SIM card's logo in the window).

To insert your SIM card into the phone, locate the slot, which is usually on the side of the phone or behind the battery. Turning on the phone, you'll be prompted to enter the "SIM PIN" (a code number that came with your card).

If you have an unlocked smartphone, you can look for a European SIM card that covers both voice and data. This is often much cheaper than paying for data roaming through your home provider.

LANDLINE TELEPHONES AND INTERNET CAFÉS

If you prefer to travel without a smartphone or tablet, you can still stay in touch using landline telephones, hotel guest computers, and Internet cafés.

Landline Telephones

Phones in your **hotel room** can be great for local calls and for calls using cheap international phone cards (described in the sidebar). Many hotels charge a fee for local and "toll-free" as well as long-distance or international calls—always ask for the rates before you dial. Since you'll never be charged for receiving calls, it can be more affordable to have someone from the US call you in your room.

While **public pay phones** are on the endangered species list, you'll still see them in post offices and train stations. Pay phones generally come with multilingual instructions. Most public phones work with insertable phone cards (described in the sidebar).

You'll see many cheap **call shops** that advertise low rates to faraway lands, often in train-station neighborhoods. While these target immigrants who want to call home cheaply, tourists can use them, too. Before making your call, be completely clear on the rates.

Internet Cafés and Public Internet Terminals

Finding public Internet terminals in Europe is no problem. Many hotels have a computer in the lobby for guests to use. Otherwise, head for an Internet café, or ask the TI or your hotelier for the nearest place to access the Internet.

European computers typically use non-American keyboards. A few letters are switched around, and command keys are labeled in the local language. Many European keyboards have an "Alt Gr" key (for "Alternate Graphics") to the right of the space bar; press this to insert the extra symbol that appears on some keys. Italian keyboards are a little different from ours; to type an @ symbol, press the "Alt Gr" key and the key that shows the @ symbol. If you can't locate a special character (such as the @ symbol), simply copy it (Ctrl-C) from a Web page and paste it (Ctrl-V) into your email message.

Types of Telephone Cards

Europe uses two different types of telephone cards. Both types are sold at post offices, newsstands, street kiosks, tobacco shops, and train stations.

Insertable Phone Cards: These cards can only be used at pay phones: Simply take the phone off the hook, insert the card, wait for a dial tone, and dial away. The phone displays your credit ticking down as you talk. These cards are sold by Italy's largest phone company, Telecom Italia. You can buy them in €5 or €10 denominations (many phone booths have signs indicating where the nearest phone-card sales outlet is located).

Rip off the perforated corner to "activate" the card, and then physically insert it into a slot in the pay phone. It displays how much money you have remaining on the card. Then just dial away. The price of the call is automatically deducted while you talk. Each European country has its own insertable phone card—so your Italian card won't work in a French phone.

International Phone Cards: These prepaid cards can be used to make inexpensive calls—within Europe, or to the US, for pennies a minute—from nearly any phone, including the one in your hotel room. The cards come with a toll-free number and a scratch-to-reveal PIN code. If the voice prompts aren't in English, experiment: Dial your code, followed by the pound sign (#), then the phone number, then pound again, and so on, until it works.

Buy a lower denomination in case the card is a dud. Because there are so many brand names, ask for an international phone card (*carta telefonica prepagata internazionale,* KAR-tah teh-leh-FOHN-ee-kah pray-pah-GAH-tah in-ter-naht-zee-oh-NAH-lay). Tell the vendor where you'll be making most calls (*"per Stati Uniti"*—to America), and he'll select the brand with the best deal.

SECURITY OVER THE INTERNET

Whether you're accessing the Internet with your own device or at a public terminal, using a shared network or computer comes with the potential for increased security risks. Ask the hotel or café for the specific name of their Wi-Fi network, and make sure you log on to that exact one; hackers sometimes create a bogus hotspot with a similar or vague name (such as "Hotel Europa Free Wi-Fi"). It's better if a network uses a password (especially a hard-to-guess one) rather than being open to the world.

While traveling, you may want to check your online banking or credit-card statements, or to take care of other personal-finance chores, but Internet security experts advise against accessing these sites over Wi-Fi. If you need to log on to a banking website, try to do so on a secure hard-wired connection or by using your bank's app over a mobile telephone network, which is harder to hack.

If using a credit card online, make sure that the site is secure. Most browsers display a little padlock icon, and the URL begins with *https* instead of *http*. Never send a credit-card number over a website that doesn't begin with *https*.

If you're not convinced a connection is secure, avoid accessing any sites (such as your bank's) that could be vulnerable to fraud.

MAIL

You can mail one package per day to yourself worth up to $200 duty-free from Europe to the US (mark it "personal purchases"). If you're sending a gift to someone, mark it "unsolicited gift." For details, visit www.cbp.gov and search for "Know Before You Go."

The Italian postal service works fine, but for quick transatlantic delivery (in either direction), consider services such as DHL (www.dhl.com).

Transportation

If you're debating between public transportation and car rental, consider these factors: Cars are best for three or more traveling together (especially families with small kids), those packing heavy, and those scouring the countryside. Trains and buses are best for solo travelers, blitz tourists, and city-to-city travelers. While a car gives you more freedom, trains and buses zip you effortlessly and scenically from city to city, usually dropping you in the center, often near a TI. Cars are an expensive headache in places like Florence, but if you want to stay in an out-of-the-way *agriturismo* and focus on isolated hill towns, having your own wheels will save you time and headaches.

If your itinerary mixes cities and countryside, arrange your car rental strategically: Wait to pick up your car until the last big city you visit, then use it for lacing together the hill towns and exploring the countryside.

TRAINS

To travel by train affordably in Italy, you can simply buy tickets as you go. Ticket machines in stations are easy to use (see "Buying Tickets," later), so you can usually avoid long lines at ticket windows. Pay all ticket costs in the station before you board, or you'll pay a penalty on the train. For travelers ready to lock in dates and times weeks or months in advance, buying nonrefundable tickets online can cut costs in half.

Types of Trains: Most trains in Italy are operated by the state-run **Trenitalia** company (www.trenitalia.com, a.k.a. Ferrovie dello

Public Transportation in Tuscany

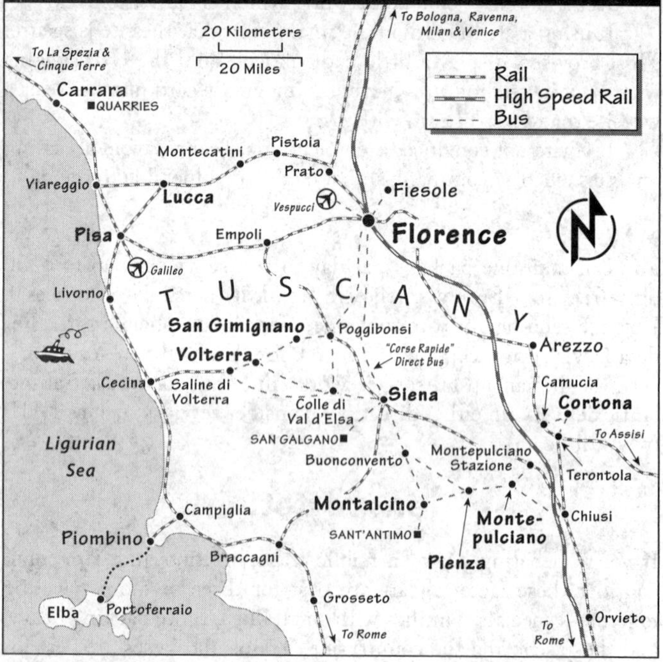

Stato Italiane, abbreviated *FS* or *FSI*). Since ticket prices depend on the speed of the train, it helps to know the different types of trains: pokey R or REG *(regionali);* medium-speed RV *(regionale veloce)*, IR (InterRegio), D *(diretto)*, and E *(espresso);* fast IC (InterCity) and EC (EuroCity); and super-fast Frecce trains: the Frecciabianca ("White Arrow"), faster Frecciargento ("Silver Arrow"), and Frecciarossa ("Red Arrow"). If you're traveling with a rail pass, note that reservations are required for EC and international trains (€5) and Frecce trains (€10). Reservations are optional for rail-pass holders on IC trains, and you can't make reservations for regional trains, such as most Pisa-Cinque Terre connections.

On high-speed routes between major cities (Venice-Padua-Bologna-Florence-Rome and Turin-Milan-Bologna-Florence-Rome), Trenitalia has a private competitor called **Italo.** Their trains run at more or less the same speed as Trenitalia's high-speed trains, but with fewer departures, and they also offer discounts for tickets booked well in advance. In some cities (most notably Rome and Milan), its trains use a secondary station rather than the main one—if taking an Italo train, pay attention to which station you need. Italo does not currently accept rail passes, but its affordable fares make it worth considering for long-haul point-to-point

Italy's Public Transportation

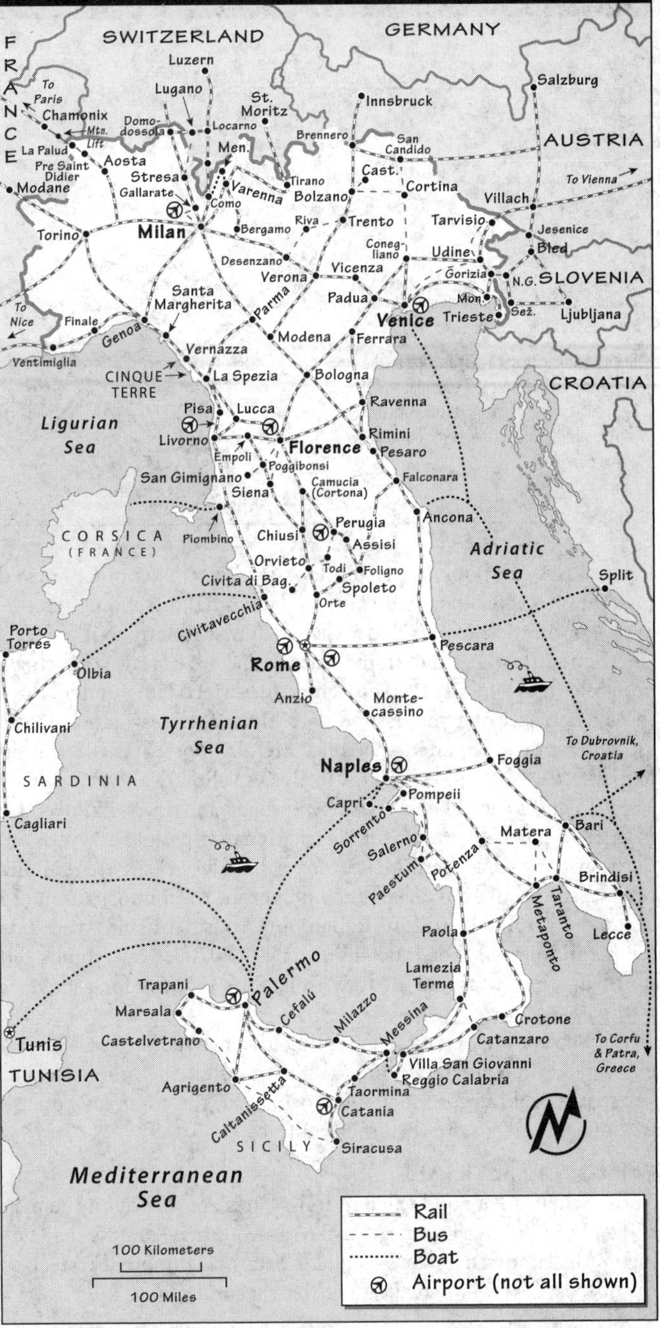

Train Costs in Italy

Map key: Approximate point-to-point one-way second-class rail fares in US dollars. First class costs 50 percent more.

Before deciding to get a railpass, add up the approximate ticket costs for your itinerary. If you'll be making short, inexpensive trips each day, you'll probably find it's cheaper to buy tickets as you go in Italy.

tickets. You can book in person (look for Italo ticket offices or red machines—tickets not sold through Trenitalia), by phone (tel. 06-0708), or on their user-friendly website (www.italotreno.it).

Schedules: At the train station, the easiest way to check schedules is at a handy ticket machine (described later, under "Buying Tickets"). Enter the desired date, time, and destination to see all your options. Printed schedules are also posted at the station (departure—*partenzi*—posters are always yellow).

On the Web, check www.trenitalia.it and www.italotreno.it (domestic journeys only); for international trips, use www.bahn.de (Germany's excellent all-Europe schedule website). Trenitalia offers a single all-Italy telephone number for train information (24 hours daily, tel. 892-021, in Italian only, consider having your hotelier call for you). For Italo trains, call 06-0708. Newsstands sell up-to-date regional and all-Italy timetables (€5, ask for the *orario ferroviaro*).

Be aware that Trenitalia and Italo don't cooperate at all. If you buy a ticket for one train line, it's not valid on the other. Even if you're just looking for schedule information, the company you ask will most likely ignore the other's options.

Point-to-Point Tickets

Train tickets are a good value in Italy. Fares are shown on the map above, though fares can vary for the same journey, mainly depending on the time of day, the speed of the train, and more. **First-class** tickets cost 30 to 50 percent more than **second-class.**

Le Frecce and Italo express trains each offer several classes of service, all with seats reserved: Standard, Premium, Business, or Executive on Frecciarossa; Smart, Prima, or Club on Italo; the standard first and second on other trains. Buying up gives you a little more elbow room, or perhaps a better chance at seating a group together, if you're buying on short notice. Ticket price levels for both companies are Base (full fare, easily changeable or partly refundable before scheduled departure), Economy (one schedule change allowed before departure, for a fee), and Super Economy or Low Cost (sells out quickly, no refund or exchange). Discounted fares typically sell out several days before departure.

Speed vs. Savings: For point-to-point tickets on mainline routes, fast trains save time, but charge a premium. For example, super-fast Florence-Rome trains run hourly, cost €45 in second class, and make the trip in 1.5 hours, while infrequent InterCity trains (only 1-2/day) cost €35 and take 3 hours.

Discounts: Families with young children can get price breaks—kids ages 4 and under travel free; ages 4-11 at half-price. Ask for the "Offerta Familia" deal when buying tickets at a counter (or, at a ticket machine, choose "Yes" at the "Do you want ticket issue?" prompt, then choose "Familia"). With the discount, families of three to five people with at least one kid (age 12 or under) get 50 percent off the child fare, and 20 percent off the adult fare. The deal doesn't apply to all trains at all times, but it's worth checking out.

Discounts for youths and seniors require purchase of a separate card (Carta Verde for ages 12-26 costs €40; Carta Argento for ages 60 and over is €30), but the discount on tickets is so minor (10-15 percent respectively for domestic travel), it's not worth it for most.

Buying Tickets: Avoid train station ticket lines whenever possible by using the ticket machines found in station halls. You'll be able to easily purchase tickets for travel within Italy (not international trains), make seat reservations, and even book a *cuccetta* (koo-CHEH-tah; overnight berth). If you do use the ticket windows, be sure you're in the correct line. Key terms: *biglietti* (general tickets), *prenotazioni* (reservations), *nazionali* (domestic), and *internazionali*.

Trenitalia's ticket machines (usually green-and-white, marked *Biglietto Veloce/Fast Ticket*) are user-friendly and found in all but the tiniest stations in Italy. You can pay by cash (they give change) or by debit or credit card (even for small amounts). Select English, then your destination. If you don't immediately see the city you're traveling to, keep keying in the spelling until it's listed. You can choose from first- and second-class seats, request tickets for more than one traveler, and (on the high-speed Frecce trains) choose an aisle or window seat. Don't select a discount rate without being sure

Open or Non-Reserved Ticket—Need to Validate

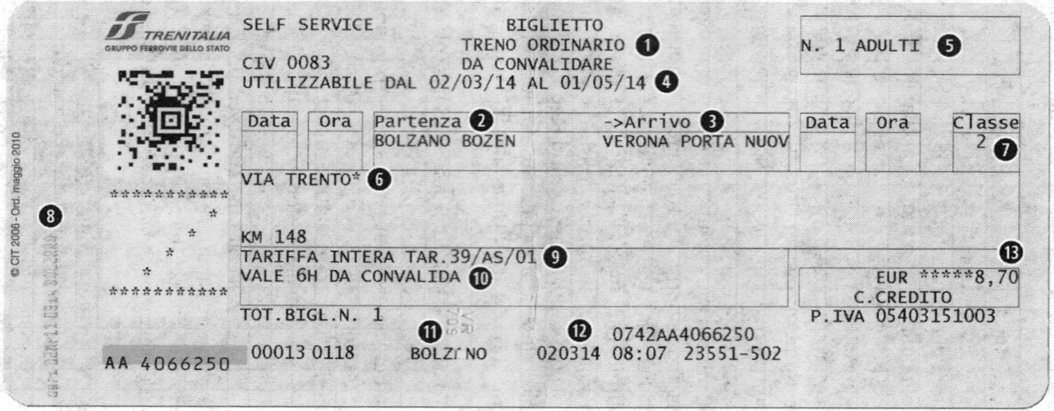

1. Open ticket for non-express train, must be validated
2. Point of departure
3. Destination
4. Period in which ticket is valid (1 use, within 2 months of purchase)
5. Number of passengers
6. Route
7. Class of travel (1st or 2nd)
8. Validation stamp
9. Full fare for non-express train
10. Ticket good for 1 trip within 6 hours after validation
11. Location of ticket sale
12. Date of ticket purchase
13. Ticket cost

Reserved Ticket (Fast Train)—Need Not Validate

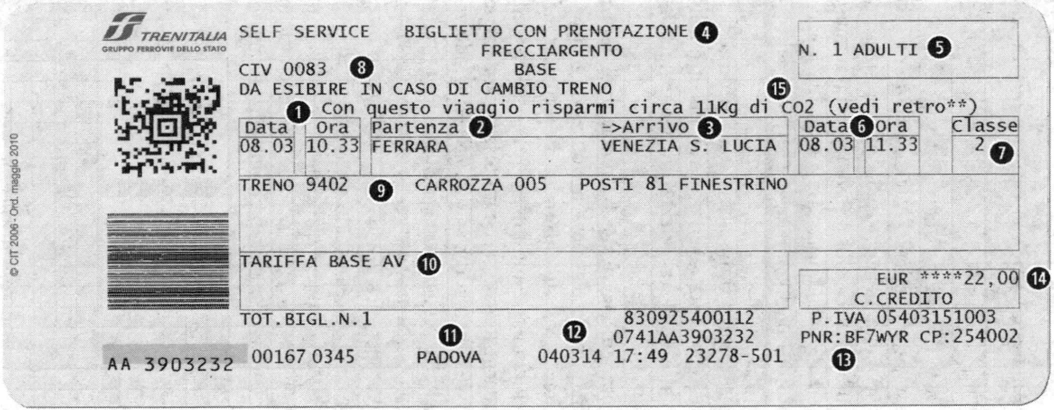

1. Departure date & time
2. Point of departure
3. Destination
4. "Ticket with reservation"
5. Number of passengers
6. Arrival date & time
7. Class of travel (1st or 2nd)
8. "Present to official if changing trains"
9. Train, car & seat numbers (finestrino = window seat)
10. Fast-train fare
11. Location of ticket sale
12. Date of ticket purchase
13. Booking ID
14. Ticket cost
15. Amount of CO^2 usage reduced by this train trip

that you meet the criteria (for example, Americans are not eligible for certain EU or resident discounts). Rail-pass holders can use the machines to make seat reservations. If you need to validate your ticket, you can do it in the same machine if you're boarding your train right away.

For nearby destinations only, you can also buy tickets from the older, gray-and-blue machines marked *Rete regionale* (cash only, push button for English).

It's cheaper to buy Trenitalia tickets in advance, either at the station or online at www.trenitalia.it. Advance planning gives you the best shot at Economy and Super Economy fares, and express trains can sell out on busy weekends or holidays. But because most Italian trains run frequently and prices are reasonable, you can also keep your travel plans flexible by purchasing full-fare tickets on the day of travel.

To buy tickets for **Italo** trains, look for a dedicated service counter (in most major rail stations), or a red ticket machine labeled *Italo.* You can also book Italo tickets by phone (tel. 06-0708) or online (www.italotreno.it).

You can't buy international tickets from machines; for this and anything else that requires a real person, you must go to a ticket window. A good alternative, though, is to drop by a local travel agency. Agencies sell domestic and international tickets and make reservations. They charge a small fee, but the language barrier (and the lines) can be smaller than at the station's ticket windows.

Validating Tickets: If your ticket includes a seat reservation on a specific train *(biglietto con prenotazione)*, you're all set and can just get on board. An open ticket with no seat reservation (it may say *da convalidare* or *convalida*) must always be validated—stamp it before you board in the machine near the platform (usually marked *convalida biglietti* or *vidimazione*). Once you validate a ticket, you must complete your trip within the timeframe shown on the ticket (within 6 hours for medium-distance trips; within 1.25 hours for short rides under 6 miles). If you forget to validate your ticket, go right away to the train conductor—before he comes to you—or you'll pay a fine.

Rail Passes

The **Italy Pass** for the Italian state railway may save you money if you're taking three long train rides or prefer first-class travel, but don't count on it for hop-on convenience on every train. Use the price map on page 674 to add up your ticket costs (ticket prices on the map are for the fastest trains on a given route, many of which have reservation costs built in). Remember that rail passes are not valid on Italo-brand trains.

Rail pass travelers must make separate seat reservations for

Rail Passes

Prices listed are for 2014 and are subject to change. For the latest prices, details, and train schedules (and easy online ordering), see www.ricksteves.com/rail.

"Saver" prices are per person for two or more people traveling together. "Youth" means under age 26. The fare for children 4–11 is half the adult individual fare or Saver fare. Kids under age 4 travel free.

ITALY PASS

	Individual 1st Class	Individual 2nd Class	Saver 1st Class	Saver 2nd Class	Youth 2nd Class
3 days in 2 months	$307	$250	$262	$213	$204
Extra rail days (max 7)	32-37	26-30	26-30	22-26	22-25

FRANCE–ITALY PASS

	Individual 1st Class	Individual 2nd Class	Saver 1st Class	Saver 2nd Class	Youth 2nd Class
4 days in 2 months	$428	$364	$364	$310	$280
Extra rail days (max 6)	45-51	38-44	38-44	33-37	29-33

Be aware of your route. Direct Paris–Italy trains (day and overnight) and trains via Switzerland aren't covered by this pass. Connections through Nice are ok.

GREECE–ITALY PASS

	Individual 1st Class	Individual 2nd Class	Saver 1st Class	Saver 2nd Class	Youth 2nd Class
4 days in 2 months	$407	$327	$347	$279	$266
Extra rail days (max 6)	37-40	30-32	32-34	26-27	25-27

Covers deck passage on overnight Superfast Ferries between Patras, Greece and Bari or Ancona, Italy (starts use of one travel day). Does not cover travel to or on Greek islands. Very few trains run in Greece.

SPAIN–ITALY PASS

	Individual 1st Class	Individual 2nd Class	Saver 1st Class	Saver 2nd Class	Youth 2nd Class
4 days in 2 months	$428	$364	$364	$310	$280
Extra rail days (max 6)	45-51	38-44	38-44	33-37	29-33

Note: Pass does not cover trains in France.

SELECTPASS

This pass covers travel in four adjacent countries.

	Individual 1st Class	Saver 1st Class	Youth 2nd Class
5 days in 2 months	$582	$495	$379
6 days in 2 months	635	540	414
8 days in 2 months	739	629	482
10 days in 2 months	845	719	551

the fastest trains between major Italian cities (€10 each). Rail pass travelers can just hop on InterCity trains (optional €5 reservation) and regional trains (no reservations possible). Making a reservation at a train station or travel agency is the same as the process to buy a ticket, so you may need to stand in line either way. Reservations for berths on overnight trains cost extra, aren't covered by rail passes, and aren't reflected on the ticket cost map.

A **Global Pass** can work well throughout most of Europe, but it's a bad value for travel exclusively in Italy. A cheaper version, the **Select Pass,** allows you to tailor a pass to your trip, provided you're traveling in four adjacent countries directly connected by rail or ferry. For instance, with a four-country pass allowing 10 days of train travel within a two-month period (about $850 for a single adult in 2014), you could choose France-Switzerland-Italy-Greece or Benelux-Germany-Austria-Italy. A **France and Italy Pass** combines just those two countries. Note that none of these passes covers direct day or night trains between Italy and Paris, which require a separate ticket. Before you buy a Select Pass or France and Italy Pass, consider how many travel days you'll really need. Use the pass only for travel days that involve long hauls or several trips. Pay out of pocket for tickets on days you're taking only short, cheap rides.

For more detailed advice on figuring out the smartest train-ticket or rail-pass options for your trip, visit the Trains & Rail Passes section of my website at www.ricksteves.com/rail.

Train Tips

This section contains information on making seat reservations, storing baggage, avoiding theft, and dealing with strikes.

Seat Reservations: Trains can fill up, even in first class. If you're on a tight schedule, you'll want to reserve a few days ahead for fast trains (see "Types of Trains," earlier). Purchasing tickets or passholder reservations onboard a train comes with a nasty penalty. Buying them at the station can be a time waster unless you use the ticket machines.

If you don't need a reservation, and if your train originates at your departure point (e.g., you're catching the Florence-Rome train in Florence), arriving at least 15 minutes before the departure time will help you snare a seat.

On the platforms of some major stations, posters showing the train composition *(composizione principali treni)* indicate where first- and second-class cars will line up when the trains arrive (letters on the poster are supposed to correspond to letters posted over the platform—but they don't always). Other stations may post the order of the cars on video screens along the track shortly before the train arrives. Since most trains now allow you to make reservations up to the time of departure, conductors post a list of the reservable

Deciphering Italian Train Schedules

At the station, look for the big yellow posters labeled *Partenze—Departures* (ignore the white posters, which show arrivals). In stations with Italo service, the posted schedules also include the FS or Italo logos.

Schedules are listed chronologically, hour by hour, showing the trains leaving the station throughout the day. Each schedule has columns:

- The first column *(Ora)* lists the time of departure.
- The next column *(Treno)* shows the type of train.
- The third column *(Classi Servizi)* lists the services available (first- and second-class cars, dining car, *cuccetta* berths, etc.) and, more importantly, whether you need reservations (usually denoted by an R in a box). All Frecce trains, many EuroCity (EC) trains, and most international trains require reservations.
- The next column lists the destination of the train *(Principali Fermate Destinazioni),* often showing intermediate stops, followed by the final destination, with arrival times listed throughout in parentheses. Note that your final destination may be listed in fine print as an intermediate destination. For example, if you're going from Florence to Cortona, scan the schedule and you'll notice that many trains that terminate in Rome stop in Cortona en route (and fast trains stop in Terontola, near Cortona). Travelers who read the fine print end up with a far greater choice of trains.
- The next column *(Servizi Diretti e Annotazioni)* has pertinent notes about the train, such as "also stops in..." *(ferma anche a...),* "doesn't stop in..." *(non ferma a...),* "stops in every station" *(ferma in tutte le stazioni),* "delayed..." *(ritardo...),* and so on.
- The last column lists the track *(Binario)* the train departs from. Confirm the *binario* with an additional source: a ticket seller, the electronic board that lists immediate departures, TV monitors on the platform, or the railway officials who are usually standing by the train unless you really need them.

For any odd symbols on the poster, look at the key at the end. Some of the phrasing can be deciphered easily, such as *servizio periodico* (periodic service—doesn't always run). For the trickier ones, ask a local or railway official, try your *Rick Steves' Italian Phrase Book & Dictionary,* or simply take a different train.

You can also check schedules—for trains anywhere in Italy, not just from the station you're currently in—at the handy ticket machines. Enter the date and time of your departure (to or from any Italian station), and you can view all your options.

and non-reservable seat rows (sometimes in English) in each train car's vestibule. This means that if you board a crowded train and get one of the last seats, you may be ousted when the reservation holder comes along.

Baggage Storage: Many stations have a *deposito bagagli* where you can safely leave your bag for about €6 per 5-hour period or €17 per 24 hours (payable when you pick up the bag, double-check closing hours; they may ask to photocopy your passport). Because of security concerns, no Italian stations have lockers.

Theft Concerns: In big cities, train stations are rife with thieves and con artists. Italy remains in economic straits, and unemployed people lurk around the station trying to skim tips (or worse) from unsuspecting tourists. If someone helps you to find your train or carry your bags, be aware that they are not an official porter; they are simply hoping for some cash. And if someone other than a uniformed railway employee tries to help you use the automated ticket machines, it's safest to politely refuse.

Italian trains are famous for their thieves. Never leave a bag unattended. Police do ride the trains, cutting down on theft. Still, for an overnight trip, I'd feel safe only in a *cuccetta* (a bunk in a special sleeping car with an attendant who keeps track of who comes and goes while you sleep—approximately €20 in a six-bed compartment, €26 in a less-cramped four-bed compartment, €50 in a more private, double compartment).

Strikes: Strikes, which are common, generally last a day. Train employees will simply explain, "*Sciopero*" (strike). But in actuality, sporadic trains, following no particular schedule, lumber down the tracks during most strikes. When a strike is pending, travel agencies (and hoteliers) can check online for you to see when the strike goes into effect and which trains will continue to run. Revised schedules may be posted in Italian at stations, and station personnel still working can often tell you what trains are expected to run. If I need to get somewhere and know a strike is imminent, I leave early (before the strike, which often begins at 9:00), or I just go to the station with extra patience in tow and hop on anything rolling in the direction I want to go.

BUSES

You can usually get anywhere you want to in Italy by bus, as long as you're not in a hurry and you plan ahead using bus schedules (pick up at local TIs). For reaching small towns, buses are sometimes the only option if you don't have a car. In many hill towns, trains leave you at a station in the valley far below, while buses more likely bring you right up into the thick of things. (If the bus stop or station is below town, sometimes an escalator or elevator helps get you up into town—ask around.)

Larger towns have a long-distance bus station *(stazione degli autobus)*, with ticket windows and several stalls (usually labeled *corsia*, *stallo*, or *binario*). Smaller towns—where buses are more useful—just have a central bus stop *(fermata)*, likely along the main road or on the main square, and maybe several more scattered around town. In small towns, buy bus tickets at newsstands or tobacco shops (with the big *T* signs). When buying your ticket, confirm the departure point *("Dov'è la fermata?")*, and once there, double-check that the posted schedule lists your destination and departure time. In general, orange buses are local city buses, and blue buses are for long distances.

Once the bus arrives, confirm the destination with the driver. You are expected to stow big backpacks underneath the bus (open the luggage compartment yourself if it's closed).

Sundays and holidays are problematic; even from large cities, schedules are sparse, departing buses are jam-packed, and ticket offices are often closed. Plan ahead and buy your ticket in advance. Most travel agencies book bus (and train) tickets for just a small fee.

RENTING A CAR

If you're renting a car in Italy, bring your driver's license. You're also required to have an International Driving Permit—an official translation of your driver's license (sold at your local AAA office for $15 plus the cost of two passport-type photos; see www.aaa.com). While that's the letter of the law, I've often rented cars in Italy without having this permit. If all goes well, you'll likely never be asked to show the permit—but it's a must if you end up dealing with the police.

Rental companies require you to be at least 21 years old and to have held your license for one year. Drivers under the age of 25 may incur a young-driver surcharge, and some rental companies do not rent to anyone 75 or older. If you're considered too young or old, look into leasing (covered later), which has less-stringent age restrictions.

Research car rentals before you go. It's cheaper to arrange most car rentals from the US. Call several companies or look online to compare rates.

Most of the major US rental agencies (including Avis, Budget, Enterprise, Hertz, and Thrifty) have offices throughout Europe. Also consider the two major Europe-based agencies, Europcar and Sixt. It can be cheaper to use a consolidator, such as Auto Europe/Kemwel (www.autoeurope.com) or Europe by Car (www.europebycar.com), which compares rates at several companies to get you the best deal. Because you're working with a middleman, it's especially important to ask in advance about add-on fees and restrictions.

Regardless of the car-rental company you choose, always read the fine print carefully for add-on charges—such as one-way drop-off fees, airport surcharges, or mandatory insurance policies—that aren't included in the "total price." You may need to query rental agents pointedly to find out your actual cost.

For the best deal, rent by the week with unlimited mileage. To save money on fuel, ask for a diesel car. I normally rent the smallest, least-expensive model with a stick shift (generally much cheaper than an automatic). Almost all rentals are manual by default, so if you need an automatic, request one in advance; be aware that these cars are usually larger models (not as maneuverable on narrow, winding roads). Roads and parking spaces are narrow in Tuscany, so you'll do yourself a favor by renting the smallest car that meets your needs.

Figure on paying roughly $200 for a one-week rental. Allow extra for insurance, fuel, tolls, and parking. For trips of three weeks or more, look into leasing; you'll save money on insurance and taxes. Big companies have offices in most cities; ask whether they can pick you up at your hotel. Small local rental companies can be cheaper but aren't as flexible.

Compare pickup costs (downtown can be less expensive than the airport) and explore drop-off options. Always check the hours of the location you choose: Many rental offices close from midday Saturday until Monday morning and, in smaller towns, at lunchtime.

When selecting a location, don't trust the agency's description of "downtown" or "city center." In some cases, a "downtown" branch can be on the outskirts of the city—a long, costly taxi ride from the center. Before choosing, plug the addresses into a mapping website. You may find that the "train station" location is handier. On the other hand, returning a car at a big-city train station or downtown agency can be tricky; get precise details on the car drop-off location and hours, and allow ample time to find it. And be aware that most Italian cities have a "ZTL" limited traffic zone that's carefully monitored by cameras. If your drop-off point is near this zone, get very clear directions on how to get there without crossing the line and getting a big fine.

When you pick up the rental car, check it thoroughly and make sure any damage is noted on your rental agreement. Find out how your car's lights, turn signals, wipers, radio, and fuel cap function, and know what kind of fuel the car takes (diesel vs. unleaded). When you return the car, make sure the agent verifies its condition with you. Some drivers take pictures of the returned vehicle as proof of its condition.

Navigation Options

When renting a car in Europe, you have several alternatives for your digital navigator: Use your smartphone's online mapping app, download an offline map app, or rent a GPS device with your rental car (or bring your own GPS device from home).

Online mapping apps used to be prohibitively expensive for overseas travelers—but that was before most carriers started offering affordable international data plans. If you're already getting a data plan for your trip, this is probably the way to go (see "Using Your American Smartphone in Europe," earlier).

A number of well-designed apps allow you much of the convenience of online maps without any costly demands on your data plan. City Maps 2Go is one of the most popular of these; OffMaps, Google Maps, and Navfree also all offer good, zoomable offline maps for much of Europe (some are better for driving, while others are better for navigating cities).

Some drivers prefer using a dedicated GPS unit—not only to avoid the data-roaming fees, but because a stand-alone GPS can be easier to operate (important if you're driving solo). The major downside: It's expensive—around $10-30 per day. Also your car's GPS unit may only come loaded with maps for its home country—if you need additional maps, ask. Make sure your device's language is set to English before you drive off. If you have a portable GPS device at home, you can take that instead. Many American GPS devices come loaded with US maps only—you'll need to buy and download European maps before your trip. This option is far less expensive than renting a GPS unit.

Car Insurance Options

Accidents can happen anywhere, but when you're on vacation, the last thing you need is stress over car insurance. When you rent a car, you're liable for a very high deductible, sometimes equal to the entire value of the car. Limit your financial risk in case of an accident by choosing one of these two options: Buy Collision Damage Waiver (CDW) coverage from the car-rental company (figure roughly 30 percent extra), or get coverage through your credit card (free, but more complicated).

In Italy, most car-rental companies' rates automatically include CDW coverage. Even if you try to decline CDW when you reserve your Italian car, you may find when you show up at the counter that you must buy it after all.

While each rental company has its own variation, basic CDW costs $10–30 a day and reduces your liability, but does not eliminate it. When you pick up the car, you'll be offered the chance to "buy down" the deductible to zero (for an additional $10–30/day;

this is sometimes called "super CDW" or "zero-deductible coverage").

If you opt for credit-card coverage, there's a catch. You'll technically have to decline all coverage offered by the car-rental company, which means they can place a hold on your card for up to the full value of the car. In case of damage, it can be time-consuming to resolve the charges with your credit-card company. Before you decide on this option, quiz your credit-card company about how it works.

For more on car-rental insurance, see www.ricksteves.com/cdw.

Theft Insurance: Note that theft insurance (separate from CDW insurance) is mandatory in Italy. The insurance usually costs about $15–20 a day, payable when you pick up the car.

Leasing

For trips of three weeks or more, consider leasing (which automatically includes zero-deductible collision and theft insurance). By technically buying and then selling back the car, you save lots of money on tax and insurance. Leasing provides you a brand-new car with unlimited mileage and a 24-hour emergency assistance program. You can lease for as little as 21 days to as long as five and a half months. Car leases must be arranged from the US. One of many companies offering affordable lease packages is Europe by Car (www.europebycar.com/lease).

DRIVING

Driving in Italy can be scary—a video game for keeps, and you only get one quarter. Italian drivers can be aggressive. They drive fast and tailgate as if it were required. They pass where Americans are taught not to—on blind corners and just before tunnels. Roads have narrow shoulders or none at all. Driving in the countryside is less stressful than driving through urban areas or on busy highways, but stay alert. On one-lane roads, larger vehicles have the right-of-way. If you're on a truckers' route, stifle your Good Samaritan impulse when you see provocatively dressed women standing by camper-vans at the side of the road; they're not having car trouble. (For more on driving in Tuscany, see page 683.)

Road Rules: Stay out of restricted traffic zones or you'll risk huge fines. Car traffic is restricted in many city centers, including all of the major destinations in this book (Florence, Siena, Pisa, Lucca, Volterra, San Gimignano, Montepulciano, Montalcino, Pienza, and Cortona). Don't drive or park anywhere

Driving in Tuscany: Distance & Time

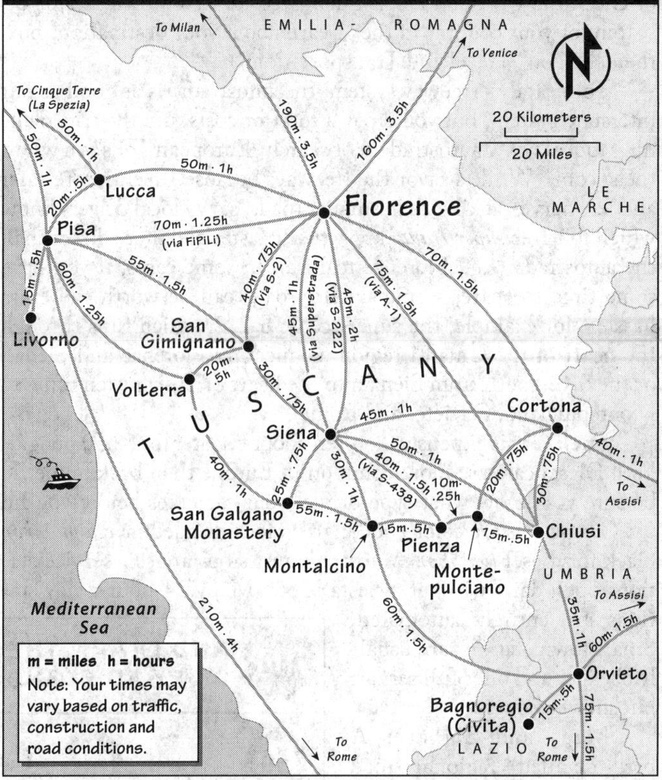

with signs reading *Zona Traffico Limitato* (*ZTL*, often shown above a red circle; see image). If you do, your license plate will likely be photographed and a hefty (€100-plus) ticket mailed to your home without you ever having met a cop. Bumbling in and out of these zones can net you multiple fines. If your hotel is within a restricted area, it's best to ask your hotelier to direct you to parking outside the zone. (Although your hotelier can register your car as an authorized vehicle permitted to enter the zone, this usually isn't worth the hassle.) If you get a ticket, it could take months to show up (see www.bella-toscana.com/traffic_violations_italy.htm for details).

Be aware of typical European road rules; for example, many countries require headlights to be turned on at all times, and it's generally illegal to drive while using your mobile phone without a hands-free headset. Seatbelts are mandatory and children under 12 must ride in child-safety or booster seats. In Europe, you're not allowed to turn right on a red light, unless there is a sign or signal specifically authorizing it, and on expressways it's illegal to pass drivers on the right. Ask your car-rental company about these rules, or check the US State Department website (www.travel.state.gov, search for your country in the "Learn about your destination" box, then click on "Travel and Transportation.").

Tolls: Italy's freeway system, the autostrada, is as good as our interstate system, but you'll pay a toll (for costs, use the trip-planning tool at www.autostrade.it or search "European Tolls" on www.theaa.com). While I favor the freeways because I feel they're safer and less nerve-racking than smaller roads, savvy local drivers know which toll-free *superstradas* are actually faster and more direct than the autostrada (e.g., Florence to Pisa). In some cases, if you have some time to spare, scenic smaller roads can be worth the extra hassle—for example, the super-scenic S-222, which runs through the heart of the Chianti region (connecting Florence and Siena); or the SR2-south from Siena into the heart of Tuscany (en route to Montepulciano, Orvieto, and Rome).

Fuel: Gas is expensive—often about €2/liter (or $8.50 per gallon). Diesel cars are more common in Europe than back home, so be sure you know what type of fuel your car takes before you fill up. Gas pumps are color-coded: green for unleaded *(senza piombo)*, black for diesel *(gasolio)*. Autostrada rest stops are self-service stations open daily without a siesta break. Many 24-hour-a-day stations are entirely automated. Small-town stations are usually cheaper and offer full service but shorter hours.

Maps and Signage: A big, detailed regional road map (buy one at a newsstand, gas station, or bookstore) and a semiskilled navigator are essential. Learn the universal road signs (see illustration). Although roads are numbered on maps, actual road signs give just a city name (for example, if you were heading west out of Montepulciano, the map would be marked "route S-146"—but you'd follow signs to Pienza, the next town along this road). The signs are inconsistent: They may direct you to the nearest big city or simply the next town along the route.

Theft: Cars are routinely

vandalized and stolen. Thieves easily recognize rental cars and assume they are filled with a tourist's gear. Be sure all of your valuables are out of sight and locked in the trunk, or even better, with you or in your room.

Parking: White lines generally mean parking is free. Yellow lines mean that parking is reserved for residents only (who have permits). Blue lines mean you'll have to pay—usually around €1.50 per hour (use machine, leave time-stamped receipt on dashboard). You'll usually pay at a centrally located pay-and-display machine, then put the receipt in your windshield. Study the signs. Often the free zones have a 30- or 60-minute time limit. Signs showing a street cleaner and a day of the week indicate which day the street is cleaned; there's a €100 tow-fee incentive to learn the days of the week in Italian.

Zona disco has nothing to do with dancing. Italian cars come equipped with a time disc (a cardboard clock), which you can use in a *zona disco*—set the clock to your arrival time and leave it on the dashboard. (If your rental car doesn't come with a *disco,* pick one up at a tobacco shop or just write your arrival time on a piece of paper and place it on the dashboard.)

Garages are safe, save time, and help you avoid the stress of parking tickets. Take the parking voucher with you to pay the cashier before you leave.

FLIGHTS

The best comparison search engine for both international and intra-European flights is www.kayak.com. For inexpensive flights within Europe, try www.skyscanner.com or www.hipmunk.com; for inexpensive international flights, try www.vayama.com.

Flying to Europe: Start looking for international flights four to five months before your trip, especially for peak-season travel. Off-season tickets can be purchased a month or so in advance. Depending on your itinerary, it can be efficient to fly into one city and out of another. If your flight requires a connection in Europe, see our hints on navigating Europe's top hub airports at www.ricksteves.com/hub-airports.

Flying within Europe: If you're considering a train ride that's more than five hours long, a flight may save you both time and money. When comparing your options, factor in the time it takes to get to the airport and how early you'll need to arrive to check in.

Well-known cheapo airlines include easyJet (www.easyjet.com) and Ryanair (www.ryanair.com). Budget airlines out of Florence (airport code: FLR) include Belle Air (www.belleair.it), Darwin Airline (www.darwinairline.com), and Vueling (www.vueling.com). Cheaper airlines use Pisa (airport code: PSA), including the

Italian-based discount airline Air One (www.flyairone.com). Airport websites may list small airlines that serve your destination.

Remember that Florence is well-connected by train to plenty of airports—giving you more options—including Parma, Perugia, Bologna, and Rimini (which all have budget flights available). Rome, Milan, and Venice are only a two-hour train ride away.

Be aware of the potential drawbacks of flying on the cheap: nonrefundable and nonchangeable tickets, minimal or nonexistent customer service, treks to airports far outside town, and stingy baggage allowances with steep overage fees. If you're traveling with lots of luggage, a cheap flight can quickly become a bad deal. To avoid unpleasant surprises, read the small print before you book.

Resources

RESOURCES FROM RICK STEVES

Rick Steves' Florence & Tuscany 2015 is one of many books in my series on European travel, which includes country guidebooks, city guidebooks (Rome, Venice, Paris, London, etc.), Snapshot Guides (excerpted chapters from my country guides), Pocket Guides (full-color little books on big cities, including Florence), and my budget-travel skills handbook, *Rick Steves Europe Through the Back Door.* Most of my titles are available as ebooks. My phrase books—for Italian, French, German, Spanish, and Portuguese—are practical and budget-oriented. My other books include *Europe 101* (a crash course on art and history designed for travelers); *Mediterranean Cruise Ports* and *Northern European Cruise Ports* (how to make the most of your time in port); and *Travel as a Political Act* (a travelogue sprinkled with tips for bringing home a global perspective). A more complete list of my titles appears near the end of this book.

Video: My public television series, *Rick Steves' Europe,* covers European destinations in 100 shows, with 17 episodes on Italy, including four on Florence and Tuscany. To watch full episodes online for free, see www.ricksteves.com/tv. Or to raise your travel I.Q. with video versions of our popular classes, such as Michelangelo's Italy and Italy Travel Skills, see www.ricksteves.com/travel-talks.

Audio: My weekly public radio show, *Travel with Rick Steves,* features interviews with travel experts from around the world. I've also produced free, self-guided **audio tours** of the top sights and

Begin Your Trip at www.RickSteves.com

My **website** is *the* place to explore Europe. You'll find thousands of fun articles, videos, photos, and radio interviews on European destinations; money-saving tips for planning your dream trip; monthly travel news; my travel talks and travel blog; my latest guidebook updates (www.ricksteves.com/update); and my free Rick Steves Audio Europe app. You can also follow me on Facebook and Twitter.

Our **Travel Forum** is an immense yet well-groomed collection of message boards, where our travel-savvy community answers questions and shares their personal travel experiences (www.ricksteves.com/forums).

Our **online Travel Store** offers travel bags and accessories that I've designed specifically to help you travel smarter and lighter. These include my popular bags (rolling carry-on and backpack versions), money belts, totes, toiletries kits, adapters, other accessories, and a wide selection of guidebooks, planning maps, and DVDs.

Choosing the right **rail pass** for your trip—amid hundreds of options—can drive you nutty. Our website will help you find the perfect fit for your itinerary and your budget: We offer easy, one-stop shopping for rail passes, seat reservations, and point-to-point tickets.

Want to travel with greater efficiency and less stress? We organize **tours** with more than three dozen itineraries and more than 700 departures reaching the best destinations in this book...and beyond. Our Italy tours include "the best of" in 17 days, Village Italy in 14 days, South Italy in 13 days, Sicily in 11 days, Venice-Florence-Rome in 10 days, the Heart of Italy in 9 days, My Way: Italy "unguided" tour in 13 days, and a week-long Rome tour. You'll enjoy great guides, a fun bunch of travel partners (with small groups of 24 to 28 travelers), and plenty of room to spread out in a big, comfy bus. You'll find European adventures to fit every vacation length. For all the details, and to get our Tour Catalog and a free Rick Steves Tour Experience DVD (filmed on location during an actual tour), visit www.ricksteves.com or call us at 425/608-4217.

RICK STEVES AUDIO EUROPE ™

neighborhoods in Florence: the Renaissance Walk, Accademia, and Uffizi Gallery. All of this audio content is available for free at Rick Steves Audio Europe, an extensive online library organized by destination. Choose whatever interests you, and download it for free via the Rick Steves Audio Europe app, www.ricksteves.com/audioeurope, iTunes, or Google Play.

MAPS

The black-and-white maps in this book are concise and simple, designed to help you locate recommended places and get to local TIs, where you can pick up more in-depth maps of cities and regions (usually free). Better maps are sold at newsstands and bookstores. Before you buy a map, look at it to be sure it has the level of detail you want.

RECOMMENDED BOOKS AND MOVIES

To learn more about Florence and Tuscany past and present, check out a few of these books or films.

Nonfiction

Among the classics of Italian literature with particular relevance to Florence are Niccolò Machiavelli's *The Prince* and *Florentine Histories.*

For a historical overview of the whole city, try *The City of Florence* (R. W. B. Lewis), which has a biographer's perspective. In *Florence: A Portrait,* Michael Levey writes with a curator's expertise. *The Stones of Florence* bubbles with Mary McCarthy's wit. *Dark Water* (Robert Clark) vividly recounts the determination of the Florentines in the face of the city's destructive floods.

Architecture fans should consider reading the novel-like *Brunelleschi's Dome* (Ross King) or *The Architecture of the Italian Renaissance* (Peter Murray), which presents a (not too dry) textbook overview. *The Lives of the Artists* offers anecdote-filled biographies from Giorgio Vasari, a 16th-century author/painter/architect who was the contemporary of many of his subjects. For a more academic take on Italian art history, try *Italian Renaissance Art* (Laurie Schneider Adams).

Christopher Hibbert tells of the intrigues of Florence's first family in *The House of Medici* (his *Florence* is also recommended). *Fortune Is a River* (Roger D. Masters) describes a scheme between Machiavelli and da Vinci to re-route the Arno (which, thankfully, never happened).

If you'll be traveling to the area outside of Florence, consider the sensuous travel memoir *The Hills of Tuscany* (Ferenc Máté). Also worthwhile is *A Tuscan Childhood* (Kinta Beevor), about growing up in a sun-drenched villa. *Under the Tuscan Sun* was a bestseller for Frances Mayes (and is better than the movie of the same name). Another memoir on the adventure of renovating a Tuscan farmhouse is *A Small Place in Italy* (Eric Newby).

Fiction

Florence was a favorite destination for European aristocrats and artists in the 19th and early 20th centuries. The Italian influence lives on in classics written during that time, including George Eliot's *Romola* and E. M. Forster's *A Room with a View*.

For a modern read, consider *The Passion of Artemisia,* by Susan Vreeland (who also wrote the bestselling *Girl in Hyacinth Blue*) and *The Sixteen Pleasures* (Robert Hellenga), set during the great floods that wracked the city in 1966. *Birth of Venus,* by Sarah Dunant, is set during Savonarola's reign, and *Galileo's Daughter* (Dava Sobel) is based on the real-life letters between the scientist and his daughter.

Page-turning mysteries set in Florence include *A Rich Full Death* (Michael Dibdin), *Death of an Englishman* (Magdalen Nabb), *The Dante Game* (Jane Langton), and *Bella Donna* (Barbara Cherne). For a fun Michelangelo potboiler, try *The Agony and the Ecstasy* (Irving Stone).

The Light in the Piazza (Elizabeth Spencer), the story of a mother and daughter visiting in the 1950s, was a movie (from 1962) and later became an award-winning Broadway musical.

And for the lover of classical tales, Giovanni Boccaccio's *Decameron,* written in the mid-1300s, is set in plague-ridden medieval Florence.

Films

For a well-done Shakespeare flick that was filmed in Tuscany, try *Much Ado About Nothing* (1993), which is actually set in Sicily. *A Room with a View* (1986) captures the charm of the book of the same name (described earlier). *Under the Tuscan Sun* (2003)—filled with eye-candy views—falls flat in comparison. The Oscar-winning Holocaust tragicomedy *Life Is Beautiful* (1997) has sections set in a Tuscan town. The warm-hearted Italian epic *Best of Youth* (2003) takes place in several Italian locations, including Florence and rural Tuscany.

For an excellent PBS docudrama about Florence's first family, look for *Medici: Godfathers of the Renaissance* (2005); its fine website is at www.pbs.org/empires/medici.

If Siena is on your itinerary, try *Palio* (1932), *Stealing Beauty* (1996), and *Up at the Villa* (2000), which also has scenes set in Florence. *The English Patient* (1996) was partially shot in and near Montepulciano, as was the vampire romance *New Moon* (2009, part of the *Twilight* series). Filmed in Lucca, *The Triumph of Love* (2001) has a Baroque feel, while *The Portrait of a Lady* (1996) stays true to Henry James' bleak novel.

If bound for San Gimignano, consider watching films set in that locale: *Prince of Foxes* (1949), *Where Angels Fear to Tread* (1991), and two of Franco Zeffirelli's films, *Brother Sun, Sister Moon* (1972) and *Tea with Mussolini* (1999).

Although it's not a film, the video game *Assassin's Creed II* takes place in Renaissance Florence, San Gimignano, and other real Tuscan locations. The action is violent (hence the title), but you spend the game exploring astonishingly detailed, fully interactive 3-D models of the towns at their Renaissance peak. Leonardo da Vinci, Machiavelli, and other real-life Florentines are characters in the game, and when you approach a famous landmark, historical information about the place pops up on the screen.

APPENDIX

Contents

Useful Contacts

Emergency Needs

English-Speaking Police Help: 113
Ambulance: 118
Road Service: 116

Embassies and Consulates

US Embassy: 24-hour emergency line—tel. 06-46741, non-emergency—tel. 06-4674-2406 (by appointment only, Via Vittorio Veneto 121, Rome, www.usembassy.it)
US Consulate: Tel. 055-266-951 (Mon-Fri 9:00-12:30, closed Sat-Sun, Lungarno Vespucci 38, Florence, http://florence.usconsulate.gov)
Canadian Embassy: Tel. 06-854-441 (Mon-Fri 9:00-12:00, closed Sat-Sun, Via Zara 30, Rome, www.italy.gc.ca)

Directory Assistance

Telephone Help (in English; free directory assistance): 170
Directory Assistance (for €0.50, an Italian-speaking robot gives the number twice, very clearly): 12

Holidays and Festivals

This list includes selected festivals in Florence, plus national holidays observed throughout Italy. Many sights and banks close on national holidays—keep this in mind when planning your itinerary. Before planning a trip around a festival, verify its dates by checking the festival's website or TI sites (www.italia.it and www.firenzeturismo.it).

In Florence, hotels get booked up on Easter weekend (from Good Friday through Monday), April 25 (Liberation Day), May 1 (Labor Day), May 14 (Feast of the Ascension Day), June 24 (St. John the Baptist), November 1 (All Saints' Day), and on Fridays and Saturdays year-round. Some hotels require you to book the full three-day weekend around a holiday.

Jan	Florence fashion convention
Jan 1	New Year's Day
Jan 6	Epiphany
Early Feb-Early March	Carnival Celebrations/Mardi Gras in Florence (costumed parades, street water fights, jousting competitions)
April	Italy's Cultural Heritage Week (check www.beniculturali.it for dates)
April 5	Easter Sunday. Explosion of the Cart (Scoppio del Carro) in Florence (fireworks, bonfire in wooden cart)
April 6	Easter Monday
April 25	Italian Liberation Day
May 1	Labor Day
May 14	Ascension Day
Mid-May	Cricket Festival in Florence (music, entertainment, food, crickets sold in cages)
Mid-Late May	Gelato Festival, Florence
June	Florence fashion convention

2015

JANUARY

S	M	T	W	T	F	S
				1	2	3
4	5	6	7	8	9	10
11	12	13	14	15	16	17
18	19	20	21	22	23	24
25	26	27	28	29	30	31

FEBRUARY

S	M	T	W	T	F	S
1	2	3	4	5	6	7
8	9	10	11	12	13	14
15	16	17	18	19	20	21
22	23	24	25	26	27	28

MARCH

S	M	T	W	T	F	S
1	2	3	4	5	6	7
8	9	10	11	12	13	14
15	16	17	18	19	20	21
22	23	24	25	26	27	28
29	30	31				

APRIL

S	M	T	W	T	F	S
			1	2	3	4
5	6	7	8	9	10	11
12	13	14	15	16	17	18
19	20	21	22	23	24	25
26	27	28	29	30		

MAY

S	M	T	W	T	F	S
					1	2
3	4	5	6	7	8	9
10	11	12	13	14	15	16
17	18	19	20	21	22	23
24/31	25	26	27	28	29	30

JUNE

S	M	T	W	T	F	S
	1	2	3	4	5	6
7	8	9	10	11	12	13
14	15	16	17	18	19	20
21	22	23	24	25	26	27
28	29	30				

JULY

S	M	T	W	T	F	S
			1	2	3	4
5	6	7	8	9	10	11
12	13	14	15	16	17	18
19	20	21	22	23	24	25
26	27	28	29	30	31	

AUGUST

S	M	T	W	T	F	S
						1
2	3	4	5	6	7	8
9	10	11	12	13	14	15
16	17	18	19	20	21	22
23/30	24/31	25	26	27	28	29

SEPTEMBER

S	M	T	W	T	F	S
		1	2	3	4	5
6	7	8	9	10	11	12
13	14	15	16	17	18	19
20	21	22	23	24	25	26
27	28	29	30			

OCTOBER

S	M	T	W	T	F	S
				1	2	3
4	5	6	7	8	9	10
11	12	13	14	15	16	17
18	19	20	21	22	23	24
25	26	27	28	29	30	31

NOVEMBER

S	M	T	W	T	F	S
1	2	3	4	5	6	7
8	9	10	11	12	13	14
15	16	17	18	19	20	21
22	23	24	25	26	27	28
29	30					

DECEMBER

S	M	T	W	T	F	S
		1	2	3	4	5
6	7	8	9	10	11	12
13	14	15	16	17	18	19
20	21	22	23	24	25	26
27	28	29	30	31		

June 1-30	Annual Flower Display in Florence (carpet of flowers on the main square, Piazza della Signoria)
June 2	Anniversary of the Republic
June 16-17	Festival of St. Ranieri in Pisa
June 24	Festival of St. John the Baptist in Florence (parades, dances, boat races). Also Calcio Fiorentino (costumed soccer game on Florence's Piazza Santa Croce)
Late June-early Sept	Florence's annual outdoor cinema season (contemporary films)
June-July	Florence Dance Festival (www.florencedance.org)
July 2	Palio horse race in Siena

Aug 15	Assumption of Mary (Ferragosto)
Aug 16	Palio horse race in Siena
Early Sept	Festa della Rificolona in Florence (children's procession with lanterns, street performances, parade)
Sept 13-14	Volto Santo in Lucca (procession and fair)
Oct	Musica dei Popoli Festival in Florence (ethnic and folk music and dances)
Nov 1	All Saints' Day
Dec 8	Feast of the Immaculate Conception
Dec 25	Christmas
Dec 26	St. Stephen's Day

Conversions and Climate

NUMBERS AND STUMBLERS

- Europeans write a few of their numbers differently than we do. 1 = 1, 4 = 4, 7 = 7.
- In Europe, dates appear as day/month/year, so Christmas is 25/12/15.
- Commas are decimal points, and decimals are commas. A dollar and a half is $1,50, one thousand is 1.000, and there are 5.280 feet in a mile.
- When counting with fingers, start with your thumb. If you hold up your first finger to request one item, you'll probably get two.
- What Americans call the second floor of a building is the first floor in Europe.
- On escalators and moving sidewalks, Europeans keep the left "lane" open for passing. Keep to the right.

METRIC CONVERSIONS

A kilogram is 2.2 pounds, and 1 liter is about a quart, or almost four to a gallon. A kilometer is six-tenths of a mile. I figure kilometers to miles by cutting them in half and adding back 10 percent of the original (120 km: 60 + 12 = 72 miles, 300 km: 150 + 30 = 180 miles).

1 foot = 0.3 meter	1 square yard = 0.8 square meter
1 yard = 0.9 meter	1 square mile = 2.6 square kilometers
1 mile = 1.6 kilometers	1 ounce = 28 grams
1 centimeter = 0.4 inch	1 quart = 0.95 liter
1 meter = 39.4 inches	1 kilogram = 2.2 pounds
1 kilometer = 0.62 mile	32°F = 0°C

ROMAN NUMERALS

In the US, you'll see Roman numerals—which originated in ancient Rome—used for copyright dates, clocks, and the Super Bowl. In Italy, you're likely to observe these numbers chiseled on statues and buildings. If you want to do some numeric detective work, here's how: In Roman numerals, as in ours, the highest numbers (thousands, hundreds) come first, followed by smaller numbers. Many numbers are made by combining numerals into sets: V = 5, so VIII = 8 (5 plus 3). Roman numerals follow a subtraction principle for multiples of four (4, 40, 400, etc.) and nine (9, 90, 900, etc.); the number four, for example, is written as IV (1 subtracted from 5), rather than IIII. The number nine is IX (1 subtracted from 10).

Rick Steves Florence & Tuscany 2015—written in Roman numerals—would translate as *Rick Steves Florence & Tuscany MMXV.* Big numbers such as dates can look daunting at first. The easiest way to handle them is to read the numbers in discrete chunks. For example, Michelangelo was born in MCDLXXV. Break it down: M (1,000) + CD (100 subtracted from 500, or 400) + LXX (50 + 10 + 10, or 70) + V (5) = 1475. It was a very good year.

M = 1000	XL = 40
CM = 900	X = 10
D = 500	IX = 9
CD = 400	V = 5
C = 100	IV = 4
XC = 90	I = duh
L = 50	

CLOTHING SIZES

When shopping for clothing, use these US-to-European comparisons as general guidelines (but note that no conversion is perfect).

- Women's dresses and blouses: Add 30
  (US size 10 = European size 40)
- Men's suits and jackets: Add 10
  (US size 40 regular = European size 50)
- Men's shirts: Multiply by 2 and add about 8
  (US size 15 collar = European size 38)
- Women's shoes: Add about 30
  (US size 8 = European size 38-39)
- Men's shoes: Add 32-34
  (US size 9 = European size 41; US size 11 = European size 45)

FLORENCE'S CLIMATE

First line, average daily high; second line, average daily low; third line, average days without rain. For more detailed weather statistics

APPENDIX

for destinations in this book (as well as the rest of the world), check www.wunderground.com.

J	F	M	A	M	J	J	A	S	O	N	D
40°	46°	56°	65°	74°	80°	84°	82°	75°	63°	51°	43°
32°	35°	43°	49°	57°	63°	67°	66°	61°	52°	43°	35°
25	21	24	22	23	21	25	24	25	23	20	24

TEMPERATURE CONVERSION: FAHRENHEIT AND CELSIUS

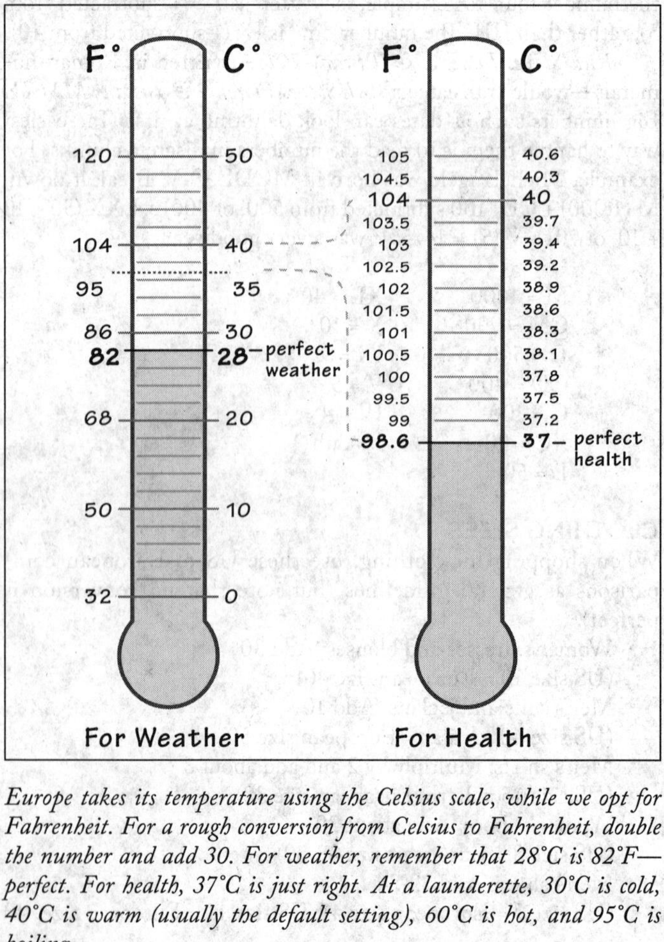

Europe takes its temperature using the Celsius scale, while we opt for Fahrenheit. For a rough conversion from Celsius to Fahrenheit, double the number and add 30. For weather, remember that 28°C is 82°F—perfect. For health, 37°C is just right. At a launderette, 30°C is cold, 40°C is warm (usually the default setting), 60°C is hot, and 95°C is boiling.

Packing Checklist

Whether you're traveling for five days or five weeks, you won't need more than this. Pack light to enjoy the sweet freedom of true mobility.

Clothing

- ❑ 5 shirts: long- & short-sleeve
- ❑ 2 pairs pants or skirt
- ❑ 1 pair shorts or capris
- ❑ 5 pairs underwear & socks
- ❑ 1 pair walking shoes
- ❑ Sweater or fleece top
- ❑ Rainproof jacket with hood
- ❑ Tie or scarf
- ❑ Swimsuit
- ❑ Sleepwear

Money

- ❑ Debit card
- ❑ Credit card(s)
- ❑ Hard cash ($20 bills)
- ❑ Money belt or neck wallet

Documents & Travel Info

- ❑ Passport
- ❑ Airline reservations
- ❑ Rail pass/train reservations
- ❑ Car-rental voucher
- ❑ Driver's license
- ❑ Student ID, hostel card, etc.
- ❑ Photocopies of all the above
- ❑ Hotel confirmations
- ❑ Insurance details
- ❑ Guidebooks & maps
- ❑ Notepad & pen
- ❑ Journal

Toiletries Kit

- ❑ Toiletries
- ❑ Medicines & vitamins
- ❑ First-aid kit
- ❑ Glasses/contacts/sunglasses (with prescriptions)
- ❑ Earplugs
- ❑ Packet of tissues (for WC)

Miscellaneous

- ❑ Daypack
- ❑ Sealable plastic baggies
- ❑ Laundry soap
- ❑ Spot remover
- ❑ Clothesline
- ❑ Sewing kit
- ❑ Travel alarm/watch

Electronics

- ❑ Smartphone or mobile phone
- ❑ Camera & related gear
- ❑ Tablet/ereader/media player
- ❑ Laptop & flash drive
- ❑ Earbuds or headphones
- ❑ Chargers
- ❑ Plug adapters

Optional Extras

- ❑ Flipflops or slippers
- ❑ Mini-umbrella or poncho
- ❑ Travel hairdryer
- ❑ Belt
- ❑ Hat (for sun or cold)
- ❑ Picnic supplies
- ❑ Water bottle
- ❑ Fold-up tote bag
- ❑ Small flashlight
- ❑ Small binoculars
- ❑ Insect repellent
- ❑ Small towel or washcloth
- ❑ Inflatable pillow
- ❑ Some duct tape (for repairs)
- ❑ Tiny lock
- ❑ Address list (to mail postcards)
- ❑ Postcards/photos from home
- ❑ Extra passport photos
- ❑ Good book

Italian Survival Phrases

English	Italian	Pronunciation
Good day.	*Buon giorno.*	bwohn **jor**-noh
Do you speak English?	*Parla inglese?*	**par**-lah een-**gleh**-zay
Yes. / No.	*Si. / No.*	see / noh
I (don't) understand.	*(Non) capisco.*	(nohn) kah-**pees**-koh
Please.	*Per favore.*	pehr fah-**voh**-ray
Thank you.	*Grazie.*	**graht**-see-ay
You're welcome.	*Prego.*	**preh**-go
I'm sorry.	*Mi dispiace.*	mee dee-spee-**ah**-chay
Excuse me.	*Mi scusi.*	mee **skoo**-zee
(No) problem.	*(Non) c'è un roblema.*	(nohn) cheh oon proh-**bleh**-mah
Good.	*Va bene.*	vah **beh**-nay
Goodbye.	*Arrivederci.*	ah-ree-veh-**dehr**-chee
one / two	*uno / due*	**oo**-noh / **doo**-ay
three / four	*tre / quattro*	tray / **kwah**-troh
five / six	*cinque / sei*	**cheeng**-kway / **seh**-ee
seven / eight	*sette / otto*	**seh**-tay / **oh**-toh
nine / ten	*nove / dieci*	**noh**-vay / dee-**ay**-chee
How much is it?	*Quanto costa?*	**kwahn**-toh **koh**-stah
Write it?	*Me lo scrive?*	may loh **skree**-vay
Is it free?	*È gratis?*	eh **grah**-tees
Is it included?	*È incluso?*	eh een-**kloo**-zoh
Where can I buy / find...?	*Dove posso comprare / trovare...?*	**doh**-vay **poh**-soh kohm-**prah**-ray / troh-**vah**-ray
I'd like / We'd like...	*Vorrei / Vorremmo...*	voh-**reh**-ee / voh-**reh**-moh
...a room.	*...una camera.*	**oo**-nah **kah**-meh-rah
...a ticket to ____.	*...un biglietto per ____.*	oon beel-**yeh**-toh pehr ____
Is it possible?	*È possibile?*	eh poh-**see**-bee-lay
Where is...?	*Dov'è...?*	doh-**veh**
...the train station	*...la stazione*	lah staht-see-**oh**-nay
...the bus station	*...la stazione degli autobus*	lah staht-see-**oh**-nay **dehl**-yee **ow**-toh-boos
...tourist information	*...informazioni per turisti*	een-for-maht-see-**oh**-nee pehr too-**ree**-stee
...the toilet	*...la toilette*	lah twah-**leh**-tay
men	*uomini / signori*	**woh**-mee-nee / seen-**yoh**-ree
women	*donne / signore*	**doh**-nay / seen-**yoh**-ray
left / right	*sinistra / destra*	see-**nee**-strah / **deh**-strah
straight	*sempre dritto*	**sehm**-pray **dree**-toh
What time does this open / close?	*A che ora apre / chiude?*	ah kay **oh**-rah ah-**pray** / kee-**oo**-day
At what time?	*A che ora?*	ah kay **oh**-rah
Just a moment.	*Un momento.*	oon moh-**mehn**-toh
now / soon / later	*adesso / presto / tardi*	ah-**deh**-soh / **preh**-stoh / **tar**-dee
today / tomorrow	*oggi / domani*	**oh**-jee / doh-**mah**-nee

In an Italian Restaurant

English	Italian	Pronunciation
I'd like...	*Vorrei...*	voh-**reh**-ee
We'd like...	*Vorremmo...*	vor-**reh**-moh
...to reserve...	*...prenotare...*	preh-noh-**tah**-ray
...a table for one / two.	*...un tavolo per uno / due.*	oon **tah**-voh-loh pehr **oo**-noh / **doo**-ay
Is this seat free?	*È libero questo posto?*	eh **lee**-beh-roh **kweh**-stoh **poh**-stoh
The menu (in English), please.	*Il menù (in inglese), per favore.*	eel meh-**noo** (een een-**gleh**-zay) pehr fah-**voh**-ray
service (not) included	*servizio (non) incluso*	sehr-**veet**-see-oh (nohn) een-**kloo**-zoh
cover charge	*pane e coperto*	**pah**-nay ay koh-**pehr**-toh
to go	*da portar via*	dah **por**-tar **vee**-ah
with / without	*con / senza*	kohn / **sehnt**-sah
and / or	*e / o*	ay / oh
menu (of the day)	*menù (del giorno)*	meh-**noo** (dehl **jor**-noh)
specialty of the house	*specialità della casa*	speh-chah-lee-**tah deh**-lah **kah**-zah
first course (pasta, soup)	*primo piatto*	**pree**-moh pee-**ah**-toh
main course (meat, fish)	*secondo piatto*	seh-**kohn**-doh pee-**ah**-toh
side dishes	*contorni*	kohn-**tor**-nee
bread	*pane*	**pah**-nay
cheese	*formaggio*	for-**mah**-joh
sandwich	*panino*	pah-**nee**-noh
soup	*zuppa*	**tsoo**-pah
salad	*insalata*	een-sah-**lah**-tah
meat	*carne*	**kar**-nay
chicken	*pollo*	**poh**-loh
fish	*pesce*	**peh**-shay
seafood	*frutti di mare*	**froo**-tee dee **mah**-ray
fruit / vegetables	*frutta / legumi*	**froo**-tah / lay-**goo**-mee
dessert	*dolce*	**dohl**-chay
tap water	*acqua del rubinetto*	**ah**-kwah dehl roo-bee-**neh**-toh
mineral water	*acqua minerale*	**ah**-kwah mee-neh-**rah**-lay
milk	*latte*	**lah**-tay
(orange) juice	*succo (d'arancia)*	**soo**-koh (dah-**rahn**-chah)
coffee / tea	*caffè / tè*	kah-**feh** / teh
wine	*vino*	**vee**-noh
red / white	*rosso / bianco*	**roh**-soh / bee-**ahn**-koh
glass / bottle	*bicchiere / bottiglia*	bee-kee-**eh**-ray / boh-**teel**-yah
beer	*birra*	**bee**-rah
Cheers!	*Cin cin!*	cheen cheen
More. / Another.	*Di più. / Un altro.*	dee pew / oon **ahl**-troh
The same.	*Lo stesso.*	loh **steh**-soh
The bill, please.	*Il conto, per favore.*	eel **kohn**-toh pehr fah-**voh**-ray
Do you accept credit cards?	*Accettate carte di credito?*	ah-cheh-**tah**-tay **kar**-tay dee **kreh**-dee-toh
tip	*mancia*	**mahn**-chah
Delicious!	*Delizioso!*	day-leet-see-**oh**-zoh

For more user-friendly Italian phrases, check out *Rick Steves' Italian Phrase Book & Dictionary* or *Rick Steves' French, Italian, and German Phrase Book.*

INDEX

C

INDEX

INDEX

INDEX

INDEX

M

INDEX

INDEX

INDEX

INDEX

INDEX

MAP INDEX

Our website enhances this book and turns

Explore Europe

At ricksteves.com you can browse through thousands of articles, videos, photos and radio interviews, plus find a wealth of money-saving travel tips for planning your dream trip. And with our mobile-friendly website, you can easily access all this great travel information anywhere you go.

TV Shows

Preview the places you'll visit by watching entire half-hour episodes of Rick Steves' Europe (choose from all 100 shows) on-demand, for free.

Rick Steves®

EUROPE GUIDES

Best of Europe
Eastern Europe
Europe Through the Back Door
Mediterranean Cruise Ports
Northern European Cruise Ports

COUNTRY GUIDES

Croatia & Slovenia
England
France
Germany
Great Britain
Ireland
Italy
Portugal
Scandinavia
Spain
Switzerland

CITY & REGIONAL GUIDES

Amsterdam, Bruges & Brussels
Barcelona
Budapest
Florence & Tuscany
Greece: Athens & the Peloponnese
Istanbul
London
Paris
Prague & the Czech Republic
Provence & the French Riviera
Rome
Venice
Vienna, Salzburg & Tirol

SNAPSHOT GUIDES

Berlin
Bruges & Brussels
Copenhagen & the Best of Denmark
Dublin
Dubrovnik
Hill Towns of Central Italy
Italy's Cinque Terre
Krakow, Warsaw & Gdansk
Lisbon
Madrid & Toledo
Milan & the Italian Lakes District
Munich, Bavaria & Salzburg
Naples & the Amalfi Coast
Northern Ireland
Norway
Scotland
Sevilla, Granada & Southern Spain
Stockholm

POCKET GUIDES

Amsterdam
Athens
Barcelona
Florence
London
Paris
Rome
Venice

Rick Steves guidebooks are published by Avalon Travel, a member of the Perseus Books Group.

Credits

RESEARCHERS

To update this book, Rick and Gene relied on principal research by Cameron Hewitt, with help from Virginia Agostinelli and Trish Feaster.

Virginia Agostinelli

Virginia was born and raised in Abruzzo, in central Italy. After graduation she moved to Seattle, where she teaches Italian at the University of Washington while continuing her studies. Besides travel and teaching, Virginia has a passion for Italian cinema and detective fiction. When not leading a Rick Steves tour, she spends time in the Pacific Northwest swimming, reading, and sipping a cappuccino at the nearest coffeehouse.

Trish Feaster

As a high-school Spanish teacher, Trish enjoyed taking her students on summer trips to Europe, sharing her passion for language, history, culture, and cuisine. She later earned a degree in French and now uses her language and teaching skills as a travel blogger, tour guide, and guidebook researcher. She and her partner enjoy traveling together, barbecuing on their deck, and playing *pétanque* in their hometown of Edmonds.

Cameron Hewitt

Cameron writes and edits guidebooks for Rick Steves, specializing in Eastern Europe. To update this book, he comparison-shopped leather jackets in Florence, taste-tested gelato and *bici* across the region, and dug deep into the Tuscan countryside—unearthing welcoming wineries, mysterious monasteries, and postcard-perfect panoramas. When he's not traveling, Cameron lives in Seattle with his wife, Shawna.